Y0-BVQ-719

Retirement & Welfare Benefit Plans

A Guide to Understanding
the
Tax Implications

1990 Addendum to

RETIREMENT AND WELFARE BENEFIT PLANS

Michael G. Kushner, Virginia L. Briggs, Patrick M. Rockelli

Section 89 Retroactively Repealed: (Book pages 361-367). The Debt Limit Extension Act, P.L. 101-140, repealed the section 89 nondiscrimination rules for health, group-term life insurance and other welfare benefit plans and generally reinstated the pre-section 89 rules. Because of delayed effective dates for section 89, it is as if the former rules have always been in effect and section 89 never existed. However, plans that would have been nondiscriminatory under section 89 for their 1989 plan years will be treated as complying with the reinstated health benefit rules for that plan year. See Statement by Ways & Means Chairman Rostenkowski, 135 Cong. Rec. H8093 (daily ed. Nov. 7, 1989).

Group-Term Life Insurance Plans: (Book pages 340-343). The repeal of section 89 resurrects the section 79(d) rules prohibiting discrimination in favor of key employees, i.e., if the plan discriminates the key employees [generally as defined in section 416(i)] lose the section 79 exclusion from gross income and the Table I rates.

Health Plans: (Book pages 343-346). Due to the repeal of section 89, no nondiscrimination tests apply to section 105 insured employer-sponsored medical plans. However, benefits provided to highly compensated employees under self-insured medical plans are excludable only to the extent the plan does not discriminate in favor of those employees. Self-insured plans discriminate if they favor highly compensated employees as to eligibility or benefits.

Group Legal Services Plans: (Book pages 346-347). The Omnibus Budget Reconciliation Act of 1989 (OBRA 1989), P.L. 101-239, reinstated and extended the section 120 exemption for group legal service organizations until September 30, 1990. The maximum annual exclusion per employee is $70.

Educational Assistance Programs: (Book pages 348-349). OBRA 1989 retroactively reinstated the section 127 exclusion for employer-provided educational assistance ($5,250 per year per employee maximum) until September 30, 1990.

Dependent Care Assistance Programs: (Book pages 349-351). For plan years beginning after 1988, only highly compensated employees must include benefits in gross income if a program fails to meet the nondiscrimination rules. Also, the average benefits provided to non-highly compensated employees must be at least 55% of the average benefits provided to highly compensated employees.

Employee Stock Ownership Plans (ESOPs): (Book pages 272-286). OBRA 1989 repealed many of the provisions that conferred favorable tax treatment on ESOPs and modified other ESOP rules. These changes include:

• For decedents dying after its enactment date, OBRA 1989 repealed the section 2057 estate tax deduction for sales of employer securities to an ESOP or worker-owned cooperative and the section 2210 liability for payment of estate tax.

• Effective generally for loans made after July 10, 1989, OBRA 1989 made the section 133 interest exclusion unavailable for interest paid during a period in which an ESOP does not own at least 50% of each class of stock of the corporation issuing the employer securities, or 50% of the value of all outstanding stock of that corporation, on or after the date the ESOP acquires the stock.

• For years beginning after July 12, 1989, the OBRA 1989 repealed the special section 415(c)(6) annual addition limits for ESOPs.

• For sales of stock to an ESOP after July 10, 1989, the OBRA 1989 made the section 1042 rule permitting the deferral of gain recognition for certain sales of employer securities to an ESOP available only if the transferor holds the securities for three years before the sale.

• Other OBRA 1989 ESOP provisions relate to reporting requirements, voting rights on employer securities, the maximum permissible term of a securities acquisition loan (a 15-year limit was imposed), excise taxes, and the dividends-paid deduction.

Qualified Plans: (Book pages 15-17). Effective generally for contributions made after October 3, 1989, OBRA 1989 amended section 401(h) to codify the IRS's rule for determining whether contributions to fund medical and life insurance benefits provided under qualified pension or annuity plans are "incidental," i.e., 25% of employer contributions made after the insurance was provided. The amendment clarifies that this calculation is based on plan contributions, not costs.

Retirement & Welfare Benefit Plans

A Guide to Understanding the Tax Implications

MICHAEL G. KUSHNER
VIRGINIA L. BRIGGS
PATRICK M. ROCKELLI

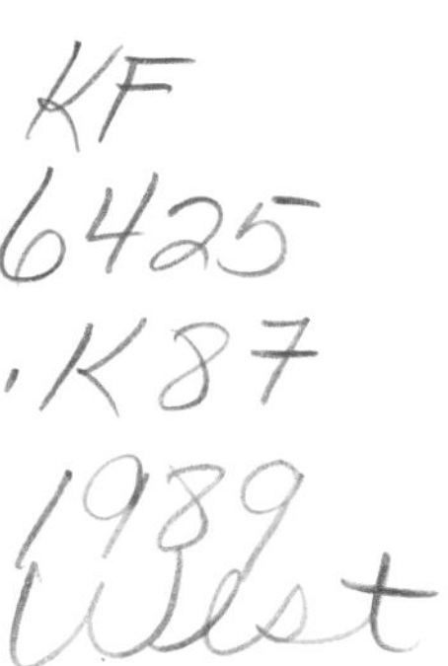

The Bureau of National Affairs, Inc., Washington, D.C. 20037

Library of Congress Cataloging-in-Publication Data

Kushner, Michael G.
Retirement and welfare benefit plans: a guide to understanding the tax implications/ Michael G. Kushner, Virginia L. Briggs, Patrick M. Rockelli. p. cm.
ISBN 0-87179-622-8
1. Pension trusts—Taxation—Law and legislation—United States. 2. Employee fringe benefits—Taxation—Law and legislation—United States. 3. Deferred compensation—Taxation—Law and legislation—United States. I. Briggs, Virginia L. II. Rockelli, Patrick M. III. Title.
KF6425.K87 1989
343.7305'24—dc20 89-36332
[347.303524] CIP

Published by BNA Books
1231 25th Street, N.W., Washington, D.C. 20037

International Standard Book Number: 0-87179-622-8
Printed in the United States of America

Introduction

Employer-sponsored deferred compensation and welfare benefit plans are playing much greater roles today in employees' overall compensation packages. This is attributable to a number of factors. First, tax reform, particularly the compression of the individual income tax rates and the expansion of the tax base, has intensified the search for ways to compensate employees while minimizing the parties' resulting tax burden. Second, personal savings programs, already at low levels, have been undermined by external forces such as market instability. Third, the social security system remains vulnerable to changes in national demographics, inflation, and politics. As a result of these factors, in many situations, employer-sponsored plans are becoming the chief means of ensuring employees' retirement security.

As the popularity of deferred compensation and welfare benefit plans has increased, so has the complexity of the law in this area. This is not surprising since the law governing these plans is drawn from a number of diverse areas, including tax, labor, trust, and fiduciary law. Moreover, since ERISA was enacted in 1974, there have been many changes in the law requiring constant redrafting of plans and reevaluations of planning strategies. Keeping pace with these changes is a formidable task for plan designers and administrators.

This book is designed to help employee benefits professionals, including lawyers, administrators, accountants, actuaries, and fiduciaries, fit qualified and nonqualified deferred compensation arrangements and welfare benefits into employee compensation packages so as to maximize the ultimate financial benefits and minimize the related costs. Special attention is devoted to the tax aspects of such arrangements due to the inherent complexity of the Internal Revenue Code and its potential impact.

Before examining the law in detail, a brief review of ERISA, its enforcing agencies, and the benefits of establishing retirement plans is necessary.

The Employee Retirement Income Security Act

In 1974, Congress enacted the Employee Retirement Income Security Act (ERISA), a wide-ranging piece of legislation regulating the organization and operation of private sector retirement and welfare benefit plans. In the years following its enactment, Congress modified the statute in several significant respects. Among the most notable modifications were those brought about by the Multiemployer Pension Plan Amendments Act of 1980, the Economic Recovery Tax Act of 1981, the Tax Equity and Fiscal Responsibility Act of 1982, the 1984 Tax Reform Act, the 1984 Retirement Equity Act, the Single Employer Pension Plan Amendments Act, and the 1986 Tax Reform Act. Despite these revisions, however, the essential enforcement structure established by ERISA remains intact.

This book examines the structure, scope, and content of ERISA and offers practical suggestions on the design and installation of deferred compensation, welfare benefit, and similar plans in light of the needs of the sponsoring employer and participating employees and the requirements of applicable law.

The Three Agencies That Administer ERISA and Their Roles

The authority for administering ERISA is divided among three agencies: the Internal Revenue Service (IRS), the Department of Labor (DOL), and the Pension Benefit Guaranty Corporation (PBGC).

The IRS, generally, is charged with administering the tax-qualification requirements imposed by the Internal Revenue Code. Favorable federal income tax results flow from a determination that a plan "qualifies" under Code §401(a).

The IRS also administers the Code provisions governing the taxation of nonqualified deferred compensation arrangements, welfare benefits, and other types of employee benefit plans, such as stock option and stock ownership plans, which receive favorable federal income tax treatment. The IRS has further authority to impose penalty taxes in certain situations, *e.g.*, for violations of the Code's prohibited transaction provisions, for underfunding defined benefit plans, and for other purposes.

The Labor Department is responsible for administering ERISA's non-tax provisions. The DOL supervises compliance with ERISA's reporting and disclosure and prohibited transaction rules. In the prohibited transactions area, the Department has authority to issue exemptions from ERISA's prohibited transaction rules. The DOL also promulgates regulations in many areas, such as crediting service to plan participants. It also enforces ERISA's civil and criminal sanctions and has an advisory role (to the IRS) concerning the tax qualification of retirement plans.

ERISA enacted identical provisions, in many areas, in both its labor title and the Internal Revenue Code. For instance, the Code provisions governing participation, vesting, and accrual have their analogues in the labor title. Similarly, Code §4975, imposing a penalty tax on certain prohibited transactions, has its parallel provisions in the labor title. Although IRS jurisdiction over §401(a) plans is triggered by a plan's attempt to seek tax-qualification, and the Labor Department's jurisdiction arises when an employee pension or welfare benefit plan is in interstate commerce, it is rare that a plan will be tax-qualified but not in interstate commerce. The converse is not necessarily true, however; a nonqualified plan generally will be subject to DOL jurisdiction because it is in interstate commerce. Such a plan would be subject to ERISA's labor title, but not to the Code's qualification rules. Most qualified plans, however, come under the concurrent jurisdiction of the IRS and the DOL.

The PBGC is a quasi-governmental insurance corporation established by ERISA. Its function is to ensure that, should certain qualified defined benefit pension plans—which are funded on an actuarially estimated basis—terminate with insufficient assets to pay participants statutorily guaranteed benefits, such amounts will be paid. The PBGC, thus, acts as insurer of the private pension system. It adopts regulations and assesses covered plans an annual per participant premium that is not yet experience-rated with respect to specific plans (although many commentators have urged this). If a single employer or multiple employer defined benefit pension plan covered by the PBGC termination insurance provisions terminates with insufficient assets, the PBGC will pay statutorily-guaranteed benefits. In return, the PBGC is given a right of recovery against the employer. The termination scheme for single and multiple employer plans was drastically revised by the Single Employer Pension Plan Amendments Act (P.L. 99-272), discussed in Chapter 11.

Until 1980, multiemployer pension plans were covered under the same insurance system as that for single and multiple employer plans. The Multiemployer Pension Plan Amendments Act of 1980 changed this, substituting an insurance system whereby employer liability is triggered by a sponsoring employer's withdrawal, or partial withdrawal, from a multiemployer plan. This liability will accrue even though the plan may continue to function with the remaining employers. Among the perceived evils MPPAA was designed to address was the tendency of employers in multiemployer plans experiencing financial difficulty to "race for the door," *i.e.*, to withdraw in an attempt to foist termination liability upon the employers remaining in the plan.

Why Establish a Retirement-Type Plan?

The chief reason for an employer to consider adopting a retirement, welfare benefit, or similar plan is to attract and retain competent employees in a competitive labor market. Employee benefit plans can also perform other functions, such as providing the employer with a source of working capital, *e.g.*, through sale of its securities to a stock plan. It can provide employees with productivity incentives through an incentive stock option plan or a §274 employee award program. As recently as 30 years ago, employers did not believe that the private sector bore the responsibility of providing for the retirement security of long-term employees. This perception has rapidly changed over the past generation to the point where, in today's labor market, private retirement plans are an integral part of most compensation packages.

The need for employer-sponsored retirement plans has been enhanced by the funding difficulties experienced by the social security system in recent years. In the Social Security Amendments of 1983, Congress acted to broaden the base of the Social Security tax to encompass more forms of compensation and to increase employment tax rates to insure that projected actuarial shortfalls would not render the Social Security system unable to pay benefits when due.

With today's changing career patterns, *e.g.*, an increasing number of single heads of household and two-earner married couples in the work force and, generally, a more mobile work force, the trend toward augmenting the basic compensation package by providing retirement, incentive, and welfare benefits has escalated. With the recent tax law changes making it more expensive than ever to provide tax-qualified deferred compensation, many employers have turned to non-tax-qualified plans to make their compensation packages competitive. Further, notwithstanding the increasing costs of establishing and maintaining qualified plans, the Internal Revenue Code still confers advantageous tax treatment on a variety of pension and welfare benefits.

In addition, Congress has conferred favored tax status upon a group of benefits that employees themselves may use to save for their retirement. These include individual retirement arrangements (IRAs), stock options and stock ownership plans, and §401(k) cash-or-deferred arrangements (CODAs).

Thus, today, the pattern of our federal laws reflects the sharing among employers, the federal government, and employees of the responsibility of providing for employees' retirement income security. Towards this end, employer-provided and employer-sponsored retirement-type arrangements are arguably the most significant component.

Summary Contents

3. Stock Plans, Salary Reduction, and Other Deferred Compensation Arrangements

4. Welfare Plans

Detailed Contents

4. Welfare Plans

List of Parallel ERISA/U.S.C. Sections

Subtitle B — Joint Pension, Profit-Sharing, and Employee Stock Ownership Plan Task Force; Studies

Title IV — Plan Termination Insurance

Subtitle A — Pension Benefit Guaranty Corporation

Subtitle B — Coverage

Subtitle C — Terminations

1

Qualified Plans—Tax Implications

1

Qualified Plans and Qualification Requirements

Qualified Plans—In General

The Internal Revenue Code provides many advantages to tax-qualified retirement plans. In contrast to nonqualified arrangements, where the employer may not deduct its contributions until the employee takes the benefits into income, an employer may deduct contributions to a qualified plan in the year they are made, subject to the limits of Code §404.

Code §404(a)(1) provides that employer contributions to a qualified stock bonus, pension, or profit-sharing plan are deductible under Code §404 and not Code §§162 or 212. This is somewhat misleading, however, because such contributions, to be deductible under §404, must also be deductible under either §§162 or 212, relating to reasonable compensation. Thus, the deferred compensation, when added to the other compensation paid the employee, must be reasonable in relation to the value of the services rendered.

Employees for whom contributions are made, however, do not realize income until their benefits are actually distributed, generally several years in the future. This result is not changed by the fact that the benefits credited to an employee may become nonforfeitable. Before the Economic Recovery Tax Act of 1981,[1] a participant would be taxed if he or she had an unrestricted right to receive benefits currently. ERTA repealed this language. The repeal of the constructive receipt language, however, does not mean that a qualified plan may permit unrestricted distributions. A defined benefit plan may never permit in-service withdrawals;[2] defined contribution plans, within certain confines, may permit in–service withdrawals.

In addition to these benefits, the assets of a qualified plan, while held in the plan's trust, grow tax-free. The effect of this tax-free compounding can be dramatic.

One way of viewing the advantages afforded by a qualified plan is to think in terms of the time value of money. In a non-qualified arrangement, the employer cannot take a compensation deduction until the employee includes the compensation in income. By permitting the employer to deduct contributions when paid, the resulting tax savings frees funds for the employer to invest. From the employee's standpoint, in addition to the benefits of tax deferral and tax-free compounding, Code §402(e) provides favorable federal income tax treatment to lump sum distributions under qualified plans that may reduce the employee's tax on retirement benefits.

The favorable income tax treatment accorded qualified plans is not without its price. Qualified plans must satisfy standards concerning coverage, participation, vesting, benefit accrual, and funding. These rules seek to prevent qualified plans from discriminating in favor of highly compensated employees.

Code §401(a)(4) contains the general antidiscrimination rule. Under this rule, a plan will not qualify if it discriminates as to benefits or contributions in favor of highly compensated individuals.

Code §414(q), as added by the 1986 Tax Reform Act,[3] defines a highly compensated individual as an employee who, during the current or the preceding year: (1) was at any time a five percent owner of the employer; (2) received annual compensation from the employer in excess of $75,000 (as adjusted for inflation); (3) received annual compensation from the employer in excess of $50,000 (as adjusted for inflation) and was in the "top-paid group," defined as the top 20 percent of employees, ranked in terms of compensation; or (4) was at any time an officer of the employer and received compensation in excess of 50 percent of the defined benefit plan §415 dollar limit for the year.[4]

Certain interpretive rules apply to the definition of highly compensated employee. For instance, whether an employee is a five percent owner is determined by that term's definition in the top-heavy plan rules.[5] Further, in determining which employees are officers, no more than 50 employees may be counted or, if lesser, the greater of three employees or 10 percent of all employees. At least one employee must be considered an officer in any year, however.

Under another special rule, if an employee is a family member of a five percent owner, or is a family member of an employee who is ranked among the top 10 percent in terms of compensation for the year, any compensation paid or owed the family member is added to the employee's compensation in determining whether the employee is a member of the prohibited group.[6] Thus, in effect, the government offers employers a bargain: If an employer establishes a qualified plan providing broad-based coverage to all employee income groups, the federal government will indirectly subsidize the plan by affording favorable income tax treatment.

The system is designed to preserve the voluntary nature of the employer's decision to establish a retirement plan while providing tax incentives to employers that help provide retirement income security for their employees.

Congress, in passing the Employee Retirement Income Security Act of 1974 (ERISA), balanced a number of policy considerations. Key among these was the goal that the qualification rules not be so stringent as to render the cost of maintaining a qualified plan prohibitive. In considering the specific qualification requirements, it is often helpful to attempt to relate them to the underlying policy considerations Congress was attempting to effectuate.

Notwithstanding the tax incentives, many employers find nonqualified plans more suited to their needs. If an employer wishes for business reasons to provide retirement benefits to its rank-and-file employees, the tax qualification requirements may not prove especially onerous. Where this is not the case, the benefits of tax qualification may be outweighed by the related cost. A nonqualified arrangement can benefit those employees the employer selects, in the amounts it chooses. Sometimes, some combination of qualified and nonqualified arrangements will best suit the employer's needs.

Defined Contribution vs. Defined Benefit Plans

Qualified retirement plans fall into two basic categories: defined benefit and defined contribution plans. A defined contribution plan is conceptually the easier to understand.

The name "defined contribution" derives from the fact that the employer's annual contribution obligation is spelled out in the plan document. The plan need not specify that a particular dollar figure or a percentage of compensation will be contributed; it need merely provide a method whereby the employer's contribution obligation may be determined with specificity. For example, a profit-sharing plan which provides that the employer's board of directors will vote an annual contribution of between 1 and 15 percent of compensation out of the employer's profits will suffice.[7] The terms "defined contribution plan" and "individual account plan" are synonymous. A defined contribution plan's trust consists of individual accounts for participating employees. Employer contributions are allocated among employees' accounts according to the formula contained in the plan. The benefit to which any participant is entitled at any given time is that participant's nonforfeitable (vested) portion of his account balance. The account can contain both employer and employee contributions, depending on the plan's terms. Thus, participating in a defined contribution plan is somewhat like maintaining a bank account—an employee's benefit is measurable by his account balance. The trustee of a defined contribution plan generally invests the plan's assets, although self-direction by participants may be permitted. Any investment return is credited to participants' accounts and they bear the incidence of any investment loss. Amounts credited to participants' accounts that are later forfeited due to the occurrence of some event, such as layoff or other separation from service, either may be reallocated to the accounts of participants remaining in the plan or may be held in suspense until a later plan year. At that time, they may be used to decrease the employer's contribution obligation. The method of allocating contributions, investment gains or losses, and forfeitures depends upon the plan's terms, subject to the general rule that such methods may not discriminate in favor of highly compensated employees.

Examples of defined contribution plans include profit-sharing plans (generally plans designed to enable employees to participate in the employer's profits), stock bonus plans, employee stock ownership plans[8] and, to some extent, money purchase pension plans (although, for funding purposes, money purchase plans are treated as defined benefit plans).

Individual retirement arrangements (IRAs) and simplified employee pensions (SEPs) also operate on the defined contribution plan model.

In contrast, defined benefit plans may be said to work backward. That is, in a defined benefit plan, as the name suggests, the benefit to which an employee will be entitled upon retirement is specified in the plan. For example, a provision that "a participant shall be entitled to a normal retirement benefit of one percent of his annual career average compensation for each year of service with the employer" would constitute a defined benefit plan formula. An annual benefit of $500 per year of service would also qualify.

Thus, in a defined benefit plan the benefit is spelled out. It is the employer's annual contribution obligation that may fluctuate from year to year. The employer must contribute annually an amount necessary to make reasonably certain that the benefits promised will be available when employees become eligible to receive them. The annual funding calculation is made by an actuary, who must consider the likely level of forfeitures, the possibility that some employees may leave the plan without earning a benefit, the life expectancies of employees and their beneficiaries, the form of benefit payment, the level of future compensation, and so forth. In a defined contribution plan, all that is specified is how much the employer will contribute. Factors such as the level of forfeitures, the level of employer contributions, and the rate of return on the plan's investments determine how large a retirement benefit will be available. Another way of expressing this is that, in a defined contribution plan, the investment risk (of gain or loss) falls on employees, while, in a defined benefit plan, it falls on the employer.

One disadvantage of establishing a defined benefit plan that must be considered is the cost of retaining a qualified actuary—a cost a defined contribution plan does not have.

The actuary's calculations must be reasonable in the aggregate. This means that individual assumptions may be unreasonable so long as all the assumptions, taken together, produce a reasonable result.[9] As conditions change, e.g., the plan's rate of return on investment increases or decreases, the actuary will have to adjust the plan's assumptions to take experience into account. These adjustments will result in variances from year to year in the employer's annual contribution obligation. Thus, another disadvantage of a defined benefit plan from an employer's standpoint is the lack of certainty as to the annual contribution obligation. From the employee's standpoint, the converse is true, i.e., the benefit is guaranteed and therefore the employee is more secure than under a defined contribution plan.

Note that one way employers may minimize their risk while maintaining a defined benefit-type plan is to establish a target benefit plan. A target benefit plan essentially works on the defined benefit plan model except that the actuarial assumptions that are in effect when the plan is established are the ones that remain in effect throughout the life of the plan. Thus, the benefit which is defined in the plan document is the one that will be paid if the actuarial assumptions conform to experience. Where there is a variance between assumed and actual experience, it will produce a gain or loss, i.e., a benefit that is higher or lower than the one targeted by the plan document. Where this occurs, gain or loss will be reflected in higher or lower retirement benefits.

A money purchase pension plan follows, in many respects, the defined contribution plan model although, for funding purposes, money purchase plans are treated as defined benefit plans. A money purchase plan is essentially one in which the employer agrees to make annual contributions that are not based on profits. The contributions are divided among participants' accounts according to a formula contained in the plan in the same manner as under a profit-sharing plan. A participant's benefit is the annuity or similar benefit that can be purchased with his account balance upon retirement.

Stock bonus plans are similar to money purchase plans in that they are defined contribution plans where the employer's annual contribution obligation is not based on profits. Stock bonus plans, however, are designed to hold their assets in the form of stock of the sponsoring employer.

General Requirements

Definitions

What is a qualified plan? In addition to satisfying specific mathematical nondiscrimination rules, a qualified plan must satisfy certain definitional requirements imposed by Code §401(a). The regulations state that a defined benefit or a money purchase plan (collectively known as "pension plans"): "is a definite written program and arrangement which is communicated to employees and which is established and maintained by an employer . . . to provide for the livelihood of the employees or their beneficiaries after retirement of such employees through the payment of benefits determined without regard to profits."[10] The regulations add that:

"A pension plan within the meaning of § 401(a) is a plan established and maintained by an employer to provide systematically for the payment of definitely determinable benefits over a period of years, usually for life, after retirement. Retirement benfits are usually measured by, and based on, such factors as years of service and compensation received by employees. The determination of the amount of retirement benefits and the contribution to provide such benefits are not dependent on profits."[11]

A profit-sharing plan is defined as:

"[A] definite written program and arrangement which is communicated to the employees and which is established and maintained by an employer . . . to enable employees or their beneficiaries to participate in the profits of the employer's trade or business, or in the profits of an affiliated employer who is entitled to deduct his contributions to the plan under § 404(a)(3)(B), pursuant to a definite written formula for allocating the contributions and for distributing the funds accumulated under the plan. . . ."[12]

The regulations add:

"A profit-sharing plan is a plan established and maintained by an employer to provide for the participation in his profits by his employees or their beneficiaries. The plan must provide a definite predetermined formula for allocating the contributions made to the plan among participants for distributing the funds accumulated under the plan for a fixed number of years, the attainment of a stated age, or upon prior occurrence of some event such as layoff, illness, disability, retirement, death, or severance of employment."[13]

Note that the 1986 Tax Reform Act added Code § 401(a)(27), which provides that a profit-sharing plan which satisfies the other qualification requirements of § 401(a) shall not fail to qualify merely because the employer does not have current or accumulated earnings and profits or because the employer is tax-exempt. Thus, contributions to a profit-sharing plan need not come from current or accumulated earnings and profits. Before the 1986 TRA, the requirement that the employer have current or accumulated earnings and profits precluded many start-up companies from adopting a profit-sharing plan. Also, before the 1986 Act, it was arguable that a nonprofit tax-exempt employer could not adopt a profit-sharing plan because the concept of current or accumulated earnings and profits was antithetical to the purposes of such an organization.

The 1986 TRA ratified pre-1986 administrative precendent under which the IRS has approved profit-sharing plans for the employees of tax-exempt employers on the grounds that such entities could have theoretical earnings and profits for qualified plan purposes despite the fact that they had no tax or financial earnings and profits. The 1986 TRA, however, prospectively overruled prior administrative authority which had allowed governmental and tax-exempt employers to establish §401(k) cash-or-deferred arrangements as part of a profit-sharing plan. Preexisting §401(k) plans of governmental and tax-exempt employers were allowed to continue in effect.

Specific Requirements

Written Plan and Trust

ERISA[14] requires, generally, that a qualified retirement-type plan be in writing and that, except for certain annuity plans where the annuity contract acts as the governing document, the plan's assets be held in trust by one or more trustees. Each trustee must be named in the trust or plan instrument or appointed by a named fiduciary.

The plan and trust are often incorporated in a single document, with the trust provisions contained in a separate article or articles. Generally, the plan provisions, whether or not contained in a separate document from the trust, deal with such matters as participation, vesting, benefit accrual, retirement eligibility, and so on. The trust provisions govern such matters as the trustee's standard of fiduciary responsibility, powers, and investment duties. The trust document also generally contains the anti-alienation rule of Code §401(a)(13). That paragraph provides that a trust shall not be a qualified trust unless the plan of which it is a part prohibits the assignment or alienation of plan benefits. This rule helps assure that the plan benefits will be available for distribution to participants and beneficiaries upon retirement. The 1984 Retirement Equity Act[15] created a limited exception to the general anti-alienation rule for certain qualified domestic relations orders.

A qualified trust is a trust created or organized in the United States.[16] Nothing in this rule prohibits a U.S. trust from holding foreign assets although, with certain exceptions, the trustee must hold the plan's assets in a manner that renders them subject to the jurisdiction of the United States district courts.[17] An example of a written plan and trust document is provided in Appendix A.

Plan Must Be Established by Employer

A qualified plan must be established and maintained by an employer.[18] This does not mean that employee contributions cannot be allowed. Indeed, a qualified plan can consist entirely of employee contributions so long as it is established by an employer. Further, this requirement does not prohibit an affiliated group of employers from establishing a common plan and, in the case of a profit-sharing plan, it does not prohibit profitable members of the group from making certain "make-up" contributions on behalf of the employees of an employer that failed to make a profit for the plan year.

The employer must act affirmatively to adopt the plan. For corporations, this generally means that the adoption of the plan must comply with the relevant state requirements for similar corporate acts. This usually means that the plan should be presented to the board of directors at an annual or special meeting to be held before the proposed effective date. The plan can then be adopted by a board resolution.

Generally, such a resolution must also be approved by the shareholders. Once the plan is formally adopted, the board may delegate day-to-day administrative authority, including securing a favorable determination letter from the IRS, to the plan's attorney or actuary or to a subcommittee of the full board.

Plan Must Be Communicated to Employees

The existence of the plan and its basic terms must be communicated to employees. This communication is to be "written in a manner calculated to be understood by the average plan participant and . . . sufficiently accurate and comprehensive to reasonably apprise such participants and beneficiaries of their rights and obligations under the plan."[19]

The IRS has not been overly stringent in enforcing this requirement and, in some offices, the statement on the application for determination, Form 5300 or 5301, that the plan was communicated orally at an employee meeting has been allowed to suffice.

The statute literally requires a written notice, however, and employers should adhere to the written form. This is so both from the IRS standpoint and from an employee relations standpoint—i.e., statements made at an employee meeting are subject to misconstruction to a greater extent than are written statements that have been carefully perused. The ERISA § 102(a)(1) notice requirement is different from the one which requires that employees be provided a Summary Plan Description (SPD).[20] Generally, however, the employer will satisfy both requirements by providing employees with an appropriately drafted SPD as notification of the plan's terms. Thus, the employer can save time and money, and assure itself of consistency in its representations, if it fulfills the ERISA § 102 notice requirement by providing employees with an SPD. SPDs can, and generally do, contain disclaimer language to the effect that any inconsistencies between the SPD and the plan will be controlled by the plan. This protective language can help minimize the effects of SPD drafting mistakes. Such mistakes may result from the difficulty of taking into account all the contingencies presented in the complex plan document while still using terms general enough to be understood by the layman. The SPD usually provides a general description of the plan terms and, where a significant exception applies, either states the exception or makes employees aware of it and refers them to the plan for details.

A plan's basic terms must be communicated to each participant or beneficiary receiving benefits within 90 days after an employee becomes a participant or a beneficiary begins to receive benefits, or 120 days after the plan becomes subject to ERISA's disclosure requirements, if later. In the case of a new plan, the requirement is that the information be supplied to participants within 120 days after the plan is established.[21]

The Exclusive Benefit Rule

Under a qualified plan's trust, it must be impossible, at any time prior to the satisfaction of all liabilities with respect to employees and their beneficiaries, for any part of the trust income or corpus to be diverted to purposes other than for the provision of benefits to covered employees or their beneficiaries.[22] The trust instrument must "definitely and affirmatively" make it impossible for the prohibited diversion to occur, whether by operation or termination of the trust, by power of revocation or amendment, by the happening of a contingency, by collateral amendment, or by any other means.[23] This does not mean, however, that the employer must relinquish the right to modify or terminate the trust. Almost all qualified plans routinely afford the employer this right. In addition, the exclusive benefit rule does not prevent the employer from including in the plan the statement that the plan's assets will be returned to the employer to the extent that (1) the plan fails to receive an initial letter of tax qualification from the IRS; (2) a contribution, once made, is later determined to have been made by mistake of fact (in the case of single and multiple employer plans) or law (in the case of multiemployer plans); or (3) the contribution was contingent upon its deductibility under Code §404 and the deduction is disallowed. (Where this occurs, the employer has one year from the disallowance of the deduction to obtain a reversion of plan assets).

Note that even though a reversion is permitted under the exclusive benefit rule, a reversion may still be subject to the 10 percent penalty excise tax imposed on reversions of excess plan assets. This excise tax was enacted by the 1986 Tax Reform Act.

The exclusive benefit rule does not prevent a plan from using its assets to pay plan administrative expenses. While the provisions authorizing such reversions or payments are generally found in different paragraphs of the plan from the one that incorporates the exclusive benefit rule, the paragraph invoking that rule should at least acknowledge that it does not supersede such other provisions. A sample of such a provision is set forth below:

> "It shall be impossible for the assets of this plan and trust to be used for any purpose other than for the satisfaction of all liabilities of this plan to participants and their beneficiaries. Nothing in this paragraph, however, shall preclude the employer from obtaining a reversion of plan assets upon the failure of this plan to receive an IRS favorable determination letter or upon a determination by the plan's trustee that a contribution was made by mistake of fact. Further, nothing herein shall prohibit the plan's trustee from using plan assets to pay the reasonable administrative expenses of this plan and nothing herein shall prevent the employer, after all liabilities of this plan have been satisfied to participants and their beneficiaries, upon a termination of this plan, from receiving a reversion of any remaining assets pursuant to the terms of this plan and in compliance with ERISA."

Plan Permanence Requirement

The term "plan" implies a permanent, as distinguished from a temporary, program. The regulations explain:

"Thus, although the employer may reserve the right to change or terminate the plan and to discontinue contributions thereunder, the abandonment of the plan for any reason other than business necessity within a few years after it has taken effect will be evidence that the plan, from its inception was not a bona fide program for the exclusive benefit of employees in general. Especially will this be true if, for example, a pension plan is abandoned soon after pensions have been fully funded for persons in favor of whom discrimination is prohibited under §401(a)."[24]

The permanency of the plan will be indicated by the surrounding facts and circumstances, including the likelihood of the employer's ability to continue contributions as provided under the plan. In other words, when the plan is established, the employer must have a present intent to establish a permanent program or arrangement. Only unforeseen business occurrences, such as bankruptcy, casualty loss or recession, will enable the taxpayer to overcome the presumption of nonpermanency where a plan terminates within a few years of its adoption. The regulations make it clear that, in a profit-sharing plan, this does not mean that the employer must contribute every year.[25] The regulations warn, however, that a qualified plan must not be a mere subterfuge to funnel earnings and profits of the employer to its owners in a tax-favored manner.[26]

A finding that the plan, at its inception, was not intended to be a permanent program can have disastrous effects for both the employer and the employees. The employer may lose deductions for its past contributions (unless such amounts would have been deductible anyway as nonqualified deferred compensation payments), the trust assets will be subject to taxation on their investment growth from the disqualification date, and employees will have to take into gross income any benefits that are substantially vested or transferable.

Practitioners having clients in the early termination situation should stress the following factors, if present, in rebutting an IRS nonpermanency argument:

(1) A substantial, unanticipated business reversal or change in the structure of the business, such as a financial reversal,

or a takeover or asset sale, has occurred since the plan was adopted;

(2) When the plan was adopted, prudent business judgment would have concluded that it was reasonable that the employer would have the ability to continue to maintain the plan; and

(3) Substantial changes in the law since the plan's adoption have rendered it significantly more costly to maintain the plan than when the plan was adopted.[27]

Incidental Benefits

The principal purpose of a defined benefit plan must be to provide pensions to employees at retirement. A profit-sharing plan, on the other hand, generally is a plan that enables employees to share in the profits of their employer.

These definitions, however, do not prohibit a plan from carrying limited amounts of life, health, and accident insurance on behalf of covered employees, if the provision of such coverage is incidental to the main purpose of the plan.

IRS Publication 778 provides that, in a pension or annuity plan funded with insurance contracts, life insurance benefits are incidental where the plan provides a preretirement death benefit that is no greater than 100 times the monthly annuity benefit provided under the plan.[28] Thus, a preretirement death benefit of $50,000 or less would be permissible if the participant's monthly annuity under the plan were $500. A money purchase pension plan may use this standard or may elect to use the standard applicable to defined contribution plans.

The publication also states that a pension or annuity plan's postretirement death benefit will be considered incidental if the death benefit does not exceed 50 percent of the participant's base salary in effect in the year preceding the year of retirement, provided that the postretirement death benefit accounts for less than 10 percent of the plan's cost, exclusive of the death benefit. It goes on to state that the death benefit payable under a qualified pension plan to the surviving spouse of an employee who died prior to attaining normal retirement age will be incidental where the death benefit's value does not exceed the death benefit that would have been payable "had the benefit been funded under a typical retirement income contract." The publication adds that, where the pension or annuity plan is funded with ordinary life insurance plus an auxiliary fund, it may permit a preretirement death benefit equal to the greater of: (a) the proceeds of the ordinary life insurance contracts, or (b) the sum of (i) the reserve under the life insurance contracts and (ii) the employee's account in the auxiliary fund. The publication cautions, however, that a death benefit equal to the sum of the proceeds of the ordinary life insurance contracts and the amount of the employee's account in the auxiliary fund would exceed the death benefit under a typical level premium retirement income contract with a face amount of 100 times the anticipated monthly retirement benefit. Therefore, such a death benefit would prevent the plan from qualifying.

Different rules apply to a profit-sharing plan that carries life insurance. Life insurance carried by a profit-sharing plan will be considered incidental where the trust funds used to purchase the insurance have not been accumulated for more than two years if (1) the total life insurance premiums for each participant are less than half the total of the contributions allocated to that participant's account at any point in time; and (2) the plan requires the trustee to convert the entire value of the contract, at or before retirement, into cash, or to provide periodic income, such as an annuity, so that no portion of such value may be used to continue life insurance protection beyond retirement, or that the trustee distribute the contract to the participant at retirement.[29]

Where a contract is distributed at retirement and the total of all premiums is not fully paid by that time, the participant may either continue to pay the premiums or cash-in the policy. Where whole life insurance is provided in a qualified plan, the "premium" is taxed to covered employees annually, despite the general nontaxable nature of benefits under a qualified plan until they are distributed. Thus, before the Tax Equity and Fiscal Responsibility Act of 1982,[30] many employers found it more advantageous to provide group-term life insurance through a Code §79 plan because the first $50,000 of such coverage was tax-free. This remained so after TEFRA, but TEFRA's addition of nondiscrimination rules applicable to group-term life insurance plans has, in some cases, discouraged the use of §79 plans.

There are several planning considerations involved in deciding whether a qualified plan should have an insurance-funded death benefit. Despite the newer, investment-oriented, life insurance contracts, life insurance generally affords a lower rate of return than other available investments. If the employee group is a younger group, it may not place that much importance on life insurance benefits and would prefer that the trustee invest the plan's assets to maximize current growth. This will also be the case where the employees have other avenues of obtaining insurance protection, whether through the employer's § 79 plan or otherwise.[31]

Where the employee group contains a number of older members who lack current life insurance and are likely to be poor actuarial risks, providing insurance through the plan (including the option to have the contract transferred to the participant upon retirement) may be a significant benefit.

A profit-sharing plan may, in addition to providing incidental life insurance, provide incidental accident and health insurance to participants, although such insurance is generally provided under Code § 105 plans.[32] The planning considerations involved in deciding to invest plan assets in health and accident insurance are similar to those involved in deciding to have the plan purchase life insurance.

Accident and health insurance coverage provided under a profit-sharing plan will be incidental where the profit-sharing funds have been accumulated for at least two years and total distributions to purchase such insurance do not exceed 25 percent of the funds allocated to the participant's account. If such funds are used to purchase ordinary life insurance in addition to accident and health insurance, the sum of the amounts spent on accident and health insurance plus 50 percent of the amount spent on ordinary life insurance cannot exceed 25 percent of the employee's account balance.[33] After the 1984 Tax Reform Act,[34] where a qualified plan provides preretirement medical benefits for employees who are key employees of the employer, the plan must provide a separate medical benefit account from which medical benefits of such employees, their spouses, and dependents may be paid.[35] The rule applies to plan years beginning after March 31, 1984. Medical benefits provided under a defined benefit plan must also meet the general nondiscrimination standards.[36] The 1984 TRA amended Code § 415 to provide that contributions allocated to an individual medical account[37] must be treated as an annual addition to a defined contribution plan in applying the limits of § 415(c).[38]

Qualification Requirements

Code §401(a)

Code §401(a) sets forth requirements for qualified retirement plans. The section, in many instances, acts as a directory, referring to other Code sections for specific requirements. For instance, §401(a)(3) states that a qualified plan must satisfy the minimum participation standards of §410, and §401(a)(7) states that a qualified plan must satisfy the §411 vesting requirements. A provision is not a qualification requirement unless it is referred to in §401(a).

Code §401(a)(4) contains the general antidiscrimination rule. Under that rule, a qualified plan must not discriminate as to benefits or contributions in favor of highly compensated employees.[39] A plan must satisfy the general rule both on paper, (that is, the plan document, by its terms, must not discriminate), and in operation.

Plan draftsmen should be alert to provisions that, although permissible on their face, could cause the plan to discriminate in operation. If, in operation, the plan discriminates, it will be disqualified. This is so even where the plan has received a favorable determination letter.[40] As a practical matter, defined contribution plans have the potential to discriminate as to contributions (or by the reallocation of forfeitures). Defined benefit plans have the potential to discriminate in terms of benefits. The following example shows how a plan might discriminate in operation but not on paper.

> *Example:* Defined contribution plan B contains a vesting schedule that applies equally to all participants and satisfies the requirements of Code §§401(a)(7) and 411. The vesting schedule calls for an employee to be 100% vested after four years of service. Over time, a disproportionately large number of nonhighly compensated employees relative to highly compensated employees leave the employer before becoming vested. As a result, there is a pattern of forfeitures from the accounts of nonhighly compensated employees to the employees who remain in the plan, and who largely tend to be members of the prohibited group. Highly compensated employees' account balances thus disproportionately benefit from reallocated

forfeitures. Where this effect is pronounced, it can constitute discrimination.

Several precautions can be taken against this sort of discrimination where employee census data indicates that a discriminatory forfeiture pattern is likely to occur. For example, the plan can provide a method of reallocating forfeitures that is skewed in favor of nonhighly compensated employees. Thus, in a plan where the employer's contributions are allocated to employee accounts based on a fixed percentage of each employee's compensation, the plan can provide that forfeitures are to be divided equally among remaining participants. This will allocate a lower percentage of forfeitures to highly compensated employees than would occur under the plan's general formula for allocating contributions.

In extreme cases, the plan might provide that, where the reallocation of a forfeiture to the account of a highly compensated employee would result in that employee's account balance rising above a specified percentage of compensation, the employee will not share in the reallocation of forfeitures. Alternatively, the plan might provide that forfeitures will not be reallocated to participants' accounts, but rather will be held in a suspense account and reallocated from that account in a future year to decrease the employer's annual contribution obligation. Another possibility might be to amend the plan to provide a more liberal vesting schedule, that is, one that does not produce such a pattern of forfeitures by nonhighly compensated employees.

The general Code §401(a)(4) rules act as a backstop to the specific qualification rules. A plan, to be tax-qualified, must satisfy both the specific mathematical antidiscrimination rules and the § 401(a)(4) general antidiscrimination rule. Practitioners should therefore consider whether a particular plan provision that appears legal on its face might, under appropriate circumstances, violate the general antidiscrimination rule. Conservative draftsmanship and prudent oversight, especially when the demographics of the covered group fluctuate dramatically, can help prevent this type of problem. In the following chapters, the specific mathematical antidiscrimination rules are examined. It is helpful in understanding these rules to remember their purpose—to assure that tax-qualified plans provide benefits to nonhighly compensated employees without making such plans so costly that employers will decline to sponsor them.

Notes

1. P.L. 97-34, (ERTA).
2. Treas. Regs. § 1.401-1(b)(1).
3. P.L. 99-514 (1986 TRA).
4. Code § 414(q).
5. Code § 416(i), discussed below.
6. For this purpose, a family member includes an employee's spouse, dependents, and lineal descendants. Before the 1986 TRA, the § 401(a)(4) prohibited group consisted of officers, shareholders, and certain highly compensated individuals. The 1986 TRA definition is effective with respect to retirement-type plans for years beginning after 1986. For welfare benefit plans, it is effective for years beginning after 1987.
7. Profit-sharing plans are unique in their ability to provide that the employer's annual contribution obligation will be discretionary. Other types of qualified plans must provide for a specific contribution obligation.
8. ESOPs.
9. In various private letter rulings, however, the IRS has come close to saying that certain assumptions, such as an interest rate that is dramatically below market rates, may be unreasonable per se.
10. Treas. Regs. § 1.401-1(a)(2).
11. Treas. Regs. § 1.401-1(b)(1)(i).
12. Treas. Regs. § 1.401-1(a)(2).
13. Treas. Regs. § 1.401-1(b)(1)(ii).
14. ERISA §§ 402(a)(1) and 403(a).
15. P.L. 98-397 (REA).
16. Treas. Regs. § 1.401-1(a)(3)(i).
17. ERISA § 404(b).
18. Treas. Regs. § 1.401-1(a)(2).
19. ERISA § 102(a)(1). This general notification obligation should not be confused with the ERISA § 3001 requirement that employees be notified of the plan's application for a favorable determination letter. This latter communication has been stylized by the Department of Labor. Where the § 3001 notice is concerned, employers should not deviate from the approved DOL language.
20. ERISA § 104(b)(1). The SPD, like the notice, is supposed to be a document that explains the plan in layman's language.
21. ERISA § 104(b)(1) (A) and (B). *See* 352 T.M., *Profit-Sharing Plans—Qualification.*
22. Code § 401(a)(2).
23. Code § 401(a)(2); Treas. Regs. § 1.401-2(a)(2).
24. Treas. Regs. § 1.401-1(b)(2).
25. Treas. Regs. § 1.401-1(b)(2).
26. Treas. Regs. § 1.401-1(b)(3).
27. For an analysis of the factors the IRS will look to in determining whether a plan that terminates within a few years of its adoption will satisfy the permanency requirement, see Rev. Rul. 60-24, 1969-1 C.B. 110 and Rev. Rul. 69-25, 1969-1 C.B. 113.
28. *Guides for Qualification of Pension, Profit-Sharing, and Stock Bonus Plans,* at 8. *See also* Rev. Rul. 74-307, 1974-2 C.B. 126.

29. P.L. 97-248 (TEFRA). *See* Rev. Rul. 54-51, 1959-1 C.B. 147, as amplified by Rev. Rul. 57-213, 1957-1 C.B. 1957 and Rev. Rul. 60-84, 1960-1 C.B. 159.
30. *Id.*
31. For example, many professional organizations privately sponsor insurance plans for members of the profession at favorable group rates. The taxation of the deemed premium amount to employees is a factor to be considered but, generally, this will not be that significant.
32. *Supra*, note 29.
33. *See* Rev. Rul. 61-164, 1961-2 C.B. 99; IRS Pub. 778 at 9.
34. P.L. 98-369 (1984 TRA).
35. Code §401(h).
36. *See* H.R. REP. NO. 432, 98th Cong., 2d Sess. 1295 (1984).
37. Described in Code §401(h)(6).
38. H. R. REP. NO. 432, 98th Cong., 2d Sess. (1984), states that the IRS may issue regulations under which medical benefits provided under defined benefit plans before the effective date of the TRA may be reallocated to §401(h)(6) individual medical accounts without reducing the §415 limit.
39. As defined in Code §414(q). *See* the definition of highly compensated employee in text at note 4, above.
40. IRS determination letters are discussed in Chapter 11.

2

Participation and Coverage

Participation

Participation refers to the eligibility of employees to be covered by a plan. Code §410, which governs participation, contains two sets of rules. The age and length-of-service rules establish minimum age and service requirements. The coverage rules measure a plan's coverage relative to the employer's entire work force.

In addition to these sets of rules, Code §410 has specific requirements for "leased" employees and for members of an "affiliated service group" or a group of businesses under common control.

Age and Length-of-Service Rules

The minimum age and service rules are designed to ensure broad employee participation in qualified plans while helping contain employers' plan costs by allowing them to decline to cover employees at initial stages of their careers or those who only remain with the employer for a short time. Once these rules are satisfied, an employee must be admitted to participation, i.e., enrolled in the plan as an individual eligible to receive benefits, by the first plan "entry date" after he has satisfied the requirements.

A plan may allow employees to participate earlier than the minimum age and service rules provide. The participation rules merely set forth the maximum period a plan can delay admitting an employee to participation and remain a qualified plan. The maximum period is generally one year.[1] A special rule allows a plan to impose a two-year service requirement if an employee's accrued benefit attributable to employer contributions becomes 100 percent vested (nonforfeitable) after two years of service.[2]

The general minimum age requirement is age 21.[3] Certain tax-exempt educational institutions' plans that confer 100 percent vesting after one year of service may use age 26 as their minimum age.[4] This rule is designed to suit the needs of universities where, particularly in the case of academic personnel, very young employees are generally not long-term employees who look to the university as a principal source of retirement income.

Where employees who remain with the employer two or more years are likely to remain long-term, the two-year option may, like the age 26 option for educational institutions, help a plan save administrative costs while permitting the employer to principally benefit those employees it wishes to retain. A qualified plan's age and service requirements must be set forth in the plan document. A plan that does not specifically provide an age or service requirement must admit all employees to participation immediately upon their employment, regardless of their age or service.

Definition of "Year of Service"

For participation purposes, a "year of service" is a consecutive 12-month period during which an employee is credited with not less than 1,000 hours of service.[5] Again, a plan may be more liberal than this. For example, a qualified plan could credit an employee with a year of service if the employee completed 900 hours of service in the applicable computation period. Labor Department regulations define an hour of service as any hour for which the employee is, directly or indirectly, entitled to compensation either by reason of the performance of duties or for certain reasons unrelated to the performance of duties, such as vacation or sick leave.[6]

Breaks in Service

A one-year break in service will occur, for participation purposes, when an employee is credited with 500 hours of service or less during a 12-month computation period.[7] Again, a plan can be more liberal than this.

For participation purposes, where a participant has incurred a one-year break in service, the plan may decline to count service rendered before the break year until the employee has returned to employment and completed a year of service.[8] This is known as the "one year hold out rule." This rule is designed to help contain a plan's administrative costs by allowing the employer to see if the employee is going to remain employed for a substantial period before reinstating the employee to active participant status. To apply this rule, the plan document must specifically so provide.

> *Example:* Plan C requires that an employee complete one year of service before being admitted to participation. Employee X satisfies this requirement and is admitted to participation for the plan year beginning January 1, 1988. Employee X works for the employer until December 31, 1990, earning benefits under the plan in which he has become vested. At the end of 1990, X leaves the employer's service and, for the plan year 1990–91, incurs a one-year break in service. X returns to work for the employer January 1, 1992. The employer may require that X complete a year of service before being readmitted to participation. Once X has satisfied this requirement and been readmitted to participation, he must be retroactively given vesting and accrual credit for the 1992 plan year as if he had been readmitted to participation on January 1, 1991.

In computing years of service, a year in which an employee is credited with 501–999 hours of service does not have to be counted as either a year of service or a year of break. Such a year may be treated as a neutral year, having no effect on the employee's eligibility to receive benefits. As is the case with ERISA requirements generally, a plan may credit service more generously than the law requires. For instance, a plan that credited an employee with a year of service for a 12-consecutive month computation period during which he completed 900 hours of service would qualify.

Certain maternity or paternity-related leaves of absence may not be treated as breaks in service. Under this rule, a leave of absence cannot cause a break in service if the period of absence occurred:

(1) By reason of the pregnancy of the individual;

(2) By reason of the birth of a child of the individual;

(3) By reason of the placement of a child with the individual in connection with the adoption of such child by such individual; or

(4) For purposes of caring for such child for a period beginning immediately following such birth or placement.

In addition, solely for purposes of determining whether a break in service has occurred, the following hours must be counted as hours of service:[9]

(1) The hours of service which would normally have been credited to the individual before such absence; or

(2) If the plan cannot determine the hours described in (1), eight hours of service per day of absence not to exceed 501 hours.

Thus, a qualified maternity or paternity leave of absence may not give rise to a one-year break in service. Such absence, however, will not give rise to a credited year of service. Rather, the absence will give rise to a neutral year, effectively precluding a plan from using the one year hold out rule with respect to the individual.

Equivalencies

Labor Department regulations permit plans to use certain "equivalencies" in computing hours of service for participation, vesting, and accrual purposes. Equivalencies are designed to enable an employer to keep track of hours of service where detailed records are unavailable or are burdensome to maintain. A situation where an equivalency might be helpful would be where actual hours worked are irregular, such as the retail sales industry. The regulations approve the following equivalencies:[10]

(1) Hours worked;[11]

(2) Regular time hours;[12]

(3) Days of employment;[13]

(4) Weeks of employment;[14]

(5) Semi-monthly periods of employment;[15]

(6) Months of employment;[16]

(7) Shifts of employment;[17]

(8) Equivalencies based on earnings;[18] and

(9) The elapsed time method.[19]

Under an hours worked equivalency, only hours for which services are performed are counted. Thus, the employer may ignore such hours as vacation or sick leave. Since this will result in employees being credited with fewer hours of service, where this equivalency is used, the plan must count 870 hours worked as 1,000 hours of service and 435 hours worked as 500 hours of service. Note that the employer does not have to apply this ratio ratably to each hour worked. When 435 hours are accumulated, however, they must be rounded up to 500. Using this equivalency can relieve the plan of the burden of keeping track of the different types of paid but unworked hours. This can be especially helpful where different groups of employees have different benefit packages or working schedules.

An employer may use different equivalencies for different groups of employees, provided there is a reasonable business justification for this and the different treatment is consistently applied and does not discriminate in favor of highly compensated employees. For instance, there might be a legitimate, nondiscriminatory business reason for different treatment for part-time and full-time employees or for different treatment for outside sales personnel. Further, different equivalencies can be used to compute hours of service for participation, accrual, and vesting. Again, the different treatment must not discriminate in operation. Where different equivalencies are used, the plan must be continually monitored for discrimination in operation in light of the demographics of the employer's work force.

Under a regular time hours equivalency, only hours worked are counted. Unlike the hours worked equivalency, however, nonregular time hours, such as overtime hours, are disregarded. Again, where there are significant nonregular time hours worked, this equivalency can help reduce recordkeeping. Where the regular time equivalency is used, the employer must count 375 regular time hours as 500 and 750 hours as 1,000.

Where a days of employment equivalency is used, an employee must be credited with 10 hours of service for each day in which he performs an hour of service. Thus, actual hours worked need not be recorded. This can be helpful where the workday varies from day to day or from employee to employee.

In most cases, the hours worked equivalency will result in an employee being credited with more hours of service than hours actually worked. For instance, an employee who works only one hour in a day will receive 10 hours of service credit. In rare circumstances, where the workday exceeds 10 hours, however, the employee will lose hours under this equivalency, since the maximum amount of hours credited for a day is 10.

A weeks of employment equivalency credits an employee with 45 hours of service for every week in which he or she performs an hour of service. Again, where the equivalency is used, employees will usually benefit, although, unlike the days worked equivalency, there may be a significant number of cases where the customary work week exceeds 45 hours and the employee actually loses hours under this equivalency.

A semi-monthly equivalency credits an employee with 95 hours of service for each semi-monthly period in which an hour of service is performed. Under a months worked equivalency, 190 hours of service are credited to an employee who performs at least one hour of service in a calendar month. A shifts-of-employment equivalency credits an employee with the number of hours that are included in one shift for each shift in which the employee performs an hour of service.

Where an equivalency based on earnings is used, the employee's total earnings during a computation period are divided by the employee's hourly rate of pay during that period. Where no hourly rate is available, the lowest rate of pay applicable to employees performing comparable jobs is used. Alternatively, the employer may mathematically convert the employee's salary to a deemed hourly rate by dividing the total salary for the computation period by the lowest rate of hourly compensation applicable to that employee during the period. Where an earnings equivalency is used, 750 hours must be counted as 1,000 hours of service and 375 hours as 500.

Under the elapsed time method, an employee's hours are disregarded and service is credited based on the total period of time for which the employee is employed. An employee's service must be counted for this purpose from the time he first performs an hour of service for the employer until he severs employment. Under the elapsed time method, a break in service occurs when the employee severs employment and does not return within a 12-consecutive month period. The IRS regulations note that temporary absences that are not related to severance from service, such as a three-week vacation, must be counted as service under the elapsed time method.[20]

Under the service spanning rules applicable to the elapsed time method, a plan must also credit certain periods of severance from service lasting 12 months or less for purposes of participation and vesting. Under the first service spanning rule, if an employee separates from service as a result of quitting, discharge, or retirement and returns to the employer's service within 12 months, the period of severance must be counted as service. The second service spanning rule deals with the situation where an employee is absent for reasons other than quitting, discharge, retirement, or death and, during the period of absence, the employee quits, is discharged, or retires. In this situation, the second service spanning rule requires a plan to count the period between the severance from service and the first anniversary of the date on which the employee was first absent, if the employee returns to service on or before this anniversary date.[21]

In addition to the equivalencies provided by the regulations, a plan may devise its own equivalency so long as it credits service at least as liberally as one of the approved methods, does not discriminate, and is uniformly applied.[22]

In choosing a method of crediting service, the employer should take into account the payroll records it customarily keeps. If no hourly records are kept, for instance, the use of an equivalency can prevent the employer's having to maintain such records solely for purposes of the plan.

Special Break-in-Service Rules

The Code provides a special break-in-service rule for employees covered under a plan that provides two-year 100 percent vesting.[23] Under this rule, where an employee incurs a one-year break in service, pre-break service need not be counted after the employee returns to service if the employee was not vested in his accrued benefit when the break occurred. Note that this only applies to an employee's accrued benefit attributable to employer contributions. An employee must always be 100 percent vested in any accrued benefit attributable to his or her own contributions.[24]

Under the "rule of parity," if a participant has no vested right to his accrued benefit when a break occurs, pre-break service does not have to be counted when the employee returns to work for purposes of the minimum participation and vesting requirements if the number of consecutive one-year breaks in service equals or exceeds the aggregate number of such years of service before such break and the number of consecutive years of break is at least five. A plan may only invoke this rule if, at the time the break occurred, the participant had no vesting whatsoever in his benefit attributable to employer contributions.[25]

> *Example:* Employee X is a nonvested participant in Plan D, which uses the rule of parity. At the time X incurred a break in service, he had four total years of service. If X incurred a five consecutive year break in service, the plan would not have to count his pre-break service, since his number of consecutive years of break equals or exceeds his total pre-break service. If, however, X incurred only a four-year break, his pre-break service would have to be aggregated with his post-break service in computing service for participation and vesting purposes. If, after the four-year break, X returned to work for one year, giving him a total of five years of service, his next break would have to be for at least six consecutive years before the plan could disregard his prior service under the rule of parity.

Note that, where an employee has any percentage of vesting whatsoever in employer contributions, the rule of parity may not be applied. Further, a plan may only apply the rule of parity where the plan document specifically so provides. A plan using the rule of parity should explain it to participants and beneficiaries in the Summary Plan Description.

Eligibility Computation Periods

The initial eligibility computation period that must be used for participation purposes is the 12-consecutive month period beginning with the date the employee begins work for the employer (the "employment commencement date") and ending with the first anniversary thereof. After the first such 12-month period, the plan, for administrative convenience, may compute subsequent years of service for participation purposes based on plan years.[26] Where a plan so converts the computation period, an employee who has performed 1,000 hours of service in each of the overlapping periods must be credited with two years of service even though this may result in double counting of certain hours.

Example: Plan E uses a calendar year as its plan year and converts the participation computation period to the plan year after the initial year. Employee X begins work for the employer on July 1, 1988, and completes 1,000 hours of service by the first anniversary of his employment commencement date, July 1, 1989. Of these 1,000 hours, 500 are attributable to the period beginning January 1, 1989, and ending July 1, 1989. The plan then converts X to the plan year. Between July 2, 1989 and December 31, 1989, X completes another 500 hours of service, giving him 1,000 hours for the 1989 plan year. X must be credited with two years of service, even though 500 of his hours were counted in each of the two overlapping periods.

The above rule can have a significant impact on a plan that has a two-year participation requirement. Practitioners drafting plans that use a two-year service requirement should consider the potential interaction of the plan's eligibility and service counting rules before adopting a rule of convenience that converts participants to the plan year for years after the initial year.

Parallel rules to those described above for initial eligibility computations apply where an employee is re-employed after a break in service. In this case, the initial eligibility period following the employee's return to service must be the 12-month period beginning with the employee's return to service (the "re-employment commencement date") and ending with the first anniversary thereof. Thereafter, the plan can again convert the employee to plan years for participation purposes.

Where an employee's employment commencement date cannot be determined because of lack of employer records, a plan may use a period of up to 31 days more than the usual 12-month period. If the plan in this situation does not switch to plan years after the initial eligibility computation period, successive computation period will overlap by up to 31 days.[27]

Plan Entry Dates

The Code and the regulations require that a qualified plan admit an employee who has satisfied the age and length-of-service requirements no later than the earlier of the following dates:[28]

(1) The first day of the first plan year beginning after the date on which the employee first satisfied the requirements; or

(2) The date six months after the date on which the employee satisfied the requirements.

Generally, plans comply with this requirement by providing for two annual entry dates, the first falling on the first day of the plan year and the second six months thereafter. A plan that ostensibly complies with the age and service requirements, however, may nonetheless be disqualified because the effect of its entry dates creates a de facto participation requirement which exceeds the applicable limit.

> *Example:* Plan F uses an age 21 and one-year of service requirement. Plan F provides for one annual entry date, corresponding to the first day of the plan year. Plan F will not qualify since it is possible to posit a case where the plan's entry date rules would cause it to fail to satisfy the age and service requirements. For instance, if Employee X turns 21 and completes the service requirement on January 2 where the plan year is the calendar year, he would not be admitted to participation until January 1 of the succeeding plan year, a date which is later than the earlier of the first day of the next plan year or six months after X has satisfied the plan's age and service requirements. Providing for two annual entry dates, the first falling on the first day of the plan year and the other six months after that date would cure this problem with respect to all potential participants.

A plan may use a single annual entry date and still qualify, provided the age and service requirements are adjusted downward accordingly.

> *Example:* Plan G is a calendar year plan. It has an age 21 requirement and a one-year service requirement. It has one annual entry date, corresponding to the first day of the plan year. Plan G qualifies because all employees will be admitted by the earlier of the first day of the plan year after they have attained age 21 and performed one year of service or a date which is six months after they have satisfied such requirements. Although an employee could be age 21 by the time he or she was admitted, this is permissible under

the age and service rules because it effectively guarantees that an employee will be admitted to participation within the earlier of six months after attaining age 21 or the first day of the first plan year after attaining age 21.

Employers generally wish to limit the number of plan entry dates for administrative convenience and cost containment. Where the administrative requirements are not unduly burdensome, such as in the case of a small plan, and the employer wishes to cover employees as soon as possible after they satisfy the age and service requirements, multiple entry dates could be used. Theoretically, a plan may provide for as many as 365 annual entry dates.

Special Industry Rules

Although, generally, a year of service for participation purposes is a 12-month eligibility computation period during which an employee is credited with 1,000 hours of service, ERISA provides special rules for industries that do not readily lend themselves to the application of the general rule.[29]

For seasonal industries, a year of service is to be determined under Labor Department regulations.[30] In the maritime industry, 125 days of service are considered 1,000 hours of service.[31]

Maximum Age Requirements

Formerly, defined benefit plans could prescribe maximum age limits for participation. Such plans could prohibit participation by employees who began employment with the employer no more than five years before the plan's qualified normal retirement age. Because funding of an employee's benefit under a plan is based on the number of years between the employee's employment commencement date and his normal retirement date, this rule was designed to remove a disincentive to hiring older workers, i.e., the prohibitive cost of funding their retirement benefits over a short period. In most cases, such employees will have already earned a pension under the plan of a former employer. The Omnibus Budget Reconciliation Act of 1986 (OBRA 1986) eliminated this rule, effective generally with respect to plan years beginning after 1987 as to employees who have one or more hours of service in any plan year to which the amendments apply. Under the revised rule, plans are completely prohibited from decreasing accrued benefits of any participant on account of any increase in age or service.[32] This prohibition, however, does not apply to plan benefits that commence before the employee is entitled to benefits payable under title II of the Social Security Act, provided such plan benefits do not exceed the employee's Social Security benefits and terminate when Social Security benefits commence.[33]

Under the revised rules, a defined benefit plan cannot cease, or reduce the rate of, an employee's benefit accrual because of the attainment of any age. Notwithstanding this general rule, a defined benefit plan may impose (without regard to age) a limit on the amount of benefits that the plan will provide or a limit on the number of years of service or participation which are counted for benefit accrual purposes. Further, when an employee covered by a defined benefit plan reaches normal retirement age two rules apply to continued accruals:

(1) If the plan has begun to distribute benefits to the employee during the plan year, the continued accrual requirement will be satisfied to the extent of the actuarial equivalent of in-service distributions; and

(2) If benefit distributions to an employee have not begun for the plan year pursuant to Code §401(a)(14)(C) and the employee's benefits are not suspended, the continued accrual rules will be satisfied to the extent the plan actuarially adjusts the benefit payable to take into consideration the delay in benefit payments that has occurred after the employee has attained normal retirement age.

In applying these continued accrual rules, the subsidized portion of an early retirement benefit is disregarded.[34] Similar rules apply to defined contribution plans.[35]

Coverage

A qualified plan must cover a significant portion of an employer's nonhighly compensated employees.[36] Before the effective date of the 1986 Tax Reform Act amendments to the minimum coverage rules, a plan would qualify if it satisfied either: (1) the 70 percent test; (2) the 70/80 percent test; or (3) the nondiscriminatory classification test.

A plan would meet the 70 percent test if it benefited 70 percent or more of an employer's employees. A plan would meet the 70/80 test if 70 percent or more of an employer's employees were eligible to participate and 80 percent of eligible employees actually participated.

If the plan did not satisfy either the 70 percent test or the 70/80 test, it could still qualify if it benefited employees under a classification set up by the employer that did not discriminate in favor of certain officers, shareholders and highly paid individuals as defined in pre-1986 TRA Code §401(a)(4) (referred to herein as "prohibited group" employees).

Effective generally for plan years beginning after 1988, the 1986 TRA completely revised the coverage rules.[37] After the effective date of the 1986 TRA amendments, a qualified plan must satisfy at least one of three coverage tests.

Under the first test, a plan must benefit 70 percent or more of all nonhighly compensated employees. For this purpose, all eligible employees are considered to benefit under the plan. In a §401(k) cash or deferred arrangement, or a plan under which employees may voluntarily contribute or may receive employer matching contributions, all employees who are eligible to contribute will be considered to benefit.[38]

Under the second, or "ratio" test, a plan must benefit a classification of employees which does not allow more than a reasonable difference between the percentage of highly compensated employees who are covered and a similarly computed percentage for nonhighly compensated employees.[39]

Under the third test, known as the "average benefits test," a plan will qualify if: (1) it benefits employees under a classification that the IRS finds not to be discriminatory; and (2) the average benefit percentage for nonhighly compensated employees is at least 70 percent of the average benefits percentage for highly compensated employees.[40]

For this purpose, the average benefit percentage for a group is the sum of all employer contributions and benefits under the plan provided to the group, expressed as a percentage of pay for all such employees.[41] The average benefits percentage may be computed on the basis of the current plan year or as a rolling average of the immediately preceding three plan years (the last being the current plan year). An employer may elect whether to use only the current plan year or the three immediately preceding years. Once such an election is made, however, it may be revoked only with IRS consent.[42]

In applying the coverage tests, certain employees must be excluded. These are:

(1) Employees covered by a collective bargaining agreement where retirement benefits have been the subject of good faith bargaining;

(2) Employees whose customary duties are performed aboard an aircraft in flight who are covered under a plan maintained pursuant to a collective bargaining agreement between employers and airline pilots in accordance with title II of the Railway Labor Act;

(3) Nonresident aliens with no United States source earned income; and

(4) Employees excluded under the plan's qualified minimum age and service requirement.[43]

If the employer operates "separate lines of business," it may apply the coverage tests separately to each line of business, provided the plan for each separate line benefits a nondiscriminatory classification of employees.[44]

Code §414(r) provides that, to be considered a separate line of business, the line of business must be operated separately for valid business reasons. Further, it must have at least 50 employees who are not excluded by virtue of the fact that they have not satisfied certain minimum service requirements contained in Code §414(q) and must meet any IRS guidelines on point. If the employer seeks to classify an operating unit as a separate line of business, Code §414(r) requires the employer to notify the IRS of its intent to treat the unit as such.

A plan that provides broad general coverage amongst employees at all levels of compensation which cannot satisfy the percentage tests because only employees in one division are eligible would be an example of a plan that might satisfy the nondiscriminatory classification test.

After the effective date of the 1986 TRA amendments, a plan

will not be disqualified due to failure to meet the §410(b) coverage rules.[45] Rather, the vested benefits of highly compensated employees as of the close of the year under such plan will be taxed as if they were provided under a nonqualified plan.[46] This rule, however, will not cause the same benefits to be taxed to employees more than once, should the plan not meet the coverage tests in more than one year.

In addition to the foregoing rules, after the effective date of the 1986 TRA amendments, a qualified plan must benefit at least the lesser of: (1) 50 employees; or (2) 40 percent or more of all employees of the employer. This rule will, as Congress intended, make it difficult in many cases for small plans of corporate partners of a partnership, including professional corporations (PIPIC), to qualify.[47]

Plans Exempted From the Participation and Coverage Rules

Code §410(c) provides that neither the age and length-of-service nor the coverage rules apply to certain types of plans. These are:

(1) Government plans;[48]

(2) Church plans;[49]

(3) Plans that have not, after ERISA's enactment date,[50] provided for employer contributions; and

(4) Plans established by certain tax-exempt organizations calling for no employer contributions.[51]

Such plans will be treated as satisfying the participation requirements if they satisfied the pre-ERISA participation requirements on the day before ERISA's enactment date, i.e., September 1, 1974.

Notes

1. Code §410(a)(1)(A)(i).
2. Code §410(a)(1)(B)(i).
3. Before the Retirement Equity Act of 1984 (P.L. 98-397) the minimum age requirement was 25 (30 for educational institutions). The REA lowered the requirements to 21 and 26, respectively (effective generally for plan years beginning after 1984). The REA changes were designed to assure that certain groups of employees who enter the work force early, such as women who may subsequently leave to have children, be covered under their employers' plans. The lower participation age, coupled with stricter break-in-service rules, attempted to provide this.
4. Generally, this includes tax-exempt universities and other similar institutions of higher education within the meaning of Code §170(b)(1)(A)(ii).
5. Code §410(a)(3)(A).
6. Hours for which an employee must be credited with an hour of service include periods (regardless of whether the employment relationship has terminated) of vacation, holiday, illness, incapacity, layoff, jury duty, military duty, or leave of absence. See 351 T.M., *Pension Plans—Qualification*, 29 C.F.R. §2530.200b-2(a).
7. 29 C.F.R. §2530.200b(a)(1). See also Code §410(a)(5)(C), which uses the vesting definition of a year of service contained in Code §411(a)(6)(A).
8. Code §410(a)(5)(C).
9. Code §410(a)(5)(E)(ii).
10. 29 C.F.R. §2530.200b-3 *et seq.*
11. 29 C.F.R. §2530.200b-3(d)(1).
12. 29 C.F.R. §2530.3(d)(2).
13. 29 C.F.R. §2530.200b-3(e)(1)(i).
14. 29 C.F.R. §2530.200b.3(e)(1)(ii).
15. 29 C.F.R. §2530.200b-3(e)(1)(iii).
16. 29 C.F.R. §2530.200b-1(e)(1)(iv).
17. 29 C.F.R. §2530.200b-3(e)(2).
18. 29 C.F.R. §2530.200b-3(f)(1).
19. See 351 T.M. (BNA), *Pension Plans—Qualification*. See also former Temp. 29 C.F.R. §2530.200b-9(a)(3)(ii). The elapsed time method regulations were issued, under IRS authority pursuant to Reorganization Plan No. 4 of 1978, which transferred jurisdiction from the Department of Labor to the Department of the Treasury. The final regulations were issued by IRS. See Treas. Regs. §1.410(a)–7(a)(3).
20. See Treas. Regs. §1.410(a)-7(a)(3)(iv).
21. See Treas. Regs. §1.410(a)-7(a)(3)(vi). Temp. Treas. Regs. §§1.410(a)-7T(a) and (b) provide special rules for applying the elapsed time method to maternity and paternity-related leaves of absence as described in post-REA §410(a)(5)(E). Under the regulations, the severance from service date of an employee who is absent from service beyond the first anniversary of his absence, or the first day of absence attributable to maternity or paternity leave, is the second anniversary of the first date of such absence. The period between the first and second anniversaries is neither a period of service nor a period of break in service.

22. *Standard Oil of California v. Comm'r*, 78 T.C. 541 (1982).
23. Code § 410(a)(4)(B), effective generally for plan years beginning after 1988. For plan years beginning before 1989, the plan need only provide 3-year 100% vesting.
24. Code § 411(a)(1).
25. Code § 410(a)(5)(D).
26. 29 C.F.R. §§ 2530.202b-2(a) and (b).
27. 29 C.F.R. § 2530.202-2(e).
28. Code §§ 410(a)(4)(A) and (B) and Treas. Regs. § 1.410(a)-4(b)(1).
29. ERISA § 203(b)(2)(C) define these industries as ones where the customary period of employment is less than 1,000 hours in a calendar year.
30. Code § 410(a)(3)(B). At this writing the Labor Department had not yet published such guidance.
31. Code § 410(a)(3)(D).
32. Code § 411(b)(1)(G).
33. Such benefits are known as Social Security supplements. Social Security supplements are an increased benefit under a qualified plan that is provided for a limited period (until the employee becomes eligible for Social Security benefits). These supplements are used to help employees retire before Social Security benefit payments begin.
34. Code § 411(b)(1)(H).
35. Code § 411(b)(1)(H)(2).
36. Code § 410(b).
37. The provisions are effective with respect to plans maintained pursuant to collective bargaining agreements ratified before March 1, 1986, as of the later of: (1) the later of January 1, 1989, or the date on which the last of such collective bargaining agreements terminates without regard to any extension after February 28, 1986; or (2) January 1, 1991. See 1986 TRA, P.L. 99-514, § 1112(e)(2).
38. Code § 410(b)(1)(A).
39. Code § 410(b)(1)(B).
40. Code § 410(b)(2).
41. Code § 410(b)(2)(B).
42. Code § 410(b)(2)(C).
43. Code §§ 410(b)(3)(A)–(C) and (b)(4). Employees excluded for failure to meet the plan's age and service requirements will not be counted for this purpose if they are covered under another plan that imposes valid age and service requirements. See § 410(b)(4)(B).
44. Code § 414(r). In general, § 414(r) requires that the line of business must be operated separately for bona fide business reasons. Section 414(r)(2) requires that, to be treated as a separate line of business, the line of business must have at least 50 employees who are not excluded under § 414(q)(8). Further, the employer must notify the IRS that the line of business is being treated as a separate line of business and the line of business must satisfy the guidelines to be established by the IRS or receive an IRS determination that the line of business may be treated separately. The statute also contains a "safe harbor" rule. If the employer satisfies the safe harbor, it need not comply with the IRS guidelines/determination requirement. The safe harbor will be met if the "highly compensated employee percentage" with respect to the line of business is not less than half, nor more than twice, the per-

centage which highly compensated employees are of all employees of the employer. For this purpose, the term "highly compensated employee percentage" means the percentage which highly compensated employees performing services for the line of business are of all employees of the employer. An employer will be treated as satisfying the "not less than half" prong of the safe harbor rule if at least 10% of all highly compensated employees of the employer perform services solely for such line of business.

45. Code § 402(b)(2).
46. Benefits under nonqualified plans, discussed at Chapter 16, are taxed under Code § 83.
47. Before the 1986 TRA, organizing a professional business such as law or accounting as a partnership with each partner owning his or her own corporation and the corporation owning the partnership interest, allowed professional employees to individually tailor their retirement plans to suit their needs.
48. Within the meaning of Code § 414(d).
49. Within the meaning of Code § 414(e).
50. September 2, 1974.
51. Exempted from tax under Code § 501(c)(8) or (9).

3

Benefit Accrual

Benefit accrual refers to the rate at which employees earn benefits under a plan. In a defined contribution plan, an employee's accrued benefit is simply his or her account balance at any point in time. In a defined benefit plan, one must look to the benefit formula to determine an employee's accrued benefit. Usually, in a defined benefit plan, an employee will accrue benefits at a specified rate for each year of service, e.g., one percent of compensation per year of service.

Sometimes for purposes of the tax law it is necessary to distinguish which part of an employee's total accrued benefit is attributable to employee contributions and which part is attributable to employer contributions.[1] Where a defined contribution plan maintains separate accounting for employee and employer contributions, making this determination is relatively easy. In a defined benefit plan, the accrued benefit attributable to employee contributions is determined by:

(1) Dividing the total of employee contributions, less withdrawals, by the total of employer contributions, less withdrawals, and

(2) multiplying the result by the employee's total accrued benefit.

The result is the employee's accrued benefit attributable to employee contributions. Whatever amount of the employee's total benefit remains is the employee's accrued benefit attributable to employer contributions.

There are two sets of accrual rules—the general rules of Code §411(b), which apply only to defined benefit plans and the "top-heavy" minimum benefit/contribution requirements of Code §416(c), which require top-heavy plans to provide certain minimum accruals to "non-key employees." The top-heavy rules apply to both defined benefit and defined contribution plans. These terms are examined in more detail below and in Chapter 6.

Code §411(b) Benefit Accrual Rules

Introduction

The Code §411(b) regular accrual rules apply to defined benefit plans, but not defined contribution plans. Section 411(b) seeks to protect rank-and-file participants in defined benefit plans from discrimination due to excessive "backloading" of plan benefits. A plan that is backloaded is one that provides low benefit accruals in an employee's early years with the employer with escalating accruals in the later years. Since highly compensated employees generally tend to remain with the employer longer, delaying benefit accrual to the later years can disproportionately benefit the highly paid. This potential usually does not exist in defined contribution plans which generally allocate the employer's annual contribution to the accounts of employees based on a specified percentage of each employee's compensation for the year. The benefit formulas in defined benefit plans, however, tend to be geared to the length of an employee's service with the employer. As a result, to qualify under Code §401(a), a defined benefit plan must satisfy one of three §411(b) accrual rules designed to prevent excessive backloading. A plan cannot qualify by satisfying one rule one year and another the next, but must satisfy one rule over all plan years for all plan participants. The three rules are:

(1) The 3% method;

(2) The 133⅓% method; and

(3) The fractional method.

The Three Methods

The 3% Method

A defined benefit plan satisfies the 3% method if the accrued benefit to which a participant is entitled upon separation from service is not less than:

(1) 3 percent of the normal retirement benefit to which the participant would be entitled if he or she began participation at the earliest possible entry age under the plan (where there is no minimum age requirement, the earliest possible entry age is deemed to be zero) and worked continuously until the earlier of age 65 or the plan's normal retirement age, multiplied by

(2) the number of years (not to exceed 33⅓) of the individual's participation in the plan.[2]

Basically, the 3% method takes the maximum benefit that a participant could accrue if he or she entered the plan at the plan's earliest possible entry age and remained in the employer's service until the earlier of age 65 or the plan's normal retirement age. For example, if a plan had an entry age of 20 and a normal retirement age of 60, the rule would have to be tested over a theoretical working career that spanned this period. Since the rule requires that only 33⅓ years be counted, however, only the first 33⅓ years would be taken into account. To pass this test, the plan must be able to satisfy the 3% test at any point in time with respect to any theoretical participant. Thus, for example, after six years of service, a participant would have to have accrued at least 18% of his or her normal retirement benefit, after seven years, at least 21 percent, and so on.

In applying the 3% test, possible future adjustments to the plan's benefit formula, such as a change in Social Security benefits (in the case of an integrated plan) and changes in the consumer price index (in the case of a plan that is indexed to the CPI) are ignored. These benefits are treated as remaining constant from the year being tested to all future years. Further, if the plan provides a benefit that is based on compensation, the number of years of compensation that is considered in applying the 3% method cannot exceed the 10 consecutive years in a participant's career for which his or her compensation was the highest.[3] This prevents a plan from reducing the benefit to which a participant is entitled by considering only compensation from the participant's early (low compensation) years of service. The example below illustrates the application of the 3% method:

> *Example (1):* Defined benefit plan H has an entry age of 20 and a normal retirement age of 60. Under the plan, a participant accrues a benefit equal to 1.25% of compensation for the first 15 years of service. In years 16–30, the annual accrual increases to 1.5% of compensation. After the 30th year, the participant accrues benefits at the rate of 1.75% of compensation per year. The following computational steps show why this plan would fail the 3% test:
>
> *Step (1): Determine the Normal Retirement Benefit for Purposes of the 3% Test:*

(1.25% × 15 years =)	18.75%	
+ (1.50% × 15 years =)	22.50%	
+ (1.75% × 3⅓ years =)	5.83%[4]	
	47.08%	= (normal retirement benefit for purposes of the 3% test)

> *Step (2): Multiply the Result of Step (1) by 3% and Compare With Plan's Benefit Formula:*

$$47.08\% \times .03 = 1.41\%$$

Because the plan fails to provide a benefit of at least 1.41% of compensation in years before the 15th year, it will fail the 3% test. If the plan had provided a benefit of at least 1.41% of compensation in all possible years during the first 33⅓ years, it would have passed the test. Note that the normal retirement benefit for purposes of this test, 47.08% of compensation, is less than the normal retirement benefit that a participant could accrue under the plan if he started at the earliest entry age, 20, and worked until normal retirement age, age 60, because only the first 33⅓ years are considered.

The 133⅓% Method

The 133⅓% rule compares all earlier years of a participant's participation in a plan to all subsequent years to limit excessive backloading. Under this method, a plan must satisfy two requirements:

(1) The plan's accrued benefit at normal retirement age must equal the plan's normal retirement benefit; and

(2) The annual rate at which any individual who is, or could be, a participant can accrue retirement benefits payable at normal retirement age must not be more than 133⅓% of the annual rate at which the individual can accrue benefits in any prior plan year.[5]

Thus, under this test, when a plan's accrual rate increases in a later year, that rate must be compared with all prior years of a participant's participation to see whether the benefit a participant accrued in the later year is more than 133⅓% of the benefit in any earlier year. This general rule is subject to certain caveats. These are:

(1) Any plan amendment that is in effect for the current year is treated as having been in effect for all other plan years.[6]

This rule prevents the prohibition on excessive backloading from impeding plans from granting benefit increases. For instance, if an amendment were passed in plan year 15, increasing prospectively the benefit of all participants by .5% of compensation per year, this amendment would be treated as having been in effect for all prior plan years. Thus, for planning purposes, some effective level of backloading may be obtained by waiting until a future year (before highly paid employees will retire) to increase benefits, as this increase will be "grandfathered," *i.e.*, treated as if it had been in effect for all prior plan years, for purposes of the 133⅓% test.

(2) The fact that benefits under the plan may be payable to certain employees before normal retirement age is disregarded.[7]

This rule allows a plan to ignore such benefits as early retirement, disability, and death benefits in applying the test. It is intended to avoid discouraging employers from providing these benefits.

(3) Any change in a plan's accrual rate that does not apply to any individual who is or could be a participant in the current year is disregarded.[8]

Under this rule, for example, an amendment retroactively increasing the accrual rate for 1988 could not affect the application of the test for 1990 if no participant in the plan in 1990 had been covered in 1988.

(4) Social Security, compensation, and all other factors used in computing benefits are treated as remaining constant in all future years.[9]

Under the 133⅓% method, as under the 3% method, deeming compensation to remain constant can result in backloading due to increases in compensation in the later years of an employee's career. The following example illustrates the application of the 133⅓% method:

> *Example (2):* Assume the same facts as in Example (1), above, i.e., accruals at a rate of 1.25% for the first 15 years, 1.5% for the next 15, and 1.75% thereafter. Testing the highest possible accrual year against all earlier years will show that the plan, as drafted, would fail the 133⅓% test. This is so because 1.25% × 1.33 = 1.66%, and the plan provides for accruals at a level higher than 1.66% of compensation in years 30 and thereafter. If the plan provided a benefit in those years of 1.66% of compensation or less, it would pass the test. Note that, if the plan started out by providing 1.25% for the first 15 years and 1.5% thereafter, but later was amended to provide the benefit structure described above, the amendment increasing benefits would be treated as if it were in effect for all prior years and the plan would pass the test.

The Fractional Method

Under the fractional method, the annual benefit to which a participant is entitled upon separation from service before normal retirement age must be at least a ratable share of the benefit to which the individual would have been entitled under the plan had he or she worked until normal retirement age. The test considers the number of years of an employee's participation relative to the total years the employee would have participated if not for the pre-normal retirement age separation from service.[10]

Thus, for example, an employee who began working 40 years before normal retirement age, worked 10 years and then left would have to be given a benefit of at least 10/40 (25 percent) of his or her normal retirement benefit under the plan. Again, compensation is assumed to remain constant in applying the test. Further, if average compensation, rather than actual compensation, is used by the plan to determine benefits, the number of years averaged cannot exceed the 10 years of service immediately preceding the employee's separation from service. This latter rule prevents back-loading by considering only the earliest years of an employee's career (presumably also the lowest paid years). For purposes of this test, Social Security and all other factors used to determine benefits are assumed to remain constant for all future years.

The following example illustrates the application of the fractional rule.

> *Example (3):* Assume the same facts as in Examples (1) and (2), i.e., 1.25% accruals in years 1–15, 1.5% in years 16–30, and 1.75% thereafter. This plan would fail the fractional test. Consider employee A who separated from service after 10 years and who began work for the employer at age 20 (remember, normal retirement age is 60 under the plan). A should, for the plan to pass the test, be entitled to 10/40, or 25% of A's normal retirement benefit at separation from service. Instead, A will only have earned 21.3% of this amount. Note that, in making this calculation, all 40 possible years of an employee's career are considered, as opposed to the 3% method, which only considers the first 33⅓ years. This can result in the normal retirement benefit being different for purposes of this test than for purposes of the 3% test. This will be the case whenever it is possible for an employee entering the employer's service at the earliest possible entry age under the plan to be more than 33⅓ years away from normal retirement age. Where this is not the case, the normal retirement benefit for purposes of both tests is the same. In this example, the fractional rule calculation is:

Step (1): Determine the Normal Retirement Benefit:

$$
\begin{array}{lr}
 & (1.25\% \times 15 \text{ years} =)\ 18.75\% \\
+ & (1.50\% \times 15 \text{ years} =)\ 22.50\% \\
+ & (1.75\% \times 10 \text{ years} =)\ 17.50\% \\
\hline
 & 58.75\%
\end{array}
$$

Step (2): Determine the Employee's Benefit at Separation From Service as a Percentage of the Normal Retirement Benefit:

12.50% (benefit after 10 years) ÷ 58.75%
(benefit after 40 years) = 21.30%

Step (3): Determine the Ratable Amount of the Normal Retirement Benefit to Which the Employee Would Be Entitled Based on Years of Service at Separation:

$$58.75\% \times .25 = 14.69\%$$

The benefit at this point in A's career is less than the required benefit under the fractional rule, i.e., 25%. Therefore, the plan fails the fractional test.

Note that the plan in examples (1)–(3) failed all three tests. Therefore, it would not qualify under §401(a).

Rev. Rul. 81-11 shows how the IRS will calculate the lowest accrued benefit that will satisfy the fractional rule for participants who continue participation following an accrual computation period in which they complete less than a full year of accrual service.[11] Under this method, the participant's accrued benefit at any time equals the "fractional rule benefit" multiplied by an "accrual ratio." The fractional rule benefit is the benefit to which the participant would be entitled if he or she continued to earn annually, until his or her normal retirement date, the same rate of compensation upon which the employee's normal retirement benefit would be computed. The accrual ratio is the sum of:

(1) The prior accrual ratio at the end of the last accrual computation period (N) in which the participant did not earn a full year of service, and

(2) The product of
  (a) one minus the prior accrual ratio determined under (1) above, and
  (b) a fraction equal to the number of years of participation subsequent to N, divided by the number of years of participation the participant would have earned after N if he or she separated from service at normal retirement age.

Rev. Rul. 81-11 also furnishes an alternative method for computing the accrual ratio which yields an accrued benefit slightly greater than the lowest accrued benefit. Under this method, a participant's accrual ratio in years following an accrual computation period in which a full year of accrual service was not earned is a fraction. The numerator is the number of credited years of participation (including partial years). The denominator is the sum of the numerator as of the end of the prior accrual computation period and the number of years from such time to normal retirement age.

Special Rules

Accrued Benefit May Not Decrease on Account of Increasing Age or Service

Even if a plan passes one of the three tests, it will not qualify if it decreases a participant's accrued benefit on account of increasing age or service.[12] Further, a qualified plan may not exclude an employee from participation on account of being hired too close to normal retirement age. Before the Omnibus Budget Reconciliation Act of 1986 (OBRA (1986))[13] defined benefit plans could exclude an employee from participation (and, hence, benefit accrual) if the employee was within five years of the plan's normal retirement age when hired. Effective generally for plan years beginning after 1988, however, OBRA (1986) added Code §411(b)(1)(H), providing that an employee's benefit under a defined benefit plan may not be discontinued or reduced in rate because the employee has attained a specified age.[14]

A defined contribution plan will satisfy this requirement if allocations to employees' accounts are not ceased or reduced by virtue of the employee's attainment of a specified age. For this purpose, any subsidized portion of an early retirement benefit may be disregarded.[15] This presumably means that plans still may provide through Social Security supplements a higher level of benefits to retirees before their Social Security benefits commence and then decrease the level of benefit payments by the amount of Social Security to which the retirees are entitled once they begin to receive Social Security. Social Security supplements allow employees to retire before they become eligible for Social Security by providing an additional benefit equal to the benefit to which they will become entitled under Social Security when they reach Social Security retirement age. The supplement terminates when Social Security benefits begin.[16]

The application of this provision to collectively bargained plans is to be determined under Treasury regulations.

Notwithstanding OBRA (1986), a defined benefit plan may impose, without regard to age, a limit on the amount of benefits that the plan provides or a limit on the number of years of service or years of participation that are taken into account in determining benefit accrual. OBRA (1986) also amended the Code to provide that, when a participant begins participation within five years of normal retirement age, the participant's normal retirement age will be deemed to be the fifth anniversary of his or her commencement of participation.[17] This latter amendment applies to plan years beginning after January 1, 1988, but only with respect to service performed on or after that date.

Note that, if a plan has to be amended to comply with the above OBRA (1986) amendments, the plan amendment must be made before the first plan year beginning after 1988 if:

(1) During the period after the amendment takes effect and before the first plan year after 1988, the plan is operated in accordance with such amendment, and

(2) The amendment applies retroactively to the period after the amendment takes effect and such first plan year.

A plan will not fail to provide definitely determinable benefits or to be operated in accordance with its terms (as required by ERISA) merely because it operates in accordance with this provision.[18]

Rules Relating to Years of Service

A plan will not fail to satisfy the accrual rules merely because it provides that an employee must have two continuous, (i.e., not separated by a break in service) years of service with the employer before being entitled to accrue benefits.[19]

A year of service for accrual purposes is defined as a 12-consecutive month computation period in which the employee completes 1,000 hours of service or such lesser amount as the plan provides, after the employee has been admitted to participation.[20] Part-time employees must be given a proportionate amount of the accruals to which they would have been entitled had they worked full-time.[21] This however, does not prevent a plan from not counting as a year of service any 12-month computation period during which an employee performs less than 1,000 hours of service.[22]

In general, a year of service for accrual purposes is the same as for participation purposes—it may be any 12-consecutive month period selected by the plan in which an employee earns 1,000 hours of service. Where the plan's participation computation period is different than its accrual computation period, however, an employee, once admitted to participation, must accrue benefits retroactive to his admission date. This means that, if a plan has a one-year participation hold-out rule for former employees who return to work for the employer, such an employee will have to be given retroactive accrual credit for the hold-out year once he or she is re-admitted to participation.

A plan, if it so provides, may require employees to perform 2,000 hours of service in a 12-month computation period before crediting them with a full year of service for accrual purposes, provided it calls for at least ratable benefit accrual for any employee who completes less than 2,000, but more than 1,000, hours of accrual service.[23] Where the plan's method of crediting service for accrual purposes has the effect, however, of prorating benefits to reflect less than full-time service or less than maximum compensation, such as a benefit that is based on a percentage of average compensation times years of participation, the plan may not reduce accruals by crediting less than full years of participation, as this would result in double proration (once for only earning compensation for part of a year and again for failing to accrue a full year of service during the computation period).[24] A plan may use any of the equivalencies approved by the Labor Department for counting service for participation purposes in determining accrual service. Further, a plan need not use the same equivalency for accrual purposes that it uses for participation or vesting.[25]

A plan may change its accrual computation period by plan amendment so long as participants receive at least a partial year of credit for any partial accrual computation periods resulting from the amendment.[26]

Seasonal and Maritime Industry Rules

For employees employed in a seasonal industry, the plan may provide that a year of service will be determined according to Labor Department regulations. For this purpose, a seasonal industry is one in which employees customarily perform less than 1,000 hours of service in a calendar year.[27]

For the maritime industry, 125 days of service in a calendar year is treated as a year of service for accrual purposes.[28]

Special Rule for Defined Benefit Plans Providing for Employee Contributions

A defined benefit plan that provides a benefit derived from employee contributions which is based on a participant's separate account will:

(1) For purposes of Code §410 (relating to minimum participation standards) be treated as a defined contribution plan, and

(2) For purposes of Code §411(a)(7)(A) (defining the term "accrued benefit" for purposes of the accrual rules) be treated as consisting of a defined contribution plan to the extent benefits are based on the separate account and as a defined benefit plan as to any remaining benefits.[29]

The IRS applied this rule to a plan funded with a participating deferred annuity contract in Rev. Rul. 79-259 and concluded that the plan was not entitled to be treated as part of a defined contribution plan for accrual purposes.[30]

Other Special Accrual Rules

Two other special accrual rules deserve mention. First, the Code exempts certain insured defined benefit plans from having to satisfy one of the Code §411(b) benefit accrual methods.[31] To qualify for this exemption, the plan must be funded exclusively through the purchase of insurance contracts and must satisfy the requirements of Code §§412(i)(2)–(3) concerning the funding of certain insurance contract plans. The exception only applies if, under the plan, an employee's benefit at any point in time would not be less than the cash surrender value of the insurance policy.[32]

Second, the Code provides that the general accrual tests do not apply to pre-ERISA years of service if the accrued benefit of any participant for such years is not less than the greater of:

(1) The participant's pre-ERISA accrued benefit; or

(2) Half the amount that would have been required under the three tests if they had applied to pre-ERISA years.[33]

Top-Heavy Minimum Contribution and Benefit Accrual Rules

For plan years beginning after 1983, Code §416(c) requires that certain minimum contributions (in the case of a defined contribution plan) or minimum benefits (in the case of a defined benefit plan) be provided to all non-key employees for any year for which the plan is top-heavy.[34] In a defined benefit plan, for any top-heavy plan year, each non-key employee must be credited with an accrued benefit attributable to employer contributions equal to the "applicable percentage" multiplied by the participant's average compensation during the statutory "testing period" which is the average of the participant's highest five consecutive top-heavy plan years.[35]

The applicable percentage is the lesser of:

(1) 2 percent multiplied by the participant's number of years of service with the employer; or

(2) 20 percent.[36]

Thus, the total minimum accrued benefit, in general, that must be given to a non-key employee participant for all top-heavy plan years cannot exceed 20% of such participant's average compensation for the testing period.

The defined contribution plan minimum contribution for a top-heavy plan year is 3 percent of compensation unless the key employee who receives the highest contribution expressed as a percentage of compensation receives less than 3 percent, in which case each non-key employee must receive the same percentage of compensation as that key employee.

Note that, in a defined benefit plan, the fact that the top minimum benefit that must be provided to a non-key employee is 20 percent of average testing period compensation does not mean that, after an employee has 10 top-heavy years of service and corresponding benefit accruals, the employer's cost of funding minimum benefits for that employee will terminate. Rather, because testing period compensation is a floating five-year average, increases in compensation in a future top-heavy plan year may trigger further funding obligations. This extra funding obligation does not apply to a defined contribution plan, where minimum accruals are determined solely as a percentage of compensation accrued in the current top-heavy plan year. This can be a significant advantage of choosing to provide minimum contributions under defined contribution plans, rather than under defined benefit plans, whenever possible. How this may be done where an employee is covered under both a top-heavy defined contribution and defined benefit plan of the same employer is discussed below. In extreme cases, the prohibitive cost of providing defined benefit plan minimum benefits has forced employers sponsoring such plans to terminate them and replace them with defined contribution plans.[37]

The years of service in the testing period for a defined benefit plan need not be consecutive calendar years; they are the consecutive years for which the plan is top-heavy.[38] Thus, if the plan was top-heavy in 1984 and 1986–90 but not in 1985, the years in the testing period would consist of the years 1984 and 1986–90, but not 1985. Plan years beginning before 1984 (the first year to which the top-heavy rules applied) are not included in the testing period.[39]

For purposes of the minimum contribution/benefit requirement of Code §416, the vesting rules of Code §§411(a)(4)–(6) will control.[40] Thus a plan, if it so provides, can disregard:

(1) Service rendered before age 18;[41]

(2) Service for years for which the employee declined to make contributions to a contributory plan;[42]

(3) Years of service for which the employer did not maintain the plan or the plan of a predecessor employer;[43]

(4) Service not required to be taken into account under the vesting break-in-service rules of §411(a)(6);[44]

(5) Pre-1971 service where the employee did not complete three years of service after 1970;[45]

(6) Years of service that would not have needed to be counted under the pre-ERISA vesting rules;[46] and

(7) Certain post-withdrawal or post-termination service under a multiemployer plan.[47]

Where an employer maintains a defined benefit plan and a defined contribution plan covering the same employees, only one plan need provide for Code §416(c) minimum accruals even if both are top-heavy. Since the vesting rules apply in crediting service for minimum contribution/benefit purposes, in a defined benefit plan, service would have to be credited for minimum accrual purposes retroactive to the date an employee first became a participant.

Thus, for instance, if a plan held an employee out of participation for two years, as the law allows, and, in the third year he or she became eligible for minimum benefits under the employer's defined benefit plan, the employee would, at that time, have to be immediately credited with three years of accruals, i.e., 6 percent of testing period compensation.[48] If the employer elected instead to make minimum contributions under the defined contribution plan, this would be calculated on a year-by-year basis.[49]

As previously indicated, however, the defined contribution plan minimum contribution for a top-heavy plan year is 3 percent of compensation unless the key employee who receives the highest contribution expressed as a percentage of compensation receives less than 3 percent, in which case each non-key employee must receive the same percentage of compensation as that key employee. In most cases, this will be less expensive than providing the minimum benefit under a defined benefit plan, since minimum contributions to defined contribution plans do not retroactively credit prior service. A target benefit plan is treated as a defined contribution plan for purposes of the top-heavy rules.[50]

For top-heavy purposes, compensation has the meaning given that term by Code §415 and—as is the case for all other qualified plan purposes—no more than $200,000 of compensation may be taken into account.

All employees who are participants in a top-heavy defined contribution plan who have not separated from service by the end of the plan year must receive the defined contribution minimum (unless otherwise provided under the safe harbors for multiple top-heavy plans of the same employer discussed below). Non-key employees who have become participants but who subsequently fail to complete 1,000 hours of service (or the equivalent) for an accrual computation period must receive the minimum. A defined contribution plan cannot fail to provide non-key employees with minimum accruals because:

(1) The employee is excluded from participation (or accrues no benefit) merely because the employee's compensation is less than a stated amount; or

(2) The employee is excluded from participation (or accrues no benefit) merely because of a failure to make mandatory employee contributions or, in the case of a §401(k) plan, elective contributions.[51]

In a top-heavy defined benefit plan, each non-key employee who has at least 1,000 hours of service (or the equivalent under Labor Department regulations)[52] for an accrual computation period must accrue minimum benefits for that period. If the accrual computation period is different than the plan year, a minimum benefit must be provided, if required, for both accrual periods within the top-heavy plan year. If a top-heavy defined benefit plan does not base accruals on accrual computation periods, service must be credited for all periods of service that must be counted for purposes of benefit accrual.[53] A non-key employee may not be denied a minimum benefit in a top-heavy defined benefit plan because either:

(1) The employee is excluded from participation (or accrues no benefit); or

(2) The employee is excluded from participation (or accrues no benefit) merely because the employee does not make mandatory employee contributions.[54]

Neither the defined contribution nor the defined benefit minimum may be integrated with Social Security.[55]

Same Non-Key Employee Covered Under Both Top-Heavy Defined Contribution and Defined Benefit Plans

Code §416(f) provides for regulations to be promulgated to prevent duplication of minimum contributions/benefits where a non-key employee is covered by both a defined benefit plan and a defined contribution plan of the same employer and both plans are top-heavy for the plan year. The regulations provide four alternative safe harbors that a plan may use in determining which minimum benefit must be provided to a non-key employee in this situation.

Under the first safe harbor, since minimum benefits under a defined benefit plan are generally more valuable than minimum contributions under a defined contribution plan, providing the employee with the defined benefit plan minimum will satisfy Code §416(c).

The second safe harbor uses a "floor offset" approach.[56] Under this approach, the minimum benefit would be provided in the defined benefit plan but would be offset by any benefits provided under the defined contribution plan.

The third safe harbor uses a comparability analysis set forth in Rev. Rul. 81-202.[57] If the plan can prove, using such an analysis, that the defined contribution plan is providing benefits at least equal to the defined benefit plan minimum, the plans will satisfy Code §416(c).

Under the fourth approach, which avoids the complexity of the other approaches, a safe harbor minimum contribution of 5 percent of compensation for each non-key employee to the defined contribution plan for each plan year the plan is top-heavy will be presumed to satisfy Code §416.[58]

Where one of the safe harbor methods is used, an employer may not use a different method each year to satisfy Code §416 unless the plan is amended to reflect the change.[59]

Where a non-key employee is covered by both a top-heavy defined benefit and a top-heavy defined contribution plan, and the employer wishes to use a factor of 1.25 in computing the denominators of the defined contribution and defined benefit plan fractions under Code §415(e), the employer may use the above safe harbor rules, subject to certain modifications. These are:

(1) The defined benefit plan minimum benefit must be increased by one percentage point of the participant's average compensation for the year up to a maximum of 10 percentage points—i.e., to 3 percent per year not to exceed 30 percent of testing period compensation for each year of service that must be counted for top-heavy minimum benefit purposes.[60]

(2) The defined contribution plan minimum is increased to 4 percent of compensation.[61]

(3) If the floor offset or comparability analysis approach is used, the defined benefit minimum must be increased by one percentage point (up to a maximum of 10 percentage points), as described in (1), above.[62]

If the employer maintains two top-heavy defined contribution plans, if one provides the defined contribution minimum for each non-key employee who participates in both plans, the other plan need not provide any additional contributions for such employees. The other plan, however, must provide top-heavy accelerated vesting in conformity with Code §416(b).[63]

Insurance Contract Plans

The regulations provide special rules for determining the required minimum benefit under a plan funded exclusively with level premium insurance contracts within the meaning of Code §412(i).[64]

The regulations note that the non-key employee's accrued benefits under such a plan may fail to provide a benefit that satisfies the defined benefit minimum because of the lower cash values in early years under most level premium contracts and because such contracts usually provide for level payments until normal retirement age. The regulations provide, however, that a plan will not violate §412(i) merely because it funds certain benefits through either an auxiliary fund or deferred annuity contracts if the following conditions are satisfied:

(1) The targeted normal retirement benefit under the contract takes into account the defined benefit minimum that would be required assuming the current top-heavy (or non-top-heavy) status of the plan continues until normal retirement age; and

(2) The benefits provided by the auxiliary fund or deferred annuity contracts do not exceed the excess of the defined benefit minimum benefits over the benefits provided by the level premium insurance contract.

If these conditions are satisfied, the plan will continue to be exempt from the Code §412 minimum funding requirements and may still use the special accrual rule of Code §411(b)(1)(F), subject to the following modifications:

(1) Although the portion of the plan funded by the level premium annuity contract is exempt from the minimum funding requirements, the part funded with the auxiliary fund is subject to the minimum funding rules;[65] and

(2) The accrued benefit for any participant may be determined

under Code §411(b)(1)(F), but must not be less than the defined benefit minimum.[66]

Special Rules

Employee Pay-All Defined Benefit Plans

The defined benefit plan minimum benefit in an employee pay-all plan is the same as that for a plan that has employer contributions.[67]

Waiver of Minimum Funding Standard for a Defined Contribution Plan

Where the IRS waives the application of the minimum funding standard for a defined contribution plan that is subject to the standard, such as a money purchase plan, the waiver will not apply to the employer's obligation to provide minimum benefits for any top-heavy plan year. The regulations provide that, where the minimum funding standard is waived for such a plan, the minimum benefit that must be provided is the benefit that the plan would have had to provide if not for the waiver (i.e., the plan cannot take advantage of the rule that allows the employer to contribute a lesser amount if no key employee received 3 percent of pay for the year solely because no contributions were required due to the waiver).[68]

Notes

1. For instance, the characterization of a benefit as attributable to either employer or employee contributions has implications when applying the vesting rules. An employee must always be 100% vested in his or her accrued benefit attributable to employee contributions. Accrued benefits attributable to employer contributions may vest less rapidly.
2. Code §411(b)(1)(A).
3. Code §411(b)(1)(A) (flush language).
4. Remember that the 3% method only counts 33⅓ years; therefore subsequent years, i.e., years from age 53 to age 60, are ignored.
5. Code §411(b)(1)(B).
6. Code §411(b)(1)(B)(i).
7. Code §411(b)(1)(B)(iii).
8. Code §411(b)(1)(B)(ii).
9. Code §411(b)(1)(B)(iv).
10. Code §411(b)(1)(C).

11. 1981-1 C.B. 227.
12. Code §411(b)(1)(G).
13. P.L. 99-509.
14. In the case of benefits accrued under a plan maintained pursuant to a collective bargaining agreement, the effective date is either:
    (1) the later of (a) January 1, 1988, or (b) the date on which the last of such collective bargaining agreements terminate determined without regard to any extension thereof after February 28, 1986, *or*
    (2) January 1, 1989,
    whichever is earlier.
15. Code §411(b)(2).
16. Social Security supplements are not to be confused with Social Security integration, discussed in Chapter 10. A Social Security supplement is a benefit that is provided for a limited period *in addition to* the normal plan benefit. As a plan drafting technique, the provision of Social Security supplements may become of increasing importance where the employer wishes to encourage early retirement because the 1983 Social Security Amendments Act increased the normal retirement age under Social Security. Encouraging early retirement through the provision of Social Security supplements can help an employer accomplish a reduction in force (RIF) through attrition rather than through discharge.
17. See Code §411(a)(8).
18. OBRA (1986), P.L. 99-509, §9204.
19. Code §411(b)(1)(E); Treas. Regs. §1.411(b)-1(d)(1).
20. Code § 411(b)(3)(A).
21. Code §411(b)(3)(B).
22. Code §411(b)(3)(C).
23. 29 C.F.R. §§2530.200b-1(a) and .204-2(c)(1) and (2).
24. 29 C.F.R. §2530.204-2(d).
25. See 29 C.F.R. §§2530.200–204.
26. 29 C.F.R. §2530.204-2(e).
27. Code §411(b)(3)(D).
28. Code §411(b)(3)(E).
29. Code §414(k).
30. 1979-2 C.B. 197.
31. Code §411(d)(1)(F).
32. Under Code §§412(i)(4)–(6).
33. Code §411(b)(1)(D).
34. Top-heavy plans are qualified plans in which more than 60% of the benefits or contributions go to certain highly paid individuals and owners of the employer who are collectively known as "key employees." The top-heavy rules are examined in Chapter 6.
35. Code §416(c)(1)(A).
36. Code §416(c)(1)(B).
37. Of course, in such a decision, other factors must be considered. For example, the termination of a defined benefit plan (either outright or by amending it to convert it into an individual account plan) requires full and immediate vesting in all accrued benefits attributable to employer contributions. Where there are substantial nonvested amounts, this could prove costly. The defined benefit plan minimum benefit is a benefit payable annually in the form of a

straight life annuity (with no ancillary benefits) commencing at the normal retirement age under the plan. If the form of the benefit provided under the plan is other than a single life annuity, the employee must receive an amount that is the actuarial equivalent of the minimum single life annuity benefit. If the benefit commences at a date other than normal retirement age, the employee must receive at least an amount that is the actuarial equivalent of the minimum single life annuity benefit commencing at normal retirement age. Thus, an employee may receive a lower benefit if benefit payments begin before normal retirement age. If benefits start after normal retirement age, the employee must receive a higher benefit. Treas. Regs. §1.416-1, Q&A M-3. See also H.R. Rep. 760, 97th Cong., 2d Sess. 629 (1982).

38. Code §416(c)(1)(C)(ii). See Treas. Regs. §1.416-1, Q&A M-2. The regulations further provide that, for this purpose, years of service in which the employee did not earn a year of service under §§411(a)(4), (5), and (6) are to be disregarded.
39. Code §416(c)(1)(C)(iii).
40. Code §416(c)(1)(C)(i).
41. Code §411(a)(4)(A).
42. Code §411(a)(4)(B).
43. Code §411(a)(6)(C).
44. Code §411(a)(6)(D).
45. Code §411(a)(6)(E).
46. Code §411(a)(6)(F).
47. Code §411(a)(6)(G).
48. See H.R. REP. NO. 760, 97th Cong., 2d Sess. 620 (1982).
49. Under Code §416(c)(2).
50. Treas. Regs. §1.416-1, Q&A M-15.
51. *Id.* at Q&A M-10.
52. 29 C.F.R. §2530.200b-3.
53. See Treas. Regs. §1.410(a)(7).
54. *Id.*
55. *Id.* at Q&A M-11. Social Security integration is a method whereby benefits under qualified plans may be reduced to take into account employees' Social Security benefits. It is discussed in Chapter 9.
56. See Rev. Rul. 76-259, 1976-2 C.B. 111.
57. 1981-2 C.B. 93.
58. Treas. Regs. §1.416-1, Q&A M-12.
59. Treas. Regs. §1.416-1, Q&A M-15.
60. Treas. Regs. §1.416-1, Q&A M-2.
61. *Id.* at Q&A M-14.
62. *Id.*
63. *Id.* at Q&A M-8.
64. *Id.* at Q&A M-17.
65. *Id.* The regulations note that this means that such a plan would have to set up a funding standard account and file a Schedule B to IRS Form 5500 with respect to the portion of the plan that is subject to Code §412.
66. *Id.*
67. *Id.* at Q&A M-7.
68. *Id.* at Q&A M-9.

4

Vesting Rules

When a participant attains a nonforfeitable right to part or all of his or her accrued benefit in a qualified plan, the participant is said to be "vested" in the nonforfeitable amount. A participant in a Code §401(a) plan must, at all times, have a 100 percent vested right to accrued benefits attributable to his or her own contributions, whether voluntary or mandatory.[1] Further, if an employee continues in an employer's service until normal retirement age, the plan must vest the participant 100 percent in any accrued benefits attributable to employer contributions at that time, regardless of what percentage of vesting the participant had attained beforehand.[2]

For this purpose, normal retirement age is the earlier of:

(1) The time a participant attains normal retirement age under the plan; or

(2) The latest of—(a) the participant's 65th birthday; (b) in the case of a participant who begins participation within five years of the plan's normal retirement age, the fifth anniversary of the commencement of participation; or (c) in the case of any participant not described in (b), the tenth anniversary of the participant's commencement of participation.[3]

The benefit that must vest in the participant is his or her "normal retirement benefit." For this purpose, the normal retirement benefit is the greater of the early retirement benefit under the plan, or the benefit under the plan commencing at normal retirement age.[4] Thus, where a plan's nominal "early retirement benefit" is greater than the purported normal retirement benefit, the early retirement benefit is deemed to be the normal retirement benefit for this purpose. Since, under Code §411(b), a plan cannot reduce a participant's accrued benefit on account of age or length-of-service, for all practical purposes, the normal retirement benefit will be the benefit denominated as such because it will at least equal the early retirement benefit.[5] The normal retirement benefit generally includes all benefits payable at normal retirement age, but does not include plan medical benefits and disability benefits provided such benefits do not exceed the plan's qualified disability benefit.[6]

There are two sets of vesting rules. The first is a set of rules imposed by Code §411(a). The second set is the top-heavy vesting rules of Code §416(b), which, for any top-heavy plan year, supersede the §411 rules and provide for more rapid vesting. Both sets of rules apply to defined benefit and defined contribution plans.

Code §411(a) Rules

Under Code §411(a), a plan must provide a schedule under which a participant who separates from the employer's service before normal retirement age will vest in his or her accrued normal retirement benefit attributable to employer contributions that is at least as liberal as one of the statutory vesting schedules.[7] Even if a plan meets the §411(a) requirements for a non-top-heavy plan year, it is not an absolute guarantee that the plan's method of vesting will qualify. This can occur where the vesting schedule, despite literal compliance with the statute, has the effect of producing a discriminatory pattern of forfeitures.

Effective for plan years beginning after 1988, the 1986 Tax Reform Act revised the Code §411 vesting rules. Because of the potential applicability of the pre-1986 TRA rules to open taxable years and because of their historical significance, this section discusses both the pre- and post-1986 TRA rules. To qualify, a Code §401(a) plan must provide vesting that is at least as rapid as is provided under one of the statutory schedules in §411(a) for any non-top-heavy plan year. A plan cannot satisfy a schedule by falling behind its requirements in one year and then making it up in a future year. Further, a qualified plan cannot satisfy one schedule in one year and another in a subsequent year; it must satisfy the same statutory schedule in all years. The 1986 TRA did not modify the top-heavy vesting schedules of Code §416.

Code §411 "Regular" Vesting Schedule

"Cliff" Vesting

Under pre-1986 TRA law, a non-top-heavy plan could satisfy §411(a) by providing for "10-year cliff vesting." This schedule derived its name from the tendency, before ERISA, of certain employers to push employees off the employment "cliff" by terminating their employment just before they became vested. Pre-ERISA plans provided for 20 and sometimes even 30-year cliff vesting. Under ERISA as originally enacted, plans were no longer permitted to be more restrictive than 10-year cliff vesting. Under 10-year cliff vesting, an employee would not be entitled to any vesting before completing 10 years of service. In the tenth year, the employer would have to vest the employee 100 percent in his or her accrued normal retirement benefit attributable to employer contributions.

Effective generally for plan years beginning after 1988, the 1986 TRA replaced 10-year cliff vesting with five-year cliff vesting. Multiemployer plans are subject to special effective-date rules and may retain 10-year cliff vesting for employees who have completed at least 10 years of service.[8] The 1986 TRA vesting amendments do not apply to participants who do not have one year of service after the effective date of the Act's amendments.

As can be seen, the potential for forfeitures where cliff vesting is employed is great. Cliff vesting is therefore generally not advisable where sharp distinctions between the length of the average career of rank-and-file employees and of members of the prohibited group may result in a disproportionate number of rank-and-file employees failing to vest. Cliff vesting is most likely to cause discrimination problems for small closely held corporations where the potential for forfeiture is extreme based on the demographics of the covered group. Cliff vesting, however, is attractive to many employers because it is the least expensive regular vesting schedule. In addition to considering the potential for discrimination in operation where cliff vesting is employed, however, employers need to take into account the possibility that cliff vesting will result in a plan becoming top-heavy, triggering faster vesting and the application of the Code §416 minimum benefit requirements.[9]

"Graded" Vesting

The second permissible regular vesting schedule is "graded" vesting. Before the 1986 TRA, 5-to-15 year graded vesting was permitted. Under this schedule employers were required to grant 25 percent vesting after five years of service. Vesting then increased in five percent annual increments in years six through 10 to the point where, after 10 years, a participant was 50 percent vested. It then increased in 10 percent annual increments in years 11 through 15, so that, after 15 years, an employee was 100 percent vested.

Effective generally for plan years beginning after 1988 (subject to a special delayed effective date for collectively bargained plans), the 1986 TRA replaced 5-to-15 year graded vesting with seven-year graded vesting. Under seven-year graded vesting, a plan must provide at least 20 percent vesting after three years, 40 percent after four, 60 percent after five, 80 percent after six and 100 percent after seven years.

The potential for discrimination in operation under graded vesting is much less than under cliff vesting, as the increments in which vesting occurs are more gradual and, after three years of service, all employees are granted some vesting.

Other Pre-1986 TRA Vesting Schedules

Before the 1986 TRA, qualified plans had two other statutory vesting schedules that could be satisfied. The first was known as "rule-of-45" or "age-related" vesting. This schedule was so named because it took into account a participant's age. It was rarely used. Under this rule, when a participant's age plus length of service equaled 45, he was entitled to 50 percent vesting. Thereafter, for every annual increment of two years, i.e., age plus service, the participant had to become vested an additional 10 percent. Thus, when age plus service equaled 55, the participant had to be 100 percent vested.[10]

The second alternative regular vesting schedule under pre-

1986 TRA law was "class-year" vesting. Class-year plans were special types of profit-sharing, stock bonus, or money purchase plans that treated each year's employer contribution as a separate "class" for vesting purposes. Under these plans, a plan year's contributions had to be 100 percent vested no later than five years after the end of the plan year for which the contribution was made. Class-year vesting was repealed by the 1986 TRA amendments to the Code §411 vesting rules.[11]

Year of Service for Vesting

The "year of service" concept used to measure vesting is similar to the one used in determining participation and accrual. A year of service is, unless a plan provides a more liberal standard, a 12-consecutive month period during which an employee is credited with 1,000 hours of service.[12] Again, the plan has complete freedom in selecting the relevant period but, if the period selected is different from the one used for determining participation, the plan will have to count hours of service rendered before the individual became a participant once the individual has been admitted to participation. For vesting purposes, a plan can use any of the equivalencies set forth in the Department of Labor regulations. Further, as is the case with participation and accrual, where the plan changes its vesting computation period, double credit must be given where the employee earns a year of service in both of the overlapping years. A plan may provide that a one-year period in which less than 500 hours of service are credited will constitute a one-year break in service,[13] and a year where the employee is credited with between 501 and 999 hours of service can be considered a neutral year, i.e., neither a year of break nor a year of service.

Certain Permitted Forfeitures

In general, a plan can allow forfeitures of an employee's accrued vested normal retirement benefit attributable to employer contributions whenever the forfeiture would not result in the plan's falling behind the applicable vesting sechedule. For instance, a plan that vested an employee 50 percent after two years and 100 percent after five years could forfeit the 50 percent vested benefit for any reason before year five because, even with the forfeiture, the vesting schedule would still be at least as liberal as five-year cliff vesting. Regardless of the normal requirements for regular vesting schedules, the Code allows a plan to provide for certain forfeitures.[14]

Forfeitures Upon Death of the Employee

The first such rule provides that an accrued benefit attributable to employer contributions shall not be treated as forfeitable solely because the plan provides that it is not payable if the participant dies (except where the Code requires that a survivor annuity be provided to the participant's surviving spouse).[15] Thus, a plan that is not subject to the joint and survivor requirements may reduce the cost of providing benefits to other participants by forfeiting a deceased participant's accrued but unpaid benefit attributable to employer contributions instead of providing a death benefit.

Suspension of Benefit Upon Reemployment of a Retiree

The second permissible forfeiture is the suspension of benefit payments (but not benefit accruals) upon the re-employment of a retiree.[16] Where this rule is invoked, it can reduce the current cost of returning a valued retiree to service. Where the plan invokes this rule but wishes to exempt a specific employee from its provisions, practitioners might consider returning the employee to service as an independent contractor and creating a plan provison that denies coverage to independent contractors. Of course, such a rule would have to be applied in a nondiscriminatory manner.

Withdrawal of Certain Mandatory Contributions

Another exception to the regular vesting rules applies to employee withdrawals from the plan of certain mandatory employee contributions.[17] Under this rule, the plan can forfeit an employee's vested benefit attributable to employer contributions if the employee, when employer contributions are less than 50 percent vested, withdraws his or her mandatory employee contributions.[18] A plan cannot provide for such forfeitures, however, unless it also allows an employee who has withdrawn his or her mandatory employee contributions to "buy back" the employer-provided benefit by repaying the withdrawn amounts plus interest. The right to repurchase may not be denied:

(1) in the case of a withdrawal on account of separation from service, before the earlier of five years after the first date on which the participant is subsequently re-employed by the employer, or the close of the first period of five consecutive one-year breaks in service commencing after the withdrawal, or

(2) in the case of any other withdrawal, five years after the date of the withdrawal.[19]

In a class-year plan, withdrawals of mandatory employee contributions are treated as occurring on a plan year by plan year basis, in succeeding order of time.

In a plan that calls for mandatory employee contributions, a provision calling for the forfeiture of benefits upon a withdrawal of employee contributions can aid a plan's trustees in developing a long-term investment strategy since it creates a deterrent to the withdrawal of such contributions. When the plan is assured that withdrawals will be kept to a minimum, it is easier for the trustees to plot the plan's investment program; it is less likely that the plan will run into a liquidity crisis based on the withdrawal of mandatory employee contributions. Further, with mandatory employee contributions added to the investment pool, the plan may find available to it certain investment vehicles guaranteeing a favorable rate of return, such as "jumbo" certificates of deposit. These vehicles might not be available because of minimum investment requirements where the plan has lesser amounts to invest. Where the employer still wishes to make funds available to employees for emergency purposes, a plan can allow participant loans. Further, a defined contribution plan can include a hardship withdrawal provision.

Retroactive Amendments Upon Business Necessity Under Code §412(c)(8)

Another exception to the regular vesting rules provides that a participant's right to an accrued benefit derived from employer contributions shall not be considered forfeitable solely because plan amendments decreasing accrued benefits may be given retroactive application under Code §412(c)(8).[20] Section 412(c)(8) allows certain retroactive amendments decreasing accrued benefits where it appears that the plan will not be able to continue to operate unless permission is given by the Secretary of Labor to retroactively reduce benefits accrued in the most recent plan year.

Special Forfeiture Provisions Relating to Multiemployer Plans

Two other exceptions to the regular vesting rules deserve mention. Both apply to multiemployer plans. The first provides that the benefits accrued to a participant under a multiemployer plan that are attributable to service rendered for one of the sponsoring employers before that employer had an obligation to make contributions to the plan shall not be treated as forfeitable solely because the employer ceases contributions to the plan.[21] This provision is designed to encourage employers to grant past service credits under multiemployer plans by giving them a limited "out" from having to fund such credits after they have ceased contributing to the plan. The second exception allows a multiemployer plan to reduce accrued benefits that are not guaranteed by the PBGC under Code §418D or ERISA §4281,[22] or which are suspended under Code §418E or ERISA §4281 (relating to insolvent plans).[23]

Service That May Be Disregarded for Vesting Purposes

If a plan so provides, it may disregard certain service for vesting purposes. Specifically, a plan may disregard:

(1) Years of service rendered before age 18;[24]

(2) Years of service during which an employee failed to make mandatory employee contributions;[25]

(3) Years of service for the employer in which the employer did not maintain the plan or the plan of a predecessor employer;[26]

(4) Years of service not required to be taken into consideration under the "rule of parity;"[27]

(5) Pre-1971 service if the participant did not complete three years of post-1970 service;[28]

(6) Pre-ERISA years of service if, under the applicable pre-ERISA break-in-service rule, the plan could disregard such service;[29] and

(7) For multiemployer plans, service rendered after the participant's employer completely withdraws from the plan; service rendered after the employees' collective bargaining representative has been decertified in a National Labor Relations Board proceeding; and service rendered for an employer after the plan has terminated.[30]

Planning Implications of the Service Disregard Rules

The above years of service may not be disregarded unless the plan so provides. Where substantial service is rendered by employees before age 18, invoking the pre-age 18 service rule can help an employer contain costs without incurring significant employee relations problems, since retirement benefits are seldom a consideration for very young employees. After the REA's institution of the five-year break requirement, invoking the rule of parity with respect to nonvested participants is chiefly a housecleaning measure. By invoking this rule, a plan can wipe credited service off the books once an employee has incurred five consecutive one-year breaks in service and the number of consecutive break years equals or exceeds the total number of years of pre-break service. In a plan that provides no vesting in an employee's early years, this can be a helpful administrative measure because it reduces the employer's recordkeeping responsibilities. After the REA, however, it will seldom prove to be an effective cost containment measure, especially since, under class year vesting, vesting may be deferred no later than five years (the rule of parity may not be invoked when an employee has any level of vesting in employer contributions).[31]

The rule referred to above concerning years when the employer did not maintain the plan or a predecessor plan is simply another way of saying that the provision of a past service credit is discretionary with the employer unless Code §414(a) requires the crediting of such service.

Often, an employer will wish to reward past service when a plan is established. Although past service credits may be given under a defined contribution plan by gearing the plan's allocation formula to include past service, this form of credit is most often given in a defined benefit plan. This is because defined benefit plans, under certain actuarial funding methods, may spread the funding of a past service credit over a number of years, making past service credit more affordable to employers. Where an employer grants a past service credit, the practitioner should consult with the plan's actuary to make sure that the funding method selected for the plan is one under which the employer can afford to fund the past service credit. The pre-1971 vesting service disregard rule was intended to give employers a fresh start in crediting service for employees who did not have significant post-ERISA service. As the years pass, its value as a cost containment tool will wane significantly. Presently, in certain circumstances, it can still be an effective cost containment device.

The rule covering years when an employee declined to make mandatory contributions to a contributory plan, as previously indicated, helps assure that these contributions are made and stay in the plan. Note the interaction of this rule with the rule permitting forfeitures when an employee who is less than 50 percent vested withdraws his or her mandatory employee contributions. The service disregard rule can effectively be combined with this rule permitting forfeitures to assure that a larger percentage of employees who withdraw their mandatory employee contributions will not become 50 percent vested and, hence, will be subject to the forfeiture penalty.[32]

Rule of Parity and Similar Rules

Under the rule of parity, a plan, if it so provides, may forfeit a nonvested employee's benefit when the number of consecutive one-year breaks in service exceeds the greater of:

(1) The employee's total number of years of pre-break service; or

(2) Five years.[33]

A rule similar to the rule of parity is the special rule for certain breaks in service under defined contribution plans.[34] Since defined contribution plans maintain separate accounts for each participant, this rule, which requires the plan to effectively maintain separate subaccounts for pre- and post-break years, lends itself to these types of plans. Before the REA, this rule allowed a defined contribution plan to disregard service rendered before a one-year break in service in determining a participant's vested percentage for any pre-break service. In other words, a participant's pre-break benefit would be frozen at his level of vesting before the break. Pre-break service would have to be counted in determining a participant's vested level in amounts attributable to post-break accruals, however, if the employee returned to service. Nevertheless, for plan years beginning after 1984, the break must be for five years before the plan can apply this rule.

> *Example*: Plan H calls for vesting in 20 percent annual increments over the first five years of an employee's career. Employee X becomes a participant in 1989 and works three years, during which time he accrues a benefit of $10,000 attributable to employer contributions (which are 60 percent vested). He then incurs a five-year break in service from 1990–1994, and returns in 1995. In 1995, he completes another year of service, raising him to 80 percent on the vesting ladder and accrues another $500 attributable to employer contributions. The plan, if it so provides, may credit X with 60 percent vesting in the $10,000 attributable to pre-break accruals. This amount will be frozen, i.e., it will not be increased by post-break service and the nonvested 40 percent ($4,000) may be forfeited. If the company contributes $5,000 to X's account for 1995, X will be 80 percent vested in this amount and, if he performs another year of service before incurring another break that is recognizable under the rule of parity, will become 100 percent vested in this amount.

Before the REA, this rule could be extremely helpful to a plan in containing its vesting costs with respect to employees who returned to service after a break. It also simplified plan administration because a plan, after a one-year break, could forfeit the nonvested portion of a participant's benefit attributable to employer contributions and distribute it to employees remaining in the plan or hold it in a suspense account until a future year. In that year, it would be released to reduce the employer's annual contribution obligation, depending on what treatment the plan provided. Although invoking the post-REA rule can still provide some of these benefits, the rule's utility was sharply curtailed for post-1984 plan years by the REA.[35]

A final service disregard rule that practitioners may wish to consider in limiting an employer's vesting costs is provided in Code §411(a)(6)(B). This rule is somewhat similar to the one-year participation hold-out rule. It can be applied when an employee incurs a one-year break in service. Pre-break service need not be counted for purposes of vesting in any accruals, whether pre- or post-break, until the employee completes a year of service after returning. Upon completion of the year of service, the employee must be given retroactive credit for the post-return year for vesting purposes. The REA did not modify this rule. For it to be available, the plan must specifically so provide.

Maternity and Paternity-Related Leaves of Absence

The REA instituted special rules to diminish the possibility that a maternity or paternity absence will give rise to a break in service.[36] Under these provisions, a plan must credit, solely for purposes of determining whether a one-year break in service has occurred, the hours of service which otherwise would normally have been credited to an individual but for the maternity or paternity absence or, if the plan cannot determine such hours, eight hours of service per day of such absence. The maximum number of hours that must be credited in any year under these provisions is 501. These hours must be credited to the year in which the absence begins, if the participant would be prevented from incurring a one-year break in service solely by reason of the crediting of the hours of leave to that year. In any other case, these hours must be credited to the immediately following year.

The foregoing crediting rules apply to a leave of absence caused by a pregnancy, a birth or an adoption of a child. They also apply to the period, beginning immediately after the birth or adoption of the child, which is used for purposes of caring for such child. A plan may require that the individual furnish the administrator with such timely information as may be reasonably required to establish that the absence is maternity- or paternity-related and the length of such absence.

Voluntary and Involuntary Cashouts

Under certain circumstances, a plan may elect to distribute an employee's accrued vested benefit upon his or her termination of participation in the plan. Where this occurs, the employee's account is wiped off the books of the plan. The circumstances in which such cashouts may occur vary depending upon whether the cashout was voluntary, i.e., at the employee's election, or involuntary, i.e., without the employee's consent.[37]

A plan, for administrative convenience, may involuntarily

cashout a participant where the present value of the participant's accrued benefit is $3,500. Where the accrued benefit exceeds $3,500, the participant's (and spouse's where the plan is subject to the joint and survivor rules) consent must be obtained before the plan may cashout the benefit. "Accrued benefit," for this purpose, means:

(1) For a defined benefit plan, the employee's accrued benefit determined under the plan, except as provided in Code §411(c)(3), expressed in the form of an annual benefit commencing at normal retirement age,[38] or

(2) For a defined contribution plan, the employee's account balance.[39]

For this purpose, present value is to be determined by reference to the PBGC's interest rate at the date of the distribution used for determining the present value of lump sum distributions upon plan termination. For vested accrued benefits of $25,000 or less, the plan may not use a rate that exceeds the PBGC rate. Where the benefit is more than $25,000, the interest rate used may not exceed 120 percent of the PBGC rate.[41] The REA also added Code §417(e) that requires the consent of both the participant and the participant's spouse to an involuntary cashout of a qualified joint and survivor annuity where the present value of such annuity exceeds $3,500.

Code §411(a)(7)(C) provides that, where a participant receives a cashout of his accrued vested benefit which is less than the present value of that benefit, and later resumes employment with the employer before a five-year break in service occurs, the participant must be given the right to buy back his credited service under the plan by repaying the cashed out amounts to the plan. In a defined benefit plan, the repayment must be with interest.

Certain Changes in the Vesting Schedule

Where a plan amendment reduces the vested percentage of any employee in his or her accrued benefit attributable to employer contributions determined as of the later of the date the plan amendment was adopted or became effective, and the vested percentage of any participant is less than it would have been if not for the amendment, the plan will fail to satisfy the vesting rules.[42] Further, where an amendment changes the vesting schedule, any participant having at least three years of service (five for plan years beginning before 1989) must be allowed to elect coverage under the old vesting schedule.[43]

Top-Heavy Vesting Rules

For any top-heavy plan year, Code §416(b) requires that plans provide more rapid vesting in participants' accrued benefits attributable to employer contributions than is otherwise required under the regular vesting rules of Code §411(a). The §416(b) rules may be provided in a separate vesting schedule that will supersede the regular schedule for any top-heavy plan year. Alternatively, the plan, for simplicity, may provide a single vesting schedule for all plan years that satisfies the requirements of both §§411(a) and 416(b).

Code §416(b) provides two alternative top-heavy vesting schedules. The first is three-year cliff vesting. Under this schedule, no vesting need be provided until an employee has three years of vesting service, at which time he or she must be 100 percent vested.[44]

Note that, before the 1986 TRA, where a plan used this schedule, it could contain costs by imposing a three-year participation requirement under Code §410(a)(5)(B). For plan years beginning after 1988, the plan may only delay participation until the completion of two years of service if it provides full and immediate vesting after not more than two years of service. For this purpose, if an employee incurs a one-year break in service before completing the two-year requirement and later returns to the employer, pre-break service need not be counted in applying the participation service requirements.[45]

The second permissible top-heavy vesting schedule is six-year graded vesting. Under this alternative, an employee must be 20 percent vested after completing two years of service, and vesting increases in 20 percent annual increments to the point where the employee is 100 percent vested after six years.[46]

In determining vesting under the top-heavy rules, except to the extent inconsistent therewith, the vesting rules of Code §411 apply.[47]

The top-heavy vesting rules, where they apply, supersede

the plan's regular vesting schedule. Thus, for instance, if a participant was 20 percent vested in employer contributions when the plan became top-heavy, under the plan's six-year graded top-heavy schedule, the participant would be entitled to 40% vesting and would be credited with 40% vesting in all employer contributions for years prior to, and including, the top-heavy year. Where a participant was already entitled to a greater level of vesting than the top-heavy schedule would provide, he or she will not be divested of a benefit by virtue of the top-heavy rules. If, in the example above, the plan then became non-top-heavy in a succeeding year, it could return to the non-top-heavy vesting schedule as to any future accruals.

Notes

1. Code §411(a)(1).
2. Code §411(a) (prefatory language).
3. Code §411(a)(8).
4. Code §411(a)(9).
5. For this purpose, under Code §411(a)(9)(B) the "early retirement benefit" under a plan is to be determined without regard to any Social Security supplements, i.e., benefits that begin before a participant receives benefits under title II of the Social Security Act and that (1) do not exceed Social Security benefits, and (2) terminate when Social Security benefits commence.
6. Section 411(a)(9)(B) defines "qualified disability benefit" as a disability benefit provided by a plan which does not exceed the benefit which would be provided for the participant if he or she separated from service at normal retirement age.
7. Contained in Code §411(a)(2)(B).
8. Under this special effective date provision, in the case of a multiemployer plan maintained pursuant to a collective bargaining agreement that was ratified before March 1, 1986, the 1986 TRA vesting amendments apply as of the earlier of:

   (1) the later of—(a) January 1, 1986, or (b) the date on which the last of such collective bargaining agreements terminates (determined without regard to any post-February 28, 1986 extension), or

   (2) January 1, 1991.

   See 1986 TRA, P.L. 99-514, §§1113(e)(2) and (3).
9. Before TEFRA, many IRS district offices had taken the administrative position, based on ERISA's legislative history, that, where the facts indicated that 10-year cliff vesting would produce discrimination, they would not issue a favorable determination letter unless the plan was amended to provide for "4/40" vesting. This schedule vests employees 40% after 4 years of service, increasing in 5% annual increments in years 5 and 6,

and then increasing in 10% annual increments in years 7 through 11, to the point where, after 11 years of service, the employee is fully vested.

10. Age-related vesting protected the interest of senior workers. To minimize the harsh effects of this schedule on junior employees, a special schedule was incorporated into the rule-of-45 schedule. This schedule required that, after 10 years of service, employees be given vesting that was at least as liberal as the last 5 years under 5-to-15 year graded vesting, i.e., 50 percent after 10 years, increasing in increments to 100 percent after 15 years. Although rule-of-45 vesting sought to protect senior workers, it had the potential to carry with it certain unintended consequences. The most notable of these was the schedule's cost—it could require rapid vesting, by virtue of the age factor, for senior employees who have performed the bulk of their career service for another employer. This, in turn, could become a deterrent to hiring senior workers.

    There was no analogue in the top-heavy vesting rules to age-related vesting because they were based on cliff and graded vesting principles. Indeed, in many situations, under age-related vesting, employees could have more vesting than required by the top-heavy schedule. Where the top-heavy schedule was more liberal, employees in plans using an age-related vesting schedule as is discussed below, had to be given the benefit of the more favorable schedule when the plan became top-heavy. In other words, the top-heavy vesting rules then, as now, will not divest an employee of the benefit in which he has become vested under the plan's regular schedule. Thus, in some cases, the use of age-related vesting could mean that the employer's cost would not rise sharply in top-heavy plan years. With the repeal of age-related vesting, this issue is moot except insofar as it applies to open years.

11. One advantage for employers of class-year vesting was that it always provided for some level of forfeiture until an employee reached normal retirement age. This could operate as an incentive to employees to remain with the employer until normal retirement age. Note that, as with age-related vesting, there was no class-year top-heavy vesting schedule. Accordingly, for any plan year for which a class-year plan was top-heavy, it had to abandon the class-year schedule in favor of one of the top-heavy schedules.
12. Code §411(a)(5).
13. Code §411(a)(6)(A).
14. Code §411(a)(3).
15. Code §411(a)(3)(A).
16. Code §411(a)(3)(B).
17. Code §411(a)(3)(D).
18. Code §411(a)(3)(D)(i).
19. Code §411(a)(3)(D)(ii). For contributions that accrued before ERISA's enactment date (September 2, 1974), the plan may provide, where the employee withdraws mandatory employee contributions, that a proportionate amount of the employee's accrued benefit attributable to employer contributions will be forfeited, regardless of his or her vested percentage at the time of the withdrawal. This rule, however, does not apply to any plan to which any mandatory employee contribution is made after September 2, 1974.

20. Code §411(a)(3)(C).
21. Code §411(a)(3)(E).
22. Code §411(a)(3)(F)(i).
23. Code §411(a)(3)(F)(ii).
24. Code §411(a)(4)(A). This was age 22 for years before the Retirement Equity Act. The REA provisions are effective for plan years beginning after 1984.
25. Code §411(a)(4)(B).
26. Code §411(a)(4)(C).
27. Code §411(a)(4)(D). The rule of parity is set forth in Code §411(a)(6). Before the REA, a plan could apply the rule of parity when a nonvested participant had more consecutive years of break in service than total years of pre-break service. After the REA, the break must be for at least 5 consecutive years for the rule of parity to apply.
28. Code §411(a)(4)(E).
29. Code §411(a)(4)(F).
30. Code §411(a)(4)(G).
31. Code §411(a)(5)(C).
32. In counting vesting service, a defined contribution plan or an insured defined benefit plan which satisfies the requirements of Code §411(b)(1)(F) may disregard service under the rule of parity discussed below.
33. Code §411(a)(6)(D).
34. Code §411(a)(6)(C).
35. Temp. Treas. Regs. §1.410(a)-5T provides two illustrations of the transitional rules under the REA with respect to the 5-year break-in-service rules. One example assumes a plan is a calendar plan year and disregards years of service as permitted by Code §§410(a)(5)(D) and 411(a)(6)(D) as in effect on August 22, 1984. If an employee completed 2 years of service in 1981 and 1982, and then incurred 2 consecutive one-year breaks in service in 1983 and 1984, the plan may disregard the prior years of service even though the employee did not incur 5 consecutive one-year breaks in service. The second example assumes the employee completed 3 consecutive years of service beginning in 1980, and incurred 2 one-year breaks in service in 1983 and 1984. Because the years of service credited before 1983 could not be disregarded as of December 31, 1984, the question as to whether the plan may subsequently (after the REA's effective date) disregard those years of service (because the break continued thereafter, e.g., for a total of five consecutive years) will be governed by post-REA law.
36. Code §§410(a)(5)(E) and 411(a)(6)(E).
37. See Code §411(a)(7).
38. Code §411(c)(3) provides special rules for the situation in a defined benefit plan, where, an employee's accrued benefit is to be determined as an amount other than an annual benefit commencing at normal retirement age, or where the accrued benefit derived from employee contributions is to be determined with respect to a benefit other than an annual benefit in the form of a single life annuity (with no ancillary benefits) commencing at normal retirement age. Where this occurs, employee's accrued benefit, or the accrued benefit derived from employee contributions, as the case

may be, will be the actuarial equivalent of such benefit or amount determined under §§411(c)(1) or (2).

39. Code §§411(a)(7)(A)(i) and (ii).
40. Retirement Equity Act, P.L. 98-397, §205(a), adding Code §411(a)(11).
41. Post-REA Code §411(a)(11)(B).
42. Code §411(a)(10)(A).
43. Code §411(a)(10)(B).
44. Code §410(a)(1)(B).
45. Code §410(a)(5)(B).
46. Code §416(b)(1)(B).
47. Code §411(b)(2). Thus, for instance, years of service that the plan may disregard for §411(a) purposes may be disregarded for §416(b) purposes.

5

Limitations on Benefits and Contributions Under Qualified Plans

Code §415 places limitations on benefits and contributions allowed under Code §401(a) qualified plans. It applies to all §401(a) defined benefit and defined contribution plans.[1] In addition, it applies to §403(b) annuity plans, §403(a) annuity contracts, and §408(k) simplified employee pensions (SEPs).[2] Section 415 limits the benefits a participant can accrue under a defined benefit plan and the "annual additions" that may be made to a participant's account under a defined contribution plan.[3] The section also limits the total benefits a participant can accrue under one or more defined benefit plans and one or more defined contribution plans maintained by the same employer. The Tax Equity and Fiscal Responsibility Act of 1982 severely cut back the §415 limits, effective generally beginning in 1982.[4] This trend was continued by the 1984 and 1986 Tax Reform Acts. The 1984 TRA extended the moratorium on post-TEFRA indexation of the defined benefit and defined contribution §415 dollar limits until 1988 (and provided that, beginning in 1988, these limits are to be adjusted for post-1986 inflation).[5] The 1986 TRA froze the §415 limits on defined contribution plans until the defined benefit plan dollar limit reaches $120,000, at which time the two limits are to move in tandem so that the defined benefit plan dollar limit will always be four times the defined contribution plan dollar limit.

For an employee who separates from service, the high three-years average limit of Code §415(b)(1)(B) is adjusted for inflation in the manner in which the $90,000 limit is adjusted for inflation with respect to all defined benefit plan participants. Those limits are to be adjusted, beginning in 1988, for post-1986 inflation in accordance with the indexation of the Social Security Primary Insurance Amount (PIA) for the year(s) in question.

Code §415(b) Defined Benefit Plan Limits

Code §§415(b)(1)(A)-(B) limit the maximum annual benefit that can accrue to a participant under a defined benefit plan. That benefit cannot exceed the lesser of:

(1) $90,000; or

(2) 100 percent of the participant's average compensation for his three consecutive most highly compensated years of service with the employer.

Adjustments to the Code §415(b) Limits

The "annual benefit" for purposes of the §415(b) limits means a benefit payable annually in the form of a straight-life annuity (with no ancillary benefits) under a plan to which employees do not contribute and to which no rollover contributions are made.[6] Where the benefit under consideration is different, the Code requires certain adjustments to the limits. These adjustments must be made where:

(1) Ancillary benefits are provided;

(2) The form of the benefit is other than a straight-life annuity; or

(3) Rollover contributions are allowed.[7]

Further, where benefit payments begin before or after the social security retirement age, the applicable dollar limit is reduced or increased to the actuarial equivalent of the $90,000 (as indexed for inflation) benefit payable at the Social Security retirement age.[8]

The IRS is to reduce a benefit beginning before Social Security retirement age in a manner that is consistent with the reduction for old age insurance benefits commencing before Social Security retirement age under the Social Security Act. The only statutory guidance given with respect to benefits that begin after the Social Security retirement age is that they be the "actuarial equivalent" of a $90,000 annual benefit commencing at Social Security normal retirement age. Where an adjustment is to be made for an alternate form of benefit or for a benefit beginning before Social Security retirement age, the interest rate assumption used in making the adjustment cannot be less than the greater of 5 percent or the rate specified in the plan.[9]

An employer may not fund for a projected future increase in the Code §415 defined benefit plan dollar limit before the year that such an adjustment takes effect.[10]

A defined benefit plan may, however, provide certain cost-of-living protection. Where this is done, any employee contribution to fund such protection is not considered an annual addition for purposes of the §415(c) limits for defined contribution plans (although it is so counted for purposes of applying the combined plan limit of §415(e)). For this purpose, a "qualified cost-of-living arrangement" is an arrangement under a defined benefit plan which:

(1) Provides a cost-of-living adjustment to a benefit provided under the plan or a separate plan subject to the minimum funding standard of Code §412; and

(2) Satisfies the following requirements:[11]
(a) The arrangement must be based on increases in the cost of living incurred by participants after their "annuity starting date." Further, on average, cost-of-living increases must be determined with reference to one or more indexes prescribed by the Treasury Secretary, except that the arrangement may provide that the increase will not exceed 3% of the retirement benefit per year (determined without regard to the increase);[12]
(b) The arrangement must be elective and must be made available on the same terms to all participants. Further, the arrangement must provide that the election may be made in: (i) the year in which the participant attains the earliest retirement age under the plan[13] or separates from service; or (ii) both of the years described in (i), above;[14] and
(c) The arrangement cannot be part of a plan which discriminates as to participation.[15]

Finally, for the arrangement to qualify, no key employee may participate.[16]

Note that, in determining whether a distribution from a defined benefit plan qualifies for lump sum distribution treatment, any amount transferred from a qualified defined contribution plan to fund a qualified cost-of-living arrangement under a defined benefit plan is not taken into account.[17]

Where an employee has less than 10 years of participation in a defined benefit plan, the dollar limit is reduced ratably by multiplying it by a fraction. The numerator of this fraction is the number of years (or parts thereof) that the employee has participated in the plan. The denominator is 10.[18] A similar reduction applies to the high-three years' average compensation limit for defined benefit plans, except that this latter reduction is based on the employee's number of years of service with the employer, rather than years of participation in the plan.

Notwithstanding the general defined benefit plan §415 limits, including the ratable reduction rule described in the preceding paragraph, an employee may accrue an annual benefit of $10,000 if the employer has not, at any time, maintained a defined contribution plan in which the employee participated.[19]

Benefits Under Collectively Bargained Plans

The statute provides an exception to the application of the high-three years' average rule to certain benefits provided under collectively bargained plans. Under this exception, the high-three years' average prong of the defined benefit Code §415 limit does not apply and the greater of $68,212 or one-half the §415(b) defined benefit plan dollar limit is substituted for the regular defined benefit plan dollar limit. The exception applies to benefits with respect to a participant under a defined benefit plan which:

(1) Is maintained for the year in question under a collective bargaining agreement;

(2) At all times during the year had at least 100 participants;

(3) Determines benefits solely by reference to length of service, which year the service was rendered, age at retirement, and date of retirement;

(4) Provides that an employee who has at least four years of

service is 100 percent vested in his or her accrued benefit derived from employer contributions;

(5) Requires, as a condition of participation, that an employee complete a period of not more than 60 consecutive days of service with the employer or employers maintaining the plan.[20]

The exception for collectively bargained plans does not apply to a participant whose compensation for any three years during the 10-year period immediately preceding the year he or she separates from service exceeded the average compensation for such three years for all participants in the plan. The exception also does not apply for any year in which the individual involved participated in another collectively bargained plan maintained by the same employer.[21]

Special Rule for Commercial Airline Pilots

Code §415(b) also contains a special rule for defined benefit plans which benefit commercial airline pilots. This rule imposes a $75,000 floor on the defined benefit plan dollar limit if a pilot retires before the then-current Social Security retirement age. Further, if, when the pilot retires, the Federal Aviation Administration's mandatory retirement age for commercial airline pilots is after age 60 but before Social Security normal retirement age at that time, the Code's rules for reducing the defined benefit plan dollar limit (after applying the $75,000 floor) are applied by substituting the FAA's then mandatory retirement age for the then-current Social Security retirement age. If a commercial airline pilot separates from service before age 60, the rules applicable to state and local governments and tax-exempt organizations (i.e., a $75,000 floor for benefits beginning at age 55 and the substitution of age 62 for Social Security retirement age) apply.[22]

Code §415(c) Defined Contribution Plan Limits

In a defined contribution plan, the maximum "annual addition" that may be made to an employee's account for the year cannot exceed the lesser of:

(1) $30,000; or

(2) 25 percent of the participant's compensation.[23]

As in the case of defined benefit plans, the dollar limit is to be adjusted for changes in the cost of living. The 1986 TRA, however, deferred the indexation of the Code §415 dollar limit for defined contribution plans until the regular defined benefit plan §415(b) dollar limit has risen to four times the defined benefit plan dollar limit. Thus, indexation of the defined contribution plan dollar limit will not begin until the defined benefit plan dollar limit reaches $120,000.[24]

An annual addition with respect to a participant for a year is the sum of:

(1) Employer contributions allocated to the participant's account;

(2) Forfeitures allocated to the participant's account; and

(3) Employee contributions made by the participant.[25]

For purposes of applying the percentage-of-compensation limits, compensation is the participant's compensation from the employer for the year.[26] For self-employed individuals, earned income from self-employment constitutes compensation for this purpose.[27]

Under a special rule contained in Code §415(c)(3)(C), an employer may continue to make contributions to a defined contribution plan on behalf of an individual who is totally and permanently disabled. Where this is done, the disabled participant's compensation is deemed to continue at the annual rate that was in effect immediately before the disability occurred. For years beginning before 1989, the disabled employee must not be an officer, owner, or highly compensated employee for this provision to be available. For years beginning after 1988, the Code §414(q) definition of highly compensated employee is substituted as the prohibited group for this purpose. Disability, for this purpose, means total and permanent disability within the meaning of Code §22(e)(3). For the special disability rule to apply, employer contributions attributable to deemed compensation during the period of disability must be nonforfeitable when made.[28]

There are various plan drafting techniques that can be employed to assure that a defined contribution plan will not exceed the limit on annual additions with respect to any participant. These techniques involve drafting plan provisions that effectively cap the allocation to a participant for a year. One form that this cap may take is that of a reallocation clause. In a typical reallocation provision, the plan would initially make allocations to participants' accounts based on the plan's general formula for allocating contributions—usually a level percentage of compensation. The plan can then provide that, to the extent the normal allocation formula would cause any participant's account to have an excess annual addition for the year when added to forfeitures and employee contributions, the excess shall be reallocated to the remaining participants based on their relative compensation or as a level dollar amount. Alternatively, the plan may provide that excess amounts will be held in a suspense account until a future year, at which time they will be allocated to participants' accounts as part of the employer's annual contribution obligation for the year.

Simplified Employee Pensions (SEPs)

For Code §415 purposes, Simplified Employee Pensions within the meaning of Code §408(k) are treated as defined contribution plans. Code §415(l), as added by the 1984 TRA, provides that for Code §415 purposes, contributions to an individual medical benefit account for a more-than-five-percent owner in a defined benefit plan will be treated as annual additions to a defined contribution plan.

Special Rules for Certain Types of Plans

Tax-Deferred Annuities (TDAs)

Code §415 recognizes the unique nature of Code §403(b) tax-deferred annuities. It therefore provides a special set of limits on amounts contributed to fund TDAs.[29] These rules recognize certain provisions that are unique to TDAs, such as the exclusion ratio rule. The special rules give a TDA participant three different types of elections. The participant may elect only one of the provisions and, once made, the election is irrevocable.[30]

Under the first TDA rule, a participant in a Code §403(b) plan maintained by a qualifying organization[31] may elect, in the year of the participant's separation from service, to substitute for the defined contribution plan percentage-of-compensation limit (which would otherwise apply to a TDA) the exclusion allowance that would be available to the participant under §403(b)(2) for the participant's year of separation from the employer's service. For purposes of determining the relevant amount of exclusion allowance available to a participant, only years of service (not to exceed 10) with the employer during the period preceding the separation from service may be counted.[32]

Under the second elective rule, for any year, a TDA participant who works for a qualifying organization may elect to substitute for the defined contribution plan percentage-of-compensation limit, the lesser of:

(1) 25 percent of the participant's includible compensation,[33] plus $4,000;

(2) The amount of the participant's exclusion allowance for the year;[34] or

(3) $15,000.[35]

Under the third elective rule, a TDA participant may elect to waive the application of the exclusion ratio rule of Code §403(b)(3)(A).[36]

Employee Stock Ownership Plans (ESOPs)

In an ESOP[37] where no more than one-third of the contributions deductible by an employer under Code §404(a)(9) for a year are allocated to the accounts of highly compensated employees,[38] the defined contribution plan dollar limit for the year is replaced by the sum of:

(1) The Code §415(c) defined contribution plan dollar limit for the year, plus

(2) The lesser of such defined contribution plan dollar limit or the amount of employer securities[39] contributed (or purchased with cash contributed) to the ESOP.[40]

In addition, where no more than one-third of the employer's deductible contributions under Code §404(a)(9) to an ESOP are allocated to highly compensated employees, the Code §415(c) defined contribution plan limits do not apply to:

(1) Forfeitures of employer securities under the ESOP if such securities were acquired with the proceeds of a loan described in Code §404(a)(9), or

(2) Employer contributions to an ESOP which are deductible under Code §404(a)(9)(B) (relating to interest on certain loans to acquire employer securities) and charged against the participant's account.

Combined Plan Limit

Where an employer maintains one or more defined benefit plans and one or more defined contribution plans covering the same participants, a special combined plan limit applies.[41] The limit is imposed by the "combined plan fraction," a number which is composed of the sum of the "defined benefit plan fraction" and the "defined contribution plan fraction."[42]

For this purpose, the defined benefit plan fraction for any year has as its numerator a participant's projected annual benefit under the plan determined at the close of the plan year.[43] The denominator is the lesser of:

(1) 1.25 multiplied by the Code §415(b)(1)(A) defined benefit plan dollar limit in effect for the year, or

(2) 1.4 times the Code §415(b)(1)(B) percentage of compensation limit for the year.[44]

The defined contribution plan fraction has as its numerator the sum of the annual additions to the participant's account as of the close of the year.[45] The denominator is the lesser of:

(1) 1.25 times the §415(c)(1)(A) dollar limit in effect for the year and each prior year of service with the employer; or

(2) 1.4 times the §415(c)(1)(B) defined contribution plan percentage-of-compensation limit in effect for such years.[46]

The sum of these two fractions cannot exceed 1.0 for any participant for any year.[47] This equation has the effect of mathematically producing a combined plan limit that is equal to 100 percent of 1.25 times the applicable dollar limit or 1.4 times the applicable percentage-of-compensation limit, whichever is less.

For a top-heavy plan, "1.0" is substituted for "1.25" in the denominators of the respective fractions.[48] This has the effect of reducing the combined plan limit to 100 percent of the lesser of 1.0 times the dollar limit or 1.4 times the percentage-of-compensation limit.

A top-heavy plan can, in effect, "buy back" the right to use the regular 1.25 times the dollar limit component of the relevant fractions if it provides an additional top-heavy minimum benefit, over and above the regular top-heavy benefit guaranteed to non-key employees by Code §416.[49] For a defined benefit plan, this is done by providing each non-key employee with an extra 1 percent of "testing period" compensation (i.e., the participant's average annual compensation for his five consecutive top-heavy plan years for which his compensation was the highest) for each top-heavy plan year.

Thus, a defined benefit plan using the buy back option would have to provide each non-key employee in every top-heavy plan year a benefit of 3 percent of testing period compensation per year, not to exceed 30 percent of such compensation for any employee.[50]

For a defined contribution plan, the buy back requires the employer to provide an additional minimum contribution of 1 percent to each non-key employee for any top-heavy plan year. Thus, a defined contribution plan would have to provide non-key employees with the lesser of 4 percent of compensation or such lesser percentage as is provided to the key employee for whom the employer's contribution for the year is the greatest.[51]

The right to buy back the higher limits, however, is denied to a "super top-heavy plan."[52] A super top-heavy plan, for this purpose, is a plan under which more than 90 percent of the benefits (in the case of a defined benefit plan) or the contributions (in the case of a defined contribution plan) inure to the benefit of key employees.

When the applicable combined plan fraction is exceeded during a year with respect to any employee, one or more of the affected plans will be disqualified.[53] Defined contribution plans usually avoid this problem by providing that no amount will be allocated to a participant's account if the amount would, when combined with the benefit the participant earns under the employer's defined benefit plan, cause the combined plan fraction to be exceeded for the year. Although technically, this is probably a forfeiture, the IRS will generally allow the legal fiction that such excess was never, in fact, allocated to the participant's account (as opposed to being allocated under the plan's general allocation formula and then reallocated).

Special Transition Rule for Computing Defined Contribution Plan Fraction

Planners should also be aware of the availability of a special transitional rule for computing the defined contribution plan fraction for years ending after 1982. Under this rule, the plan administrator may elect to compute the plan's defined contribution plan fraction by using the "transition fraction."[54] Specifically where this rule is elected, the defined contribution plan fraction for all years ending before 1983 is deemed to be equal to the product of the applicable defined contribution plan denominator—*i.e.*, the lesser of 1.25 times the dollar limit of 1.4 times the percentage limit—times the transition fraction.[55] The transition fraction is a fraction having as its numerator the lesser of:

(1) $51,875; or

(2) 1.4 times 25 percent of the participant's compensation for the year ending in 1981.[56]

The denominator of the transition fraction is the lesser of:

(1) $41,500; or

(2) 25 percent of the participant's compensation for the year ending in 1981.

Despite its complexity, the purpose of this transitional rule is chiefly to spare plans administrative expense. Since the numbers for pre-TEFRA years are assumed, detailed recordkeeping for these years is not necessary. Where accurate pre-TEFRA records are not available, using the transitional rule may be the only alternative for a plan.

Under another transitional rule, the application of the special "1.0" rule to top-heavy plans will not apply with respect to any individual so long as there are no (1) Employer contributions, forfeitures, or voluntary nondeductible contributions allocated to such individual; or (2) Accruals for such individual under the defined benefit plan until either the 1.0 limit is met or the combined plan denominator is increased to 1.25 times the dollar limits by virtue of the plan's ceasing to be top-heavy.[57] Practitioners should not overlook the potential usefulness of these two transitional rules in situations where they could apply.

For purposes of applying the combined plan fraction test, all defined contribution plans of one employer are treated as one plan. The same rule applies to all defined benefit plans.[58] Thus, no Code §415(e) benefit can be gained by an employer's use of multiple plans of the same type. This rule also applies to the individual plan limits of Code §§415(b) and (c).[59]

Notes

1. Code §§415(a)(1)(A) and (B).
2. Code §415(a)(2).
3. Code §§415(b)(1)(A) and (B) (benefit limitations) and Code §§415(c)(1)(A) and (B) (annual additions). For this purpose, a participant's high 3 years are the period of consecutive calendar years (not to exceed 3) during which the participant both was an active participant in the plan and had the greatest aggregate compensation from the employer. For a self-employed individual, earned income from self employment (determined without regard to any exclusion under Code §911) is used instead of "compensation from the employer." See §415(b)(3).
4. The defined benefit dollar limit as originally enacted by ERISA was $75,000, indexed for post-1974 inflation. That indexation, by the time TEFRA was enacted, had raised the dollar limit to $136,425. TEFRA cut back the dollar limit to $90,000 effective with respect to plans that were not in existence on July 1, 1982, for years ending after July 1, 1982. For plans that were in existence on July 1, 1982, the reduced dollar limit applied to years beginning after 1982. TEFRA §235(g)(1)(B)(ii) provided a transition rule that a plan would not fail to qualify merely because it provided for benefits in excess of the Code §415 limits for any year beginning before January 1, 1984. This relief did not apply to plans that exceeded the §415 limits before their reduction by TEFRA. TEFRA cut back the indexed dollar limit for defined contribution plans from $46,475 to $30,000.
5. The moratorium had originally been scheduled to expire in 1986. Thereafter, the limits were to be adjusted for post-1984 inflation.
6. Code §415(b)(2)(A).
7. Code §415(b)(2)(B). The adjustments are to be made in accordance with Treasury regulations.
8. Code §§415(b)(2)(C)–(D). Section 415(b)(8) defines "Social Security retirement age" for this purpose as the age used as the retirement age under §216(1) of the Social Security Act, except that such section is to be applied: (1) without regard to the age increase factor, and (2) as if the early retirement age under the Social Security Act were 62.

   Note that, for "qualified participants" in plans maintained by governments and tax-exempt organizations and "qualified merchant marine plans", the reduction in the dollar limit begins when benefits start before age 62, rather than the Social Security retirement age. In addition, a $75,000 floor is placed under the dollar limit so that, regardless of the discounting calculation, it cannot fall below this amount. These provisions applied to all plans under TEFRA. Code §415(b)(2)(H) defines a "qualified participant" for purposes of the governmental and tax-exempt plan rule as a participant (i) in a defined benefit plan which is maintained by a state or political subdivision thereof, (ii) with respect to whom the period of service taken into account in determining the amount of benefit under such defined benefit plan includes at least 20 years of service of the participant as: (I) a full-time employee of a police department or fire department which is organized and operated by a state or political subdivision maintaining such defined benefit plan to provide police protection, firefighting services, or emergency medical services for any area within the jurisdiction of such state or political subdivision, or (II) a member of the U.S. armed forces. A "qualified merchant marine plan" is a plan in existence on January 1, 1986, the participants in which are merchant marine officers holding licenses issued by the Secretary of Transportation under title 46 of the United States Code. *See* §415(b)(2)(F). For "qualified police or firefighters," §415(b)(2)(G) establishes a $50,000 floor below which the dollar limit cannot be reduced.

9. Code §415(b)(2)(E).
10. Code §415(b)(2)(E)(iii).
11. Code §§415(k)(2)(C)–(F).
12. Code §415(k)(2)(C).
13. Determined without regard to any separation from service.
14. Code §415(k)(2)(D).
15. Code §415(k)(2)(E).
16. In general, a key employee for this purpose is an individual described in §416(i), although certain modifications to the definition apply.
17. Code §402(e)(4)(N). The 1986 TRA amendments providing for qualified cost-of-living arrangements in defined benefit plans are effective generally for years beginning after 1986. A special effective date applies to collectively bargained plans. Another transitional rule protects an employee's current accrued benefit in certain situations. Under this rule, if, as of the first day of the first year to which the 1986 TRA amendments to Code §415 apply, an individual was a participant in a defined benefit plan that was in existence on May 6, 1986, and such plan met the §415 limits at that time for all plan years, then, for purposes of the defined benefit plan limit and the combined plan limit, the individual's benefit is deemed to satisfy the defined benefit plan dollar limit. Under the transitional rule, for purposes of determining an individual's accrued benefit, no changes in the plan after May 5, 1986, may be considered, including cost-of-living adjustments occurring after that date. A similar transitional rule protects plans from inadvertently violating the §415(e) combined plan limit by virtue of the 1986 TRA amendments to §415.
18. Code §415(b)(5)(A).
19. Code §415(b)(4)(A).
20. Code §§415(b)(7)(A)–(E).
21. Code §415(b)(7).
22. Code §415(b)(9).

23. Code §§415(c)(1)(A) and (B). Before TEFRA, the dollar limit was $25,000, indexed for post-1974 inflation to the point where, for 1981, the applicable dollar limit had risen to $46,475. The dollar limit for defined contribution plans, before the 1986 TRA, was always one-third of the dollar limit for defined benefit plans. Whether the ultimate retirement benefit that a participant will receive under a defined contribution plan that is designed to be the equivalent of a particular defined benefit plan will be greater than or less than the benefit that would be provided under the defined benefit plan depends largely on the defined contribution plan's investment experience.
24. 1986 TRA, P.L. 99-514, §1106.
25. Before the 1986 TRA, employee contributions were only counted to the extent of the lesser of (a) one-half of employee contributions to the participant's account for the year; or (b) the excess of such employee contributions over 6% of the participant's compensation for the year. The 1986 TRA, effective generally for years beginning after 1986, made employee contributions count dollar-for-dollar for purposes of computing annual additions. Under a transitional rule added to prevent plans from being disqualified because of the repeal of the partial exclusion for employee contributions, recomputation of the §415(e) combined plan limit for any year beginning before 1987 is not required.
26. Code §415(c)(3)(A).
27. Code §415(c)(3)(B). For this purpose, a participant's compensation within the meaning of Code §401(c)(2) is used, without regard to any exclusion under Code §911.
28. Code §415(c)(3)(C).
29. Code §415(c)(4).
30. Code §415(c)(4)(D).
31. I.e., an educational organization, a hospital, a home health service agency, a health and welfare service agency, or a church, convention or association of churches, or an organization described in Code §414(e)(3)(B)(ii). These are the qualifying organizations with respect to all three of the TDA §415 elections.
32. Code §415(c)(4)(A).
33. As defined in Code §403(b)(3).
34. Determined under Code §403(b)(2).
35. Code §415(c)(4)(B).
36. Code §415(c)(4)(C). For special rules under which contributions to church plans are treated as not exceeding the applicable annual addition limit, see Code §415(c)(7).
37. Within the meaning of Code §4975(e)(7) or a tax-credit employee stock ownership plan. See §415(c)(6)(B).
38. Within the meaning of §414(q), see §415(c)(6)(A).
39. Within the meaning of §409, see §415(c)(6)(B)(ii).
40. Code §415(c)(6)(A).
41. Code §415(e).
42. Code §415(e)(1).
43. Code §415(e)(2)(A).
44. Code §415(e)(2)(B).
45. Code §415(e)(3)(A).

46. Code §415(e)(3)(B).
47. Code §415(e)(1).
48. Code §415(h)(1).
49. Code §416(h)(2).
50. Code §416(h)(2)(A)(ii)(I).
51. Code §416(h)(2)(A)(ii)(II).
52. Code §416(h)(1)(B).
53. Code §415(g).
54. Code §415(e)(6).
55. Code §415(e)(6)(A).
56. Code §415(e)(6)(B)(i).
57. Code §416(h)(3).
58. Code §415(f)(1).
59. *Id.* Under another plan aggregation rule contained in Code §415(h), in applying the individual plan limits of §§415(b) and (c), the §414 controlled group rules are to be applied by substituting "more than 50%" for "at least 80%" each place it appears in Code §1563(a)(1). Thus, it takes a lower level of interlocking ownership to trigger the controlled group rules for §415 purposes than is generally the case for the purposes of other Code provisions.

6

Parity and Top-Heavy Rules

The Tax Equity and Fiscal Responsibility Act of 1982 made sweeping changes in the tax law governing qualified plans—the most sweeping since ERISA was enacted in 1974. The major TEFRA changes fall into two categories: the "parity" provisions and the "top-heavy" rules.

In enacting the parity provisions, Congress sought to rectify a disparity in the tax treatment that existed between the qualified plans of corporate and unincorporated entities. This disparity had arisen because, in 1962, Congress had enacted H.R. 10, the bill which gave its name to the qualified plans of unincorporated entities (known as "H.R. 10" or "Keogh" plans). The body of law concerning the taxation of the qualified plans of unincorporated entities then developed independently of the qualified plan rules and, in 1982, generally afforded much less attractive benefits to the plans of unincorporated entities than those of corporations. In enacting the parity provisions, Congress sought to make qualified plan considerations tax-neutral in deciding in what form to operate a business entity. It did so by bringing corporate plans within the coverage of certain rules that had previously applied only to H.R. 10 plans, by eliminating certain of the H.R. 10 plan requirements, and by enacting the top-heavy plan rules which, in many respects, were drawn from the H.R. 10 plan rules but which were now applied to all qualified plans.

The top-heavy rules, contained in Code §416, provide certain additional requirements that qualified plans must satisfy where a disproportionate amount of the plan's benefits inures to certain highly compensated individuals known as "key employees." These changes were enacted to buttress the regular nondiscrimination rules of Code §401(a). Congress felt that these changes were necessary because, notwithstanding the regular nondiscrimination rules, in certain plans (often involving closely held businesses), benefits were still going disproportionately to the highly paid. The top-heavy rules were designed to insure that a tax-qualified plan provide at least a minimum level of universal coverage to the sponsor's employees.

Although both the parity and top-heavy rules are discussed elsewhere, this chapter provides an explanation of the legislative intent behind, and an overview of, these rules.[1]

Parity Rules

Before TEFRA, more favorable income tax benefits were available under a "corporate" retirement plan than under the plans of unincorporated entities (partnerships, proprietorships and, for this purpose, S corporations). Under pre-TEFRA law, unincorporated entities could maintain only H.R. 10 plans. H.R. 10 plans benefiting one or more "owner-employees"[2] were subject to certain restrictive rules. For instance, in 1981, the maximum annual addition that could be made to the account of a self-employed individual in a defined contribution H.R. 10 plan was the lesser of $15,000 or 15 percent of compensation. This contrasted with the then Code §415(b)(1) limit on corporate defined contribution plans of the lesser of 25 percent of compensation or $45,475. In addition, the corporate dollar figure was adjusted annually for inflation but this was not the case for H.R. 10 plans. The H.R. 10 plan rules were also stricter in the areas of vesting, distributions, trusteeship (an individual could not be his own plan's trustee in an H.R. 10 plan, but could in a corporate plan), benefit accrual, and so on.

The H.R. 10 plan restrictions generally applied only to entities having one or more shareholder-employees or owner-employees (collectively known as "self-employed individuals"). Conceptually, the H.R. 10 plan rules applied *on top of* the regular Code §401(a) qualification rules (H.R. 10 plans were also §401(a) plans). Only where a more restrictive H.R. 10 plan rule was imposed over a regular qualification rule did it take effect. In these instances, the regular rule was not so much null and void as rendered dormant. Where the H.R. 10 plan rule only applied to the self-employed individuals covered by the plan, it was still theoretically possible for an employer to be as liberal as the corporate plan limits would allow with respect to rank-and-file employees. Despite this, however, the practical effect was usually that the more restrictive rules also applied to rank-and-file employees, since business owners rarely conferred better benefits on rank-and-file employees than on themselves.

It was possible, however, for an unincorporated entity not to be subject to the H.R. 10 rules because it employed no self-employed individuals. An example would be a partnership where no partner owned a 10 percent capital or profits interest. These plans of unincorporated entities were not subject to the major H.R. 10 restrictions and were known as "super-Keogh" plans.

TEFRA repealed the H.R. 10 plan restrictions effective generally for plan years beginning after 1983. In the area of the annual contribution/benefit limit, it lowered the former corporate plan limits and raised the former H.R. 10 plan limits to a point in between both old limits. The limits are now, in most respects, identical regardless of whether the business is incorporated or unincorporated and regardless of whether there is a self-employed individual participating. In the case of a self-employed individual, however, the compensation on which a benefit may be based is net self-employment income, taking into account the plan contribution deduction. Thus, for instance, where a corporate defined contribution plan benefited a shareholder/employee, such an individual earning $100,000 per year could be allocated an annual addition of $25,000 (lesser of 25 percent of compensation or $30,000).

As a result of the disparate treatment that existed before TEFRA, many businesses incorporated solely to avail themselves of the more liberal corporate limits. After TEFRA, the plans of unincorporated entities have parity with those of incorporated entities. Specifically, TEFRA repealed the H.R. 10 plan requirements that:

(1) All employees having three years' service be 100 percent vested in their employer's contributions;[3]

(2) Employer contributions on behalf of an owner-employee in excess of the special limits imposed by Code §404(e) be prohibited by the plan;[4]

(3) Voluntary or mandatory contributions by an owner-employee *as an employee* be prohibited by the plan where the plan only benefited owner-employees;[5]

(4) The plan prohibit employer contributions on behalf of an owner-employee for the five taxable years following a premature withdrawal of such contributions by such employee;[6]

(5) The trustee of an H.R. 10 plan be a bank, credit union, or other financial institution subject to government supervision;[7]

(6) An H.R. 10 profit-sharing plan set a definite contribution formula for employees who are not owner-employees;[8] and

(7) A consent to participate be obtained from owner-employees before such employees could be allowed to participate in the H.R. 10 plan.[9]

In addition, TEFRA extended the H.R. 10 plan rules that it did not repeal, in their old or, in some cases, modified, form, to all plans, provided such plans were top-heavy for the plan year. Specifically, TEFRA applied the following H.R. 10 plan rules to all top-heavy plans:

(1) The minimum required distribution rules;[10]

(2) The rule that limited defined contribution H.R. 10 plans to the applicable Old Age Survivors' and Disability premium in integrating such plans with Social Security (this rule was applied generally to all defined contribution plans);[11]

(3) The rule that limited to $200,000 the compensation which could be considered in providing a benefit;[12] and

(4) The three-year, 100 percent vesting requirement formerly applicable to H.R. 10 plans (this was made one of the optional vesting schedules that could be adopted with respect to a top-heavy plan year).[13]

Top-Heavy Rules

The top-heavy rules, contained in Code §416, generally assure that, where the benefits under a qualified plan inure disproportionately to certain highly compensated individuals or owners of the sponsoring employer, rank-and-file employees will receive certain minimum benefits. TEFRA made satisfaction of the top-heavy rules a qualification requirement for all Code §401(a) plans. Even a non-top-heavy plan must contain these rules, unless specifically exempted under Treasury regulations.[14] The top-heavy rules apply *in addition to* the regular qualification requirements.

Consequences of Top-Heaviness

A top-heavy plan must satisfy certain minimum vesting[15] and minimum benefit/contribution requirements.[16] The top-heavy vesting requirements require that, for any top-heavy plan year, the plan either provide for 100 percent vesting after an employee has completed three years of service or that it provide for vesting in 20 percent annual increments over six years. These alternatives are known as "three-year cliff vesting" and "six-year graded vesting." They are more stringent than the regular vesting requirements for Code §401(a) plans.

The minimum contribution/benefit requirements require that a top-heavy defined contribution plan provide each non-key employee with a benefit equal to 3 percent of annual compensation or such lesser percentage as may be provided the key employee who receives the highest percentage of compensation for the plan year. A top-heavy defined benefit plan must provide each non-key employee with an accrued benefit equal to 2 percent of such employee's compensation earned during a statutory testing period, not to exceed 20 percent of such testing period compensation with respect to any non-key employee for all top-heavy plan years.[17]

Note that the regulations specify that, if an employee has ceased employment before a plan becomes top-heavy, the employer is not required to provide the employee with minimum accruals, contributions, or vesting unless the individual returns to employment with the employer.[18]

Finally, if a plan is top-heavy, the "combined plan limitation" on the accrual of benefits by an employee who participates in one or more defined benefit plans and one or more defined contribution plans maintained by the same employer is decreased.

Determining Top-Heavy Status

The 60% Test

A defined benefit plan is top-heavy for a plan year if, as of the "determination date," the present value of the accrued benefits under the plan for key employees exceeds 60 percent of the present value of accrued benefits under the plan for all employees.[19] A defined contribution plan is a top-heavy plan for a plan year if, as of the determination date, the value of the accounts of key employees exceeds 60 percent of the value of the accounts of all employees under the plan.[20]

The "determination date" for any plan year is (1) The last day of the preceding plan year, or (2) For the first plan year of any plan, the last day of the plan year.[21]

The determination date is, in effect, a snapshot of the accumulated benefits accrued under a plan taken at a designated point in time. If a plan is a calendar year plan, for example, the determination date for the January 1, 1989–December 31, 1989 plan year would be December 31, 1988. If the plan was top-heavy on that date, the top-heavy rules would apply for the entire ensuing plan year, regardless of whether, during that year, the accrued benefits of key employees fell to 60 percent or less. Similarly, if, on December 31, 1988, the plan was not top-heavy, the top-heavy rules would not apply to the plan until, at the earliest, the 1990 plan year, even if the benefits of key employees rose above 60 percent during the 1989 plan year.

In determining the level of benefits of both key employees and all employees under the plan, the present value of the accrued benefit of any employee (in a defined benefit plan) or the account value of any employee (in a defined contribution plan) is increased by the value of any distributions made with respect to such employee under the plan during the five-year period ending on the determination date.

Because key employees are often individuals who are in a position to control the timing of distributions to themselves or their beneficiaries, the five-year lookback rule makes it more difficult for a plan to avoid top-heavy classification by planned distributions to key employees. The statutory phrase "with respect to such employee" makes it clear that all distributions of amounts credited to the employee under the plan are to be counted, regardless of whether they are distributed to the employee or to the employee's spouse or other beneficiary.

In determining whether the 60 percent test is met, certain special rules apply. For example, except to the extent provided by the regulations, any "rollover" contribution (or similar transfer) to a plan initiated by the employee is not counted in applying the 60 percent test to the recipient plan.[22] (A rollover is a tax-free transfer of an employee's interest in a qualified plan or IRA to another qualified plan or IRA. Rollovers are explained in greater detail in Chapter 10.)

Another special rule provides that, if an employee was a key employee in a prior plan year but ceased to be a key employee as of the determination date for the current plan year, the benefits such individual earned under the plan will not be counted in the top-heavy determination.[23]

This rule means that such benefits are not counted in either the numerator or the denominator of the top-heavy plan fraction. It will be as if this individual was not a participant in the plan for the year. This prevents individuals who had been key employees in past years from divesting themselves of key employee status, in an effort to prevent the plan from being top-heavy. While there is still some potential to use this device to escape top-heavy status (since it will effectively prevent the benefits earned by such an individual from being counted in either the numerator or the denominator of the equation) the rule at least prevents the plan from counting the benefits accrued by the former key employee as benefits earned by a non-key employee in the year or years after the individual loses key employee status.

Although the regulations provide that the top-heavy ratios need not be computed each year to determine whether a plan is top heavy, the administrator has the responsibility for knowing the status of the plan.[24] If the IRS questions the plan's status, the employer may show, by using calculations that are "not precisely in accordance" with §416, that the plan is not top-heavy.[25] The regulations provide as an example estimating benefits for key employees in a manner that overstates such benefits. The IRS also provides in regulations three methods of estimating that may be used to make the top-heavy calculation.[26] These are:

(1) If the top-heavy ratio, computed by taking into account all key employees but not all non-key employees is less than 60 percent, the employer need not accumulate employee data concerning any remaining non-key employees.

(2) If the employer knows the number of key employees but not their identity, the numerator may be calculated using a hypothetical "worst case" basis. Thus, for instance, if the numerator of the top-heavy fraction for all key employees was computed based on the assumption that all key employees will accrue a benefit equal to the maximum accruable benefit under Code §415 and the ratio so computed was less than 60 percent, the plan would not be top heavy.

(3) If the employer's figure for the present value of accrued benefits of employees under a defined benefit plan differs from the present value figure that would be derived under the regulations[27] solely due to the inclusion of a withdrawal assumption, the employer may adjust the present value figures for key employees. The regulations provide a formula for making this adjustment that takes into account the likelihood that an employee will withdraw from the plan prior to attaining normal retirement age.[28]

The regulations specify that these calculation procedures may also be used in determining whether a plan is "super top-heavy" (a term discussed below) for the plan year.

Who Are the Key Employees?

Key employees are defined differently from highly compensated employees for Code §401(a)(4) purposes, although many key employees will also be highly compensated. A key employee is any participant who, at any time during the plan year or any of the four preceding plan years, is (or was) in one of four categories, described below.[29] Under Code §416(i)(2), a non-key employee is simply any employee other than a key employee.

Officers. This category includes any employee who is an officer of the employer. For this purpose, no more than 50 employees (or, if lesser, the greater of three or 10 percent of the employees) shall be treated as officers.[30]

Example: Corporation A has 450 employees, 60 of whom are classified as officers. Under the general rule, no more than 50 of these individuals will be counted as officers for purposes of the key employee test. Further, 10 percent of all the employees of the employer is 45. Since this number is less than 50 and greater than three, the second test will apply. Thus, 45 of the 60 will be considered officers. The 45 who will be counted will be the 45 officers earning the highest compensation.

Only those individuals performing actual officer functions are counted as officers. Thus, an individual could have an officer title and yet not be an officer for this purpose if it can be demonstrated that the person does not perform duties typical of an officer. An example might be the officers of a bank where, for nontax reasons, many individuals are given officer titles who do not perform the duties generally associated with corporate officers. Similarly, an employee who lacks an officer title but performs officer duties will be considered an officer. An officer will only be considered a key employee if the officer has annual compensation from the employer that is greater than 150 percent of the dollar amount in effect under Code §415(c)(1)(A) for the year ($30,000 for 1988, to be indexed for inflation).

If an individual is employed by a controlled group of corporations, officer status will be determined with respect to the corporation by which the employee is directly employed, and not by reference to the employee's services with respect to the entire group.

For purposes of Code §416, unincorporated entities are considered to have officers. A partner in a partnership will not be considered an officer merely because he or she owns a capital or profits interest in the partnership, exercises voting rights as a partner, and may, for limited purposes, be authorized to, and does in fact, act as an agent for the partnership.[31]

Top 10 Owners of the Employer. A key employee under this category is one of the 10 employees owning[32] during the plan year containing the determination date or any of the four preceding plan years a certain level of interest in the employer. This interest must be both more than a .5 percent ownership interest in value and the largest percentage ownership interest by value of any of the employers required to be aggregated under Code §414(b), (c), or (m).[33]

Ownership for each plan year is determined on the basis of the employee's percentage of ownership in total ownership value, and not in terms of dollar amounts. Thus, for instance, an employee whose stock interest in Year #1 was valued at $15,000, and constituted 15 percent of the corporation's total stock value, would be ranked higher than an employee whose percentage interest in the corporation in Year #3 was 5 percent, even though that interest was worth $50,000.

Under the regulations, if an employee's ownership interest changes during a plan year, the employee's ownership interest for the year is considered to be the largest interest owned at any time during the year. If two or more employees have the same ownership interest in the employer during the testing period, the employee with the highest annual compensation from the employer for the plan year is considered to have the largest equity interest.[34]

A 5 Percent Owner of the Employer. For this purpose, if the employer is a corporation, a 5 percent owner is any employee who owns (or is considered as owning under Code §318) more than 5 percent of the value of the outstanding stock of the corporation or stock possessing more than 5 percent of the total combined voting power of all stock of the corporation. If the employer is unincorporated, a 5 percent owner is any employee who owns more than 5 percent of the capital or profits interest in the employer. In determining who is a 5 percent owner, the aggregation rules of Code §§414(b), (c), and (m) do not apply.[35]

A 1 Percent Owner of the Employer With Annual Compensation of More Than $150,000. Under this test, an employee who owns 1 percent or more of the employer and who receives compensation from the employer in excess of $150,000 is considered a key employee.[36]

In determining 1 percent ownership for this purpose, rules similar to those set forth with respect to 5 percent owners above apply.[37]

Key Employee Aggregation Rules. The regulations provide that, in determining ownership percentages for purposes of the top-heavy rules, each employer that would otherwise have to be aggregated under Code §§414(b), (c), or (m) will be treated as a separate employer.[38] In determining whether an employee has $150,000 of compensation, however, or whether an individual is a key employee by virtue of officer or top 10 percent status, each entity that has to be considered under the aggregation rules is taken into account. The regulations provide the following example:

"*Example*: An individual owns 2% of the value of a professional corporation, which in turn owns a 1/10th of 1% interest in a partnership. The entities must be aggregated in accordance with §414(m). The individual performs services for both the professional corporation and the partnership. The individual receives compensation of $125,000 from the professional corporation and $26,000 from the partnership. The individual is considered to be a key employee with respect to the employer that comprises both the professional corporation and the partnership because he has a 2% interest in the professional corporation and because his combined compensation from both the professional corporation and the partnership is more than $150,000."[39]

Other Special Rules. In addition to the foregoing, the following special rules apply in determining which employees are key employees:

(1) A self-employed individual is treated as an employee for purposes of the definition of key employee and such individual's earned income is treated as compensation.[40]

(2) The top-heavy minimum benefit and vesting rules will not apply to any employee included in a collective bargaining unit where the Secretary of Labor finds that retirement benefits were the subject of good faith bargaining.[41]

(3) For purposes of the definition of key employee, the terms "employee" and "key employee" include their beneficiaries.[42]

Top-Heavy Plan Aggregation Rules

In testing for top-heaviness, each plan required to be included in an aggregation group will be considered a top-heavy plan if the aggregation group is considered to be a "top-heavy group." A top-heavy group can be any aggregation group if the sum (as of the determination date) of the present value of the cumulative accrued benefits for key employees under all defined benefit plans included in such group and the aggregate of the accounts of key employees of all defined contribution plans included in such group exceeds 60 percent of a similar sum so determined for all employees.[43]

Again, as in the regular top-heavy determination, the various special rules, such as the five-year distribution lookback rule, apply in determining each employee's benefit under the various plans.

Code §416(f)(2) breaks down aggregation groups into two types:

(1) Required aggregation groups; and

(2) Permissive aggregation groups.

As their names suggest, the employer must combine all plans in a required aggregation group in testing for top-heaviness, but need not (although it may elect to) also aggregate plans within a permissive aggregation group.

A required aggregation group is defined as:

(1) Each plan of the employer in which a key employee is a participant; and

(2) Each plan of the employer that enables any plan having a key employee participant to satisfy the general antidiscrimination rule of Code §401(a)(4) or the participation rules of Code §410.[44]

An employer, under Code §416(g)(2)(A), may also elect to include in the group plans that are not required to be part of the group if the expanded group would continue to satisfy Code §401(a)(4) and §410. This expanded group is called the "permissive aggregation group."

There are several factors to consider in determining whether to aggregate plans from a permissive aggregation group. Whether the election should be made will depend on the particular facts involved. If the employer's required aggregation group is top-heavy, it is possible that, by including the permissive aggregation group, the combined group will not be top-heavy. Where this is so, plans in the required aggregation group that would otherwise have been considered top-heavy by virtue of their membership in a top-heavy group, but which were not themselves top-heavy, could be freed from top-heavy status where the combined group is not top-heavy. Where both the required aggregation group and the combined required and permissive aggregation group are top-heavy, an election to include the permissive group will taint all the plans within the permissive group with top-heavy status, however, regardless of whether they are top-heavy individually.

Where an individual plan is top-heavy, it will not escape the Code §416 requirements merely because its required or combined group is not top-heavy. Top-heavy group status can turn non-top heavy plans into top-heavy plans, but a top-heavy plan cannot escape the application of the rules because it is a member of a group that is not top-heavy.

Where the employer wishes to keep a plan out of a required aggregation group (for instance because the plan is not, itself, top-heavy but, when combined with other plans in the required group, produces a top-heavy group), it may wish to exclude key employees entirely from participation in the non-top-heavy plan. This type of provision will prevent the plan in which key employees do not participate from being included in the required aggregation group. The exclusion can be accomplished by including in the plan document an appropriately drafted participation provision and, since such employees are generally also members of the Code §401(a)(4) prohibited group, is not likely to result in discrimination. Exclusion of key employees from the required aggregation group in this manner will be preferable to using the permissive aggregation rules where the permissive group is top-heavy. Where necessary, the excluded key employee can be compensated for being left out of the second plan by an increase in salary or through nonqualified deferred compensation. Where a limited number of key employees are involved, the savings in terms of not having to provide rapid vesting or minimum benefits can be substantial.

A permissive aggregation group includes any plan that does not have to be included in a required aggregation group if the required aggregation group would continue to satisfy the Code §401(a)(4) general antidiscrimination rule and the Code §410 participation rules with such plan being taken into account.[45]

The regulations provide rules as to when, in the case of an aggregation group, the determination of whether the group is top-heavy is to be made. Under these rules, when two or more plans constitute an aggregation group in accordance with Code §416(g)(2), the present value of accrued benefits (including distributions to key employees and all employees) is first determined separately for each plan as of each plan's determination date. The plans are then aggregated by adding together the results for each plan as of the determination dates for such plans that fall within the same calendar year. The combined results will determine whether the aggregated plans are top-heavy.[46]

The regulations provide the following example of how this determination is made:

"An employer maintains Plan A and Plan B, each containing a key employee. Plan A's plan year commences July 1 and ends June 30. Plan B's plan year is the calendar year. For Plan A's plan year commencing July 1, 1984, the determination date is June 30, 1984. For plan B's plan year in 1985, the determination date is December 31, 1984. These plans are required to be aggregated. For each of these plans as of their respective determination dates, the present value of the accrued benefits for key employees and all employees are separately determined. The two determination dates, June 30, 1984, and December 31, 1984, fall within the same calendar year. Accordingly, the present values of accrued benefits as of each of these determination dates are combined for purposes of determining whether the group is top-heavy. If, after combining the two present values, the total results show that the group is top-heavy, Plan A will be top-heavy for the plan year commencing July 1, 1984, and Plan B will be top-heavy for the 1985 calendar year."[47]

Effect of Top-Heaviness on Combined Plan Fraction

The fact that a plan is top-heavy or "super top-heavy" (a plan is super top-heavy when more than 90 percent of contributions or benefits go to key employees) will affect the application of the Code §415 rules on maximum benefits and contributions to the plan.

Where an employer maintains one or more defined benefit plans and one or more defined contribution plans covering the same participants, a special combined plan limit applies. The limit is imposed by the combined plan fraction. This fraction is the sum of the defined benefit plan fraction and the defined contribution plan fraction.

For this purpose, the defined benefit plan fraction for any year has as its numerator the projected annual benefit of the participant under the plan determined at the close of the plan year. The denominator is the lesser of 1.25 multiplied by the Code §415 defined benefit plan dollar limit in effect for the year or 1.4 times the §415 defined benefit plan percentage-of-compensation limit for the year, whichever is less. The defined contribution plan fraction has a numerator of the sum of the annual additions to the participant's account as of the close of the year. The denominator is the lesser of 1.25 times the defined contribution plan §415(c) dollar limit in effect for the year and each prior year of service with the employer or 1.4 times the §415(c) defined contribution plan percentage-of-compensation limit in effect for such years.

The sum of these two fractions ordinarily cannot exceed 1.0 for any participant for any year.

In the case of a top-heavy plan, "1.0" is substituted for "1.25" in the denominators of the respective fractions. This has the effect of reducing the combined plan limit to 100 percent of the lesser of 1.0 times the dollar limit or 1.4 times the percentage-of-compensation limit.

A top-heavy plan can, however, effectively "buy back" the right to use the regular 1.25 times the dollar limit component of the relevant fractions if it provides an additional top-heavy minimum benefit over and above that regularly required under Code §416.

In a defined benefit plan, this is done by providing each non-key employee with 3 percent (rather than 2 percent) of testing period compensation for the top-heavy plan year (not to exceed 30 percent of such compensation for any employee). In a defined contribution plan, this is done by providing for a minimum contribution equal to the lesser of 4% (rather than 3%) of compensation or such lesser percentage as is provided to the key employee participant for whom the employer's contribution for the year is the greatest when expressed as a percentage of compensation.

The right to buy back the higher limits, however, is denied to a super top-heavy plan. A super top-heavy plan is a plan under which more than 90 percent of the benefits (in a defined benefit plan) or more than 90 percent of the contributions (in a defined contribution plan) inure to key employees. Thus, top-heavy plans that have between 60 and 90 percent of their benefits inuring to key employees are provided with this buy back option, but not plans where over 90 percent of the benefits go to key employees.

Special Top-Heavy Rules

In addition to the foregoing general discussion, practitioners should be aware of the following special rules relating to top-heavy plans:

Simplified Employee Pensions (SEPs). For purposes of the top-heavy rules, a simplified employee pension is considered a defined contribution plan. An employer that sponsors a SEP may elect to have only employer contributions counted (instead of the aggregate of employee accounts) in applying the 60 percent test and the top-heavy aggregation rules.[48]

Frozen and Terminated Plans. For purposes of the top-heavy rules, a "frozen" plan (one in which accruals have ceased but which still remains in existence to distribute its assets to participants and beneficiaries) is treated as if it were not frozen. Thus, such a plan must contain top-heavy provisions. Further, if it is top-heavy, it must provide minimum accruals and top-heavy vesting provisions.

Although no additional top-heavy vesting, accruals, or contributions need be provided for participants in a terminated plan, for all other top-heavy purposes the regulations treat a terminated plan as if it were still active. For this purpose, a terminated plan is one that has been formally terminated, has ceased crediting service for benefit accrual and vesting purposes, and has been, or is, distributing its assets to participants and beneficiaries as soon as is administratively feasible. Such a plan must be aggregated with other plans of the employer if it was maintained within the last five years ending on the determination date for the plan year in question and would, but for the fact that it terminated, be part of a required aggregation group for the plan year. Distributions that have taken place within the five-year period ending on the determination date must be accounted for pursuant to Code §416(g)(3).[49]

Aggregation of Collectively Bargained Plans. The top-heavy minimum benefit accrual and vesting rules do not apply to a plan that the Secretary of Labor finds to be established under a collective bargaining agreement between employee representatives and one or more employers if there is evidence that retirement benefits were the subject of good faith collective bargaining. The regulations provide, however, that a collectively bargained plan that includes a key employee of an employer must be included in the required aggregation group for that employer. A collectively bargained plan that does not include a key employee may be included in a permissive aggregation group.[50]

Multiple and Multiemployer Plans. The regulations provide that multiemployer plans described in Code §414(f) and multiple employer plans described in Code §413(c) to which an employer makes contributions on behalf of its employees are treated as plans of that employer to the extent that benefits under the plan are provided to employees of the employer because of service with that employer.[51] An employer may permissively aggregate multiple employer plans and multiemployer plans (as well as SEPs) with a plan covering key employees or with a required aggregation group if the contributions or benefits provided under the multiemployer plan, multiple employer plan, or SEP are comparable to the contributions or benefits provided under the plan covering key employees or the plans in the required aggregation group.[52]

Certain Plans Not Required to Contain Top-Heavy Rules. Although the Code makes the top-heavy requirements applicable to almost all qualified plans, certain types of plans are statutorily exempted. IRS regulations identify certain circumstances in which a plan is not required to contain provisions that comply with these rules. The IRS felt that these situations contained little potential for abuse and that these types of plans were unlikely to become top-heavy anyway.

The Code exempts governmental plans within the meaning of §414(d) from the top-heavy requirements.[53] In addition, IRS regulations exempt plans that satisfy the following criteria:

(1) The plan is not top-heavy, and

(2) It covers only employees who are included in a unit of employees covered under a collective bargaining agreement, provided retirement benefits were the subject of good faith bargaining.

The regulations require that the criteria of Code §7701(a)(46) must be met before an agreement will be considered a collective bargaining agreement.[54]

In addition, the regulations provide that, where an employer has no employee who has participated in, or who is eligible to participate in, both a defined benefit and a defined contribution plan (including a SEP) of the employer, certain otherwise required top-heavy provisions may be omitted from the plan document. The provisions that may be omitted in this situation include:

(1) Provisions describing the defined benefit or defined contribution fraction for purposes of Code §415; and

(2) Provisions for determining whether a plan is super top-heavy or modifying certain other plan provisions should the plan become super top-heavy.

When the plan provides a single benefit structure that satisfies the top-heavy minimum contribution, benefit, and vesting requirements in all conceivable cases, the plan need not include separate provisions to determine whether it is top-heavy.[55]

Where the employer maintains or has maintained both a defined benefit and a defined contribution plan (or a SEP) and some participants do, or could, participate in both types of plans, the plans must contain more top-heavy provisions than in the situation where no employee is participating, or could participate, in both types of plans.

Nonetheless, plans of this type need not contain rules for determining whether the plan is top-heavy (or that apply if the plan becomes top-heavy) if both plans contain benefit structures that, in all conceivable cases, satisfy the top-heavy rules. In addition, if such plans, by their terms, will always produce a combined plan fraction for Code §415 purposes that is less than 1.0, such plans need not contain rules for determining if the plan is super top-heavy or that apply if it is.[56]

Notes

1. See Chapters 3 and 4 relating to vesting and benefit accrual. See also 353 T.M., *Owner Dominated Plans—Top-Heavy and H.R. 10 Plans.*
2. Owner employees are defined as sole proprietors, partners who own 10% or more of either the profits or capital interest in a partnership and 5%-or-more shareholder-employees of an S corporation.
3. Formerly contained in Code §401(d)(3)(A).
4. Former Code §401(d)(5)(A).
5. Former Code §401(d)(5)(B).
6. Former Code §401(d)(5)(C).
7. Former Code §401(d)(1).
8. Former Code §401(d)(2)(B).
9. Former Code §401(d)(4)(A).
10. This requirement was formerly found in Code §401(d)(7). The revised rule became §401(a)(9).
11. The old rule was found in pre-TEFRA Code §401(d)(5). The 1986 Tax Reform Act imposed further restrictions on Social Security integration. These included a rule limiting integration of a defined contribution plan to the old age portion of the OASDI premium.

12. Before the 1986 TRA, this limit applied only to top-heavy plans. The TRA extended the $200,000 limit to all qualified plans.
13. See Code § 416(b).
14. Code § 401(a)(10)(B).
15. See Code § 416(a)(1). The top-heavy vesting rules are set forth in § 416(b).
16. See Code § 416(a)(2). These requirements are set forth in § 416(d).
17. The computation of testing period compensation is discussed in text at nn. below.
18. Treas. Regs. § 1.416-1, Q&A T-43.
19. Code § 416(g)(1)(A)(i).
20. Code § 416(g)(1)(A)(ii).
21. Code § 416(g)(4)(C).
22. Code § 416(g)(4)(A).
23. Code § 416(g)(4)(B).
24. Treas. Regs. § 1.416-1, Q&A T-39.
25. *Id.*
26. *Id.*
27. Treas. Regs. § 1.416-1, Q&A T-25.
28. Treas. Regs. § 1.416-1, Q&A T-39.
29. Code § 416(i)(1).
30. Code § 416(i)(1)(A).
31. Treas. Regs. § 1.416-1, Q&A T-13.
32. Or considered as owning due to the application of the ownership attribution rules of Code § 318.
33. Code § 416(i)(1)(A)(ii); Treas. Regs. § 1.416-1, Q&A T-19.
34. Treas. Regs. § 1.416-1, Q&A T-19.
35. Code § 416(i)(1)(A)–(B); Treas. Regs. § 1.416-1, Q&A T-17.
36. Code § 416(i)(1)(A)(iv).
37. Code § 416(i)(1)(B)(ii). Thus, for instance, in applying the constructive ownership rules of Code § 318 for purposes of both this and the 5 percent ownership test, Code § 416(i)(1)(B)(iii) provides that § 318(a)(2)(C) shall be applied by substituting "5 percent" for "50 percent" and, in the case of unincorporated employers, ownership will be determined under regulations that apply principles similar to those contained in § 318.
38. Code § 416(i)(1)(C).
39. Treas. Regs. § 1.416-1, Q&A T-20.
40. Code § 416(i)(3).
41. Code § 416(i)(4).
42. Code § 416(i)(5).
43. Code § 416(g)(1)(B).
44. Code § 416(g)(2)(A)(i).
45. Code § 416(g)(2)(A)(ii).
46. Treas. Regs. § 1.416-1, Q&A T-23.
47. *Id.* at Q&A T-23.
48. Code § 416(i)(6)(B).
49. Treas. Regs. § 1.416-1, Q&A T-4 and 5.
50. *Id.* at Q&A T-3.
51. *Id.* at Q&A T-2.

52. *Id.* at Q&A T-8. As indicated above, in applying this latter rule in the case of a SEP, only the employer's contribution may be counted.
53. Code § 401(a)(10)(B).
54. Treas. Regs. § 1.416-1, Q&A T-39.
55. *Id.* at Q&A T-36.
56. *Id.*

7

Limits on Employer and Employee Contributions

Deductibility of Employer Contributions Under Code §404

One of the principal advantages of establishing a tax-qualified plan is that the employer may, within certain limits, deduct its contributions currently, while participants need not recognize taxable income until they actually receive a distribution. The deductibility of a contribution by an employer depends on whether the contribution satisfies two tests. First, the contribution must be an ordinary and necessary business expense within the meaning of Code §§162 or 212.[1] Second, the contribution must fall within the limits of Code §404.

Generally, for an employer to deduct contributions to a qualified plan for a taxable year, the plan must have been in existence, i.e., the formalities of plan adoption must have been completed, before the end of the taxable year. Thus, the employer can evaluate its financial position as its taxable year draws to a close and determine if it would be beneficial to establish a qualified plan in that year. Such factors as a healthy profitability picture coupled with the potential of having excess retained corporate earnings (in the case of a corporation) are among those that an employer might consider in deciding whether to establish a plan, in addition to the obvious ones of providing for the retirement needs of employees.

Once the plan is adopted, the employer's contribution for the taxable year must be made before the due date of its federal income tax return for the year, including any extensions, if the employer is to take a deduction for a contribution in the taxable year to which the return relates.[2] Corporate tax returns are usually due two and one-half months after the close of the taxable year, with extensions of up to six months readily available. Where a contribution is made after the close of the taxable year that is intended to relate back to the prior year, the employer must note this fact on its federal income tax return; otherwise, the IRS will treat the contribution as if it were attributable to the employer's taxable year in which it was made.

Generally, for deductibility purposes, the employer's contribution may take any form, for example, cash, securities, or other property. This general rule is subject to an important limitation, however: the contribution, to be deductible, cannot take the form of the employer's unsecured promissory note, even if the employer is on the accrual method of accounting. Further, as discussed in Chapter 12, ERISA's fiduciary duty rules limit the ability of certain qualified plans to hold employer securities or employer real property.

Under general principles of taxation, when the employer contributes property that has a fair market value exceeding its adjusted basis, the employer will have to recognize taxable gain to the extent of the difference. This is because the employer's contribution obligation is being extinguished with a piece of property having a lesser basis than the obligation to contribute to the plan. An example would be the extinguishing of a $10,000 obligation with the contribution of property having an adjusted basis of $6,000 and fair market value of $10,000. This sort of difference between a piece of property's adjusted basis and its fair market value is usually the result of the fact that the employer's depreciation deductions have exceeded the actual diminutions of the property's market value over time.

The converse of this situation, however, does not produce a loss deduction, e.g., where a $6,000 obligation is extinguished with the contribution of property having a $10,000 basis and a $6,000 fair market value. This is because Code §267 denies taxpayers deductions for losses incurred in transactions between related parties (in this case, the employer and the plan's trust). In this situation, it would be advisable for the employer to sell the property, recognize the loss, and make a deductible cash contribution of

$6,000. This is especially so since, for taxable years beginning after 1986, plan sponsors are subject to a nondeductible 10 percent penalty tax if they make nondeductible contributions to a qualified plan for a taxable year.[3]

Note that there also may be situations where the *plan* will have to sell property that has been contributed to provide sufficient liquidity to pay benefits when they fall due.

For single employer plans, only the employer sponsoring the plan is entitled to a Code §404 deduction for contributing to it. An exception exists for multiple employer and multiemployer plans. Also, where an affiliated group of corporations maintains a profit-sharing plan, and a group member is unable to contribute to the plan because it lacks profits, the remaining employers may make such contributions on the nonprofitable member's behalf up to the percentage of that member's employees' compensation that would have been contributed. (Note, however, that, after the 1986 Tax Reform Act, profits are not a prerequisite to an employer's contributing to a profit-sharing plan). Where the affiliated group does not file a consolidated return for the taxable year in question, the contributions that may be made up by each remaining employer may not exceed each employer's proportionate share of total employer contributions that were made to the profit-sharing plan for the year in which the "make-up" contribution is made.[4]

The employer's applicable Code §404 deduction limit for the year will depend upon the type of plan involved.

Defined Benefit Plans

Code §404(a)(1) provides three alternative methods that a defined benefit pension plan may use in computing the employer's maximum allowable annual deductible contribution.[5] These alternative limits are subject to the overall rule that the annual deductible amount must be computed using the funding method and the actuarial assumptions that the plan uses for purposes of the Code §412 minimum funding standard rules. Further, in no year may the deductible amount exceed the amount that is necessary to satisfy the full funding limitation of §412.[6]

The first alternative method may be called the "minimum funding standard method." Under this method, the employer may deduct annually the amount necessary to satisfy the Code §412 minimum funding standard (defined generally as the excess, if any, of charges over credits to the plan's §412 funding standard account) if this amount is greater than the amount deductible under the second and third alternatives described below.[7]

The second method is the "individual level premium method." Under this method, the employer may deduct the amount necessary to fund the remaining unfunded cost of the plan's past service credits and any current service credits under the entry age normal funding method, distributed as a level amount (or a level percentage of compensation) over the projected remaining future service of each participant.[8]

Where the individual level premium method applies, if the unfunded cost with respect to any three individuals covered by the plan is more than 50 percent of the total remaining unfunded cost for the plan, the amount of unfunded cost attributable to those individuals must be spread out for deductibility purposes over at least five years.[9] This prevents the use of the plan as a device to rapidly fund the benefits of highly compensated participants with deductible contributions.

The third alternative is the "normal cost plus 10-year amortization method." Under this method, the employer may deduct an amount equal to the plan's normal costs plus any supplemental liability, e.g., past service liability, experience losses, and so forth. The supplemental liability must, however, be amortized in equal annual installments over a period of 10 years.[10]

Note that, when an employer makes an excess contribution for a year to a defined benefit plan, i.e., an amount that cannot be deducted in the current year because of the Code §404 limits, the excess amount may be carried forward indefinitely and deducted in any future year to the extent that the employer's contribution for that year is less than the amount allowable under §404 as a deduction for that year. Such excess amounts are to be carried forward to future years in succeeding order of time.[11] When a plan terminates with unused carryovers, deductions may be carried forward to the year of termination or a later year, but the deduction for such carryovers in any year cannot exceed the amount that would be deductible under the normal cost plus 10-year amortization method. Since, at this point, the plan's normal costs will be zero, the result will be that the carryforwards will be deductible in equal annual installments over the next 10 years.

In a conforming change necessitated by the more rigorous funding rules imposed on defined benefit plans by OBRA (1987),[12] if a defined benefit plan (other than a multiemployer plan) has more than 100 participants for the plan year, the maximum amount deductible under Code §404 will not be less than the plan's "unfunded current liability," as determined under Code §412(l).[13] This provision was needed to ensure that an employer will not be required to make a contribution under the revised minimum funding standard, while being denied the right to deduct the required contribution.

Profit-Sharing and Stock Bonus Plans

Generally, an employer may deduct annually, with respect to contributions made, an amount equal to 15 percent of the compensation paid or accrued to participants in a profit-sharing or stock bonus plan.[14] Contributions in excess of the deductible limits arising in taxable years beginning before 1987 may be carried forward indefinitely to future years in succeeding order of time, subject to the restriction that the amount carried forward cannot exceed 15 percent of participant compensation paid or accrued in the year to which the deduction is carried. Further, the combined deductions for the current year plus any deductions carried over to that year may not exceed 25 percent of participant compensation paid or accrued in the year to which the excess contribution is carried.[15]

For contributions in excess of the deductible limits arising in taxable years beginning after 1986, the total deductible amount in the carryforward year, consisting of amounts carried forward from a prior year plus the current year's deduction, cannot exceed 15 percent of compensation paid or accrued to participants in the carryforward year.[16]

Limits Applicable to Combinations of Plans

Where an employer maintains two or more defined benefit plans or two or more defined contribution plans, the applicable Code §404 limit is applied to all plans of the same type in the aggregate. In other words, the employer does not get extra tax deductions for maintaining multiple plans of the same type that cover the same employees. If the employer maintains one or more pension or annuity plans and one or more profit-sharing or stock bonus plans, however, the individual limit is superseded by the combined plan limit of Code §404(a)(7). That paragraph limits the employer's annual deductible contribution to the greater of:

(1) 25 percent of compensation paid to or accrued during the taxable years to the participants in such plans; or

(2) The amount of contributions made to defined benefit plans to the extent such contributions do not exceed the amount needed to satisfy the minimum funding standard for the plan year which ends with or within the employer's taxable year (or any prior plan year).[17]

A money purchase pension plan, when combined with a profit-sharing or stock bonus plan, will also be subject to the Code §404(a)(7) combined plan limit. This is because, for §404 purposes, money purchase plans are treated as defined benefit plans. The minimum funding standard in the case of a money purchase plan is the employer's annual contribution obligation, as money purchase plans do not have deferred supplemental liabilities. Therefore, the §404(a)(7) combined plan limit for combinations of plans that involve defined contribution plans and one or more money purchase plans will be the 25 percent of compensation limit. Code §404(a)(7) does not limit the amount otherwise deductible under the §404(a) individual plan limits where the plans involved have no common participants.[18]

Where a contribution is not deductible due to the application of the combined plan limit of Code §404(a)(7), the nondeductible amounts may be carried forward and deducted in future taxable years in succeeding order of time. The total amount deductible in any such carryforward year (carryforward amounts plus that year's regular contribution), however, may not exceed 25 percent of compensation paid or accrued during the taxable year to participants under the plan.

Partially as a result of the combined plan rules, in a business' early years when profits may be uncertain, employers often adopt a profit-sharing plan with a discretionary annual contribution formula. When, in later years, the business becomes more stable, employers often add a money purchase or defined benefit pension plan and take advantage of the increased deduction available under the combined plan limits.

Code §404(j): Coordination of §404 and §415 Limits

Before TEFRA, there was no coordination between the maximum benefit or annual addition that could be earned under Code §415 and the maximum deductible employer contribution under Code §404. TEFRA enacted Code §404(j), which limits the amount of the employer's annual deductible contribution to the applicable annual §415 limit. Thus, an employer maintaining a defined benefit plan may not deduct a contribution that exceeds the permissible projected annual benefit accrual under §415(b) with respect to all participants for the year. For a defined contribution plan, the Code §404(j) limit is geared to the maximum annual addition allowable under §415 with respect to all participants.

Section 404(j) also prevents an employer from deducting contributions made to fund in advance a cost-of-living adjustment under a defined benefit plan.

Special Limits

Self-Employed Individuals

A self-employed individual is treated as an employee for purposes of the Code §404 deduction rules, and the §404(a) limits apply to plans which benefit such individuals. The compensation of a self-employed individual for this purpose is the earned income of the individual derived from the trade or business maintaining the plan.[19] Contributions to a qualified plan on behalf of a self-employed individual are considered to satisfy the reasonable compensation requirements of Code §§162 and 212 if they do not exceed the net earned income (gross income less allocable deductions other than the deduction for plan contributions) of the individual from the trade or business, provided the amount is not used to purchase life, health, or accident insurance for the self-employed individual through the plan.

Employee Stock Ownership Plans (ESOPs)

Code §404(a)(9) contains a special rule designed to encourage employers to sponsor "leveraged ESOPs." A leveraged ESOP is, generally, one that borrows money (often with the employer acting as guarantor on the loan) to acquire securities of the employer corporation. Under the special ESOP rule, the regular §404(a) deduction limits do not apply to contributions made by the employer to the ESOP that are used by the ESOP to repay the principal amount of a securities acquisition loan. Instead, such contributions are deductible up to 25 percent of compensation paid or accrued to the ESOP participants for the year. Further, any contributions to the plan that are used to pay the interest on a securities acquisition loan are deductible in their entirety, regardless of amount.

Limits on Employee Contributions

Voluntary Nondeductible Employee Contributions

If a qualified plan so provides, employees may be permitted to make voluntary contributions. Permitting voluntary nondeductible employee contributions will not adversely affect a plan's tax qualification, provided such contributions are limited to a reasonable amount.[20] An amount will usually be considered reasonable if it does not exceed 10 percent of the participant's total compensation.[21] From an income tax standpoint, voluntary nondeductible employee contributions must first be reported as wages or other income to employees when those amounts are earned; the employee is not entitled to deduct his voluntary contributions.

Permitting voluntary nondeductible employee contributions provides the employee with tax-free growth on the funds contributed and provides the plan with a larger investment fund, which may result in a higher rate of return (for example, because the plan is able to purchase "jumbo" certificates of deposit or other investments with a minimum investment requirement). One major disadvantage exists to permitting such contributions: these contributions are counted in determining whether a plan is top-heavy or super top-heavy.[22] Therefore, in plans that border on becoming top-heavy or super top-heavy, the employer may wish to restrict voluntary employee contributions where they tend to come disproportionately from key employees.

Limit on Mandatory Employee Contributions

A plan can require employees to make mandatory contributions as a precondition to plan participation or to continued employment. The IRS, concerned that such an obligation might discourage rank-and-file employees from participating in plans, has limited the amount which can be required as a mandatory employee contribution to 6 percent of compensation.[23] Thus, a plan may require mandatory employee contributions of 6 percent of employee compensation and permit voluntary contributions of 10 percent of compensation, for a total of 16 percent, where such a requirement does not produce prohibited discrimination.

Qualified Voluntary (Deductible) Employee Contributions (QVECs)

The Economic Recovery Tax Act of 1981[24] permitted participants in tax-qualified employer or governmental plans to make qualified voluntary (deductible) employee contributions ("QVECs") to an individual retirement account (IRA). Alternatively, if the employee's employer or governmental plan permitted, the employee could make deductible IRA contributions directly to such a plan. Qualified recipient plans, for this purpose, were plans described in Code §401(a), §403(a) annuity plans, §405(a) retirement bond plans (before that section's repeal by the 1984 TRA), §403(b) annuity contracts, §408(k) Simplified Employee Pensions and governmental plans of the United States, a state or political subdivision thereof, or any agency or instrumentality of the foregoing. Although these amounts did not have to be held in separate plan accounts, separate accounting was required.

Plans accepting qualified voluntary employee contributions may need to contain certain protective provisions. For instance, IRA contributions cannot be invested in life insurance. If a plan holds life insurance, this can present a problem. A plan "ordering" provision, however, will generally cure this. An ordering provision can provide that, should the plan's assets be invested in life insurance, the amounts so invested will be considered to come first from employer contributions, second from voluntary nondeductible employee contributions or mandatory employee contributions (if applicable), and lastly from QVECs.

Unlike voluntary nondeductible employee contributions, QVECs are not counted in determining whether a plan is top-heavy or super top-heavy. Further, a plan that holds QVECs may pool them with the plan's general assets and conceivably earn a greater investment return, subject to the requirement that QVECs not be invested in life insurance.

The 1986 Tax Reform Act repealed the QVEC provisions effective for years beginning after 1986. After the 1986 TRA, deductible contributions under Code §219 cannot be made to a qualified plan. The QVEC rules are still significant, however, because, for years to come, many plans will still hold such amounts among their assets.

Code §402(g): $7,000 Limit on Elective Deferrals

To curb the use of Code §401(k) and other salary reduction arrangements by highly compensated individuals to defer large amounts of income, the 1986 Tax Reform Act enacted Code §402(g), providing a $7,000 annual cap (adjusted for inflation—the limit for 1988 was $7,313) on elective salary reduction (i.e., after-tax) deferrals by employees. The limit applies to elective deferrals under §401(k) cash-or-deferred arrangements (CODAs), Simplified Employee Pensions (SEPs) and Code §403(b) tax-deferred annuities (TDAs). For amounts deferred under TDAs, the limit is increased to $9,500.[25]

Under Code §402(g), if an employee's elective deferrals under all covered plans for the year exceed the annual dollar limit, a correcting distribution of the excess may be made to the affected employee on or before April 15th of the year following the year of the excess deferral. If such amounts are not distributed by two and one-half months after the close of the plan year, the *employer* will be subject to a 10 percent excise tax on excess contributions.[26] The fact that an excess employee deferral has been made, however, will not disqualify a §401(k) plan if the correcting distribution of the amount involved plus any growth thereon is made to the affected employee prior to the last day of the following taxable year.[27]

Code §402(g) is effective generally for taxable years beginning after 1986. Special effective date rules were provided for collectively bargained plans and for deferrals under CODAs in 1987 attributable to services performed in 1986.

Where a correcting distribution is made under Code §402(g) before the April 15th following the close of the taxable year, no penalty tax on premature distributions will apply and the employee will take the amount incorrectly deferred into income for the year in which the excess deferral was made. Any earnings on the excess deferral will be taxed to the employee in the year they are actually distributed.[28] Under a special provision, not later than the March 1st following the close of a taxable year, an individual who has made excess deferrals under §402(g) among multiple plans (the dollar limit applies to all deferrals in the aggregate made by the individual for the year), may allocate the amount of such excess deferrals among the plans to which the deferrals were made and notify each plan of the portion allocated to it. Once a plan has this information, it can then make the correcting distribution.

Code §401(m): Nondiscrimination Rules for Employee and Matching Contributions

In addition to enacting Code §402(g), discussed above, the 1986 Tax Reform Act added Code §401(m), establishing nondiscrimination tests for matching and employee contributions under all §401(a) plans, including §401(k) cash-or-deferred arrangements. To remain tax-qualified, §401(m) requires a plan to satisfy the "contribution percentage requirement" as to all employer matching and all employee contributions for a plan year. Section 401(m) defines a matching contribution as (1) Any employer contribution made to the plan on behalf of an employee on account of an employee contribution by such employee, and (2) Any employer contribution to the plan on behalf of an employee on account of an employee's elective deferral.[29]

Also, to the extent provided in Treasury regulations, an employer may elect to take into account in computing the §401(m) contribution percentages, any elective deferrals (i.e., pre-tax contributions) and "qualified nonelective contributions" (i.e., ones where the employee may not elect to take payment in cash).[30]

Code §401(m) tests the contribution percentage for highly compensated employees[31] against that of all other employees eligible to participate in the plan. Section 401(m) applies a test similar to that used under §401(k) to determine if a cash-or-deferred arrangement discriminates. Specifically, a plan that provides for employee or matching contributions will satisfy §401(m) if, for each plan year, the contribution percentage (employee and matching contributions expressed as a percentage of compensation) for eligible highly compensated employees does not exceed the greater of:

(1) 125 percent of such percentage for all other eligible employees, or

(2) The lesser of 200 percent of such percentage for all other eligible employees, or such percentage for all other employees plus two percentage points.[32]

The Code §401(k) "actual deferral percentage" tests are discussed in Chapter 16. Note that there is one significant difference between the §401(m) "actual contribution percentage" test and the §401(k) "actual deferral percentage" test. Under §401(k), the deferral percentages of the highly compensated and all other eligible employees are compared *in the aggregate*. That is, individual members of the highly compensated group may defer more than is allowed under the §401(k) test so long as the average deferral percentages of the two groups satisfy the test. Under §401(m), however, *each* eligible highly compensated employee cannot defer an amount that exceeds the amount under the two-prong test. This is a more restrictive standard than that used by §401(k).

Under Code §401(m), if two or more plans maintained by an employer to which employee or matching contributions are made are treated as one plan for purposes of §410(b) (relating to the minimum coverage rules), then all such employee and matching contributions are aggregated in applying §401(m).[33] Further, if a highly compensated employee participates in two or more plans of an employer to which such contributions are made, all such contributions are aggregated in applying §401(m).

Section 401(m) contains a "savings" feature which provides that a plan will not be disqualified for any plan year if, before the close of the following plan year, any excess aggregate contributions (i.e., contributions in excess of those allowable under the percentage test) and the income attributable thereto are distributed or, if forfeitable, are forfeited. Such correcting distributions may be made without regard to any other provision restricting distributions from qualified plans. For instance, the Code §72(t) penalty excise tax on premature distributions does not apply to such correcting distributions.

Section 401(m) applies generally to years beginning after 1986. A special effective date rule applies to collectively bargained plans.

Penalty for Overstatement of Pension Liabilities

The 1986 Tax Reform Act added Code §6659A, providing a penalty tax applicable to understatements of employer tax liabilities that are attributable to overstatements of pension liabilities. Under the provision, an overstatement of pension liabilities occurs if the actuarial determination of liabilities taken into account for purposes of computing the employer's deduction under Code §§404(a)(1) or (2) (relating to defined benefit plans and employees' annuities, respectively) exceeds the amount that the IRS determines to be the correct amount of such liability.

Section 6659A was a legislative response to the perceived abuse by certain defined benefit plans that attempted to produce artificially higher employer deductions by using unrealistic actuarial assumptions. This provision, coupled with the provision added to the minimum funding rules by OBRA (1987) that requires individual plan actuarial assumptions to be reasonable, should curtail this practice.

The amount of tax imposed depends on what percentage the valuation of pension liabilities claimed is of the amount that is determined to be the correct valuation. If the incorrect valuation exceeds the correct one by 150 percent, but not more than 200 percent, the penalty is 10 percent. If the mistaken valuation exceeds the proper one by more than 200 percent, but not more than 250 percent, the penalty is 20 percent. If the mistaken valuation exceeds the proper one by more than 250 percent, the penalty is 30 percent.

The penalty percentage is applied to the taxpayer's regular tax for the year due under Chapter 1 of the Code and applies in addition to such tax. The penalty is the applicable percentage, above, times the amount of the understatement of tax liability that was attributable to the overstatement of pension liabilities.

For the penalty tax to apply, the understatement of tax liability resulting from the overstatement must be at least $1,000. The IRS may waive all or part of the penalty tax if the taxpayer shows that there was a reasonable basis for the valuation claimed on the return and that the return was made in good faith.

Section 6659A applies to overstatements occurring after the 1986 Tax Reform Act's enactment date (October 22, 1986).

Notes

1. That is, the contribution, taken together with all other compensation paid the participant for the year, must represent reasonable compensation for services rendered.
2. Code § 404(a)(6).
3. See Code § 4972, as enacted by § 1131 of the 1986 TRA (P.L. 99-514).
4. Code § 404(a)(3)(B). Make-up contributions can only be made to the extent of the profitable corporations' earnings and profits. An "affiliated group" for this purpose is defined in Code § 1504.
5. See Code §§ 404(a)(1)(A)(i)–(iii).
6. Code § 404(a)(1)(A) (flush language). The minimum funding rules of Code § 412 are discussed in Chapter 8.
7. Code § 404(a)(1)(A)(i).
8. Code § 404(a)(1)(A)(ii).
9. *Id.*
10. Code § 404(a)(1)(A)(iii).
11. Code § 404(a)(1)(E).
12. P.L. 100-203.
13. Code § 404(a)(1)(D). The Code § 412(l) amount is determined without regard to any reduction by the credit balance in the funding standard account. Further, for purposes of this rule, all defined benefit plans maintained by the same employer or any member of such employer's controlled group (within the meaning of § 412(l)(8)(C)) are treated as one plan, but only employees of such member or employer may be taken into account. Section 404(a)(1)(D) is effective for "years" beginning after 1987.
14. Code § 404(a)(3).
15. Code § 404(a)(3)(A)(v).
16. Code § 404(a)(3)(A)(ii).
17. Code § 404(a)(7)(A).
18. Code § 404(a)(7)(C).
19. Code § 404(a)(8)(D).
20. See IRS Publication 778, Part 2(g).
21. *Id.*, at Part 4(h). See also Rev. Rul. 69-217, 1969-1 C.B. 115; Rev. Rul. 70-658, 1970-2 C.B. 86; Rev. Rul. 72-349, 1972-2 C.B. 219; and Rev. Rul. 69-627, 1969-2 C.B. 92.
22. See the discussion of the consequences of a plan being top-heavy or super top-heavy in Chapter 6.
23. See IRS Pub. 778, Part 4(g). See also Rev. Rul. 70-658, 1970-2 C.B. 86 and Rev. Rul. 72-349, 1972-2 C.B. 219.
24. P.L. 97-34, (ERTA).
25. Code § 402(g)(4).

26. Code §4979(f).
27. Code §401(k)(8).
28. Code §402(g)(2)(C).
29. Code §401(m)(4). Section 401(m)(4)(B) defined "elective deferral" for this purpose by reference to Code §402(g)(3)(A).
30. Code §§401(m)(3)–(4).
31. Within the meaning of §414(q).
32. Code §§401(m)(2)(A)(i)–(ii).
33. Code §401(m)(2)(B).

8

Minimum Funding Standard: Code §412

Defined benefit and money purchase pension plans must satisfy the minimum funding standard of Code §412.[1] In general, to satisfy this standard, a plan must not have an "accumulated funding deficiency" in its funding standard account. An accumulated funding deficiency is defined as an excess of charges over credits in the funding standard account.[2] If a plan has a deficiency in the funding standard account for any year, it can seek to satisfy the regular or the "alternative" minimum funding standard. OBRA (1987)[3] significantly tightened the minimum funding standard rules, imposing more stringent funding requirements on plans subject to §412.

Before examining the items that constitute charges or credits to the funding standard account, some background on plan actuarial methods is necessary. Basically, under ERISA, defined benefit plans may employ different IRS-approved actuarial methods in determining how they are to be funded. Different actuarial methods allocate different amounts of plan liabilities to "normal costs" (generally, the cost of funding projected benefits accrued by participants during the current plan year) and "supplemental liabilities" (generally, the sum of all other costs not allocated to normal costs under the plan's actuarial method). In general, accepted actuarial methods for funding defined benefit plans fall into two broad categories:

(1) Accrued benefit cost methods; and

(2) Projected benefit methods.

Accrued benefit cost methods consider the entire amount necessary to fund a plan's past service liability to be due in the first plan year in which that liability arises.[4] Thus, for a plan with significant past service liabilities, these methods accelerate the rate at which the employer must fund this type of liability. This can be desirable where the employer needs a large current deduction because employer deductions under Code § 404 for defined benefit plans are geared to the amount necessary to satisfy the minimum funding standard.

In contrast, projected benefit methods generally treat past service liability as accruing over an employee's entire career. Projected benefit methods, thus, even out the employer's annual liability more than accrued benefit cost methods, avoiding large jumps in liability in the year a past service liability arises.[5]

Since normal costs and supplemental liabilities (including past service costs) are treated differently under Code § 412, different actuarial methods create different patterns of charges and credits to the funding standard account.

The Funding Standard Account

The funding standard account is a recordkeeping system that plans subject to Code § 412 must maintain. Certain items, such as payments, are credited to the account. Certain expenses, relating to the funding of benefits, are charged to the account and amortized in level annual installments over a statutory period. Plans subject to the minimum funding standard generally may select a more rapid amortization period for a particular type of liability than is required.

If, at the end of a plan year, there is a negative balance in the funding standard account, Code § 4971 imposes an initial penalty excise tax on the employer equal to 10 percent of the accumulated funding deficiency.[6] An additional 100 percent penalty excise tax is imposed if the deficiency is not corrected within the "correction period." The correction period begins with the end of the plan year and ends on the later of:

(1) 90 days after the IRS mails the employer a notice of deficiency; or

(2) The date on which a Tax Court decision regarding the funding deficiency becomes final.[7]

Credits and Charges to the Funding Standard Account

The following items are charged to the funding standard account:[8]

(1) Normal costs for the plan year;

(2) The amount needed to amortize, in equal annual installments over 30 years, any unfunded past service liability arising in connection with services rendered before the plan was adopted;

(3) The amount needed to amortize in equal annual installments over 30 years, separately for each plan year, any net increase in the plan's unfunded past service liability arising from plan amendments adopted in that year;

(4) The amount needed to amortize in equal annual installments over five (15 for years beginning before 1988) years,[9] separately for each plan year, any "net experience loss" under the plan;

(5) The amount needed to amortize, in equal annual installments over 10 years, (30 for years beginning before 1988)[10] separately for each plan year, any net loss resulting from changes in the plan's actuarial assumptions;

(6) The amount needed to amortize, in equal annual installments over 15 years, each waived funding deficiency the plan obtains under Code §412(d)(3); and

(7) The amount needed to amortize, in equal annual installments over five years, the amount credited under Code §412(b)(3)(D) that is attributable to a plan's change back to the regular minimum funding standard from the alternative minimum funding standard.[11]

The credit side of the funding standard account is basically the mirror image of the charge side. The following amounts are credited to the funding standard account:

(1) The amount considered to be contributed by the employer for the plan year;

(2) The amount needed to amortize in equal annual installments over 30 years, separately for each plan year, any net decrease in the plan's unfunded past service liability attributable to plan amendments adopted during the year;

(3) The amount needed to amortize in equal annual installments over five years (15 for years beginning before 1988), separately for each plan year, any "net experience gain" for the plan year;

(4) The amount needed to amortize in equal annual installments over 10 years (30 for years beginning before 1988), separately for each plan year, any net gain attributable to changes in actuarial assumptions;

(5) The amount of any waived funding deficiency for the plan year;[12] and

(6) When the plan has been using the alternative minimum funding standard, the amount needed to amortize, over five years, the excess, if any, of the deficit balance in the funding standard account over the deficit balance in the alternative minimum funding standard account.[13]

Under Code §412(b)(5) the items in the funding standard account are charged or credited (depending on whether the items are charges or credits) with interest at a rate determined by the Treasury Secretary that is "consistent with the rate or rates of interest used under the plan to determine costs."

Requirement That Actuarial Assumptions Be Reasonable

Under pre-OBRA (1987) law (which still applies to multiemployer plans), a plan's actuarial assumptions were subject only to the requirement that they be "reasonable in the aggregate." Thus, individual unreasonable assumptions could be used so long as their net effect was reasonable.

OBRA (1987) amended the Code to provide that, in addition to the requirement that actuarial assumptions be reasonable in the aggregate, individual assumptions for single and multiple employer plans also be reasonable.[14] The change continues a pattern in several pre-OBRA (1987) Technical Advice Memoranda involving closely held professional corporations where the IRS came close to ruling that certain actuarial assumptions were unreasonable per se (such as an interest rate assumption below the prevailing rate on fully insured governmental securities). After OBRA (1987), a plan subject to this provision may also satisfy the requirements for individual assumptions if the level of contributions called for under all the plan's actuarial assumptions is equivalent to that which would have resulted had all individual assumptions been reasonable. Multiemployer plans remain subject only to the requirement that assumptions be "reasonable in the aggregate."

The assumptions, whether for single or multiemployer plans, must constitute the actuary's best estimate of anticipated experience under the plan.[15]

The OBRA (1987) amendments reduce employers' ability to raise the level of deductible contributions by changing actuarial assumptions.

OBRA (1987) also limited the "permissible range" within which the interest rate used for funding purposes may fall. In general, the permissible range will be limited to a rate that is not more than 10 percent above or below the weighted average of interest rates on 30-year Treasury securities during the four-year period ending on the last day before the beginning of the plan year. The OBRA (1987) change is effective for years beginning after 1987. It limits an actuary's ability to change interest rates in a manner that will significantly effect a plan's funding requirements. If the IRS determines that the interest rate so determined is unreasonably high, it may prescribe a lower rate but, in all events, the rate may not fall below 80 percent of the rate on 30-year Treasury securities for the four-year computation period, as described above.[16]

The Conference Report to OBRA (1987) states that no rate outside the permissible rate will be allowed "under any circumstances."[17] The report further states that the guideline corridors are not intended to provide a safe harbor. Thus, if an interest assumption falls within the range of allowable rates but is not reasonable in light of conditions prevailing at the time the assumption was made, a deduction based on an inappropriate interest assumption could still be denied.

Where it is more advantageous for one or more plan years, a plan may use the alternative minimum funding standard.[18] The alternative minimum funding standard account is charged with the sum of:

(1) The lesser of the normal cost under the plan's funding method for the plan year or normal costs determined under the "unit credit" actuarial cost method;

(2) The excess, if any, of the present value of accrued benefits under the plan over the fair market value of such assets; and

(3) The excess, if any, of credits to the alternative minimum funding standard account over charges to that account for all prior plan years.

The account is credited with the amount considered contributed by the employer for the plan year. Thus, where plan assets are large relative to liabilities, employers may wish to consider using the alternative minimum funding standard for one or more years. In doing so it will be important to consider the adjustment in future years that will have to be made to the regular minimum funding standard account if the plan goes back on the regular standard. Use of the alternative minimum funding standard may not be necessary, however, where the full funding limitation applies. The full funding limitation, discussed later in this chapter, effectively caps the amount an employer can be required to contribute to satisfy the minimum funding standard.

Special Rules Added by OBRA (1987) for Plans With More Than 100 Participants

OBRA (1987) tightened the funding rules for single and multiple employer defined benefit plans, requiring that such plans be more rapidly, and more fully, funded.[19] The revised rules, where they apply, generally supersede the parallel provisions of pre-OBRA (1987) law. Certain OBRA (1987) provisions discussed in this section do not apply to any plan that, on no day during the preceding plan year, had more than 100 participants and only apply in part to plans that had between 101 and 150 participants on every day in the preceding plan year. For this purpose all plans of a controlled group are aggregated. Steel companies are subject to special rules.

Under the revised funding rules, past service costs (a plan's liability for benefits relating to service rendered before the plan's effective date), referred to as "unfunded old liabilities," generally must be amortized over 18 years instead of 30, as otherwise allowed under the minimum funding standard. In addition, plans subject to the OBRA rules must amortize their "unfunded new liability" under a formula based on the amount by which they are underfunded and must amortize a liability added by OBRA: the "unpredictable contingent event amount."

If a defined benefit plan has a funded ratio (the ratio of plan assets to plan liabilities) of less than 100 percent, a statutory lien will arise against the employer (and other members of its controlled group) 60 days after the due date of any unpaid contribution or installment. The amount of the lien is the total contributions that have been missed that are in excess of $1 million. The employer and all members of its controlled group are liable for the contributions under these rules. For plans with more than 100, but no more than 150, participants during the preceding year, the amount of additional required contribution is determined by multiplying the otherwise applicable additional required contribution for plans with more than 150 participants by 2 percent for each participant in excess of 100.[20]

If a single or multiple employer defined benefit plan has an "unfunded current liability" for the plan year, the plan's funding standard account, in addition to the regular charges, is charged with the sum of:

(1) The excess (if any) of:
(a) the "deficit reduction contribution" for the plan year, over
(b) charges to the funding standard account other than experience losses and losses due to changes in actuarial assumptions, plus

(2) The "unpredictable contingent amount benefit" for the plan year (if any).

The increase only applies to the extent necessary to increase the "funded current liability percentage" to 100 percent.

Deficit Reduction Contribution

The "deficit reduction contribution" is the sum of:

(1) The "unfunded old liability amount," plus

(2) The "unfunded new liability amount."[21]

Unfunded Old Liability Amount. The "unfunded old liability amount" is the amount needed to amortize any "unfunded old liability" (generally any supplemental liabilities) in equal annual installments over 18 plan years starting with the first plan year that begins after 1988.[22] "Unfunded old liability," in turn, is defined as the plan's unfunded current liability as of the beginning of the first plan year that begins after 1987, determined without regard to any plan amendment increasing liabilities that was adopted after October 16, 1987.

Unfunded New Liability Amount. The "unfunded new liability amount" is the "applicable percentage" times the plan's "unfunded new liability."[23] "Unfunded new liability," in turn, is defined as the plan's unfunded current liability for the plan year, determined without regard to:

(1) The unamortized portion of any unfunded old liability, and

(2) The liability with respect to any unpredictable contingent event benefits, determined without regard to whether the event has occurred.

For this purpose, the "applicable percentage" is 30 percent, reduced by the product of .25 multiplied by the number of percentage points (if any) by which the "funded current liability percentage" exceeds 35 percent.[24]

> *Example*: Plan A's funded liability percentage is 40 percent. Its unfunded current liability is \$7,000,000. Of this, \$2,000,000 is attributable to unamortized old liability or unpredictable contingent event benefit liability. Plan A's unfunded new liability amount is \$1,437,500, computed as follows:
>
> $$(\$7{,}000{,}000 - \$2{,}000{,}000) \times (30\% - [.25 \times 5]\%) = \$1{,}437{,}500.$$

"Unpredictable Contingent Event Amount." The unpredictable contingent event amount includes plant shut-down benefits and any other benefits that are not based on age, service, compensation, death, or disability and that are not "reasonably and reliably predictable."

The additional contributions required to fund the unpredictable contingent event amount are generally equal to the greater of:

(1) The "applicable percentage" of—
(a) 100 percent, reduced, but not below zero, by the funded current liability percentage for the plan year, (i.e., the unfunded current liability percentage) multiplied by
(b) the amount of unpredictable contingent event benefits paid during the plan year (regardless of the form in which paid), including (except as provided by regulations) any payment for the purchase of an annuity contract on a participant's or beneficiary's behalf with respect to unpredictable contingent event benefits, or

(2) the amount needed to amortize unpredictable contingent event benefit liabilities in equal annual installments over seven plan years beginning with the year in which the event occurred.

Under a special rule, unless the employer elects otherwise, the unpredictable contingent event amount for the first year in which the liability arises is equal to 150 percent of the amount determined under (1), above. Where this rule applies, the IRS is to provide rules making appropriate adjustments to the amount derived under (2), above.

The Applicable Percentage. The "applicable percentage" to be plugged into (1) in the above formula for determining the unpredictable contingent event amount is:

TABLE 1

Rate	*Plan Years Beginning In*
5%	1989 and 1990
10%	1991
15%	1992
20%	1993
30%	1994
40%	1995
50%	1996
60%	1997
70%	1998
80%	1999
90%	2000
100%	2001

The "applicable percentage" rates in the above table go into effect for plan years beginning after 1989. For plan years beginning in 1988, unpredictable contingent event benefits are subject to the OBRA (1987) provisions relating to the amortization of experience gains and losses.

The rules on unpredictable contingent event benefits do not apply to any unpredictable contingent event benefit (and liabilities attributable thereto) for which the event occurred before October 17, 1987.[25]

When Unpredictable Contingent Event Benefits Are Taken Into Account. Unpredictable contingent event benefits are not taken into account until the contingent event occurs.[26] The contingent event is generally not deemed to occur until all events on which the event is contingent have occurred. If the event on which the benefit is contingent occurs during a plan year and plan assets equal or exceed current liability (calculated as if the event had occurred), the employer may continue to fund unpredictable contingent event benefits without regard to the special OBRA (1987) provision. This would treat the event as an experience loss. The OBRA rule, however, will apply in this situation if the plan's level of funding later fell below the plan's level of current liability.[27]

Examples of Unpredictable Contingent Events. An "unpredictable contingent event benefit" is any benefit contingent on an event other than:

> "(I) age, service, compensation, death, or disability, or
> (II) an event which is reasonably and reliably predictable . . . ."[28]

The Conference Report states that unpredictable contingent event benefits include benefits that depend on contingencies that, like facility shutdowns or contractions in workforce, are not "reliably and reasonably predictable."[29] The report states that an event will not be considered reasonably and reliably predictable merely because there is an actuarial possibility that it will occur. It also provides the following guidelines:

(1) If an employer offers a "window" benefit to encourage early retirement, the window benefit will be considered reasonably and reliably predictable.[30]

(2) A benefit that is contingent on employer profitability or the employer's stock not dropping below a certain level is

not considered reasonably and reliably predictable unless the contingency is, in fact, illusory.

(3) A benefit dependent on marital status, such as a joint and survivor annuity, is contingent on an event that is reasonably and reliably predictable.

(4) A benefit that depends on an event that has a substantial certainty of occurring is considered reasonably and reliably predictable.

Unpredictable contingent event benefits for which the event has occurred before October 17, 1987, are not subject to the post-OBRA (1987) rules.

Special Rules for Collectively Bargained Plans. For a plan maintained pursuant to a collective bargaining agreement that was ratified before October 17, 1987, the plan's unfunded old liability amount will be increased by the amount needed to amortize over 18 years in equal annual installments any "unfunded existing benefit increase liability."[31] For this purpose, any extension, amendment, or other modification of a collective bargaining agreement after October 16, 1987, is not taken into account. In general, such amortization must begin with the plan year with respect to which the liability arises. At the taxpayer's election, however, amortization may begin with the first plan year beginning after 1988.

"Unfunded existing benefit increase liabilities" means, for any benefit increase under the agreement that takes effect after the first plan year beginning after 1987, the plan's unfunded current liability determined:

(1) By taking into account only liabilities attributable to such benefit increase, and

(2) By determining the value of plan assets under Code §412(c)(2) without regard to any benefit increases described in (1), above.[32]

In general, if an employee is covered under a collectively bargained defined benefit plan but is not subject to the collective bargaining agreement, any liability increases with respect to the individual are not counted for purposes of the special rule for collectively bargained plans. If, however, 75 percent or more of the employees covered by the plan on October 16, 1987, are subject to the agreement, the "unfunded existing benefit increase liability" includes liabilities attributable to any covered employee, provided such employee's benefits are determined directly or indirectly by reference to the collective bargaining agreement. For purposes of the special collective bargaining rule, separate plans may not be treated as a single plan, even if benefits are coordinated between them.[33]

The Full Funding Limitation

The full funding limitation applies when, despite the fact that a plan has an accumulated funding deficiency in its funding standard account for the plan year, plan assets are actually rather large relative to liabilities. Where this situation exists, the full funding limitation "caps" the minimum funding standard and also caps the employer's deductible contribution under Code §404 for the plan year.

Where the full funding limitation applies, the funding standard account is credited with the amount of its accumulated funding deficiency that exceeds its full funding limitation. Further, all amortizable charges to the funding standard account are considered to be fully amortized. This brings the account deficit balance back to zero for future plan years.

The theory behind the full funding limitation is that employers should not be required to fund (and should not be allowed to deduct contributions to) plans where, despite a negative balance in the funding standard account, the value of plan liabilities exceeds the value of plan assets by less than this negative balance. Where it applies, the full funding limitation is mandatory, not elective. It is designed to prevent the employer from incurring excessive funding costs and/or a penalty excise tax when plan assets are insufficient to pay plan liabilities when they fall due and to prevent the employer from deducting, and sheltering from tax, excessive contributions when the plan is adequately funded. In calculating the employer's annual funding obligation for a year, the full funding limitation should always be calculated as well to see if it applies.

Note that, for purposes of determining the employer's contribution for the year, in applying both the minimum funding standard and the alternative minimum funding standard, as well as the full funding limitation, employer contributions made after the last day of the plan year are considered to have been made for the preceding plan year if they are made no later than two and a half months after the close of the plan year (the normal time for filing the corporate income tax return for the year). This coincides with a similar provision for determining deductibility of the employer's annual contribution under Code §404. The minimum funding standard rule, however, is not geared to the actual due date for filing the employer's tax return. Thus, although IRS may grant extensions of up to six months, such extensions are not automatic with the grant of an extension of time to file the employer's tax return. If the employer is in a current liquidity crisis that will end shortly, for instance by the receipt of a large receivable, it should consider applying for a six-month extension under Code §412. Where this is done, however, the employer should have a contingency plan to avoid the imposition of the penalty excise tax on underfunding should the application be denied.

OBRA (1987) dramatically revised the full funding limitation for all plans subject to the minimum funding standard. Pre-OBRA law defined the full funding limitation as the excess (if any) of the plan's accrued liability (including its liability for normal costs) over the lesser of the fair market value of the plan's assets or the value of such assets determined under reasonable actuarial methods.

The OBRA (1987) revised full funding limitation is effective for years beginning after 1987.[34] The revised limit applies both for purposes of the funding requirements and for determining the deduction limits under Code §404.

The revised full funding limit is the difference between the value of plan assets (determined under Code §412(c)(2) or at their fair market value, whichever is less) and the lesser of:

(1) 150 percent of the plan's "current liability;" or

(2) The plan's accrued liability (including normal costs) (determined under the entry age normal method if the plan's funding method does not permit accrued liability to be directly calculated).

"Current liability" for this purpose is essentially the amount the plan would have to pay out as benefits on termination, calculated in accordance with certain limits on actuarial assumptions and interest rates that may be used and only taking into account unpredictable contingent event benefits when the event upon which they are contingent occurs.[35]

Under a special rule for participants who, when they became

participants (1) had not accrued any other benefit under any defined benefit plan (whether or not terminated) maintained by the employer or a member of its controlled group; and (2) entered in a plan year beginning after 1987, the amount of current liability taken into account under the plan is the amount of current liability otherwise computed, multiplied by the "applicable percentage" set forth in Code §412(l)(7)(D). These percentages are determined as follows:

TABLE 2

If Years of Participation Are	*The Applicable Percentage Is*
1	20%
2	40%
3	60%
4	80%
5 or more	100%

The IRS may issue regulations adjusting the 150 percent prong of the revised full funding limitation, discussed above, to take the ages and length of service of participants into account.[36] The IRS may also prescribe alternative methods other than current liability which plans may use in applying the limits.[37]

Options When Employer Lacks Funds to Make Contributions

Waived Funding Deficiencies

One technique that can be used if it appears that the employer will not have adequate funds to make its required contribution by the due date is to obtain a variance from the minimum funding standard from the IRS. Code §412(d) authorizes the IRS to waive the minimum funding standard for a year in which the employer incurs certain substantial business hardships. An employer is eligible for this waiver if it, or in the case of a multiemployer plan, 10 percent of contributing employers, is unable to satisfy the minimum funding standard for the year without substantial business hardship and "if application of the (minimum funding) standard would be adverse to the interests of plan participants in the aggregate." The waiver may be made with respect to all or part of the minimum funding standard liability for the year.

"Substantial business hardship," for this purpose, includes situations where:

(1) The employer is operating at an economic loss;

(2) There is substantial unemployment or underemployment in the employer's trade or business or in the relevant industry;

(3) Sales and profits of the industry concerned are depressed or declining; and

(4) It is reasonable to expect that the plan will be continued only if the waiver is granted.

It is reasonable to assume that the impairment of the employer's general line of credit by securing a loan to make the plan contribution will generally not constitute a substantial business hardship except where the impairment would render the employer unable to secure the funds to continue to operate its business. Therefore, generally, in applying for a waiver, the employer should first attempt to obtain the needed financing through a loan while continuing to operate its business, unless this is impractical. The representation that the employer has tried unsuccessfully to borrow the funds to contribute to the plan should be helpful in obtaining a waiver, as will a demonstration that such borrowing could not be done without rendering the employer unable to continue to conduct its business. To protect the interests of participants, the PBGC may terminate a plan that is experiencing financial difficulty.

Because the PBGC felt that funding waivers had been granted too frequently and in situations where it generally increased the ultimate PBGC liability, it sought restrictions on employers' ability to obtain funding waivers.

OBRA (1987) added a requirement that the funding waiver be requested within two and a half months after the close of the year and limited waivers to temporary substantial business hardship.[38] (The circumstances required to be present under pre-OBRA law, discussed above, must also be demonstrated).

The temporary hardship must apply to the entire controlled group of which the employer is a member. OBRA (1987) also reduced the frequency with which a funding waiver may be obtained from five to three years in any 15-year period. Interest on the makeup of the funding waiver will be calculated at 150 percent of the applicable federal (mid-term) rate (AFR).[39] This is the federal government's rate on its obligations (such as Treasury bills) with terms of between three and nine years. Participants must be given notice of the funding waiver. The IRS may require security for the funding waiver in certain situations.

The revised funding waiver rules apply to single and multiple employer plans, but not multiemployer plans. The OBRA (1987) changes are effective generally as to waiver requests submitted after December 17, 1987, and waivers granted pursuant to such applications. For non-multiemployer plans, however, the number of prior waivers granted is to be determined without regard to waivers granted with respect to plan years beginning before 1988.

OBRA (1987) also broadened the notice requirement for funding waivers. Under pre-OBRA law, an employer that applied for a waiver of the minimum funding standard or an extension of amortization periods for supplemental liabilities only had to provide notice of the application to any employee organization representing employees covered by the plan.[40] As revised, effective for applications submitted more than 90 days after OBRA (1987)'s enactment date, the notice requirement is extended to each individual participant, beneficiary, and any alternate payee under a qualified domestic relations order.[41] The notice must describe the extent to which benefits guaranteed under Title IV of ERISA are funded and the plan's existing benefit liabilities.

When a waiver is granted, the waived amount is deemed to have been contributed, and is reflected as a credit, to the funding standard account for the year. The amount of the waiver is then charged back to the account over 15 years. Thus, a plan has up to 15 years to repay the waived amounts, and the possibility of incurring a penalty excise tax on the waived amounts in the year of the waiver is eliminated. Of course, the penalty excise tax, particularly the second-tier 100 percent tax, is to be avoided at all costs.

Extension of Amortization Periods

A second planning device that is available when the employer lacks the funds to make its annual required contribution is to obtain an extension of the plan's amortization periods for amortizable charges to the funding standard account under §412(e). That subsection provides that the Secretary of Labor (note that it is the Secretary of the Treasury who has the authority to grant a waiver) may extend the amortization period for any amortizable liability by up to 10 years. To grant an extension, the Secretary of Labor must find that the extension would help carry out the purposes of ERISA and would provide adequate protection to participants and beneficiaries. The Secretary must, further, find that the failure to grant an extension would:

(1) Result in a substantial risk that the plan would not be continued or a substantial curtailment of pension benefits and/or wage levels would result; or

(2) Be adverse to the interests of participants in the aggregate.

The request for an extension of amortization periods is not subject to the restriction that it can only be granted a particular number of times in a given period. Further, the standard here is more liberal than the substantial business hardship standard applicable to waivers. Where the employer's inability to pay the year's liability is chiefly attributable to amortizable liabilities and not to normal costs, this route can be preferable, since it extends the payment period for almost as long as a waiver (10 as opposed to 15 years) and leaves the door open in future years for the plan to apply for a waiver. Under Code §412(f), a plan cannot increase its benefit accrual rate or adopt a more liberal vesting schedule during any year when a waiver or extension is in effect.

Certain Retroactive Plan Amendments Reducing Benefits

In general, under ERISA, a plan amendment that retroactively deprives participants of an accrued benefit (as opposed to a benefit to be accrued in the future—i.e., a mere expectation) will cause the plan to be disqualified. A limited exception applies, however.[42] Under this exception, where the Secretary of Labor approves the amendment (or fails to act on the application for approval within 90 days), a plan may adopt an amendment after the close of the plan year reducing accrued benefits as of the first day of the plan year. Before approving the amendment, the Secretary must find that the amendment is required due to substantial temporary business hardship and that a waiver of the minimum funding standard is unavailable or inadequate. The use of "temporary" here means that if there is no hope that the employer will recover from the hardship, the amendment will not be approved.

The amendment, in the case of a single employer or multiemployer plan, must be adopted within two and a half months of the close of the plan year. For multiemployer plans, this is extended to two years. The amendment must not reduce the accrued benefit of any participant determined as of the beginning of the first plan year to which the amendment applies, and, further, must not reduce the accrued benefit of any participant determined as of the time of the amendment's adoption, except to the extent required by circumstances.

The rule prohibiting increases in benefits also applies where such a retroactive amendment is in effect.[43] The rule against benefit increases applies in the retroactive amendment situation where such an amendment has been made at any time in the preceeding 12 months (24 months in the case of multiemployer plans). In all cases, certain exceptions are allowed. Under the exceptions, the prohibition on benefit increases will be lifted where:

(1) The Secretary of Labor determines that the increase is reasonable and that it provides for only *de minimis* increases in the plan's liability;

(2) The benefit increase is only attributable to the repeal of a Code §412(c)(8) amendment that retroactively reduced benefits; or

(3) The amendment is required to keep the plan tax qualified.[44]

In regard to the general prohibition on plan amendments decreasing accrued benefits,[45] Code §411(d)(6)(B) treats certain amendments as decreasing accrued benefits. These amendments are ones that:

(1) Eliminate or reduce an early retirement benefit or a "retirement-type subsidy;" or

(2) Eliminate any optional form of benefit with respect to benefits that accrued before the amendment.

With respect to a retirement-type subsidy, the prohibition will not apply with respect to a participant who, at the time of the amendment, had not qualified for the subsidy.

Special Rules for Multiemployer Plans

In addition to the foregoing, certain special rules apply to multiemployer plans.[46] Under these rules, withdrawal liability paid by a multiemployer plan sponsor is considered an amount contributed by the employer under the plan for Code §412 purposes. Further, when a multiemployer plan in financial difficulty enters reorganization status under the Multiemployer Pension Plan Amendments Act of 1980, all charges or credits to the minimum funding standard account will be eliminated by an offsetting credit or charge and amortized in equal annual installments over 30 years.

Where a plan sets up a supertrust[47] to insure certain liabilities not guaranteed under the PBGC's regular multiemployer plan insurance program, amounts paid by the plan to fund the supertrust will be applied to reduce the amount considered contributed by employers for the plan year. Any amount paid by a withdrawing employer in a multiemployer plan as an interim payment of withdrawal liability until the actual withdrawal liability is computed (and later refunded by the plan) is charged to the plan's funding standard account in accordance with Treasury regulations. For purposes of applying the full funding limitation to a multiemployer plan, benefits that are not nonforfeitable shall, unless the plan provides to the contrary, not be counted in determining the plan's accrued liability.[48] Note that the 1980 MPPAA reduced certain amortization periods that applied to charges to the funding standard accounts of multiemployer plans to bring those periods into line with the then-applicable periods for nonmultiemployer plans. For pre-1980 MPPAA liabilities, the former (longer) amortization periods continue to apply.

Other OBRA (1987) Amendments to the Funding Rules

In addition to the changes described above, OBRA (1987) added certain additional funding requirements to the Code. These amendments include a provision requiring that employers provide security for certain underfunded plans, a requirement that employers make quarterly contributions of estimated liability to plans subject to the minimum funding standard, and the extension of the uniform capitalization rules of Code §263A to past service costs. These amendments are described below.

Security for Underfunded Plans

OBRA (1987), added a provision requiring that if a defined benefit plan (other than a multiemployer plan) that has a less-than-60 percent funded current liability percentage as of the plan year in which the amendment takes effect adopts an amendment that has the effect of increasing its current liabilities, the contributing employer (and any members of its controlled group) must provide the plan with a bond or other security for that increase in liability before the amendment can become effective.[49]

For this purpose, "unfunded current liability" has the meaning supplied by Code §412(l), except that any unamortized portion of the plan's "unfunded old liability amount" is disregarded.[50]

The security may take the form of:

(1) A corporate surety bond by a company that is acceptable under ERISA §412,

(2) Cash or federal obligations having a maturity of three years or less held in escrow by a bank, or

(3) Such other security as Treasury and the parties agree upon.

The security generally is not required unless the increase in liability exceeds $10 million. The amount of the security must equal the excess of:

(1) The lesser of—
(a) the amount needed to increase the plan's funded current liability percentage to 60 percent (including liability brought about by the amendment), or
(b) the amount by which the plan's current liability increases as a result of the amendment, over

(2) $10 million.

The employer also must notify participants annually (on the annual report) of the plan's funding status if it is less than 60 percent unfunded.

Once the plan's funding of current liability returns to 60 percent or more, the security can be released. The IRS may issue regulations providing for partial releases of security.

These provisions are generally effective for amendments adopted after December 22, 1987. In the case of collectively bargained plans, the amendments do not apply to amendments adopted pursuant to collective bargaining agreements if the agreement was ratified before December 22, 1987.

Quarterly Contributions Required

Effective generally for plan years beginning after 1988 but subject to a four-year phase-in, OBRA (1987) requires employers maintaining plans other than multiemployer plans subject to ERISA's funding requirements, i.e., defined benefit and money purchase plans, to make quarterly estimated plan contributions.[51] An employer that fails to make the required quarterly payments will have to pay interest to the plan at the rate of 175 percent of the mid-term applicable federal rate (AFR) in effect for the first month of the plan year or the rate at which the funding standard account is charged with interest (under Code §412(b)(5)), whichever is greater on the amount of the underpayment for the period of underpayment.

For this purpose, the amount of underpayment is the excess of the required installment over the amount (if any) of the installment contributed to or under the plan, determined without regard to the time limits set forth in Code §412(c)(10).[52] The "period of underpayment" runs from the due date of the installment to the date on which the installment is paid, determined without regard to §412(c)(10).[53]

The first installment is due April 15th, the second July 15th, the third October 15th, and the fourth on January 15th of the following year. In addition, plans must make their "required annual payment" by the end of the plan year. For this purpose, contributions made within eight and a half months of the end of the plan year are treated as if they were made on the last day of the plan year.

The amount of any required installment is defined as the "applicable percentage" of the "required annual payment."[54] The "required annual payment" is:

> "the lesser of—
> "(i) 90 percent of the amount required to be contributed . . . for the

plan year under §412 (without regard to any waiver under subsection (c) thereof), or

"(ii) 100 percent of the amount so required for the preceding plan year."[55]

The 100 percent safe harbor described in (ii), above, is not available where the prior plan year was less than 12 months.

The "applicable percentage" for this purpose is:[56]

TABLE 3

For Plan Years Beginning in	*The Applicable Percentage Is*
1989	6.25%
1990	12.50%
1991	18.75%
1992 and thereafter	25.00%

The Act extended the liability to make required contributions to the sponsoring employer and all members of its controlled group. Under Code §404, however, only the sponsoring employer may take a deduction for its plan contributions.

Further, OBRA (1987) increased the 5 percent initial excise tax on failure to satisfy the minimum funding standard to 10 percent. The required installments must total either 100 percent of the required contribution for the preceding year or 90 percent of the required contribution for the current year.

Changes in the Code §404 Deduction Limits

Under OBRA (1987) the maximum amount deductible under Code §404 will not be less than the plan's unfunded current liability as determined under Code §412(l), discussed above.[57] This requirement applies to single and multiple employer plans with more than 100 participants for the plan year (except as provided in regulations). Unfunded current liability is determined without regard to any reduction by the credit balance in the funding standard account. Also, all defined benefit plans of an employer, or of a member of its controlled group, are treated as a single plan, but only employees of such member or employer are to be taken into account. The foregoing changes are effective for "years" beginning after 1987.

Interest on Mandatory Contributions

Pre-OBRA (1987) law required defined benefit plans to credit mandatory employee contributions with interest of 5 percent per year. OBRA (1987) increased this rate to 120 percent of the applicable federal mid-term rate.[58] The change is effective for plan years beginning after 1987.

Capitalization of Pension Costs

The 1986 Tax Reform Act required that all pension costs, except past service costs, "with respect to property," be capitalized instead of deducted currently under the normal deduction rules applicable to pension contributions. Under these rules, pension costs that were associated with capital construction projects or inventory items must be capitalized. If associated with inventory, the pension costs are recovered as the inventory is sold and, if associated with a capital asset, the costs are recovered through depreciation.

OBRA (1987) modified these rules so that the capitalization requirements apply to all pension costs, including past service costs. The rules permit a four-year spread of any adjustments that are required as a result of a change in accounting practice but otherwise are generally effective for costs incurred after 1987.[59]

Notes

1. Money purchase plans are technically subject to the minimum funding standard, but, since these plans do not generally have past service costs or other supplemental liabilities, the significance of this is generally to impose a penalty excise tax if the employer's obligation to contribute an amount annually that is necessary to fund normal costs for the plan year is not met.
2. Code §412(a). The funding standard account is a recordkeeping system that plans subject to Code §412 must maintain.
3. The Omnibus Budget Reconciliation Act of 1987 (P.L. 100-203).
4. See Canan, Qualified Retirement Plans (West's Handbook Series), West Publishing Co. 1977, ch. 12. See also the 1987 revision of that book by Michael J. Canan and David Baker.
5. *Id.* The "entry age normal" method is the most commonly used form of projected benefit cost methods. The IRS rules on what methods constitute reasonable funding methods are set forth in Treas. Regs. §1.412(c)(3).
6. Five percent before the amendments enacted by OBRA (1987).
7. Code §4971(c)(3).

8. Certain charges must be amortized more rapidly than under this general rule after the effective date of the OBRA (1987) amendments with respect to plans having more than 100 participants. The OBRA requirements are detailed below.
9. See OBRA (1987), §9307(a), amending Code §§412(b)(2)(B) and (b)(3).
10. *Id.*
11. Code §412(b).
12. Under Code §412(d)(3), treating waivers in cases of substantial business hardship.
13. *Id.*
14. OBRA (1987), §9307(b), amending Code §412(c)(3), effective generally as to "years" beginning after 1987.
15. Under Code §412(c)(3)(B).
16. See Code §412(b)(5) as amended by OBRA (1987), §9307.
17. H.R. Rep. No. 495, 100th Cong., 1st Sess. 854 (1987), hereinafter "OBRA (1987) Conference Report."
18. Under Code §412(g).
19. OBRA (1987), §9303, adding Code §412(l).
20. See Code §412(l)(6)(B).
21. Code §412(l)(2).
22. See Code §412(l)(3)(A).
23. Code §412(l)(4).
24. Code §412(l)(4)(C).
25. See Code §412(l)(5)(C).
26. Code §412(l)(7)(B).
27. See OBRA (1987) Conference Report, at 857.
28. Code §412(l)(6)(B)(ii).
29. OBRA (1987) Conference Report, at 855.
30. A window benefit is typically an election period (the "window period" prior to normal retirement age, where an employee may elect to retire without reduced benefits for having retired early, or with less of an early retirement reduction than would otherwise apply. Employers use window benefits to encourage reductions in force through voluntary attrition.
31. Code §412(l)(3)(C).
32. Code §412(l)(3)(C)(ii).
33. See OBRA (1987) Conference Report, at 856–57.
34. OBRA (1987), §9301 amending Code §412(c).
35. "Current liability" is defined by reference to Code §412(d)(7) without regard to paragraph (D) thereof. The interest rate used may not exceed that of Code §412(b)(5), i.e., the interest rate used to determine plan costs.
36. Code §412(c)(7)(D).
37. Treasury was instructed by OBRA (1987), §9301(c)(2) to promulgate regulations interpreting the revised full funding limitation by Aug. 15, 1988. Treasury was also instructed to submit a study of the effect of these amendments on defined benefit plans to the House Ways and Means and Senate Finance Committees by Aug. 15, 1988.
38. OBRA (1987), §9306.
39. Under Code §1274.
40. Under Code §412(f)(4).
41. OBRA (1987)'s enactment date is Dec. 22, 1987.

42. Under Code §412(c)(8).
43. Code §412(f)(1).
44. Code §§412(f)(2)(A)–(C).
45. Code §411(d)(6).
46. Code §412(b)(7)(E).
47. Under ERISA §4222.
48. Code §412(c)(7).
49. OBRA (1987), §9341, adding Code §401(a)(29).
50. See discussion of this term, above, in text following n. 22.
51. OBRA (1987), §9304, adding Code §412(m).
52. Code §412(m)(2)(A).
53. Code §412(m)(2)(B).
54. Code §412(m)(4).
55. Code §412(m)(4)(B).
56. Code §412(m)(4)(C).
57. OBRA (1987), §9307, adding Code §404(a)(1)(D).
58. Under Code §1274. See OBRA (1987), §9346, amending Code §411(c)(2).
59. OBRA (1987), §10204, amending Code §263A.

9

Social Security Integration

Social Security integration is a method by which qualified plans may reduce participants' benefits to take into account the employer's contributions to Social Security on behalf of its employees without violating the Code's qualification rules, including the §401(a)(4) general antidiscrimination rule. Since Social Security taxes are regressive (a flat rate is applied until an employee's wages equal the Social Security wage base in effect for the year and, for subsequent remuneration, no further taxes are due), integrating a plan has the effect of directing benefits away from rank-and-file employees and towards the highly paid.

Where a plan covers employees whose remuneration is subject to the Railroad Retirement Tax Act, plan benefits may be integrated with that tax. Defined benefit plans are integrated based on the employee's benefit while defined contribution plans are integrated based on the employer's contribution obligation.

The 1986 Tax Reform Act significantly tightened the integration rules—permitting employers less latitude in directing benefits to the highly paid. A further effective restriction on the use of integration comes from the top-heavy rules. That is, a plan that is integrated will be more likely to be top-heavy, triggering additional benefit and more rapid vesting requirements for non-key employees. The top-heavy plan rules are discussed in Chapter 6.

For plan years beginning before 1989, most of the specific rules for integrating qualified plans are contained in Rev. Rul. 71-446, and subsequent IRS rulings modifying the 1971 ruling.[1] The statutory authority allowing integration of qualified plans is found in Code §§401(a)(5) and 401(l).

This chapter will examine pre-1986 TRA law first because of its applicability to open taxable years and because IRS' interpretation of the pre-1986 Act integration rules in revenue rulings provides useful insight into how the IRS may interpret the revised rules.

Pre-1986 TRA Law

Definitions

To understand integration, it is first necessary to understand some of the terminology used in this area. Rev. Rul. 71-446, §2.02, defines an "integrated plan" as one that is not considered discriminatory because of the fact it provides disproportionate benefits due to offsetting for Social Security benefits or contributions.

"Covered compensation" is the amount of annual wages with respect to which Old Age Survivors and Disability Insurance (OASDI) benefits would be provided under Social Security for an employee if, for each year until he attains Social Security normal retirement age, his annual compensation is at least equal to the taxable wage base.[2]

The Social Security "taxable wage base,"*i.e.*, the wages on which FICA taxes are imposed and on which Social Security benefits are based, is an amount established annually under §230 of the Social Security Act.

A plan's "integration level" is the compensation level below which, under the plan's benefit formula, compensation is excluded or reduced in the computation of benefits or contributions.[3] Thus, for example, a defined benefit plan that provided a benefit of 30 percent of pay on compensation below $30,000 and 40 percent of pay on compensation above that amount would have an integration level of $30,000. Under pre- (and post-) 1986 TRA law, an integrated plan may use an integration level that exceeds the taxable wage base but, where it does, it must proportionately reduce the applicable integration "spread" factor (*i.e.*, the permitted disparity in benefits above and below the integration level expressed as a percentage of compensation). For instance, under pre-1986 TRA law, if a plan integrated at a level that was 4/3 of the wage base, the integration "spread" factor would have to be reduced to 3/4 of what would otherwise be allowable. After the 1986 TRA, these reductions are to be accomplished pursuant to a table in the Code §401(l) regulations, discussed below. Also, under pre-1986 TRA law, a plan could use a lower, *i.e.*, more liberal, level than the wage base. No positive adjustment may be made to the applicable "spread" factor where this is done, however. After the 1986 TRA, defined contribution plans generally may not use an integration level below the wage base, although defined benefit plans may.

A plan's "normal retirement age," for integration purposes, is the lowest age specified in a plan at which the employee has the right to retire without the employer's consent and receive retirement benefits based on service up to the date of retirement at the full rate for such service set forth in the plan, *i.e.*, without actuarial reduction because of retirement before some later specified age. A plan's normal retirement age is not the same as Social Security normal retirement age, which is fixed by the Social Security Act.

"Normal retirement benefits" are the benefits payable under a plan after retirement at any age no earlier than the plan's normal retirement age.

The applicable revenue rulings set forth different rules for integrating defined contribution and defined benefit plans due to the inherently different structure of such plans. These specific requirements will be examined next.

Defined Benefit Plans

Rev. Rul. 71-446 distinguishes between "flat" benefit plans and "unit" benefit plans and makes a further distinction based on whether a defined benefit plan is integrated on the "excess" or the "offset" method.

A flat benefit plan provides an employee with a specific benefit, regardless of that employee's length of service with the employer at retirement. An example would be a plan that provides all employees who retire at normal retirement age with a benefit of 30 percent of career average compensation, or one that provides a benefit of $30,000 per year.

A unit benefit plan's benefit formula is based on some unit, usually years of service. An example would be a plan that provides a benefit of 2 percent of career average compensation per year of service with the employer.

An "excess" plan is one under which benefits are provided at a specified rate below the plan's integration level and at another, higher, rate above that level. Where at least some level of benefits is provided both above and below the integration level, the plan is also known as a "step-rate" plan. A step-rate plan may have more than one "step" in the ladder. For instance a plan could provide a benefit of 5 percent of pay on the first $20,000 of compensation, 10 percent on the next $20,000 and 15 percent above that. A plan with multiple steps will qualify if the disparity between the top and bottom rates does not exceed the maximum permitted disparity for plans of its type.

An "offset" plan is one that provides a specified level of benefits to all participants initially, but then reduces (offsets) that benefit by a percentage of a participant's Social Security benefit.

General Rules

Section 4 of Rev. Rul. 71-446 specifies some conditions that apply to all integrated defined benefit plans. Under the ruling, a defined benefit plan will integrate only if it satisfies the following conditions:

(1) No benefits are payable when the employee dies before retirement unless, if such benefits are payable, the otherwise applicable integration "spread" (the disparity between benefits below and above the integration level, expressed as a percentage of compensation) limit is adjusted.[4]

(2) The form of retirement benefit is a straight-life annuity unless, if there are other forms, the benefit payments are adjusted so that the total value of such other forms is the same as the maximum allowable straight-life annuity.[5]

(3) Normal retirement age is not less than Social Security normal retirement age unless, if benefits of any kind other than disability are payable in the case of retirement or severance from employment before that age, such benefits are appropriately adjusted[6] and, if disability benefits are payable, the otherwise applicable limit is also adjusted.[7]

Flat-Benefit Excess Plans

Under pre-1986 TRA law, a flat-benefit excess plan will integrate if the integration level applicable to an active participant is his covered compensation or a stated dollar amount that applies uniformly to all active participants and that does not exceed the "covered compensation" of any individual who is or may become an active participant.[8]

Covered compensation for this purpose is determined in accordance with a table in Rev. Rul. 71-446, which takes into account the annual limits for all the years of an employee's career until the employee reaches Social Security normal retirement age.[9] Since this is a "rolling" type of average, each employee will have a different level of covered compensation.

For retired participants, a flat-benefit excess plan can provide a normal annual retirement benefit that does not exceed the following percentage of the participant's "average annual compensation" in excess of the applicable integration level:

(1) 37½ percent for employees with 15 or more years of service with the employer at normal retirement age, or

(2) 2½ percent for each year of service with the employer, for employees with less than 15 years of service with the employer at normal retirement age, but not to exceed 37½ percent.

Example (1): Flat benefit excess Plan A has an integration level equal to each employee's covered compensation. All employees will receive at normal retirement age a benefit of 30 percent of average annual compensation up to the integration level. Participant X, whose average annual compensation exceeds covered compensation and who has worked for the employer for more than 15 years will earn an additional benefit of 65 percent of so much of his average annual compensation as exceeds his covered compensation. The plan will integrate under pre-1986 TRA law with regard to Participant X (assuming no applicable reduction factors) because the "spread" above and below the wage base is less than 37½ percent. Participant Y, who has 10 years of service at retirement, will also earn a benefit of 30 percent of so much of his average annual compensation as does not exceed his covered compensation. Y will also receive a benefit of 53 percent of so much of his average annual compensation as exceeds covered compensation. The plan will integrate with respect to Participant Y because the "spread" for Y above and below the integration level (23 percent) is less than the permitted disparity (10 × 2½% = 25%)—again assuming no applicable reduction factors.

The following example shows how such a calculation would work if a reduction factor under Rev. Rul. 71-446 applied to the plan. Although this example uses a flat benefit excess plan, the method by which reduction factors diminish the permissible "spread" factor applies to all types of integrated qualified plans.

> *Example (2)*: Assume the same facts as in Example (1) except that, because of the type of ancillary benefits that are available under the plan, a reduction factor of .9 applies to it. The plan will not integrate with respect to Participant X because the actual spread (35 percent) exceeds the adjusted permissible spread (37.5% × .9 = 33.75%). Similarly, the plan will not integrate with respect to Participant Y because the actual spread (23 percent) is greater than the adjusted allowable spread (2.5% × 10 × .9 = 22.5%). The plan, therefore, will not qualify.

Note that, to qualify, a plan must integrate with respect to all participants. Under pre-1986 TRA law, "average annual compensation" is an employee's average compensation over a period of at least five consecutive years, under a formula which is uniform for all employees. Where an employee has less than five years of total service, the plan may use his actual years of service. A plan may not, however, define average annual compensation as the average of the five highest (nonconsecutive) years within any period of more than five years, or as the annual compensation during any one year, even though that year precedes the plan's normal retirement date by more than five years, unless such compensation is limited to that averaged over the five consecutive years of service that will produce the highest average for each employee.

If the sponsor of a flat benefit excess plan does not wish to keep records of each employee's covered compensation, it will integrate under pre-1986 TRA law if the applicable percentages (above) are multiplied by a fraction.[11] The numerator of that fraction for an active participant is the covered compensation of the oldest individual who is or may become a participant. For a retired participant, it is his covered compensation. The denominator is the plan's integration level applicable to the participant.

Unit-Benefit Excess Plans

Under pre-1986 TRA law, a unit-benefit excess plan will integrate, in the case of a plan that bases its benefits on actual compensation, if the integration "spread" above and below the integration level does not exceed 1.4 percent. For example, a plan that provided a benefit of 1 percent of compensation per year of service below the integration level and 2.4 percent above that level would qualify.[12] Where the plan bases benefits on average annual compensation, "1 percent" replaces "1.4" percent in this formula. An excess plan may employ multiple integration levels provided that the plan, when tested as a whole, does not provide a spread factor of more than the applicable limit.[13]

> *Example:* Unit benefit excess plan B bases its benefits on actual compensation. Employees earn a benefit of 1.3 percent of compensation per year of service on wages at or below the integration level (which is equal to or less than covered compensation) and 2.5 percent per year of service on covered compensation in excess of the integration level. Plan B will integrate (assuming no applicable reduction factors) because the actual disparity above and below the integration level (1.2 percent) does not exceed the maximum permitted disparity for plans of this type (1.4 percent). If plan B based its benefits on average annual compensation and the facts otherwise remained the same, it would not integrate because the actual disparity (1.2 percent) would exceed the permitted disparity (1.0 percent) for plans of this type.

Offset Plans

Under pre-1986 TRA law, an offset plan integrates if the rate at which the offset is applied to any employee's benefit does not exceed 83⅓ percent, if the offset is computed based on the Social Security Act as in effect when the offset is first applied.[14] The permissible spread is adjusted where the plan's benefit formula is based on the Social Security Act as in effect at some other point in time.[15] Thus, for example, a benefit of 50 percent of compensation reduced by 83⅓ percent of the benefit to which the employee is entitled under the Social Security Act as in effect when the offset is first applied would qualify. Under pre-1986 TRA law, offset plans have special adjustment factors for early retirement.[16]

Defined Contribution Plans

Defined contribution plans, as might be expected, are integrated based on the employer's annual contribution obligation. The test is applied to each year's contribution individually.

Under pre-1986 TRA law, for a defined contribution plan, the applicable integration level, for any year, may be an amount up to the Social Security wage base (or, if a level above the wage base is used, the allowable "spread" factor must be appropriately adjusted).

Under pre-1986 TRA law, the allowable spread factor for compensation above and below the wage base is the applicable employer premium level for the year for the Old Age Survivors and Disability Insurance (OASDI) employer portion of the Social Security tax premium for the year.

> *Example:* The Social Security wage base for the year is $45,000. This is also the plan's integration level. The plan provides a benefit of 4 percent of compensation at or below the integration level and 8 percent above it. The OASDI rate for employers for the year is 5.7 percent. The plan will integrate because the spread (8% − 4% = 4%) is less than 5.7 percent.

Post-1986 TRA Law

Effective generally for plan years beginning after 1988 (a special effective date applies to collectively bargained plans, however), the 1986 Tax Reform Act substantially restricted the use of Social Security integration in qualified plans. The discussion below examines the revised rules.

Defined Benefit Plans

Excess Plans

After the 1986 TRA, defined benefit excess plans are integrated based upon an "excess benefit percentage."[17] This percentage is the permissible benefit level above and below the allowable integration level, expressed as a percentage of compensation. Under the revised rules, this percentage cannot exceed the "base benefits percentage" by more than the "maximum excess allowance."[18]

The base benefits percentage is the percentage of compensation provided with respect to compensation that does not exceed the integration level.

For excess plans, the maximum excess allowance for any year of service taken into account under the plan is the lesser of:

(1) The base benefits percentage; or

(2) ¾ of 1 percent (.75 percent).[19]

When computing the maximum excess allowance for *total benefits* under an excess plan, the maximum excess allowance is the lesser of:

(1) The base benefits percentage; or

(2) .75 percent times the participant's number of years of service taken into account under the plan, not to exceed 35.[20]

Example: Flat benefit excess plan C has an integration level that is equal to or less than covered compensation. No reduction factors apply. The base benefits percentage for all compensation at or below the integration level is 20 percent of compensation. Benefits are provided on compensation above the integration level at a rate of 35 percent of compensation. Participant W has 36 years of service at normal retirement age. Plan C integrates with respect to Participant W because the actual spread above and below the integration level (15 percent) is less than the maximum excess allowance with respect to Participant W (lesser of the base benefits percentage [20 percent] or the maximum excess allowance [35 × .75 = 26.25%]). Note that, although W has 36 years of service, only 35 are considered for this purpose.

Proposed regulations promulgated by the IRS under post-1986 TRA law provide that the disparity between the excess benefit percentage and the base benefits percentage must be uniform with respect to all participants.[21] Similar rules apply to offset plans. The proposed regulations, however, include an exception from the general uniformity requirement for differences in disparities that result solely from differences in employees' Social Security retirement ages.

The foregoing rules apply to both final average pay excess

benefit plans and career average pay excess benefits plans. A year of service is treated as being taken into account under the plan if a benefit accrues to the participant for that year. The maximum excess allowance also applies to a flat benefit final pay plan and a unit benefit final pay plan.

The statute directs the IRS to prescribe regulations under which the .75 percent factor is to be reduced where a plan uses integration levels in excess of covered compensation.[22] This is similar to the proportionate reduction rule discussed above under pre-1986 TRA law, except that the reduction factors are to be based on brackets of compensation. The IRS, in proposed regulations, has prescribed these reduction factors (see discussion at nn. 31–37, below).

If an option, such as a lump sum distribution election based upon certain calculations, is provided to employees having compensation above the integration level, then such option must be provided below the integration level as well.[23]

Excess plans may employ multiple integration levels.[24] Note that, for all plans, the definition of "integration level" used under pre-1986 TRA law was codified by the 1986 Act.[25]

Offset Plans

Post-1986 TRA law defines an "offset plan" as one under which the employer-provided benefit for each participant is reduced by an amount specified in the plan that does not exceed the applicable "maximum offset allowance."[26]

This allowance, with respect to any year of service taken into account under the plan, is the lesser of:

(1) 50 percent of the benefit that would have accrued to the participant without regard to the plan's offset reduction; or

(2) .75 percent of the participant's final average compensation, multiplied by the participant's years of service (not to exceed 35) taken into account under the plan.[27]

An offset plan must base benefits on average annual compensation for at least the lesser of:

(1) The participant's highest average annual compensation for at least three consecutive years; (years, for this purpose,

may be any 12 consecutive month period specified in the plan)[28] or

(2) The participant's "final average compensation" (defined for this purpose as the participant's average annual compensation for the three consecutive year period ending with the current year, or if shorter, the participant's full period of service).[29]

Example: Flat benefit offset plan D bases its benefits on average annual compensation as defined above. It uses covered compensation as its integration level. Plan D provides a benefit of 50 percent of average annual compensation, but reduces benefits below the integration level to 25 percent of such average annual pay. Participant Z retires with 40 years of service. The plan integrates with respect to Participant Z (assuming no reduction factors apply) because the offset that applies to Z (25 percent) *does not exceed* the maximum offset allowance (lesser of [50% × ½ = 25%] or [35 × .75 = 26.25%]).

The proposed regulations require that any offset in a defined benefit offset plan be uniform with respect to all participants.[30]

Code §401(l)(5)(F) authorizes the IRS to prescribe regulations requiring a reduction in the .75 percent factor in the maximum excess and offset allowances for defined benefit excess/offset plans that provide for benefits (other than certain disability benefits) beginning before a participant has reached his or her Social Security retirement age. The proposed regulations provide tables that set forth the reduced maximum excess and offset allowances.[31] These tables are set forth below:

TABLE 4

If the integration level—

Is more than	*But not more than*	*.75% factor is reduced to:*
Covered Comp.	125% of Covered Comp.	.69%
125% of Covered Comp.	150% of Covered Comp.	.60%
150% of Covered Comp.	175% of Covered Comp.	.53%
175% of Covered Comp.	200% of Covered Comp.	.47%
200% of Covered Comp.		.42%

The proposed regulations clarify that the maximum excess and offset allowance rules apply only to employer-derived benefits under the plan. Benefits attributable to employee contributions are not taken into account in determining whether defined benefit excess or offset plans properly integrate.[32] In general, the rules of Code §411(c) and the regulations thereunder apply to determine whether a particular benefit is attributable to employer or employee contributions.[33]

Post-1986 TRA law preserves the rule contained in pre-1986 TRA revenue rulings whereby the applicable spread factor is to be reduced when the employee's benefit under a defined benefit excess or offset plan is payable before the participant attains Social Security normal retirement age. Under the table contained in the proposed regulations, the .75 percent spread factor is to be reduced as shown in Table 5.[34]

For purposes of this rule, the "benefit commencement date" is the first day of the period for which the benefit is paid under the plan.[35] For purposes of applying the maximum excess and offset allowances, no reduction in the .75 percent factor is to be made solely because the plan provides for benefits payable before a participant's Social Security retirement age.[36] Benefits attributable to employee contributions to a defined benefit plan are not taken into account in determining whether a plan integrates.[37]

Under a special rule contained in the proposed regulations, if one of two tests are satisfied, a "uniform factor" can be applied in determining whether a plan integrates with Social Security, disregarding benefits attributable to employee contributions. The uniform factor for a plan year is a factor determined for an age equal to the average attained age for all participants minus the average years of participation under the contributory plan for all participants.[38]

The first test is the "minimum percentage test." This test is met if:

(1) More than 40 percent of the participants who are not highly compensated employees have attained ages at least equal to the plan's "target age;" and

(2) More than 20 percent (rounded up to the next whole number) of the participants who are not highly compensated employees have attained ages at least equal to the average attained age of participants who are highly compensated employees.

TABLE 5

Social Security Retirement Age 67		*Social Security Retirement Age 66*		*Social Security Retirement Age 65*	
Age at which Benefits Commence	*Annual Factor in Maximum Excess Allowance and Maximum Offset Allowance*	*Age at which Benefits Commence*	*Annual Factor in Maximum Excess Allowance and Maximum Offset Allowance*	*Age at which Benefits Commence*	*Annual Factor in Maximum Excess Allowance and Maximum Offset Allowance*
66	.70%	65	.70%	64	.70%
65	.65%	64	.65%	63	.65%
64	.60%	63	.60%	62	.60%
63	.56%	62	.55%	61	.55%
62	.52%	61	.51%	60	.50%
61	.48%	60	.47%	59	.46%
60	.44%	59	.43%	58	.42%
59	.40%	58	.39%	57	.38%
58	.37%	57	.36%	56	.35%
57	.34%	56	.33%	55	.32%
56	.31%	55	.30%		
55	.28%				

The target age for a plan is the lesser of:

(1) Age 50, or

(2) The average attained age of highly compensated participants, minus "X years" where X is the following amount:

20 − (5 × the employee contribution rate under the plan expressed as a percentage × 100).

For purposes of this equation, however, "X years" may never be less than zero."[39]

Example: Under a defined benefit plan, the average attained age of highly compensated participants is 53 years. The employee contribution rate is 2 percent of compensation. The plan's target age is 43 years (53 − [20 − (5 × 2)]).

The second test is the "ratio test." This test is met if the number of non-highly compensated participants who have attained ages that are at least equal to the average attained ages of highly compensated participants, stated as a percentage of all nonhighly compensated employees, is at least 70 percent of the number of highly compensated participants, stated as a percentage of all highly compensated employees. For purposes of this test, an employer may assume that 50 percent of its highly compensated participants have attained ages at least equal to the average attained age of highly compensated participants.[40]

For purposes of both the minimum percentage test and the ratio test, a highly compensated participant's "attained age" is the per capita average of the attained ages for the participants who are highly compensated employees, determined as of the beginning of the plan year.[41]

Flat Dollar Excess and Offset Plans

The IRS's proposed regulations also provide rules for plans that use a flat dollar limit on the compensation that is to be taken into account in determining the offset amount for purposes of integrating a defined benefit offset plan. Under these rules, the flat dollar offset either may be specified in the plan or may be determined pursuant to a formula set forth in the plan. In general, the flat dollar offset may not exceed the greater of:

(1) $10,000, or

(2) One-half of the covered compensation of an individual who reached Social Security retirement age in the current plan year.

Alternatively, a flat dollar excess or offset plan may qualify by satisfying both the "attained age requirement" and the "nondiscrimination requirement."[42]

The "attained age requirement" is satisfied only if the average attained age of nonhighly compensated employees is not greater than the greater of:

(1) Age 50, or

(2) The average attained age of highly compensated employees, plus five years.

For purposes of this test, the attained age of participants is to be determined as of the beginning of the plan year.

The "nondiscrimination requirement" is satisfied if the plan passes at least one of three tests.

The first test, known as the "minimum percentage test" is satisfied only if more than 50 percent of nonhighly compensated participants have compensation that is at least equal to 120 percent of the "uniform dollar amount" (this amount is the amount determined above, i.e., the greater of $10,000 or half the compensation of an individual who reached Social Security retirement age in the current plan year).

The second test is the "ratio test." This test is satisfied if nonhighly compensated participants who have compensation that is at least equal to 120 percent of the uniform dollar amount, expressed as a percentage of all nonhighly compensated employees, is at least 70 percent of the number of participants who are highly compensated, expressed as a percentage of all highly compensated employees of the employer.[43]

The third test is the "high dollar amount" test. This test is satisfied only if the uniform dollar amount exceeds 150 percent of the covered compensation of an individual who attains Social Security retirement age in the current plan year.

Integration of Defined Benefit Plans Limited to Primary Insurance Amount Actually Paid

A significant amendment made by the 1986 TRA limits the amount that an employer may reduce a participant's benefit to the employer-derived Social Security Primary Insurance Amount (PIA) actually paid.[44] Under this provision, a defined benefit plan (whether excess or offset) cannot reduce a retirement benefit based upon a participant's final average pay by more than the Social Security primary insurance amount actually paid on behalf of the participant and attributable to service of the participant with that employer. For this purpose, the primary insurance amount is deemed to accrue over 35 years and is computed without regard to auxiliary benefits such as spousal benefits, survivor benefits, children's benefits, and disability benefits. The employer-derived primary insurance amount attributable to service by the participant for the employer is determined by multiplying the employer-derived portion of the participant's projected primary insurance amount by a fraction (not exceeding one). The numerator is the participant's number of complete years of covered service for the employer under the Social Security Act and the denominator is 35.[45] A further restriction provides that this limit on integration cannot be applied either to reduce benefits that have already accrued under a plan or to reduce minimum benefits that must be supplied to non-key employees under the top-heavy plan rules.

Defined Contribution Plans

After the 1986 TRA, a defined contribution plan will integrate if its "excess contributions percentage" (the percentage of pay that is contributed above the integration level) does not exceed its "base contributions percentage" (the percentage contributed on compensation below the integration level) by more than the lesser of:

(1) The "base contribution percentage;" or

(2) The greater of (a) 5.7 percent or (b) the applicable Old Age Insurance tax rate in effect under Code §3111(a) for the year.[46]

The disparity between the excess contribution percentage and the base contribution percentage must be uniform with respect to all participants.[47]

> *Example:* Defined contribution plan E integrates at or below the Social Security wage base for the year. The Old Age component of OASDI for the year is 4.35 percent. Plan E provides a "base contributions percentage" on all compensation at or below the integration level of 5 percent of pay and a contribution on compensation above the integration level of 10.5 percent. No reduction factors apply. Plan E will not integrate for the year because its excess contributions percentage exceeds its base contributions percentage (10.5% − 5% = 5.5%) by more than the maximum allowable disparity of 5% (lesser of (1) base contribution percentage, 5%, or (2) the greater of [5.7% or 4.35%—*i.e.*, 5.7%]).

Under post-1986 TRA law, for a defined contribution plan, the integration level may not exceed the taxable wage base for the plan year.[48] A defined contribution plan must specify an integration level for a plan year that equals the taxable wage base in effect at the beginning of the plan year.[49] Thus, a defined contribution plan will not satisfy Code §401(l) if it has for a plan year an integration level that is less than the wage base as of the beginning of the plan year. This change, supplied by the proposed regulations, represents a departure from the IRS' interpretation of the law in effect prior to the 1986 TRA. The Preamble to the proposed regulations explains the IRS' view that:

> "Such a lower integration level creates a significant potential for discrimination in favor of highly compensated employees and thus such a plan may not rely on sections 401(a)(5)(C) and 401(l) to disregard its disparity. Instead, such a plan will be required to demonstrate that it is nondiscriminatory under the general section 401(a)(4) analysis."

The proposed regulations clarify that a defined contribution plan will not violate §401(l)(2) merely because it provides for the payment of benefits to participants for reasons other than retirement, death, disability, or other separation from service.[50]

Note that the revised integration rules define "covered compensation" as, with respect to an employee, the average of the contribution and benefit bases in effect under §230 of the Social Security Act for each year in the 35-year period ending with the year in which the employee reaches age 65. The determination for any year preceding the year in which the employee reaches age

65 is to be made by assuming that there is no increase in the bases described above after the determination year and before the employee reaches age 65.[51]

Combinations of Plans

Carrying over a principle that applied pursuant to Rev. Rul. 71-446 under pre-1986 TRA law, post-1986 TRA Code §401(l)(5)(F)(ii) requires the IRS to prescribe regulations to prevent the multiple use of the permitted disparity limits with respect to employees who participate in more than one plan maintained by an employer. The proposed regulations contain rules under which employer contributions and forfeitures under defined contribution plans and employer-derived benefits under defined benefit plans that are provided under two or more plans maintained by an employer in which an employee participates or may participate are combined for purposes of applying:

(1) The maximum excess allowance for defined contribution and defined benefit excess plans; and

(2) The maximum offset allowance for defined benefit offset plans.[52]

Coordination of §§401(l) and 401(a)(4)

The IRS' proposed regulations make it clear that the mere fact that a plan is in compliance with Code §401(l) does not constitute an automatic safe harbor for determining whether a plan discriminates within the meaning of §401(a)(4) in this area. Rather, the Preamble to the proposed regulations explains the interaction between §§401(a)(4) and 401(l) as follows:

"Section 401(l) is more narrowly directed at the question of whether, in the case of an excess plan, the disparity in the explicit formula for contribution allocation or benefit rates with respect to compensation below and above a specified level may be disregarded, by reason of section 401(a)(5)(C), in determining whether the plan satisfies the nondiscrimination rule of section 401(a)(4). Similarly, in the case of an offset plan, section 401(l) is directed at determining whether the benefit offset provided under the explicit formula in the plan (i.e., the reduction or offset of the benefit that otherwise would have been earned under the positive portion of the formula) may be disregarded, by reason of section 401(a)(5)(C), in determining whether the plan satisfies the nondiscrimination rule of section 401(a)(4).

"This general relationship is reflected by the focus under section 401(l) on the treatment of the disparity in the rates of contributions or benefits with respect to participants' compensation below and above a specified level and the disparity among the rates of contributions or benefits among plan participants that is solely the result of a specified benefit offset under the plan's benefit formula. Section 401(l) does not directly address the disparity in contribution or benefit rates between highly compensated and nonhighly compensated employees.

"Thus, for purposes of applying section 401(a)(4) to a defined benefit excess plan that satisfies section 401(l), a participant may generally be treated as having a benefit equal to the excess benefit percentage under the plan formula applied to all compensation taken into account under the plan even though, because of the permitted rate disparity, the participant actually earns a smaller benefit. Similarly, in applying section 401(a)(4) to an offset plan that satisfies section 401(l), a participant may generally be treated as having earned the full benefit under the positive portion of the benefit formula under the plan even though, because of the permitted offset, the participant actually earns the positive benefit reduced by the permitted offset.

"However, although the rate disparity of benefit offset provided under the contribution allocation or benefit formula in a plan satisfies section 401(l) and is therefore permitted disparity under such section, the plan nevertheless may not satisfy the nondiscrimination rules of section 401(a)(4). In other words, disregarding the disparity in allocations or benefits that results solely from the permitted disparity in allocation or benefit rates or from the permitted offset does not provide assurance that the plan, or the amounts of contributions or benefits provided thereunder, will be nondiscriminatory under section 401(a)(4)."

The Preamble goes on to explain that Code §§401(a)(5)(C) and 401(l) are intended to provide the only permitted disparities in benefit rates that may be disregarded in applying §401(a)(5). Therefore, the proposed regulations clarify that a plan that provides for a benefit disparity that is not allowable under §§401(a)(5) and 401(l) will be tested for discrimination under §401(a)(4), without disregarding any benefit disparities. Nonetheless, the Preamble points out that a plan that fails to satisfy §401(l) may still satisfy §401(a)(4) if it can demonstrate under a §401(a)(4) analysis that it does not discriminate in favor of highly compensated employees.

Notes

1. 1971-2 C.B. 187. See, e.g., Rev. Rul. 75-480, 1975-2 C.B. 131, modifying Rev. Rul. 71-446, 1971-2 C.B. 187, in light of the enactment of ERISA; see also Rev. Rul. 79-236, 1979-2 C.B. 160, analyzing the application of Rev. Rul. 71-446 to a controlled group that maintains separate plans for different business entities; Rev. Rul. 81-157, 1981-1 C.B. 170; Rev. Rul. 83-53, 1983-1 C.B. 88 (amplifying §8.01 of Rev. Rul. 71-446 to clarify the applicable adjustment factor in the case of preretirement death benefits); Rev. Rul. 83-97, 1983-2 C.B. 72; and Rev. Rul. 83-110, 1983-2 C.B. 70 (modifying Rev. Rul. 71-446 in light of TEFRA's enactment of Code §401(l)).
2. The OASDI tax is the largest component of the Social Security payroll tax (which is known as the FICA tax). The other key component of the tax is hospital insurance (i.e., medicare).
3. Rev. Rul. 71-446, §2.05.
4. The adjustments are to be made in accordance with §8; see Rev. Rul. 71-446, §4.01. Section 8 reduces the otherwise applicable integration rate by 8/9 for preretirement death benefits and also contains a reduction factor where a plan provides spousal annuity benefits.
5. Section 9 contains a list of reduction factors to be applied where other forms of benefits are provided. For instance, where an optional form of retirement benefit is available in the form of an annuity for five years certain and life thereafter, the otherwise applicable integration rate must be reduced to 97% of what it would be if the plan only provided straight-life annuity benefits. If the optional form is an annuity for 10 years certain and for life thereafter, the reduction factor is 90% of the otherwise applicable limit.
6. Under Rev. Rul. 71-446, §10 or 11.
7. Under §12.
8. Rev. Rul. 71-446, §5.01.
9. *Id.* at §3.02.
10. *Id.* at §5.02.
11. Under §5.04 of Rev. Rul. 71-446.
12. *Id.* at §6.02.
13. Under §19 of Rev. Rul. 71-446.
14. *Id.* at §7.01.
15. *Id.* at §7.04.
16. *Id.* at §11.
17. Code §401(l)(3).
18. See Code §§401(l)(3) and (4).
19. Code §401(l)(4)(A).
20. *Id.*
21. Prop. Treas. Regs. §1.401(l)-3(b)(2).
22. Code §401(l)(4)(C).
23. Code §401(l)(3)(A)(i)(II).
24. Code §401(l)(5)(iv).
25. Code §401(l)(5)(A).
26. Code §401(l)(3)(B). The proposed regulations clarify that a defined benefit plan that provides a benefit to each participant will not be considered an offset plan merely because benefits provided under the plan are offset on

account of benefits provided under another qualified plan maintained by the employer.

27. Code §401(l)(4)(B).
28. See Prop. Treas. Regs. §1.401(l)-1(b)(8).
29. Code §§401(l)(3)(B); (l)(5)(C), and (l)(5)(D)(ii). Note that the statute limits final average compensation by requiring that wages in excess of the Social Security wage base for the year in question be disregarded.
30. Prop. Treas. Regs. §1.401(l)-3(c)(2).
31. Prop. Treas. Regs. §1.401(l)-3(e)(3).
32. Prop. Treas. Regs. §1.401(l)-3(g).
33. Prop. Treas. Regs. §1.401(l)-3(g)(1). Note, however, that Prop. Treas. Regs. §1.401-3(g)(2) provides a special rule that certain plans may use to determine which benefits are attributable to employee contributions.
34. Prop. Treas. Regs. §1.401(l)-3(e)(3).
35. Prop. Treas. Regs. §1.401(l)-3(e)(5).
36. Prop. Treas. Regs. §1.401(l)-3(f).
37. Prop. Treas. Regs. §1.401(l)-3(g).
38. Prop. Treas. Regs. §1.401(l)-3(g)(2)(i). In applying these tests, participants who would be excludable employees but for the fact that they (and similarly situated employees) benefit under the plan (or another plan of the employer) may be disregarded if the plan would satisfy Code §410(b) coverage tests without regard to such participants.
39. Prop. Treas. Regs. §1.401(l)-3(g)(iv).
40. Prop. Treas. Regs. §1.401(l)-3(g)(2)(iii).
41. Prop. Treas. Regs. §401(l)-3(g)(v).
42. Of Prop. Treas. Regs. §§1.401(l)-3(c)(4)(B) (attained age) and 1.401(l)-3(c)(4)(C) (nondiscrimination).
43. The proposed regulations provide that, except as provided in Prop. Treas. Regs. §1.401(l)-3(c)(4)(iii)(A), the ratio test is to be applied on a basis that is consistent with the §401(b) qualified plan coverage rules and the regulations under that provision.
44. Code §401(l)(4)(C)(ii).
45. Prop. Treas. Regs. §1.401(a)(5)-1(a)(3)(ii).
46. Code §§401(l)(2)(B)(i) (excess contributions percentage), 401(l)(2)(B)(ii) (base contributions percentage), and 401(l)(2)(A).
47. Prop. Treas. Regs. §1.401(l)-2(b)(3).
48. Code §401(l)(5)(A)(ii).
49. Prop. Treas. Regs. §1.401(l)-2(b)(4).
50. Prop. Treas. Regs. §1.401(l)-2(b).
51. Code §401(l)(5)(E).
52. Prop. Treas. Regs. §1.401(l)-4.

10

Taxation of Distributions From Qualified Plans

Distributions from qualified plans to participants and beneficiaries may take many forms. Among the most common are the lump sum distribution, the straight-life annuity, the annuity for a fixed term of years, and the qualified joint and survivor annuity. The only form of benefit distribution imposed on plans as a matter of law is the requirement that certain qualified plans provide that, absent an election to the contrary, a married participant will receive normal retirement benefits in the form of a "qualified joint and survivor annuity" and that spouses of certain vested participants who die before retirement receive their benefits in the form of a "qualified preretirement survivor annuity." For both these benefits, the participant's spouse must also waive the right to receive joint and survivor benefits.

Note that, after the Supreme Court's decision in *Arizona Governing Committee for Tax Deferred Annuity and Compensation Plans v. Norris*, plans may not differentiate on the basis of gender in calculating amounts payable under annuities.[1] Before *Norris*, a plan could pay a female participant a lesser annual annuity amount than a male participant because of the longer life expectancy of women (requiring that payments be made over a longer period). After *Norris*, plans must use gender-neutral or "blended" annuity tables in computing benefits.

The Code contains rules governing when a participant's benefit under a qualified plan must be distributed to the participant, the participant's spouse, or the participant's beneficiary.[2] A penalty excise tax of 50 percent of the amount that should have been distributed under these rules, but was not, is imposed upon distributees. Certain excess retirement distributions and excess retirement accumulations are also subject to excise taxes.

Code §402 provides special rules that allow the recipient of a lump sum distribution under a qualified plan to receive favorable income tax treatment or to roll over the distributed amounts taxfree to a qualified recipient plan. Where a rollover occurs, the recipient will not be taxed until the amount rolled over is distributed from the recipient plan.

Finally, Code §2039 governs the federal estate tax treatment of interests in qualified plans. Before TEFRA, §2039 provided an unlimited estate tax exclusion for these amounts.[3] TEFRA limited the exclusion to $100,000 per estate. The 1984 Tax Reform Act repealed the estate tax exclusion entirely, subject to certain transition rules for participants in pay status.

Qualified Joint and Survivor Annuity Requirement

The Code requires that, where a qualified plan provides benefits in the form of a life annuity, the plan must presume, where the participant and the participant's spouse have been married for at least one year on the annuity starting date that, absent an election to the contrary, normal retirement benefits will be provided in a form having the effect of a qualified joint and survivor annuity.[4]

A "qualified joint and survivor annuity" (J&S) is an annuity for the life of the participant with a survivor annuity for the life of the participant's spouse that is not less than 50 percent, nor greater than 100 percent, of the amount of the annuity payable during their joint lives, and which is the actuarial equivalent of a single life annuity for the participant. The definition also encompasses any mode of payment that, in form, has the effect of such an annuity.[5] An annuity is not a qualified joint and survivor annuity if payments to the spouse of a deceased participant are terminated or reduced because that spouse remarries. A qualified joint and survivor annuity must be at least the actuarial equivalent of the normal form of life annuity or, if greater, of any optional form of life annuity offered under the plan.[6]

A "life annuity," for this purpose, is defined as an annuity that provides retirement payments and requires the survival of the participant or the participant's spouse as one of the conditions for any payment or possible payment under the annuity. Thus, an annuity that provides payments for 10 years or until death, whichever occurs later, would be a life annuity.

A provision allowing a plan to involuntarily cash out annuity benefits having a present value not in excess of $3,500, however, will not violate the joint and survivor or preretirement survivor annuity rules.[7] This is because Code §417(f) allows qualified plans to distribute benefits in lump sum to a participant if the present value of such benefits do not exceed $3,500. Benefits in excess of this amount may be cashed out only with the participant's consent. In determining present value under this rule, if the benefit is under $25,000 (using this rate), the applicable interest rate to be used is the rate used by the PBGC in calculating the value of lump sum distributions upon plan termination. If the vested benefit exceeds $25,000, the interest rate to be used in calculating present value may not exceed 120 percent of such PBGC rate.

Pre-REA Law

Before the 1984 Retirement Equity Act, a plan that included an early retirement age did not have to provide a presumption in favor of joint and survivor annuity benefits for married participants who elected early retirement.[8] Such a plan did, however, have to give a participant who took early retirement the option of affirmatively electing an "early survivor annuity."[9]

Thus, under pre-REA law, a plan providing life annuity benefits had to allow a married participant who retired at normal retirement age the opportunity to elect "out" of joint and survivor annuity treatment, while a married participant who retired early had to be given the opportunity to elect "in" to early survivor annuity benefits.

Post-REA Law: Code §417

The REA continued the trend of the *Norris* decision in making the qualification rules for Code §401(a) plans more responsive to the concerns of women. In so doing, the REA made sweeping changes to §401(a)(11) and added Code §417. In general, the REA amendments apply to plan years beginning after 1984, except that the REA rules do not apply to any participant who does not have one hour of service after the REA's enactment date (August 23, 1984).

As amended by the REA, Code §401(a)(11) provides that, except as provided in §417, a plan will not qualify under §401(a) unless it provides for benefits to be paid in the form of a joint and survivor annuity or a "pre-retirement survivor annuity."

Section 401(a)(11) applies to:

(1) Any defined benefit plan;

(2) Any defined contribution plan that is subject to the minimum funding standards of Code §412, *e.g.*, money purchase pension plans; and

(3) In the case of a defined contribution plan, to any participant in such plan unless (a) the plan provides that the participant's nonforfeitable accrued benefit is payable in full on the participant's death to the participant's surviving spouse; (b) the participant does not elect to receive benefits in life annuity form; and (c) with respect to the participant, the defined contribution plan is not a direct or indirect transferee of a defined benefit plan or a defined contribution plan subject to Code §412.[10]

Certain Employee Stock Ownership Plan (ESOP) benefits are also excepted from Code §401(a)(11). The ESOP exception applies to certain tax-credit ESOPs as defined in Code §409(a), and ESOPs as defined in Code §4975(e)(7). For such plans, Code §401(a)(11)(A) does not apply to that portion of an employee's accrued benefit to which the requirements of §409(h) (relating to an employee's right to demand benefit distributions in the form of employer securities) apply, provided the other requirements of (3), above, are met.[11]

In general, plans to which Code §401(a)(11) applies must provide married vested participants who retire under the plan with benefit payments in the form of a qualified joint and survivor annuity.[12] If a vested participant dies before his or her annuity starting date and has a surviving spouse, the plan, if covered by §401(a)(11), must provide the spouse with a "qualified preretirement survivor annuity."[13]

A qualified preretirement survivor annuity is a survivor annuity for the life of the participant's surviving spouse that satisfies certain conditions. First, the payments to the spouse must not be less than the amounts that would be payable as a survivor annuity under the plan's joint and survivor annuity (or the actuarial equivalent thereof) if certain criteria were met. These criteria are:

(1) If a participant dies after attaining the plan's earliest retirement age, the annuity must be as great as the survivor annuity that would have been payable to the spouse under the plan's joint and survivor annuity if the participant had retired with an immediate qualified joint and survivor annuity on the date of death.

(2) If a participant dies on or before the date he would have attained the plan's earliest retirement age, the annuity must be as great as the survivor portion of the plan's joint and survivor annuity if the participant had:
(a) separated from the employer's service on his date of death;
(b) survived to the plan's earliest retirement age;
(c) retired with an immediate qualified joint and survivor annuity at the plan's earliest retirement age; and
(d) died on the day after the day on which he would have attained the plan's earliest retirement age.[14]

In addition the earliest period for which a surviving spouse may receive a payment under the preretirement survivor annuity must not be later than the month in which the participant would have attained the earliest retirement age under the plan.[15]

In a defined contribution plan, however, the plan must permit the surviving spouse to direct the commencement of benefit payments within a reasonable time of the participant's death.[16]

A special exemption from the joint and survivor rules is provided for defined contribution plans. That exception applies to:

(1) Any defined contribution plan subject to the minimum funding standard of Code §412, or

(2) Any participant in any defined contribution plan unless—
(a) The plan provides that the participant's vested benefit (reduced by any security interest held by the plan in respect of a participant loan) is payable on the participant's death to the surviving spouse or, if there is no spouse, (or

there is a spouse, but such spouse consents), to the participant's designated beneficiary,
(b) The participant does not elect life annuity benefits, and
(c) With respect to such participant, the plan is not a direct or indirect transferee in a post-1984 transfer of a plan described in (a) or (b), above.[17]

Note that (c), above, only applies to a participant to the extent of the transferred assets if the plan accounts separately for such assets and the income therefrom.

The temporary regulations provide that a defined contribution plan is a transferee plan with respect to a particular participant if it is a direct or indirect transferee of benefits that were held on the participant's behalf on or after January 1, 1985, by:

(1) A defined benefit plan,

(2) A defined contribution plan subject to the minimum funding standard, or

(3) A defined contribution plan that is subject to the J&S rules with respect to that participant.[18]

Pre-1985 transfers and any rollover contribution made *at any time*, do not subject a plan to the J&S requirements. The temporary regulations provide that the J&S requirements do not apply to other participants solely because a plan is a transferee plan with respect to one or more of its participants. They add, however, that it may be necessary to provide J&S and preretirement annuities to other participants to prevent discrimination.

A plan, in general, may decline to provide a qualified joint and survivor annuity or a preretirement survivor annuity where the participant and the participant's spouse have not been married throughout the one-year period ending on the earlier of:

(1) The participant's annuity starting date; or

(2) The date of the participant's death.[19]

This rule reflects a determination that public policy does not require that survivor benefits be provided to spouses who marry participants late in life. The rule was carried over from pre-REA law. The REA, however, added an exception for certain marriages that occur within one year of the participant's annuity starting date.[20] Under that exception, for purposes of the J&S provisions (but not for purposes of the preretirement survivor annuity rules), if (1) the participant and the spouse have been married within a one-year period before the participant's annuity starting date, and (2) the couple have been married for at least a one-year period ending on or before the participant's date of death, the marriage requirement will be deemed satisfied.[21]

Where the J&S rules apply, a plan must provide that each participant may elect, at any time during the "applicable election period," to waive the qualified joint and survivor form of benefit and that the participant may revoke such a waiver election during that period as well.[22] Where a waiver election is made, the plan must provide that the waiver will not be effective unless the spouse consents. This consent must be in writing.[23] The spouse's consent must acknowledge the effect of the waiver election and must be witnessed by a plan representative or a notary public.[24] Alternatively, an election will be given effect if it is established to the satisfaction of a plan representative that the spouse's consent cannot be obtained because:

(1) There is no spouse,

(2) The spouse cannot be located, or

(3) Of such other reasons as the Treasury, by regulations, may prescribe.[25]

Any spousal consent, or deemed consent, is effective only as to the spouse involved.[26]

In addition to the foregoing, to qualify under Code §401(a), the plan must, within a reasonable time before the annuity starting date, provide a written explanation of the joint and survivor benefit.[27]

The explanation must include a description of the terms and conditions of the qualified joint and survivor annuity.[28] This, presumably, includes an explanation of its economic effect in light of the benefits offered under the plan when contrasted with other optional modes of benefit payment. The explanation must also apprise the participant of the right to waive the joint and survivor annuity and of the rights of the participant's spouse in connection with such a waiver.[29] The explanation must also apprise the participant of his right to make, and the effect of, a waiver election or a revocation of such waiver with regard to joint and survivor benefits.[30]

Further, a qualified plan must provide each participant, within the period beginning with the first day of the plan year in which he or she attains age 32, and ending with the close of the plan year in which he or she attains age 35, a written explanation of the qualified preretirement survivor annuity comparable to that which is required for the qualified joint and survivor annuity.

The "applicable election period" during which the joint and survivor or preretirement survivor annuity waiver election can be made is:

(1) For the regular joint and survivor annuity, a 90-day period ending on the annuity starting date, and

(2) For the preretirement survivor annuity, a period beginning with the first day of the plan year in which the participant attains age 35 and ending on the date of the participant's death.[31]

Where a participant has separated from the employer's service, the preretirement election as to benefits accrued before the date of separation may not begin later than the separation date.[32] A special exception to the election and notification requirements applies to subsidized J&S or preretirement survivor benefits. Under this exception, neither the J&S nor the preretirement survivor annuity requirement applies if (1) the benefit (J&S or preretirement) may not be waived (or another beneficiary may not be selected); and (2) the plan "fully subsidizes" the cost of the benefit. A plan will be considered to fully subsidize a benefit if the participant's failure to waive the benefit will not cause a reduction in any plan benefit with respect to the participant and would not result in increased contributions by the participant.[33]

Note that the J&S rules apply to benefits derived from employee as well as employer contributions, but an exception is provided for benefits attributable to accumulated deductible employee contributions within the meaning of Code §72(o).[34] In a defined benefit plan, the survivor annuity requirements apply only to benefits in which a participant was vested immediately before death. They do not apply to benefits in which a participant becomes vested by reason of death or to the proceeds of a life insurance contract maintained by the plan for the participant to the extent such proceeds exceed the present value of the participant's vested accrued benefits immediately before death. However, in a defined contribution plan that is subject to the survivor annuity requirements, all vested benefits are covered, whether vested before or upon death, including life insurance contract proceeds.

A spousal consent to a waiver of joint and survivor benefits need not be irrevocable. However, a plan may preclude a spouse from revoking consent once given.[35] In addition, the spousal consent requirement applies to a participant's election of a nonspouse beneficiary. For example, if a spouse consents to a participant's election not to receive a preretirement survivor's annuity, but instead to have the benefits payable to their children upon the participant's death, the participant may not subsequently change beneficiaries without the spouse's consent. Any spousal consent to a nonspouse beneficiary must acknowledge the nonspouse beneficiary, including any class of beneficiaries or contingent beneficiaries.[36]

The REA's survivor annuity provisions are generally effective for plan years beginning after 1984. An exception is provided for plans maintained pursuant to a collective bargaining agreement ratified before August 23, 1984.[37] The post-REA survivor annuity requirements, however, generally only apply to participants having at least one hour of service under the plan, or at least one hour of paid leave, on or after August 23, 1984.[38]

Minimum Required Distribution Rules

Code §401(a)(14) requires that a qualified plan must provide for the payment of benefits to participants, absent the participant's election to the contrary, no later than the 60th day following the close of the plan year in which the latest of the following events occurs:

(1) The participant attains age 65;

(2) The participant completes 10 years of service with the employer; or

(3) The participant separates from the employer's service.[39]

TEFRA and the 1984 TRA

TEFRA added Code §401(a)(9), providing mandatory distribution rules for qualified plans. These rules were later amended by the 1984 and 1986 Tax Reform Acts.

For plan years beginning after 1983, TEFRA required that two sets of mandatory distribution rules be included in qualified plans. One was for distributions occurring before the death of the participant. The second was for post-death distributions.

TEFRA required that, with respect to pre-death distributions, a qualified plan provide that the entire interest of an employee be distributed to him no later than the taxable year in which he attained age 70½ or retired, whichever was later. For key employees participating in top-heavy plans, distributions had to begin when the employee attained age 70½, regardless of when he retired. Once required distributions commenced, benefits were required to be distributed in accordance with Treasury regulations over one of the following periods:

(1) The life of the employee or the lives of the employee and the employee's spouse, or

(2) The life expectancy of the employee or the life expectancies of the employee and the employee's spouse.[40]

This rule, retained in modified form after the 1984 and 1986 Tax Reform Acts, effectively requires that distributions be made according to a schedule over one of the permissible periods. For example, if distributions had to commence at age 70½ and the employee's then life expectancy was 10 years, he would have to receive 1/10 of his benefit in the first year, 1/9 of any remaining benefits in the next year, and so on.

Where an employee died before his entire interest was distributed to him or distribution had commenced under the required distribution rules to the employee's surviving spouse and the spouse died before the entire interest had been distributed, TEFRA required that the entire interest (or any remaining part thereof) be distributed within five years after the participant's (or spouse's) death to the participant's beneficiary. The five-year rule did not apply where distributions had already commenced over one of the permitted periods.

The 1984 TRA amended the required distribution rules to provide, for plan years beginning after 1984, that a qualified plan must require distributions to begin no later than April 1st of the calendar year following the plan year in which the participant attained age 70½ or retired (known as the "required beginning date"). Where the participant was a 5 percent owner of the employer, distributions had to begin at age 70½, regardless of retirement.

This change liberalized the more restrictive TEFRA "key employee in top-heavy plan" requirement.

Alternatively, the 1984 Act allowed a plan to begin to make benefit payments to participants on their required beginning date and make payments over:

(1) The participant's life,

(2) The joint lives of the participant and the participant's spouse,

(3) The life expectancy of the participant, or

(4) The joint life expectancy of the participant and the participant's spouse.

For post-death distributions, the 1984 TRA introduced a rule requiring that the remaining portion of the participant's interest be distributed at least as rapidly as distributions would have occurred under the method that was in effect before the participant died. Where distributions had not commenced at the time of death, the participant's interest had to be distributed, in general, within five years of death. Exceptions to the five-year rule were provided, however. One exception allows the distributions to be over the life or life expectancy of a designated beneficiary if such distributions commence within one year of the participant's death. The second allows a plan to distribute the participant's interest over the life expectancy of the participant's surviving spouse, provided distributions begin no later than the date on which the participant would have attained age 70½ had he lived. The 1984 Act also amended the IRA rules to direct the IRS to promulgate similar minimum distribution requirements in regulations for IRAs.[41]

1986 TRA Modifications to the Required Distribution Rules

Distribution Rules Made Uniform

Effective generally for years beginning after 1988, the 1986 Tax Reform Act extended the minimum distribution rules that, before the Act, applied only to 5 percent owners and IRA participants to all participants in tax-favored retirement arrangements, including qualified plans, IRAs, tax-sheltered annuities, and custodial accounts. Thus, after the 1986 TRA amendments, distributions from all qualified plans must begin no later than April 1st of the calendar year following the year in which the employee reaches age 70½, regardless of whether the employee retires.

The 1986 TRA imposed a 50 percent excise tax on amounts that were required to have been distributed during the taxable year under the minimum distribution rules but were not distributed.[42] Before the 1986 Act, the penalty for failure to comply with these rules was plan disqualification. Because Congress felt it was inappropriate to penalize all participants for a failure to make minimum required distributions to a particular individual, the excise tax was substituted as the sanction for noncompliance. The excise tax is imposed on the person receiving the distribution if the distribution is less than the required minimum distribution amount for the year. The tax is applied to the amount by which the minimum required distribution exceeds the actual amount distributed during the taxable year.

The 1986 Act did not specifically define "minimum required distribution." Rather, the IRS was granted the authority to define the term in regulations. The IRS has issued proposed minimum distribution regulations.

The 1986 TRA Conference Report states that Congress intended that, if a participant selects a permissible distribution option, the minimum required distribution in any year will be the amount required to be distributed in that year under the option selected.

The Report states that, under a defined contribution plan, the minimum distribution must be determined under pre-1987 law. For a defined benefit plan, if the participant selects an impermissible payout option and designates a beneficiary, the minimum required distribution in any year is the amount that would have been distributable to the participant in that year had the participant selected a joint and survivor annuity payable over the joint life expectancies of the participant and the designated beneficiary. In applying this rule, the ages of the beneficiary and the participant at the required beginning date must be taken into account. The Conference Report adds that the survivor benefit is assumed to be the maximum percentage of the annuity payable during the participant's lifetime that will not violate the incidental benefit rule, but may not exceed 100 percent of the benefit payable to the participant. The Report provides that, even if the distribution option is described in the plan and the plan receives a favorable determination letter, the penalty tax will still apply.

The Report states that, where the participant selects an impermissible payout option and does not designate a beneficiary, the minimum requried distribution in any year will be the amount that would have been distributable to the participant in that year had the participant selected an annuity payable over the participant's life expectancy, taking into account the participant's age on the required beginning date.

Excise Tax on Failure to Make Required Distributions

As previously indicated, effective generally for years beginning after 1988, the 1986 Act replaced the sanction of plan disqualification for failure to satisfy the minimum distribution rules with a 50 percent excise tax. The tax is imposed on the difference between the amount that should have been distributed and the amount that was actually distributed. The IRS may, in certain circumstances, waive the tax for any taxable year. To obtain a waiver, the taxpayer must show that the shortfall in the amount distributed was due to reasonable error and that reasonable steps are being taken to remedy it.

Restrictions on Withdrawals From §401(k) Plans

The 1986 TRA added certain restrictions on withdrawals from Code §401(k) cash-or-deferred arrangements (CODAs). The Act also imposed a revised tax on certain "early" distributions.

After the 1986 Act, withdrawals from a CODA are only permitted on:

(1) Separation from service, death, or disability;

(2) The termination of the plan if there is no successor plan;

(3) The sale by a corporation of substantially all of its assets used in a trade or business[43] where its employees continue employment with the corporation acquiring its assets;

(4) A corporation's sale of its interest in a subsidiary[44] with respect to an employee who continues employment with the subsidiary,

(5) In the case of a profit-sharing or stock bonus plan, the attainment of age 59½, or

(6) In the case of a profit-sharing or stock bonus plan which

allows voluntary employee deferrals, upon the hardship of the employee.

Effective generally for plan years beginning after 1988, only the actual amount of §401(k) plan contributions (and not the investment growth thereon) may be distributed on account of hardship.[45]

Code §72(t) Penalty Tax on Premature Withdrawals

Effective generally for plan years beginning after 1988, the 1986 TRA imposed on additional income tax of 10 percent on the amounts includable in income as a result of an early distribution.[46] This tax applies to distributions (including involuntary cashouts) from qualified retirement plans[47] unless made:

(1) After the participant attains age 59½;

(2) On account of the death or disability of the employee;

(3) In annuity form for the participant's life;

(4) To an employee following a separation from the employer's service after reaching age 55; or

(5) From dividend distributions from an Employee Stock Ownership Plan (ESOP) under Code §404(k).[48]

Additional exceptions to the 10 percent tax apply to:

(1) Amounts used for medical expenses that do not exceed the deduction allowable under Code §213 for such expenses;[49]

(2) Pre-1990 distributions from ESOPs[50] to the extent that, on average, the majority of assets in the plan have been invested in employer securities[51] for the five-plan-year period preceding the plan year in which the distribution is made;[52] and

(3) Payments to "alternate payees" under qualified domestic relations orders (QDROs).[53]

Qualified Domestic Relations Orders

Before the 1984 Retirement Equity Act (REA), there was a conflict in authority as to whether a court's award, pursuant to a divorce decree, of a portion of a participant's benefit in a qualified plan to the participant's former spouse, was an anticipatory assignment or alienation of pension benefits in violation of Code §401(a)(13). The REA amended Code §401(a)(13) to provide an exception to the general anti-alienation rule in the case of certain "qualified domestic relations orders" (QDROs). The REA provided relief to plan administrators and practitioners since, before the change, these individuals had to exercise their judgment on the basis of conflicting authority, running the risk of plan disqualification or suit by the former spouse for choosing one alternative rather than the other.

Under post-REA Code §401(a)(13) the general anti-alienation rule does not apply to a qualified domestic relations order.

A "qualified domestic relations order" is a domestic relations order of a court that creates or recognizes the existence of an alternate payee's right to receive all, or part of, the benefits payable with respect to a participant under a plan, provided the requirements of Code §414(p)(2) and (3) are met.

The term "domestic relations order" for purposes of defining "qualified domestic relations order" means any judgment, decree, or order (including approval of a property settlement agreement) which relates to the provision of child support or alimony payments, or the marital property rights of a spouse, child, or other dependent of the participant. Further, the order must be made pursuant to a state domestic relations law (including a community property law).[54]

A domestic relations order must contain certain provisions to be a QDRO. These are:

(1) The name and the last known mailing address (if any) of the participant and of each alternate payee covered by the order;

(2) The amount or percentage of the participant's benefits to be paid by the plan to each such alternate payee, or the manner in which such amount or percentage is to be determined;

(3) The number of payments or the period to which the order applies; and

(4) Each plan to which the order applies.[55]

A QDRO cannot require a plan to alter the amount or form of benefits or to make payment to an alternative payee when a previous order has already required the plan to make such payments to a different alternate payee.[56] The statute provides an exception to the general definition of QDRO for certain payments after the participant has attained the plan's earliest retirement age. An order will not fail to be a QDRO solely because, after the participant has separated from the employer's service on or after the plan's earliest retirement date, it requires that payments be made to an alternate payee:

(1) On or after the date on which the participant attains (or would have attained) the plan's earliest retirement age;

(2) As if the participant had retired on the date on which such payment is to begin under such order (but taking into account only the present value of benefits actually accrued and not taking into account the present value of any employer subsidy for early retirement);[57] and

(3) In any form in which such benefits may be paid under the plan to the participant (other than in the form of a joint and survivor annuity with respect to the alternate payee and his or her subsequent spouse).[58]

To the extent provided in any QDRO, the former spouse of a participant, rather than the current spouse, will be treated as the participant's surviving spouse for purposes of the joint and survivor annuity rules, provided the participant and the former spouse were married for at least one year.[59]

This provision enables courts to craft their domestic relations orders in the form of a requirement that the participant elect a joint and survivor annuity benefit naming the former spouse as beneficiary. Thus, a QDRO can make a divorced spouse eligible to give or withhold consent to the joint and survivor benefit waiver under the usual joint-and-survivor rules.

The QDRO rules make it necessary in many cases where retirement benefits are considered part of the marital estate (a position that includes all community property jurisdictions and a growing number of noncommunity property ones) for domestic relations counsel to retain an actuary to determine a participant's expected pension benefits. This determination is by no means cut-and-dry. Different actuarial assumptions can produce different results.

The plan administrator must promptly notify the participant and any alternative payee of the receipt of a domestic relations order and of the plan's procedures for determining whether such an order is a QDRO. Within a reasonable period thereafter, the administrator must make this determination and notify the participant and any alternate payees of the result.[60]

Plans must establish reasonable procedures to make this determination.[61] The procedures need not be made part of the plan document but should be in writing. The procedures should allow the individual who will decide whether the order qualifies (usually the plan administrator) to seek an opinion of counsel if necessary.

While a determination on the qualified status of a domestic relations order is pending, the administrator must separately account for the amounts that would be payable to the alternate payee should the order be determined to be a QDRO. If, within 18 months of the date on which the first payment would be required under the order, the order is found to be qualified, the payee is to be given the separately accounted-for amounts, (referred to as the "segregated amounts") plus interest. If the order is found not to be a QDRO or if the issue is not resolved within the 18-month period, the administrator must pay the segregated amounts, plus interest, to the person who would be entitled to them (usually the participant) as if there had been no order. Any determination that the order is a QDRO that is made after the end of the 18-month period is to be given prospective effect only, i.e., amounts that were payable before the determination are not to be paid to the payee.[62]

The amount paid to an alternate payee under a QDRO is includable in the payee's gross income under Code §402(a) if the payee is the participant's former spouse.[63] Distributions to a nonspousal alternate payee are included in the participant's gross income. The participant's basis in his or her pension benefit is to be allocated ratably between the amount paid a spousal alternate payee and any other benefits under the plan to which the participant may be entitled.[64] If the alternate payee is not a spouse or former spouse, the investment in the contract (basis) is not allocated and may be recovered only by the participant under the Code §72 basis-recovery rules. This would mean, for instance, that an alternate payee who is the participant's child would not have any basis in the portion of the participant's benefit that was allocated to him.

For purposes of the lump sum distribution rules, amounts payable to an alternate payee under a QDRO do not make the participant ineligible for the favorable income tax treatment accorded such distributions if the distribution otherwise qualifies for such treatment.[65] Also, if the amounts payable to the alternate payee otherwise satisfy the taxfree rollover requirements, such amounts will be considered a taxfree rollover. To qualify for this rule, where property is distributed, the actual property must be rolled over.[66]

The taxfree rollover rule appears to apply not only to the original alternate payee, but also to any beneficiary of the payee should the payee die before receiving a qualifying distribution.

In addition, the Technical and Miscellaneous Revenue Act of 1988 made favorable tax treatment afforded lump sum distributions from qualified plans (discussed later in this chapter) available for distributions to an alternate payee who is a spouse or former spouse of the employee. Specifically, the Act provided that, if a distribution of the balance of the credit to an employee would constitute a lump sum distribution, then a distribution of the balance to the credit of an alternate payee will also constitute a lump sum distribution. In determining whether the distribution consists of the balance to the credit of the alternate payee (a prerequisite to favorable tax treatment of a lump sum distribution under §402(e)), only the interest of the alternate payee is taken into account.

Taxation of Distributions From Qualified Plans

The Code §72 Annuity Rules

In general, periodic payments distributed from a qualified plan will be taxable under Code §72 (relating to annuities).[67] For this purpose, the amount that is considered distributed does not include any net unrealized appreciation on securities of the employer corporation attributable to employee contributions (other than QVECs). The net unrealized appreciation attributable to employer securities purchased with nondeductible employee contributions will generally, absent an election to the contrary, be taxed to the employee when the securities are sold or disposed of. The gain on such sale or disposition generally will constitute capital gain.

Before the 1986 TRA, Code §72 contained two basic rules for taxing annuities. The first, contained in §72(b), is known as the "exclusion ratio method." After the effective date of the 1986 TRA amendments, this became the only method for taxing annuities. The second method, repealed by the 1986 TRA, was known as the "three-year basis recovery rule."

Under the exclusion ratio method, a fraction is established. The numerator of the fraction is the employee's investment in the annuity contract. The denominator is the projected return under the contract. For qualified plan purposes, only amounts that were previously taxed to the employee, such as voluntary nondeductible employee contributions, are considered an investment in the contract. Once this fraction is established, it is applied to distributions under the annuity to determine the taxable and nontaxable portions thereof.

> *Example:* Employee X makes $50,000 of nondeductible employee contributions to plan K. X elects to receive a life annuity under plan K commencing at age 65. When X turns 65, he is eligible to receive $20,000 per year for life. At that time, X's life expectancy is 15 years. The projected return on the contract is $300,000, determined as follows: ($20,000 × 15 = $300,000). Of that $300,000, X has contributed $50,000 ÷ $300,000 (the fraction), or 16.7 percent. Therefore, for every annual distribution of $20,000, 16.7 percent ($3,340) is nontaxable and the remainder is taxable. Where the annuity is for a term of years, the actual term is used in place of life expectancy in computing projected return. Where the annuity is a joint and survivor annuity, the combined life expectancies of the annuitant and the designated beneficiary are used.

The three-year recovery method, before its repeal, applied where part of the annuity was attributable to employee contributions and where, during the first three years of payments under the annuity, the total amount receivable was equal to or greater than the amount contributed by the employee. In this situation, the employee was allowed to fully recover his basis before any of the annuity distributions became taxable to him.

The 1986 TRA made all periodic distributions subject to the exclusion ratio method. The repeal of the three-year basis recovery rule is effective with respect to individuals whose annuity starting date is after July 1, 1986.

The 1986 TRA also provided uniform rules governing amounts

received as an annuity both before and after the annuity starting date. After the 1986 TRA, all such amounts are subject to pro rata basis recovery under the exclusion ratio method. Formerly, the participant could recover his basis up-front when amounts were received prior to the annuity starting date.

The 1986 TRA also provided that an employee's recovery of his basis in an annuity contract is limited to the employee's investment in the contract (i.e., employee contributions). Before the Act, if an employee outlived his life expectancy, he could continue to exclude a portion of all annuity payments received, even if this resulted in recovering more than 100 percent of the original investment. The 1986 TRA also provided that, should an employee die before recovering his entire basis, the employee may deduct on his final income tax return all basis that remained unrecovered as of the date of death. Before the TRA, if an employee had not fully recovered his basis at death, no deduction was allowed.

The post-1986 TRA basis recovery rules are effective generally for individuals whose annuity starting date is after 1986.

Lump Sum Distributions

Lump sum distributions are given favorable income tax treatment designed to reduce the tax impact when an employee receives his entire distribution in a single year, forcing him into a higher marginal tax bracket. As originally enacted in ERISA, the portion of a lump sum distribution that was attributable to pre-ERISA (pre-1974) benefit accruals received long-term capital gains treatment. The portion of a lump sum distribution attributable to post-ERISA accruals was eligible for special favorable tax treatment known as "10-year forward averaging." The 1986 TRA replaced 10-year forward averaging with five-year averaging and phased out capital gains treatment on the pre-1974 portion of a distribution. Both changes are subject to certain transitional rules.

Definition of Lump Sum Distribution

For purposes of Code §402, a lump sum distribution is defined as the distribution or payment of the balance of an employee's account, in a single taxable year, to the recipient that becomes payable:

(1) On account of the employee's death;

(2) After the employee has attained age 59½;

(3) On account of the employee's having become disabled; or

(4) On account of the employee's separation from the employer's service.[68]

The separation from service category does not apply to a self-employed individual as defined in Code §401(c)(1). The reason for this rule is that it is difficult to tell when an individual has separated from his own service where there is not a corporate entity interposed. An individual may merely have ceased doing business temporarily. Shareholder-employees of a "C" (regular) corporation are not considered self-employed. Thus, even after TEFRA's parity provisions, this advantage of C corporation status remains. As indicated earlier in this chapter, an "alternate payee" of a qualified domestic relations order may also be eligible for the favorable tax treatment afforded lump sum distributions where a distribution to the alternate payee otherwise qualifies for such treatment.

The taxpayer must affirmatively elect favorable lump sum tax treatment. The taxpayer will not always be the participant; sometimes it will be the participant's beneficiary. To be eligible to elect the favorable tax treatment, the employee must have been a participant in the plan for five or more (not necessarily consecutive) years preceding the year of the distribution.[69] Once lump sum tax treatment is elected, all distributions from qualified plans to the recipient for that year must use this treatment (eliminating the potential for further tax reduction by making multiple distributions in the same year but only using lump sum treatment for some).

In determining whether a distribution is a lump sum distribution, all trusts of one plan are considered a single trust and all plans of the same type maintained by the employer, e.g., pension, profit-sharing, or stock bonus, are treated as one plan.

Forward Averaging and Capital Gains Treatment

The purpose of forward averaging is to reduce the employee's tax on lump sum distributions. Code §402(e) does this by treating the distribution as if it were a separate "taxpayer" from the recipient similar to the manner in which trusts are taxed. This avoids bunching the distribution with the taxpayer's other income for the taxable year and thus generally yields a lower overall effective rate. The effect of this before the reduction in, and compression of, tax brackets by the 1986 TRA was much more pronounced. Another benefit of forward averaging is that it taxes the distribution as if it had been spread out over several taxable years. This also can help avoid the bunching of income. The tax rate that is applied to the distribution is the Code § 1(c) rate for single taxpayers, regardless of the recipient's filing status.

Note that forward averaging does not allow the taxpayer to pay the tax on the distribution over several years. The tax is paid in the year of the distribution. The tax payable, however, will be the tax that would have resulted had the distribution been spread out in equal annual increments over the statutory period (assuming that tax rates remain constant). The resulting tax is generally much less than the tax would have been on a single lump-sum distribution in one taxable year.

Note also that, before the 1984 TRA repealed the estate tax exclusion for qualified plan distributions, taxpayers had to choose between the estate tax exclusion and forward averaging/capital gains treatment. For open years under the old rules, the estate tax exclusion continues to apply to certain participants whose benefits were in pay status as of a particular date. In such situations, this choice continued to be a significant consideration, requiring practitioners to calculate the tax savings under both alternatives before advising clients. Where the former law applies, however, a taxpayer can sometimes get the best of both worlds by disposing of the qualified plan interest in such a manner as to qualify it for the estate tax marital deduction or the unified credit. In this situation, favorable income tax treatment may still be elected without subjecting the benefit to federal estate tax.

Effective generally for post-1986 distributions, the 1986 TRA limited the tax break for lump sum distributions. The TRA replaced the former law provision permitting 10-year forward averaging with one permitting five-year forward averaging. Five-year averaging is basically identical to the pre-TRA 10-year rule, except that, in making the computation, the distribution is considered to have been made over five, rather than 10, taxable years. This revision, plus the 1986 TRA's phaseout of capital gains treatment for the part of a lump sum attributable to pre-1974 participation, however, will not necessarily result in a higher incidence of tax on lump sums, in light of the Act's reduction in tax rates.

Under post-TRA law, an individual may make only one forward averaging election per lifetime. This election must be made after the individual reaches age 59½. Under pre-TRA law, an individual could make an unlimited number of elections before reaching age 59½, but was limited to one post-59½ election.[70] Under a transition rule, individuals who reached age 50 before January 1, 1986, may elect to have pre-1986 TRA law (10-year forward averaging and pre-1987 tax rates, plus capital gain at a 20 percent rate on any pre-1974 portion) apply to a lump sum distribution. A participant who makes this election may not make any further forward averaging or capital gains elections with respect to lump sum distributions.

As previously indicated, the 1986 TRA also phased out capital gains treatment for the portion of a lump sum distribution attributable to pre-1974 participation. Under the phaseout, effective for post-1986 distributions, capital gains treatment applies to 95 percent of the eligible portion of a distribution in 1988, 75 percent in 1989, 50 percent in 1990 and 25 percent in 1991. Capital gain treatment fully phases out in 1992.

Under a transitional rule for individuals receiving lump sum distributions before 1992 who reached age 50 before 1986, similar to the one described above for 10-year forward averaging, an eligible individual may elect capital gains treatment for the pre-1974 portion of the distribution. Individuals making this election will have their pre-1974 portion taxed at a flat 20 percent rate regardless of their individual rate. Where the capital gains election is made, the requirement that an individual have attained age 59½ to be eligible for favorable tax treatment does not apply.

Note that, where the participant makes a transitional rule election of 10-year forward averaging, he automatically gets capital gains treatment (and a 20 percent rate) for any pre-1974 portion of the distribution. This election may be made even if the distribution is made after 1992. The special capital gains election that is limited to the capital gains portion need only be considered if the recipient does not wish to have 10-year forward averaging apply to the post-1973 portion of a distribution (something that might be desirable if the individual's post-1986 marginal tax rate is lower than the individual's pre-TRA rate, even taking into account 10-year forward averaging). As is the case with the all-encompassing general 10-year averaging/capital gains election, however, if a participant makes the special capital gains election, he is deemed to have exhausted his one-time lump sum distribution election under Code §402(e), i.e., he cannot make a 10- or five-year forward averaging election with respect to the current, or any other, lump sum distribution.

The transitional rules will play an important part in planning for the receipt of lump sum distributions. Planners will have to calculate an individual's probable rate of tax under pre-TRA rates and 10-year forward averaging and contrast this with the projected tax due under post-TRA rates and five-year averaging. In addition, post-TRA law places a premium on choosing which distribution should be the subject of a 10- or five-year averaging election, as this will be the taxpayer's only chance to avail himself of these provisions. A client might be in a better position by choosing to forego an election with respect to a current distribution, despite the fact that making it would reduce his current tax due, because he might save even more by using the one-time election on a subsequent distribution. In calculations such as these, however, the time value of money should also be considered. Time value of money considerations may mean that a taxpayer's tax savings realized in an earlier year will be more valuable than even greater tax savings which must be realized in a later year.

With the purpose of the capital gains/forward averaging rules in mind, the formula in Code §402(e) can now be examined. In doing so, it is important to define some terms.

The "total taxable amount" (TTA) is the balance to the credit of an employee that is distributed in a distribution qualifying for lump sum treatment, less employee contributions previously included in gross income and the net unrealized appreciation on any securities of the sponsoring employer included in the distribution (whether derived from employer or employee contributions).[71]

The "minimum distribution allowance" (MDA) is an exemption amount that reduces the TTA. The allowance varies depending on the amount of the distribution. It is defined as the lesser of (1) $10,000; or (2) One-half of the TTA.

The relevant amount, however, is reduced 20 cents on the dollar for each dollar by which the TTA exceeds $20,000.[72] Thus, for distributions of over $70,000, there is no MDA.

The "ordinary income portion" of a distribution is computed by multiplying the TTA by a fraction. The numerator is the employee's time under the plan as an active participant after 1973, in months. The denominator is the participant's total time as an active participant in the plan (computed for pre-1974 service in years and for post-1973 service in months). Multiplying this fraction times the TTA results in the ordinary income portion (OIP). This is the amount that will be eligible for forward averaging. The remainder will be eligible for long-term capital gains treatment, subject to the phase-out rules enacted by the 1986 TRA, as discussed above.

The "initial separate tax" (IST) is the tax, using the rates in Code § 1(c), on the ordinary income portion.

The following example shows how the total tax is computed on a lump-sum distribution. Assume that the total distribution is $60,000, of which $10,000 is attributable to employee contributions already taxed to the employee and the unrealized appreciation on employer securities. The employee accrued no benefits attributable to pre-1974 participation. This example is based on 1988 tax rates.

Step 1: Determine the total taxable amount (TTA):

($60,000 (LSD)) − 10,000 (Employee contributions and unrealized appreciation on employer securities) = $50,000

Step 2: Determine the minimum distribution allowance (MDA):

Lesser of $10,000 or half the TTA ($50,000 × 1/2 = $25,000).

In this case, $10,000 is the lesser amount. This amount is then reduced by 20 cents on the dollar for each dollar by which the TTA exceeds $20,000:

($50,000 (TTA)) − $20,000 = $30,000 × .2 = $6,000;
$10,000 − $6,000 = $4,000 (MDA)

Step 3: Subtract the minimum distribution allowance from the Total Taxable Amount:

($50,000 − $4,000 = $46,000).

Step 4: Divide the amount derived from Step #3 by 5:

($46,000/5 = $9,200).

Step 5: Apply the tax rate from § 1(c) to the result of Step #4:

$9,200 × .15 = $1,380.

Step 6: Multiply the result of Step #5 by 5:

$1,380 × 5 = $6,900.

The result of Step 6, $6,900, is the amount of tax due.

In the foregoing example, if the taxpayer could not, or did not, use five-year forward averaging and had no other income for the year other than the $50,000 taxable portion of the distribution, the tax imposed by Code § 1(c) would be $11,679.50. If the taxpayer had other taxable income, the tax attributable to this distribution would be even higher.

Planners should also note that an election is available under Code §402(e)(4)(L) to treat pre-1974 participation as post-1973 participation, i.e., to elect to use forward averaging, not capital gains treatment, for both the pre- and post-ERISA portions of the distribution.

Distributions that include employer securities are treated differently from other distributions. There are two rules with respect to such distributions. The first provides that, where employer securities are part of a lump-sum distribution, the employee will only be taxed on the basis of such securities at the time they were contributed to the plan. Any appreciation thereon (except that which is attributable to QVEC contributions) will be taxed to the employee only when he sells or disposes of the securities in a taxable transaction.[73] This can defer the tax for a number of years. Further, if, at that time, the long-term capital gains holding period has been satisfied, the appreciation will be taxed as long-term capital gain. Where the distribution of employer securities is not part of a lump-sum distribution, only the appreciation attributable to nondeductible employee contributions escapes tax until later sale or disposition.[74]

Penalty Taxes on Excess Distributions

Effective generally for post-1986 distributions, another factor that planners will have to consider for large distributions is whether the client will incur a penalty tax on excess distributions.[75] For lifetime distributions, the penalty tax is equal to 15 percent of any "excess distribution" from a qualified retirement plan, tax-sheltered annuity plan or an individual retirement arrangement. Choosing to have the excess amount distributed at death through the participant's estate will generally not help avoid this tax, however, as the 1986 TRA also enacted a 15 percent penalty estate tax on the portion of a decedent's gross estate attributable to an "excess retirement accumulation."[76] Further, since the 15% estate tax is an excise tax, none of the traditional methods of reducing estate tax is available to offset it, such as the unified credit, the marital deduction, or any other credit or deduction.

The penalty income and estate taxes are imposed on the individual in respect of whom the distribution is made. The tax, however, is reduced by any amount of the 1986 TRA-enacted penalty tax on premature distributions that has been imposed under Code §72(t). In applying the 15% tax, amounts attributable to after-tax employee contributions and distributions not includable in income by reason of a rollover are excluded. For periodic distributions, the amount which exceeds the greater of (1) $150,000, or (2) $112,500, as adjusted for inflation in any year is subject to the tax. Thus, until inflation adjustments drive the $112,500 limit over $150,000, the latter amount will be the relevant limit.

Where the distribution is a lump sum distribution, the penalty tax is imposed on the amount in excess of five times the applicable periodic payment annual limit. In applying the tax, all qualified plan distributions made with respect to an individual for a year are aggregated.[77] Also, where distributions with respect to an individual are received by the individual and one or more persons, all such distributions are aggregated in applying the penalty tax for the year.[78] The 1986 Act gives participants an election to grandfather benefits (i.e., exempt them from the penalty tax) if they were earned before August 1, 1986. The Conference Report to the 1986 Act provides the following example of Congress' view of the proper applicaton of this rule:

> "[A]ssume that at the time of a distribution of $250,000 an individual's grandfathered benefit is equal to 80% of the individual's accrued benefit on such date under all plans or programs subject to the tax. Under the grandfather, $200,000 (80% of $250,000) would be exempt from the tax. The remaining $50,000 would be subject to the tax because the grandfathered amounts are taken into account in determining whether the distribution exceeds the $112,500 limit."

IRS regulations have given taxpayers electing grandfather treatment three optional methods that may be used in determining the grandfathered portion of their benefit: the 10% method, the attained age method and the 100% discretionary method. In general, in advising clients who are eligible to elect grandfather treatment, the planner will have to make various assumptions about inflation, the rate of return on plan investments, and the life expectancy of the recipient to project whether grandfathering treatment under any of the three methods is advisable.

To be eligible to elect the grandfather rule, the individual must have an accrued benefit as of August 1, 1986 of at least $562,500. The election must be made on a return for a year beginning no later than January 1, 1988. In applying the grandfather rule, only the $112,500 limit is used, not the greater of $112,500 as indexed for inflation or $150,000.

The penalty estate tax is imposed on "excess retirement accumulations," defined as the value of an individual's interest in all qualified and individual retirement plans that exceeds the present value of an annuity for a term certain equal to the decendent's life expectancy at date of death and calling for annual payments equal to the Code §4974(c) limits. These limits, as previously indicated, are the lesser of $112,500, as indexed for inflation or $150,000.

The penalty estate tax applies generally to estates of decedents dying after 1986. Certain special transitional rules apply.

Tax-Free Rollovers

Code §402(a)(5) provides an alternative tax planning tool for individuals who receive certain single sum distributions known as "qualifying rollover distributions" within a single taxable year. If the distribution qualifies, the participant may retransfer that amount, or any part thereof, within 60 days of receipt, to an "eligible retirement plan." No income tax will be due on the retransferred amounts until they are distributed from the recipient plan. The IRS interprets the 60-day rule literally, and generally allows no extensions, even if the failure to meet the deadline was not the recipient's fault. Nondeductible employee contributions cannot be part of a tax-free rollover, although QVECs may be.[79] Where the recipient plan is an IRA, the distribution will not be eligible for forward averaging/capital gains treatment. The taxpayer, however, will be eligible to defer the tax until the IRA must begin making distributions under the minimum distribution rules.

Where the IRA is a "conduit IRA," however, i.e., one that is used only as a temporary repository of a lump sum distribution until those amounts can be retransferred to a Code §401(a) or § 403(a) plan, the distribution will not lose its eligibility for lump sum treatment when it is distributed from the recipient plan. Before the 1984 TRA, a qualifying rollover distribution had to be of the entire balance to an employee's credit in the distributing plan. The 1984 TRA reduced this requirement to 50 percent of such amount. Any diversification distribution from an ESOP under Code §401(a)(28)(B)(ii) is considered to qualify as a partial distribution. Before the 1986 TRA, partial rollovers could not be made if the distribution was part of a series of periodic payments. The 1986 Act removed this restriction, effective generally for post-1986 distributions.

Except where the distribution is being made pursuant to a QDRO, the rolled over amount need not be the same property received in the distribution. So long as the amount of the rollover does not exceed the amount of the distribution, QVECs can be rolled over, but other employee contributions cannot.[80]

To qualify for rollover treatment, the total or partial distribution must be made within a single taxable year of the recipient. The distribution must:

(1) Have been made on account of one of the events in Code §402(e)(4) that can give rise to a lump sum distribution, i.e., death, disability, separation from service, or attaining age 59½;

(2) Be on account of plan termination, or the total cessation of contributions to a profit-sharing or stock bonus plan; or

(3) Constitute a distribution (in whole or in part) of accumulated QVECs under the plan.[81]

Eligible recipient plans are IRAs, individual retirement annuities, §401(a) plans and §403(b) annuity plans, except that §401(a) plans and §403(b) annuity plans cannot take rollovers of an owner-employee that were accrued under an H.R. 10 plan.[82]

Federal Estate Taxation of Qualified Plan Distributions

Before the 1984 TRA, Code §2039 provided a $100,000 exclusion per estate (unlimited before TEFRA for estates of decedents dying before 1982) from the federal estate tax for amounts attributable to employer contributions and QVECs distributed from qualified plans. A similar rule applied to IRAs. Former Code §2039(f) made forward averaging unavailable for federal income tax purposes where the estate tax exclusion was used.

The 1984 Act provided transitional rules allowing certain estates to use the former exclusion. Under one exception, in the case of the estate of a decedent who irrevocably elected the form of the benefit before July 18, 1984 (the TRA's enactment date), and was in pay status on December 31, 1984, the $100,000 exclusion will apply. For recipients in pay status on December 31, 1982, who irrevocably elected the form of the benefit before January 1, 1983, the pre-TEFRA unlimited estate tax exclusion will apply.[83]

Discrimination by Provision of Alternate Benefit Forms

In Rev. Rul. 85-59, the IRS considered whether a qualified plan could discriminate by restricting the right to receive a lump sum benefit that was the actuarial equivalent of the plan's normal retirement benefit to certain classes of employees.[84]

The ruling considered four situations. In situation #1, the lump sum option was available to highly compensated employees only. The Service ruled that this limit would cause the plan to discriminate within the meaning of Code §401(a)(4).

In situation #2, only employees having a certain net worth at retirement could receive a lump sum. In situation #3, only employees who could provide an attorney's or accountant's letter that receiving a lump sum was in the employee's best interests could receive a lump sum. In these two situations, the Service ruled that the lump sum option was not discriminatory per se but could violate Code §401(a)(4) if, in operation, it caused discrimination.

The final situation involved three different plans, each of which gave its trustees the discretion to determine who would be eligible to receive a lump sum. Although the plans did not specify the selection criteria, the trustees consistently applied the standards in situations #1, #2, and #3, above, respectively. The Service ruled that the provision giving the trustees discretion in each of the three plans was not per se discriminatory but could discriminate in operation if the trustees' selection practices favored the prohibited group.

The Service later formalized the principles of Rev. Rul. 85-59 in "alternate form of benefit" regulations.[85] The regulations define an alternate benefit form as a benefit form that differs in timing or mode of payment from another benefit form. The regulations prohibit discrimination within the meaning of Code §401(a)(4) in the availability of alternate forms of benefits under qualified plans.

In determining discrimination, the regulations applied the nondiscriminatory coverage tests of (pre-1986 TRA) Code §410(b)(1), i.e., an alternate form must be available to either 70 percent of all employees or a fair cross-section of employees. Note that the term "employees" was used rather than "participants," making it impossible to use the 70/80 percent test of pre-1986 TRA Code § 410(b) in this context.

The second aspect of the regulations, and the one which has drawn the heaviest criticism, is the provision that benefit options, the availability of which are subject to employer discretion or employer consent, are per se discriminatory. In this regard, the regulations go considerably beyond the position taken in Rev. Rul. 85-59 which generally indicated that, unless the criterion upon which such discretion or consent would be based clearly discriminated, such provisions would not be considered discriminatory per se, but rather would be evaluated for discrimination in operation. Many commentators urged the IRS to modify its position, arguing that, if all the benefit options offered under a plan are actuarially equivalent, it should not be discriminatory per se to offer alternative benefit forms.

The regulations are generally effective for plans in existence when the original proposed regulations were promulgated as of the first day of the second plan year beginning on or after January 30, 1986. Additional time was provided for collectively bargained plans. Amendments necessary to comply with the proposed regulations were required to be adopted before the effective date. The regulations were effective immediately with respect to new plans. Limited relief from the anti-cutback rule of Code §411(a)(6) was originally provided for plans that wished to delete a benefit option the discretionary provisions of which would violate the original proposed regulations.

Participant Loans

Before TEFRA, Code §4975 (the prohibited transaction rules) provided the only limits in the Code on loans by a plan to participants and beneficiaries. Section 4975 provides that loans meeting the following tests will not be considered prohibited transactions:

(1) The loans must be made available to all participants and beneficiaries on a reasonably equivalent basis;

(2) The plan must not discriminate in its loan policy;

(3) There must be a provision authorizing participant loans in the plan document;

(4) The loans must bear a reasonable rate of interest; and

(5) The loans must be adequately secured.

TEFRA added to these requirements certain dollar limits restricting the amount of participant loans made after August 13, 1982. Under Code §72(p), an excess loan will be treated as a constructive distribution to the recipient in the year the loan is made. A plan loan will not be treated as includable in an employee's income where the aggregate loan amount plus the amount of all other outstanding loans to the participant does not exceed the lesser of:

(1) $50,000, reduced by the excess (if any) of
(a) The highest outstanding balance of loans from the plan during the one-year period ending on the day before the date on which such loan was made, over
(b) The outstanding balance of loans from the plan on the date on which such loan was made, or

(2) The greater of:
(a) One-half of the participant's vested accrued benefit, or
(b) $10,000.

To qualify under Code §72(p), the loan terms must provide that it will be repaid within five years unless it is used to acquire a dwelling unit which is to be used within a reasonable time (determined when the loan is made) as the participant's principal residence. A loan will not qualify under the rules for nonhousing loans unless the loan, by its terms, must be repaid within five years. The repayment period is determined when the loan is made. If a repayment period of less than five years is subsequently extended beyond that time, the balance payable at the extension date is considered a constructive distribution. Further, if payments due within five years are not, in fact, paid, the unpaid balance will also be a constructive distribution. If a loan with a repayment term of more than five years is, in fact, repaid within that period, the early repayment will not change the fact that the loan, by its terms, is to be treated as a constructive distribution.[86] Violating the Code §72(p) limits will not disqualify a plan.

After the 1986 TRA, payments on plan loans, to satisfy §72(p), must be amortized in level payments over the term of the loan and payments must be made no less frequently than quarterly.

The availability of loans may help a plan attract employee contributions, since the participants will be assured that they can get their money back if the need arises. This can be critical in a Code §401(k) cash-or-deferred arrangement, where contributions from nonhighly compensated employees are necessary to meet the actual deferral percentage tests. Under Code §72(p)(3), however, if a loan that violates any of the §72(p)(2) standards discussed above is made to a key employee within the meaning of Code §416(i) or is secured by elective deferrals to a §§401(k) or 403(b) plan, no deduction for interest paid or accrued on the loan will be allowed. Further, plan loans are subject to the 1986 TRA rules denying taxpayers a deduction on consumer interest unless the interest fits within one of the exceptions to those rules, such as that for qualified residence interest.

In considering whether to adopt a participant loan policy, sponsors should consider the downside of such a decision. For instance, where a plan adopts a loan policy, it must avoid discrimination. Further, allowing loans creates an administrative burden involved in determining what constitutes adequate security and a reasonable interest rate. Finally, a participant loan program can put the employer in the awkward position of being a creditor to its employees.

Participant loans are an exception to the general rule of Code §401(a)(13) that plan benefits cannot be assigned or alienated. A plan loan provision, as indicated above, may require that employees pledge their vested account balances as collateral. Where this is not enough, the employer may require additional collateral on a nondiscriminatory basis. This, in turn, can impose additional recordkeeping requirements on the plan.

The employer may, if it chooses, limit plan loans for a specific purpose or purposes or to an amount that is less than the Code §72(p) limit. Plans generally do not specify the exact interest rate for loans. Rather, the plan document usually delegates this authority to the administrator or to the plan's trustees.

As discussed above, the REA requires that spousal consent be obtained when a qualified plan that is subject to the joint-and-survivor and preretirement annuity rules makes a distribution other than in the prescribed form. Under IRS regulations, a plan loan will not be treated as a distribution for purposes of the spousal consent requirement. However, when an account balance or the present value of an accrued benefit is reduced in order to satisfy a participant's loan repayment obligation, the loan repayment reduction is treated as a distribution to the participant requiring the consent of the participant and spouse (if any).

The regulations further provide that a plan may require the participant and spouse to consent to a loan and the possible reduction in the accrued benefit within the 90-day period before the making of the loan. If this advance consent procedure is used, no subsequent consent will be required if the loan is eventually set off by a participant's accrued benefit. For example, if an unmarried participant provides the advance consent when the loan is made, no additional consent will be required at the time of any benefit offset even if the participant is married when the offset occurs.

Although the advance consent procedure is not mandatory, the temporary regulations state that failure to obtain consent when a loan is made could cause the loan to be treated as not having been adequately secured for purposes of Code §§401(a)(13) and 4975. Accordingly, the adoption of an advance consent procedure by plans that permit loans seems highly advisable.

Notes

1. 463 U.S. 1075 (1983).
2. See Code §401(a)(9).
3. Tax Equity and Fiscal Responsibility Act of 1982, P.L. 97-248.
4. Code §§401(a)(11) and 417. Before *BBS Associates v. Comm'r*, 74 T.C. 1118 (1980), *aff'd*, in unpublished opinion No. 80-2851 (3d Cir. 1981), IRS regulations interpreted this requirement to mean that, whenever a plan provided a life annuity benefit, even if only as an optional benefit form, it had to provide the joint and survivor presumption. The Tax Court, in *BBS*, determined that the statute only required that, where the plan provided life annuity benefits, *and the participant elected to receive benefits in this form and made no further specification*, benefits had to be provided in joint and survivor form. Under this holding, a defined contribution plan (other than a money purchase pension plan), which is not required by law to provide life annuity benefits could, as was true before *BBS*, decline to offer joint and survivor benefits. Also, as a result of *BBS*, such a plan could provide a life annuity option but decline to extend joint and survivor benefits unless the participant elected life annuity benefits but did not specify which of several forms of life annuity benefits he wanted. Since defined benefit plans must generally have a life annuity benefit as their normal form of benefit (automatically triggering the joint and survivor presumption, even under *BBS*), the effect of *BBS* was chiefly upon defined contribution plans.

5. Code §417(b).
6. Treas. Regs. §1.401(a)-11(b)(2).
7. Code §417(e).
8. Code §401(a)(11)(B), before amendment by the REA.
9. An early survivor annuity was defined as an annuity for the life of the participant's spouse calling for the payment of the amount that would have been payable to the spouse under a qualified joint and survivor annuity if the participant elected the early survivor annuity before retirement and retired on the day before his death.
10. Code §401(a)(11)(B)(i)-(iii).
11. Code §401(a)(11)(C).
12. Code §401(a)(11)(A). IRS regulations provide that, for an unmarried participant, the qualified joint and survivor annuity rules will be applied by substituting a life annuity for the term "qualified joint and survivor annuity."
13. Code §417(c)(1)(A).
14. Code §417(c)(1)(A)(ii)(I)-(IV).
15. Code §417(c)(1)(B).
16. Code §417(c)(2).
17. Code §401(a)(11)(B)(iii).
18. Treas. Regs. §1.401(a)-11, Q&A-7.
19. Code §417(d)(1)(A)-(B).
20. "Annuity starting date," for this purpose, is the first day of the first period during which annuity payments commence. Thus, if the annuity were a monthly annuity and the first payment was made January 15th, January 1st would be the annuity starting date.
21. Code §417(d)(2)(A)-(B).
22. Code §§417(a)(1)(A)(i) and (ii).
23. Code §417(a)(2).
24. Code §417(a)(2)(A).
25. Code §417(a)(2)(B).
26. Code §417(a)(2) (flush language).
27. Code §417(a)(3)(A).
28. Code §417(a)(3)(A)(1).
29. Code §§417(a)(3)(ii) and (iii).
30. Code §417(a)(3)(iv).
31. Code §417(a)(5)(A) (regular J&S), §417(a)(5)(B) (preretirement survivor annuity). See the definition of "annuity starting date" at n.20, above.
32. Code §417(a)(5) (flush language).
33. Code §417(a)(4).
34. These contributions are no longer allowed, but plans may still hold assets that are attributable to such contributions.
35. Where this is done, the plan document and Summary Plan Description should make it clear.
36. It is advisable to explain the effect of an election not to take benefits in joint and survivor form on the document by which the participant and spouse will waive the joint and survivor form of benefits, in order to show that the effect of the waiver was made clear to the spouse.

37. Under this exception, the application of these REA rules may be delayed for plan years beginning before the earlier of (i) the date on which the last of the collective bargaining agreements relating to the plan terminates, or (ii) Jan. 1, 1987.
38. Under a transitional rule, any participant meeting the foregoing hour-of-service requirement who dies on or after Aug. 23, 1984, and before the first day of the first plan year beginning after 1984, must be provided with the preretirement survivor annuity feature. Additional transitional provisions apply to participants who separated from service before Aug. 23, 1984. The first rule provides that, if the participant meets 4 conditions, the participant may elect to have the pre-REA version of Code §401(a)(11) apply. The four conditions are:

    (1) The participant has had at least one hour of service under the plan on or after Sept. 2, 1974;

    (2) The participant was not otherwise eligible for the qualified joint and survivor annuity enacted by ERISA;

    (3) The participant is not covered by the amendments made by the REA to the joint and survivor annuity rules; and

    (4) As of Aug. 23, 1984, the participant's annuity starting date had not occurred and the participant was living.

    Under the second transitional rule, a participant who had at least one hour of service in the first plan year beginning after 1975 may elect the application of the preretirement survivor annuity provisions if, when the participant separated from service, the participant had at least 10 years of service under the plan and was vested in all or a portion of the participant's accrued benefit derived from employer contributions and, as of Aug. 23, 1984, the participant's annuity starting date had not occurred and the participant was still living.

    The elections provided under the foregoing two transitional rules for a separated participant may be made by the participant during the period beginning on Aug. 23, 1984, and ending on the earlier of (i) the participant's annuity starting date, or (ii) the date of the participant's death. A plan must give notice of the foregoing transitional provisions in accordance with rules to be prescribed by the Treasury Secretary. A plan is subject to penalty (up to $2,500) for failure to comply with this notice requirement.
39. Code §401(a)(14).
40. Code §401(a)(9)(A)(ii).
41. Of Code §§401(a)(9), 403(b)(10), 408(a)(6), 408(b)(3), or 457(d)(2).
42. Code §4974.
43. Within the meaning of Code §409(d)(2).
44. Within the meaning of Code §409(d)(3).
45. Code §401(k)(2)(B)(i)(V). *See* 358 T.M., *Cash or Deferred Arrangements.*
46. Code §72(t).
47. As defined in §4974(c), i.e., plans qualifying under Code §§401(a), 403(a), 403(b), and IRAs.
48. Code §72(t)(2)(A).

49. Code §72(t)(2)(B). The amount of medical expense deductions is determined without regard to whether the employee itemizes deductions.
50. As defined in Code §4975(e)(7).
51. Within the meaning of Code §409(l).
52. Code §72(t)(2)(C). This provision does not apply to assets that have not been invested in employer securities at all times during the five-plan-year period preceding the plan year in which the distribution is made.
53. Code §72(t)(2)(D).
54. Code §414(p)(1)(B).
55. Code §414(p)(2).
56. Code §414(p)(3).
57. For purposes of determining the present value of an employer subsidy, the discount interest rate to be used must be the interest rate specified in the plan or, if no interest rate is specified, 5%.
58. Code §414(p)(4)(A)(i)-(iii). For this purpose, §414(p)(4)(B) defines "earliest retirement age" as the earliest of: (1) the date on which the participant is entitled to a distribution under the plan, or (2) the later of (a) the date on which the participant attains age 50, or (b) the earliest date on which the participant could begin receiving benefits from the plan if the participant separated from service.
59. Code §414(p)(5).
60. Code §414(p)(6).
61. Code §414(p)(6)(B).
62. Code §414(p)(7).
63. Code §402(a)(9). Section 414(p)(8) defines "alternate payee" as any spouse, child, or other dependent of a participant who is recognized by a domestic relations order as having a right to receive all, or a portion of, the benefits under a plan. Thus, child support orders can create rights in a participant's pension benefits.
64. Code §402(a)(10).
65. Code §402(e)(4)(M).
66. Code §402(a)(6)(F).
67. Code §402(a)(1).
68. Code §402(e)(4)(A)(i)-(iv).
69. Code §402(e)(4)(H).
70. The taxpayer, however, before age 59½, could take lump sum distribution treatment on multiple distributions, subject to a six-year "lookback" rule which grossed up the amount of an individual's lump sum distributions for the immediately preceding six taxable years in calculating the forward averaging tax on the current distribution and then subtracted out any forward averaging tax previously paid. This had the effect of pushing the current distribution into a higher tax bracket, i.e., it prevented participants from further reducing their tax by spreading out their lump sum distributions over several taxable years.
71. Code §402(e)(4)(D).

72. Code §402(e)(1)(C).
73. Code §402(e)(4)(J).
74. Code §402(a)(1).
75. Code §4981A.
76. Code §4981A(d).
77. Code §4981A(c)(1).
78. Code §4981A(c)(3).
79. Code §402(a)(5)(B). The employee would owe no tax on nondeductible employee contributions anyway, but might wish to make a rollover to obtain taxfree investment growth or a higher rate of return in the recipient plan because a larger amount was invested.
80. Code §402(a)(5)(B).
81. Code §402(a)(5)(E).
82. *Id.*
83. 1984 TRA, §425, P.L. 98-369.
84. 1985-1 C.B. 135.
85. Treas. Regs. §1.401(a)(4).
86. H.R. Rep. 97-760, 98th Cong., 2d Sess. 619 *et seq.* (1982). As enacted by TEFRA, the Code §72(p) rules apply to loans, assignments, and pledges made after Aug. 13, 1982, except that the balance of any loan outstanding as of that date which was renegotiated, extended, renewed, or revised after that date is treated as a new loan on the modification date. TEFRA further required that the outstanding balance of any loan, regardless of whether it was made before the effective date, must be aggregated with any post-effective date loans in determining whether a post-effective date loan exceeds the §72(p) limits.

2

IRS Application Process, Reporting and Disclosure, Fiduciary Duty, and Plan Terminations

11

IRS Application Process; Reporting and Disclosure Requirements

The IRS Application Process

Although it is not a prerequisite to plan qualification, it is almost always advisable to submit a plan to the IRS for a determination letter concerning the plan's tax qualification either prior to, or shortly after, a plan is adopted. A favorable determination letter will assure the plan sponsor that the IRS will treat the plan as qualified so long as the law does not change and the plan is operated in accordance with its express terms. The determination letter does not afford the sponsor protection from disqualification due to either discrimination in operation of the plan or its failure to comply with subsequent legislative or regulatory developments.

The IRS, upon receipt of an application for a determination letter, either will issue a favorable letter or, if the plan must be amended to conform to the law or regulations, will issue a letter of comment, informing the sponsor of what changes must be made to bring the plan into compliance so that a favorable letter may issue.

When significant changes in the law occur or significant plan amendments are made, it is advisable to resubmit the plan to the IRS for a letter of continuing qualification. When a plan terminates, an application for a "termination determination" letter should be submitted. This latter type of letter states that nothing in the proposed termination will adversely affect the plan's prior tax-qualified status.

Plans may, prior to their adoption, be submitted to the IRS in proposed form. Where this occurs, the IRS approval letter may be issued conditionally pending formal adoption of the plan if proof of such adoption is submitted to the IRS within 30 days after the issuance of the letter or within the "remedial amendments period."

Because the IRS may require that a plan, as submitted, be amended, it is often beneficial to submit the plan in proposed form to avoid going through a formal amendment process twice. When this is done, the plan, as finally approved by the IRS, can then be submitted one time to the board of directors or other governing body of the sponsor for its approval. Where pre-submission is not possible, the board can delegate to the plan's representative, such as an attorney or a subcommittee of the sponsor's board of directors, the authority to make amendments required to obtain tax qualification.

The remedial amendments period also governs the time for amendment of a plan that is submitted to the IRS after it is placed in operation. Under Code §401(b), a stock bonus, pension, profit-sharing, or annuity plan will qualify from the date it was put into effect, or for the period beginning with the earlier of the date on which there was adopted or put into effect any amendment that caused the plan to fail to satisfy Code §401(a), and ending with the time prescribed by law for filing the employer's tax return for the taxable year in which the defective amendment was adopted (including extensions) if the appropriate corrective amendments are made within this period. All provisions of the plan that are needed to satisfy § 401(a) must be in effect by the end of the above period and must have been made effective for the entire period. ERISA §3001 requires, before the application can be processed, that the sponsor notify all employees who are "interested parties" of the pendency of the application and of their right to submit comments on it, within certain prescribed time limits, to the IRS.

Requests for a favorable determination letter on a defined benefit plan are made on IRS Form 5300; for defined contribution plans, application must be made on Form 5301. Both forms must be accompanied by employee census information on Form 5302. Form 5302 is a confidential document, not for public inspection. Forms 5300 and 5301 are public documents. Generally, if the employer is being represented before the IRS, IRS Form 2848, *Power of Attorney*, must also be submitted. IRS Form 5307 may be used as a short form to obtain approval of certain plan amendments and for employer-requested approval of master, prototype, and model plans. Such applications may also be submitted on Form 6406.

Applications for approval of amendments to collectively bargained plans, however, must be made on Form 6406. IRS Form 5310 is used to apply for favorable termination determination letters.

For single employer plans, application is made to the IRS Key District Office in which the sponsor's (employer or employee organization's) principal place of business is located. For plans maintained by more than one employer, applications go to the District Director for the Key District in which the principal place of business of the association, committee, joint board of trustees, or other similar group of representatives of those who established or maintain the plan is located.

A District Director's adverse decision may be reviewed by the relevant IRS Regional Office and, from there, may be appealed to the National Office. Applications can also reach the National Office on a request by a District Director for technical advice. After administrative remedies have been exhausted, the taxpayer may petition the United States Tax Court to reverse the IRS' decision by granting declaratory judgment. The petition may cite either an adverse determination letter or the failure to act on an application for a determination.[1] The petition must be filed in the Tax Court within 90 days of receipt of an adverse determination, or, if there has been no IRS response, within 270 days after request for a determination was made.

Applications for determination letters must include Form 5300, Schedule T, which requests certain information on how the plan complies with TEFRA, the 1984 TRA, and the 1984 REA.

The IRS may extend the remedial amendments period administratively. It did this numerous times to give noncomplying plans the chance to come into compliance with TEFRA, the 1984 TRA, and the REA. Finally, the IRS, in an effort to prevent mass disqualifications of plans, issued Notice 86-3.[2] Instead of disqualification, the notice took the novel approach of treating a plan as a nonqualified arrangement with respect to any key employee participants (i.e., requiring that such individuals be taxed on their benefits under Code §83). This sanction was phased in in stages, with the amount of a key employee's benefit to be treated in this manner to be determined based on the number of months a plan failed to comply with the three Acts. Whether a similar approach will be taken with respect to subsequent legislation remains to be seen.

To facilitate compliance with the 1986 Tax Reform Act, Congress provided in § 1140 of that Act that TRA-required amendments will not have to be made before the first plan year beginning on or after January 1, 1989, if:

(1) During the period after the amendment takes effect and before such first plan year, the plan is operated in accordance with the requirements of the amendment or in accordance with an IRS model amendment adopted by the plan, and

(2) The amendment applies retroactively to the period required by law.

The IRS has issued model amendments for different types of qualified plans as was contemplated by TRA § 1140. A plan sponsor may rely on a pre-1986 TRA favorable determination letter if it adopts the mandatory provisions of the applicable amendment (certain provisions are optional) and operates the plan in accordance with the amendment's terms. The amendments relate to changes brought about by the 1986 Act that are effective before 1989. The IRS will not process applications for a determination letter with respect to these provisions, so sponsors are left with only one course of action—to adopt the mandatory provisions of the applicable model amendment word-for-word. Examples of such model amendments appear as amendments to the plans contained in Appendix A.

Reporting and Disclosure

ERISA requires that plans make certain reports to the IRS, the Department of Labor, and the PBGC and disclose certain information to participants and beneficiaries. The penalties for failing to make required reports and disclosures range from fines to criminal sanctions and civil actions, brought by the Department of Labor and/or participants, to compel compliance.

In general, ERISA's reporting and disclosure requirements apply to "employee pension benefit plans" and "employee welfare benefit plans." ERISA defines an employee pension benefit plan to include all plans maintained by employers or labor organizations, or both, that provide either retirement benefits or the deferral of income by employees for periods extending to the termination of covered employment or beyond.[3] The following types of plans are exempt from the requirements of Title I and, therefore, from reporting and disclosure:[4]

(1) Governmental plans;[5]

(2) Church plans;[6]

(3) Plans maintained solely for the purpose of complying with applicable workers' compensation laws or unemployment compensation or disability insurance laws;

(4) Plans maintained outside the U.S. primarily for the benefit of nonresident aliens; and

(5) Unfunded excess benefit plans.[7]

ERISA defines an "employee welfare benefit plan" as any plan, fund, or program established or maintained by an employer, a labor organization, or both, to the extent it was established or maintained for the purpose of providing participants or beneficiaries, through the purchase of insurance or otherwise, with:

(1) Medical, surgical, or hospital care or benefits, or benefits in the event of sickness, accident, disability, death or unemployment, or vacation benefits, apprenticeship or other training programs, or day care centers, scholarship funds, or prepaid legal services; or

(2) Any benefit described in §302(c) of the Labor Management Relations Act of 1947 (other than pensions on retirement or death, and insurance to provide such pensions).[8]

In addition to the statutory exceptions, Labor Department regulations exclude a number of plans and practices from the reporting and disclosure rules.[9] Among the types of practices exempted are the giving of holiday gifts and the establishment and maintenance of employee first aid stations, employee dining facilities, and on-premises recreation facilities. The types of plans exempted include certain voluntary group insurance programs, plans having no employees, severance pay plans, employee bonus programs, IRAs that are not sponsored by the employer, profit-sharing plans that do not defer income until termination of employment or retirement, and Code §403(b) tax-sheltered annuities.

Specific Reporting and Disclosure Requirements

With respect to reporting, ERISA requires the administrator of a covered plan to file with the Secretary of Labor:

(1) An annual report;

(2) A plan description and a summary plan description (generally, plan sponsors choose to draft a more detailed summary plan description to enable them to satisfy both of these requirements with a single document—as the Labor Department allows);

(3) A report of certain modifications and changes in the plan; and

(4) Certain terminal and supplementary reports.[10]

The first requirement to be examined will be the requirement that plans file annual reports.[11]

Annual Returns and Reports

The various requirements that plans file annual information returns with the IRS and annual reports with the Department of Labor and the PBGC have been consolidated in practice. The agencies have developed IRS Form 5500, which needs to be filed only with the IRS. The IRS will then forward any pertinent information disclosed on the form to the other two agencies. Form 5500 reports are public documents, open for general inspection.

Pension and welfare plans having fewer than 100 participants do not need to file Form 5500. They may file Form 5500-R (registration statement for small plans) annually and Form 5500-C (the equivalent of the Form 5500 return/report for small plans) every three years as well as for the first and last plan years of the plan.

Unfunded "top hat" plans and unfunded or insured "top hat" welfare plans, i.e., plans that only provide benefits for a select group of management employees, need not file Form 5500. Further, welfare plans having fewer than 100 participants do not have to file the form where:

(1) Benefits are paid only as needed from the employer's general assets;

(2) The plan is funded with insurance contracts or policies; or

(3) Both.

This exception applies to most insured medical reimbursement plans of small employers.

In general, the plan administrator must sign and date all Form 5500 series reports. For a single employer plan, the employer (if different from the administrator) must also sign. When a plan is run by a joint employer-union board of trustees, at least one employer representative and one union representative must sign. All participating employers in a multiemployer plan must sign Form 5500 series reports but, in this case, the plan administrator's signature is not required.

A two and a half month extension of time to file the Form 5500 reports will be granted if a request is timely filed on Form 5558. Additional requests for extensions will be evaluated on a case-by-case basis. Single employer plans and plans of a controlled group of corporations are automatically granted an extension until the due date of the employer's tax return for the year, including any extensions, if the following conditions are met:

(1) The plan year and the employer's taxable year coincide;

(2) The single employer or the controlled group has been granted an extension of time to file its federal income tax return to a date that is later than the normal due date for the 5500 report; and

(3) A copy of the approved IRS extension of time to file the federal income tax return is attached to each 5500 report.

The instructions to Form 5500 specify that an extension of time to file the return/report does not automatically extend the due date of PBGC Form PBGC 1 (discussed below). Where all the assets of a plan (including insurance/annuity contracts) have been distributed to participants and beneficiaries, the administrator is instructed to check the box marked "final return" at the top of the form. The year of a complete distribution of plan assets is the last year for which a 5500 report must be filed. For this purpose, a complete distribution will be deemed to have occurred where a defined benefit plan's assets are brought under the PBGC's control.[12]

The more significant items on Form 5500 concern:

(1) The number of participants in a plan, broken down as to whether such participants are vested and whether they are retired or terminated participants whose benefits are in pay status;

(2) Any amendments made to a pension plan (but not to a welfare plan) during the plan year and whether the plan has filed the appropriate Department of Labor documents in connection with such amendments;

(3) Certain termination information that must be provided by terminated welfare plans;

(4) An indication of whether there has been a merger, consolidation, or asset transfer involving the plan during the plan year.

(5) Funding arrangements, e.g., trust, custodial account, and so forth.

(6) Compensation received by persons who rendered services to the plan during the plan year;

(7) Audited financial statements of plan assets, liabilities, and transactions during the year; for plans with 100 or more participants, this information must be completed by a licensed public accountant.

In generating the financial statements described in (7) above, the plan's accountant may rely on representations in the plan's actuarial report if he specifies that he is relying on this information. Conversely, the actuary may rely on the representations of the accountant if he so specifies. Where the actuary or the accountant cannot obtain independent first-hand verification of material facts on which his calculations are to be based, he should either state on whose representations he is relying or, if the representations are made by someone other than a person on whom he is entitled to rely under ERISA, he should decline to sign the form unless the employer uses its best efforts to supply the information that would be needed to perform the calculations. Where the employer is unable to supply this documentation, the accountant or actuary should disclose the information on which he relies as a footnote to the form as a matter of self-protection.

Other questions on Form 5500 concern insurance and annuity contracts held by the plan, bonding of the plan, census information about the employer, and information concerning any party-in-interest transactions engaged in during the plan year.

Certain schedules must be attached to Form 5500 where they apply. The most significant ones will be noted here.

(1) Schedule A requires the plan to disclose any insurance contracts that it holds, including the names of any agent or brokers and the amount of their commission, and information concerning the amount and allocation of any premiums.

(2) Schedule B, the actuarial statement, must be completed by an enrolled actuary (an accreditation created by ERISA) for any defined benefit plan required to file an annual report. The actuarial statement must be supplied annually. The actuary must perform a valuation of plan assets and liabilities at least once every three years.

(3) Schedule SSA must be filed by a plan having separated participants with deferred vested benefits. It is a registration statement that identifies such individuals, sets forth their Social Security numbers, and describes the type and amount of payment they are entitled to receive. The plan must disclose on Schedule SSA whether the separated participant has been notified of his benefit.

Numerous penalties under the Code and ERISA apply to a person charged with the responsibility of filing Form 5500 reports who either fails to give complete information on such reports or who fails to file them in a timely manner. The penalty for not filing a required return/report for a plan is $25 per day up to a maximum of $15,000.[13] A penalty of $1 per day is imposed for failing to report a change in plan status.[14] A $1,000 penalty applies to any failure to file actuarial information on Schedule B.

The instructions to Form 5500 advise that, under appropriate circumstances, the IRS will waive a penalty that would otherwise apply. The instructions suggest that, where a penalty for failure to file or disclose may apply, the preparer should attach to the report an explanation of the reason for the failure in order to enable the IRS to determine if the penalty should be wiaved.

Among the factors that might persuade the IRS to waive a penalty are:

(1) The fact that the current failure to file is the first involving this particular plan or individual;

(2) The fact that the filing was only a few days late;

(3) The fact that the failure to file or disclose was due to the failure to transmit all the necessary information to the individual responsible for making the filing;

(4) The fact that the late filing was caused by denial of a request for an extension of time to file which the individual reasonably believed would be granted; and

(5) Any other factor not within the individual's control that could not have reasonably been contemplated in advance.

In addition to the foregoing penalties, ERISA provides a penalty of up to one year's imprisonment, a $5,000 fine, or both, for an individual who willfully violates Part I of Title I of ERISA (relating to reporting and disclosure) or an order issued pursuant to that part.[15] If the violation is by a person other than a natural person, a fine of up to $100,000 may be imposed.[16] Further, ERISA imposes a penalty of up to five years' imprisonment, a $10,000 fine, or both, on a person who makes any false statement or representation on a report or who knowingly conceals or fails to disclose any fact that ERISA requires to be disclosed.[17] In addition, ERISA §502 allows a participant, beneficiary, or fiduciary to maintain a civil action to enjoin any act or to obtain other appropriate relief for any violation of Title I of ERISA or of the terms of the plan.

Summary Annual Reports

In addition to the requirement that the administrator of a covered plan file with the Secretary of Labor an annual report containing the information described in ERISA §103,[18] ERISA also requires the administrator to furnish participants and pay status beneficiaries a summary of the statements and schedules included in the annual report that are described in ERISA §103(b)(3)(A) and (B) and such other information as is necessary to fairly summarize this data.[19] This information consists of, essentially, the schedules of the plan's assets and liabilities, as well as its receipts and disbursements, for the fiscal year. The Labor Department has streamlined this process by promulgating two fill-in-the-blank forms, one for welfare plans and one for pension plans, which the administrator must use to satisfy this "summary annual report" (SAR) requirement.[20] The administrator need not fill in the blanks that do not apply to the plan, but must provide any further information that may be necessary to fairly summarize the data that must be disclosed. The actual statements and schedules need not be furnished to participants and pay status beneficiaries, but must be provided upon request.[21]

The SAR must be furnished within nine months of the close of the plan year unless an extension has been obtained with respect to the annual report. Where it has, the SAR must be furnished within two months after the expiration of the extension. Certain unfunded welfare plans and unfunded "top hat" pension plans are exempt from the requirement that a SAR be provided.[22]

Plan Description and Summary Plan Description (SPD)

ERISA requires the plan administrator to file a Summary Plan Description (SPD) with the Labor Department.[23] The administrator must also furnish the SPD to each participant and each beneficiary who is receiving benefits.[24] As previously indicated, ERISA § 101(b) also requires that plans provide the Labor Department with a more detailed plan description. In practice, DOL allows plans to satisfy both requirements by providing the relevant parties (participants, beneficiaries and the Labor Department) with a single document that satisfies the requirements of both ERISA §§ 101(a) and (b). Since this consolidated document is generally called a "Summary Plan Description," that term will be used in this discussion to describe the consolidated document.

The SPD is, essentially, a document that describes the most significant features of the plan. Most SPDs state that, to the extent the SPD is inconsistent with the provisions of the plan, the plan will control. Including this type of provision is helpful since, given the complexity of the law, it is difficult to fully present the rule in every given case, especially where there is a general rule and a number of minor exceptions. To the extent every possible situation is covered by the SPD, the document can become exceedingly complex and unwieldy. This, in turn, could violate ERISA's requirement that the SPD "shall be written in a manner calculated to be understood by the average plan participant."[25]

In practice, SPDs are often written at a level of complexity that makes them difficult to understand unless the reader has had some training in employee benefits. In certain circumstances, this is a necessary by-product of the complexity of the law and the plan provisions that the SPD must explain. The draftsman must balance the concerns for completeness against the risk that the document will not be understandable by participants. Where the attempt to comply with both sets of requirements is reasonable, however, the Labor Department will extend latitude to the drafter.

Persons responsible for drafting SPDs should also be aware that other documents disseminated by the employer or the plan administrator may legally constitute SPDs where it is not intended that they do so. This is most common in the case of employer-generated promotional materials that are distributed in connection with plans that depend on voluntary employee participation, e.g., a §401(k) cash-or-deferred arrangement. Where such materials are sent out, they should be carefully scrutinized for accuracy and should be clearly marked to the effect that they are not the plan's SPD. The legend should also inform employees of how they may obtain the SPD.

The SPD must contain, among other things, the following information:

(1) The plan sponsor's name and the type of administration, *e.g.*, trust, insurance contracts, etc.;

(2) The name and address of the plan's designated agent for receipt of legal process if this person is different than the plan administrator;

(3) The name and address of the administrator, and any plan trustees if they are different from the administrator;

(4) A description of the relevant provisions of any applicable collective bargaining agreement;

(5) The plan's requirements concerning eligibility and benefits;

(6) A description of the plan's vesting provisions;

(7) The source of financing of the plan and the identity of any entity through which plan benefits are provided;

(8) The date of the end of the plan year and whether the plan's records are kept on a calendar, fiscal, or policy year basis; and

(9) The procedures to be followed in presenting benefit claims

under the plan and the remedies available for redress of claims that are denied in whole or part (including the benefit claims procedures required by ERISA §503).[26]

In addition, Labor Department regulations require that the SPD detail:

(1) The availability of joint and survivor benefits under the plan and any elections that may be made with respect thereto (including, presumably, a description of the spouse's waiver election);

(2) Any provisions in the plan that could lead to ineligibility to receive benefits, including any forfeiture provisions or provisions for suspension of benefits (such as a provision for suspension of benefits upon the reemployment of a retiree);

(3) Whether the plan is subject to the PBGC's termination insurance provisions and, if so, a summary of how those provisions work;

(4) The manner in which the plan computes service and its computation periods; and

(5) The plan's early termination rule.[27]

This last requirement was added in 1984 and applies only to SPDs filed after it was added.

SPDs must contain an explanation of the top-heavy provisions, including the plan's rules on top-heavy vesting and minimum benefits/contributions.

The SPD must be furnished to participants and the Labor Department:

(1) Within 90 days after (the individual) becomes a participant, or (in the case of a beneficiary) within 90 days after he first receives benefits; or

(2) If later, within 120 days after the plan becomes subject to the reporting and disclosure rules.[28]

Further, every fifth year after the plan becomes subject to the reporting and disclosure rules, the administrator must furnish an updated SPD that integrates all plan amendments made in the five-year period to each participant and beneficiary receiving benefits.[29] Where there have been no plan amendments in the five-year period, an updated SPD is not required; but due to the rapid pace of changes in the law, this is unlikely. Even if there are no amendments, however, the SPD must be furnished to participants and beneficiaries in pay status at least every 10 years after the plan becomes subject to the reporting and disclosure rules.

Where a plan is changed significantly and a revised SPD is not issued, the plan must send participants and pay status beneficiaries a document known as a "Summary of Material Modifications" (SMM) describing the changes. The "calculated to be understood by the average participant" requirement also applies to a Summary of Material Modifications.[30] The SMM must be furnished to participants and beneficiaries (and filed with the Department of Labor) no later than 210 days (seven months) after the close of the plan year in which the change is adopted.

For retirees in pay status, Labor Department regulations prescribe an alternative method of compliance that allows certain information to be omitted. The information supplied must either contain a statement that current benefits will continue to be paid or describe any benefit reductions that might occur.[31] In addition, a copy of the updated SPD does not have to be provided to a retiree, a vested separated participant, or a pay status beneficiary if, on or before the retirement or separation date or the date benefits commence, whichever applies, the individual is furnished with a copy of the most recent SPD and any subsequent SMMs. Where this method is used, the material disseminated must contain a statement that the individual's rights are those that were set forth in prior SPDs and SMMs and that an updated SPD may be obtained from the plan administrator.[32]

The above information does not have to be supplied where the amendment cannot possibly affect the individual.[33]

The administrator of a terminated plan does not have to furnish SPDs to participants and beneficiaries.[34] Generally, a pension plan is considered terminated when all distributions have been completed.[35] A welfare plan is generally considered terminated where no benefit claims can be incurred that will give rise to liability.[36]

A plan administrator who fails to supply a beneficiary or participant with information, such as an SPD or SMM, to which the individual is entitled can be fined up to $100 per day for each day after 30 days that the failure continues, unless the administrator can demonstrate that matters reasonably beyond his control caused the failure.[37] Mailing the requested material to the individual's last known mailing address constitutes compliance.[38] This fine can attach to any failure of the administrator to supply information that an individual is entitled to under Title I of ERISA.

Terminal and Other Reports

ERISA §101(c) requires the administrator of an employee benefit plan which is winding up its affairs to file such terminal reports as the Secretary of Labor and the PBGC require. The Secretary is also authorized to require such a plan to file a supplementary or terminal report with the plan's annual (Form 5500) report in the year the plan terminates. If the plan is a defined benefit plan that is subject to the termination insurance provisions of Title IV of ERISA, the Secretary may also require the plan to file a copy of any such supplementary or terminal report with the PBGC.[39]

Reporting of Participants' Benefit Rights

ERISA requires the administrator of every employee pension benefit plan to furnish to any participant or beneficiary, upon request, a written statement indicating, on the basis of the latest available information:

(1) The total benefits accrued; and

(2) The nonforfeitable benefits that have accrued or the earliest date on which the benefits will become nonforfeitable.[40]

A participant or beneficiary may only make one such request in a 12-month period.[41] Further, where an administrator is required to register under Code §6057, he must provide any participant, within the time prescribed for filing the registration statement, a copy of the information that must be included in the registration statement.

PBGC Reporting Requirements

PBGC Form 1 must be filed annually by a defined benefit plan subject to ERISA's termination insurance provisions, and must be accompanied by a tendering of the plan's annual per participant premium for termination insurance. Certain reports must also be filed with the PBGC when a covered plan terminates.

Claims Procedure

ERISA requires that every covered plan provide adequate notice in writing to any participant or beneficiary whose claim for benefits under the plan has been denied, setting forth the specific reasons for the denial.[42] Such notice must be written in a manner calculated to be understood by the participant or beneficiary. Further, the administrator must afford a reasonable opportunity for a full and fair review of the decision denying the claim to any participant or beneficiary whose claim for benefits has been denied.[43]

Notes

1. Code §7476.
2. 1986-19 I.R.B. 21.
3. ERISA §3(2).
4. ERISA §4(b).
5. As defined in ERISA §3(32). This section, in turn, defines a "governmental plan" as a plan established or maintained for its employees by the U.S. government, the government of any state or political subdivision thereof, or an agency or instrumentality of any of the foregoing. The section also includes within the definition of "governmental plan" any plan to which the Railroad Retirement Act of 1935 or 1937 applies and that is financed by contributions required under that Act. Also exempted is any plan of an international organization that is exempt from taxation under §501 of the International Organizations Immunities Act (59 Stat. 669).
6. Church plans are defined in ERISA §3(33). Section 3(33)(A) provides that the term "church plan" means "a plan established and maintained (to the extent required in clause (ii) of subparagraph (B)) for its employees (or their beneficiaries) by a church or by a convention or association of churches which is exempt from tax under §501 of the Internal Revenue Code of 1954." Clause (ii) of subparagraph (B) requires that "substantially all" of the employees covered by the plan be employees of the church or convention of churches and/or their beneficiaries. Section 3(33)(B) excludes from the definition of "church plan" plans that are maintained primarily for the benefit of individuals employed by the church or convention of churches in an unrelated trade or business as that term is defined in §513, and plans where the above-referenced "substantially all" requirement has not been met.
7. Excess benefit plans are defined in ERISA §3(36) as plans maintained "by an employer solely for the purpose of providing benefits for certain employees in excess of the limitations on contributions and benefits imposed

(5) Excess plans (plans designed to provide employees with benefits in excess of the Code §415 limits);

(6) Unfunded "top hat" plans, i.e., plans for key executives; and

(7) Certain plans[11] that provide for payments to retired or deceased partners of a partnership.[12]

Written Plan Instrument and Named Fiduciary Requirements

ERISA requires that an employee benefit plan subject to its provisions be maintained pursuant to a written instrument and that the instrument must name a person who will serve as the plan's "named fiduciary."[13] The named fiduciary will be liable for the operation and administration of the plan. A plan may designate more than one person as the named fiduciary. If it does so, the persons so designated will be jointly and severally liable for the plan's operation and administration.[14] The named fiduciary may, however, designate one or more persons to carry out specific responsibilities with respect to the plan.[15] This includes the authority to appoint a person to act as investment manager for the plan's assets.[16]

Establishment of a Trust and Plan Trustee Requirements

In general, the assets of an employee benefit plan covered by ERISA must be held in trust by one or more trustees.[17] The trustee or trustees must be named in either the plan document or trust instrument or be named by the named fiduciary. Generally, the trustee has exclusive authority to manage and control plan assets unless:

(1) The plan provides that the trustee shall be subject to the direction of a nontrustee fiduciary; or

(2) Authority to manage the plan's assets has been delegated to one or more investment managers pursuant to ERISA §402(c)(3).[18]

The requirements concerning the naming of the trustee and

the requirement that the trustee manage the plan's assets do not apply to:

(1) Plan assets held in the form of insurance contracts;

(2) Plan assets held by an insurance company;

(3) IRA assets held in custodial accounts;

(4) Plans not covered under parts 2 and 3 of Title I of ERISA, i.e., participation, funding, vesting, accrual, and so on, or under Title IV of ERISA (relating to termination insurance);

(5) §403(b) tax-sheltered annuities where the assets of the plan are held in custodial accounts; and

(6) Certain plans of employee-owned corporations to compensate employees for retirement benefits lost due to forfeiture.

Duties of the Fiduciary

A fiduciary must discharge his duties with respect to the plan solely in the interest of its participants and beneficiaries.[19] Those duties must be discharged for the exclusive purpose of:

(1) Providing benefits to participants and their beneficiaries; and

(2) Defraying reasonable expenses of administering the plan.[20]

Prudence

A fiduciary must also satisfy the "prudent man rule." This rule requires that a fiduciary discharge his duties "with the care, skill, prudence, and diligence under the circumstances then prevailing that a prudent man, acting in a like capacity and familiar with such matters would use in the conduct of an enterprise of a like character and with like aims."[21]

It is not entirely clear whether, in certain cases, a fiduciary will be held to the standard of the "prudent expert," rather than that of the "prudent layman." Clearly, where the fiduciary does not have experience in the matter under consideration, it can be

Duties Retained by the Fiduciary in a Self-Directed Plan

The regulation provides that ERISA §404(c) does not relieve a fiduciary of liability for implementing a participant's instruction that results in a transaction between the plan and a plan sponsor or an affiliate of the sponsor or that results in the acquisition or sale of any employer security or employer real property.

A plan may satisfy §404(c) if it provides for the investment of a participant's accounts in one of the investments within the "safe" category discussed above in the absence of affirmative instructions from the participant. To invoke this rule, however, the plan must take reasonable steps to inform the participant about the option that will be selected in the absence of his or her affirmative direction.

The proposed regulation takes the position that a plan fiduciary, as a general matter, does not have the duty to inform the participant as to the suitability of a particular investment choice or the advisability of retaining an investment that has been made.

Where a participant exercises independent control, he will not be considered a fiduciary merely because of the exercise of such control.[26] Thus, the prohibited transactions rules and the cofiduciary liability provisions of ERISA would not apply to the participant merely because the participant exercised independent control of the investment of the assets in his or her account. Under ERISA §404(c), plan fiduciaries are relieved of potential liability for any losses that *result from* the participant's exercise of control over his or her account pursuant to a self-direction option. This determination will be made on a case-by-case basis. The proposed regulation, however, only relieves a fiduciary of responsibility for the *direct and necessary consequences* of a participant's exercise of control. Therefore, a fiduciary could still be held liable for imprudence in implementing a self-direction choice. Where a fiduciary implements one participant's self-direction election, the fiduciary will be relieved of his duty with respect to that participant (provided no supervening breach occurred). Following the participant's instructions will not, however, relieve the fiduciary of his statutory duty with respect to any other participant.

The proposed self-direction regulation does not impose any fiduciary duty that does not otherwise exist under ERISA. Thus, for example, the decisions of an investment company under the Investment Company Act of 1940 would not be treated as resulting from the participant's decision to invest in the company because such companies are not fiduciaries under ERISA in the first place.

Notwithstanding the general rule relieving a fiduciary from potential liability in a self-directed plan, a fiduciary will not be relieved of his or her duty with respect to participant instructions which:

(1) Would not comply with the terms of the plan's documents and governing instruments;

(2) Would cause the fiduciary to maintain the indicia of ownership of plan assets outside the jurisdiction of the U.S. district courts;[27]

(3) Would jeopardize the plan's qualified status; or

(4) Would result in a direct or indirect acquisition, sale, or lease of property (including employer securities or employer real property) between a participant and a plan sponsor or an affiliate of the sponsor, or in a direct or indirect loan between the participant and the sponsor or an affiliate. Further, a fiduciary is not relieved of any responsibility with respect to any sale, acquisition, or lease of employer securities or employer real property, regardless of whether the employer is involved in the transaction.

To the extent relief is granted under ERISA §404(c) and the regulations thereunder, a fiduciary is relieved of any liability he or she might otherwise incur for engaging in a prohibited transaction within the meaning of ERISA §406 or any cofiduciary liability that might be imposed under ERISA §405 to the extent that the fiduciary's action was a "direct and necessary" consequence of the participant's exercise of control.

Note that nothing in the proposed regulation exempts a "disqualified person" from the excise tax that may be imposed on prohibited transactions under Code §4975. Further, the proposed regulation does not impose cofiduciary liability on an individual where the participant has engaged in self-direction under §404. The preamble cites as an example of this principle the situation where the participant chooses an investment manager who imprudently invests plan assets. While the investment manager will not be relieved of liability in this instance (because the loss was not the direct and necessary result of the choices made by the participant), the other cofiduciaries will be relieved of any liability that would otherwise be imposed under ERISA §405 even if, for example, they had knowledge of the manager's imprudence. Such a cofiduciary would, however, be required to take the manager's imprudence into account in determining whether to continue the designation of the manager.

Liability for Breach by a Cofiduciary

In addition to any other liability that a fiduciary may incur under Title I of ERISA, ERISA §405 provides that a fiduciary will be liable for any breach by another fiduciary under the following circumstances:

(1) If he participates knowingly in, or knowingly undertakes to conceal, an act or omission of such other fiduciary, knowing such act or omission constitutes a breach;

(2) If, by his failure to comply with ERISA §404(a)(1) in the administration of his specific responsibilities which gave rise to his status as a fiduciary, he has enabled such other fiduciary to commit a breach; or

(3) If he has knowledge of a breach by such other fiduciary, unless he makes reasonable efforts under the circumstances to remedy the breach.[28]

In general, when more than one trustee is responsible for the plan's assets, each must use reasonable care to prevent a cotrustee from committing a breach of fiduciary duty.[29] This does not prevent a plan from allocating responsibility for certain plan assets to one fiduciary and away from any others.[30] Where this is done, no cofiduciary liability will attach to a trustee to the extent he is not responsible for the assets with respect to which the breach has been committed.[31] Further, no cofiduciary liability will arise for a trustee whom the plan makes subject to the direction of a named fiduciary.[32] In addition, a named fiduciary who has properly allocated a duty under the plan to another will not be liable for such other's breach unless the allocation of responsibilities itself violated the ERISA §404 standard of fiduciary duty.[33] A trustee will not be liable for the acts or omissions of a properly appointed investment manager.[34]

ERISA's cofiduciary liability provisions are similar to provisions commonly found in corporate and securities law that can make an officer or director of a corporation liable for failing to detect or acting to remedy improper conduct by a fellow officer or director. The standard in ERISA §405 points up the need for a fiduciary to attend all meetings of plan officials held with respect to assets for which he is responsible and to make his dissent to any actions taken by a cofiduciary a matter of record where he believes that the cofiduciary is breaching his duty. In extreme cases, legal action, such as seeking a temporary restraining order against a course of conduct by a cofiduciary, may be appropriate.

Prohibited Transactions

ERISA §406 prohibits certain transactions between a plan and a "party-in-interest," and subjects such transactions to various penalties. Code §4975 contains parallel provisions, but uses the term "disqualified person." The sanction provided by the Code is a two-tiered excise tax, the second tier of which is a 100 percent penalty if the prohibited transaction is not corrected within a statutory "correction period." For ease of reference, the citations in this section to the prohibited transactions provisions are to ERISA, although there are parallel provisions in the Code.

"Party-in-Interest"

As a threshold matter, it is necessary to define the term "party-in-interest" which describes persons having certain specified relationships to the plan.[35] Specifically, a party-in-interest is:

(1) Any fiduciary (including, but not limited to, an administrator, officer, trustee, or custodian), counsel or employee of such employee benefit plan;

(2) A person providing services to such plan;

(3) An employer any of whose employees are covered by such plan;

(4) An employee organization any of whose members are covered by such plan;

(5) An owner, directly or indirectly, of 50 percent or more of (i) the combined voting power of all classes of stock entitled

to vote or the total value of shares of all classes of stock of a corporation, (ii) the capital interest or the profits interest of a partnership, or (iii) the beneficial interest of a trust or unincorporated enterprise which is an employer or an employee organization described in (3) or (4), above;

(6) A relative of any individual described in (1), (2), (3), or (5), above;

(7) A corporation, partnership, trust or estate of which (or in which) 50 percent or more of (i) the combined voting power of all classes of stock entitled to vote or the total value of shares of all classes of stock of such corporation, (ii) the capital interest or profits interest of such partnership, or (iii) the beneficial interest of such trust or estate, is owned, directly or indirectly, or held by persons described in (1), (2), (3) (4), or (5), above;

(8) An employee, officer, director (or an individual having powers or responsibilities similar to those of officers or directors), or a 10 percent or more shareholder, directly or indirectly, of a person described in (2), (3), (4), (5), or (6), above, or of the employee benefit plan; or

(9) A 10 percent or more (directly or indirectly in capital or profits) partner or joint venturer of a person described in (2), (3), (4), (5), or (6), above.[36]

In addition, the Secretary of Labor, after consulting with the Secretary of the Treasury, may impose a percentage lower than 10 percent with respect to categories (5), (7), (8), or (9).[37]

Some commentators have suggested that Congress went too far in ERISA in identifying who is a party-in-interest and in creating a detailed list of prohibited transactions. This criticism generally takes the view that the relationships that make one a party-in-interest (or disqualified person) with respect to a plan can often be quite attenuated, especially where ownership is attributed through another person or entity, and that the prohibited transaction provisions prohibit a number of ordinary business transactions that are necessary to the plan's economic health. For example, the necessary process of applying to the Labor Department for an exemption from the prohibited transaction rules is extremely time consuming. Although the Labor Department has attempted to expedite the process by promulgating class exemptions for common transactions, critics of the prohibited transaction rules, however, point out that, where a plan must act quickly to take advantage of an investment opportunity, the prohibited transaction rules often make this impossible, with the resultant loss of the opportunity. Loss of such opportunities may adversely affect participants and beneficiaries. One can argue from this that the statute has created a framework for "defensive investing" by plans, i.e., that fiduciaries, precluded from acting aggressively to maximize investment return, in many instances are left to insulate themselves against potential breaches of fiduciary duty by assuring that the diversification, exclusive benefit, and other requirements are satisfied.

Specific Prohibited Transactions

ERISA §408 (Code §4975) enumerates specific prohibited transactions. Section 408 provides that a fiduciary shall not cause a plan to enter into a transaction if he knows or should have known that the transaction constitutes a direct or indirect:

(1) Sale or exchange, or leasing, of any property between the plan and a party-in-interest;

(2) Lending of money or other extension of credit between the plan and a party in interest;

(3) Furnishing of goods, services, or facilities between the plan and a party-in-interest;

(4) Transfer to, or use by or for the benefit of, a party-in-interest, of any assets of the plan; or

(5) Acquisition, on behalf of the plan, of any employer security or employer real property in violation of ERISA §407(a).[38]

Rules Governing Employer Securities and Employer Real Property

ERISA §407(a), in general, prevents any plan that is not an individual account plan from holding as more than 10 percent of its assets "employer securities" or "employer real property." Employer securities are securities issued by the sponsoring employer or an affiliate. Employer real property is any real property (and any related personal property) that is leased from the plan to the sponsoring employer or an affiliate.

Notwithstanding the general 10 percent rule for nonindividual account plans, a plan cannot hold employer securities or employer real property other than "qualifying employer securities" or "qualifying employer real property."

ERISA §§407(d)(5) and (e) define qualifying employer security. This definition is designed to assure that the plan acquires the security over a recognized securities exchange or otherwise, at a price no less favorable to the plan than an arm's length buyer would pay.

ERISA §407(d)(4) defines qualifying employer real property. It requires that the parcels of property be geographically dispersed, that the property be suitable for more than one use, and that the acquisition or retention of the property otherwise meets the requirements of Title I of ERISA (other than the diversification requirement).

Exemptions From Prohibited Transaction Rules

ERISA §408 sets forth the exemptions to the prohibited transaction rules. Section 408(a)(1) authorizes the Secretary of Labor to grant specific exemptions to the prohibited transactions provisions if he finds that the exemption is:

(1) Administratively feasible;

(2) In the interests of participants and beneficiaries; and

(3) Protective of the rights of participants and beneficiaries.

Before granting an exemption, the Secretary must have the proposed exemption published in the Federal Register for the purpose of soliciting public comments.

In addition, ERISA §408(b) exempts certain specific transactions from the prohibited transactions rules. Section 408(b)(1) allows a plan to make loans to participants and beneficiaries if such loans meet the following criteria:

(1) They are available to all participants and beneficiaries on a reasonably equivalent basis;

(2) They are not made available to Code §401(a)(4) prohibited group employees in an amount greater than that made available to other employees;

(3) They are made in accordance with a specific plan provision;

(4) They bear a reasonable interest rate; and

(5) They are adequately secured.

Notwithstanding Code §72(p), which allows participant loans to the extent they satisfy certain criteria and do not exceed certain dollar limits, in order to avoid engaging in a prohibited transaction, a plan must conform its loan policy to the above requirements. The only function of §72(p) is to assure the recipients of plan loans that the loan will not trigger the constructive receipt of income. Section 72(p) is not a plan qualification requirement, and compliance with its provisions does not insulate a transaction against the application of the prohibited transaction rules.

ERISA §408(b)(2) creates a significant exception to the prohibited transaction rule concerning parties-in-interest providing services to a plan. The exemption allows a plan to contract or to make reasonable arrangements with a party-in-interest for office space, or legal, accounting, or other services that are necessary for the establishment or operation of the plan, provided no more than reasonable compensation is paid. For example, this exception would allow a plan administrator, investment manager, or trustee to share office space with the plan to promote the plan's effective operation.

ERISA §408(b)(3) allows certain loans from a party-in-interest to an Employee Stock Ownership Plan (ESOP). The loan must be primarily for the benefit of participants and beneficiaries, and the interest rate must not exceed a reasonable rate. The only collateral the plan may offer for such a loan is "qualifying employer securities." This exemption allows leveraged ESOPs to finance the purchase of qualifying employer securities from the plan sponsor or from a financial institution (in the latter case, often involving the employer's guarantee of the loan to the plan).

ERISA §408(b)(4) provides an exemption for the plans of certain banks. Under this exemption, a bank party-in-interest may act as a depositary institution for all or part of a plan's assets, provided they bear a reasonable rate of return. The depositary institution must be a bank or similar institution supervised by the United States or a state. The exemption applies where the plan covers only employees of the bank or other institution and its affiliates and the investment of plan assets is authorized either by the plan document or by the plan's fiduciary if, under the plan terms, he has the responsibility to direct the trustee as to plan investment. This exemption prevents banks from having to deposit their plans' funds with unrelated banks.

ERISA § 408(b)(5) allows a plan to enter into a contract for life or health insurance or annuities with a party-in-interest that is an insurer qualified to do business in a state. The insurer can be the sponsoring employer or a party-in-interest that is owned by the employer or by a party-in-interest. The premiums on insurance written by such an insurer for the plan cannot exceed, for any year, 5 percent of the total premiums for all lines of insurance written by the insurer for the year. This figure does not include premiums or annuity considerations written by the employer maintaining the plan.

ERISA § 408(b)(6) exempts the provision of certain ancillary bank services. The services must be provided by a bank or similar institution supervised by the United States or a state if the bank or other institution is a fiduciary with respect to the plan. Further, the institution must have adopted "adequate internal safeguards which assure that the providing of such ancillary services is consistent with sound banking and financial practice, as determined by Federal or State supervisory authority." In addition, the extent to which such services are provided must be subject to specific guidelines issued by the institution, and adherence to such guidelines must be sufficient to "reasonably preclude" the services from being provided in an excessive or unreasonable manner or in a manner that would be inconsistent with the best interests of participants and beneficiaries.

ERISA § 408(b)(7) allows a plan to exercise a privilege to convert securities if the plan receives no less than adequate consideration pursuant to the conversion.

ERISA § 408(b)(8) allows transactions between a plan and:

(1) A common or collective trust or pooled investment fund maintained by a party-in-interest which is a bank or trust company supervised by a state or federal agency; or

(2) A pooled investment fund of an insurance company qualified to do business in a state, if (i) the transaction is a sale or purchase of an interest in the fund, (ii) the bank, trust company, or insurance company receives not more than reasonable compensation, and (iii) such transaction is expressly permitted by the instrument under which the plan is maintained, or by a fiduciary (other than the bank, trust company, or insurance company, or an affiliate thereof) who has authority to manage and control the plan's assets.

Finally, ERISA §408(b)(9) allows a fiduciary to distribute plan assets in accordance with the plan's terms, provided the asset allocation requirements of ERISA §4044 are satisfied.

ERISA §408(c) specifies that nothing in the prohibited transaction rules shall be construed to prohibit a fiduciary from receiving his normal benefit as a participant or beneficiary under a plan, receiving reasonable compensation for services rendered, or receiving reimbursement for expenses properly and actually incurred, or from serving as a fiduciary in addition to being an officer, employee, agent, or other representative of a party-in-interest.[39]

Notwithstanding the general prohibited transaction rules and exemptions, ERISA §408(d) prohibits a plan from lending plan assets, paying compensation for personal services rendered, or purchasing or selling any property to an owner-employee (as defined in Code §401(c)) or a family member thereof (as defined in Code §267) or to certain persons related to, or controlled by, such person.

This prohibits a sole proprietorship or partnership plan from making a loan to an owner-employee. It represents one of the few areas where parity does not exist between the plans of corporations and those of unicorporated entities.

Liability Under ERISA for Breach of Fiduciary Duty

ERISA §409 imposes liability for a breach of fiduciary duty. It provides that a fiduciary who breaches any responsibility, obligation, or duty imposed by Title I of ERISA will be personally liable to make good to the plan any losses resulting from the breach and to restore any profits he made through the use of plan assets. The statute also provides that the breaching fiduciary will be subject to such equitable or other remedial relief as the court deems appropriate. This may include the removal of the fiduciary. Further, a court may remove a fiduciary because of his involvement in one of the crimes enumerated in ERISA §411.[40] Under ERISA, no fiduciary will be liable for any breach of fiduciary duty where the breach was committed before the person became a fiduciary or after he ceased to be one.[41]

ERISA §410 prohibits the use of exculpatory agreements that purport to relieve a fiduciary from his statutory liability, other than a provision allocating responsibilities between trustees pursuant to ERISA §405(b)(1) or a provision relieving a trustee of responsibility for the acts or omissions of an investment manager pursuant to

§405(d). ERISA §410(b) provides, however, that this prohibition does not preclude a plan from purchasing insurance for its fiduciaries or itself to cover liability or losses arising from acts or omissions if the insurance permits recourse by the insurer against the fiduciary.[42] A fiduciary may also purchase insurance to cover liability "from and for his own account."[43] Further, an employer or employee organization may purchase insurance to cover potential liability of one or more persons who serve in a fiduciary capacity with regard to an employee benefit plan.[44]

Penalty Taxes Under the Internal Revenue Code

Code §4975 also imposes a set of sanctions on prohibited transactions. Where a party-in-interest (disqualified person) engages in a prohibited transaction, §4975(a) imposes a tax on the disqualified person equal to 5 percent of the "amount involved." If the transaction is not corrected within a statutory correction period (known as the "taxable period"), an additional penalty tax, equal to 100 percent of the amount involved, will be imposed.

The taxable period is the period beginning with the date on which the prohibited transaction occurred and ending on the earliest of:

(1) The date the IRS mails a notice of deficiency for the 5 percent tax;

(2) The date the 5 percent tax is assessed; or

(3) The date on which the prohibited transaction is completely corrected.[45]

Prohibited transactions must be reported to the IRS and the Department of Labor on the plan's annual 5500 series report. IRS Form 5330, which provides the basis for computing the amount involved and, hence, the amount of tax due, must also be filed with the IRS.

ERISA §411: Prohibition Against Certain Persons Holding Certain Positions

ERISA prohibits persons who are convicted of committing certain crimes from acting, for a specified period of time, as an administrator, fiduciary, officer, trustee, custodian, counsel, agent, or consultant to an employee benefit plan. The crimes include those involving controlled substances, murder, rape, kidnaping, perjury, assault with intent to kill, certain violations of the 1940 Investment Company Act, violations of any provision of ERISA, violations of §302 of the Labor-Management Relations Act of 1947, or the Labor-Management Reporting and Disclosure Act of 1959, and certain other crimes, as well as conspiracy or attempts to commit any of the enumerated crimes. The list also includes any crime in which an enumerated crime is an element of the offense.

The prohibition on holding office will be imposed during the five-year period after the conviction or after the end of imprisonment, whichever is later, unless, before the end of the period, the person's citizenship rights, which have been revoked as a result of the conviction, have been fully restored or the Board of Parole of the Department of Justice determines that the person's service will not be contrary to the purposes of Title I of ERISA. Anyone who intentionally violates ERISA §411 is subject to a fine of up to $10,000 or up to one year's imprisonment, or both.[46]

Bonding

ERISA §412 requires that every fiduciary of an employee benefit plan and every person who handles the funds or other property of such a plan (known for purposes of §412 as a "plan official") be bonded, except as provided in §412(a). Section 412(a)(1) exempts a plan from the bonding requirements where the only assets from which benefits are paid are the general assets of a union or an employer. In that case, the plan administrator, its officers, and its employees are exempt from the bonding rules. Furthermore, no bond is required of a fiduciary or of any director, officer, or employee of the fiduciary, if such fiduciary:

(1) Is a corporation organized and doing business under the laws of the United States or of any state;

(2) Is authorized under such laws to exercise trust powers or to conduct an insurance business;

(3) Is subject to supervision or examination by federal or state authority; and

(4) Has at all times a combined capital and surplus in excess

of such a minimum amount as may be established by regulations issued by the Secretary (of Labor), which amount shall be at least $1,000,000.[47]

This latter exception applies to a bank or other financial institution authorized to exercise trust powers where deposits are not guaranteed by the FDIC. The institution must meet the bonding requirements of state law; the Secretary of Labor will determine whether these particular state requirements are at least equivalent to those imposed on banks by federal law.[48]

Where bonding is required, the amount of the bond is to be fixed at the beginning of the plan's fiscal year.[49] It must be at least 10 percent of the amount of funds handled, but not less than $1,000 or more than $500,000.[50] However, after notice to interested parties, the Secretary may prescribe a bond in excess of the 10 percent and $500,000 limits.[51] ERISA §412(b) makes it unlawful for a plan official who must be bonded to "receive, handle, disburse, or otherwise exercise custody or control of any of the funds or other property of any employee benefit plan" without being properly bonded or to permit another to exercise such functions without proper bonding. ERISA §412(c) makes it unlawful to procure a bond from anyone in whom the plan has a "significant financial interest," whether direct or indirect.

ERISA §413: Statute of Limitations

ERISA §413 imposes a general statute of limitations on the commencement of any legal action relating to a breach of fiduciary duty under Title I. The limitations period is the earlier of:

(1) Six years after (i) the date of the last action which constituted a part of the breach or violation, or (ii) in the case of an omission, the latest date on which the fiduciary could have cured the breach or violation, or

(2) Three years after the earliest date (i) on which the plaintiff had actual knowledge of the breach or violation, or (ii) on which a report from which he could reasonably be expected to have obtained knowledge of such breach or violation was filed with the Secretary (of Labor);

In the case of fraud or concealment, legal action may be commenced no later than six years after the date of discovery of the breach or violation.

Administration and Enforcement

Part 5 of Title I of ERISA provides for both criminal and civil sanctions for violations of that Title. Civil actions may be brought by the Secretary of Labor, a participant, or a beneficiary. ERISA §504 grants the Secretary investigative authority to determine if there has been a violation of the Title.

ERISA Preemption

ERISA §514 preempts certain state laws that govern employee benefits plans to the extent that ERISA governs the matter. In general, preemption will not relieve a plan from its duty to comply with state banking, insurance, or securities laws.[52] The statute provides, however, that neither a covered employee benefit plan (other than one established primarily to provide health benefits), nor any trust of a covered plan, shall be deemed to be an insurance company, insurer, or bank for state insurance law purposes or for purposes of state laws regulating banks, trust companies, or investment companies.[53]

Notes

1. Under former Code §503.
2. Under Code §4975.
3. ERISA §3 (21).
4. It is not always clear what constitutes a "plan asset." For instance, when a plan invests in a limited partnership that owns real estate, is the plan asset the limited partnership interest or the underlying real property it owns? The Labor Department has promulgated regulations on the definition of "plan asset." See 29 C.F.R. §2510.3-101 *et seq.*
5. ERISA §3 (21) (A).
6. ERISA §405 (c) (1) (B).
7. Described in ERISA §3 (21) (A), discussed above.
8. ERISA §3 (21) (B).
9. *Id.*
10. *Id.*
11. Described in Code §736.
12. ERISA §401 (a).

13. ERISA §402 (a) (1).
14. ERISA §402 (a) (1).
15. Under ERISA §405.
16. ERISA §402 (c) (2).
17. ERISA §403 (a).
18. *Id.*
19. ERISA §404 (a) (1).
20. ERISA §§404 (a) (1) (A) and (B).
21. ERISA §404 (a) (1) (B).
22. ERISA §404 (a) (1) (C).
23. ERISA §404 (b).
24. ERISA §§404 (c) (1) and (2).
25. 29 C.F.R. §2550.404c *et seq.*
26. ERISA §404 (c) (1).
27. Except as allowed under ERISA §404 (b).
28. ERISA §§405 (a) (1)-(3).
29. ERISA §405 (b) (1) (B).
30. ERISA §405 (b) (1) (B).
31. *Id.*
32. ERISA §405 (b) (3) (B).
33. ERISA §405 (c) (2).
34. ERISA §405 (d) (1).
35. Contained in §3 (14) of Title I (the labor title) of ERISA and paralleled in Code §4975, where the term used is "disqualified person."
36. ERISA §§3 (14) (A)-(I).
37. ERISA §3 (14) (flush language).
38. ERISA §§406 (a) (1) (A)-(E).
39. ERISA §§408 (c) (1)-(3). The statute prevents "double dipping," i.e., no additional compensation for services can be paid to someone who already receives compensation from an employer, an association of employers, or a labor organization whose employees or members are covered by the plan except as reimbursement for expenses properly and actually incurred.
40. ERISA §409 (a).
41. ERISA §408 (b).
42. ERISA §410 (b) (1).
43. ERISA §410 (b) (2).
44. ERISA §410 (b) (3).
45. Code §§4975 (f) (2) (A)-(C).
46. ERISA §411 (b).
47. ERISA §§412 (a) (2) (A)-(D).
48. *Id.*
49. *Id.*
50. *Id.*
51. *Id.*
52. ERISA §514 (a) (2) (A).
53. ERISA §514 (a) (2) (B).

13

Plan Terminations

Single Employer Plan Terminations

When an employer decides it no longer desires to maintain the plan it has in place or if the plan becomes a severe financial burden, the employer may turn to a mechanism known as plan termination.

Title IV of ERISA provides that in the case of single employer and multiple employer plan terminations, certain benefits will be paid to the participants even where the plan lacks adequate assets to make such payments. Subject to certain limitations,[1] the Pension Benefit Guaranty Corporation guarantees the payment of all nonforfeitable benefits under defined benefit single employer plans covered by the termination insurance.[2] In return for paying certain benefits, the PBGC receives a lien on 30 percent of the employer's net worth from which the amounts paid out may be recouped.[3] Since a defined contribution plan provides individual accounts for each participant and benefits are based solely on the amount contributed to that account, a participant's benefit is always fully funded, and termination insurance is not required for these plans.[4]

Under ERISA §4041(a)(1), a defined benefit plan may be voluntarily terminated only in a "standard termination" or a "distress termination." In addition, the PBGC may initiate an involuntary plan termination, if the employer's financial condition demands such an action in order to inhibit further losses.[5] In a standard termination, all benefit liabilities, including those for nonguaranteed benefits, must also be met.[6]

For plan terminations for which a notice of intent to terminate was filed with the PBGC before January 1, 1986, standard and distress terminations were not the only forms of voluntary termination available. A voluntary termination could be completed at any time that certain procedural requirements (e.g., filing a notice of intent to terminate, satisfaction of PBGC sufficiency determination rules) were met.[7] When a plan terminated with insufficient assets, the employer became responsible to the PBGC for the insufficiency rather than having the termination discontinued.[8]

In such a termination, the PBGC's basic determination was whether the plan assets were sufficient to meet all plan obligations for basic benefits when due.[9] If the plan was clearly insufficient, the PBGC would issue a notice of inability to determine sufficiency to the administrator and would place the plan into trusteeship. If the plan was not clearly insufficient, the PBGC would notify the administrator and inform the administrator of the procedure for determining plan sufficiency.[10] The PBGC would subsequently issue a notice of sufficiency directing the administrator to close out the plan, unless the value of the plan assets was less than plan benefits in "priority categories 1 through 4," in which case the PBGC would issue a notice of inability to determine plan sufficiency and place the plan into trusteeship.

The Single-Employer Pension Plan Amendments Act of 1986 (SEPPAA), which applies to voluntary terminations initiated on or after January 1, 1986, changed the PBGC rules for single-employer plan terminations, insurance premiums, procedures, employer liability for unfunded benefits, enforcement, and related provisions.[11]

Standard Terminations

Under a SEPPAA standard termination, a plan administrator must provide a notice of intent to terminate to affected parties. This notice must be given at least 60 days and no more than 180 days before the proposed termination date.[12] Each affected party must receive notice either by hand delivery, by first class mail, or by courier service to his or her last known address.[13] The regulations define affected party as each participant, beneficiary of a deceased participant, alternate payee under a QDRO, or employee organization representing participants. The notice must set forth the name of the plan and the contributing sponsor, the sponsor's Employer Identification Number and the Plan Number, or a statement that the number does not exist, the name, address and telephone number of a person who may be contacted regarding the termination, a proposed termination date, a statement that if the termination is not completed, the administrator will notify affected parties, a statement that affected parties who are individuals will receive written notice of the benefits which they will receive, and, for retirees, a statement that periodic benefits will not be affected by the termination.[14]

A separate termination notice must be sent to the PBGC. ERISA §4041(b)(2) provides that a standard termination notice must be sent as soon as practicable after the date on which the notice of intent to terminate was sent to the affected parties. Regulations clarify, however, that the standard termination notice must be provided no later than 60 days after the proposed termination date.[15]

Before the 1987 Omnibus Budget Reconciliation Act, an employer was liable to participants in a terminated defined benefit plan to meet benefit commitments. Benefit commitments were defined as benefits guaranteed by the PBGC under ERISA §4022, benefits which would be guaranteed under ERISA §4022 but for the operation of §4022(b), and early retirement supplements or subsidies, and plant closing benefits for which a participant or beneficiary had satisfied all entitlement conditions before the termination date. OBRA 1987 increased this liability to the full amount of benefit liabilities.[16] Benefit liabilities are defined as those liabilities described under Code §401(a)(2), i.e., all benefits promised under the plan up to the date of plan termination (including contingent liabilities and benefits not protected under Code §411(d)(6)).

ERISA §4041(b)(2)(B) provides that the administrator must send a notice of full benefit liabilities, called the notice of plan liabilities, to each participant or beneficiary under the plan not later than the date the standard termination notice is sent to the PBGC. This notice must set forth the participant's full benefits under the plan.[17]

The notice must be sent to all persons who, as of the proposed termination date, are participants in the terminating plan and to all beneficiaries of deceased participants or alternate payees under a QDRO (and in the case of a spin-off termination, participants and beneficiaries in the ongoing plan).[18]

The content of the notice of benefit liabilities includes the name of the plan, the sponsor's EIN, the name, address and telephone number of a person to contact concerning the person's benefits, the proposed termination date, a statement that the benefit commitments given are only estimates but that benefits will not be less than that amount (the employer will be bound by the figure given in the notice of benefits), a statement, if applicable, that greater benefits may be paid if assets are adequate. The requirements apply to three different categories, (1) persons in pay status, (2) participants not in pay status whose benefit form and starting date are known, and (3) other participants not in pay status.[19]

In a standard termination, the PBGC does not have to take any action for the termination to become effective. The PBGC generally has 60 days[20] after the filing of a standard termination notice to issue a notice of noncompliance.[21] The 60 day period begins on the day following the filing of a standard termination notice and includes the 60th day. The PBGC may provide, in writing, an extension.[22]

If the PBGC does not issue a notice of noncompliance within the 60 day period, the plan administrator has 30 days to make a final distribution of plan assets.[23] If the administrator fails to make the final distribution because of an insufficiency of plan assets, the termination is nullified. A failure to distribute for any other reason nullifies the termination, unless the administrator makes a written request to the PBGC for an extension of time before the 30-day period expires.[24]

If the PBGC issues a notice of noncompliance, the termination process is stopped, and the plan is treated as an ongoing plan. Note that a notice of noncompliance may be appealed; the notice becomes effective when the period for appeals expires. The administrator must notify affected parties that the plan is not going to terminate.[25]

Distress Terminations

A distress termination is required when a plan has insufficient assets to meet benefit liabilities. In a distress termination, the employer is liable to the PBGC for all unfunded benefit liabilities as of the plan termination date along with reasonable interest from the termination date.[26] Four events may bring about a distress termination: (1) liquidation in bankruptcy,[27] (2) reorganization in bankruptcy,[28] (3) demonstration that, absent plan termination, the employer will be unable to continue in business, or (4) demonstration that solely as a result of employment of covered employees, the costs of providing coverage have become unreasonably burdensome.[29]

A notice of intent to terminate must be provided to the PBGC as well as affected parties.[30] This notice must provide the specific date on which the plan will be terminated and a statement that benefits under the plan are guaranteed by the PBGC. It must describe the guaranteed benefits and include a statement that participants and beneficiaries may receive benefits in excess of guaranteed benefits. The notice to retirees must state that the benefits may be reduced to guaranteed levels or below the guaranteed level.[31] The notice filed with the PBGC must give other information with respect to, among other things, premium payments, multiple employer plan status, and participants in pay status who are not receiving benefits.[32]

The PBGC must review the notice of intent to terminate in a distress termination and advise the administrator as to whether it satisfies the regulations.[33] If the PBGC decides that all criteria appear satisfied, it must notify the administrator in writing of the initial determination (which is subject to reversal after review of the distress termination notice).[34] If the notice of intent to terminate does not comply with the regulations, the PBGC will advise the administrator that the proposed termination is nullified and the plan is an ongoing plan. The decision may be appealed by the administrator; this stays any effects until after the appeal.[35]

In addition, a distress termination notice must be filed by the administrator with the PBGC within 60 days of the proposed termination date. It must contain proof of distress and various plan data that the PBGC may request.[36] Under certain circumstances, the PBGC may request participant data schedules be filed with the distress termination notice. However, the plan administrator may delay the submission of those schedules until 20 days after the PBGC has reviewed the distress termination notice and advised the administrator that the plan may terminate.[37]

The PBGC will determine whether the criteria for the distress termination have been met and, if they have been met, will notify the administrator that the participant data schedules must be filed.[38] If the administrator failed to properly issue the notice of intent to terminate or the distress termination notice, or if the distress criteria have not been met, the PBGC will notify the administrator of this determination and the basis of the determination and will advise him or her the termination is nullified and the plan is an ongoing plan. If a timely filed distress termination notice is incomplete, the PBGC will notify the administrator of the problem which must be corrected no later than the 60th day after the proposed termination date, or the 20th day after the date of the PBGC notice, whichever is later.[39] The PBGC determination may be appealed.[40] After receiving the participant data schedules, the PBGC will determine the degree to which the plan is insufficient and notify the administrator of this in writing.[41] Before making the final distribution of assets, the administrator must verify to the PBGC whether the plan is still able to pay benefits at the level determined by the PBGC.[42] The administrator will receive a final distribution notice from the PBGC and must make the final distribution of plan assets within 30 days of receiving that notice. Within 30 days of the final distribution, the administrator must file a post-distribution certification with the PBGC.[43]

Multiemployer Plan Terminations

The 1980 Multiemployer Pension Plan Amendments Act (MPPAA) removed multiemployer plans from the termination insurance system that governs single and multiple employer plans and substituted a system that imposes liability for certain unfunded vested benefits when an employer partially or totally withdraws from a multiemployer plan.[44] Under MPPAA, a multiemployer plan is one where more than one employer must make contributions to a plan that is maintained pursuant to a collective bargaining agreement.[45]

ERISA §4201(a) provides that a complete withdrawal has occurred either when there is a permanent cessation of the employer's contribution obligation or when, despite the fact that the employer literally still has an obligation to make contributions, e.g., under the collective bargaining agreement, the employer no longer has operations that are covered by the plan. ERISA §4204 also treats certain employer asset sales as a withdrawal, but creates an exception for arm's-length sales where the buyer assumes the seller's contribution obligation and the buyer either purchases a bond or places in escrow sufficient funds to cover the seller's contribution obligation for one year. This bond or escrow account must be maintained for five years after the asset sale.[46] It insures the plan should the buyer withdraw or default on its contribution obligation. For purposes of this rule, the seller's contribution history is attributed to the buyer.[47]

A "partial withdrawal" will also give rise to withdrawal liability. A partial withdrawal will occur when there is a 70 percent decline in the employer's "contribution base units" (CBUs), e.g., the units on which an employer's contribution obligation is calculated, such as work days) over a three-year period. The CBUs in this period are compared with the employer's average contribution obligation in its two highest years of the five years preceding the three-year period being tested.[48] The closing of an employer facility or the termination of a collective bargaining agreement can also give rise to partial withdrawal liability.[49] MPPAA contains various special rules for those industries that calculate partial withdrawals differently. Further, any multiemployer plan may choose among several methods of determining withdrawal liability.[50]

Under the "presumptive rule" of ERISA §4211(b)(3), annual changes in unfunded vested benefits (UVBs) are allocated ratably to employers based on each employer's share of UVBs during the current year and the immediately preceding four years, with a reduction of each employer's share of 5 percent for each passing year, i.e., 20-year amortization. Different rules apply to employers that were in the plan in plan years ending before April 29, 1980, and those that were not.[51] Further, under the presumptive rule, when an employer is unable to pay its share of UVBs, its share is reallocated to employers remaining in the plan.

Instead of using the presumptive rule, which will apply if the plan does not specify an alternative, a plan may use certain statutory alternative rules. Under the first alternative rule of ERISA §4211(c)(2), pre-1980 UVBs are allocated in the same manner as they are under the presumptive rule. Post-1980 UVBs are allocated to employers in a block, but not, however, on a year-by-year basis. Thus, this rule is less favorable to new employers entering the plan than the presumptive rule.[52] Under the second alternative method of §4211(c)(3), no distinction is made between pre- and post-1980 UVBs. Thus, this rule is even less favorable to new entrants than the first alternative, although it is comparatively easy to administer. A plan might wish to use the first or second alternative methods where attracting new employers is not a significant concern. The second alternative method is especially helpful where administrative costs are a significant issue.

The third alternative method is known as "the attributable

rule." As its name suggests, this rule attempts to trace each employer's obligation to the service performed by its employees under the plan. Where such service cannot be traced, each employer is allocated a share of this "unattributable liability." The attributable rule promotes fairness in dividing liability among employers, but is the most complex to administer.

Note that an employer's liability for a partial withdrawal is a proportionate share of the liability that it would have incurred had it totally withdrawn. When a partially withdrawing employer resumes its prior level of contributions, the statute provides that partial liability will be reduced ("abated") for subsequent years.[53] A *de minimis* rule allows small employers to escape partial withdrawal liability. Further, under ERISA §4210, a plan may adopt a "free look" rule, which allows an employer to enter the plan and withdraw within six years without incurring withdrawal liability. This rule has the effect of encouraging new employers to enter the plan. Under the 20-year cap of ERISA §4219, an employer's withdrawal liability obligation is limited to payments over 20 years unless a "mass withdrawal," as defined in §4219(c)(1)(D), took place. Other special restrictions on partial withdrawal liability apply for pre-April 28, 1980, partial withdrawals, insolvent employers, cases of liability of employers to multiple plans, and successive withdrawals.

Under MPPAA, when a withdrawal occurs, the plan sponsors must notify the employer within a reasonable time of the amount of liability and provide a schedule for its payment.[54] The employer may request a review of this determination before payments begin. Payments are made based on the number of contribution base units in the average year of the three highest years in the previous 10 years, multiplied by the employer's highest contribution rate within the 10 year period. The payments are made in equal annual installments and are subject to the 20-year cap.[55]

ERISA §4223 allows the employers in a multiemployer plan to create a "supertrust" that is exempt from tax under Code §501(c)(22). This trust will pay any liabilities accruing by statute that are not guaranteed by the PBGC. An example of such a liability might be the employers' shares of "unattributable liability" or liability that cannot be collected from a withdrawing employer because of the operation of one of the MPPAA rules limiting liability, such as the 20-year cap or the *de minimis* rule. The supertrust assesses participating employers a premium and is administered by a joint employer-union board of trustees. The supertrust's investments must be limited to certain government securities and time deposits. The bankruptcy of an employer could also be an event that could be insured by a supertrust. In addition to the supertrust, ERISA §4222 directs the PBGC to create a supplemental insurance fund to pay uncollectable liabilities of multiemployer plans. These devices are intended to provide greater economic stability for multiemployer plans. Arbitration for disputes between an employer and the plan sponsor over withdrawal liability is provided under ERISA §4221.

When a plan is experiencing financial difficulty, it will go into reorganization status under MPPAA. A plan will go into this status when its "vested benefits charge" exceeds the charges to its funding standard account under Code §412. The vested benefits charge is the amount necessary to amortize benefits in pay status over 10 years and any other vested benefits over 25 years.

A plan in reorganization must be funded more rapidly than under Code §412. Specifically, the plan must be funded annually to the extent of the vested benefits charge plus any increases in normal costs due to plan amendments while the plan was in reorganization. This amount is called the "minimum contribution requirement."[56]

The minimum contribution requirement is subject to two caps. Under one limit, imposed by ERISA §4243(d), the minimum contribution requirement cannot increase by more than 7 percent per year. This is known as the "107% safe-harbor." In addition, the minimum contribution requirement can be reduced by the "overburden credit" under ERISA §4244. The overburden credit applies to plans that are overburdened with increasing contribution obligations. It will apply where the number of pay status participants for the plan year exceeds the average number of participants in that year and the two preceding years and where the employer contribution rate is at least equal to the rate for the preceding year or for the year before reorganization.[57] The amount of the overburden credit is computed by taking half the monthly PBGC-guaranteed benefit for all pay status participants for the year and multiplying this by the "overburden factor." The overburden factor is the average number of participants who were in pay status for the plan's "base year" (for determining reorganization status) minus the average number of such participants for the base year and the two preceding years.[58] A plan in reorganization status can reduce benefits to the level guaranteed by the PBGC. Reorganization status is determined annually.

14

Stock Plans

While Congress has gradually whittled away the benefits available under qualified plans, in one area—plans that invest their assets in the stock of the sponsoring employer—the trend has been the other way, i.e., towards providing and expanding the tax incentives for establishing and maintaining such plans. This trend reflects Congress' desire to encourage employee ownership of businesses as well as a desire to provide a channel whereby employers may raise capital. Stock plans remain one of the areas of the tax law where full parity between corporate and unincorporated entities does not exist—because of their nature, only corporations can sponsor stock plans. In addition, because of state professional corporation laws which limit stock ownership to licensed professionals in the area of the corporation's business, these plans are generally not available to professional corporations. The discussion below examines the two most widely used stock plans: Employee Stock Ownership Plans (ESOPs) and Incentive Stock Options (ISOs). While ESOPs are subject to nondiscrimination rules (because they are Code §401(a) plans), ISOs are not. Because of this, ISOs are chiefly a technique of executive compensation.[1]

In addition to the two types of plans discussed here, the reader should also be aware of the existence of three other types of stock-related plans:

(1) *Stock Bonus Plans:* These plans are similar to profit-sharing plans except that contributions are not usually related to the employer's profitability, and plan assets are invested in the common stock of the sponsoring employer. A Code §401(k) cash-or-deferred

arrangement (discussed in Chapter 17) may be operated as part of a stock bonus plan, giving employees the right to choose between cash compensation and a contribution of cash to the plan.

(2) *Employee Stock Purchase Plans:* These plans are governed by Code §423. Their objective is to give employees a systematic manner of purchasing the common stock of the sponsoring employer.

(3) *Nonqualified Stock Options (NQSOs):* These are stock options that do not satisfy the requirements of Code §422A (relating to ISOs). If a NQSO has a readily ascertainable fair market value when it is granted (it usually does not) it will be taxed under Code §83, and the employer may take a corresponding compensation deduction, subject to the restriction that the employee's total compensation be reasonable compensation for services rendered.

In addition to the foregoing, individual account plans may invest freely in the employer's common stock (subject to the fiduciary duty rules of ERISA).[2] Defined benefit plans are limited in their ability to invest plan assets in employer common stock.

Employee Stock Ownership Plans (ESOPs)

ESOPs have gone through several incarnations in the Code. They antedated ERISA and were codified by that Act. TRASOPs (Tax Reduction Act stock ownership plans) were introduced by the 1975 Tax Reduction Act, and the rules for these plans were modified the next year by the 1976 Tax Reform Act. The 1979 Technical Corrections Act then changed the terminology in this area, renaming the conventional ESOP designed to obtain an investment tax credit for the sponsoring employer as a TRASOP.

Thus, after the 1979 Act, "TRASOP" referred to a plan that was designed to procure an investment tax credit for the employer, while "ESOP" came to mean a "leveraged employee stock ownership plan," a type of plan that finances its aquisition of employer securities with loans from a third party such as a bank, with the employer typically guaranteeing the loan. The Economic Recovery Tax Act again modified the ESOP/TRASOP rules, effectively eliminating the term "TRASOP" from the tax lexicon and substituting a tax credit that was based on the sponsoring employer's covered payroll rather than upon its investment in "§38 (investment tax-credit) property." The change was designed to make ESOPs more attractive to labor-intensive industries by gearing the tax credit to payroll rather than to capital investment. Thus, after ERTA, there are ESOPs (also sometimes referred to as "TCESOPs" due to the payroll-based tax credit) and "leveraged ESOPs."[3] ERTA also permitted employers to take an unlimited deduction for contributions of interest payments used to amortize the plan's loan in the case of a leveraged ESOP. The 1984 TRA again significantly amended the ESOP rules by freezing the payroll-based credit at .5 percent of payroll through 1987 (it was scheduled to increase to .75 percent in 1985) and by providing various tax incentives to encourage employee stock ownership.

The 1986 TRA repealed the ESOP credit effective for compensation paid or accrued after 1986. Because many TCESOPs which are still in existence have not either been terminated or amended and restated as leveraged ESOPs or some other type of qualified plans (many of these TCESOPs are being administered as frozen plans with wasting trusts), the TCESOP qualification rules are still significant for the ongoing qualification of such plans. Accordingly, they are discussed below.[4]

Tax Treatment of ESOPs

TCESOPs

The TCESOP rules appear in Code §409. Sections 409(a)(1)-(3) define a tax-credit employee stock ownership plan as a defined contribution plan that:

(1) Meets the requirements of Code §401(a);

(2) Is designed to invest primarily in "employer securities;" and

(3) Meets the requirements of Code §§409(b)-(h) and (o).

Section 409(l) defines "employer securities" for this purpose. In general, the term means common stock issued by the employer or by a corporation that is a member of the same controlled group of corporations as the employer and that is readily tradable on an established securities market.[5] Where the employer has no common stock that meets this definition, i.e., it is not traded on an established securities market, "employer securities" means common stock issued by the employer or by a corporation that is a member of the same controlled group as the employer and that has a combination of voting power and dividend rights equal to or in excess of:

(1) That class of common stock of the corporation having the greatest voting power; and

(2) That class of stock of the corporation having the greatest dividend rights.[6]

Noncallable preferred stock that is convertible, at a reasonable price, into stock which meets the requirements of §409(l)(3) constitutes employer securities. Code §409(l)(4) contains rules governing the application of the definition of employer securities to a controlled group of corporations.

As previously indicated, ESOPs must satisfy the Code §401(a) requirements, such as vesting, participation, and so on, which apply to defined contribution plans, in addition to meeting the requirements of Code §409.

The first specific qualification requirement relates to the required allocation of employer securities. For the plan year, a TCESOP must provide for an allocation of all employer securities transferred to it or purchased by it to the accounts of all participants who are entitled to share in the allocation.[7] The allocation must be made according to a participant's ratable share of the compensation of all participants for the plan year.[8] For purposes of allocating employer securities according to compensation, compensation in excess of $100,000 per year must be disregarded.[9] Notwithstanding the general rule, allocation of employer securities to participants' accounts to obtain the basic employee plan credit or the tax credit allowed under Code §41 may be suspended if the suspension is to allow the plan to satisfy the Code §415 limits on annual additions to the accounts of participants in defined contribution plans.[10]

A TCESOP participant must be completely vested in all employer securities allocated to his account at all times.[11] This rule is more restrictive than the Code §411 vesting rules or the §416 top-heavy vesting rules and, to that extent, supersedes the general vesting qualification requirements of §401(a).[12]

Code §409(d) restricts the distribution of employer securities from the plan. In general, the securities must stay in the plan for 84 months after they are allocated to a participant's account. Exceptions exist for distributions on account of death, disability, separation from service, plan termination and transfers of a participant pursuant to a buyout of all the assets of the sponsoring employer. In addition, there is an exception and with respect to the stock of a parent corporation that sells stock in a subsidiary which employs the participant, where the participant continues employment with the subsidiary. The 1986 TRA added a sentence to §409(d) making it clear that, where the §409(d) rules conflict with the minimum required distribution rules of Code §401(a)(9), the §409(d) rules govern.

A TCESOP must pass through to participants certain voting rights in the employer securities. Where the employer has a "registration-type" class of securities, each participant and beneficiary must be able to direct the plan as to how any employer securities allocated to his account are to be voted. Where the employer does not have a registration-type class of securities, the participants and beneficiaries must be entitled to direct the plan as to how shares allocated to their accounts are to be voted with regard to the approval or disapproval of any merger or consolidation, recapitalization, reclassification, liquidation, dissolution, sale of substantially all of the assets of a trade or business, or such similar transactions as the IRS may define in regulations. For this purpose, a "registration-type class of securities" is a class of securities for which SEC registration is required under the 1934 Securities Exchange Act and any class of securities that would have been required to be registered if not for the exception contained in §12(g)(2)(H) of the 1934 Act.[13]

The voting rights pass-through requirement can make a TCESOP useful in resisting a hostile takeover bid. By getting the voting rights into the hands of a broad cross-section of employees, it may become more difficult for an acquiring corporation to muster the votes necessary to effectuate a takeover. The 1986 TRA added a rule, effective October 22, 1986, which provides that an ESOP will satisfy the voting rights pass-through requirements if the plan permits each participant one vote with respect to each issue on which voting rights must be passed through and the plan's trustee votes the shares held by the plan accordingly.[14]

The rules concerning when a TCESOP must be established in order for an employer to make deductible contributions for the taxable year are slightly more liberal than the general Code §401(a) rules for qualified plans. To this extent, Code §409 provides a limited exception to the general §401(a) rule that, for an employer to claim a deduction for contributions, the plan must have been established prior to the close of the employer's taxable year for which the deduction is claimed.

A TCESOP may be established for a taxable year at any time up to the due date (including extensions) of the employer's tax return for the year.[15]

Securities that are placed in the plan must remain in the plan, and those allocated to participants' accounts must remain so allocated, even where the contribution was made to obtain an ESOP tax credit and the amount of that credit is later recaptured or redetermined.[16]

A TCESOP must provide for certain employee "put" options with respect to the employer securities in his account. A put option, basically, is the right of an individual (in this case, the employee) to require someone (in this case, the employer) to purchase his securities. A TCESOP will qualify if the employee has the right to demand a distribution of his benefits in the form of employer securities. Where the securities are not readily tradable on an established securities market, however, an employee put option that requires the employer to repurchase the securities from the employee under a fair valuation formula must be provided. A put option must be available for a statutory period of at least 60 days after the stock is distributed. If the option is not exercised in this period, it must again be provided for a period of at least 60 days during the following plan year.[17]

The 1986 TRA modified the ESOP rules to provide rules governing installment payments by the employer when the employer repurchases its securities under an employee put option. For a total distribution of employer securities that are put to the employer, the employer must pay the participant the option price in substantially equal installments over a period that does not exceed five years. This period must begin no more than 30 days after the put option is exercised. The employer must provide adequate security where installment payments are made. A total distribution is a distribution of the account balance under the plan within one taxable year of the recipient.[18] If the put option is exercised as part of an installment distribution, the employer must pay the option price within 30 days after the option is exercised. The 1986 TRA also extended the put option requirement to stock bonus plans.[19]

Notwithstanding the general rule that allows a participant to demand that his benefit be distributed in the form of employer securities, a TCESOP may, in certain cases, distribute the benefit in the form of cash. If the plan otherwise qualifies, but its charter or bylaws restrict the ownership of substantially all of its employer securities to employees, or to a trust described in Code §401(a), the plan may distribute the participant's benefit in the form of cash.

Plans maintained by banks that are prohibited by law from redeeming or purchasing their own securities may also distribute benefits in the form of cash where the plan so provides.[20]

When the tax credit was available, a TCESOP could have allowed the employer, for the year the plan was established, to withhold from required contributions the expenses incurred in establishing the plan so long as those expenses did not exceed the sum of:

(1) 10 percent of the first $100,000 that the employer was required to transfer to the plan to obtain the credit; and

(2) 5 percent of any amount in excess of $100,000 required to be transferred to obtain the credit.[21]

In addition, the employer could withhold from its annual contribution, or the plan could itself pay, certain plan administration expenses. For any taxable year, these amounts could not exceed the lesser of:

(1) The sum of—
(a) 10 percent of the first $100,000 of the dividends paid to the plan with respect to the stock of the employer during the plan year ending with or within the employer's taxable year; and
(b) 5 percent of such dividends in excess of $100,000; or

(2) $100,000.[22]

Under certain conditions, the employer could make conditional contributions to a TCESOP that could be returned. Such contributions could be made if:

(1) The contribution to the plan was conditioned on an IRS determination that the plan was qualified;

(2) An application for a favorable determination letter was made no later than 90 days after the date on which the employee plan credit was claimed; and

(3) The contribution was returned within one year after the date on which the IRS issued a notice to the employer that the plan did not qualify under Code § 409.[23]

The sponsor of a TCESOP recognized no gain or loss on the transfer of employer securities to the TCESOP to the extent the transfer was required to obtain the tax credit when it existed.[24]

Leveraged ESOPs

A leveraged ESOP is a defined contribution plan that is:

(1) A stock bonus plan qualified under Code §401(a) or a §401(a) money purchase plan or both; and

(2) Is designed to invest primarily in qualifying employer securities that meet the requirements of Code §409 relating to voting rights, payment of benefits in the form of employer securities, and employee put options.

This type of ESOP, in general, borrows money from an outside lender to finance its acquisition of employer securities. The employer then guarantees the loan. Leveraged ESOPs are exempt from the prohibited transaction rules with respect to their loans, provided certain conditions are met.

In general, for the ESOP loan to be exempt from the prohibited transaction rules:

(1) The plan must be primarily for the benefit of participants and beneficiaries;

(2) The loan must bear a reasonable interest rate;

(3) The collateral posted by the plan must consist solely of qualifying employer securities;

(4) The loan proceeds must be used within a specified period of time after their receipt to acquire qualifying employer securities or to repay the loan or a prior exempt loan;

(5) The loan must be without recourse against the ESOP, except to the extent of the employer securities acquired with the loan (or with the proceeds of an outstanding exempt loan to the extent that such loan is repaid with the loan proceeds), contributions made to meet the ESOP's obligation under the loan, and earnings attributable to such employer securities and contributions;

(6) The collateral must be released in installments over the loan term in accordance with a schedule that appears in the Code §4975 regulations;

(7) The loan must be a term loan, not a demand loan. A leveraged ESOP may not make loan payments other than from contributions made to enable it to meet its loan ob-

ligations and from the earnings on such contributions. (If there is a default on the loan, it may be accelerated, unless the loan is from a "disqualified person."[25] In this case, the default may be only to the extent of the plan's failure to meet the payment schedule); and

(8) The loan terms must be at least as favorable to the ESOP as the terms of a comparable loan resulting from an arm's-length transaction between independent parties; e.g., the interest rate may be variable.

The leveraged ESOP, unlike the TCESOP, does not have to satisfy the rules regarding allocation of securities to participants' accounts, the 84-month distribution rule, or the rules concerning the date of plan establishment. A leveraged ESOP that does not have a registration-type class of securities does not have to pass through voting rights under Code §409. (One that does is subject to the pass-through requirements of §409(e)). Pass-through is required for an employer that does not have a registration-type class of securities, however, where it is required of a Code §401(a) defined contribution plan that holds employer securities. Thus, pass-through is only required where:

(1) There is a major corporate issue at stake;

(2) The employer's stock is not publicly traded; and

(3) After acquiring the securities from the employer, more than 10 percent of the plan's assets are held in the form of employer securities.

A leveraged ESOP is subject to certain percentage restrictions on the amount of any outstanding issue of the employer stock that it may hold.

From a tax perspective, the leveraged ESOP allows the plan and the employer to use outside funds to finance the acquisition of employer securities. They thus are a potential source of capital for the employer. Further, as the loan is paid off, the employer may deduct both the principal and the interest. Normally only interest is deductible on a loan. For a leveraged ESOP, however, Code §404(a)(9) provides that, notwithstanding the general rules restricting the deductibility of employer contributions to qualified plans, principal amounts are deductible up to 25 percent of compensation paid or accrued during the taxable year by employees covered by the ESOP. Excess contributions may be carried forward and deducted in a future year if there is "room" (i.e., the difference between the maximum deductible amount and amounts contributed) under the 25 percent limit in that year.

Further, employer contributions to a leveraged ESOP that are used by the plan to pay interest on the loan by which it acquired qualifying employer securities are deductible in their entirety for the taxable year for which made, provided they are made no later than the due date of the employer's tax return for the taxable year, including any extension.[26]

The leveraged ESOP places the securities acquired with the third-party loan in a suspense account. As the loan principal is repaid from employer plan contributions, a pro rata amount of employer securities must be released from the suspense account and allocated to the accounts of participants based on relative compensation.

Distributions to participants and beneficiaries from a leveraged ESOP are eligible for lump sum distribution (forward averaging/capital gains) income tax treatment. Where the distribution is in the form of employer securities and qualifies for lump sum treatment, the net unrealized appreciation on the employer securities is excluded from the total taxable amount. Therefore, if the securities have appreciated in the plan, only the value of the securities at the time they were contributed to the trust (or purchased by the trust) is included in the employee's taxable income at the time of the distribution. The net unrealized appreciation is taxed as capital gains (long or short-term depending on the holding period) when the securities are sold or disposed of in a taxable transaction. If the distribution does not qualify for lump sum treatment, only the portion of the net unrealized appreciation attributable to employee contributions is unrecognized until subsequent sale or taxable disposition. Under a provision added by the 1986 TRA, the recipient of a lump-sum distribution that contains employer securities may elect to be taxed immediately on the appreciation element. If he does so, his basis in the stock will increase accordingly.[27]

Among the consequences of rolling over a lump sum distribution from an ESOP to an IRA is the fact that the employee cannot elect to take forward averaging/capital gain treatment on a distribution from an IRA. Further, in such cases, the unrealized gain attributable to appreciation on the employer securities will be included in its entirety in employee gross income when the securities are distributed from the IRA. Provisions in certain corporate charters restricting the ownership of corporate stock may also prevent the IRA from holding the securities. In this case, the employee will have to sell the stock and contribute the proceeds to the IRA or other qualfied recipient plan within the 60-day rollover period.

Special ESOP Incentives in the Code

The 1984 and 1986 Tax Reform Acts added a number of provisions that made ESOPs more attractive. These changes are examined below.

Code §1042: Tax-free Treatment on Certain Sales of Employer Securities to an ESOP

Enacted by the 1984 TRA, Code §1042 generally allows the proceeds from the sale of a business to be rolled over tax-free to an ESOP or to certain worker-owned cooperatives if the sales proceeds are reinvested in the securities of another business and, immediately after the sale, the ESOP owns 30 percent of the value of the employer securities. The seller must elect §1042 treatment for this tax-free rollover rule to apply.

To prevent the ESOP from being used as a conduit to sell employer stock, Congress added Code §4978, imposing an excise tax on the sponsoring employer of an ESOP that disposes of stock within three years of acquiring it under §1042 if:

(1) The total number of shares the ESOP holds after the §1042 sale is less than the total number of employer securities it held immediately before the sale; and,

(2) Except to the extent provided by regulations, the value of qualified securities held by the ESOP is less than 30 percent of the total value of all employer securities as of the date of the disposition.[28]

The tax is generally equal to 10 percent of the amount realized on the disposition. The amount realized, however, will not be deemed to exceed that portion allocable to qualified securities acquired in a sale to which Code §1042 applied (determined as if the §1042 securities were the first ones disposed of). For purposes of the excise tax, the amount realized on any distribution to an employee for less than fair market value is determined as if the security had been sold to the employee at fair market value.[29]

Certain dispositions are exempt from the excise tax. They are distributions made by reason of the employee's death, disability, separation from service (for at least a one-year break in service), and retirement after age 59½. Securities disposed of in a tax-free reorganization under Code §368(a)(1) are also exempt from the tax.[30]

Code §404(k): Deduction on Dividends Paid on ESOP Stock

The second 1984 TRA change was the enactment of Code §404(k). Section 404(k) supersedes the general rule that a payor corporation is not entitled to take a deduction for dividends paid. Section 404(k) allows the payor corporation to deduct dividends paid on stock held by an ESOP, provided:

(1) It is paid in cash;

(2) The dividend is paid to the plan and is distributed in cash to participants or their beneficiaries no later than 90 days after the close of the plan year in which it was paid; or

(3) The dividend with respect to employer securities is used to make payments on an ESOP loan described in Code §404(a). (In this latter case, the corporation may deduct the dividend in the taxable year in which it is used to repay the loan).

Code §404(k) provides that a dividend made under its provisions will not violate §§401, 409 (including the rules governing distributions) or 4975.

To be eligible for the dividend deduction under §404(k), the stock must be held by an ESOP maintained by the distributing corporation or a member of its affiliated group.

Code §133: Exemption From Income for Certain Interest Payments on ESOP Loans

The third 1984 TRA change was the enactment of Code §133. Section 133 allows banks, insurance companies, regulated investment companies, and other corporate commercial lenders to exclude from gross income 50 percent of the interest received on loans to finance an ESOP's acquisition of employer securities (known as a "securities acquisition loan").

For this purpose, a "securities acquisition loan" is:

(1) Any loan to a corporation or an ESOP to the extent that the proceeds are used to acquire employer securities for the plan, or are used to refinance such a loan, or

(2) Any loan to a corporation to the extent that, within 30 days, employer securities are transferred to the plan in an amount equal to the loan proceeds and the securities involved are allocated to participant accounts within one year after the loan is made (This latter provision does not apply where the loan's commitment period exceeds seven years).[31]

The following types of loans cannot qualify as "securities acquisition loans:"

(1) Loans between members of the same controlled group of corporations; or

(2) Any loan between an ESOP and (a) the employer of any employees covered by the plan, or (b) a member of a controlled group of corporations that includes the employer.

A loan, however, will not fail to qualify as a securities acquisition loan if it was not originated by the employer or a member of its controlled group. Any interest received on such a loan by the employer or a member of its controlled group, however, will not be excludable under Code § 133.[32]

Further, a loan will not fail to qualify as a "securities acquisition loan" merely because its proceeds are lent to any ESOP sponsored by the employer or a member of its controlled group if the loan includes:

(1) Repayment terms that are substantially similar to the terms of such loan by one of the qualified lending institutions described in Code § 133(a); or

(2) Repayment terms providing for more rapid principal or interest payments on such loans, provided (a) allocations of securities under the ESOP that are attributable to such repayment do not disproportionately inure to "highly compensated employees" within the meaning of Code § 414(q), and (b) the loan's total commitment period does not exceed seven years.[33]

Section 6061 of the Technical and Miscellaneous Revenue Act of 1988 modified a provision in the technical corrections portion of that Act by providing that, in the case of a refinancing of a securities acquisition loan that was made before October 22, 1986, the partial interest exclusion under § 133 is available for the greater of: (1) the term of the original securities acquisition loan, or (2) the amortization period used to determine the regular payments under the original securities acquisition loan. This provision is effective on November 10, 1988, TAMRA's enactment date.

Code § 2210: Relief From Estate Tax Liability on Certain Transfers of Employer Securities to an ESOP

The final incentive for ESOPs in the 1984 TRA was the addition of Code § 2210, which permits an ESOP that acquires employer securities from a decedent's estate to elect (together with the executor) to relieve the executor of the estate tax liability with respect to the securities. The ESOP will assume the estate tax liability generated by the securities.

The stock must be acquired from a decedent by an ESOP, pass from the decedent to an ESOP, or be transferred by the executor to the ESOP. The executor must elect the application of Code § 2210 and file:

(1) A written agreement between the executor and an authorized plan representative and;

(2) A written signed agreement between the executor and the plan sponsor consenting to the employer's guaranteeing the estate tax payments assumed by the ESOP (plus interest under § 6601) before the due date of the estate tax return (including extensions).[34]

When § 2210 is elected, the ESOP pays that portion of the estate tax that is attributable to the employer securities. This amount cannot exceed the value of the employer securities transferred to the plan, nor may it exceed the amount of estate tax due under Code § 2001, reduced by any applicable credits.[35]

If the estate has properly elected to defer estate tax payments under the installment provisions of Code § 6166 (relating to certain closely held business interests), the ESOP can gain the benefit of this treatment by filing an election before the due date of the estate tax return (including extensions). In determining the portion of the business interest that is eligible for the § 6601(j) "4% portion," the amount of tax imposed on the estate for which the executor is liable under Code §2001 and the amount of such tax assumed by the ESOP are aggregated.[36]

An ESOP's assumption of estate tax liability under Code §2210 will not be considered a prohibited transaction under Code §4975.[37]

Additional ESOP Incentives Added by the 1986 TRA

Code §401(a)(28): Diversification Election. The 1986 TRA also made substantial modifications to the ESOP rules. One of the most significant planning opportunities afforded by the 1986 TRA to ESOP participants was the addition of Code §401(a)(28), adding diversification requirements applicable to the accounts of certain participants.

After the 1986 TRA, ESOPs must offer partial diversification elections to their participants who satisfy certain age and participation requirements. These individuals are known as "qualified participants."

In general, a qualified participant is one who has participated in the ESOP for at least 10 years and has attained age 55. Such a participant must be allowed annually to direct diversification of up to 25 percent of his account balance (50 percent after the participant has attained age 60). This election must be provided within 90 days of the close of the plan year and must extend through a "qualified election period."

A "qualified election period" is defined as the five-plan-year period beginning with the plan year after the plan year in which the participant reached age 55 (or if later, the plan year following the plan year in which the individual first became a qualified participant).

An ESOP will satisfy the diversification election requirements if it either:

(1) Distributes to the participant the portion of his account with respect to which an election may be made; or

(2) Offers at least three investment options to each electing participant.

The ESOP diversification election rules apply to stock acquired after 1986.

Code §2057: Estate Tax Deduction for Proceeds From Sales of Employer Securities. Another ESOP amendment brought about by the 1986 TRA that will have a significant impact upon compensation planning is the enactment of Code §2057 providing an estate tax deduction equal to 50 percent of the proceeds of certain sales of employer securities to an ESOP.

To qualify for the deduction, the proceeds must be received by the estate before the due date (including extensions) for the decedent's estate tax return. Sales of stock from Code §401(a) qualified plans do not qualify for the §2057 deduction, nor do shares acquired pursuant to nonqualified stock options, incentive stock options, restricted stock options, qualified stock options, or stock acquired pursuant to a Code §423 employee stock purchase plan. To qualify for the deduction, the executor of the decedent's estate must file a written election described in §2057(d). The §2057 deduction expires, unless renewed, for sales occurring after 1991.

Code §4978A imposes an excise tax on certain early dispositions by an ESOP of stock it acquired under §2057. The tax applies where: (1) the ESOP disposes of the stock within three years of its acquisition; (2) the stock is disposed of before it is allocated to the accounts of participants and beneficiaries; or (3) where the assets received in a §2057 transaction are used to repay any part of a securities acquisition loan. The tax is equal to 30 percent of the amount realized on the disposition or, where the tax is triggered because the proceeds are used to pay a securities acquisition loan, 30 percent of the amount on the loan that was repaid. The tax may be paid by either the employer or the ESOP. It does not apply where the disposition was made in order to satisfy the diversification requirements of Code §401(a)(28).

Section 4978A does not apply to forced dispositions occurring by operation of state law, provided the securities are readily traded on an established securities market both at the time the ESOP acquired them and at the time it disposed of them. This rule applies to taxable dispositions ((1)-(3), above), occurring after February 26, 1987.

Incentive Stock Options (ISOs)

Incentive stock options (ISOs) are a form of executive compensation accorded tax-favored status by Code §422A. The ISO rules were enacted by ERTA and represent Congress' third attempt to confer tax benefits on a type of statutory stock option. Prior attempts were known as "restricted stock options" and "qualified stock options." Nonqualified stock options—those that do not meet the requirements of Code §422A—are taxed under Code §83. Section 422A does not contain the sort of qualification requirements typically found in §401(a)-type plans. As a result of this general lack of nondiscrimination rules, nonstatutory stock options lend themselves favorably for use as incentive compensation for a selected group of executives or other key personnel. The chief benefit of ISOs for employees is the fact that they are not taxed at the time of the option grant or exercise, and, for employers, the fact that they do not have to contribute cash to the plan. The chief detriment of ISOs is the fact that the employer may not take a compensation deduction with respect to ISO stock. After the 1986 TRA, ISOs lost some of their benefits relative to nonqualified options. The impact of these changes is examined in Chapter 16.

Under Code §422A, an employee will not recognize income upon the grant or exercise of an ISO, provided he does not transfer the stock within two years after the date of the option grant or one year after option exercise. The option must otherwise satisfy the requirements of §422A.[38]

The difference between the option price (the price the employee must pay for the stock) and the stock's fair market value on the date the employee exercises the option constitutes an item of tax preference and therefore will be subject to the 21 percent "alternative minimum tax" imposed by Code §55. In determining the stock's fair market value for alternative minimum tax purposes, restrictions other than restrictions which, by their terms, will never lapse are disregarded. This rule applies Code §83 principles and was intended to overturn the result of a 1982 Tax Court case.[39] The 1984 TRA provision not only applies for alternative minimum tax purposes, but also in determining whether the stock's fair market value at date of grant does not exceed the option price, as is required by §422A.[40]

For an option to qualify as an ISO, at all times beginning on the date of option grant and ending on the date which is three months prior to the date of option exercise, the optionee must have been an employee of the grantor corporation, a parent or subsidiary of such corporation, or a parent or subsidiary of a corporation issuing or assuming a stock option in a transaction to which the definition in Code §425(a) applies.[41] The three-month employment requirement is extended to one year in the case of an employee who is disabled.[42]

An ISO, in addition, must be granted to the employee for a reason "connected with his employment with a corporation." This means that the individual's employment with the employer, its parent, or subsidiary must have caused the option to be granted.[43]

An ISO must be granted pursuant to a plan that includes an aggregate number of shares which may be issued under options and describes the employees, or class of employees, eligible to receive options. The plan must be approved by the shareholders of the grantor corporation within 12 months prior to, or following, the date the corporation adopts the plan.[44]

Once the plan is approved, the ISO must be granted within 10 years of the date of plan adoption or the date the plan is approved by the corporation's shareholders, whichever is earlier.[45] The option, by its terms, must not be exercisable after 10 years have elapsed from the date of the grant.[46]

The option price must, in general, be not less than the stock's fair market value at the date of the grant.[47] For this purpose, a good faith attempt to satisfy the fair market value requirement will suffice.[48] Where the optionee is a 10 percent shareholder, the option price at the date of the grant must be at least 110 percent of the stock's fair market value, and the option must not be exercisable later than five years after the date of the grant.[49]

An ISO, by its terms, must not be transferable by the employee other than by will or the laws of descent and distribution, and must be exercisable, during the employee's lifetime, only by him.[50]

For options granted after 1986, under the plan's terms, the total fair market value (determined at the time the option is granted) of the stock for which ISOs are exercisable for the first time by an individual for a calendar year may not exceed $100,000. This limit applies to all ISOs sponsored by the corporation and its parent or subsidiary corporations.[51]

In addition to the required provisions, an ISO may elect to include certain provisions. For example, the plan may allow the employee to pay for the ISO stock with other stock of the grantor corporation, may confer upon the employee the right to receive other property at the time the ISO is exercised, and may include any other provision that is not inconsistent with §422A.[52]

If the employee does not dispose of the stock within two years of the date of the grant and within one year of option exercise, he will recognize no income on either date and, if he holds the stock for the requisite long-term capital gains holding period, he will recognize long-term capital gain income in the year of sale or disposition. In the event of a premature disposition, the employee will recognize ordinary compensation income equal to the excess, if any, of the stock's fair market value at that time over its adjusted basis, and the employer will be allowed an offsetting compensation deduction. That is, the option will be taxed as a nonqualified option under Code § 83 and the employee will not have a tax preference item. Ordinarily, as indicated above, the employer may not take a tax deduction with respect to the grant or exercise of an ISO. An exception to the general rule requiring recognition of income upon sale or disposition of the underlying stock exists where the employee transfers the shares in a bankruptcy, insolvency, or similar proceeding.[53]

ISOs allow an employer a cost effective way of providing an employee benefit—no current cash need be provided. From the employee's standpoint, the ISO gives him an opportunity to share in the profitability of the company. This "incentive" factor may also be helpful to the employer. On the downside, unless there is a premature disposition, the employer does not get a compensation deduction for the granting or exercise of an ISO.

Notes

1. Because of certain structural changes in the law made by the 1986 Tax Reform Act, many employers are establishing nonqualified stock option plans (NQSOs), which are more flexible than ISOs and which afford the employer a tax deduction for the contributed stock. NQSOs are taxed under Code § 83. See Chapter 16.
2. The fiduciary duty rules are discussed in Chapter 12.
3. These plans are also referred to as "PAYSOPs" although they are referred to as "TCESOPs" herein.
4. After the 1984 TRA, the ESOP tax credit was governed by former Code § 41(c)(1)(B). Under that provision, if a corporation established a plan which met the requirements of Code § 409 and under which no more than one-third of employer contributions for the taxable year were allocated to officers, 10% shareholders, or employees whose compensation for the year is more than twice the applicable Code § 415 dollar limit, the corporation was eligible for the tax credit. To obtain the credit, the employer had to agree to make transfers of employer securities to a TCESOP having a total value of not more than the "applicable percentage" of the amount of aggregate compensation paid or accrued to participants by the corporation during the taxable year. Further, the employer had to actually transfer such amounts no later

than 30 days after the due date (including extensions) for the employer's corporate income tax return for the year for which the plan was established. The applicable percentage when the credit ceased to be available was .5%. Before the 1984 TRA, an employer could put up additional amounts that, if matched by employee contributions, could entitle the employer to an additional matching credit. Code § 48(n), which provided this credit, was repealed by the 1984 TRA for taxable years beginning after 1983.

5. Code § 409(l)(1). The 1986 TRA added a provision stating that nonvoting common stock of an employer in the trade or business of newspaper publishing on a regular basis will constitute employer securities where: (1) The employer's stock is not publicly traded, and (2) The employer has a class of nonvoting common stock outstanding and the specific shares that the plan acquires have been issued and outstanding for at least 24 months. Code § 409(l)(5).
6. Code § 409(l)(2).
7. Code § 409(b)(1)(A).
8. Code § 409(b)(1)(B).
9. Code § 409(b)(2). Compensation, for this purpose, has the definition accorded that term by § 415(c)(3). See § 409(b)(3).
10. Code § 409(b)(4).
11. Code § 409(c).
12. Code § 409(k) contains a special rule whereby the withdrawal of amounts contributed by the employer to obtain the matching employee plan credit will not make plan benefits forfeitable. Nor shall such a withdrawal violate the "exclusive benefit" rule where the withdrawn amounts were not matched by employee contributions or were in excess of the § 415 limits. For this purpose, the matching employee plan credit means that credit as it existed before the 1984 TRA.
13. Code § 409(e)(4). A "leveraged ESOP" (discussed later in this chapter) must also pass through voting rights if the employer has a registration-type class of securities. Where this is not the case, the § 409(e) voting pass-through rules do not apply to a leveraged ESOP. Thus, leveraged ESOPs can be used to resist a corporate takeover either where the employer has a registration-type class of securities or where the plan, even if there is no registration-type class, provides for the pass-through of voting rights. Note, however, that when the trustee of an ESOP (or any other plan containing employer stock) must vote these shares without giving effect to the directions of participants and beneficiaries, the trustee is bound by ERISA's fiduciary duty rules and the "exclusive benefit" rule contained in Code § 401(a)(2), to vote those shares solely for the purpose of providing retirement benefits for participants and beneficiaries. This may mean that the trustee must vote to accept a tender offer even where the sponsoring employer wishes to resist the offer.
14. Code § 409(e)(5) as added by the 1986 TRA, P.L. 99-514, § 1854(b)(1)(A). Section 12(g) of the 1934 Securities Act requires the registration of securities if the issuer has assets of at least $1 million and 500 or more shareholders. Note that the voting rights pass-through requirement only applies to stock that has been allocated to an employee's plan account. See 354 T.M., *ESOPs*.
15. Code § 409(f). Unless an extension is obtained, IRS Form 1120, the em-

ployer's corporate income tax return, is due within 2½ months after the close of the employer's taxable year.

16. Code § 409(g).
17. Code § 409(h).
18. Code § 409(h)(5).
19. Code § 409(h)(6).
20. Code §§ 409(h)(2)–(3).
21. Code § 409(i)(1).
22. Code § 409(i)(2).
23. Code § 409(j).
24. Code § 409(m).
25. As defined in Code § 4975. See Chapter 12.
26. Code §§ 404(a)(9)(B), and 404(a)(6).
27. See the 1986 TRA, P.L. 99-514, § 1122(g), amending § 402(e)(4)(J).
28. Code § 4978(a).
29. Code § 4978(b).
30. Code § 4978(d).
31. Code § 133(b)(1)(B).
32. Code § 133(b)(2).
33. Code § 133(b)(3).
34. Code § 2210(a), (d), and (e).
35. Code § 2210(b).
36. Code § 2210(c).
37. Code § 2210(f).
38. Code § 422A(a)(1).
39. *Gresham v. Comm'r,* 79 T.C. 322 (1982), had previously applied non-§ 83 principles in valuing an ISO for alternative minimum tax purposes.
40. *See* Code § 422A(c).
41. Code § 422A(a)(2).
42. Code § 422A(c)(7). Disability, for this purpose, is defined in § 22(e)(3).
43. Code § 422A(b) (flush language).
44. Code § 422A(b)(1).
45. Code § 422A(b)(2).
46. Code § 422A(b)(3).
47. Code § 422A(b)(4).
48. Code § 422A(c)(1).
49. Code § 422A(c)(6).
50. Code § 422A(b)(5).
51. Code § 422A(b)(7). This rule was modified by the 1986 TRA to read as above. Under pre-1986 TRA law, for options granted after 1980 and before Dec. 31, 1986, the plan had to provide that the aggregate fair market value (determined at the date of the grant) of the stock for which any employee could be granted ISOs in any calendar year by the employer, its parent, or subsidiary, could not exceed $100,000 plus any unused carryover limit for such year. In general, if $100,000 exceeded the aggregate fair market value at the date of the grant for ISOs granted after 1980 and before 1987, half of such excess could be carried over to each of the three succeeding calendar years. In applying this rule, any options granted in the current year were

first treated as using up that year's $100,000 limit and then as using up any unused carryover for that year in the chronological order of the years in which such carryovers arose.

52. Code § 422A(c)(5).
53. Code § 422A(c)(3).

15

Salary Reduction Vehicles and Individual Retirement Arrangements

As the cost of providing benefits to employees under traditional qualified plans has increased, employers have been turning to salary reduction arrangements as a means by which employees may effectively "co-insure" their retirement benefits. The most popular and widely used tax-qualified salary reduction vehicle has been the Code §401(k) cash-or-deferred arrangement (CODA). Others include Simplified Employee Pensions under §408(k) (SEPs), tax-deferred annuities under §403(b) (TDAs), and certain plans for governmental employees and the employees of tax-exempt organizations (§457 plans). In addition, individual retirement arrangements such as individual retirement accounts (IRAs) and individual retirement annuities (IRANs) provide a means by which employees may save towards their retirement on a tax-favored basis.

In the 1986 Tax Reform Act, Congress made several changes in the rules affecting these types of plans. Among the most significant were the following:

(1) Tightening the "actual deferral percentage" (ADP) test for Code §401(k) plans to make it more difficult to direct benefits towards the highly paid;

(2) Making the employees of tax-exempt and governmental organizations ineligible to participate in §401(k) plans, other than certian preexisting plans which were grandfathered;

(3) Making SEPs available as a salary reduction vehicle for certain small employers;

(4) Expanding the scope of Code §§403(b) and 457;

(5) Imposing an annual cap on the aggregate amount of tax-free deferrals an employee may take by enacting Code §402(g);

(6) Imposing nondiscrimination rules on employee and employer matching contributions by enacting Code §401(m);

(7) Restricting the deductibility of IRA and IRAN contributions for taxpayers with annual adjusted gross incomes above certain levels; and

(8) Repealing the qualified voluntary employee contribution (QVEC) rules which had allowed employees to make deductible IRA contributions to certain types of qualified plans.

In all, Congress attempted to impose stricter nondiscrimination standards on salary reduction arrangements in view of their wider use to bring them more into line with the qualified plan rules and to more effectively coordinate the Code provisions dealing with salary reduction. As a result, the salary reduction tax environment is vastly different after the 1986 TRA than before.

Chapter 7 examined the Code §401(m) employee and matching contribution rules and the §402(g) dollar limit on annual deferrals ((4) and (5), above) as well as the QVEC rules ((8), above), so these will only be mentioned in passing here. This chapter examines the types of salary reduction vehicles that are available to employers and employees on a tax-favored basis and the rules that govern them.

Code §401(k): Cash-or-Deferred Arrangements (CODAs)

"Cash-or-deferred arrangements" (CODAs) under Code §401(k) were given tax-favored status by the 1978 Revenue Act. In general, a CODA may be established as part of a profit-sharing or stock bonus plan.[1]

To qualify as a CODA, the plan must be an arrangement under

integration may not be taken into account in determining whether the ADP tests are met for a salary reduction SEP (discussed below).

A SEP must permit withdrawals of employer contributions by employees; the employer contribution must not be premised upon an employee's leaving these amounts in the SEP.[22] Contributions to a SEP must be made pursuant to a written allocation formula.[23]

The limit on annual additions to a SEP is the applicable Code §415 defined contribution plan dollar limit, or 15 percent of the employee's compensation from the employer included in gross income for the employer's taxable year (determined without regard to the SEP contribution), whichever is less.[24]

The 1986 TRA allowed SEPs of certain small employers to be used as salary reduction vehicles. Such plans are called "SARSEPs." An employer can only maintain a SARSEP if at no time during the preceding year it had more than 25 employees and if 50 percent or more of its employees elect salary reduction.[25] For purposes of the rule limiting these plans to employers with 25 or fewer employees, only employees eligible to benefit under the SEP are counted.

The 1986 Act subjected SARSEP deferrals to the 125/200 percent ADP rules. These rules are somewhat more stringent when applied to a SARSEP than to a CODA, however. In a CODA, the tests are applied to the average of the two employee groups. In a SARSEP no individual highly compensated employee can make salary reduction deferrals for the year in excess of the applicable limitations when applied to eligible nonhighly compensated employees as a group. In addition to incurring an income tax, amounts withdrawn from a SARSEP before the employer can test it for discrimination are also subject to the 10 percent tax on early distributions of Code §72(t).

Elective deferrals under a SARSEP are subject to the §402(g) $7,000 (as adjusted for inflation) annual dollar limit on elective deferrals discussed in Chapter 7.

The SEP amendments made by the 1986 TRA apply to years beginning after 1986.

Code §403(b): Tax-Deferred Annuities (TDAs)

Code §403(b) provides tax-favored status for certain annuity-type retirement plans for the benefit of employees of tax-exempt

Code §501(c)(3) organizations and public schools. Employer contributions to fund TDAs for employees are excludable from gross income up to a statutory "exclusion allowance." An employee's rights under the contract must be nonforfeitable, except for a failure to pay future premiums.[26] When payments are made under the annuity contract, the employee is taxed under Code §72.[27]

In general, the exclusion allowance for an employee for a taxable year is the excess, if any, of the amount determined by multiplying 20 percent of his or her includable compensation by the number of years of service *over* the total amount contributed by the employer for the annuity contract that was excludable from the employee's income for any prior taxable year.[28] Includable compensation, for this purpose, is compensation from the employer for the year that is includable in employee gross income, except for non-U.S. source income.[29] Employees are credited with a year of service for each full year during which the individual was a full-time employee and with partial years of service for parts of a year during which the individual was a full-time employee or for full years during which the individual was a part-time employee.[30]

Example: Employee A has $10,000 of includable compensation for the year and two years of service. The employer has made $1,000 in contributions to annuity contracts on behalf of A that were excludable in a prior taxable year. The employer contributes $4,000 to an annuity for A for the current taxable year. Under the general exclusion allowance rule, $3,000 of this amount is excludable, computed as follows:

$$\$10{,}000 \times .20 \times 2 = \$4{,}000;$$
$$\$4{,}000 - \$1{,}000 = \$3{,}000.$$

An employee may elect, instead of the general exclusion allowance described above, to have his exclusion allowance determined under the Code §415 rules for defined contribution plans.[31]

For purposes of Code §403(b), all years of service by ordained ministers or lay persons as employees of churches, or conventions or associations of churches, are treated as service for a single employer.[32] Section 403(b) provides a floor under which the exclusion allowance of these individuals may not fall, known as the "alternative exclusion allowance." The alternative allowance provides that the general exclusion allowance for an employee who is an ordained minister or lay person employed by a church, association of churches, or convention of churches shall not be less than the lesser of (1) $3,000; or (2) the includable compensation of such individual.[33]

This rule, however, does not apply to any taxable year for which such an individual had adjusted gross income in excess of $17,000. For foreign missionaries, includable compensation includes any amount contributed for the year by a church or convention or association of churches with respect to the individual.

Code § 403(b) provides the rollover rules for distributions from TDAs.[34] In general, if any portion of the balance to the credit of an employee in a TDA contract is paid to him and the employee transfers any portion of this amount to an individual retirement account or an individual retirement annuity and, in the case of a distribution of property other than money, the amount transferred consists of the property distributed, the distribution (to the extent so transferred) is not includable in the recipient's gross income in the year the distribution was paid. The statute provides that rules similar to the general rollover rules will apply to rollovers involving TDAs.

For plan years beginning after 1988, in a highly significant change designed to equalize the tax treatment afforded TDAs and that afforded § 401(a) qualified plans, the 1986 TRA applied the full array of nondiscrimination rules applicable to § 401(a) plans to TDAs, including the limit on compensation to be taken into account in determining benefits, the employee leasing rules, and the minimum participation rules. To ease the transition to the revised rules, the Technical and Miscellaneous Revenue Act of 1988 (TAMRA), for plan years beginning after 1988 and before 1992, allowed employers to perform the nondiscrimination tests based on a statistically valid cross-section of employees.

Note also that, after the 1986 TRA, tax-exempt and governmental entities cannot establish new CODAs. Thus, TDAs and Code § 457 plans will become increasingly attractive deferred compensation vehicles for these types of entities.

The 1986 TRA imposed a $9,500 annual limit on deferrals under TDAs. This limit is greater than the regular Code § 402(g) dollar limit for CODAs and SEPs as enacted by the 1986 Act.[35] Further, under a special catch-up rule, this limit is increased by the lesser of:

(1) $3,000;

(2) $15,000 reduced by amounts not included in income in prior taxable years under this rule; or

(3) The excess of $5,000 times the number of years of service of the employee with the organization sponsoring the annuity over employer contributions made for the employee by the organization for all prior taxable years.[36]

Where a TDA program provides for elective deferrals, that portion of the program is subject to a special nondiscrimination rule added by the 1986 TRA. Under this rule, the TDA will be considered discriminatory with respect to elective deferrals unless the opportunity to make such deferrals is available to all employees of the entity sponsoring the TDA program. Elective deferrals consist of all amounts made pursuant to a salary reduction agreement with the employer to the extent these contributions are excludable from the employee's gross income.

Code §457 Plans

For taxable years beginning before 1989, Code §457 applied only to the deferred compensation plans of state and local governments. The 1986 TRA, effective generally for taxable years beginning after 1988, expanded the scope of §457 to include the deferred compensation plans of tax-exempt organizations and expanded its requirements.

Under §457, in the case of any participant in an "eligible deferred compensation plan," any amount deferred and any income thereon will only be taxed to the participant in the taxable year in which such amounts are paid or otherwise made available to the participant or the participant's beneficiary.[37]

Section 457 plans are subject to a limit of $7,500 per year on employee salary reduction deferrals. This amount is reduced dollar for dollar by any CODA, SARSEP, or TDA deferral made by the employee for the year. The penalty imposed on an employee who exceeds this limit is that his plan benefit is taxed to him immediately—as if it were provided under a funded nonqualified deferred compensation arrangement.

To be an "eligible deferred compensation plan," the plan must be established by an "eligible employer."[38] Eligible employers are states, subdivisions of states, instrumentalities or political subdivisions of a state, and any other entity other than a governmental unit that is exempt from federal income tax.[39]

A plan, to qualify under §457, must only admit to participation individuals who perform service for the employer.[40] In general, the plan must provide that the maximum amount which may be deferred for a taxable year may not exceed the lesser of $7,500 or 33⅓ percent of the participant's "includable compensation."[41] A §457 plan, notwithstanding the above limit, may provide that, for one or more of a participant's last three taxable years ending before he attains normal retirement age under the plan, the usual $7,500/33⅓ percent ceiling will be the lesser of:

(1) $15,000; or

(2) The sum of—
(a) the applicable ceiling under the regular rule, above, and
(b) so much of the applicable ceiling under the regular rule for past taxable years as had not been used up by the participant in such prior years.[42]

To qualify under §457, a plan must provide that compensation will be deferred for a calendar month only if an agreement providing for the deferral had been entered into before the beginning of the month.[43]

A §457 plan must also satisfy certain minimum distribution requirements. These rules, in general, apply principles similar to the minimum distribution rules applicable to qualified plans of §401(a)(9). Further, amounts may not be made available from a §457 plan earlier than: (1) the calendar year in which the participant reaches age 70½, (2) when the participant separates from the employer's service; or (3) when the participant has an unforeseeable emergency.[44]

A rule that required that at least two-thirds of a participant's benefit be payable during the participant's lifetime was repealed by TAMRA.[45]

Where a plan fails to qualify under §457, Code §83 principles (taxation when there is no substantial risk of forfeiture) will govern the timing of the employee's receipt of gross income and Code §72 principles will govern the amount.[46]

Section 457 does not apply to a §401(a) plan, a §403 annuity plan (including a TDA), property that is §83 property, or property transferred to a trust for a nonqualified deferred compensation plan to which §402(b) applies.[47]

Individual Retirement Arrangements: IRAs and IRANs

Individual retirement accounts and individual retirement annuities are collectively referred to as individual retirement arrangements. For ease of reference, however, unless otherwise specified, "IRA," as used herein, refers to an individual retirement account and "IRAN" to an individual retirement annuity. Before the 1984 TRA, there were also individual retirement bonds (federal government bonds set up to parallel the IRA provisions), but these provisions, together with the qualified bond purchase plan rules of Code §405 were repealed by that Act.

Code §408 governs the qualification requirements for IRAs and IRANs, while §219 governs the deductibility of employee contributions to these plans.

Section 408(a) provides that an individual retirement account is a trust organized or created in the United States for the exclusive benefit of an individual or his beneficiaries which satisfies certain criteria. Except for rollover contributions, the IRA must provide that no contribution will be accepted for a taxable year in excess of $2,000 on behalf of any individual.[48] The trustee must be a bank or such other person that demonstrates to the IRS' satisfaction that it is capable of administering IRAs in accordance with §408.[49] No part of an IRA may be invested in insurance contracts (although, of course, an IRAN may invest in annuities).[50] The interest of the IRA owner in his account must be nonforfeitable at all times.[51] The assets of the IRA must not be commingled with any other property except in a common trust fund or a common investment fund.[52] Finally, an IRA must provide for mandatory distributions under principles similar to those employed for qualified plans in Code §401(a)(9).[53]

An IRAN is an annuity contract or an endowment contract issued by an insurance company that meets certain requirements. The contract must not be transferable by the owner.[54] Under the contract, the premiums must not be fixed, the annual premium must not exceed $2,000, and any refund of premiums must be applied, before the close of the calendar year following the year of the refund, toward the payment of future premiums or the purchase of additional benefits.[55] The owner's entire interest must be nonforfeitable.[56] As with IRAs, §401(a)(9) principles apply to distributions from IRANs.[57]

In addition to the traditional type of individually-established IRA, under §408(c), employers and employee associations may establish IRAs for the benefit of employees. These IRAs must satisfy the general qualification requirements of §408(a) and must provide for separate accounting for the interests of each employee or member, or spouse thereof.[58]

In general, IRA distributions are includable in the recipient's gross income in the taxable year in which they are paid.[59] The recipient's basis in his account is always zero.[60] Distributions from IRANs are taxed under Code §72, with the recipient's investment in the contract deemed to be zero.[61]

IRAs, in addition to receiving Code §219 contributions, may receive taxfree rollovers from other qualified plans, provided certain requirements described in §§402(a)(5), 402(a)(7), 403(a)(4), or 403(b)(8) are met, as well as from certain other IRAs or IRANs. Such amounts will not be taxed until they are distributed from the IRA or IRAN. Lump-sum distributions from IRAs or IRANs, however, are not eligible for forward averaging/capital gains treatment. With respect to amounts distributed from other IRAs or IRANs, to receive taxfree treatment, the amount received must be recontributed, in whole or in part, within 60 days after the payment or distribution.[62]

In the case of a distribution of the entire amount received from a Code §401(a) plan or a §403(a) annuity plan, an IRA or IRAN can shield the distribution from tax by acting as a "conduit" IRA (or IRAN).[63] To receive the taxfree treatment where the conduit IRA is used, the entire amount must be paid into another §401(a) plan or §403(a) annuity plan no later than 60 days after the initial distribution was made, together with any earnings thereon.[64] An IRA or IRAN can also shield a rollover contribution from tax where the entire amount received (including money or other property) represents the entire interest in an IRA or IRAN, no amount is attributable to any source other than a rollover contribution from a §403(b) tax-deferred annuity plan, and the entire amount is rolled over to another §403(b) annuity within 60 days after the initial payment or distribution from the §403(b) plan.[65] An individual can only take one tax free rollover per year under these provisions.[66] The rollover rules do not apply to inherited IRAs or IRANs.[67]

Code §408(d)(4) provides an exception to the general rule of taxation for certain excess contributions returned from the IRA or IRAN before the due date of the taxpayer's return for the year. A deduction must not have been claimed for the excess contributions.

The rule allowing for such correcting distributions with respect to excess contributions also applies to SEPs.[68] The transfer of an interest in an IRA or IRAN incident to a divorce decree is not considered a taxable distribution and, after the transfer, the IRA or IRAN is considered to be maintained for the recipient former spouse.[69]

In general, like a qualified plan, an IRA or IRAN is exempt from federal income tax.[70] Where the IRA and the employee engage in a prohibited transaction within the meaning of Code §4975, however, the IRA is disqualified and the entire account is deemed to be distributed to the employee as of the first day of the taxable year in which the prohibited transaction took place.[71] Disqualification also results when the employee borrows any money from, or by use of, an IRAN.[72] Where the individual for whom an IRA is maintained pledges a portion of the IRA for a loan, the amount pledged is deemed distributed in that taxable year.[73] Further, where the assets of an IRA are used to purchase an endowment contract, any amounts under such contract that are attributable to life, health, or accident insurance are deemed to be distributed.[74]

Premature distributions from IRAs and IRANs are subject to the Code §72(t) 10 percent penalty tax.[75]

IRA contributions must be made in cash to be deductible. Rollover contributions, which are not deductible, but are excludable from gross income, may be made in the property distributed. Alternatively, the distributed property may be sold and the proceeds rolled over, provided the other rollover requirements are satisfied.

The basic annual deductible limit for IRA contributions is the lesser of $2,000 or 100 percent of compensation included in the individual's gross income for the taxable year.[76] Items of passive investment income, such as rents and royalties, cannot be counted in determining an individual's compensation for this purpose.

Where an employee's spouse has no earned income for a taxable year, the employee may make deductible contributions to a "spousal IRA." A spousal IRA is a regular IRA with two subaccounts, one for each spouse. For a spousal IRA, the maximum annual deductible contribution is the lesser of $2,250 or 100 percent of compensation.[77] The amounts may be allocated between the subaccounts in any manner the individual chooses, except that no more than $2,000 per year may be allocated to any subaccount. The spousal IRA deduction is only available where the married couple files a joint federal income tax return for the year for which the spousal IRA deduction is claimed.[78] In general, if both spouses have compensation income, they may not establish a spousal IRA for the year (except that certain spouses with *de minimis* compensation may elect to be treated as having no compensation for the year). Rather, both spouses will be eligible to make deductible contributions to a regular IRA to the extent allowed under the general individual limit. This can produce a deduction of up to $4,000 per year per couple.

ERTA introduced the concept of IRAs for divorced individuals based on the qualified alimony received by the divorced spouse for the taxable year. The measure was intended to enable divorced women to provide for their retirement savings at a time they might lack compensation income because they were involved in training to reenter the work force. Under these rules, all qualifying alimony is considered compensation for IRA purposes and the alimony recipient may make deductible contributions up to the usual IRA limits for the taxable year.

Note that, on IRS Form 1040, the IRA contribution is deducted above the line, *i.e.*, it is treated as an exclusion that is subtracted from gross income in arriving at adjusted gross income. It is not reported as a miscellaneous deduction on Schedule A. This has the effect of allowing an individual to take the full allowance for the IRA deduction even where he does not itemize deductions on his tax return. It also has the effect of reducing adjusted gross income which, in turn, reduces the threshold deductible limit for such partially deductible items as the Code §213 medical expense deduction—which is based on adjusted gross income for the taxable year.

ERTA also prohibited IRAs from investing their assets in "collectibles" such as stamps, rare coins, and so forth.[79] This change was enacted to force IRAs to invest in more actively-traded assets to promote capital formation in the economy. No deduction is allowed to an individual for a contribution to an "inherited IRA," e.g., one acquired through a bequest. An individual cannot make deductible IRA contributions after he has attained age 70½, if this age is attained before the close of the taxable year for which the deduction is claimed.[80] IRA contributions, to be deductible for an employee's taxable year, must have been made prior to the due date for filing the individual's federal income tax return for the year for which the deduction is claimed.

The 1986 TRA limited the deductibility of IRA contributions for certain "active participants" in qualified plans. After the 1986

TRA, if an employee (or the employee's spouse) is a participant for the year in a qualified employer plan, their otherwise allowable IRA deduction (the lesser of $2,000 or 100 percent of compensation for an individual, the lesser of 100 percent or $2,250 for a spousal IRA) will be reduced. For single individuals, the phase-out begins at $25,000 of adjusted gross income and reduces the allowable deduction by 20 cents for every dollar of adjusted gross income in excess of this amount, to the point where the ability to make deductible IRA contributions is fully phased out at $35,000. For married individuals, the phase-out begins at $40,000 of combined adjusted gross income and phases out 20 cents on the dollar to the point where it is fully phased out at $50,000.

The Technical and Miscellaneous Revenue Act of 1988, to remove an incentive for married taxpayers to file separate returns that existed under prior law, added Code §219(g)(4). That paragraph provides that, in computing the allowable IRA deduction for a married taxpayer, if the taxpayer and his or her spouse lived together at any time during the year, the active participant status of both spouses is to be considered in determining the deductibility of IRA contributions.

This provision, however, treats individuals who did not live with their spouse at any time during the year and who filed separately as unmarried for purposes of computing the IRA deduction limit. Code §219(g)(4) is effective generally for taxable years beginning after 1987, except that a taxpayer may elect to have it apply to any taxable year beginning in 1987.

Under Code §408(o), an individual who makes a nondeductible IRA contribution for the year, either because of the application of the adjusted gross income limit or by electing to treat an otherwise deductible contribution as nondeductible, must provide certain required information on the taxpayer's tax return for the year in question. The information that may be required includes, but is not limited to: (1) the amount of designated nondeductible contributions for the taxable year; (2) the amount of distributions from individual retirement plans for the taxable year; (3) the aggregate amount of designated nondeductible contributions for all preceding taxable years which have not been withdrawn; and (4) the aggregate balance of all IRAs of the individual as of the close of the calendar year with or within which the taxable year ends.

Under these rules, an individual who overstates the amount of designated nondeductible contributions for a year is subject to a $100 penalty for each overstatement unless the individual can show that there was reasonable cause for the overstatement. No separate penalty, however, was provided in the 1986 TRA for a failure to file the applicable form.

Effective for years beginning after 1988, TAMRA remedied this defect by adding to Code §6693(b) a $50 penalty for each failure to file the required information, unless the taxpayer can show that the failure was for reasonable cause. To take account of non-calendar year taxpayers, the 1988 Act provided that the required information includes the aggregate balance of all IRAs of the taxpayer as of the close of the calendar year in which the taxpayer's taxable year begins (rather than the calendar year with or within which the taxable year ends).

Notes

1. Code §401(k)(1). Pre-ERISA money purchase plans and plans of rural electric cooperatives may also contain a §401(k) cash-or-deferred feature.
2. Code §401(k)(2).
3. Within the meaning of Code §409(d)(2).
4. Within the meaning of Code §409(d)(3).
5. Code §401(k)(2)(B)(i). For plan years beginning before 1989, salary reduction deferrals may not be distributed to participants or beneficiaries earlier than retirement, death, disability, separation from service, hardship, or the attainment of age 59½.
6. Code §401(k)(2)(B)(ii) and (C).
7. Code §401(k)(2)(D).
8. Code §401(k)(4)(A).
9. Before the 1984 TRA, a CODA could qualify if it failed to meet the "actual deferral percentage" tests (discussed below), provided it was nondiscriminatory within the meaning of Code §401(a)(4). Since §401(a)(5) permits §401(a) plans to be integrated with Social Security, this allowed CODAs to have Social Security integration if §401(a)(4) was not violated. This provision was repealed by the 1984 TRA, effective generally for plan years beginning after 1984. After the TRA, the actual deferral percentage tests became the exclusive tests for determining whether a CODA discriminates.
10. Code §401(k)(3)(A)(ii). Under pre-1986 TRA law, a CODA would pass the actual deferral percentage tests if the actual deferral percentage of the top third did not exceed the actual deferral percentage of the bottom two-thirds by more than 150%. Alternatively, the CODA would qualify if the actual deferral percentage of the top third did not exceed that of the bottom two-thirds by more than 250%, provided the spread between the deferral percentage of the top third and the bottom two-thirds did not exceed 3 percentage points.
11. Code §401(k)(3)(A) (flush language).
12. See (former) Prop. Treas. Regs. §1.401(k)-1.
13. Code §401(a)(8).

14. Code § 401(a)(8)(D).
15. Section 4979 applies to excess deferrals under CODAs, tax-deferred annuities under § 403(b), salary reduction SEPs (SARSEPs) and certain plans described in § 501(c)(18).
16. Code § 408(k)(1)(A).
17. Code § 408(k)(1)(B).
18. Code § 408(k)(2).
19. Code § 408(k)(3)(A).
20. Code § 408(k)(3)(B).
21. Code § 408(k)(3)(C)(i).
22. Code § 408(k)(4).
23. Code § 408(k)(5).
24. Code § 219(b)(2).
25. Code § 408(k)(6).
26. Code § 403(b)(1).
27. *Id.*
28. Code § 403(b)(2)(A).
29. Code § 403(b)(3).
30. Code § 403(b)(4).
31. Code § 403(b)(2)(B).
32. Code § 403(b)(2)(C).
33. Code § 403(b)(3)(D).
34. Code § 403(b)(8).
35. Code § 402(g)(4).
36. Code § 402(g)(8).
37. Code § 457(a).
38. Code § 457(b).
39. Code § 457(e)(1). In Notice 88-68, 1988-26 I.R.B. 5, the IRS announced that § 457 did not apply to bona fide vacation leave, sick leave, compensatory time, severance pay, disability pay, and death benefit plans. In Notice 88-98, 1988-35 I.R.B. 26, the IRS announced that § 457 does not apply to compensation deferred under a written, nonqualified, nonelective deferred compensation plan that was in existence on Dec. 31, 1987, and that is maintained pursuant to one or more collective bargaining agreements, until the earlier of: (1) the effective date of any material modification of such nonelective plan (other than modifications entered into on or before Dec. 31, 1987, to agreements entered into on or before such date), or (2) Jan. 1, 1991.

    The Technical and Miscellaneous Revenue Act of 1988 (TAMRA), (P.L. 100-647), codified the grandfathering relief granted in Notice 88-98, except that, under the Act, the grandfathering protection does not expire on Jan. 1, 1991—i.e., it is made open-ended.

    Specifically, Act § 6064(d)(3) provided that § 457 does not apply to certain nonelective deferred compensation deferred:

    (1) pursuant to agreements in effect on July 14, 1988, or

    (2) if such amounts are deferred from periods on or after July 14, 1988, pursuant to an agreement: (i) which was in writing on that date, (ii) on that date provided for a deferral for each taxable year covered by the agreement of a fixed amount or an amount determined under a fixed formula, and (iii) where the individual with respect to whom the deferral is made was

covered by the agreement on that date.

The grandfather provision does not cease to apply merely because of a modification to the agreement prior to Jan. 1, 1988, which does not increase the benefits of participants in the plan.

The 1988 Act (§8064(a), adding Code §457(e)(11)) also codified IRS Notice 88-68. Section 457(e)(11) is effective generally for taxable years beginning after 1987 with a special effective date for certain collectively bargained plans. The 1988 Act also added Code §457(e)(12), clarifying that § 457 does not apply to nonelective deferred compensation provided to individuals other than in their capacity as employees (e.g., as independent contractors).

40. Code §457(b)(1).
41. Code §457(b)(2). "Includable compensation" for this purpose is defined in §457(e)(5) to mean compensation for service performed for the employer which (taking into account the provisions of §457 and the other income tax provisions of the Code) is currently includable in gross income.
42. Code §457(b)(3).
43. Code §457(b)(4).
44. Code §457(d).
45. P.L. 100-647, §1011(e), repealing the restriction formerly contained in Code §457(d)(2)(B)(i).
46. Code §457(f)(1).
47. Code §457(f)(2). *See also* the plans which are not subject to §457 in note 39, *supra*.
48. Code §408(a)(1). As discussed below in text at note 77, a "spousal IRA" can receive $2,250 per year, but no more than $2,000 may be allocated to either of the spouses.
49. Code §408(a)(2).
50. Code §408(a)(3).
51. Code §408(a)(4).
52. Code §408(a)(5).
53. Code §408(a)(6).
54. Code §408(b)(1).
55. Code §408(b)(2).
56. Code §408(b)(4).
57. Code §408(b)(3).
58. Code §§408(c)(1) and (2).
59. Code §408(d)(1).
60. *Id.*
61. Code §408(d)(2).
62. Code §408(d)(3)(A).
63. Code §408(d)(3)(A)(ii).
64. *Id.*
65. Code §§408(d)(3)(A)(iii)(I)-(III).
66. Code §408(d)(3)(B).
67. Code §408(d)(3)(C)(i).
68. Code §408(d)(5).
69. Code §408(d)(6).
70. Code §408(e)(1).
71. Code §408(e)(2).

72. Code §408(e)(3).
73. Code §408(e)(4).
74. Code §408(e)(5).
75. Code §4974(c)(4)-(5).
76. Code §219(b)(1).
77. Code §219(c)(2).
78. *Id.*
79. Code §408(m). Section 6057 of TAMRA amended §408(m)(3) to provide that coins issued under the laws of any state are also not to be treated as collectibles for this purpose, so long as the coins are held by a person independent of the IRA owner. This provision is effective with respect to state coins acquired by the IRA after Nov. 18, 1988, TAMRA's enactment date.
80. Code §219(d)(1).

16

Nonqualified Deferred Compensation Arrangements

This chapter examines the law governing the taxation of nonqualified deferred compensation arrangements. Because numerous pieces of tax legislation in the 1980s have restricted the benefits and increased the compliance costs of qualified plans, nonqualified arrangements are taking on an increasingly important role in executive compensation packages. The tax advantages and disadvantages of qualified plans can perhaps best be appreciated by examining the taxation of nonqualified arrangements. As a threshold matter, it is important to gain an understanding of the taxation of nondeferred compensation.

Code §§162 and 61: Reasonable Compensation

Under Code §162, an employer is allowed a deduction for all the ordinary and necessary expenses incurred during the taxable year in carrying on its trade or business. This includes a reasonable allowance for salaries and other compensation for personal services actually rendered.[1]

The Code §162 regulations deny a compensation deduction for any amount paid in the form of compensation which is not in fact related to the purchase price of services. The regulations indicate that, where an excessive amount of ostensible compensation is paid to a shareholder for services rendered to a corporation, the excess over reasonable compensation may be recharacterized as a dividend. Dividends are not deductible by the payor but are ordinary income to the recipient. Another possible recharacterization of excessive compensation for services is to treat the excess as being, in part, payment for property. The regulations indicate that the IRS may so recharacterize compensation where, for example, a partnership sells out to a corporation, stating:

> "In such a case it may be found that the salaries of the former partners are not merely for services but in part constitute payment for the transfer of their business."[2]

Whether compensation is reasonable depends on the facts and circumstances. In general, the IRS will consider compensation paid or incurred to be reasonable if the amount involved would ordinarily be paid by a similar business for like services under similar circumstances to those that existed when the contract for services was made.[3]

The regulations specify that it is the date of contracting for services, not the date when the payment is questioned by the IRS which controls. When compensation in respect of a particular taxable year is considered excessive, the taxpayer may argue that a certain portion is attributable to services rendered in an earlier year for which he was not adequately compensated. The employer can also defend the reasonableness of its compensation payments by demonstrating that the employee made a special contribution to business development or in some other way contributed to the worth of the business.

Where a payor corporation lacks earnings and profits, IRS recharacterization of an ostensible compensation payment as a distribution "in respect of stock" (*i.e.*, one that is made by virtue of an individual's stock ownership) will not produce dividend treatment. Distributions in respect of stock that are not characterized as dividends are first applied to reduce a taxpayer's basis in his stock. After the basis is reduced to zero, any additional amounts are treated as a gain from the sale or exchange of property.[4]

Under Code §61, (employee) gross income includes all income from whatever source derived, including "compensation for services, including fees, commissions, and similar items."[5] Thus, there is a symmetry on both sides of the accounting ledger when compensation payments are made. The employer may deduct reasonable compensation payments under Code §162 when such amounts are paid or incurred, and the employee must include such amounts in gross income when received.

Code §83: Property Transferred in Connection With Performance of Services

This parallel treatment of deduction and inclusion in income also exists where a non-tax-qualified deferred compensation arrangement is involved. Code §83 governs the deductibility by employers and the inclusion in gross income by employees (and independent contractors) of payments under nonqualified deferred arrangements.

Code §83(a) provides that if, in connection with the performance of services, property is transferred to anyone other than the person to whom such services are rendered, the excess of the fair market value of the property transferred over the amount the employee paid for it (if any) is included in the employee's gross income at the time the property becomes freely transferable by the employee or not subject to a substantial risk of forfeiture.

Fair Market Value Under Code §83: Lapse and Nonlapse Restrictions

In determining fair market value under §83, restrictions on the property other than restrictions that, by their terms, will never lapse are disregarded.[6] Where a nonlapse restriction allows the employee to sell the property only under a price determined under a formula, e.g., stock subject to a corporate cross-purchase agreement, the formula price is considered the property's fair market value unless the IRS establishes otherwise.[7]

When a nonlapse restriction is canceled, the cancellation is treated as compensatory unless the taxpayer establishes that it was not and that the employer did not take a compensation deduction. The amount to be included in income in this situation is the property's fair market value (computed without regard to the restriction) at the time of cancellation *less* the sum of:

(1) The property's fair market value (computed by taking the

restriction into account) immediately before the cancellation; and

(2) Any amount paid by the employee for the cancellation of the restriction.[8]

Timing of Deduction and Receipt Under Code §83: Transferability and Forfeiture Restrictions

Under §83(a), the employer may deduct, and the employee must include in income, property transferred in connection with the performance of services if the employee's rights in the property are transferable or are not subject to a substantial risk of forfeiture, whichever applies. This contrasts with the tax treatment of property transferred under qualified plans whereby the employer may obtain an immediate tax deduction for its contribution, but the employee may be able to defer the recognition of income for many years. Further, although nonqualified plan assets may be invested in vehicles that produce tax-exempt income, barring that, either the employer or the employee will have to pay tax on the earnings on the property in such an arrangement.

The general §83(a) rule of transferability/nonforfeitability will not apply where the employee sells or disposes of the property before his rights therein become transferable or nonforfeitable.

An employee's rights in property are subject to a substantial risk of forfeiture if the rights to full enjoyment of the property are conditioned upon the performance of substantial services.[9]

Forfeiture restrictions can take many forms. For instance, an employer might give an employee rights in property but, to give the employee an incentive to remain with the employer, might provide in the employment contract that the property will be forfeited if the employee leaves the employer before the expiration of a specified period or goes to work for a competitor. Forfeitability restrictions can also be used as productivity incentives, e.g., a provision that the property will become nonforfeitable if certain performance goals are satisfied. These restrictions can also be useful in controlling the timing of both the employee's receipt of income and the employer's deduction. This can be especially helpful to an employee who wishes to spread his income from the property among several taxable years to avoid bunching of income. Where this is the case, and the employer is agreeable to deferring its deduction in whole or in part, a vesting schedule can be employed.

Another technique that the parties may use to control the tax consequences in this area is the §83(b) election (discussed below). The §83(b) election, however, will, to the extent it minimizes the employee's receipt of income, correspondingly reduce the employer's compensation deduction. Deferring the receipt of income and the timing of deductions by using forfeiture restrictions can have a similar effect, i.e., to the extent the employer cannot take a deduction "up front," it loses the time value of money (the opportunity cost of not having the money the deduction would produce available for investment in an earlier taxable year). This may not be important to an employer that, in the earlier years, has little or no taxable income and therefore could not utilize the deduction anyway. Further, when forfeitability restrictions defer the taxable event in the case of appreciating property, the employer may get a larger deduction if the restrictions lapse in a year when the property's fair market value is higher. Of course, where this is the case, the employee will have to recognize more income at that time than if the restrictions had lapsed earlier. The employee may find this agreeable, however, where, in such a year, he has less taxable income than in the earlier year or where the tax laws call for a reduction in personal marginal tax rates over a period of several years.

Restrictions on the transferability of property can also be used to control the tax consequences to the parties. A restriction on transferability is somewhat circularly defined in §83(c)(2), which states that a person's rights in property are freely transferable when they are not subject to a substantial risk of forfeiture.

These planning considerations are examined in greater detail in the section on tax planning involving nonqualified plans after the 1986 and 1987 tax acts, below.

The Economic Recovery Tax Act of 1981 (ERTA)[10] added Code §83(c)(3). Section 83(c)(3) applies a special rule when the property transferred consists of securities which may be the subject of a suit under §16(b) of the 1934 Securities Exchange Act (the provision that requires certain corporate "insiders" to disgorge profits taken on sales and purchases, or purchases and sales, of securities within six months of each other). Section 83(c)(3) states that, where there is a possibility that the insider trading restrictions could subject the employee to suit under §16(b), the employee's rights in the securities are considered to be nontransferable and subject to a substantial risk of forfeiture. Section 83(c)(3) was enacted in response to cases such as *Horwith v. Commissioner.*[11] The Tax Court, in *Horwith*, came up with the rather inequitable result that stock which was subject to §16(b) was taxable to the employee immediately. Reading the statute literally, it reasoned that a six-month restriction did not pose a substantial risk of forfeiture. In the court's opinion, it also did not amount to a restriction on transferability. Of course, a restriction that expires in six months could not be considered a restriction which, by its terms, will never lapse. Therefore, absent §83(c)(3), a §16(b) restriction also could not be said to affect valuation. The result was that the taxpayer in *Horwith* had to pay the tax on the restricted stock despite the fact that he could not be assured of retaining any profit he might take if he had to sell it before the insider trading restrictions lapsed. Further, the taxpayer was taxed on the stock's fair market value *without regard to the insider trading restrictions*. A taxpayer in such a situation might be forced to sell the stock and subject himself to suit merely to obtain the cash to pay the tax on the stock. Section 83(c)(3) reversed this result as to post-1981 transfers and, with it, reversed the IRS' position.[12] ERTA did not amend the Code, but did enact a similar rule where the property transferred is subject to the Securities and Exchange Commission's pooling of interest accounting rules. Thus, for post-1981 transfers of such restricted securities, the taxpayer does not recognize income, and the employer may not take a compensation deduction, until the §16(b) or accounting restrictions cease to apply. At that time, the securities will be taxed at their current fair market value.

Code §83(b) Election

Code §83(b) allows the employee to disregard the general taxation scheme of §83 and instead elect to be taxed on the transferred property in the year of the transfer, regardless of whether forfeiture or transferability restrictions apply. If the election is made, the taxpayer will be taxed on the current fair market value of the property less any consideration paid for the property. The §83(b) election must be made no later than 30 days after the property is transferred and may not be revoked without IRS consent.[13]

The §83(b) election is a gamble. If the employee believes that the property will significantly appreciate, an election will be to his advantage, since he will only be taxed on the property's fair market value at the time of the transfer. The employee, however, will be taxed regardless of whether the property is later forfeited. Therefore, under §83(b), it is possible that the employee will pay tax on property which he is never able to control.

Further, the employer's offsetting compensation deduction, where the election is made, will be the property's fair market value at the time of the transfer, not at the time the restrictions lapse. If the employer anticipated that the property would appreciate, the resulting deduction could be less than it had planned on. Note that the §83(b) election is totally at the employee's prerogative. Further, where the election is made, it is the employee, not the employer, who controls the timing of the receipt of gross income and the compensation deduction. This, again, could upset the employer's financial plans. Where a successful (from the employee's standpoint) §83(b) election is made, however, the employee will be able to defer the gain on the transferred property until it is subsequently sold or disposed of—an event that usually will be within the employee's control. If, at the time of the subsequent taxable disposition, the property is a capital asset in the hands of the employee, and the long-term capital gains holding period has been satisfied, any gain will be taxed to the employee as long-term capital gain. An employee who forfeits §83 property may only take a loss deduction to the extent he has basis in the property (usually by supplying some consideration).

An interesting twist on the §83(b) election, and one that practitioners should bear in mind when advising clients, was provided by *Alves v. Commissioner.*[14] In *Alves*, a new corporation transferred stock to a key person at its current fair market value. The corporation's stock was restricted so that it could only be purchased by employees of the corporation. Because of favorable business prospects, the stock was expected to appreciate significantly in the future. The Tax Court held that the stock was subject to §83 because the underlying facts indicated that it was transferred "in connection with the performance of services" even though there was no "present bargain element" to the transfer, *i.e.*, it was arguably noncompensatory—the employee had paid full fair market value for the stock. The Tax Court noted that, had Congress intended that §83 only apply to transfers having a present bargain element, (*i.e.*, transfers where the employee is given the right to buy something for less than its full fair market value because of his employment status), it could have so provided in the statute. Instead, the statute refers to "property transferred in connection with the performance of services," a broader term than "compensation." This, the Court found, meant that even if there was no bargain element at the time the right was granted (because the employee was only given the right to buy property at its then fair market value) §83 would apply to the transaction if the reason the employer gave the employee the right to buy the property was his or her employee status. Further, in the *Alves* situation, it is not clear that there is not a present compensatory element to the transfer, since the employee, by virtue of the employment relationship, was given a valuable right to buy property which was likely to substantially appreciate in the future. Clearly, in *Alves*, if it were not for the rendering of services, the property would not have been available for the employee to purchase.

The result of *Alves* is that taxpayers in this situation will usually want to make the §83(b) election so as to defer gain on the appreciating property and remit any tax due at that time.

Nonqualified Deferred Compensation Strategies After the 1986 and 1987 Tax Acts

The 1986 Tax Reform Act and the 1987 Omnibus Budget Reconciliation Act made substantial changes in the tax law that should have a dramatic impact upon tax planning strategies involving nonqualified deferred compensation arrangements. This section examines some strategies that may be coming to the forefront in the post-1987 tax environment.

One of the most visible trends in tax legislation in the 1980s has been the reduction in the benefits available under, and the increase in the cost of maintaining, qualified plans. In light of these increasing costs, employers have shown a willingness to use nonqualified plans. Key among the developments which have helped fuel this trend are:

(1) The enactment of the top-heavy plan rules by TEFRA,[15]

(2) The reduction in, or freezing of, the §415 limits by TEFRA, the 1984 TRA,[16] and the 1986 TRA;[17]

(3) The revision of the joint and survivor annuity rules by the REA;[18]

(4) The revision of the qualified plan coverage rules by the 1986 TRA;[19]

(5) The tightening of the Social Security integration rules by TEFRA and the 1986 TRA;[20] and

(6) The tightening of the defined benefit plan funding requirements by OBRA (1987).[21]

The state of flux in the law has also, in itself, imposed increased compliance costs and made corporate long-term financial planning difficult.

In addition, certain basic structural changes brought about by the 1986 TRA have dramatically affected tax planning involving nontax qualified arrangements. Key among these are the compression of federal income tax brackets from 14 to two (three, including the "hidden" 33 percent bracket), the dramatic reduction in the top marginal income tax rate for individuals, the repeal of the capital gains differential, and the relative rate changes which, for the first time in modern history, place the top corporate marginal rate above the top rate for individuals.

Nonqualified Arrangements

As can be seen from the foregoing, it has generally become progressively more costly to maintain qualified plans in the 1980s and qualified plans have been restricted in their ability to direct benefits to highly compensated employees. Further, these two trends show no signs of abating.

Nonqualified arrangements, if appropriately structured, can ameliorate some of these problems. For example, nonqualified arrangements generally allow an employer to benefit the employees it chooses in the amounts it chooses, without regard to the nondiscrimination rules applicable to qualified plans. In addition, if the nonqualified arrangement comes within one of the recognized exceptions, such as that provided for "top-hat" or "excess" plans, or if the arrangement is not funded, it will be exempt from the application of Title I of ERISA, including the reporting and disclosure rules. Finally, although nonqualified plan assets are not held in a taxfree trust (as are qualified plan assets), investing in taxfree vehicles such as municipal bonds and variable annuity contracts (where the inside buildup is taxfree) can produce a similar result.

Nonqualified plans also offer employers flexibility. If the employer uses a funded arrangement, a variety of vehicles are available, including trusts, escrow accounts, time deposits, brokerage accounts, and insurance products.

While funded arrangements help secure the employer's promise to pay benefits, unfunded arrangements can also provide attractive benefits. Where the arrangement is unfunded, the employee effectively becomes a creditor of the employer, however, so the employer's creditworthiness and stability become key here. If the employer does not have a strong economic track record and/or currently needs the funds to operate its business, it may have to offer increased future benefits to induce top personnel to incur the risks inherent in an unfunded arrangement.

Nonqualified arrangements can be structured to accommodate a variety of employer goals. For instance, forfeiture restrictions can be used as an incentive to key employees to remain with the employer or to meet certain productivity standards. Further, through forfeiture and transferability restrictions, the parties can manipulate the timing of the employer's deduction and the employee's recognition of income to their mutual advantage.

Nonqualified plans can also be used to protect key executives against the effects of a hostile takeover ("golden parachutes"), to discourage key employees from going to work for a competitor ("golden handcuffs") or to supplement qualified plan benefits.[22] They can even be used to make the sponsor a less attractive takeover target by automatically triggering deferred compensation liabilities that deplete corporate reserves in the event of a takeover. These types of arrangements have become more popular in recent years due to the trend towards corporate takeovers and the increased mobility of the executive workforce.

Nonqualified plans are also used to circumvent the Code §415 limits on the amount of benefit an employee can earn under a qualified plan.[23] This has become especially significant in light of the fact that, as previously indicated, Congress has repeatedly reduced the §415 limits since 1982.

Taxation Under Code §83

As discussed in the preceding section, §83 governs the deductibility by employers and the inclusion in income by employees (and independent contractors) of payments under nonqualified arrangements. Section 83(a) provides that if, in connection with the performance of services, property is transferred to anyone other than the person to whom such services are rendered, the excess of the fair market value of the property transferred over the amount the employee paid for it will be included in the employee's income when the property is transferable by the employee or not subject to a substantial risk of forfeiture. The employer may not take a deduction for compensation paid or accrued until its taxable year with or within which the employee's taxable year of income recognition ends.[24]

In determining fair market value under §83, restrictions on the property other than restrictions that, by their terms, will never lapse are disregarded. Nonlapse restrictions are considered in determining the property's fair market value, however. Where a nonlapse restriction allows the employee to sell the property only under a formula price (e.g., stock subject to a cross-purchase agreement), the formula price is considered the property's fair market value unless the IRS establishes otherwise. Such a restriction can help the employer retain control of its business, by giving it a right of first refusal to repurchase its own stock at a fixed price while controlling (and making predictable) the tax consequences to employer and employee by allowing fair market value to be established in advance for both income and estate tax purposes. Formula price restrictions can be used in conjunction with cross-purchase and buy-sell agreements to provide for the orderly continuation of a business after an employee separates from service. Where planning is being done to protect the company upon the death of a key executive, the cross-purchase, buy-sell, or other redemption agreement can be funded with life insurance.

Use of Forfeiture and Transferability Restrictions to Control Tax Consequences

Restrictions on the right to obtain the property held in a nonqualified plan may take many forms. For instance, an employer might give an employee rights in property but provide that the property will be forfeited if certain events occur. Alternatively, the employee can be given a forfeitable right that becomes nonforfeitable when certain goals are achieved. Forfeiture restrictions that are based on productivity or profitability goals, in addition to providing an incentive, are "profit sensitive," i.e., they assure the employer that plan benefits will only have to be funded if the performance objectives are achieved.

Where benefits are geared to performance objectives, however, it is important to craft the plan so that the desired result is encouraged. For example, a plan that provides benefits to division managers based on the profitability of their division might not encourage managers to incur advertising expenses aimed at attracting new sales, research and development expenses, or other costs that decrease short-term profitability but further the enterprise's long-range interests. In designing a plan, it is important to precisely identify the desired objective. Of course, if the objective is more precisely defined, this may generate higher administrative costs connected with monitoring performance, resulting in less money being available to fund benefits. This tradeoff should be examined in advising clients about their arrangements.

As discussed in the preceding section, forfeiture and transferability restrictions can also help control the timing of both the employee's recognition of income and the employer's compensation deduction, which are governed by §83. Formerly, the conventional wisdom was that the longer the compensation was deferred, the greater the benefit to the employee. This was based on the assumption, however, that the employee would, at retirement, be in a lower marginal tax bracket than during his or her working career. With the compression of tax brackets and the lowering of individual tax rates, together with the expectation that future rate increases for individuals are inevitable, the conventional wisdom has changed. The soundness of using short-term deferrals is particularly suspect due to the possibility that rates will increase in the future.

Another significant factor changing the considerations involved in the deferral of compensation is the fact that, for the first time in modern history, the top marginal corporate rate is higher than the top rate for individuals. This situation, together with the repeal of the capital gains differential, has necessitated the reexamination of compensation strategies. The change in the relative marginal rates may make it beneficial for the employer to seek "up front" deductions (i.e., deductions in the current year or for short-term deferrals only), since, by so doing, it will gain the advantage of the time value of money—having the tax savings around for a longer period to reinvest in its business. Due to the lower individual rates, however, employees may not desire short-term deferrals for 1988 and beyond, creating a tension between employer and employee interests. This problem is further complicated by the employee's ability to elect under §83(b) to be taxed currently on property transferred in connection with a nonqualified arrangement. An employee's §83(b) election, however, will also trigger the employer's compensation deduction.

Planning Involving the Code §83(b) Election

If the employee prefers to be taxed immediately upon the receipt of plan benefits (usually because he believes the property will appreciate substantially in the future and that he will not sell or dispose of the property in a taxable transfer for some time), §83(b) provides an additional planning tool. Where the employee elects to be taxed immediately on the property's fair market value at the date of transfer, the tax on subsequent appreciation will be deferred until the property is sold or disposed of. Where the employee makes a §83(b) election, the employer's deduction is accelerated but is limited to the amount the employee must include in income (which is generally lower when the §83(b) election is made than when the restrictions lapse).

The §83(b) election can be a useful planning tool where the employee's and employer's interests are congruent but, where they are not, the possibility that an employee might make the election is a contingency that employers must consider. This unpredictability remains one of the key disadvantages of nonqualified deferred compensation.

The adverse effect of the possibility of a §83(b) election being made, however, is somewhat mitigated by the fact that the election must be made within 30 days of the date property is transferred. Thereafter, the tax consequences of the transaction are more predictable.

The tension between the interests of employee and employer will be most acute if the property is likely to appreciate substantially in the future, since the §83(b) election taxes the employee on the property's current fair market value. Optimally for both parties, the employer, in this situation, might benefit somewhat from an employee's making the election because this will entitle the employer to take its deduction up-front. The employer will have to weigh this against the projected benefit from the deduction that it believes it would be able to take in future years if no §83(b) election were made. In other words, the employer generally must weigh the benefit of a smaller current deduction against a larger one in later years, since property with the potential for appreciation is usually the subject of a §83(b) election. The employer's preference will depend on its current need for cash as well as its expectations about future changes in corporate tax rates.

From the employee's viewpoint, the repeal of the capital gains differential may have taken away some of the incentive to make a §83(b) election (because postelection appreciation of a capital asset may not be taxable at favorable rates, at least for the immediate future). The lowering of the tax rates has, however, in some cases, created a new reason for electing under §83(b): the assumption that the tax burden on individuals is as low as it is ever likely to be.

Further, the possibility that the capital gains differential will be reinstituted in future years is a factor that might make an employee elect under §83(b) if the property is a capital asset in the employee's hands, as this will allow the employee to realize future appreciation as capital gain, rather than ordinary income.

One possibility that might be used to control the use of the §83(b) election is to provide in the plan that an employee will forfeit all or part of the benefit if he or she makes a §83(b) election. If the parties bargained for such a provision, arguably it could withstand legal challenge.

ISOs vs. Nonqualified Options

The change of the marginal rates, together with the repeal of the capital gains differential has, at least temporarily, made incentive stock options (ISOs) less attractive relative to nonqualified options. Many practitioners have suggested that a nonqualified option, which allows a corporate level deduction on option exercise (provided the option did not have a readily ascertainable fair market value at date of grant), is a superior vehicle from the employer's perspective than an ISO (where no corporate deduction is allowed). Both employers and employees like the fact that nonqualified options are not subject to the price and term restrictions applicable to ISOs. From the employee's perspective, of course, the ISO still has significant advantages, most notably the fact that an ISO does not generate income recognition either at grant or exercise. Many employers, however, are considering substituting nonqualified options for ISOs and offering, as an inducement to employees, to share their tax savings with their employees in the form of higher benefits.

"Rabbi Trusts"

Another vehicle which has drawn much attention recently is the "Rabbi trust." This arrangement derives its name from the fact that the first one to be approved by the IRS in a private letter ruling was established for a Rabbi by his congregation. Subsequently, Rabbi trusts have come to be used as a tool of executive compensation. If a Rabbi trust or similar arrangement satisfies IRS standards, it will provide the following tax results:

(1) Benefits will not be taxed to employees until they become freely transferable or not subject to a substantial risk of forfeiture;

(2) Until benefits become taxable to the employee, investment growth will be taxed to the employer under the grantor trust rules; and

(3) In the case of an unfunded arrangement, until funding occurs the assets may be used in the employer's business.

To have the desired tax effects, a Rabbi trust or similar arrangement cannot provide the employee a right to sell, pledge, assign, or alienate his or her benefit, as this will trigger constructive receipt. This has the same effect on nonqualified plan benefits as the Code §401(a)(13) anti-alienation rule has on qualified plan benefits, except that a domestic relations order does not have to be a "qualified domestic relations order" within the meaning of Code §414(p) to be enforceable against a nonqualified plan. In addition, various other court orders may, despite a nonqualified plan's anti-alienation language, be enforceable against a participant's nonqualified plan interest.

Pure life insurance is also generally unsuitable for these arrangements because, under the "economic benefit doctrine," the employee could be charged currently with gross income on the theory that insurance protection is a benefit of value that is being provided currently.

Note that the economic benefit doctrine makes it more beneficial to provide insurance either outside the nonqualified arrangement, through Code §79 group-term life insurance or a qualified plan (although the qualified plan "incidental benefit" rule may make this impractical, especially since qualified preretirement survivor annuity benefits will be counted against the amount of insurance benefit that may be provided).

The IRS, in the last two years, has ended its temporary moratorium on the issuance of private letter rulings concerning the tax consequences of Rabbi trusts. One issue that the Service has not addressed in the postmoratorium period is whether the employee may secure the otherwise unsecured promise of future compensation in a Rabbi trust by purchasing a surety bond insuring the benefit against employer default. One premoratorium ruling approved the use of such a bond if the premium were paid entirely with fresh funds provided by the employee. Of course, such tracing is difficult to administer; employers might increase an employee's compensation gradually over a period of time to reimburse the employee for the funds used to acquire the bond. As a practical matter, however, the IRS' resolution of this issue is likely to make little difference since such bonds, where available, carry prohibitive premiums, presumably in recognition of the possibility that the employer and employee could collude to trigger a forfeiture, foisting the liability to pay deferred compensation onto the suretor. Thus, one of the main problems with Rabbi trusts is likely to remain the risk of forfeiture if, for instance, the employer were to go into bankruptcy. For that reason, Rabbi trusts as a planning tool are generally more suited to established companies with records of consistent growth over a prolonged period of time. For a start-up company, stock options and performance incentives (including performance share plans and stock appreciation rights) are more likely to prove effective in attracting and retaining qualified personnel since, under options, the employee controls the timing of when the option will be exercised and when the underlying stock will be sold or disposed of. This provides some measure of security to an employee of a company without a proven track record.

Other Developments Accelerating the Use of Nonqualified Arrangements

Termination of Defined Benefit Plans

A common occurrence in the 1980s has been the termination of single employer defined benefit plans and their replacement with defined contribution arrangements, often with a cash-or-deferred feature.

This trend has been the result of a number of changes, including the enactment of the top-heavy rules, the increased funding requirements brought about by OBRA (1987), and the fact that, due to double-digit inflation in the 1970s, many of these plans found themselves overfunded in the 1980s, and, as such, constituted a ready source of operating capital for employers.

For employees who are relatively young and in the early stages of their career, the conversion from defined benefit to defined contribution plan probably will not adversely affect total retirement benefits, provided the replacement plan is comparable to the terminated one and investment experience is not adverse. For senior highly compensated employees, however, the conversion to a defined contribution plan can often mean a loss of expected retirement benefits. This is largely because such employees' benefits under a defined benefit plan generally increase rapidly in the later years of an employee's career due to benefit formulas that are based on the employee's most highly compensated years. In a defined contribution plan, this effect is not as pronounced. In addition, instead of the 1:3 ratio that existed between the defined contribution and defined benefit plan Code § 415 dollar limits under pre-1986 TRA law, after 1987, the defined contribution plan dollar limit will remain frozen until the defined benefit plan limit reaches $120,000, at which point the two limits will be adjusted in tandem to preserve the 1:4 ratio. This new ratio further limits the capacity of defined contribution plans to approximate the accruals an executive could expect under a defined benefit plan in his or her most highly compensated years.

An employer that terminates a defined benefit plan and replaces it with a defined contribution plan can compensate the employees who are disadvantaged by the switch by establishing nonqualified plans for them. Where this is done, the employer may wish to provide a vesting schedule, or forfeiture conditions (such as a provision that the employee will forfeit a portion of his benefit if he goes to work for a competitor) in the nonqualified arrangement. Since the employee is likely to be fully vested in both the terminated and the replacement qualified plans, the employer can gain added leverage by compensating the employee for lost benefits through the nonqualified plan. If the same benefit were provided through the new defined contribution plan, similar benefits would have to be provided to all employees covered by that plan. Under the revised coverage rules, discussed below, this can be costly.

Nonqualified arrangements constitute a means by which the employer can make its key people whole without incurring the additional costs attributable to fulfilling the qualified plan nondiscrimination requirements.

Tighter Coverage Rules

Another factor forcing employers to take a second look at the merits of nonqualified arrangements is the stricter coverage rules for qualified plans enacted by the 1986 TRA.

Under these rules, effective generally for plan years beginning after 1988, a qualified plan must satisfy at least one of three coverage tests. Under the first, the plan must benefit 70 percent or more of all nonhighly compensated employees. For this purpose, all eligible employees are considered to benefit.

Under the second test, a plan must benefit a classification of employees which does not allow more than a reasonable difference between the percentage of highly compensated employees who are covered and a similarly computed percentage for nonhighly compensated employees. This is known as the "ratio test."

Under the third test, a plan will qualify if:

(1) It benefits employees under a nondiscriminatory classification; and

(2) The average benefits percentage for nonhighly compensated employees is at least 70 percent of the average benefits percentage for highly compensated employees. This is known as the "average benefits test."

The revised coverage rules make it much more difficult to direct qualified plan benefits to highly compensated employees without similarly increasing benefits for the rank-and-file. Benefits for executives are now, more than ever, tied to the benefits provided nonhighly compensated employees.

In addition to revising the general coverage rules of Code §410(b), the 1986 Act added a new coverage requirement. Under this requirement, a qualified plan must benefit at least the lesser of: (1) 50 employees; or (2) 40 percent or more of all employees of the employer.

The 50/40 percent coverage rule will make it difficult for small plans of a partnership including professional corporations (PIPIC) to qualify. Before the 1986 TRA, organizing a professional business as a partnership with each partner owning his or her own corporation and the corporation owning the partnership interest, allowed professional employees to individually tailor their retirement plans to suit their needs. Since the plans of related employers are aggregated in applying the coverage rules, this option is generally no longer viable. One technique that can be used to retain the flexibility that was formerly available in this situation is to establish a base qualified plan for the entire partnership and add nonqualified arrangements for the individual partners.

This technique can also be used to help an employer satisfy the revised coverage rules of §410(b), by keeping the ratios between benefits provided to highly paid employees and the rank-and-file under the employer's qualified plan within the prescribed limits. Adding a nonqualified arrangement for key executives, as opposed to trying to benefit these individuals under a qualified plan, can be particularly helpful when the plan is relying on the "average benefits" test of §410(b) to qualify.

Code §401(k) Plans and Raising Capital

Another area in which nonqualified arrangements may be used to replace the benefits lost under the qualified plan rules is in the Code §401(k) area. Formerly, an employee could defer up to 15 percent of compensation in a §401(k) plan, provided the defined contribution plan dollar limit was not exceeded and the actual deferral percentage tests were met. After the 1986 TRA, a dollar limit on annual employee deferrals was imposed; for 1988 it is $7,313. In addition, the actual deferral percentage tests were tightened and similar nondiscrimination rules were imposed on employer matching contributions. Thus, employers and employees are increasingly looking to nonqualified arrangements to make up the difference.

Where an existing §401(k) plan has been operated as part of a stock bonus plan, an employer whose stock is not publicly traded may find that it has lost a ready (tax-favored) market for its securities and that, as a result, its ability to raise capital has become impaired.

Granting nonqualified stock options can help make up the difference, allowing employees to acquire stock at bargain prices while compensating the employer for selling the stock at less than fair market value by means of a tax deduction.

Similarly, in the defined benefit plan area, corporate sponsors may be driven to terminate their plans by considerations relating to raising capital. Since the Financial Accounting Standards Board promulgated FASB 87, qualified plan sponsors have been required to reflect their liability for plan benefits on the corporation's financial statements. In many cases, this has made the corporation appear significantly less attractive to prospective investors. Again, nonqualified arrangements, coupled with freezing or terminating the plan that gives rise to the balance sheet liability, can help the corporation continue to raise capital while making whole employees who suffer a loss of benefits due to the plan termination or freeze.

Social Security Integration

The revised integration rules are another factor forcing employers to look outside the qualified plan context for ways to compensate key employees. For example, prior to the 1986 TRA, a flat benefit excess plan could provide a Code §401(a)(4) prohibited group employee with a benefit that exceeded the benefit provided to rank-and-file employees by as much as 2.5 percent of compensation per year of service not to exceed 37.5 percent for employees with 15 or more years of service. For example, a plan that provided rank-and-file employees with a benefit of 20 percent of high-five-years' average compensation could generally provide prohibited group employees with a benefit of 57.5 percent. Thus, an executive with high-five years' average compensation of $100,000 could receive at retirement a single life annuity commencing at age 65 of $57,500 per year. Under the revised rules, the maximum "spread" between the highly compensated and the rank-and-file under such plans cannot exceed .75 percent per year up to 35 years of service. Thus, if a 57.5 percent of compensation benefit were to be provided to an executive, the benefit provided to long-service rank-and-file employees would have to be at least 31.25 percent. Rather than continue such a plan, employers are considering freezing accruals prospectively or terminating the plan, coupled with compensating the executive for loss of benefits through a combination of defined contribution and nonqualified arrangements.

Distributions, Penalty Taxes, and Estate Planning Considerations

An area in which nonqualified arrangements may help employees involves avoiding certain excise taxes on distributions and benefits provided under qualified plans such as the penalty taxes on excess retirement distributions and accumulations. After the 1986 TRA, in fact, nonqualified arrangements in many cases will constitute a better estate planning vehicle than qualified plans.

For post-1986 distributions, for instance, key employees may find the value of their retirement benefits reduced because of the 15 percent penalty excise tax on excess retirement plan distributions of Code §4980A. Employees who do not currently need the funds, however, may find themselves limited in their ability to delay distributions due to the 50 percent penalty tax on failure to make required distributions added by the 1986 TRA. No such taxes apply to distributions from a nonqualified arrangement.

Another area in which nonqualified arrangements may receive better tax treatment than nonqualified plans is in the area of estate planning. For example, if, to avoid the penalty income tax on excess retirement distributions, an executive limits the amount of retirement distributions made during his lifetime, upon his death his estate may be subject to the 15 percent penalty estate tax on excess retirement accumulations imposed by Code §4980A(d). The penalty estate tax cannot be offset by the unified credit, the marital deduction, or any other credit or deduction. Thus, where the executive is the first spouse to die, it may represent the estate's only estate tax liability. Benefit accumulations under nonqualified arrangements are subject only to the general estate tax and, as such, may be offset by both the unified credit and the marital deduction. Further, in contrast to qualified plans, when such amounts are distributed during the employee's lifetime, there is no penalty income tax. Thus, the employee can enjoy the full benefit provided under a nonqualified plan in his lifetime, or can pass it to his heirs through his estate, without fear of encountering one or more penalty taxes. The benefits of nonqualified arrangements relative to qualified plans in estate planning is further enhanced by the fact that, after the 1984 Tax Reform Act, generally no Code §2039 annuity exclusion is available for qualified plan benefits.

In addition, before the 1986 TRA, qualified plan benefits were eligible for 10-year forward averaging under Code §402(e) and for capital gains treatment on the pre-1974 portion of a distribution. The 1986 TRA, subject to certain transitional rules, replaced 10-year averaging with five-year averaging and eliminated the favorable treatment of capital gains. The 1986 Act also limited employees to one forward averaging election per lifetime. In addition, due to the compression of the tax rates, the benefit of five-year averaging relative to regular income tax treatment is significantly less than it was under pre-TRA law. Thus, notwithstanding the ability to take taxfree rollovers, the tax-favored treatment afforded qualified plan lump sum distributions has been significantly lessened relative to distributions from nonqualified plans. Some of the benefit of taxfree rollover treatment can even be partially achieved in a nonqualified plan distribution by investing the distributed amounts in taxfree vehicles. Where the benefit is distributed in the form of an annuity, the repeal of the three-year exclusion rule of Code §72(d) has also diminished the favorable tax treatment available to distributions from certain contributory plans.

Finally, as previously indicated, nonqualified arrangements can obey a property settlement or support order pursuant to a divorce decree without having to go through the validation process to determine whether the order is a "qualified domestic relations order" within the meaning of Code §414(p), and nonqualified plan benefits are not subject to the complex joint and survivor annuity rules of Code §417.

After the 1986 and 1987 Acts, nonqualified plans should play an even greater role than before in compensation planning. As the costs of maintaining qualified plans mount, more employers are turning to nonqualified plans to benefit their key executives. Although short-term deferrals are generally not advisable at this writing due to the expectation that individual income tax rates will rise in the future, long-term deferrals still make sense in many cases. Although the current low individual tax rates and the repeal of the capital gain differential may, in some cases, work against making a decision to defer compensation, since these developments are likely to be short-term in nature, the use of nonqualified arrangements to accomplish long-term deferral and to convert ordinary income into capital gain is likely to once again become significant. Nonqualified arrangements are particularly suited to replacing benefits lost by senior employees when a defined benefit plan is replaced with a defined contribution plan, to compensate employees for lost benefits under the revised Code §415 and §402(g) limits, and to avoid the numerous penalty excise taxes on qualified plan benefits and distributions enacted by the 1986 TRA. Finally, in planning for distributions either during the employee's lifetime or after his or her death, nonqualified arrangements possess many features to recommend them over qualified plans.

Notes

1. Code §162(a)(1). Note that Code §212 allows a parallel deduction for all the ordinary and necessary expenses incurred in the production of income.
2. Treas. Regs. §1.162-7(b)(1).
3. Treas. Regs. §1.162-7(b)(3).
4. See Code §301(c).
5. Code §61(a)(1).
6. Code §83(a)(1).
7. Code §83(d)(1).
8. Code §§83(d)(2)(A)-(D).
9. Code §83(c)(1).
10. P.L. 97-34, §252.
11. 71 T.C. 932 (1979).
12. Code §83(c)(3), reversing Treas. Regs. §1.83-3(h).
13. Code §§83(b)(1) and (b)(2).
14. 79 T.C. 864 (1982), *aff'd*, 734 F.2d 478 (9th Cir. 1984).
15. The Tax Equity and Fiscal Responsibility Act of 1982, P.L. 97-248. The top-heavy requirements are set forth in Code §416.
16. The 1984 Tax Reform Act, P.L. 98-369. After TEFRA, which reduced the Code §415 dollar limits to $30,000 for defined contribution plans and $90,000 for defined benefit pension plans, the respective dollar limits were to be indexed for post-1984 inflation beginning in 1986. The 1984 TRA set both of these dates back two years, *i.e.*, after the 1984 Act the limits were to be adjusted for post-1986 inflation beginning in 1988.
17. The Tax Reform Act of 1986, P.L. 99-514, which froze the indexation of the defined contribution plan dollar limit at $30,000 until the defined benefit plan dollar limit increased to $120,000. The 1986 TRA also further reduced the benefits available under defined benefit plans having an early normal retirement age—continuing a process begun by TEFRA.
18. The Retirement Equity Act of 1984, P.L. 98-397, which required spousal consent for a participant's waiver of joint and survivor benefits to be effective, added spousal notification requirements, and replaced the former optional early retirement survivor annuity rule with a mandatory (unless elected out of) preretirement survivor annuity requirement for the spouses of vested participants who die prior to retirement age.
19. The 1986 TRA added a requirement that a plan, to qualify under Code §401(a) benefit at least the lesser of 50 employees or 40% or more of all employees of the employer. See §401(a)(26).

20. The tighter integration rules, combined with the fact that an integrated plan is likely to be top-heavy, triggering the Code §416 requirements, make it considerably more difficult to direct qualified benefits towards the highly paid.
21. Omnibus Budget Reconciliation Act of 1987, P.L. 100-203.
22. Such plans are generally known as "SERPs"—supplemental executive retirement plans. SERPs are also used to induce an executive to leave his or her current position and come to work for the employer. In such cases, SERPs are often used to compensate the employee for the forfeiture of benefits that may occur under the current employer's qualified plan when the employee separates from service.
23. These plans are known as excess plans.
24. Code §83(h).

4

Welfare Plans

17

Welfare Benefit Plans

Tax-Favored Fringe Benefit Plans

Congress accorded statutory tax-favored status to a number of employer-sponsored employee fringe benefits, including group-term life insurance, medical reimbursement plans, group legal services programs (for taxable years ending before December 31, 1988), qualified transportation plans, qualified educational assistance programs (for taxable years beginning before December 31, 1988), and dependent care assistance programs, as well as certain plans that permit employees to choose their benefit options, known as "cafeteria plans."

With mounting budget deficits and an increasing portion of employee compensation being channeled into tax-favored fringe benefits, however, legislation changed direction. As a result, Congress moved to restrict the availability of certain fringe benefits that previously enjoyed tax-favored status. In this regard, Treasury followed a similar path. The trend may be said to have begun in 1982, when TEFRA added nondiscrimination rules for group-term life insurance plans.[1] The trend accelerated in the early part of 1984, when the IRS issued a news release, I.R. 84-22 (February 10, 1984), and followed it up with proposed regulations under Code §125 that restricted the growth of certain "flexible benefit plans" which, in the absence of regulatory guidance, had operated as §125 cafeteria plans.

Congress confirmed in the 1984 TRA much of what the IRS

had done in the § 125 area, although it did provide some transitional relief for existing flexible benefit plans.[2] The 1984 TRA also saw Congress act to limit the types of nonstatutory fringe benefits that may be received taxfree by employees by enacting Code § 132. In addition, Congress restricted the benefits that may be provided under a cafeteria plan to certain enumerated benefits.

The 1986 TRA called for further cutbacks in the area of fringe benefits with the creation of the Code §89 nondiscrimination provisions.[3] In addition, TAMRA allowed the education assistance and the group legal service provisions to expire at the end of 1988.[4]

Code §79: Group-Term Life Insurance Plans

When group-term life insurance is provided as a form of compensation to employees, it is deductible by the employer under Code § 162 or §212, provided it constitutes an ordinary and necessary business expense, i.e., it does not, when considered together with other compensation paid to the employee, constitute unreasonable compensation. Code §79(a) provides that, in the case of qualified group-term life insurance benefits, the employee may exclude from gross income the sum of: the premium cost of $50,000 of such insurance and any amount paid by the employee towards the purchase of such insurance.

Any benefits that are taxable to the employee under the statute are taxed at a deemed premium rate provided in Table I of the §79 regulations. Congress, in TEFRA, directed the IRS to periodically revise Table I in light of market experience.[5]

The regulations provide that insurance, to be group-term life insurance, must satisfy certain specified conditions. First the insurance must provide a general death benefit that is excludable from employee gross income under Code § 101(a).[6] Second, the insurance must be provided to a "group of employees."[7] As a general rule, this means that, at some time during the calendar year, such insurance must be provided to a group consisting of at least 10 employees.[8] For purposes of the 10-employee rule, all life insurance policies carried directly or indirectly by the employer are aggregated.[9]

The 10-employee rule, however, has certain exceptions. The rule will not apply, for instance, where the insurance is provided to all full-time employees of the employer or, where evidence of insurability affects eligibility, to all full-time employees who provide evidence of insurability satisfactory to the insurer, if the amount of insurance provided is a flat percentage of compensation or is based on certain uniform coverage brackets of the insurer, and "evidence of insurability" is limited to requiring the employee to complete a medical questionnaire that does not include a physical examination.[10]

Another exception to the 10-employee rule exists where the insurance is provided under a common plan to the employees of two or more unrelated employers; where the insurance is restricted to, but mandatory for, all employees of the employer who are members of, or represented by, an organization (such as a union) that carries on substantial activities other than obtaining insurance; and where evidence of insurability does not affect the employee's eligibility for insurance or the amount of insurance that the employee may have.[11]

For purposes of determining whether all employees are covered who have to be covered to qualify for one of the exceptions, the employer need not count employees who are held out of the plan pending the completion of a minimum period of employment—which cannot exceed six months.[12] Further, part-time employees, i.e., those working less than 20 hours per week, and seasonal employees (those working less than five months per year) may be disregarded for this purpose,[13] as may employees who have reached age 65.[14]

The third criterion that insurance must satisfy to qualify as group-term life insurance is that it must be provided under a policy that is carried directly or indirectly by the employer.[15] Finally, the amount of insurance provided to employees must be computed under a formula that precludes individual selection, although a formula based on such factors as age, length of service, compensation, or position, is allowable.[16]

Group-term life insurance may not be provided in connection with a policy that also provides whole life insurance benefits, unless the policy or the employer designates in writing the part of the death benefit provided to each employee that is group-term life insurance. The part of the death benefit that is provided to an employee and designated as group-term life insurance must not be less than the difference between the total death benefit provided under the policy and the employee's "deemed death benefit" at the end of the policy year.[17]

Code §79(b) provides that certain types of group-term life insurance will not be subject to the general $50,000 exclusion rule of §79(a). What this means is that such insurance will be taxed under pre-§79 law, i.e., it will be deductible by the employer and excludable in its entirety from employee gross income. Section 79(b) provides that §79(a) does not apply to:

(1) The cost of group-term life insurance on the life of an individual, provided under a policy carried directly or indirectly by the employer, after the individual's employment has been terminated and the individual is disabled (within the meaning of §72(m)(7));

(2) The cost of any portion of the group-term life insurance on the life of any employee provided during part or all of the taxable year of the employee under which (A) the employer is directly or indirectly the beneficiary, or (B) a person described in Code §170(c) (i.e., a charity) is the sole beneficiary, for the entire period during such taxable year for which the employee receives such insurance; and

(3) The cost of any group-term life insurance which is provided under a contract to which §72(m)(3) (relating to insurance provided in the qualified plan context) applies.

Code §79(d) contained nondiscrimination rules. The penalty for violating these rules was the loss of §79(a)'s $50,000 exclusion by any key employee involved and the inclusion of any employer-paid premiums in the income of such an employee, determined without regard to the Table I rates.[18] A key employee, for this purpose, was generally as defined in Code §416(i).[19]

A plan was considered a "discriminatory group-term life insurance plan," and hence one to which the benefits of Code §§79(a) and (c) were lost to key employees, unless the requirements of §§79(d)(2), (3), and (4) were satisfied. Section 79(d)(2) required that the plan not discriminate in favor of key employees as to eligibility to participate and that the type and amount of benefits available under the plan not discriminate in favor of key employee participants.

Section 79(d)(3) required that the plan benefit either 70 percent of all employees of the employer or a group of employees of the employer consisting of at least 85 percent non-key employees, or that the plan benefit a group of employees that the Secretary of Treasury determined to be a nondiscriminatory classification as regards key employees.[20] In the event the group-term life insurance was provided as part of a cafeteria plan, the plan was not deemed discriminatory in terms of eligibility if the requirements of Code § 125 are met.[21]

For purposes of applying the above mathematical participation tests as well as the nondiscriminatory classification test, the following were excluded: employees lacking three years of service with the employer, part-timers or seasonal employees, employees covered by a collective bargaining contract, and nonresident aliens lacking U.S.-source earned income for the taxable year.[22]

Finally, § 79(d)(4) required, for a plan to be nondiscriminatory, that all benefits that were available to key employee participants be available to all other participants. This did not make a plan discriminatory merely because the amount of life insurance provided was computed based on a uniform percentage of participant compensation.[23] For § 79 purposes, the employer aggregation rules of Code §§ 414(b), (c), and (m) applied.[24]

Note, however, that § 79 group-term life insurance plans were made subject to the uniform nondiscrimination rules for welfare plans enacted by the 1986 TRA in Code § 89. The § 89 provisions are effective generally for years beginning in 1989. The § 89 rules are discussed below. The § 89 nondiscrimination rules supersede the § 79 nondiscrimination rules for group-term life insurance plans discussed in this section.

Code § 105: Medical Reimbursement Plans

As a general rule, amounts paid by an employer, either directly or indirectly—through direct payment or a third-party insurer—to provide health care for employees, their spouses, or dependents are includable in employee gross income.[25] Code § 105(b), however, provides that, when amounts are provided by an employer, directly or indirectly, to reimburse the taxpayer for expenses incurred for medical care, as defined in Code § 213(e), for the taxpayer, his or her spouse, or dependents, those amounts are excludable from employee gross income unless a § 213 medical expense deduction was taken on the personal return for the amounts so expended.

In effect, where tax-qualified medical reimbursement is concerned, the employer may be said to "buy" the employee's personal medical expense deduction by reimbursing him. The employer will be entitled to a deduction for the reimbursed amounts under Code §§ 162 or 212 and, while the employee loses this deduction, he will not have to take the reimbursed amounts into gross income. This may be an advantageous transaction from a tax perspective since:

(1) The employer may have a greater need for the deduction, i.e., if it is in a higher marginal tax bracket than the taxpayer;

(2) The employee may get a slight "time value of money" benefit by getting the reimbursement up front from the employer rather than having to wait for a tax refund; and

(3) There is no threshold deductible limit under §§162 or 212—unlike §213, which only allows a medical expense deduction to the extent qualifying expenses exceed five percent of adjusted gross income for the employee's taxable year.

All such reimbursements, to the extent they constitute reasonable compensation, will be deductible where the employer pays them.

As is the case generally under ERISA, such favorable tax treatment is conditioned upon the plan's satisfying certain nondiscrimination standards. Originally, insured medical reimbursement plans did not have to satisfy these rules, i.e., the employer could obtain the benefits of Code §105(b) and still benefit whomever it chose among its employees if a third-party insurer was used. This was because Congress believed that the requirements of group rating would have the same effect as nondiscrimination rules where an insured plan was concerned.

A self-insured plan, however, had to satisfy the nondiscrimination rules of Code §105(h) to obtain the favorable tax treatment provided by §105(b). For eligibility purposes, §105(h) required that a self-insured plan either satisfy the 70 percent coverage test, the 70/80 test, or the nondiscriminatory classification test, i.e., the same tests that apply under Code §410 to §401(a) plans.

For purposes of applying these tests, the following employees were not counted: employees under age 25; employees with less than three years of service; part-time (less than 35 hours per week) or seasonal employees; employees covered by a collective bargaining agreement where medical benefits have been the subject of good faith collective bargaining; and nonresident aliens lacking U.S.-source earned income for the taxable year.[26]

Further, a self-insured medical reimbursement plan could not discriminate in favor of "highly compensated individuals." These individuals were the employer's five most highly paid officers, individuals who own 10 percent or more in value of the employer's stock (taking into account the ownership attribution rules of Code §318), and the 25 percent most highly compensated employees of the employer (other than employees who need not be counted in applying the coverage tests of §105(h)(3)).

If a self-insured medical reimbursement plan discriminated in favor of this prohibited group, the plan was not disqualified. Rather, the discriminatory benefits were taxed to the prohibited group employees. Under this rule, where a benefit was provided in some amount to all participants, but in greater amounts to members of the prohibited group, the excess was divided among members of the prohibited group and taxed to them proportionately.[27]

This rule could cause an inequitable distribution of taxable income—it did not look to which members of the group actually received the excess benefits.

Where a benefit was provided to the prohibited group, but not to rank-and-file employees, it was taxable to prohibited group members in its entirety.

After the parity provisions of TEFRA, tax-qualified medical reimbursement plans remain one of the few benefits that are not available outside the "C" corporation context with respect to self-employed individuals and owner-employees. This is because in Code §401(c)(1) self-employed individuals are not treated as employees for purposes of Code §105. Therefore, amounts paid by the employer as medical reimbursement on behalf of such individuals will not be eligible for the tax benefits provided by §105.[28]

The Consolidated Omnibus Budget Reconciliation Act of 1985 made certain changes in the rules concerning group health care plans.[29] These changes are effective generally for plan years beginning on or after July 1, 1986. A detailed discussion of these rules appears below.

The 1986 TRA introduced a provision designed to help provide parity between the tax-favored medical benefits provided under Code §105 and those that may be obtained by self-employed individuals. Under §162(m), as added by the 1986 TRA, self-employed individuals within the meaning of §401(c)(1) are allowed to deduct 25 percent of the amount which they paid during the taxable year for insurance for medical care for themselves, their spouses and their dependents. This deduction is limited to a taxpayer's earned income within the meaning of §401(c)(1) for the taxable year. The deduction is only available if the insurance is provided under one or more plans that would meet the fringe benefit nondiscrimination rules applicable to medical plans, enacted by the 1986 TRA in Code § 89, if the plan were treated as being maintained by an employer and the coverage were treated as an employer-provided benefit. In years before the § 89 nondiscrimination rules for fringe benefit plans took effect, the requirement that the plan satisfy any applicable nondiscrimination rule otherwise imposed by the Code is substituted for the requirement that the plan satisfy § 89. Any amount deducted under § 162(m)'s provisions cannot be deducted as a medical expense under § 213.

The provisions of § 162(m) allowing self-employed individuals to deduct 25 percent of their health insurance costs are effective generally for taxable years beginning after 1986. Unless renewed, the provision is scheduled to expire for taxable years beginning after 1989.

Code § 105 medical plans were made subject to the uniform nondiscrimination rules for welfare plans enacted by the 1986 TRA in § 89. The § 89 provisions are effective generally for years beginning in 1989. The § 89 rules are discussed below. The § 89 rules, when they apply, supersede the § 105 nondiscrimination rules for medical plans discussed in this section.

Code § 120: Group Legal Services Plans

Before 1976, prepaid group legal services were not accorded tax-favored status. In the 1976 Tax Reform Act, however, Congress enacted Code § 120, excluding from employee gross income the value of employer-provided personal legal services under a qualified group legal services plan. Congress extended the sunset provision for § 120 through the end of 1985.[30] This sunset provision was again extended through December 31, 1987, by the 1986 TRA.[31] TAMRA allowed the group legal service provision to expire for taxable years ending after December 31, 1988. Note that TAMRA restricted the use of educational assistance plans for taxable years beginning after December 31, 1987, so that they could not be used to provide payments for certain graduate level courses.[32] The following discussion is included for historical purposes.

Under Code § 120(a), an employee could exclude from gross income amounts contributed by his employer on behalf of the employee, the employee's spouse, or dependents, to a qualified group legal services plan; the value of personal legal services that the employer provides through a § 120 plan to the employee, the employee's spouse, or dependents; and amounts paid by the employer under a §120 plan for personal legal services provided to the employee, the employee's spouse, or dependents.

A §120 plan could only provide for, or reimburse employees for, the cost of "personal legal services." For this purpose, personal legal services were defined in the proposed regulations as any legal service provided to a participating employee, the employee's spouse, or dependent that was not connected with or directly pertaining to a trade or business of the employee, the employee's spouse, or dependents; the management, conservation, or preservation of property held by the employee, the employee's spouse, or dependents for the production of income; or the production or collection of income by the employee, the employee's spouse, or dependents.[33] The legal services could be provided by a lawyer or by certain nonlawyers under the direction of a lawyer.[34]

A §120 plan had to be nondiscriminatory with respect to eligibility and benefits, i.e., it could not discriminate in favor of employees who were officers, shareholders, or highly compensated, or in favor of self-employed individuals.[35] In addition, no more than 25 percent of the amounts contributed under a qualified §120 plan during the year could be provided to a class of individuals who were shareholders or owners (or their spouses or dependents), each of whom owned (on any day of the year) more than five percent of the stock (or the capital or profits interest) in the employer.[36] Note, that if Congress had extended the sunset provision for §120 plans, these plans would have become subject, at the employer's election, to the §89 nondiscrimination rules for welfare plans. These rules are discussed below.

Code §124: Qualified Transportation Provided by an Employer

Code §124(a) provides that employee gross income does not include the value of qualified transportation provided by the employer between the employee's place of residence and place of employment. For this purpose, "qualified transportation" means transportation in a commuter highway vehicle.[37] The transportation, to qualify, must be provided under a written plan that does not discriminate in favor of officers, shareholders, or highly compensated employees.[38] The plan must provide that the value of the transportation provided is in addition to (or in lieu of) any compensation otherwise payable to the employee.[39] Again, unincorporated entities cannot take advantage of this provision to confer benefits on owner-employees in a taxfree manner, since the term "employee" for § 124 purposes does not include a self-employed individual or an owner-employee.[40]

Code § 127: Educational Assistance Programs

Code § 127(a) provides that employee gross income does not include amounts paid or incurred by the employer for educational assistance pursuant to a program described in § 127(b). Although Congress extended the sunset date for Code § 127 educational assistance programs through the end of 1985, Public Law 98-611 limited to $5,000 the amount of educational assistance that an employee could receive taxfree from all employers during a taxable year.[41] After the 1986 TRA, the maximum amount of tuition assistance which an employee could receive on a tax-favored basis under § 127 was $5,250. The 1986 TRA also retroactively extended the provision for two years, through December 31, 1987. TAMRA allowed Code § 127 to expire for taxable years beginning after 1988. The following discussion is included for historical purposes.

Section 127(b) defines an educational assistance program as a separate written plan of an employer for the exclusive benefit of its employees that provides educational assistance and satisfies certain specific requirements.[42] The program must benefit a classification of employees that the Secretary of Treasury finds does not discriminate in favor of employees who are officers, owners, or highly compensated, or their dependents.[43] In applying this test, employees who are covered by a collective bargaining agreement where educational assistance benefits have been the subject of good faith collective bargaining are not considered.[44] No more than five percent of the amounts paid or incurred by the employer to provide educational assistance during any year may go to shareholders or owners (or their spouses or dependents) each of whom (on any day of the year) owns more than five percent of the stock of (or the capital or profits interest in) the employer.[45]

Furthermore, a qualified § 127 program may not provide employees with a choice between educational assistance and other remuneration includable in gross income.[46] A § 127 program does not have to be funded, i.e., it can provide reimbursement as qualified expenses are incurred without the necessity of establishing a

for sale to customers in the course of the employer's business in which the employee is performing services.[72]

A "working condition fringe" is defined as any property or services provided to an employee of the employer to the extent that, if the employee paid for such property or services, the payment would be deductible under Code § 162 (relating to ordinary and necessary trade-or-business expenses) or Code § 167 (relating to depreciation).[73] An example of this might be the use of a company car by an employee whose employment requires extensive travel.

Note that § 132(h) contains a special rule that recognizes the practice in the auto sales industry of providing a demonstration use car for auto salespersons. Such use is considered a working condition fringe if it satisfies the requirements of § 132(h)(3)(B).

De minimis fringes were exempted from taxation largely due to the administrative burden associated with keeping track of such benefits. Code § 132(e) defines a *de minimis* fringe as any property or service whose value (after taking into account the frequency with which similar fringes are provided by the employer to its employees) is so small as to make accounting for it unreasonable or administratively impractical.[74] Under § 132(e)(2), the operation by an employer of an employee eating facility is a *de minimis* fringe if the facility is located on or near the employer's business premises and revenue derived therefrom normally equals or exceeds the direct operating costs of the eating facility.[75]

Such eating facilities are a *de minimis* fringe with respect to officers, owners, or highly compensated individuals only if access to the facility is available on substantially the same terms to each member of a group of employees that does not discriminate in favor of these individuals.[76]

For purposes of the no-additional cost service and qualified employee discount rules, certain retired and disabled employees and the surviving spouses of employees are treated as employees.[77] In addition, for purposes of all § 132 fringe benefits, use of the benefit by the employee's spouse or dependent children is considered to be use by the employee.[78] The exclusion from gross income provided by § 132(a) will only apply to an officer, owner, or highly compensated employee with respect to a no-additional cost service or a qualified employee discount if the benefit is provided on substantially the same terms to a group of employees that constitutes a reasonable classification and that does not discriminate in favor of this prohibited group.[79]

The statute allows for reciprocal agreements between employers to provide fringe benefits for each other's employees. A reciprocal agreement will allow the benefits provided by one employer for the employees of the other party to the agreement to qualify for the exclusion under § 132 if the services are provided pursuant to a written agreement between the employers and neither of the reciprocating employers incurs any substantial additional cost (including foregone revenue) in providing such service or pursuant to such agreement.[80]

An example of such a reciprocal agreement might be an agreement between an airline and a hotel chain to provide free airfare and free hotel accommodations to the employees of the other when such airfare or accommodations go unbooked.

For purposes of Code § 132, employer aggregation under Code §§414(b), (c), and (m) applies.[81] The statute also contains special rules for leased sections of department stores, parking on or near the employer's business premises (which is treated as a working condition fringe), and on-premises gyms and other eating facilities.[82] The Secretary of the Treasury is directed to prescribe regulations to carry out the purposes of § 132.[83]

As indicated above, the Tax Reform Act of 1984 added § 132 to the Code to exclude from income certain fringe benefits that qualify as no-additional-cost services, qualified employee discounts, working condition fringes, and *de minimis* fringes. Under § 132, no-additional-cost services and qualified employee discounts are available to employees in the "line of business" of the employer providing discounts or services. The IRS' "new" temporary fringe benefit regulations (issued December 23, 1985, to replace those issued in January 1985), determine a line of business based on the two-digit codes contained in the Enterprise Standard Industrial Classification Manual (ESIC Manual) which is prepared by the Statistical Policy Division of the Office of Management and Budget. An employer will be considered to have more than one line of business if it offers for sale to customers property or services in more than one classification referred to in the ESIC Manual.

Special aggregation rules are provided under which employees of one line of business will be treated as employees of another line of business if it is uncommon in the employer's industry for any of the separate lines of business to be operated without the others. The rule also applies if it is common for a substantial number of employees (other than those working at the employer's headquarters or main office) to perform substantial services for more than one line of business. Separate retail lines of business located on the same premises will also be considered one line of business.

Under the new regulations, the value of employer-provided transportation provided for security reasons would be excludable as a working condition fringe to the extent the employee could deduct the payment for the service under Code §162 or §167. Under the new regulations, the value of employer-provided transportation provided for bona fide business-oriented security reasons will be excludable as a working condition fringe only if provided pursuant to an overall 24-hour security program.

The temporary regulations exclude the value of parking as a working condition fringe provided the employee makes an adequate accounting of parking expenses.

The regulations also provide special rules for the treatment of certain individuals who are nonemployees. For instance, partners performing services for a partnership will qualify for all of the fringe benefit exclusions. Under a special administrative convenience rule, directors and independent contractors may qualify for certain working condition fringes.

Code §125: Cafeteria Plans

Code §125 was added by the 1978 Revenue Act effective for taxable years beginning after 1978.[84] Code §125 accords tax-favored status to certain plans—known as cafeteria plans—that allow employees to choose between taxable and taxfree benefits. If the cafeteria plan requirements are met, an employee will not be charged with the constructive receipt of income merely because he chooses a taxfree benefit when he otherwise could have chosen a taxable one. If not for this rule, the employee would be required, according to the principles of constructive receipt, to recognize the benefit as gross income in this situation.

Between the enactment of §125 and early 1984, no IRS guidance in the form of proposed regulations or otherwise was available with respect to cafeteria plans. As a result, several arrangements arose in the business community that, arguably, pushed the interpretation of this statute to its limit. Among the sorts of arrangements were "flexible spending accounts" and "zero-based reimbursement accounts" (ZEBRAs). Basically, these arrangements allowed an employee to choose between an array of reimbursable benefits as the plan year went on. For example, if medical benefits were reimbursable under a flexible spending arrangement, and the employee incurred a medical bill during the year, he would submit this bill for reimbursement at the next available reimbursement date, which could, in the extreme case, be as early as the next pay period. If, in the next reimbursement period, the employee incurred no medical expenses, but did incur a reimbursable tuition expense, he would do likewise. The advantage afforded by these plans was not only their flexibility, but also their design—to ostensibly remove such reimbursable amounts from federal income tax withholding and from FICA and FUTA taxes.

The growth of these purported cafeteria plan arrangements led the IRS to act in early 1984. On February 10, 1984, the IRS issued I.R. 84-22 which spelled out the agency's intention to retroactively disqualify any tax benefits received under ZEBRA and flexible spending account arrangements. Consistent with I.R. 84-22, the agency promulgated proposed regulations under §125.[85] Specifically, the proposed regulations contained a "use it or lose it" rule whereby an employee would have to make an irrevocable election as to which benefits he would like to receive under the plan before the beginning of the plan year and could not carry over unused benefit amounts to a succeeding taxable year. Only certain specified changes in circumstances will justify the alteration in mid-year of such an election, e.g., marriage, divorce, death, or termination of employment.[86]

The proposed regulations confirmed that a cafeteria plan may be operated off a salary reduction arrangement, provided the employee irrevocably elected prior to the beginning of the plan year (subject to changed conditions) to forego a specified amount of compensation.[87] The proposed regulations also clarified that, if a cafeteria plan discriminated in favor of the prohibited group, members of that group would be taxed as if they had elected to receive the maximum amount of taxable benefits that they could have elected under the plan. The proposed regulations were given retroactive application. When finalized, they were to apply for cafeteria plan years beginning after 1978, the first year under the statute.

The 1984 TRA through Code §531(b) grandfathered certain past practices that were disallowed under the proposed regulations and made certain other changes to Code §125. Under the grandfather provision, a plan will not be disqualified for failure to conform to the requirements of the proposed regulations for those plans that were in existence on February 10, 1984, but failed after that date (and continued to fail thereafter) to satisfy Prop. Treas. Regs. §1.125-1. These plans will continue to qualify until the earlier of January 1, 1985, or the effective date of any plan modification that provides additional benefits after February 10, 1984 (the date of I.R. 84-22).[88]

Another special transitional rule is provided with respect to "advance election benefit banks." These arrangements will not be disqualified merely because they provided that an employee would be assured of receiving unused benefit amounts as compensation, in violation of Prop. Treas. Regs. §1.125-1. The relief only extends to benefits provided before the earlier of July 1, 1985, or the effective date of any modification to the plan that provided for additional benefits after February 10, 1984.[89] Another special transitional rule extended the grandfathering relief to plans that were not in existence on February 10, 1984, but with respect to which the employer had already incurred substantial implementation costs before that date.

The 1984 TRA also limited the types of benefits that may be provided under a cafeteria plan to, in general, cash or nontaxable benefits, subject to certain enumerated exceptions. The TRA added a limitation of 25 percent on the benefits that may be provided key employees under a cafeteria plan. A similar limit applies to the prohibited group of highly compensated employees. The TRA also imposed certain reporting requirements on employers maintaining cafeteria plans during taxable years beginning after 1984. These amendments to §125 are generally effective on January 1, 1985.

With this legislative background in mind, it is easier to understand the basic cafeteria plan rules. Code §125(a) provides the general rule that, except as provided in §125(b), no amount will be includable in the gross income of a cafeteria plan participant solely because he may choose among the benefits provided under the plan.

For this purpose, a cafeteria plan is defined as a written plan under which all participants are employees and the participants may choose among two or more benefits consisting of cash and qualified benefits.[90]

Qualified benefits are defined as any benefit that is not includable in employee gross income under Chapter 1 of the Code, except for a benefit excludable under Code §117 (relating to certain scholarships); Code § 124 (transportation assistance); Code § 127 (educational assistance); and Code § 132 (previously nonstatutory fringe benefits).[91]

For this purpose, group-term life insurance in excess of the $50,000 limit of Code § 79(a) is considered a nontaxable benefit under Chapter 1.[92] Thus, after the 1984 TRA, the only fringe benefits that may be provided under a cafeteria plan are:

- Code § 79 group-term life insurance;
- Code §§ 105–106 medical, accident, and disability benefits;
- Code § 120 group legal services; and
- Code § 129 dependent care assistance.

In addition, as under pre-TRA law, a cafeteria plan cannot permit an employee to elect to receive deferred compensation, except pursuant to a Code § 401(k) CODA.[93]

Under Code § 125(b), the general § 125(a) exclusion from constructive receipt does not apply to a highly compensated participant for any plan year for which the plan discriminates in favor of such individuals as to eligibility to participate or as to contributions or benefits.[94] For this purpose, a "highly compensated participant" is defined with reference to § 414(q).[95]

Section 125(b) also provides that in the case of a key employee,[96] any benefit provided under a plan for which the statutory nontaxable benefits attributable to key employees exceed 25 percent of the total of such benefits provided for all employees will be considered constructively received.[97]

Note that both of these rules apply to all members of the group of highly compensated or key employees, regardless of the benefit levels of individual members of that group. Thus, the benefits of certain group members can cause adverse tax consequences for all members of the group.

For purposes of applying the nondiscriminatory classification test and the key employee test, employees who may be excluded from consideration under Code § 89(h)'s age and service requirements need not be counted. Code § 89 is discussed below.

Benefits that violate the § 125(b) standards with respect to highly compensated participants or key employees will be taxed to such individuals in their taxable year in which the plan year ends. Thus, for instance, assuming the employee's taxable year is the calendar year, and the plan year where the discriminatory benefit is provided ends June 30, 1985, the amount would be included in gross income in taxable 1985.

Finally, Code § 125(g) imposes certain reporting requirements on cafeteria plans. Specifically, for plan years beginning after 1984, employers maintaining § 125 cafeteria plans must file a return at such time and in such manner as the Secretary of the Treasury prescribes, showing for the plan year:

- The number of employees of the employer;
- The number of employees eligible to participate under the plan;
- The number of employees participating under the plan;
- The total cost of the plan during the year;
- The name, address, and taxpayer identification number of the employer and the type of business in which the employer is engaged; and
- The number of highly compensated employees.[98]

Employers with cafeteria plans are required to maintain the necessary records to determine whether there has been compliance with the reporting requirements.[99] The Secretary is given discretion to require additional information and an additional return from specific employers maintaining cafeteria plans.[100]

Since the enactment of Code § 125 in 1978, there have been two main inhibitors to the widespread use of cafeteria plans:

(1) The question as to whether salary reduction could be employed in a cafeteria plan; and

(2) The problem of "adverse selection."

The first issue, salary reduction, has been addressed in the proposed regulations, i.e., so long as the salary reduction requirement satisfies the regulatory criteria, it will not disqualify the plan. The second issue is that of adverse selection. Adverse selection, basically, refers to the tendency of employees who need a particular benefit most to select that benefit where a choice is provided. For example, an employee with teenage children might be inclined to select an orthodonture benefit, whereas one with a serious medical condition might select a hospitalization benefit with a low deductible. Because of experience rating, this has tended to drive the per participant cost upward, rendering cafeteria plans extremely costly.

Two main planning techniques are available to combat this sort of adverse selection.

The first involves limiting the range of choices from which an employee may select. For instance, a plan might provide a core of basic benefits and permit employees to select incremental amounts of additional benefits over and above the core benefits. The core benefit requirement would produce a group for group rating purposes that can help contain costs. Another planning technique that can be used in addition to the core benefit technique or by itself is the technique of restricting participants' ability to alter their benefit mixes from one plan year to the next. For instance, a plan might provide that benefit A can be elected at each of five levels in ascending order of magnitude. The plan might provide that an employee can only increase or decrease his benefit by one level per year. Thus, an employee who initially elected benefits at the third level for one plan year could not elect such benefits at lower than the second, nor higher than the fourth, in the succeeding plan year. This limiting of selection can make benefit costs more predictable from year to year. Finally, employers can contain costs by providing an effective co-insurance feature. Under this type of arrangement, the employer might agree to contribute a uniform dollar amount or a uniform percentage of compensation for all employees to use in the plan. To the extent an employee's selection of benefit options exceeded this amount, he could be required to make up the difference.

These techniques are all viable alternatives to help contain the costs of cafeteria plans. These plans are certainly more complex to administer than the traditional fringe benefit package that provides specified amounts of each benefit for each employee. But, where the problems associated with cafeteria plans can be worked out to the satisfaction of the sponsoring employer and participating employees, such plans can have a tremendously beneficial impact on employee morale by tailoring each employee's benefit package to suit his or her particular needs. The impact will be especially beneficial when the plan is effectively communicated to employees. With the increasing diversity of the modern work force and concomitant diverse benefit needs, a cafeteria plan, when properly used, can be an effective tool to enable an employer to compete in hiring and retaining employees. Now that the proposed regulations have given practitioners some guidance in this area, the risk factor connected with maintaining such a plan has been greatly reduced—the main obstacles to installing a cafeteria plan now come from increased administrative costs and the problem of inverse selection. However, planning techniques are available that can reduce the impact of these problems somewhat.

Code §89: Uniform Nondiscrimination Rules for Welfare Plans

As a condition of the taxfree treatment of fringe benefits, Congress adopted various nondiscrimination rules to protect against discrimination in favor of highly compensated employees. As the rules in this area developed, each benefit was given its own set of nondiscrimination rules with its own standards and definitions. In an effort to make the varying nondiscrimination rules for the numerous statutory fringe benefits uniform, the 1986 Tax Reform Act added Code §89. The comprehensive rules and definitions set forth in this section apply to "statutory employee benefit plans" as defined in Code §89(i). The provisions are mandatory for §79 group-term life insurance plans and §105 medical plans[101] and may, at the employer's election,[102] apply to §120 group legal service plans (which, however, have expired for years beginning after 1988), §127 tuition assistance plans (which have also expired for years beginning after 1988), and §129 dependent care assistance programs. The effect of §89 is to put all the nondiscrimination rules under one Code section, to extend these rules to insured health plans and to broaden the segment of the work force covered by the rules to include highly compensated employees.[103] The general effective date of §89 is for years beginning after 1989. Special effective date rules apply to collectively bargained plans, certain group-term life insurance plans, church plans, and cafeteria plans.

The general rule under Code §89 is that if a statutory fringe benefit plan discriminates in favor of highly compensated employees, the "excess benefit" is taxable to the favored employees. Thus, §89(a) provides that the gross income of a highly compensated employee who is a participant in a discriminatory employee benefit plan during any plan year must include an amount equal to such employee's "excess benefit" under the plan for the year.[104] The inclusion in income occurs in the employee's taxable year in which the plan year ends. Section 89(b) defines the "excess benefit" of a highly compensated employee as the excess of such employee's employer-provided benefit over the highest permitted benefit.[105] "Highest permitted benefit" is defined as the benefit determined by reducing the nontaxable benefits of highly compensated employees until the plan would not be considered discriminatory if such reduced benefits were taken into account.[106] "Nontaxable benefit" is defined as any benefit covered under §89 that is excludable from gross income under the Code's income tax provisions.

The above sanction is applied to "discriminatory employee benefit plans," which §89(c) defines as any statutory employee benefit plan that does not meet the eligibility requirements of §89(d) and the benefit requirements of §89(e).

Because of the extreme difficulty employers were having trying to comply with the §89 testing scheme, TAMRA provided that good-faith compliance with a reasonable interpretation of §89 based on the statute and the legislative history would be considered reasonable compliance by the IRS. Congress noted that a taxpayer would not be considered to be acting in good faith where the taxpayer consistently resolved unclear issues in his own favor. The preamble to the proposed §89 regulations reiterates that relief.[107]

Eligibility Requirements

Code §89(d) provides that a plan will satisfy the eligibility requirements for any plan year if it meets three eligibility tests:

(1) *The 90 Percent/50 Percent Eligibility Rule:* At least 90 percent of *all* employees who are not highly compensated are eligible to participate in the plan (or in a plan of the employer of the same type), and they would (if they participated) have available to them under the plan a benefit which is at least 50 percent of the largest employer-provided benefit under all such plans of the employer to any highly compensated employee[108];

(2) *The 50 Percent Eligibility Rule:* At least 50 percent of the employees *eligible* to participate in the plan are not highly compensated employees; and

(3) *The Subjective Discrimination Test:* The plan does not contain any provision relating to eligibility to participate which,

by its terms or in operation, discriminates in favor of highly compensated employees.

In lieu of the 50 percent eligibility rule described in (2) above, a plan may satisfy an "alternative eligibility percentage test." Under this test, a plan will satisfy the second part of the three-part eligibility test if the percentage determined by dividing the number of highly compensated employees eligible to participate in the plan by the total number of highly compensated employees does not exceed the percentage similarly determined with respect to employees who are not highly compensated.[109]

Benefit Requirements

A statutory employee fringe benefit plan will be treated as discriminatory if, in addition to the eligibility requirements, it does not meet the Code §89 benefit requirements. The calculations under these requirements are generally a comparison of the benefits received by the nonhighly compensated employees to those received by the highly compensated employees. Consequently, §89(e) requires that for a plan to meet the benefit requirements for any plan year, the average employer-provided benefit received by nonhighly compensated employees under all plans of the employer of the same type be at least 75 percent of the average employer-provided benefit received by highly compensated employees under all plans of the employer of the same type.

"Average employer-provided benefit" for highly compensated employees is defined as an amount equal to (1) the aggregate employer-provided benefits received by highly compensated employees under all plans of the type being tested, divided by, (2) the number of highly compensated employees of the employer (whether or not covered under such plan). Code §89(g)(3) defines the term "employer-provided benefit" as (1) in the case of a health or group-term life insurance plan, the value of the coverage, or (2) in the case of any other plan, the value of the benefits provided during the plan year on behalf of the employee that are attributable to employer contributions.[110] A similar calculation applies in determining the average employer-provided benefit for nonhighly compensated employees.

Special 80-Percent Actual Coverage Test

Under a special rule, if at least 80 percent of the employees who are not highly compensated are covered under a health plan or group-term life insurance plan during the plan year, the health or group life plan will be treated as satisfying the eligibility and benefit requirements for the year if the plan does not contain any provision relating to eligibility to participate which, by its terms or in operation, discriminates in favor of highly compensated employees.

Plan Aggregation and Separation

In conducting the Code §89 analysis, a plan, as defined by the employer, often must be broken down into its component parts and reconfigured. The basis of the analysis is a "benefit option." Code §89(j)(11) provides that each different benefit option or variation is considered a separate plan. Under this provision, if plan benefits vary in any way, the benefit will be broken into its component parts and redefined as multiple plans. An exception under §89(j)(4)(A) provides that a group-term life insurance plan is not to be treated as two or more separate plans merely because the amount of insurance coverage varies in proportion to compensation.

Section 89(g)(1) alleviates some of the harshness of the separate plan rules by allowing aggregation of comparable health care plans for purposes of certain §89 tests (the "50% eligibility" and "80% actual coverage" tests). Plans are comparable when the smallest benefit available to any participant in the plan is at least 95 percent of the largest benefit available to any participant in the other plan.[111]

Note that §89(g)(4) provides an employer with an election to treat plans of different types as plans of the same type for purposes of applying the benefit requirements of §89(e). However, this election is not available for purposes of determining whether a health plan satisfies §89(e), except that benefits provided under health plans may be taken into account in determining whether plans of other types satisfy §89(e).

In addition, Code §89(g)(5) provides that if, under Code §414(r), an employer is treated as operating separate lines of business for a year, the employer may apply the §89 rules separately with respect to the employees of each separate line of business. This election is only available if the plan is available to a nondiscriminatory classification of employees.

Excluded Employees

Code §89(h) specifies which employees may be disregarded in testing a plan for discrimination under §89. Under this provision, employees with less than a year of service (or six months in the case of core benefits under a health plan) may be excluded until the first day of the first month beginning after they have completed the applicable period of service.

Similarly, employees who regularly work less than 17½ hours per week may be excluded from consideration along with employees who regularly work not more than six months during the year, employees under age 21, employees covered by collective bargaining agreements and nonresident aliens with no U.S.-source income. The employer may elect to substitute shorter periods and lower ages for those prescribed by statute.

If the employer excludes a particular category of employees in testing for discrimination, all employees within that category must be so excluded. Further, all such exclusions must generally be applied to all statutory employee benefit plans of the employer of the same type. An exception to this later rule applies with respect to differences in waiting periods for core and noncore benefits under a health plan. Under Code §89(h)(5), if employees are excluded from consideration due to qualified age and service requirements but are covered under another plan of the employer, the employer may satisfy the nondiscrimination rules separately with respect to such employees.

TAMRA added a special rule for the application of §89 to certain small employers. It allows employers with fewer than 10 employees to disregard certain part-time employees in applying the 80 percent actual coverage test. These employers may disregard employees who normally work 35 hours or less per week in applying this test in plan years beginning in 1989. For plan years beginning in 1990, they may disregard employees who normally work 25 hours or less per week. In 1991, the standard 17½ hours worked exclusion will again apply for these small employers.[112]

Qualification and Reporting Requirements

Code §89(k) introduces plan permanence and formality requirements for covered plans. An employee must include in income an amount equal to his or her employer-provided benefit unless the following requirements are satisfied:

(1) The plan is in writing;

(2) The employee's rights under the plan are legally enforceable;

(3) Employees are provided reasonable notification of benefits available in the plan;

(4) The plan is maintained for the exclusive benefit of the employees; and

(5) The plan was established with the intention of being maintained for an indefinite period of time.

These permanence requirements apply to any statutory employee benefit plan, qualified tuition reduction plan, cafeteria plan, fringe benefit programs providing no-additional-cost services, qualified employee discount, or employer-operated eating facilities which are excludable from income under Code §132, and Voluntary Employees' Beneficiary Associations (VEBAs) covered under the Code §505 nondiscrimination rules.

For any plan year beginning in 1989, TAMRA permits employers to comply with the requirement that a plan be in writing by completing the required written documentation by the end of that plan year if employees are given reasonable notice of the plan's essential features by the first day of the plan year and the written provisions are effective retroactively to the beginning of that plan year.[113] In addition, the proposed §89(k) regulations provide transitional relief under which a plan is not required to meet the writing requirement before the later of the beginning of the first day of the second plan year beginning after December 31, 1988, or the end of the 12-month period beginning on the first day of the first plan year that the plan is subject to §89.[114]

The employer is required to report on Form W-2 the amount of excess benefits that the employee is required to include in gross income under Code §89(a)(1) and the amount of employer-provided benefit required to be included in income under Code §89(k)(1).

An employer who fails to report such amounts is subject to a penalty in the form of an additional tax. In a rather unique enforcement mechanism, Code §6652(k) imposes a penalty for failure to provide certain information with respect to includable employee benefits. If an employer fails to report an amount on a required statement that is includable in income under §89, a tax is imposed on the employer equal to the highest rate of tax imposed on individual taxpayers for taxable years beginning in the calendar year to which the return or statement relates, multiplied by the employer-provided benefit with respect to which the failure relates. Note that the provision may be exercised for reasonable cause and only one addition to tax may apply per employee per year even if there is more than one failure with respect to the employee.

COBRA Health Care Continuation Requirements

Congress has been consistently cutting back on the benefits associated with welfare plans while also trying to provide coverage for a larger segment of the work force. If an employer desires to receive the tax benefits associated with a welfare plan, it must comply with the various restrictions and limitations enacted by Congress to ensure that the policy objective of providing essential social services to individuals who otherwise could not afford the services is met. The health care continuation provisions set forth in the Consolidated Omnibus Budget Reconciliation Act of 1985 (COBRA) are one such set of rules.[115] COBRA generally applies to plan years beginning on or after July 1, 1986.[116] As discussed below, although the consequences of ignoring COBRA were originally very harsh, TAMRA significantly reduced the penalties.[117]

Coverage Requirements

Basically, the COBRA health care continuation rule provides that a qualified beneficiary covered under an employer's group health plan who experiences a qualifying event may elect to continue that health coverage for up to 18 or 36 months (depending on the qualifying event). The provisions introduce a number of terms, the definitions of which are key to understanding and implementing the COBRA rules.

To begin, qualified beneficiaries are employees, as well as their spouses and dependents who are covered under the employer's plan.[118] Qualified beneficiaries must be covered by a health plan on the day before the qualifying event, as an employee or an employee's spouse or dependent.[119] A qualifying event is any one of the following events which would cause the individual to lose coverage under the employer's plan:

(1) The death of the employee;

(2) The termination of the employee's employment (other than for gross misconduct) or a reduction in the employee's hours;

(3) The divorce or legal separation of the employee from his or her spouse;

(4) The employee's entitlement to Medicare; and

(5) A dependent child ceasing to be a dependent under the plan.[120]

Generally exempted from the COBRA requirements are group health plans of employers that normally employ fewer than 20 employees, and plans maintained by churches, the federal government, the District of Columbia, and any territory or possession of the United States. Plans established and maintained by state and local governments which receive funds from under the Public Health Services Act must comply with the continuation provisions, although there is no specific statutory penalty for failure to comply.[121]

A group health plan is defined as an employee welfare benefit plan providing medical care to participants and beneficiaries directly or through insurance, reimbursement, or otherwise.[122] Dental and vision plans are included.[123]

Where the event ending coverage is termination of employment or a reduction in hours, group health care coverage must be offered to continue for at least 18 months after the termination or reduction in hours. For the other events, coverage must continue for at least 36 months.[124] In the event that a second qualifying event occurs during the first 18 months after the date of the initial event, coverage must be continued for up to 36 months from the first qualifying event.[125] The 18- or 36-month period runs from the date of the qualifying event even if coverage does not terminate until a later date (for example because the employer extends coverage for some other reason).[126]

The continuation coverage may be stopped, however, if any of the following interceding events occurs: the employer ceases to provide any group health coverage to its employees, the payment of premiums required under the plan fails to be made in a timely manner, or the qualified beneficiary becomes covered under any other group health plan.[127]

The continuation coverage must consist of the same coverage that is provided under the health plan to other similarly situated employees and beneficiaries who have not incurred a qualifying event. If coverage under the plan is modified for any group of similarly situated employees and beneficiaries, the coverage must also be modified for all those receiving continuation coverage.[128] COBRA requires that a qualified beneficiary be given the right to elect to buy the same coverage that he or she had immediately before the qualifying event. If a similarly situated active employee's coverage is modified, that change must be passed through to the COBRA continuees. However, the proposed regulations state that if the active employees' plan is "changed or eliminated" the COBRA continuees may opt into any other health plan that the employer maintains.[129]

Qualified beneficiaries may choose either core-only coverage, or core-plus-noncore coverage, but if noncore coverage is no more than 5 percent of the total cost, the plan need not break out the noncore benefits.[130]

The applicable premium is equal to the cost to the plan for a determination period for similarly situated beneficiaries with respect to whom a qualifying event has not occurred (without regard to whether such costs are paid by the employer or employee).[131] The employer is not required to cover the costs of the continuation coverage. The plan may require the employee or beneficiary to pay the premium, but not in excess of 102 percent of the cost to the plan for similarly situated employees or beneficiaries who have not incurred a qualifying event.[132] If so elected, the premium may be paid in monthly installments.[133] The premium must be determined for a 12-month period before the beginning of the coverage period.[134] Plan deductibles and out-of-pocket limits are continued after the qualifying event for the entire period of continuation coverage.[135] The first premiums are not due until 45 days after the COBRA election. But also note that COBRA electors must be given a grace period for payment of premiums equal to 30 days or, if longer, the period allowed for active employees or the employer to pay any premiums to the provider of coverage.[136]

Notice and Election Requirements

The group health plan must provide written notice to each employee, covered spouse and dependent child of the right to elect continuation coverage under COBRA. The notice must be given at the time coverage under the plan begins or when COBRA took effect for those who were already covered by a plan when COBRA became law.[137] Generally, the employer has an additional burden of notifying the plan administrator (if it is not the administrator) of any event which would require the extended coverage.[138] After being advised of a qualifying event, the administrator has 14 days to notify qualified beneficiaries of their rights to continuation coverage and to provide them with an opportunity to elect such coverage.[139]

The COBRA election period may begin at any time, but it must last for at least 60 days after the date the qualified beneficiary would lose coverage in absence of a COBRA election.[140] Plans do not have to pay claims for services furnished during the election period before the qualified beneficiary has elected continuation coverage and paid the premium for it, but they must make a retroactive reimbursement for such claims if the individual ultimately makes the election and pays the premium.[141] While a parent may elect COBRA on behalf of the family, each qualified beneficiary has the independent right to elect it if the employee or the spouse rejects for him or herself.[142] This also means that each qualified beneficiary has the independent right to elect core or core and noncore benefits.[143]

Note that if COBRA coverage lapses at the end of the 18- or 36-month period, the beneficiary must be given the same conversion privilege otherwise available under the plan.[144]

Sanctions

The consequences of failing to comply with COBRA were originally quite harsh and resulted in the denial of the federal income tax deduction for expenses paid or incurred for any group health plan maintained by the employer, regardless of the extent or duration and regardless of correction of the violation.[145] In addition, highly compensated employees who participated in the plan were not permitted to exclude from income the amount contributed by the employer on their behalf if any health plan of the employer failed to provide extension of coverage as required by COBRA.[146] Also, for those plans covered by ERISA, a penalty of up to $100 per day was imposed on the plan administrator, personally, for failure to provide the required notices.[147] Presumably, the Labor Department could bring enforcement procedures against a delinquent employer.[148] Employers who fail to notify of this coverage could also be subject to suits to recover medical costs associated with an injury which would otherwise have been covered by continuation coverage.[149]

For plan years beginning after December 1988, TAMRA replaced the original sanctions with an excise tax that takes into account the number of individuals for whom there has been a failure, the amount of time a failure existed, the employer's knowledge of the failure and whether there was a correction made.[150] The excise tax consists of $100 per day per qualified beneficiary during the noncompliance period, with a maximum of $200 per day imposed where a family is involved.[151] There is a total maximum liability which is the lesser of 10 percent of the total amount the employer paid during the preceding year for group health plans or $500,000.[152]

Notes

1. Tax Equity & Fiscal Responsibility Act of 1982, P.L. 97-248, adding Code §79(d).
2. The Tax Reform Act of 1984 (P.L. 98-369).
3. The Tax Reform Act of 1986 (P.L. 99-514).
4. Technical and Miscellaneous Revenue Act of 1988 (TAMRA) (P.L. 100-647).
5. *See* Treas. Regs. §1.79-3(d)(2).
6. Treas. Regs. §1.79-1(a)(1).
7. Treas. Regs. §1.79-1(a)(2).
8. Treas. Regs. §1.79-1(c)(1).
9. *Id.*
10. Treas. Regs. §§1.79-1(c)(2)(i)–(iii).
11. Treas. Regs. §§1.79-1(c)(3)(i)–(iii).
12. Treas. Regs. §1.79-1(c)(4)(i).
13. Treas. Regs. §1.79-1(c)(4)(ii).
14. Treas. Regs. §1.79-1(c)(4)(iii).
15. Treas. Regs. §1.79-1(a)(3).

16. Treas. Regs. § 1.79-1(a)(4).
17. Treas. Regs. §§ 1.79-1(b)(1)–(2). "Deemed death benefit" is defined in Treas. Regs. § 1.79-1(d)(3).
18. Code §§ 79(d)(1)(A)–(B).
19. Code § 79(d)(6).
20. Code §§ 79(d)(3)(A)(i)–(iii).
21. Code § 79(d)(3)(A)(iv).
22. Code §§ 79(d)(3)(b)(i)–(iv).
23. Code § 79(d)(5).
24. Code § 79(d)(7).
25. Code § 105(a).
26. Code §§ 105(h)(3)(A)–(B).
27. Code § 105(h)(7).
28. Code § 105(g).
29. COBRA § 10001(g).
30. Internal Revenue Code, Amendments (P.L. 98-612), 1984.
31. Under a transitional rule contained in the 1986 TRA, if, within 60 days after the 1986 TRA's enactment date, an employee elects under a Code § 125 cafeteria plan coverage for group legal benefits under § 120, this election, if the taxpayer chooses, may apply to all legal services provided during 1986. This rule was made necessary because the pre-TRA sunset provision for group legal services plans expired December 31, 1985, and was not renewed until late 1986 by the TRA. The 1986 TRA transitional rule is not available for any plan which, on August 16, 1986, offered § 120 group legal services.
32. See Code § 127(c)(1).
33. See 394 T.M. *Employee Fringe Benefits.*
34. *Id.*
35. Code § 120(c)(1)(2).
36. Code § 120(c)(3).
37. As defined in Code § 46(c)(6)(B), i.e., one with a seating capacity of at least 8 adults, where at least 80% of the mileage is for transporting employees between their residences and their place of employment and where, during trips, the number of employees comprise at least half the vehicle's adult seating capacity, not including the driver. For this purpose, the requirements of §§ 46(c)(6)(B)(iii)–(iv), relating to the date of vehicle acquisition and the employer's income tax election, are inapplicable. See Code § 124(b).
38. Code § 124(c)(1).
39. Code § 124(c)(2).
40. Code § 124(d)(2).
41. Internal Revenue Code, Amendments (P.L. 98-612), 1984.
42. Code § 127(b)(1).
43. Code § 127(b)(2).
44. *Id.*
45. Code § 127(b)(3).
46. Code § 127(b)(4). However, this paragraph provides that, for this purpose, the business practices of the employer shall be taken into account.
47. Code § 127(b)(5).
48. Code § 127(b)(6).
49. Code § 127(c)(1).
50. *Id.*

51. Code § 127(c)(2).
52. Code § 127(c)(5).
53. Economic Recovery Tax Act (ERTA), (P.L. 97-34), Code § 124(e)(1).
54. Family Support Act of 1988 (P.L. 100-485).
55. Code § 129(d)(1).
56. Code § 129(d)(2).
57. Code § 129(d)(3).
58. Code § 129(d)(5).
59. Code § 129(d)(6).
60. Code § 129(d)(7).
61. Code § 129(d)(4).
62. See Code § 129(e)(1).
63. Code §§ 129(c)(1)–(2).
64. Code §§ 129(b)(1)(A)–(B).
65. See Code §§ 129(b)(2); 21(d)(2).
66. Code §§ 132(a)(1)–(4).
67. Code §§ 132(b)(1)–(2).
68. Code §§ 132(c)(1)(A)–(B).
69. Code § 132(c)(2)(A).
70. Code § 132(c)(2)(B).
71. Code § 132(c)(3).
72. Code § 132(c)(4).
73. Code § 132(d).
74. Code § 132(e)(1).
75. Code §§ 132(e)(2)(A)–(B).
76. *Id.*
77. Code § 132(f)(1).
78. Code § 132(f)(2).
79. Code § 132(h)(1).
80. Code § 132(g)(2).
81. Code § 132(g)(1).
82. See Code §§ 132(h)(2), (4), (5).
83. Code § 132(k).
84. P.L. 95-600.
85. See Prop. Treas. Reg. § 1.125-1.
86. See 1984 T.M., *Detailed Analysis of the 1984 Tax Reform Act*, at A-411.
87. See Prop. Treas. Reg. § 1.125-1, 984 T.M. at A-411.
88. Code § 531(b)(5)(A); 984 T.M. at A-413.
89. *Id.*
90. Code §§ 125(c)(1)(A)–(B).
91. Code § 125(e).
92. *Id.*
93. Code § 125(c)(2).
94. Code § 125(b)(1).
95. Code § 125(d).
96. Within the meaning of Code § 416(i)(1).
97. Code § 125(b)(2).
98. Code § 125(h). See § 6039D(a).
99. Code § 125(h). See § 6039D(b).
100. Code § 125(h). See § 6039D(c).

101. In a conforming amendment, the special nondiscrimination rules for group-term life insurance plans contained in § 79(d) and for self-insured medical reimbursement plans in § 105(h) were repealed.
102. If an employer does elect, the Code § 89 rules apply in place of the nondiscrimination rules that otherwise would apply for that fringe benefit.
103. The Code § 89 rules have numerous difficult and sloppy areas which require technical corrections and regulations. The Technical Corrections Act of 1987 (H.R. 2636 and S. 1350) was dropped from the 1987 Omnibus Budget Reconciliation Act (P.L. 203-100). Further efforts are being made to pass technical corrections before the effective date of § 89. In addition, a number of proposed regulations are at various stages and are expected before § 89 comes into force.
104. As defined in § 414(q).
105. In computing the excess benefits, all plans of the same type are aggregated.
106. This calculation begins with the employees with the greatest nontaxable benefits.
107. See Preamble, Treas. Regs. § 1.89(a)–1.
108. Under the 50% part of the 90/50% eligibility test, salary reduction is treated as an employer contribution.
109. Note that Code § 89(g)(6) provides that, in determining whether a plan satisfies the 50 percent part of the 90/50 percent eligibility test or, for purposes of applying the special 80 percent health plan coverage rule of § 89(f), the employer may elect (1) to apply § 89 separately with respect to coverage of spouses and dependents under such plans, and (2) to take into account with respect to such coverage only those employees with a spouse or dependent.
110. Under a special rule for health plans, the value of their coverage is to be determined under regulations which will provide the values of various standard types of coverage involving a representative group. Under a special rule for determining the value of coverage for group-term life insurance plans, the amount taken into account for any employee is to be based on the insurance cost under the Table II rates of Code § 79(c) for an employee age 40.
111. When testing plans under the "75% benefit" and "90%/50% eligibility" tests, Code § 89(i)(3) aggregates all plans of the "same type."
112. Code § 89(h)(1)(B).
113. See TAMRA § 3021(c)(3), explaining § 89(k)(1)(A).
114. Proposed Treas. Regs. § 1.89(k)-1.
115. Title X of the Consolidated Omnibus Reconciliation Act of 1985 (COBRA), P.L. 99-272, as amended by § 1895(d) of the Tax Reform Act, P.L. 99-514, and § 9501 of the Omnibus Budget Reconciliation Act of 1986 (OBRA 1986), P.L. 99-509. These statutes amended ERISA §§ 601–608, 29 U.S.C. §§ 1161–68; Code §§ 106(b), 162(k); and Public Health Services Act §§ 2201–08, 42 U.S.C. §§ 300bb-1–300bb-8.
116. This means they apply to calendar plan years starting on January 1, 1987. COBRA §§ 10001(e) and 10002(d).
117. Note that the plan may offer the employee a choice between COBRA coverage and some other form of extended coverage, including retiree coverage or state law continuation coverage. Prop. Treas. Regs. §§ 1.106-1, 1.162-26, 52 Fed. Reg. 22716 (June 15, 1987).

118. Code §4980B, ERISA §607(3).
119. The term employee includes former employees (for example, retirees) as well as sole proprietors, partners, directors and independent contractors, if they were covered under a plan that also covers employees, but does not include nonresident aliens with no U.S.-source income. See Prop. Treas. Regs. §§1.106-1, 1.162-26, 52 Fed. Reg. 22716 (June 15, 1987).
120. Code §4980B.
121. Code §106(b)(2).
122. ERISA §607(1). Medical care is defined in Code §213(d).
123. Note that the term "group health plan" includes any plan maintained by an employer to provide medical care to employees, former employees and/or their families. This includes individual as well as group health insurance policies (if two or more employees) and employee-pay-all plans "if coverage under the plan would not be available at the same cost to an employee in the event that he or she were not employed by the employer." From Prop. Treas. Reg. §§1.106-1, 1.162-26, 52 Fed. Reg. 22,716 (June 15, 1987).
124. Code §4980B, ERISA §602(2). A reduction in hours includes reduction due to a strike, lockout, or layoff. Prop. Treas. Regs. §§1.106-1, 1.162-2, 52 Fed. Reg. 22,716 (June 15, 1987).
125. Prop. Treas. Regs. §162-26.
126. See Prop. Treas. Regs. §§1.106-1, 1.162-26, 52 Fed. Reg. 22,716 (June 15, 1987).
127. See Joint Committee Blue Book.
128. Code §4980B, ERISA §602(1).
129. Prop. Treas. Regs. §§1.106-1, 1.162-26, 52 Fed. Reg. 22,716 (June 15, 1987).
130. Conf. Rep. 841 at 859. Noncore refers to dental and vision plans that do not require the services of a licensed physician).
131. Code §4980B, ERISA §604(1).
132. Code §4980B, ERISA §602(3).
133. Code §4980B, ERISA §604.
134. Code §4980B, ERISA §604(3).
135. Prop. Treas. Regs. §§1.106-1, 1.162-26, 52 Fed. Reg. 22,716 (June 15, 1987).
136. *Id.*
137. Code §4980B, ERISA §606(1).
138. The employer must notify the administrator if the qualifying event is death, termination, or reduction in hours, or entitlement to Medicare. The employee must notify the administrator if the event is separation or divorce or a dependent child ceasing to be dependent. The employer has 30 days to notify the administrator. Where the employee must notify, he or she has 60 days from the date of the event.
139. Code §4980B, ERISA §605(2).
140. *Id.*
141. Prop. Treas. Regs. §§1.106-1, 1.162-26, 52 Fed. Reg. 22,716 (June 15, 1987).
142. Code §4980B, ERISA §605(2); Conf. Rep. 841 at 859.
143. Prop. Treas. Regs. §§1.106-1, 1.162-26, 52 Fed. Reg. 22,716 (June 15, 1987).
144. Code §4980B, ERISA §602(5). The qualified beneficiary must be given the right to elect conversion to an individual plan during the 180 day period ending on the expiration date of continuation coverage. See Prop. Treas. Regs. §1.162-26.

145. Code § 162(i)(2)(A); See also Prop. Treas. Regs. §§ 1.106-1, 1.162-26, 52 Fed. Reg. 22,716 (June 15, 1987).
146. Code § 102(b). Highly compensated employee is defined by reference to Code § 105(h)(5).
147. Plan administrator is defined in ERISA § 16(A).
148. ERISA § 502(a).
149. Prop. Treas. Regs. § 1.106-1.
150. Code § 4980B.
151. Code § 4980B(c)(3).
152. Code § 4980B(c)(4).

Appendix A

Model Plans

THE XYZ CORPORATION EMPLOYEES' DEFINED BENEFIT PENSION PLAN*

ARTICLE I. NAME AND PURPOSE OF PLAN

This Plan shall be known as the XYZ Corporation Employees' Retirement Plan (herein called the "Plan"). The Plan is established and adopted for the sole and exclusive benefit of eligible employees qualifying as Participants. Its purpose is to compensate and reward employees for loyal and faithful service and to secure and establish for them greater security in old age by providing income after retirement.

ARTICLE II. DEFINITIONS

The following words and terms, used in this Plan, shall have the meaning set forth below, unless a different meaning is clearly required by the context:

2.01. "Actuarially Equivalent": Actuarially equivalent benefits means benefits having equal value as determined on the basis of interest at 7% per year, compounded annually, and with mortality in accordance with the 1971 Group Annuity Mortality Tables.

2.02. "Administrative Committee": The Administrative Committee hereinafter provided for.

2.03. "Affiliated Company": A member with XYZ Corporation of a controlled group of corporations within the meaning of Section 1563(a) of the Code, determined without regard to Section 1563(a)(4) and (e)(3)(C) of the Code, or an entity under common control with XYZ Corporation within the meaning of Section 414(c) of the Code, or a member of an affiliated service group with XYZ Corporation within the meaning of Section 414(m) of the Code.

2.04. "Beneficiary": A person designated by a Participant or designated under the provisions of the Plan to receive any benefits which may be payable upon or after the Participant's death.

2.05. "Board of Directors": The Board of Directors of XYZ Corporation.

2.06 "Code" shall mean the Internal Revenue Code.

2.07. "Considered Compensation": Aggregate of the gross amounts paid to a Participant in the form of wages, salaries, commissions or other forms of current compensation for services rendered as shown by the payroll records of an Employer, including overtime payments, and bonuses, plus, in the case of any Participant who was on leave without pay for any reason within the leave provisions of XYZ Corporation's employment policies, the aggregate of the gross amounts which would have been payable to such Participant during the period of such leave, in the form of wages, salaries, commissions or other forms of compensation, including overtime payments, if such Participant had not been on leave.

2.08. "Employee": Any person employed by XYZ Corporation or any Affiliated Company which adopts the Plan with the consent of XYZ Corporation's Board of Directors.

2.09. "Employer": XYZ Corporation and every other Affiliated Company which adopts the Plan with the consent of XYZ Corporation's Board of Directors.

2.10 "ERISA" shall mean the Employee Retirement Income Security Act of 1974, as amended.

2.11. "Full-time Employee": An Employee regularly scheduled to work on a full-time basis.

2.12. "Hour of Service":

(a) Where specifically applicable under the terms of the Plan to Part-time Employees, such an Employee shall be credited with an Hour of Service for each hour for which he or she is directly or indirectly paid or entitled to payment for duties performed for XYZ Corporation, or for purposes of eligibility and vesting, any Affiliated Company (after the date of affiliation unless determined otherwise by the Board of Directors), or any predecessor corporation of XYZ Corporation or corporation merged, consolidated or liquidated into XYZ Corporation or its predecessor, or a corporation, substantially all of the assets of which were acquired by XYZ Corporation, but only if such Service otherwise meets the requirements of this paragraph and only to the extent required under regulations prescribed by the Secretary of the Treasury pursuant to Section 414(a) of the Code.

(b) The term Hour of Service also shall include each hour for which back pay, irrespective of mitigation of damages, has been awarded or agreed to by XYZ Corporation or by an Affiliated Company and each hour for which an Employee is directly or indirectly paid or entitled to payment by XYZ Corporation or an Affiliated Company for reasons (such as vacation, sickness, or disability) other than for the performance of duties, except as provided in paragraph (d).

(c) Hours for which an Employee is directly or indirectly paid, or entitled to payment, for the performance of duties shall be credited to the Employee for the period in which the duties are performed. Hours for which back pay has been awarded or agreed to shall be credited to the Employee for the period or periods to which the award or agreement pertains rather than the period in which the award or agreement is made. The period to which Hours of Service, for which an Employee is directly or indirectly paid or entitled to payment for reasons (such as vacation, sickness or disability) other than for the performance of duties, are credited pursuant to subparagraph (b), and the number of such Hours credited (and the number of Hours credited if an award of or agreement to pay back pay applies to such a period) shall be determined in accordance with Department of Labor regulations Section 2530.200b-2.

(d) For purposes of preventing a Break in Service, Hours for which an Employee is credited for maternity and paternity leave shall be credited:

(i) to the eligibility computation period or Plan Year, as the case may be, in which such leave begins if, as of the date the maternity and paternity leave begins, the Employee has completed less than 501 Hours of Service, and

(ii) in any other case, to the next eligibility computation period or Plan Year, as the case may be.

The number of Hours with which an Employee is credited for maternity and paternity leave, for purposes of preventing a Break in Service, shall be the number of hours that

*Reprinted from 351 T.M., *Pension Plans—Qualification.*

normally would have been credited to the Employee but for the maternity and paternity leave or, if the Administrative Committee is unable to determine the number of such Hours, eight Hours per day of such leave; provided, however, that no more than 501 Hours of Service shall be so credited for any single continuous period of maternity and paternity leave.

(e) For purposes of this paragraph, an Employee shall incur a one-year Break in Service for any Plan Year in which he or she completes less than 501 Hours of Service.

2.13. "Investment Committee": The Investment Committee hereinafter provided for.

2.14. "Part-time Employee": An Employee regularly scheduled to work on less than a full-time basis.

2.15. "Participant": Any Employee who becomes a Participant as provided in Article III hereof.

2.16. "Plan Year": The calendar year.

2.17. "Service": Subject to the exceptions otherwise set forth in the Plan, Service shall mean periods of employment with XYZ Corporation, or for purposes of eligibility and vesting, an Affiliated Company (after the date of affiliation unless determined otherwise by the Board of Directors), or any predecessor corporation of XYZ Corporation, or a corporation merged, consolidated, or liquidated into XYZ Corporation or its predecessor, or a corporation substantially all of the assets of which have been acquired by XYZ Corporation, but only if such Service otherwise meets the requirements of this paragraph and only to the extent required under regulations prescribed by the Secretary of the Treasury pursuant to Section 414(a) of the Code.

(a) Service shall be measured in years and days (with 365 days being equivalent to one Year of Service) from the date on which employment commences to the date on which it is severed as a result of a quit, discharge, death, retirement, or, if earlier, the expiration of a 12-month leave of absence. Notwithstanding the foregoing, the following rules will apply with respect to Part-time Employees:

For purposes of determining a Part-time Employee's eligibility to participate in the Plan, Service shall be measured on the basis of Hours of Service with the completion of 1000 Hours of Service at any time during the first 12 months of employment, or in any Plan Year, being treated as a Year of Service for these purposes.

(b) A one-year Break in Service shall mean a 12 consecutive month period after employment is severed if the Employee is not reemployed within such 12 consecutive month period. If an Employee's employment is severed but he or she is reemployed within the 12 consecutive month period commencing on the date of severance, the period of severance shall constitute Service for purposes of eligibility to participate in the Plan and the vesting of benefits.

(c) For purposes of determining an Employee's Service, all periods of Service shall be credited and aggregated, except that the following periods shall be disregarded:

Periods prior to a Break in Service if the Employee was not vested at the time of the Break and if the period of severance of employment equals or exceeds the greater of five years or the period of Service before the severance; provided that Years of Service that were disregarded as of December 31, 1984 under Plan provisions in effect at that time shall be disregarded.

(d) Notwithstanding anything herein to the contrary, for purposes of benefit accrual, a Participant shall be credited with one-half of a Year of Service for each 500 hours of unused sick leave accumulated at retirement. In the case of delayed retirement, a Participant shall be credited with one-half of a Year of Service for each 500 hours of unused sick leave accumulated at the end of the Plan Year of his or her 65th birthday or at the time of the Employee's actual retirement, whichever is less.

(e) The severance from Service date of an Employee who is absent from Service beyond the first anniversary of the first date of absence from employment by reason of maternity and paternity leave shall be the second anniversary of the first date of such absence. The period between the first and second anniversaries of the first date of absence shall be neither a period of Service nor a period of severance. The term "maternity and paternity leave" means any paid or unpaid absence from work during which no duties are performed due to the pregnancy of the Employee, the birth of a child of the Employee, the placement of a child with the Employee in connection with the adoption of such child by the Employee or the caring for such a child for a period immediately following birth or placement.

2.18. "Trust": The legal entity resulting from the Trust Agreement between XYZ Corporation and the Trustee by which the contributions of XYZ Corporation under this Plan shall be received, held, invested and disbursed.

2.19. "Trust Agreement": Trust Agreement established pursuant to Article XV hereof for the purpose of implementing the administration of the Plan.

2.20. "Trustee": Trustee named in the Trust Agreement and any duly appointed successor Trustee.

ARTICLE III. EMPLOYEES ENTITLED TO PARTICIPATE

3.01 An Employee shall be admitted to participation on the first day of the first month after the Employee has attained age 21 and completed 1,000 Hours of Service within a 12 consecutive month computation period.

3.02 Any reemployed former Participant shall recommence participation on his or her date of reemployment unless such a former Participant's Service prior to his or her reemployment was disregarded under Article II, in which case such a former Participant shall recommence participation at the same time provided under section 3.01.

ARTICLE IV. RETIREMENT DATES

4.01. NORMAL RETIREMENT DATE

The normal retirement date of a Participant shall be his 65th birthday or, at the option of the Participant, the last day of any month thereafter of the Plan Year in which he or she reaches such age. Notwithstanding any Plan provisions to the contrary, a Participant shall be 100% vested in his or her accrued retirement benefit upon attainment of age 65.

4.02. DELAYED RETIREMENT DATE

A Participant may remain in the active employ of XYZ Corporation beyond his or her Normal Retirement Date until the last day of any month in which he or she elects to retire, provided that retirement may not be deferred beyond the last day of the Plan Year in which he or she reaches age 70.

4.03. REGULAR AND SPECIAL EARLY RETIREMENT DATES

(a) A Participant who has attained age 62 and completed at least 15 Years of Service may retire on the last day of any month prior to his or her Normal Retirement Date. Such a date of retirement shall constitute a Regular Early Retirement Date.

(b) Notwithstanding the provisions of (a), above, a Participant whose age as of his last birthday, when added to his Years of Service, totals at least 85, may retire on the last day of any month prior to his or her Normal Retirement Date. Such a date of retirement shall constitute a Special Early Retirement Date.

4.04. DISABILITY RETIREMENT DATE

A Participant, who has attained the age of 55, or who regardless of age, has completed at least 20 Years of Service may retire prior to his or her Normal Retirement Date if he or she is disabled. The Participant shall be deemed to be disabled if his physical or mental condition is such as to render it impossible for the Participant to perform his or her customary duties with XYZ Corporation and to perform similar duties for any other employer, provided that such incapacity is likely to be of a continuing nature and provided, further, that such inability to perform similar duties and the likelihood that such incapacity is of a continuing nature shall be established by such evidence as the Administrative Committee may deem sufficient.

ARTICLE V. RETIREMENT BENEFITS

5.01. NORMAL AND SPECIAL EARLY RETIREMENT BENEFIT

A Participant, upon retirement on his or her Normal Retirement Date or on a Special Early Retirement Date, shall receive a retirement benefit, payable in a form provided pursuant to Article VI, which shall have the actuarial value of a monthly benefit commencing on the first day of the month following such retirement date and continuing on the first day of each month thereafter during his or her lifetime, equal to one-twelfth of one and one-tenth percent (1.1%) of the Participant's average annual Considered Compensation for the five highest Plan Years of earnings out of the ten Plan Years of Service immediately preceding his or her retirement, multiplied by the number of his or her Years of Service with XYZ Corporation at retirement. Notwithstanding the foregoing sentence, the amount of the benefit shall not be less than the amount of any Early Retirement Benefit to which the Employee would have been entitled upon retirement on any regular or special early retirement date. If the Participant has less than ten Plan Years of Service at retirement, his or her average annual Considered Compensation shall be computed by reference to the five highest Plan Years of earnings out of the Participant's total number of Years of Service, or by reference to the Participant's total number of Plan Years of Service if less than five.

5.02. DELAYED RETIREMENT BENEFIT

(a) A Participant, upon retirement at a Delayed Retirement Date, shall receive a monthly retirement benefit, payable in a form provided pursuant to Article VI, the amount of which shall be determined in the same manner as if such Delayed Retirement Date were the Participant's Normal Retirement Date, based on the Participant's Years of Service and average annual Considered Compensation as of the last day of the Plan Year in which he or she attained age 65, with no actuarial increase due to the delay of benefits, and with Service for accumulated sick leave credited in accordance with Article II; provided, however, that in the case of a Participant with less than 10 Years of Service as of the end of the Plan Year in which he or she attains age 65, such Participant's average annual Considered Compensation shall be computed as of the date of actual retirement.

(b) A Participant who remains in the active employ of XYZ Corporation after his or her Normal Retirement Date and who is credited with less than 40 Hours of Service during any calendar month in which he or she remains in active employment shall receive a monthly retirement benefit for such month in an amount determined under section 50.1, above, as if he or she had retired on his or her Normal Retirement Date.

5.03. REGULAR EARLY RETIREMENT BENEFIT

A Participant shall, upon retirement on a Regular Early Retirement Date, receive a monthly retirement benefit, commencing on the first day of the month following his or her Regular Early Retirement Date (unless the Participant elects to defer commencement of benefits until attainment of age 65 or to any date between Early Retirement Date and attainment of age 65), payable in the form provided pursuant to Article VI, computed as if his or her Early Retirement Date were his Normal Retirement Date, based on his or her Years of Service and Considered Compensation at early retirement, reduced by 0.5% for each month by which the commencement of benefits precedes his or her 65th birthday.

5.04. DISABILITY RETIREMENT BENEFIT

A Participant, upon retirement at a disability retirement date, shall receive a monthly retirement benefit, payable in the form provided pursuant to Article VI, computed as if his or her Disability Retirement Date were his or her Normal Retirement Date, based on h.such Participant's is Years of Service and Considered Compensation at disability retirement, provided, however, that if the Participant has less than 10 Years of Service at his or her Disability Retirement Date, the benefit shall be reduced by 0.5% for each month by which the Disability Retirement Date precedes his or her Normal Retirement Date.

5.05. REEMPLOYMENT

If a Participant is reemployed by an Employer, any benefit payable hereunder shall be suspended, the benefits payable to such Participant upon his or her subsequent termination of employment shall not duplicate previous benefit payments, and such subsequent benefits shall be reduced to reflect the actuarial value of benefits previously paid prior to Normal Retirement Date.

5.06. LIMITATIONS ON RETIREMENT INCOME

(a) Subject to the adjustments hereinafter set forth, the maximum annual benefit payable in the form of a life annuity to a Participant under this Plan and under any other qualified defined benefit plan maintained by XYZ Corporation or by an affiliate shall not exceed the lesser of:

(i) $90,000, or

(ii) 100% of the Participant's average compensation for the three consecutive calendar years during which he participated in the Plan and had the greatest aggregate compensation.

(b) The limitation on the maximum pension required by subparagraph (a) shall be adjusted as follows:

(i) The dollar limitation prescribed in section 5.06(a)(i) shall be adjusted annually beginning January 1, 1988 for increases in the cost of living, in accordance with the rules issued by the Secretary of the Treasury pursuant to Section 415(d) of the Code. The adjusted figure shall be effective as of January 1 of each calendar year and shall apply to limitation years that end during that year.

(ii) If a Participant's benefits are payable in any form other than a life annuity, such benefits shall be actuarially adjusted to a straight life annuity beginning at the same age, in accordance with regulations issued by the Secretary of the Treasury pursuant to Section 415(b) of the Code and based on an interest rate of 5%, or if greater, the rate specified in the Plan for determining the actuarial equivalence of such benefit; provided, however, that for purposes of this subparagraph, the portion of any joint and survivor annuity, and any ancillary benefits not directly related to retirement income benefits, shall not be taken into account.

(iii) If a Participant's benefits under the Plan become payable before age 62, the dollar limit shall be reduced in accordance with regulations issued by the Secretary of the Treasury pursuant to Section 415(b) of the Code at an interest rate equal to the greater of 5% or the rate used under the Plan to determine actuarial equivalence of a benefit payable before age 65; provided, however, that the limit shall never be reduced to less than $75,000, if the benefit becomes payable at or after age 55, nor shall it be reduced below the amount payable at age 55, determined in accordance with Code Section 415(b)(2). If benefits become payable after age 65, the dollar limit shall be increased in accordance with regulations issued by the Secretary of the Treasury pursuant to Section 415(b) of the Code at an interest rate equal to 5%. The dollar limit shall not apply (and shall not be used in computing the denominator of the defined benefit fraction under subparagraph (f) below) in the case of any Participant who was a participant in the Plan on December 31, 1982 and whose annual benefit accrued under the Plan as of such date, determined in accordance with Section 415(b)(2) of the Code, exceeds such limit. In lieu thereof, the Participant's annual accrued benefit as of December 31, 1982 shall be the applicable dollar limit.

(c) The dollar limit shall not apply to any Participant who has not at any time participated in a defined contribution plan maintained by XYZ Corporation or by an affiliate if his or her total annual retirement benefit (without regard to the age at which such benefit commences) does not exceed $10,000 in any year. For purposes of this subparagraph (c), the value of the retirement benefit payable under the Plan shall not be adjusted upward for early retirement provisions and benefits which are not in the form of a straight life annuity (whether or not directly related to the retirement benefits).

(d) The maximum annual benefit payable under this paragraph 6 to any Participant who has completed less than ten (10) Years of Service with XYZ Corporation or an affiliate shall be the amount determined under section 5.06(a) or 5.06(c), as the case may be, multiplied by a fraction, the numerator of which is the number of the Participant's Years of Service and the denominator of which is ten (10).

(e) Notwithstanding the foregoing, in the case of a Participant who participates in any qualified defined contribution plan maintained by XYZ Corporation or an affiliate, the sum of the defined benefit plan fraction and the defined contribution plan fraction for any limitation year shall not exceed 1.0. For purposes of applying the limits of this section 5.06(e), the following rules shall apply:

(i) The term defined benefit plan fraction shall mean the projected annual benefit payable under this Plan, determined without regard to subparagraphs (a) through (e), over the maximum benefit payable under Section 415(b) of the Code, increased as provided by Section 415(e)(2)(B) of the Code; provided, however, that the defined benefit plan fraction with respect to a Participant whose benefit is described in subparagraph (e) shall never be deemed to exceed one (1).

(ii) The term defined contribution plan fraction shall mean the actual aggregate annual additions to the defined contribution plans determined as of the close of the limitation year, over the aggregate of the maximum annual additions which could have been made for each year of the Participant's Service had such annual additions been limited each such limitation year to the maximum amount permitted under Section 415(c) of the Code increased as provided by Code Section 415(e)(3)(B) Code and taking into account the transition rules for years ending prior to January 1, 1983 prescribed under such defined contribution plans and under ERISA and the Tax Equity and Fiscal Responsibility Act of 1982, including, if elected by the Administrative Committee, the provisions of Code Section 415(e)(6); provided, however, that the defined contribution plan fraction shall be reduced in the manner described in IRS Notice 83-10 to the extent necessary to assure that the sum of the defined benefit and defined contribution fractions does not exceed 1.0.

(iii) The term annual addition shall mean that term as defined in Code section 415(c)(2).

(f) In the event that in any limitation year the limits prescribed under subparagraphs (a) through (e) will be exceeded for any Participant, whether under this Plan or whether under a combination of qualified plans, then prior to reducing benefits or contributions under any other Plan, the Participant's accrued benefits under this Plan shall be reduced or frozen to an amount which will satisfy the limits for that year. If, in a later limitation year, the limits are increased due to cost of living adjustments or any other factor, the reduction or freeze on the Participant's benefits shall lapse to the extent that additional benefits may be payable under the increased limits.

(g) For purposes of subparagraphs (a) through (f), the following terms shall have the following meanings:

(i) Affiliate: An Affiliated Company, as modified by Section 415(h) of the Code.

(ii) Compensation: The Participant's wages, salaries, fees for professional services, and other amounts received for personal services actually rendered in the course of employment with XYZ Corporation or an affiliate, and all other income treated as compensation pursuant to regulations issued under Section 415 of the Code.

5.06. RESTRICTIONS ON DISTRIBUTIONS

(a) Subject to subparagraph (b) hereof, distribution to a Participant shall commence not later than the latest of:

(i) The 60th day after the close of the Plan Year in which the Participant attains age 65; or

(ii) The 60th day after the close of the Plan Year in which the Participant terminates employment.

(b) Distribution to a Participant who is a 5% owner shall commence not later than the April 1 following the calendar year in which he attains age 70-1/2, regardless of whether he has terminated employment as of such date. For the purposes of this paragraph 8, the term "5% owner" means a person who owns or is considered as owning more than 5% of the outstanding stock of XYZ Corporation or stock possessing more than 5% of the total combined voting power of XYZ Corporation.

(c) Distribution to a Participant, on or after January 1, 1985 shall be made over a period not exceeding the life (or life expectancy) of the Participant or the lives (or life expectancy) of the Participant and his beneficiary.

(d) Notwithstanding anything in the Plan to the contrary, if a Participant dies before distributions to him have commenced, payments to the Participant's beneficiary or estate shall be made within five years after the death of the Participant, subject to the following exceptions:

(i) If any portion of any benefit payable after the Participant's death is payable to or for the benefit of his beneficiary, and if the distribution of such portion commences not later than one year after the Participant's death (or such later date as the Secretary of the Treasury may prescribe by regulations), such portion may be distributed over the life or life expectancy of such beneficiary.

(ii) If any portion of any benefit payable after the Participant's death is payable to or for the benefit of his surviving spouse, and if the distribution of such portion commences not later than the date on which the Participant would have attained age 70-1/2, such portion may be distributed over the life or life expectancy of the surviving spouse.

ARTICLE VI. FORM OF RETIREMENT BENEFIT

6.01. NORMAL FORM OF PAYMENT — PARTICIPANT WITH NO SPOUSE

Unless an election of an alternative form of payment is made in accordance with section 6.08, the retirement benefit to which a Participant who has no spouse on his Annuity Starting Date is entitled shall be paid in accordance with Form 1 of section 6.04.

6.02. DISABILITY RETIREMENT BENEFIT

Disability retirement benefits of a Participant shall be continued during disability, and if such disability continues until the Participant's 65th birthday, benefits will be continued thereafter in accordance with the form of benefits selected by the Participant. If the disability ceases before the Participant's 65th birthday, the disability benefit shall cease unless the cessation of the disability was due to the death of the Participant and the Joint and Survivor Option, the Life and 10 Year Certain Option, or the Life and 15 Year Certain Option described under section 6.04 is applicable.

6.03. NORMAL FORM OF PAYMENT — PARTICIPANT WITH SPOUSE

Unless an election of an alternative form of payment is made in accordance with section 6.08, a Participant who has a spouse on his Annuity Starting Date shall receive benefits in the form of the 50% Joint and Survivor Option described as Form 2 of section 6.04. The spouse of the Participant shall be the Beneficiary under such 50% Joint and Survivor Option.

6.04. ALTERNATIVE FORMS OF PAYMENT

In lieu of the form of benefit otherwise provided in the foregoing paragraphs of this Article VI, by making proper written election as prescribed in paragraph 8 on a form acceptable to and filed with the Administrative Committee, a Participant may elect to receive his pension benefits, with a value equal to the actuarial equivalent of the single life annuity commencing at normal retirement date, pursuant to any of the following forms:

- Form 1 — Life Annuity Option. A single life annuity providing monthly payments for the life of the Participant commencing on the first day of the month following his retirement date, unless otherwise deferred pursuant to paragraph 3 of Article V, and continuing on the same day each month thereafter during his lifetime.

- Form 2 — Joint and Survivor Option. A joint and survivor annuity providing actuarially reduced monthly payments for the life of the Participant with monthly payments continuing thereafter for the life of the Participant's spouse under which each monthly payment is 50% of the amount of the monthly payment during their joint lives.

- Form 3 — The Joint and Contingent Annuitant Option. A joint and contingent annuity providing actuarially reduced monthly payments for the life of the Participant with monthly payments continuing thereafter for the life of his designated Contingent Annuitant under which each monthly payment is (A) equal to, or (B) 75% of, or (C) 50% of the amount of the monthly payment during their joint lives; provided that if the Contingent Annuitant is other than the Participant's spouse the pension payable to the Contingent Annuitant shall, if necessary, be further reduced to a point which will require the Participant's pension to be at least 50% of the pension which he would have received on the life annuity basis set forth in Form 1.

- Form 4 — The Life and 10 Year Certain Option. A reduced pension payable monthly for life with monthly payments guaranteed for a period of 120 months (or such lesser number of months as will permit monthly payments of a minimum of $10.00), with the result that if the Participant dies prior to receipt of the guaranteed number of monthly payments the Beneficiary designated by the Participant will continue to receive a monthly pension until the total guaranteed number have been paid either to the Participant or to his Beneficiary.

- Form 5 — The Life and 15 Year Certain Option. A reduced pension payable monthly for life with monthly payments guaranteed for a period of 180 months (or such lesser number of months as will permit monthly payments of a minimum of $10.00), with the result that if the Participant dies prior to receipt of the guaranteed number of monthly payments, the Beneficiary designated by the Participant will continue to receive a monthly pension until the total guaranteed number have been paid either to the Participant or to his Beneficiary.

6.05. The following rules shall apply to the Joint and Survivor, Joint and Contingent, the Life and 10 Year Certain, and the Life and 15 Year Certain Options:

(a) If the spouse or the Contingent Annuitant, or the Beneficiary, as the case may be, named by the Participant dies prior to the day the Participant's pension payments are to begin, the Option will be canceled and of no effect.

(b) If the Participant dies before his Annuity Starting Date, the Option will be canceled and of no effect, and his Beneficiaries' rights, if any, shall be governed by the provisions of Article VII.

6.06. Within a reasonable time prior to the election period described in section 6.08, the Administrative Committee shall provide to each married Participant a written general explanation of the terms and conditions of Form 2, the Participant's right to make (and the effect of) and election to receive benefits in an alternative form, the requirements regarding spousal consent to an election to receive benefits in an alternative form and the right to make (and the effect of) a revocation of an election to receive benefits in an alternative form. Such general explanation may be furnished by posting on bulletin boards.

6.07. A married Participant may at any time after receipt of the general explanation of the 50% Joint and Survivor Option request a further written explanation of such Option and the financial effect upon the particular Participant's benefits of an election not to receive benefits in that form. Within 30 days of the Participant's request, the Administrative Committee shall furnish such an explanation to the Participant, including an explanation of the effect of such an election given in terms of dollars per payment.

6.08. A Participant may elect to have the retirement benefit that normally would be payable to him in accordance with Form 1 or Form 2 payable to him in accordance with any of the other Forms described in paragraph 4. An election by a Participant who has a spouse shall only be valid if received by the Administrative Committee within the 90-day period (the "election period") ending on the Annuity Starting Date. Any election of an alternative form may be revoked or changed during the election period. No election or revocation or change of election which would cause the spouse of a Participant to receive no benefit or a benefit other than the benefit such spouse would receive under Form 2 of section 6.04 shall be effective without the written and notarized consent of such spouse.

6.09. The Administrative Committee may elect to have all or part of any retirement amounts to which the Participant is entitled distributed in the form of a nontransferable annuity contract, providing benefits described in this Article.

ARTICLE VII. PRERETIREMENT SPOUSE'S BENEFIT

7.01. GENERAL RULE

If a Participant who has one Hour of Service or paid leave after August 22, 1984 and who has a vested interest under the Plan dies prior to his termination of Service or in the event that a Participant retires or terminates employment and dies prior to the receipt of any benefits, his spouse shall be entitled to a benefit under this Article. The preretirement spouse's benefit shall be a life annuity under which payments shall be equal to the payments which would have been paid to such spouse under a joint and survivor annuity, as described in Form 2 of section 6.04, determined

(a) in the case of a Participant who dies prior to attaining early retirement age, as if the Participant had terminated employment on the date of death, begun to receive his retirement benefit upon the first day of the month following the Participant's early retirement date, and died on the following day, and

(b) in the case of a Participant who died after attaining early retirement age, as if the Participant had retired on the day before his or her death.

Subject to the provisions of section 7.03, the preretirement spouse's benefit shall be payable beginning in the month following the month in which the Participant dies; provided, however, that in the case of the spouse of a Participant who dies before the Participant would have been entitled to commence receiving benefits under the Plan, the preretirement spouse's benefit shall not become payable until the date on which the Participant could have first elected to commence receiving benefits under the Plan, had he lived.

7.02. If the present value of the preretirement spouse's benefit payable hereunder shall be $3,500.00 or less, the Administrative Committee may direct that the present value of such benefit be paid in a lump sum. For the purposes hereof, present value shall be calculated in accordance with section 2.01, provided that such interest rate shall not be greater than the interest rate which would be used, as of the first day of the Plan Year in which the distribution occurs, by the Pension Benefit Guaranty corporation for determining the present value of a lump sum distribution on Plan termination.

7.03. If a spouse entitled to a preretirement spouse's benefit hereunder does not consent to commencement of such preretirement spouse's benefit at the time specified in paragraph 1 hereof, commencement of such preretirement spouse's benefit shall commence on the first day of the month following the date the Participant would have attained his normal retirement date.

ARTICLE VIII. TERMINATION OF SERVICE

8.01. If any Participant terminates employment for any reason other than retirement, death, or disability, the nonforfeitable interest of such Participant expressed as a percentage of his or her Normal Retirement Benefit determined under Article V shall be as follows:

(i)	Two or less Years of Service	—	0%
(ii)	2 - 3 Years of Service	—	20%
(iii)	3 - 4 Years of Service	—	40%
(iv)	4 - 5 Years of Service	—	60%
(v)	5 - 6 Years of Service	—	80%
(vi)	More than 6 Years of Service	—	100%

8.02. FORM AND TIME OF PAYMENT

(a) Unless an election of an alternative form of payment is made in accordance with section 8.04, the benefit payable hereunder to a Participant who terminates employment with an Employer and who has no spouse shall be paid in a lump sum, in accordance with section 8.03.

(b) Unless an election of an alternative form of payment is made in accordance with section 8.04, the benefit payable hereunder to a Participant who terminates employment with an Employer and who has a spouse shall be paid in the form of a 50% joint and survivor annuity, except as otherwise provided in paragraphs 3(a) or (b). For the purposes of this subparagraph, the term "50% joint and survivor annuity" shall mean an annuity (which is the actuarial equivalent of a single life annuity) providing monthly payments for the life of the Participant, commencing on (i) the first day of the month following his or her attainment of age 65 if he or she has less than 15 Years of Service at the date of termination of Service or (ii) if he or she has 15 Years of Service or more at the date of termination of Service, on the first day of any month following his attainment of age 62, if elected by the Participant, but no later than the first day of the month following attainment of age 65, and with monthly payments continuing thereafter for the life of the Participant's spouse under which each monthly payment is 50% of the amount of the monthly payment during their joint lives, and provided, further, that if a benefit under this subparagraph commences as of the first day of any month following the attainment of age 62, such benefit shall be reduced by 18%.

8.03. (a) If the present value of the benefit payable hereunder shall be $3,500 or less, the Administrative Committee may direct that the present value of such benefit be paid in a lump sum on the first day of the calendar quarter following termination of employment.

(b) If the present value of the benefit payable hereunder shall be in excess of $3,500, such present value may be distributed in a lump sum on the first day of the calendar quarter following termination of employment only with the consent of the Participant and with the written, notarized consent of the Participant's spouse, if any.

(c) For the purposes of this section 8.03, present value shall be calculated in accordance with section 2.01, provided that such interest rate shall not be greater than the interest rate which would be used, as of the first day of the Plan Year in which the distribution occurs, by the Pension Benefit Guaranty Corporation for determining the present value of a lump sum distribution on Plan termination.

8.04. ALTERNATIVE FORMS OF PAYMENT

In lieu of the normal form of benefit provided in section 8.02, by making proper written election as prescribed in section 8.05 on a form acceptable to and filed with the Administrative Committee, a Participant may elect to receive his or her benefit hereunder pursuant to any of the following alternative forms:

(a) LIFE ANNUITY OPTION.

A single life annuity providing monthly payments for the life of the Participant commencing (i) on the first day of the month following his attainment of age 65 if he has less than 15 Years of Service at the date of his termination of service, or (ii) on the first day of any month following his attainment of age 62, if elected by the Participant, but no later than the first day of the month following attainment of age 65, if he has 15 Years of Service or more at the date of his termination of service, provided in either case that the Participant survives to the required age; provided, however, that in the event a benefit under this subparagraph commences as of the first day of any month following the attainment of age 62, such benefit shall be reduced by 18%.

(b) LUMP SUM OPTION FOR PARTICIPANT WHO HAS A SPOUSE.

(a) *A lump sum payable in accordance with section 8.03.* A terminated participant may elect to have the benefit that normally would be payable to him in accordance with paragraph 2 payable to him in accordance with any of the other forms described in paragraph 4 of this Article. An election by a Participant who has a spouse of an alternative form shall only be valid if received by the Administrative Committee within the 90-day period (the "election period") ending on the Annuity Starting Date. Any election of an alternative form may be revoked or changed during the election period. No election or revocation or change of election which would cause the spouse of a Participant to receive no benefit or a benefit other than the benefit such spouse would receive under paragraph 2 shall be effective without the written and notarized consent of such spouse.

(b) Within a reasonable time prior to the election period described in subparagraph (a), the Administrative Committee shall provide to each married Participant a written general explanation of the terms and conditions of the 50% joint and survivor annuity, the Participant's right to make (and the effect of) an election to receive benefits in an alternative form, the requirements regarding spousal consent to an election to receive benefits in an alternative form and the right to make (and the effect of) a revocation of an election to receive benefits in an alternative form.

(c) A married Participant may at any time after receipt of the general explanation of the 50% joint and survivor annuity request a further written explanation of such annuity and the financial effect upon the particular Participant's benefits of an election not to receive benefits in that form. Within 30 days of the Participant's request, the Administrative Committee shall furnish such an explanation to the Participant, including an explanation of the effect of such an election in terms of dollars per payment.

ARTICLE IX. CONTRIBUTIONS

9.01. The entire cost of the retirement benefits payable under the Plan shall be borne by XYZ Corporation. XYZ Corporation shall make contributions in such amounts and at such times as the Board of Directors of XYZ Corporation shall determine from time to time, provided that such contributions shall at least be equal to the amounts determined by an independent actuary to be sufficient to maintain the qualified status of the Plan under the regulations of the Internal Revenue Service, and the requirements of ERISA.

9.02. All contributions by XYZ Corporation shall be irrevocable and may be used only for the benefit of the Participants; provided, however, notwithstanding anything herein to the contrary, a contribution which was made under a mistake of fact, or conditioned upon initial qualification of the Plan under the Code, if the Plan does not so qualify, shall be returned to XYZ Corporation within one year after the payment of the contribution, or the date of denial of the qualification of the Plan, whichever is applicable. The provisions of this paragraph shall be applicable only to the extent consistent with the Code.

ARTICLE X. ADMINISTRATIVE AND INVESTMENT COMMITTEES: PLAN FIDUCIARIES AND FIDUCIARY OBLIGATIONS

10.01. ADMINISTRATIVE COMMITTEE

(a) The Board of Directors of XYZ Corporation shall appoint an Administrative Committee of five members, at least one of whom shall be an employee who is neither an officer nor a supervisor. The members shall serve at the pleasure of the Board and the Board shall appoint their successors. A member of the Committee may, but need not be, a Participant hereunder.

(b) The Administrative Committee, subject to the powers of the Board of Directors specified in this paragraph, shall be charged with and all have authority for and control of the administration of the Plan, other than authority or control respecting management or disposition of Plan assets. The Committee shall be the "Named Fiduciary" under the Plan, for purposes of ERISA, with respect to such administration of the Plan. The Committee shall have all the powers necessary to enable it to carry out its duties. Not in limitation but in amplification of the foregoing, the Administrative Committee shall have the duty and authority to interpret and construe the Plan, maintain all records, and determine all questions that shall arise hereunder, including all questions relating to the eligibility of employees to become Participants, the eligibility of Participants for benefits hereunder and the amount of those benefits. All disbursements by the Trustee of benefits under the Plan shall be made upon, and in accordance with, the written instructions of the Administrative Committee. The decision of the Administrative Committee upon all matters within the scope of its authority shall be final, to the extent permitted by law.

(c) To enable the Administrative Committee to perform its functions, XYZ Corporation shall make available full and timely information to the Committee concerning all matters within the scope of the Plan relating to employees, their compensation and length of service, their retirement or other termination of employment, and such other pertinent facts as the Committee may require.

(d) The Board of Directors may employ or appoint, or may authorize the Administrative Committee to employ or appoint, agents, legal counsel, accountants, actuaries and such other experts as may be necessary or convenient in the administration of the Plan and Trust Agreement. Neither the Administrative Committee, Board of Directors, nor any other fiduciary shall be liable for the directions, actions or omissions of any such expert who has agreed to the performance of administrative duties in connection with the Plan, but shall be entitled to rely upon all certificates, reports and opinions which may be made by such experts and shall be fully protected in respect of any action taken or suffered by them in good faith in reliance upon the advice or opinion of any such expert.

(e) The Administrative Committee shall maintain full and complete records of its deliberations and decisions. Its records shall contain all relevant data pertaining to individual Participants and their rights under the Plan. It shall maintain convenient means of conference with Participants at reasonable hours and places to assure a full understanding of the rights and benefits of each. Such of its records as may pertain solely to a particular Participant shall be made available by reports or presentation for examination by such Participant.

(f) Any person dissatisfied with the Administrative Committee's determination of a claim for benefits hereunder shall be entitled to a written explanation setting forth, the specific reasons for such determination. Such person shall be given a reasonable time within which to comment, in writing, to the Committee with respect to such explanation. The Committee shall review its determination promptly and render a written decision with respect to the claim. Such decision upon matters within the scope of the authority of the Administrative Committee shall be final.

10.02. BOARD OF DIRECTOR'S CONTROL OF INVESTMENTS: APPOINTMENT OF INVESTMENT COMMITTEE

(a) The Board of Directors shall be charged with and shall have authority for and control of the management, investment and disposition of Plan assets. The Board shall be the "Named Fiduciary" under the Plan, for purposes of ERISA, with respect to such authority and control of the management, investment, and disposition of Plan assets. The Board shall issue investment policy guidelines and review the actions taken by the Investment Committee appointed under this paragraph.

(b) The Board of Directors shall appoint an Investment Committee of five members, at least one of whom shall be an employee of XYZ Corporation who shall serve at the pleasure of the Board and the Board shall appoint their successors. A member of the committee may, but need not be, a Participant hereunder.

(c) The Investment Committee shall have the duty and authority to direct the Trustee concerning the investment and reinvestment of all funds held in the trust from time to time and all funds to be related thereunder, subject to the review and control of such authority by the Board of Directors.

(d) The Investment Committee shall maintain full and complete records of its deliberations and decisions which shall be available for inspection from time to time by the Board of Directors.

(e) The Board of Directors may employ or appoint, or may authorize the Investment Committee to employ or appoint, such investment counsel or experts to render investment advice or other investment services as may be necessary or convenient in the discharge of its power and authority with respect to the management, investment and disposition of Plan assets.

(f) Notwithstanding any other provision of this Plan, the Board of Directors, in carrying out its powers and authority with respect to the management, investment and disposition of Plan assets may employ or appoint one or more Investment Managers to manage all or any portion of the Trust Fund. Such Investment Manager shall be an investment adviser registered under the Investment Advisers Act of 1940, a bank, as defined in such Act, or an insurance company qualified to manage, acquire and dispose of the assets of employee benefit plans under the laws of more than one State. An Investment Manager shall acknowledge in writing its appointment as a fiduciary of the Trust Fund, and shall serve until a proper resignation is received by the Committee, or until it is removed and/or replaced by the Board of Directors.

Other Plan fiduciaries shall be under no duty to question any direction or lack of direction of any Investment Manager, but may act, and shall be fully protected in acting in accordance with each such direction. An Investment Manager shall have the sole investment responsibility for the portion of the Trust Fund which it is appointed to manage, and no other Plan fiduciary including the Board of Directors, or the Investment Committee or the Trustee shall have any responsibility for the investment of any asset of the Trust Fund, the management of which has been delegated to an Investment Manager, or liability for any loss to or diminution in value of the Trust resulting from any action directed, taken or omitted by an Investment Manager.

10.03. PROVISIONS APPLICABLE TO BOTH COMMITTEES

(a) Each Committee shall hold meetings upon such notice, at such place or places and at such times as it may from time to time determine. A majority of the members of the Administrative Committee shall constitute a quorum for the transaction of business and two members shall constitute a quorum for the transaction of business by the Investment Committee. All resolutions or other actions taken by a Committee at any meeting shall be by vote of the majority of those present at any such meeting and entitled to vote. Resolutions may be adopted or other action taken without a meeting upon written consent signed by at least a majority of the Administrative Committee, and at least two members of the Investment Committee; provided, however, that all members of the Committee shall be notified of the proposed action and the dissent, if any, of any member shall be recorded.

(b) Each Committee shall appoint one of its members to act as its chairman and may appoint a secretary who need not be a member of the Committee, and who shall keep the minutes of the proceedings of the Committee. The Committee shall designate the person or persons who shall be authorized to sign for the Committee.

(c) No member of the Administrative Committee or the Investment Committee shall have any right to vote or decide upon any matter relating solely to himself or to any of his rights or benefits under the Plan.

(d) No bond or other security shall be required of any member of the Administrative Committee or the Investment Committee other than as affirmatively required by statute or regulation thereunder.

(e) No fee or compensation shall be paid to any member of the Administrative Committee or the Investment Committee who is an employee of XYZ Corporation for his services as a member of such Committee. Any expenses properly incurred by the Administrative Committee or the Investment Committee shall be reimbursed or paid by XYZ Corporation, including such reasonable fee or compensation, as may be determined by the Board of Directors of XYZ Corporation, for any member of the Administrative Committee or the Investment Committee who is not an employee of XYZ Corporation.

10.04. PLAN FIDUCIARIES AND FIDUCIARY OBLIGATIONS

(a) The fiduciaries under the Plan and Trust shall be the Board of Directors, the Administrative Committee, the Investment Committee, the Trustee, any Investment Manager appointed under the provisions of Paragraph 2 of Article X, and any other person who is a fiduciary under the terms of ERISA. A person may act in more than one fiduciary capacity with respect to the Plan or Trust.

(b) Each person who is a fiduciary shall discharge his duties with respect to the Plan and Trust with the care, skill, prudence and diligence under the circumstances then prevailing that a prudent man acting in a like capacity and familiar with such matters would use in the conduct of an enterprise of a like character and with like aims, and in accordance with the Plan and Trust Agreement. A fiduciary who complies with the foregoing standards shall not be liable for any loss, action or omission hereunder. A fiduciary not charged with a specific responsibility under the provisions of the Plan or Trust shall be under no duty to question any action or lack of action of another fiduciary with respect to such responsibility, and shall not be liable for a breach of such fiduciary responsibility by another fiduciary unless he participates knowingly in, or knowingly undertakes to conceal, an act or omission of such other fiduciary knowing such act is a breach, or if he has knowledge of a breach by such fiduciary, he fails to make reasonable efforts under the circumstances to remedy the breach. (c) Any Named Fiduciary and any fiduciary designated by a Named Fiduciary may use, employ, discharge or consult with one or more individuals, corporations or other entities with respect to advice regarding any responsibility, obligation or duty of such fiduciary in connection with the Plan. Any Named Fiduciary may designate other individuals, corporations or other entities who are not Named Fiduciaries, to carry out such Named Fiduciaries' responsibilities, obligations and duties with respect to the Plan, except to the extent ERISA prohibits delegation of authority and discretion to manage and control the assets of the Trust. Such delegations may be revoked or modified at any time and any such delegation, revocation or modification shall be made written instruments signed by the Named Fiduciary, if an individual, or, in the case of other entities who are Named Fiduciaries in accordance with the procedures governing the functions of such entity, and a written record shall be kept thereof. No fiduciary shall be liable for the directions, actions, or omissions of any individual, corporation, or other entity who has been designated to carry out any responsibilities, obligations or duties in connection with the Plan, but shall be fully protected by any action taken or suffered by them in good faith in reliance upon the advice or opinion of any such individual, corporation or other entity.

(d) Notwithstanding any other provision of this Plan, the Board of Directors may to the extent permitted by law, cause XYZ Corporation to indemnify any fiduciary for any liability incurred in his capacity as such fiduciary.

ARTICLE XI. INVESTMENTS AND FUNDING

11.01. Funding of the Plan and payment of retirement benefits thereunder shall be provided through the medium of a Trust Fund held by the Trustee under the Trust Agreement. Except as provided by law, in no event shall XYZ Corporation or its officers, directors or stockholders be liable jointly or severally to any person whomsoever on account of any claim arising by reason of the provisions of the Plan or any trust agreement implementing the provisions thereof. The Administrative Committee nevertheless shall have the authority in its discretion to direct the Trustee to use the funds of the Trust from time to time to purchase one or more annuity contracts covering one or more Participants and issued by any insurance company or companies designated by the Administrative Committee.

11.02. The assets of the Trust shall be invested, pursuant to a funding policy established by the Board of Directors from time to time, in any securities or other property including bonds, preferred or common stocks, whether said bonds or stocks are issued by XYZ Corporation or others, without regard to the restrictions of the laws of any jurisdiction applicable to investments of fiduciaries, other than ERISA, and shall retain such securities or other property in trust. Such assets also may be invested in one or more individual or group annuity or insurance contracts purchased from an insurance company. The Board of Directors shall seek such actuarial and other advice as it deems advisable so that needs for liquidity and diversity may be met and a long range investment policy adopted.

ARTICLE XII. AMENDMENT OR TERMINATION

12.01. XYZ Corporation shall have the right at any time and from time to time to amend the Plan in whole or in part; provided, however, that no such amendment may permit any part of the Trust to be used for or diverted for purposes other than for the exclusive benefit of Participants.

12.02. XYZ Corporation has established the Plan with the intention and expectation that the Plan will continue in force. However, XYZ Corporation realizes that circumstances not now foreseen or circumstances beyond its control may make it either impossible or inadvisable to continue the Plan. Accordingly, XYZ Corporation reserves the right to terminate the Plan at any time.

12.03. Notwithstanding any other provisions of the Plan, any modification or amendment of the Plan may be made, retroactively if necessary, when the Employer deems it necessary or appropriate to conform the Plan to or, satisfy the conditions of, any law, governmental regulation or ruling, and to permit the Plan or Trust to meet the requirements of the Code or any provisions of ERISA.

12.04. In the event of the termination of the Plan or complete discontinuance of contributions hereunder, all accrued benefits of Participants under the Plan shall be full vested and nonforfeitable to the extent funded. The assets of the Trust shall be allocated among the Participants and their beneficiaries in accordance with Section 4044(a) and (d) of the Employee Retirement Security Act of 1974 and thereafter distributed at such time and in such manner as determined by the Trustees. In the event of the partial termination of the Plan, accrued benefits of affected Participants under the Plan shall be fully vested and nonforfeitable to the extent such benefits have been partially terminated and are funded.

12.05. (a) Notwithstanding any provision of the Plan to the contrary, if the Plan is terminated or its full current costs have not been paid during the first 10 years after the Effective Date, benefits by XYZ Corporation's contributions for any one of its 25 highest-paid employees as of the time of establishment of the Plan, but excluding those whose monthly pension as of such time will not exceed $125 shall be limited to the benefits purchased by the larger of the following amounts:

(i) $20,000, or

(ii) an amount equal to 20% of the first $50,000 of the employee's average regular annual compensation multiplied by the number of years and fractions thereof since the establishment of the Plan, plus the amount of XYZ Corporation contributions (or funds attributable thereto) which would have been applied to provide such benefits for the employee if the predecessor plans of the Company had been terminated as of December 31, 1970.

(b) If the Plan is amended at any time to increase benefits, the contributions of XYZ Corporation which may be used during the first 10 years thereafter to provide such benefits for any one of its 25 highest-paid employees on the effective date of the amendment but excluding those whose monthly pension as of such date will not exceed $125, shall be limited to the benefits purchased by the largest of the following amounts:

(i) XYZ Corporation contributions (or funds attributable thereto) which would have been applied to provide benefits for the employees if such benefits under the Plan had not been increased, or

(ii) $20,000, or

(iii) the sum of:

(A) XYZ Corporation contributions (or funds attributable thereto) which would have been applied to provide such benefits for the employee if the Plan had been terminated the day before the effective date of the increase, and

(B) an amount computed by multiplying the number of years following the date of the amendment by 20% of the first $50,000 of his annual compensation, or

(iv) Effective January 1, 1984, a dollar amount equal to the present value of the maximum benefit prescribed in Section 4022(b)(3)(B) of ERISA, determined in accordance with Pension Benefit Guaranty Corporation regulations and without regard to any other limitations of Section 4022 of ERISA.

(c) Benefits payable to any of the employees described in (a) or (b) above, whichever is applicable, may not exceed such benefits described in that same section whenever:

(i) the Plan is terminated within 10 years after its Effective Date or effective date of an amendment to increase benefits, or

(ii) such benefits of any such employees become payable within 10 years after such date.

This limitation shall cease to be effective upon the expiration of 10 years from the Effective Date of the Plan or the effective date of any such amendment.

(d) If an employee described above leaves the service of XYZ Corporation or withdraws from participation in the Plan, benefits which he may receive from XYZ Corporation's contributions shall not at any time within the 10-year period after the Effective Date of the Plan or the effective date of any amendment to increase such benefits exceed the benefits described in (a) or (b) above, whichever is applicable.

(e) The Conditions in this paragraph shall not restrict the full or current payment, so long as the Plan is in full effect, of either:

(i) any insurance, death or survivor's benefits which may be provided by the Plan on account of the death of a Participant, or

(ii) the retirement benefits provided by the Plan for retired Participants.

(f) If the Plan is terminated within 10 years from the Effective Date, or within 10 years from the effective date of any amendment to increase benefits, distributions to then unretired employees, other than those described in this paragraph shall include an equitable apportionment of amounts withheld from any of the 25 highest-paid employees to each such other employee.

(g) This paragraph is included in this Plan to conform with the requirements of Treasury Regulation 1.401-4(c) and shall cease to be effective at such time as the provisions of that Regulation or any substitute therefor are no longer effective or applicable.

12.06. In the case of any merger or consolidation of this Plan or the Trust hereunder with, or transfer of the assets or liabilities of the Plan or Trust to, any other Plan, the terms of such merger, consolidation or transfer shall be such that each Participant would receive (in the event of termination of this Plan or its successor immediately thereafter) a benefit which is no less than he would have received in the event of termination of this Plan immediately before such merger, consolidation or transfer.

ARTICLE XIII. MISCELLANEOUS PROVISIONS

13.01. The adoption and maintenance of the Plan shall not be deemed a contract between XYZ Corporation and any employee. Nothing herein contained shall be deemed to give any employee the right to be retained in the employ of XYZ Corporation or to interfere with the right of XYZ Corporation to discharge any employee, nor shall anything contained herein be deemed to give XYZ Corporation the right to require any employee to remain in its employ or to interfere with the employee's right to terminate his employment.

13.02. (a) Except as provided in subparagraph (b), no benefit payable under this Plan shall be subject in any manner to anticipation, assignment, garnishment or pledge; any attempt to anticipate, assign, garnishee or pledge the same shall be void, and no such benefits shall be in any manner liable for or subject to the debts, liabilities, engagements or torts of any Participant. If any Participant shall become bankrupt or attempt to anticipate, assign or pledge any benefits (except as provided in subparagraph (b)), then such benefits shall, in the discretion of the Trustees, cease, and in such event the Trustees shall have the authority to cause the same or any part thereof to be held or applied to or for the benefit of such Participant, his spouse, his children or other dependents, or any of them, in such manner and such proportion as the Trustees may deem proper.

(b) Notwithstanding any other provisions of the Plan, in the event that the Administrative Committee determines that a domestic relations order received by it is a qualified domestic relations order (as defined in Section 414(p) of the Code), benefits shall be payable in accordance with such order and with Section 414(p) of the Internal Revenue Code. The amount payable to the Participant and to any other person other than the payee entitled to benefits under the order, shall be adjusted accordingly.

13.03. Except as otherwise expressly provided by law, all benefits payable under the Plan shall be paid or provided solely from the Trust and XYZ Corporation assumes no liability or responsibility therefor, except as expressly required by law.

13.04. The masculine gender used in the Plan shall be deemed to include the feminine gender unless the context requires otherwise.

ARTICLE XIV. THE TRUST, TRUST AGREEMENT AND TRUSTEE

XYZ Corporation has entered into a Trust Agreement with the Trustee, providing for the administration of the Trust. The Trust Agreement and any amendment thereto made in accordance with said Trust Agreement, shall be deemed to form a part of this Plan, and any and all rights or benefits which may accrue to any person under the Plan shall be subject to all the terms and provisions of said Trust Agreement and any said amendment thereto.

ARTICLE XV. TOP HEAVY REQUIREMENTS

15.01. GENERAL RULE

Effective for the first Plan Year beginning after 1983 the Plan shall meet the requirements of this Article in the event that the Plan is or becomes a Top-Heavy Plan.

15.02. TOP-HEAVY PLAN

(a) BASIC DEFINITION. Subject to the aggregation rules set forth in subparagraph (b), the Plan shall be considered a Top-Heavy Plan pursuant to Section 416(g) of the Code in any Plan Year beginning after December 31, 1983, if, as of the Determination Date, the present value of the cumulative accrued benefits of all Key Employees of the Employer exceeds 60% of the present value of the cumulative accrued benefits of all of the Employees of the Employer as of such Date, taking into account in computing the ratio any distributions made during the five consecutive Plan Year period ending on the Determination Date. Notwithstanding the foregoing, former Key Employees and except for the Plan Year beginning January 1,

1984, any Employee who has not received Compensation from the Employer maintaining the Plan during the five consecutive Plan Year Period ending on the Determination Date, shall be excluded from the above ratio. For purposes of the above ratio, the present value of a Key Employee's accrued benefit shall be counted only once each Plan Year, notwithstanding the fact that an individual may be considered a Key Employee for more than one reason in any Plan Year. Present value for the purposes of this paragraph shall be calculated using the mortality table set forth in paragraph 19 of Article II with respect to post-retirement mortality and an interest rate of 6%.

(b) AGGREGATION WITH OTHER PLANS. For purposes of determining whether the Plan is a Top-Heavy Plan and for purposes of meeting the requirements of this Article, the Plan shall be aggregated with other qualified plans in a Required Aggregation Group and may be aggregated with other qualified plans in a Permissive Aggregation Group. If such Required Aggregation Group is Top-Heavy, this Plan shall be considered a Top-Heavy Plan. If such Permissive Aggregation Group is not Top-Heavy, this Plan shall not be a Top-Heavy Plan.

15.03. DEFINITIONS

For the purpose of determining whether the Plan is Top-Heavy, the following definitions shall be applicable:

(a) DETERMINATION AND VALUATION DATES.

The term "Determination Date" shall mean, in the case of any Plan Year, the last day of the preceding Plan Year. The amount of an individual's accrued benefit and the present value thereof shall be determined as of the Valuation Date. The term "Valuation Date" means the valuation date for minimum funding purposes under the Plan which is within the 12-month period ending on the Determination Date, regardless of whether a valuation for minimum funding purposes is performed that year.

(b) KEY EMPLOYEE. An individual shall be considered a Key Employee if he is an Employee or former Employee who, at any time during the current Plan Year or any of the four preceding Plan Years:

(i) was an officer of the Employer who has annual Compensation from the Employer in the applicable Plan Year in excess of 150% of the dollar limitation under Section 415(c)(1)(A) of the Code; provided, however, that the number of individuals treated as Key Employees by reason of being officers hereunder shall not exceed the lesser of 50 or 10% of all Employees, and provided further, that if the number of employees treated as officers is limited to 50 hereunder, the individuals treated as Key Employees shall be those who, while officers, received the greatest annual Compensation in the applicable Plan Year and any of the four preceding Plan Years (without regard to the limitation set forth in Section 416(d) of the Code),

(ii) was one of the 10 Employees owning or considered as owning both more than a one-half percent interest in value and the largest interests in value in the Employer who has annual Compensation from the Employer in the applicable Plan Year in excess of the dollar limitation under Section 415(c)(1)(A) of the Code as increased under Section 415(d) of the Code;

(iii) was a more than 5% owner of the Employer; or

(iv) was a more than 1% owner of the Employer whose annual Compensation from the Employer in the applicable Plan Year exceeded $150,000.

For purposes of determining who is a Key Employee, ownership shall be determined by taking into account the constructive ownership rules of Section 318 of the Code, as modified by Section 416(i)(1) of the Code. For purposes of determining who is more than 5% or more than 1% owner, ownership shall mean ownership of the outstanding stock of the Employer or of the total combined voting power of all stock of the Employer.

For purposes of clause (ii), an Employee (or former Employee) who has at least a one-half percent ownership interest is considered to be one of the top 10 owners unless at least 10 other Employees (or former Employees) own a greater interest than such Employee (or former Employee); provided that if an Employee has the same ownership interest as another Employee, the Employee having greater annual compensation from the Employer is considered to have the larger ownership interest.

(c) NON-KEY EMPLOYEE. The term "Non-Key Employee" shall mean any Employee who is a Participant and who is not a Key Employee.

(d) BENEFICIARY. Whenever the term "Key Employee", "former Key Employee", or "Non-Key Employee" is used herein, it includes the beneficiary or beneficiaries of such individual. If an individual is a Key Employee by reason of the foregoing sentence as well as a Key Employee in his own right, both the present value of his inherited accrued benefit and the present value of his own accrued benefit will be considered his accrued benefit for purposes of determining whether the Plan is a Top-Heavy Plan.

(e) COMPENSATION AND COMPENSATION LIMITATION.

For purposes of this Article, except as otherwise specifically provided, the term "Compensation" has the same meaning as in paragraph 6(i) of Article V. In the event the Plan becomes a Top-Heavy Plan, the annual Compensation of a Key Employee taken into account under the Plan (for all Plan Years, including Plan Years before the Plan was a Top-Heavy Plan) shall not exceed $200,000, adjusted for increases in the cost of living pursuant to regulations issued under Section 416 of the Code; provided that benefits accrued before the Plan was a Top-Heavy Plan shall not be reduced.

(f) REQUIRED AGGREGATION GROUP.

The term "Required Aggregation Group" shall mean all other qualified defined benefit and defined contribution plans maintained by the Employer in which a Key Employee participates, and each other plan of the Employer which enables any plan in which a Key Employee participates to meet the requirements of Sections 401(a)(4) or 410 of the Code when considered with a Required Aggregation Group.

(g) PERMISSIVE AGGREGATION GROUP.

The term "Permissive Aggregation Group" shall mean all other qualified defined benefit and defined contribution plans maintained by the Employer that meet the requirements of Sections 401(a)(4) and 410 of the Code when considered with a Required Aggregation Group.

(h) EMPLOYER.

For purposes of determining whether the Plan is a Top-Heavy Plan, the term "Employer" shall mean the Employer and any entity required to be aggregated with the Employer pursuant to Section 414(b), (c) or (m) of the Code; provided that for purposes of Section 416(i)(1)(A) of the Code, ownership percentages shall be determined separately with respect to each entity that would otherwise be aggregated under Section 416(b), (c) or (m) of the Code.

15.04. REQUIREMENTS APPLICABLE IF PLAN IS TOP-HEAVY

In the event the Plan is determined to be Top-Heavy for any Plan Year, the following requirements shall be applicable.

(a) MINIMUM BENEFITS. The minimum Annual Retirement Benefit accrued under the Plan by each Non-Key Employee shall equal the product of such Employee's average compensation for the Testing Period and the lesser of 2% per Year of Minimum Benefit Service or 20%. The minimum Annual Retirement Benefit shall be determined without regard to an Employee's primary Social Security Benefit. All accruals derived from Employer Contributions, whether or not attributable to years in which the Plan is Top Heavy, may be used in determining whether an Employee's minimum Annual Retirement Benefit has been satisfied. The minimum Annual Retirement Benefit may not be suspended or forfeited under Sections 411(a)(3)(B) or 411(a)(3)(D) of the Code.

A Non-Key Employee shall not fail to accrue a minimum Annual Retirement Benefit because he is excluded from participation (or accrues no benefit) merely because the Employee's compensation is less than a stated amount or merely because of a failure to make mandatory employee contributions, if any are so required under the Plan. A Non-Key Employee shall not fail to accrue a minimum Annual Retirement Benefit merely because the Employee was not employed on a specified date.

(b) DEFINITIONS. For purposes of determining minimum benefits for a Top-Heavy Plan, the following definitions shall apply:

(1) YEAR OF MINIMUM BENEFIT SERVICE.

The term "Year of Minimum Benefit Service" means a year of Service within the meaning of paragraph 17 of Article II except that Years of Minimum Benefit Service shall not include years of Service completed in a Plan Year beginning before January 1, 1984 or any year of Service thereafter in the event the Plan was not a Top-Heavy Plan in the Plan Year ending during such year of Service.

(2) ANNUAL RETIREMENT BENEFIT.

The term "Annual Retirement Benefit" means a benefit derived from Employer contributions and payable annually in the form of a life annuity (with no ancillary benefits) beginning at age 65. A benefit received in a form other than a single life annuity or commencing at a date other than at age 65 shall be the actuarial equivalent of such benefit; provided, however, that no adjustment shall be made for preretirement ancillary benefits.

(3) TESTING PERIOD.

The term "Testing Period" means the number of consecutive Years of Minimum Benefit Service, not exceeding five, during which a Non-Key Employee's compensation is the highest.

(c) TOP HEAVY VESTING SCHEDULE

(1) An Employee whose employment is terminated prior to age 65 and prior to the completion of two or more full years of Service shall not be entitled to any benefits under the Plan derived from Employer contributions.

(2) Two or More Years of Service. An Employee whose employment is terminated prior to age 65 but after the completion of two or more years of Service shall be entitled to receive the actuarial equivalent of the vested percentage of his Annual Retirement Benefit, determined in accordance with the following schedule:

Two Years of Service	(20%)
Three Years of Service	(40%)
Four Years of Service	(60%)
Five Years of Service	(80%)
Six or More Years of Service	(100%)

The vesting schedule under this subparagraph (c) shall apply to an Employee's benefit under the Plan accrued before or while the Plan is a Top-Heavy Plan.

(3) VESTING PERCENTAGE. In the event that the Plan previously was a Top-Heavy Plan but subsequently is not a Top-Heavy Plan, the vesting schedule under subparagraph (c) shall be changed to the vesting schedule set forth in paragraph 1(b) of Article VIII; provided, however, that any Employee who has completed at least five or more years of Service and who had at least one hour of service while the Plan was a Top-Heavy Plan, shall be entitled to elect, within a reasonable period, which of the above two vesting schedules is applicable to his benefit.

(d) LIMITATIONS ON ANNUAL ADDITIONS AND BENEFITS. For purposes of computing the defined benefit plan fraction and defined contribution plan fraction as set forth in Sections 415(e)(2)(B) and 415(e)(3)(B) of the Code, the dollar limitations on benefits and annual additions applicable to a limitation year shall be multiplied by 1.0 rather than by 1.25.

(e) NON-DUPLICATION OF MINIMUM BENEFITS. If a Non-Key Employee is entitled to a minimum Annual Retirement Benefit under this Plan in the same Plan Year in which he is covered by a defined contribution plan of the Employer that is a Top-Heavy Plan for such Plan Year, such Non-Key Employee shall receive the minimum Annual Retirement Benefit provided under this Plan, but shall not receive any minimum benefit or minimum allocation under the defined contribution plan.

FIRST AMENDMENT TO THE XYZ CORP. DEFINED BENEFIT PENSION PLAN

(To Comply with Provisions of the 1986 Tax Reform Act That are Effective Before 1989).

Note: IRS Notice 87-2 contains model amendments that qualified plans must adopt to comply with certain provisions of the 1986 Tax Reform Act that are effective before plan years beginning after 1989. Notice 87-2 also contains certain optional amendments that plans may adopt. The amendment below is derived from Model Amendment I of Notice 87-2 (for defined benefit plans that do not provide for employee contributions). Where a provision is required (R) appears next to the title. Optional provisions are marked with the letter (O). Required provisions must be adopted verbatim in order for a plan to rely on a favorable determination letter that was obtained before the 1986 Tax Reform Act. The IRS will not rule on whether a plan qualifies under the 1986 Act, but plan sponsors that adopt the model amendments before January 1, 1988, retroactive to December 31, 1986 and administer their plans after December 31, 1986 as if the required provisions were fully effective.

SECTION I: PURPOSE AND EFFECTIVE DATE

1.1. *Purpose*. It is the intention of the Employer to amend the plan to comply with those provisions of the Tax Reform Act of 1986 that are effective prior to the first Plan Year beginning after December 31, 1988.

1.2. *Effective Date*. Except as otherwise provided, this amendment shall be effective as of the first day of the first Plan Year beginning after December 31, 1986.

SECTION II: DEFINITIONS (R)

For purposes of this amendment only, the following definitions shall apply.

2.1. "Adjustment Factor" shall mean the cost of living adjustment factor prescribed by the Secretary of the Treasury under Section 415(d) of the Code for years beginning after December 31, 1987, applied to such items and in such manner as the Secretary shall prescribe.

2.2. "Affiliated Employer" shall mean the Employer and any corporation which is a member of a controlled group of corporations (as defined in Section 414(b) of the Code) which includes the Employer; any trade or business (whether or not incorporated) which is under common control (as defined in Section 414(c) of the Code) with the Employer; any organization (whether or not incorporated) which is a member of an affiliated service group (as defined in Section 414(m) of the Code) which includes the Employer; and any other entity required to be aggregated with the Employer pursuant to regulations under Section 414(o) of the Code.

2.3. "Code" shall mean the Internal Revenue Code of 1988 and amendments thereto.

2.4. "Current Accrued Benefit" shall mean a Participant's accrued benefit under the plan, determined as if the Participant had separated from service as of the close of the last Limitation Year beginning before January 1, 1987, when expressed as an annual benefit within the meaning of Section 415(b)(2) of the Code. In determining the amount of a Participant's Current Accrued Benefit, the following shall be disregarded:

(i) any change in the terms and conditions of the Plan after May 5, 1988; and

(ii) any cost of living adjustment occurring after May 5, 1988.

2.5. "Defined Benefit Dollar Limitation" shall mean the limitation set forth in Section 415(b)(1) of the Code.

2.6. "Defined Contribution Dollar Limitation" shall mean $30,000 or, if greater, one-fourth of the Defined Benefit Dollar Limitation in effect for the Limitation Year.

2.7. "Employee" shall mean employees of the Employer and shall include leased employees within the meaning of Section 414(n)(2) of the Code. Notwithstanding the foregoing, if such leased employees constitute less than twenty percent of the Employer's nonhighly compensated workforce within the meaning of Section 414(n)(1)(C)(ii) of the Code, the term "Employee" shall not include those leased employees covered by a plan described in Section 414(n)(5) of the Code unless otherwise provided by the terms of the plan other than this amendment.

2.8. "Employee Contributions" shall mean contributions to the plan made by a Participant during the Plan Year.

2.9. "Employer" shall mean the entity that establishes or maintains the plan; any other organization which has adopted the plan with the consent of such establishing employer; and any successor of such employer.

2.10. "Limitation Year" shall mean the limitation year specified in the plan or, if none is specified, the calendar Year.

2.11. "Participant" shall mean any Employee of the Employer who has met the eligibility and participation requirements of the plan.

2.12. "Social Security Retirement Age" shall mean the age used as the retirement age for the Participant under Section 218(1) of the Social Security Act, except that such section shall be applied without regard to the age increase factor, and as if the early retirement age under Section 218(1)(2) of such Act were 62.

2.13. "Plan Year" shall mean the plan year otherwise specified in the plan.

SECTION III: PROVISIONS RELATING TO LEASED EMPLOYEES (R)

3.1. *Safe-Harbor.* Notwithstanding any other provisions of the Plan, for purposes of the pension requirements of Section 414(n)(3) of the Code, the employees of the Employer shall include individuals defined as Employees in Section 2.7 of this amendment.

3.2. *Participation and Accrual.* A leased employee within the meaning of Section 414(n)(2) of the Code shall become a Participant in, or accrue benefits under, the plan based on service as a leased employee only as provided in provisions of the plan other than this Section III.

3.3 *Effective Date.* This Section III shall be effective for services performed after December 31, 1988.

SECTION IV: LIMITATIONS ON CONTRIBUTIONS AND BENEFITS (R)

4.1. *Adjustment to Defined Benefit Dollar Limitation for Early or Deferred Retirement.*

4.1(a). *Adjustment for Early Retirement.* If the retirement benefit of a Participant commences before the Participant's Social Security Retirement Age, the Defined Benefit Dollar Limitation shall be adjusted so that it is the actuarial equivalent of an annual benefit of $90,000, multiplied by the Adjustment Factor, as prescribed by the Secretary of the Treasury, beginning at the Social Security Retirement Age. The adjustment provided for in the preceding sentence shall be made in such manner as the Secretary of the Treasury may prescribe which is consistent with the reduction for old-age insurance benefits commencing before the Social Security Retirement Age under the Social Security Act.

4.1(b) *Adjustment for Deferred Retirement.* If the retirement benefit of a Participant commences after the Participant's Social Security Retirement Age, the Defined Benefit Dollar Limitation shall be adjusted so that it is the actuarial equivalent of a benefit of $90,000 beginning at the Social Security Retirement Age, multiplied by the Adjustment Factor as provided by the Secretary of the Treasury, based on the lesser of the interest rate assumption under the Plan or on an assumption of five percent (5%) per year.

4.2. *Adjustment of Limitation for years of Service or Participation.*

4.2(a). *Defined Benefit Dollar Limitation.* If a Participant has completed less than ten years of participation, the Participant's accrued benefit shall not exceed the Defined Benefit Dollar Limitation as adjusted by multiplying such amount by a fraction, the numerator of which is the Participant's number of years (or part thereof) of participation in the Plan, and the denominator of which is ten.

4.2(b). *Other Defined Benefit Limitations.* If a Participant has completed less than ten years of service with the Affiliated Employers, the limitations described in Sections 415(b)(1)(B) and 415(b)(4) of the Code shall be adjusted by multiplying such amounts by a fraction, the numerator of which is the Participant's number of years of service (or part thereof), and the denominator of which is ten.

4.2(c). *Limitations on Reductions.* In no event shall Sections 4.2(b) and (c) reduce the limitations provided under Sections 415(b)(1) and (4) of the Code to an amount less than one-tenth of the applicable limitation (as determined without regard to this Section 4.2).

4.2(d). *Application to Changes in Benefit Structure.* To the extent provided by the Secretary of the Treasury, this Section 4.2 shall be applied separately with respect to each change in the benefit structure of the plan.

4.3. *Preservation of Current Accrued Benefit Under Defined Benefit Plan.*

4.3(a). *In General.* This section 4.3 shall apply to defined benefit plans that were in existence on May 8, 1988, and that met the applicable requirements of Section 415 of the Code as in effect for all Limitation Years.

4.3(b). *Protection of Current Accrued Benefit.* If the Current Accrued Benefit of an individual who is a Participant as of the first day of the Limitation Year beginning on or after January 1, 1987, exceeds the benefit limitations under Section 415(b) of the Code (as modified by sections 4.1 and 4.2 of this amendment), then, for purposes of Code Section 415(b) and (e), the Defined Benefit Dollar Limitation with respect to such individual shall be equal to such Current Accrued Benefit.

4.4. *Special Rules for Plans Subject to Overall Limitations Under Code Section 415(e).*

4.4(a). *Defined Contribution Plan Fraction.* For purposes of computing the defined contribution plan fraction of Section 415(e)(1) of the Code, "Annual Addition" shall mean the amount allocated to a Participant's account during the Limitation Year as a result of:

(i) Employer contributions,

(ii) Employee Contributions,

(iii) Forfeitures, and

(iv) Amounts described in Sections 415(l)(1) and 419(A)(d)(2) of the Code.

4.4(b). *Recomputation Not Required.* The Annual Addition for any Limitation year beginning before January 1, 1987 shall not be recomputed to treat all Employee Contributions as an Annual Addition.

4.4(c). *Adjustment of Defined Contribution Plan Fraction.* If the Plan satisfied the applicable requirements of Section 415 of the Code as in effect for all Limitation years beginning before January 1, 1987, an amount shall be subtracted from the numerator of the defined contribution plan fraction (not exceeding such numerator) as prescribed by the Secretary of the Treasury so that the sum of the defined benefit plan fraction and defined contribution plan fraction computed under Section 415(e)(1) of the Code (as revised by this Section IV) does not exceed 1.0 for such Limitation Year.

4.5. *Special Rules.* The provisions of this Section IV shall be modified as provided in:

(i) Section 415(b)(2)(F) of the Code for plans maintained by organizations (other than governmental units) exempt from tax under Subtitle A of the Code, and qualified merchant marine plans; and

(ii) Section 415(b)(9) of the Code for plan participants who are commercial airline pilots.

4.6 *Effective Date of Section IV Provisions.* The provisions of this Section IV shall be effective for Limitation Years beginning after December 31, 1986.

SECTION V: CALCULATION OF PRESENT VALUE FOR CASH-OUT OF BENEFITS AND FOR DETERMINING AMOUNT OF BENEFITS (R)

5.1. *In General.* This Section V shall apply to all distributions from the plan and from annuity contracts purchased to provide plan benefits other than distributions described in Section 1.417-1T(e)(3) of the Income Tax Regulations issued under the Retirement Equity Act.

5.2. *Determination of Present Value.*

5.2(a). For purposes of determining whether the present value of:

(i) a Participant's vested accrued benefit;

(ii) a qualified joint and survivor annuity, within the meaning of Section 417(b) of the Code; or

(iii) a qualified preretirement survivor annuity within the meaning of Section 417(c)(1) of the Code

exceeds $3,500, the present value of such benefits or annuities shall be calculated by using an interest rate no greater than the Applicable Interest Rate.

5.2(b). In no event shall the present value of any such benefit or annuity determined under this Section 5.2 be less than the greater of:

(i) the present value of such benefits or annuities determined under the plan's provisions for determining the present value of accrued benefits or annuities other than Sections V and IX of this amendment; or

(ii) the present value of such benefits or annuities determined using the Applicable Interest Rate.

5.3. *Determination of Amount of Benefits.*

5.3(a). For purposes of determining the amount of a Participant's vested accrued benefit, the interest rate used shall not exceed:

(i) the Applicable Interest Rate if the present value of the benefit (using such rate or rates) is not in excess of $25,000; or

(ii) 120 percent of the Applicable Interest Rate if the present value of the benefit exceeds $25,000 (as determined under clause (i)). In no event shall the present value determined under this clause (ii) be less than $25,000.

5.3(b). In no event shall the amount of the benefit or annuity determined under this Section 5.3 be less than the greater of:

(i) the amount of such benefit determined under the plan's provisions for determining the amount of benefits other than Sections V and IX of this amendment; or

(ii) the amount of such benefit determined using the Applicable Interest Rate if the value determined in Section 5.3(a) is less than $25,000 or 120 percent of the Applicable Interest Rate if the value determined in Section 5.3(a) is not less than $25,000.

5.4. *Coordination with Limitations on Contributions and Benefits.* In no event shall the amount of any benefit or annuity determined under this Section V exceed the maximum benefit permitted under Section 415 of the Code.

5.5. *Applicable Interest Rate.*

5.5(a). For purposes of this Section V, "Applicable Interest Rate" shall mean the interest rate or rates which would be used as of the date distribution commences by the Pension Benefit Guaranty Corporation for purposes of determining the present value of that Participant's benefits under the plan if the plan had terminated on the date distribution commences with insufficient assets to provide benefits guaranteed by the Pension Benefit Guaranty Corporation on that date.

5.5(b). Notwithstanding the foregoing, if the provisions of the plan other than Section 5.5 so provide, the Applicable Interest Rate shall be determined as of the first day of the Plan Year in which a distribution occurs rather than as of the date distribution commences.

5.6. *Effective Dates.*

5.6(a). In General. This Section V shall apply to distributions in Plan Years beginning after December 31, 1984, other than distributions under annuity contracts distributed to or owned by a Participant prior to September 17, 1985 unless additional contributions are made under the plan by the Employer with respect to such contracts.

5.6(b). Special Rule for Distributions Prior to 1987. Notwithstanding the foregoing, this Section V shall not apply to any distributions in Plan Years beginning after December 31, 1984, and before January 1, 1987, if such distributions were made in accordance with the requirements of the Income Tax Regulations issued under the Retirement Equity Act of 1984.

SECTION VI: DETERMINATION OF TOP-HEAVY STATUS (R)

Solely for the purpose of determining if the plan, or any other plan included in a required aggregation group of which this plan is a part, is top-heavy (within the meaning of Section 416(g) of the Code) the accrued benefit of an Employee other than a key employee (within the meaning of Section 416(i)(1) of the Code) shall be determined under (a) the method, if any, that uniformly applies for accrual purposes under all plans maintained by the Affiliated Employers, or (b) if there is no such method, as if such benefit accrued not more rapidly than the slowest accrual rate permitted under the fractional accrual rate of Section 411(b)(1)(C) of the Code.

SECTION VII: QUALIFIED VOLUNTARY EMPLOYEE CONTRIBUTIONS NOT PERMITTED

(R) — for Plans with Qualified Voluntary Employee Contributions).

The plan shall accept no Employee Contributions designated by the Participant as deductible employee contributions (within the meaning of Section 72(o)(5)(A) of the Code) for a taxable year of the Participant beginning after December 31, 1986.

SECTION VIII: EMPLOYEE CONTRIBUTIONS NOT PERMITTED (R)

The Plan shall accept no Employee Contributions which are accounted for separately (as though they were actually allocated to a separate account) after the last day of the last Plan Year beginning before December 31, 1986.

SECTION IX: REPLACEMENT OF IMMEDIATE ANNUITY RATE WITH APPLICABLE INTEREST RATE

(O — For Plans that Use PBGC Immediate Annuity Rate to Determine Amount and Present Value of Benefits)

9.1. *Replacement of Immediate Annuity Rate.* If the provisions of the plan, other than this Section IX, provide that the present value and amount of benefits under Sections 5.2 and 5.3 of this amendment are determined with reference to the immediate annuity rates used by the Pension Benefit Guaranty Corporation, the rate used for such purposes shall instead be the Applicable Interest Rate as defined in Section 5.5 of this amendment or 120 percent of that rate if the present value of the benefit exceeds $25,000 (determined using the Applicable Interest Rate) and provided that the use of 120 percent of such rate shall not reduce the present value or amount of benefits below $25,000.

9.2. *Effective Date.* This Section IX shall apply to distributions in Plan Years beginning after December 31, 1986, and shall also apply to any distributions in Plan Years beginning after December 31, 1984 and before January 1, 1987 other than:

(a) Distributions under annuity contracts distributed to or owned by a Participant prior to September 17, 1985 unless additional contributions are made under the plan by the Employer with respect to such contracts; or

(b) Distributions made in accordance with the requirements of the Income Tax Regulations issued under the Retirement Equity Act of 1984.

MODEL AMENDMENT II FOR DEFINED BENEFIT PLANS WITH CURRENT EMPLOYEE CONTRIBUTIONS

Note: This amendment is from Model Amendment II of Notice 87-2. It is to be used to comply with provisions of the 1986 Tax Reform Act that are effective before plan years beginning after 1988 if the plan currently provides for employee contributions which are separately accounted for. As is the case with the model amendment that is based on Model Amendment I, above, plan sponsors to whom this model amendment applies must adopt it verbatim in order to be able to rely on a pre-1986 TRA favorable determination letter. Required provisions are marked with the designation (R). Optional provisions are marked with the letter (O). Since the XYZ Corp. defined benefit plan does not provide for employee contributions, this amendment would not be appropriate for that plan. It is set forth here for use by plan sponsors that maintain defined benefit plans calling for current employee contributions which are separately accounted for. Many of the required provisions of Model Amendment II track the provisions of Model Amendment I, above.

SECTION I: PURPOSE AND EFFECTIVE DATE (R)

1.1. *Purpose.* It is the intention of the Employer to amend the plan to comply with those provisions of the Tax Reform Act of 1986 that are effective prior to the first Plan Year beginning after December 31, 1988.

1.2. *Effective Date.* Except as otherwise provided, this amendment shall be effective as of the first day of the first Plan Year beginning after December 31, 1986.

SECTION II: DEFINITIONS (R)

For purposes of this amendment only, the following definitions shall apply.

2.1. "Adjustment Factor" shall mean the cost of living adjustment factor prescribed by the Secretary of the Treasury under Section 415(d) of the Code for years beginning after December 31, 1987, applied to such items and in such manner as the Secretary shall prescribe.

2.2. "Affiliated Employer" shall mean the Employer and any corporation which is a member of a controlled group of corporations (as defined in Section 414(b) of the Code) which includes the Employer; any trade or business (whether or not incorporated) which is under common control (as defined in Section 414(c) of the Code) with the Employer; any organization (whether or not incorporated) which is a member of an affiliated service group (as defined in Section 414(m) of the Code) which includes the Employer; and any other entity required to be aggregated with the Employer pursuant to regulations under Section 414(o) of the Code.

2.3. "Code" shall mean the Internal Revenue Code of 1986 and amendments thereto.

2.4 "Compensation" shall mean compensation paid by the Employer to the Participant during the taxable year ending with or within the Plan Year which is required to be reported as wages on the Participant's Form W-2, and, if the provisions of the plan other than this amendment so provide, shall also include compensation which is not currently includible in the Participant's gross income by reason of the application of Sections 125, 402(a)(8), 402(h)(1)(B) or 403(b) of the Code.

2.5. "Current Accrued Benefit" shall mean a Participant's accrued benefit under the plan, determined as if the Participant had separated from service as of the close of the last Limitation Year beginning before January 1, 1987, when expressed as an annual benefit within the meaning of Section 415(b)(2) of the Code. In determining the amount of a Participant's Current Accrued Benefit, the following shall be disregarded:

(i) any change in the terms and conditions of the Plan after May 5, 1986; and

(ii) any cost of living adjustment occurring after May 5, 1986.

2.6. "Defined Benefit Dollar Limitation" shall mean the limitation set forth in Section 415(b)(1) of the Code.

2.7. "Defined Contribution Dollar Limitation" shall mean $30,000 or, if greater, one-fourth of the Defined Benefit Dollar Limitation in effect for the Limitation year.

2.8. "Employee" shall mean employees of the Employer and shall include leased employees within the meaning of Section 414(n)(2) of the Code. Notwithstanding the foregoing, if such leased employees constitute less than twenty percent of the Employer's nonhighly compensated work force within the meaning of Section 414(n)(1)(C)(ii) of the Code, the term "Employee" shall not include those leased employees covered by a plan described in Section 414(n)(5) of the Code unless otherwise provided by the terms of the plan other than this amendment.

2.9 "Employee Contributions" shall mean contributions to the plan made by a Participant during the Plan Year.

2.10. "Employer" shall mean the entity that establishes or maintains the plan; any other organization which has adopted the plan with the consent of such establishing employer; and any successor of such employer.

2.11. "Family Member" shall mean an individual described in Section 414(q)(6)(B) of the Code.

2.12. "Limitation Year" shall mean the limitation year specified in the plan or, if none is specified, the calendar Year.

2.13. "Highly Compensated Employee" shall mean an individual described in Section 414(q) of the Code.

2.14. "Non-Highly Compensated Employee" shall mean an Employee of the Employer who is neither a Highly Compensated Employee nor a Family Member.

2.15. "Participant" shall mean any Employee of the Employer who has met the eligibility and participation requirements of the plan.

2.16. "Social Security Retirement Age" shall mean the age used as the retirement age for the Participant under Section 216(1) of the Social Security Act, except that such section shall be applied without regard to the age increase factor, and as if the early retirement age under Section 216(1)(2) of such Act were 62.

2.17. "Plan Year" shall mean the plan year otherwise specified in the plan.

SECTION III: PROVISIONS RELATING TO LEASED EMPLOYEES (R)

3.1. *Safe-Harbor.* Notwithstanding any other provisions of the Plan, for purposes of determining the number or identity of Highly Compensated Employees or for purposes of the pension requirements of Section 414(n)(3) of the Code, the employees of the Employer shall include individuals defined as Employees in Section 2.8 of this amendment.

3.2 *Participation and Accrual.* A leased employee within the meaning of Section 414(n)(2) of the Code shall become a Participant in, and accrue benefits under, the plan based on service as a leased employee only as provided in provisions of the plan other than this Section III.

3.3 *Effective Date.* This Section III shall be effective for services performed after December 31, 1986.

SECTION IV: LIMITATIONS ON CONTRIBUTIONS AND BENEFITS (R)

4.1. *Adjustment to Defined Benefit Dollar Limitation for Early or Deferred Retirement.*

4.1(a). *Adjustment for Early Retirement.* If the retirement benefit of a Participant commences before the Participant's Social Security Retirement Age, the Defined Benefit Dollar Limitation shall be adjusted so that it is the actuarial equivalent of an annual benefit of $90,000, multiplied by the Adjustment Factor as provided by the Secretary of the Treasury, beginning at the Social Security Retirement Age. The adjustment provided for in the preceding sentence shall be made in such manner as the Secretary of the Treasury may prescribe which is consistent with the reduction for old-age insurance benefits commencing before the Social Security Retirement Age under the Social Security Act.

4.1(b) *Adjustment for Deferred Retirement.* If the retirement benefit of a Participant commences after the Participant's Social Security Retirement Age, the Defined Benefit Dollar Limitation shall be adjusted so that it is the actuarial equivalent of a benefit of $90,000 beginning at the Social Security Retirement Age, multiplied by the Adjustment Factor as provided by the Secretary of the Treasury, based on the lesser of the interest rate assumption under the Plan or on an assumption of five percent (5%) per year.

4.2. *Adjustment of Limitation for Years of Service or Participation.*

4.2(a). *Defined Benefit Dollar Limitation.* If a Participant has completed less than ten years of participation, the Participant's accrued benefit shall not exceed the Defined Benefit Dollar Limitation as adjusted by multiplying such amount by a fraction, the numerator of which is the Participant's number of years (or part thereof) of participation in the Plan, and the denominator of which is ten.

4.2(b). *Other Defined Benefit Limitations.* If a Participant has completed less than ten years of service with the Affiliated Employers, the limitations described in Sections 415(b)(1)(B) and 415(b)(4) of the Code shall be adjusted by multiplying such amounts by a fraction, the numerator of which is the Participant's number of years of service (or part thereof), and the denominator of which is ten.

4.2(c). *Limitations on Reductions.* In no event shall Sections 4.2(b) and (c) reduce the limitations provided under Sections 415(b)(1) and (4) of the Code to an amount less than one-tenth of the applicable limitation (as determined without regard to this Section 4.2).

4.2(d). *Application to Changes in Benefit Structure.* To the extent provided by the Secretary of the Treasury, this Section 4.2 shall be applied separately with respect to each change in the benefit structure of the plan.

4.3. *Preservation of Current Accrued Benefit Under Defined Benefit Plan.*

4.3(a). *In General.* This section 4.3 shall apply to defined benefit plans that were in existence on May 6, 1986, and that met the applicable requirements of Section 415 of the Code as in effect for all Limitation Years.

4.3(b). *Protection of Current Accrued Benefit.* If the Current Accrued Benefit of an individual who is a Participant as of the first day of the Limitation Year beginning on or after January 1, 1987, exceeds the benefit limitations under Section 415(b) of the Code (as modified by sections 4.1 and 4.2 of this amendment), then, for purposes of Code Section 415(b) and (e), the Defined Benefit Dollar Limitation with respect to such individual shall be equal to such Current Accrued Benefit.

4.4. *Revised Contribution Limitations Under Defined Contribution Plan.*

4.4(a). *Definition of Annual Additions.* For purposes of the plan, "Annual Addition" shall mean the amount allocated to a Participant's account during the Limitation Year that constitutes:

(i) Employer contributions,

(ii) Employee Contributions,

(iii) Forfeitures, and

(iv) Amounts described in Sections 415(l)(1) and 419(A)(d)(2) of the Code.

4.4(b). *Maximum Annual Addition.* The maximum Annual Addition that may be contributed or allocated to a Participant's account under the Plan for any Limitation Year shall not exceed the lesser of:

(i) the Defined Contribution Dollar Limitation, or

(ii) 25 percent of the Participant's compensation, within the meaning of Section 415(c)(3) of the Code for the Limitation year.

4.4(c). *Special Rules.* The compensation limitation referred to in Section 4.4(b)(ii) shall not apply to:

(i) Any contribution for medical benefits (within the meaning of Section 419A(f)(2) of the Code) after separation from service which is otherwise treated as an Annual Addition, or

(ii) Any amount otherwise treated as an Annual Addition under Section 415(l)(1) of the Code.

4.4(d). "Defined Contribution Dollar Limitation" shall mean $30,000 or, if greater, one-fourth of the defined benefit dollar limitation set forth in Section 415(b)(1) of the Code as in effect for the limitation year.

4.5. *Special Rules for Plans Subject to Overall Limitations Under Code Section 415(e).*

4.5(a). *Recomputation Not Required.* The Annual Addition for any Limitation Year beginning before January 1, 1987 shall not be recomputed to treat all Employee Contributions as an Annual Addition.

4.5(b). *Adjustment of Defined Contribution Plan Fraction.* If the Plan satisfied the applicable requirements of Section 415 of the Code as in effect for all Limitation Years beginning before January 1, 1987, an amount shall be subtracted from the numerator of the defined contribution plan fraction (not exceeding such numerator) as prescribed by the Secretary of the Treasury so that the sum of the defined benefit plan fraction and defined contribution plan fraction computed under Section 415(e)(1) of the Code (as revised by this Section IV) does not exceed 1.0 for such Limitation Year.

4.6. *Special Rules.* The provisions of this Section IV shall be modified as provided in:

(i) Section 415(b)(2)(F) of the Code for plans maintained by organizations (other than governmental units) exempt from tax under Subtitle A of the Code, and qualified merchant marine plans; and

(ii) Section 415(b)(9) of the Code for plan participants who are commercial airline pilots.

4.7. *Effective Date of Section IV Provisions.* The provisions of this Section IV shall be effective for Limitation Years beginning after December 31, 1986.

SECTION V: CALCULATION OF PRESENT VALUE FOR CASH-OUT OF BENEFITSAND FOR DETERMINING AMOUNT OF BENEFITS

5.1. *In General.* This Section V shall apply to all distributions from the plan and from annuity contracts purchased to provide plan benefits other than distributions described in Section 1.417-1T(e)(3) of the Income Tax Regulations issued under the Retirement Equity Act.

5.2. *Determination of Present Value.*

5.2(a). For purposes of determining whether the present value of:

(i) a Participant's vested accrued benefit;

(ii) a qualified joint and survivor annuity, within the meaning of Section 417(b) of the Code; or

(iii) a qualified preretirement survivor annuity within the meaning of Section 417(c)(1) of the Code

exceeds $3,500, the present value of such benefits or annuities shall be calculated by using an interest rate no greater than the Applicable Interest Rate.

5.2(b). In no event shall the present value of any such benefit or annuity determined under this Section 5.2 be less than the greater of:

(i) the present value of such benefits or annuities determined under the plan's provisions for determining the present value of accrued benefits or annuities other than Sections V and X of this amendment; or

(ii) the present value of such benefits or annuities determined using the Applicable Interest Rate.

5.3. *Determination of Amount of Benefits.*

5.3(a) For purposes of determining the amount of a Participant's vested accrued benefit, the interest rate used shall not exceed:

(i) the Applicable Interest Rate if the present value of the benefit (using such rate or rates) is not in excess of $25,000; or

(ii) 120 percent of the Applicable Interest Rate if the present value of the benefit exceeds $25,000 (as determined under clause (i)). In no event shall the present value determined under this clause (ii) be less than $25,000.

5.3(b). In no event shall the amount of the benefit or annuity determined under this Section 5.3 be less than the greater of:

(i) the amount of such benefit determined under the plan's provision for determining the amount of benefits other than Sections V and X of this amendment; or

(ii) the amount of such benefit determined using the Applicable Interest Rate if the value determined in Section 5.3(a) is less than $25,000 or 120 percent of the Applicable Interest Rate if the value determined in Section 5.3(a) is not less than $25,000.

5.4. *Coordination with Limitations on Contributions and Benefits.* In no event shall the amount of any benefit or annuity determined under this Section V exceed the maximum benefit permitted under Section 415 of the Code.

5.5. *Applicable Interest Rate.*

5.5(a). For purposes of this Section V "Applicable Interest Rate" shall mean the interest rate or rates which would be used as of the date distribution commences by the Pension Benefit Guaranty Corporation for purposes of determining the present value of that Participant's benefits under the plan if the plan had terminated on the date distribution commences with insufficient assets to provide benefits guaranteed by the Pension Benefit Guaranty Corporation on that date.

5.5(b). Notwithstanding the foregoing, if the provisions of the plan other than Section 5.5 so provide, the Applicable Interest Rate shall be determined as of the first day of the Plan Year in which a distribution occurs rather than as of the date distribution commences.

5.6. *Effective Dates.*

5.6(a). *In General.* This Section V shall apply to distributions in Plan Years beginning after December 31, 1984, other than distributions under annuity contracts distributed to or owned by a Participant prior to September 17, 1985 unless additional contributions are made under the plan by the Employer with respect to such contract.

5.6(b). *Special Rule for Distributions Prior to 1987.* Notwithstanding the foregoing, this Section V shall not apply to any distributions in Plan Years beginning after December 31, 1984, and before January 1, 1987, if such distributions were made in accordance with the requirements of the Income Tax Regulations issued under the Retirement Equity Act of 1984.

SECTION VI: DETERMINATION OF TOP-HEAVY STATUS (R)

Solely for the purpose of determining if the plan, or any other plan included in a required aggregation group of which this plan is a part, is top-heavy (within the meaning of Section 416(g) of the Code) the accrued benefit of an Employee other than a key employee (within the meaning of Section 416(i)(1) of the Code) shall be determined under:

(a) the method, if any, that uniformly applies for accrual purposes under all plans maintained by the Affiliated Employers, or

(b) if there is no such method, as if such benefit accrued not more rapidly than the slowest accrual rate permitted under the fractional accrual rate of Section 411(b)(1)(C) of the Code.

SECTION VII. LIMITATIONS ON EMPLOYEE CONTRIBUTIONS

(R — for Plans with Employee Contributions Accounted for Separately).

7.1. *Contribution Percentage.*

7.1(a). The Average Contribution Percentage for Eligible Participants who are Highly Compensated Employees for the Plan Year shall not exceed the Average Contribution Percentage for Eligible Participants who are Nonhighly Compensated Employees for the Plan Year multiplied by 1.25; or

7.1(b). The Average Contribution Percentage for Eligible Participants who are Highly Compensated Employees for the Plan Year shall not exceed the Average Contribution Percentage for Eligible Participants who are Nonhighly Compensated Employees for the Plan Year multiplied by 2, provided that the Average Contribution Percentage for Eligible Participants who are Highly Compensated Employees does not exceed the Average Contribution Percentage for Eligible Participants who are Nonhighly Compensated Employees by more than two (2) percentage points or such lesser amount as the Secretary of the Treasury shall prescribe to prevent the multiple use of this alternative limitation with respect to any Highly Compensated Employee.

7.2. *Definitions.* For purposes of Sections VII and IX of this amendment, the following definitions shall apply.

7.2(a). "Average Contribution Percentage" shall mean the average (expressed as percentage) of the Contribution Percentages of the Eligible Participants in a group.

7.2(b). "Contribution Percentage" shall mean the ratio (expressed as a percentage), of the Employee Contributions under the plan on behalf of the Eligible Participant for the Plan Year to the Eligible Participant's Compensation for the Plan Year.

7.2(c). "Eligible Participant" shall mean any employee of the Employer who is otherwise authorized under the terms of the plan to have Employee Contributions allocated to his account for the Plan Year.

7.3. *Special Rules.*

7.3(a). For purposes of this section, the Contribution Percentage for any Eligible Participant who is a Highly Compensated Employee for the Plan Year and who is eligible to make Employee Contributions, or to have matching contributions within the meaning of Section 401(m)(4)(A) of the Code, qualified nonelective contributions within the meaning of Section 401(m)(4)(c) of the Code or elective deferrals within the meaning of Section 402(g)(3)(A) of the Code allocated to his account under two or more plans described in Section 401(a) or arrangements described in Section 401(k) of the Code that are maintained by the Employer or an Affiliated Employer shall be determined as if all such Employee Contributions, matching contributions, qualified nonelective contributions or elective deferrals were made under a single plan.

7.3(b). In the event that this plan satisfies the requirements of Section 410(b) of the Code only if aggregated with one or more other plans, or if one or more other plans satisfy the requirements of section 410(b) of the Code only if aggregated with this plan, then this section VII shall be applied by determining the Contribution Percentages of Eligible Participants as if all such plans were a single plan.

7.3(c). For purposes of determining the Contribution Percentage of a Eligible Participant who is a Highly Compensated Employee, the Employee Contributions of such Participant shall include the Employee Contributions of Family Members and such Family Members shall be disregarded in determining the Contribution Percentage for Eligible Participants who are Nonhighly Compensated Employees.

7.3(d). The determination and treatment of the Contribution Percentage of any Participant shall satisfy such other requirements as may be prescribed by the Secretary of the Treasury.

SECTION VIII: QUALIFIED VOLUNTARY EMPLOYEE CONTRIBUTIONS NOT PERMITTED

(R — for Plans with Qualified Voluntary Employee Contributions)

The pla.. shall accept no Employee Contributions designated by the Participant as deductible employee contributions (within the meaning of Section 72(o)(5)(A) of the Code) for a taxable year of the Participant beginning after December 31, 1986.

SECTION IX: DISTRIBUTION OF EXCESS AGGREGATE CONTRIBUTIONS

(O — For plans with Employee Contributions)

9.1. *In General.* Excess Aggregate Contributions and income allocable thereto shall be distributed no later than the last day of each Plan Year beginning after December 31, 1987, to Participants to whose accounts Employee Contributions were allocated for the preceding Plan Year.

9.2. *Excess Aggregate Contributions.* For purposes of this amendment, "Excess Aggregate Contributions" shall mean the amount described in Section 401(m)(6)(B) of the Code.

9.3. *Determination of Income.* The income allocable to Excess Aggregate Contributions shall be determined by multiplying the income allocable to the Participant's Employee Contributions for the Plan Year by a fraction, the numerator of which is the Excess Aggregate Contributions on behalf of the Participant for the preceding Plan Year and the denominator of which is the sum of the Participant's account balances attributable to Employee Contributions on the last day of the preceding Plan Year.

9.4. *Maximum Distribution Amount.* The Excess Aggregate Contributions to be distributed to the Participant shall be adjusted for income and, if there is a loss attributable to the Excess Contributions shall in no event be less than the lesser of the Participant's account under the Plan or the Participant's Employee Contributions for the Plan Year.

SECTION X: REPLACEMENT OF IMMEDIATE ANNUITY RATE WITH APPLICABLE INTEREST RATE

(O — For Plans that Use PBGC Immediate Annuity Rate to Determine Amount and Present Value of Benefits)

10.1. *Replacement of Immediate Annuity Rate.* If the provisions of the plan, as adopted prior to October 22, 1986, provide that the present value and amount of benefits under Sections 5.2 and 5.3 of this amendment were determined with reference to the immediate annuity rates used by the Pension Benefit Guaranty Corporation, the rate used for such purposes shall instead be the Applicable Interest Rate as defined in Section 5.5 of this amendment or 120 percent of such rate if the present value of the benefit exceeds $25,000 (determined using such immediate interest rate) and provided that the use of 120 percent of such rate shall not reduce the present value or amount of benefits below $25,000.

10.2. *Effective Date.* This Section X shall apply to distributions in Plan Years beginning after December 31, 1986, and shall also apply to any distributions in Plan Years beginning after December 31, 1984 and before January 1, 1987 other than:

(a) Distributions under annuity contracts distributed to or owned by a Participant prior to September 17, 1985 unless additional contributions are made under the plan by the Employer with respect to such contracts; or

(b) Distributions made in accordance with the requirements of the Income Tax Regulations issued under the Retirement Equity Act of 1984.

ABC CORP. PROFIT-SHARING PLAN WITH §401(k) ARRANGEMENT*

ARTICLE I. INTRODUCTION

1.01. *Purpose of Plan.* ABC Corp. has established this Plan in order to encourage savings by its employees for retirement.

1.02. *Plan and Trust Intended to Qualify.* This Plan and its related Trust are intended to qualify as a profit sharing plan and trust under Section 401(a) of the Internal Revenue Code of 1986, and the cash or deferred arrangement forming part of the Plan is intended to qualify under Section 401(k) of the Code. Except as otherwise provided herein, no part of the corpus or income of the Trust forming part of the Plan will be used for or diverted to purposes other than for the exclusive benefit of each Participant and Beneficiary.

ARTICLE II. DEFINITIONS

Wherever used herein, a pronoun or adjective in the masculine gender includes the feminine gender, the singular includes the plural, and the following terms have the following meanings unless a different meaning is clearly required by the context:

2.01. "Accounts" mean, for any Participant, his or her Elective Contribution Account, Matching Contribution Account, and Company Contribution Account.

2.02. "Administrator" means the Company or other person appointed to administer the Plan in accordance with Article III.

2.03. "Affiliated Company" means:

(a) any corporation (other than the Company) that is a member of a controlled group of corporations (as defined in Section 414(b) of the Code) of which the Company is also a member,

(b) any trade or business (other than the Company), whether or not incorporated, that is under common control (as defined in Section 414(c) of the Code) with the Company, and (c) any trade or business (other than the Company) that is a member of an affiliated service group (as defined in Section 414(m) of the Code) of which the Company is also a member; provided, that the term "Affiliated Company" shall not include any corporation or unincorporated trade or business prior to the date on which such corporation, trade or business satisfies the affiliation or control tests of (a), (b) or (c) above.

In identifying any "Affiliated Companies" for purposes of Section 7.03, the definitions in Sections 414(b) and (c) of the Code shall be modified as provided in Section 415(h) of the Code.

2.04. "Annual Addition" means, in the case of any Participant, the sum for any Limitation Year of the Elective Contribution, Company Contribution and reallocated forfeitures (if any), made for the Participant's benefit for such Year.

2.05 "Annuity Starting Date" shall mean the first day of the first period for which a Participant (or his or her Beneficiary, if applicable) is entitled to receive annuity benefits under this Plan.

2.06. "Beneficiary" means any person entitled under Section 8.03 to receive benefits under the Plan upon the death of the Participant.

2.07. "Board of Directors" means the Board of Directors of the Company. The Board of Directors may allocate or delegate its fiduciary responsibilities, or may designate others to carry out its fiduciary responsibilities, in writing in accordance with Section 405 of ERISA.

2.08. "Code" means the Internal Revenue Code of 1986, as amended. Reference to any section or subsection of the Code includes reference to any comparable or succeeding provisions of any legislation which amends, supplements, or replaces such section or subsection.

2.09. "Company" or "Employer" means ABC Corp., a [insert name of state] corporation, and any successor to all or a major portion of its assets or business which assumes the obligations of the Company with the consent of the Trustees.

2.10. "Company Contribution" means any contribution made for the benefit of a Participant under Section 5.01.

2.11. "Company Contribution Account" means the total Company Contributions made on behalf of a Participant plus investment growth thereon.

2.12. "Computation Period" shall mean either the "Initial Participation Computation Period," or the "Regular Computation Period," depending upon the context, except that, if neither is specified, references to the Computation Period shall be taken to mean the Regular Computation Period.

The Initial Computation Period shall be the 12-consecutive month period beginning with the day the Employee first performs an Hour of Service for the Company. The Initial Participation computation Period shall be used for purposes of determining Years of Service and Breaks in Service for participation purposes during the above-referenced 12-consecutive month period. For purposes of determining eligibility to participate only, an Employee will be credited with two Years of Service for Participation purposes if he or she is credited with 1,000 Hours of Service in both the Initial Eligibility Computation Period and the First Regular Computation Period.

The Regular Computation Period shall be the 12-consecutive month period beginning with the first day of the first Plan Year which commences prior to the anniversary of the Employee's Initial Participation Computation Period. The Regular Computation Period shall be used for purposes of determining a Year of Service for vesting and benefit accrual.

2.13. "Disability" shall mean the inability to engage in any substantial gainful activity, considering the Participant's age, education, and work experience, by reason of any medically determined physical or mental impairment which can be expected to result in death or which can be expected to last for a continuous period of not less than 12 months. A Participant who becomes disabled shall be entitled to receive a Disability retirement benefit in accordance with Article VIII.

The Company shall have the right to require an Employee seeking to receive Disability retirement benefits hereunder to submit reasonable proof of such Disability, before beginning to make payments under this provision. Such proof may include a requirement that the Participant submit to a medical examination by a qualified physician selected by the Company, and that, as a condition of continuing to receive Disability retirement benefits, proof of the continuing nature of such Disability, including the requirement that the Employee submit to a physical examination by a physician selected by the Company. Such an examination shall not be required more frequently than annually.

2.14 "Early Retirement Age" means, before a Participant's Normal Retirement Date:

(a) with respect to Employees who were hired by the Company before the Effective Date of this Plan, the later of such Participant's attaining age 55 or completing six years of participation in the Plan,

*Reprinted from 352 T.M., *Profit-Sharing Plans—Qualification.*

(b) with respect to Participants who were hired by the Company after the Effective Date of this Plan, the later of such Participant's attaining age 55 or completing 10 years of Participation in the Plan.

2.15 "Early Retirement Date" shall mean the date on which a Participant attains his or her Early Retirement Age.

2.16. "Effective Date" means April 1, 1988.

2.17. "Elective Contribution" means the salary reduction contributions of a Participant made pursuant to Article V.

2.18. "Elective Contribution Account" means, for any Participant, the amount of salary reduction contributions made pursuant to Article V and any investment growth thereon.

2.19. "Employee" means any individual employed by the Company.

2.20. "Employment Commencement Date" means the first day on which the Employee performs an Hour of Service.

2.21. "ERISA" means the Employee Retirement Income Security Act of 1974, as amended, and any successor statute or statutes of similar import.

2.22. "Highly Compensated Employee" means an employee of the Company or any Affiliated Company who, during the Plan Year in question or the preceding Plan Year,

(a) was at any time a 5-percent owner (as defined in Section 416(i)(1) of the Code) of the Company or any Affiliated Company,

(b) received Total Compensation in excess of $75,000,

(c) received Total Compensation in excess of $50,000 and was in the top-paid group of employees (as defined in Section 414(q) of the Code, based upon the exclusion of all employees excludable under Section 414(q)(8)) for the Year, or

(d) was at any time an officer of the Company or any Affiliated Company and received Total Compensation greater than 150% of the amount described in Section 7.03(a).

The $75,000 and $50,000 amounts in (b) and (c) above shall be automatically adjusted if and to the extent the corresponding amounts in Section 414(q) of the Code are adjusted by the Secretary of the Treasury. No more than 50 employees of the Company and any Affiliated Companies (or, if less, the greater of three employees or 10 percent of all employees of the Company and any Affiliated Companies) shall be treated as officers for purposes of clause (d) above. An individual who was not described in (a), (b), (c), or (d) above during the preceding Plan Year shall be a Highly Compensated Employee during the current Plan Year only if he or she is described in (a) above or is among the 100 employees of the Company and any Affiliated Companies with the greatest Total Compensation for the current Plan Year.

2.23. "Highly Compensated Participant" means a Participant who is a Highly Compensated Employee.

2.24. "Hour of Service" means

(a) each hour for which the Employee is directly or indirectly paid, or entitled to payment, for the performance of duties for the Company or any Affiliated Company, each such hour to be credited to the Employee for the Computation Period in which the duties were performed;

(b) each hour for which the Employee is directly or indirectly paid, or entitled to payment, by the Company or any Affiliated Company (including payments made or due from a trust fund or insurer to which the Company or any Affiliated Company contributes or pays premiums) on account of a period of time during which no duties are performed (irrespective of whether the employment relationship has terminated) due to vacation, holiday, illness, incapacity, disability, layoff, jury duty, military duty, or leave of absence, each such hour to be credited to the Employee for the Computation Period in which such period of time occurs, subject to the following rules:

(1) No more than 501 Hours of Service will be credited under this subsection (b) to the Employee on account of any single continuous period during which the Employee performs no duties;

(2) Hours of Service will not be credited under this subsection (b) for a payment which solely reimburses an individual for medically related expenses, or which is made or due under a plan maintained solely for the purpose of complying with applicable workers' compensation, unemployment compensation, or disability insurance laws;

(3) If the period during which the Employee performs no duties falls within two or more Computation Periods and if the payment made on account of such period is not calculated on the basis of units of time, the Hours of Service credited with respect to such period shall be allocated between not more than the first two such Computation Periods on any reasonable basis consistently applied with respect to similarly situated Employees;

(c) each hour not credited under (a) or (b) above for which back pay, irrespective of mitigation of damages, has been either awarded or agreed to by the Company or any Affiliated Company, each such hour to be credited to the Employee for the Computation Period to which the award or agreement pertains; and

(d) each noncompensated hour during a period of leave of absence from the Company or any Affiliated Company for service in the armed forces of the United States if the Employee returns to work for the Company or any Affiliated Company at a time when he or she has reemployment rights under federal law.

Hours of Service to be credited to an individual under (a), (b) and (c) above will be calculated and credited pursuant to paragraphs (b) and (c) of Section 2530.200(b)-2 of the Department of Labor Regulations which are incorporated herein by reference. Hours of Service to be credited to an individual during an absence described in (d) above will be determined by the Administrator with reference to the individual's most recent normal work schedule. If the Administrator cannot so determine the number of Hours to be credited, there shall instead be credited eight Hours of Service for each day of absence.

Hours of Service will be credited for employment with other members of an affiliated service group, a controlled group of corporations or a group of trades or businesses under common control (under Code Section 414)), of which the Company is a member.

Hours of Service will also be credited for any individual considered an Employee under Code Section 414(n).

Solely for purposes of determining whether a Break in Service for participation and vesting purposes has occurred in a computation Period, and individual who is absent from work for maternity or paternity reasons shall receive credit for hours of service which would otherwise have been credited to such individual but for such absence, or, in any case in which such hours cannot be determined, eight hours of service per day of such absence. For purposes of this paragraph, an absence from work for maternity or paternity reasons means an absence:

(1) by reasons of the pregnancy of the individual,

(2) by reason of a birth of a child of the individual,

(3) by reason of the placement of a child with the individual in connection with the adoption of such child by such individual, or

(4) for purposes of caring for such child of a period beginning immediately following such birth or placement.

The Hours of Service credited under this paragraph shall be credited:

(1) in the Computation Period in which the absence begins if the crediting is necessary to prevent a Break in Service for that period, or

(2) in all other cases, in the following Computation Period.

2.25. "Limitation Year" means the Plan Year.

2.26 "Married Participant" shall mean a Participant who is legally married on his or her Annuity Starting Date.

2.27 "Matching Contributions" shall mean contributions that will be made on a Participant's behalf by the Company pursuant to Article V in the event a Participant makes Elective Contributions and has completed the requirements of Article IV relating to eligibility to receive matching contributions.

2.28 "Matching Contribution Account" shall mean an account established on behalf of each Participant who is entitled to receive Matching Contributions which shall hold such Participant's Matching Contributions plus investment growth thereon.

2.29. "Normal Retirement Age" means the later of:

(a) the date on which the Participant attains age 65,

(b) in the case of a Participant who commences participation in the plan within five years of age 65, the fifth anniversary of the date the individual commenced such participation, or

(c) in the case of a Participant not described in (b), above, the tenth anniversary of the date the individual commenced Participation.

2.30. "Normal Retirement Date" means the date on which the Participant attains Normal Retirement Age.

2.31. "Participant" means each Employee who participates in the Plan in accordance with Article IV.

2.32. "Plan" means the ABC Corp. Amended and Restated Section 401(k) Profit-Sharing Plan set forth herein, together with any and all amendments and supplements hereto.

2.33. "Plan Year/Fiscal Year" means Company's fiscal year, i.e., the twelve-month period beginning on April 1st of each year.

2.34. "Qualified Domestic Relations Order" means any judgment, decree or order (including approval of a property settlement agreement) which

(a) relates to the provision of child support, alimony payments, or marital property rights to a spouse, former spouse, child or other dependent of a Participant;

(b) is made pursuant to a State domestic relations law (including a community property law);

(c) constitutes a "qualified domestic relations order" within the meaning of Code Section 414(p).

2.35 "Qualified Joint and Survivor Annuity" means an annuity for the life or life expectancy of the participant, followed by, upon the Participant's death, an annuity for the life or life expectancy of the participant's spouse calling for payments of 50% of the amounts that were payable during the spouses' joint lives. In the case of a Participant who is not married on his or her Annuity Starting Date, the provisions of section 8.04(a) shall be interpreted by substituting "life annuity" for "Qualified Joint and Survivor Annuity."

2.36 "Qualified Preretirement Survivor Annuity" or "Preretirement Survivor Annuity" means a survivor annuity for the life of the surviving spouse of a Participant if:

(a) the payments to the surviving spouse are not less than the amounts which would be payable as a survivor annuity under the Qualified Joint and Survivor Annuity under the Plan (or the actuarial equivalent thereof) if —

(i) in the case of a Participant who dies after the date on which the Participant attained the Plan's earliest retirement age, such Participant had retired with an immediate Qualified Joint and Survivor Annuity on the day before the Participant's date of death, or

(ii) in the case of a Participant who dies on or before the date on which the Participant would have attained the earliest retirement age under the Plan, such Participant had (I) separated from service on the date of death, (II) survived until the earliest retirement age under the plan, (III) retired with an immediate Qualified Joint and Survivor Annuity at the earliest retirement age, and (IV) died on the day after the day on which such Participant would have attained the earliest retirement age, and

(b) the earliest period for which a surviving spouse may receive a payment on such annuity is not later than the month in which the Participant would have attained the earliest retirement age under the Plan.

In the case of an individual who separated from service before the date of the individual's death, subparagraph (a)(ii)(I) shall not apply.

2.37. "Taxable Compensation" means, in the case of each Participant and for each Plan Year, the Participant's wages, salaries, fees for professional services and other amounts payable for personal services actually rendered during the Plan Year in the course of employment with the Company and any Affiliated Companies, but does not include Elective Contributions, Matching Contributions, or Company Contributions or other amounts which are excluded under the definition of compensation in the Treasury Regulations promulgated under Section 415 of the Code. In no event shall the amount of a Participant's Taxable Compensation taken into account under the Plan for any Plan Year exceed $200,000 (or such larger amount as the Secretary of the Treasury may determine for such Plan Year under Section 401(a)(17) of the Code).

2.38. "Total Compensation" means, in the case of each Participant and for each Plan Year, all compensation payable to the Participant by the Company and any Affiliated Companies for services rendered during the Plan Year, including salary and any bonus for the Plan Year, overtime pay, and any other compensation payable for the Plan Year, and including any Elective Contributions or other amounts that would have been paid to the Participant for the Plan Year but for any election under Section 125, 401(k), 402(h), or 403(b) of the Code. Subject to the foregoing, "Total Compensation" does not include any contributions under this Plan or any other employee benefit plan, fund, program or arrangement, whether now or hereafter established. In no event shall a Participant's Total Compensation for any Plan Year exceed, for purposes of this Plan, $200,000 (or such larger amount as the Secretary of the Treasury may determine for such Plan Year under Section 401(a)(17) of the Code).

2.39. "Trust" means the trust established between the Company and the Trustees in connection with the Plan as set forth in Article XVIII.

2.40. "Trust Fund" means the property held in trust by the Trustees for the benefit of Participants, former Participants and their Beneficiaries.

2.41. "Trustees" means the persons appointed as Trustees pursuant to Section 6.01, any successor trustee or trustees, and any additional trustee or trustees.

2.42. "Valuation Date" means the last day of the Plan Year and such other day or days as the Administrator may determine.

2.43. "Year of Service" means, with respect to any Employee, a Computation Period during which the Employee has completed 1,000 or more Hours of Service.

ARTICLE III. ADMINISTRATION

3.01. *Administrator.* The Plan will be administered by the Company or by any person, including a committee consisting of at least three individuals, appointed from time to time by the Board of Directors to serve at its pleasure. Participants may be appointed to serve as Administrator at the discretion of the Board of Directors. Except as may be directed by the Company, no person serving as Administrator will receive any compensation for his or her services as Administrator.

If a committee is appointed to serve as Administrator, it will act by majority vote. If at any time a majority of the individuals serving on such committee and eligible to vote are unable to agree, or if there is only one such individual, any action required of the committee will be taken by the Board of Directors and its decision will be final. An individual serving on such committee who is a Participant will not vote or act on any matter relating solely to himself.

3.02. *Powers of Administrator.* The Administrator will have full power to administer the Plan in all of its details, subject, however, to the requirements of ERISA. For this purpose the Administrator's power will include, but will not be limited to, the following authority:

(a) to make and enforce such rules and regulations as it deems necessary or proper for the efficient administration of the Plan or required to comply with applicable law;

(b) to interpret the Plan, its interpretation thereof in good faith to be final and conclusive on any Employee, former Employee, Participant, former Participant and Beneficiary;

(c) to decide all questions concerning the Plan and the eligibility of any person to participate in the Plan;

(d) to compute the amounts to be distributed to any Participant, former Participant or Beneficiary in accordance with the provisions of the Plan, and to determine the person or persons to whom such amounts will be distributed;

(e) to authorize the payment of distributions;

(f) to keep such records and submit such filings, elections, applications, returns or other documents or forms as may be required under the Code and applicable regulations, or under other federal, state or local law and regulations;

(g) to appoint such agents, counsel, accountants and consultants as may be required to assist in administering the Plan; and

(h) by written instrument, to allocate and delegate its fiduciary responsibilities in accordance with Section 405 of ERISA.

3.03. *Examination of Records.* The Administrator will make available to each Participant such of its records as pertain to him or her, for examination at reasonable times during normal business hours.

3.04. *Nondiscriminatory Exercise of Authority.* Whenever, in the administration of the Plan, any discretionary action by the Administrator is required, the Administrator shall exercise its authority in a nondiscriminatory manner so that all persons similarly situated will receive substantially the same treatment.

3.05. *Reliance on Tables, etc.* In administering the Plan, the Administrator will be entitled, to the extent permitted by law, to rely conclusively on all tables, valuations, certificates, opinions and reports which are furnished by any accountant, trustee, counsel or other expert who is employed or engaged by the Administrator or by the Company on the Administrator's behalf.

3.06. *Named Fiduciary.* The Administrator will be a "named fiduciary" for purposes of Section 402(a)(1) of ERISA with authority to control and manage the operation and administration of the Plan, and will be responsible for complying with all of the reporting and disclosure requirements of Part 1 of Subtitle B of Title I of ERISA. The Administrator will not, however, have any authority over the investment of assets of the Trust.

3.07. *Claims and Review Procedures.*

(a) *Claims Procedure.* If any person believes he or she is being denied any rights or benefits under the Plan, such person may file a claim in writing with the Administrator. If any such claim is wholly or partially denied, the Administrator will notify such person of its decision in writing. Such notification will contain: (1) specific reasons for the denial, (2) specific reference to pertinent plan provisions, (3) a description of any additional material or information necessary for such person to perfect such claim and an explanation of why such material or information is necessary, and (4) information as to the steps to be taken if the person wishes to submit a request for review.

Such notification will be given within 90 days after the claim is received by the Administrator (or within 180 days, if special circumstances require an extension of time for processing the claim, and if written notice of such extension and circumstances is given to such person within the initial 90 day period). If such notification is not given within such period, the claim will be considered denied as of the last day of such period and such person may request a review of his or her claim.

(b) *Review Procedure.* Within 60 days after the date on which a person receives written notice of a denied claim (or, if applicable, within 60 days after the date on which such denial is considered to have occurred) such person (or his or her duly authorized representative) may: (1) file a written request with the Administrator for a review of the denied claim and of pertinent documents, and (2) submit written issues and comments to the Administrator.

The Administrator will notify such person of its decision in writing. Such notification will be written in a manner calculated to be understood by such person and will contain specific reasons for the decision as well as specific references to pertinent Plan provisions. The decision on review will be made within 60 days after the request for review is received by the Administrator (or within 120 days, if special circumstances require an extension of time for processing the request, such as an election by the Administrator to hold a hearing, and if written notice of such extension and circumstances is given to such person within the initial 60 day period). If the decision on review is not made within such period, the claim will be considered denied.

3.08. *Indemnification of Administrator.* The Company agrees to indemnify and defend to the fullest extent of the law any Employee or former Employee who serves or has served in the capacity of Administrator or as a member of a committee designated as Administrator against any liabilities, damages, costs and expenses (including attorneys' fees and amounts paid in settlement of any claims approved by the Company) occasioned by any act or omission to act in connection with the Plan, if such act or omission to act is in good faith.

3.09. *Costs of Administrator.* All reasonable costs and expenses incurred by the Administrator and the Trustees in administering the Plan and Trust will be paid by the Company.

ARTICLE IV. PARTICIPATION

4.01. *Participation.* Each Employee will be eligible to participate upon attaining age 21 and completing one year of service.

Once an Employee has satisfied the foregoing eligibility requirements, he or she will be admitted to participation as of the first day of the month following the month in which the Employee has satisfied such requirements.

4.02. *Notice to Participants.* The Administrator will inform each Employee who satisfies the requirements of Section 4.01 above of his or her eligibility to participate in the Plan.

4.03. *Cessation of Participation.* A Participant will cease to be a Participant as of the earlier of: (a) the date on which he or she ceases to be an Employee, or (b) the date on which the Plan terminates.

4.04. *Breaks in Participation.* If an individual who has ceased to be a Participant pursuant to Section 4.03 again becomes an Employee, he or she will become a Participant in the Plan on the first day of the first month following the date on which the individual completes one Hour of Service upon returning to employment with the Company.

ARTICLE V. CONTRIBUTIONS

5.01. For the Company's Fiscal Year during which the Plan is adopted and each Fiscal Year thereafter, the Company shall contribute to the Plan (a) The amount of all Elective Contributions of all Participants made pursuant to section 5.02(a), (b) ____________ percent of such Participant's Taxable Compensation paid during the year, plus (c) a Matching Contribution, equal to ______ times the amount the Participant validly contributed (i.e., taking into account the limits of Code sections 401(k), 402(g) and 415) for the year as an Elective Contribution, except that the total Matching Contribution in respect of a Participant for a year shall not exceed ______ percent of such Participant's Taxable Compensation for the year. The total of (a) plus (b), above shall be deemed the "Total Contribution."

Notwithstanding (a) and (b), above, however, the Total Contributions for any Fiscal Year shall not exceed the amount allowable as a deduction to the Company under the applicable provisions of Code section 404 (unless the Company is required to make minimum required contributions for top-heavy plan purposes pursuant to Code section 416). All contributions by the Company shall be made in cash or in such property as is acceptable to the Trustee.

This plan shall be eligible to receive tax-free rollover contributions and/or to receive trustee-to-trustee asset transfers from other qualified plans. Any Employee whose benefit is the subject of a trustee-to-trustee asset transfer to this Plan shall be entitled, as of the date of transfer, to receive a benefit that is no less than the benefit to which he or she would be entitled had the transferor plan terminated on the date of the asset transfer. Nothing herein, however, shall compel the Trustees to allow a specific rollover contribution or trustee-to-trustee asset transfer, provided, however, that any denial of the right to make such a rollover or transfer shall be pursuant to a uniform written policy of the Plan adopted by the Trustees which does not discriminate in favor of highly-compensated employees. Such rollovers or asset transfers shall be accounted for separately and shall, subject to the provisions of (e), below, be allocated to the accounts of the Employees whose benefits are the subject of this provision.

Any trustee-to-trustee asset transfers accepted by the Plan that exceed the benefit to which the Employees whose benefits were the subject of the transfer would be entitled under the transferee plan on a termination basis shall, as soon as is administratively practicable, be allocated to a suspense account within this Plan. Any funds so allocated shall then be released from the suspense account to reduce the Employer's annual contribution obligation hereunder until all such excess funds have been allocated to the accounts of Participants or their Beneficiaries. The Company's annual contribution obligation under Section 5.01(b), above, shall be reduced by any excess assets allocated from the suspense account to the accounts of Participants for the year.

5.02(a) *Elective Contributions.* On or before November 15th of the preceding calendar year, each Participant (including each Employee who is expected to become a Participant by the beginning of the next calendar year) may enter into a deferral agreement with the Company, in a form prescribed or approved by the Administrator, pursuant to which part of the Participant's Taxable Compensation for the succeeding Plan Year will be contributed by the Company to the Trust as an Elective Contribution in lieu of being paid to the Participant in cash. The portion of the Participant's Compensation to be contributed to the Trust shall be specified by the Participant, but shall not exceed the lesser of: (i) $7,000 (or such higher limit as may be in effect for the Plan Year under Section 402(g)(1) of the Code), reduced by any other elective deferrals (as defined in Code Section 402(g)(3)) of the Participant through the Company or any Affiliated Company for the same year, or (ii) 15 percent of the Participant's Total Compensation from the Company for the Plan Year.

This maximum percentage shall be reduced, if necessary, so that it will not exceed the highest allowable "Actual Deferral Percentage" allowed under Code Section 401(k) with respect to that Participant for the Plan Year under consideration. All Elective Contributions and any investment growth thereon will be fully vested and nonforfeitable at all times.

(b) *Withdrawals.* A Participant may not make withdrawals from his or her Elective Contribution Account other than hardship withdrawals as described in (c), below.

(c) *Hardship Withdrawals.* Any Participant who suffers a financial hardship, as defined in this paragraph, may request a withdrawal from his or her Accounts. Such request shall be made by written notice to the Administrator setting forth the amount requested and the facts establishing the existence of such hardship. Upon receipt of such a request, the Administrator shall determine whether a financial hardship exists; if the Administrator determines that such a hardship does exist, it shall further determine what portion of the amount requested by the Participant is required to meet the need created by the hardship, and shall direct the Trustee to distribute to the Participant the amount so determined to be required. For purposes of this provision, the term "financial hardship" includes any financial need arising from: (1) the education of a dependent of the Participant, (2) the purchase of a primary residence for the Participant, (3) major medical expenses of the Participant or a dependent which are not covered by insurance, or (d) any other cause which, in the Administrator's determination, has produced an immediate and heavy financial need; provided, that the Administrator may, in its sole discretion, alter the foregoing definition of financial hardship or otherwise limit the amount, time or manner of any distribution under this Section to the extent deemed necessary by the Administrator to satisfy the requirements of Section 401(k) of the Code or of the Treasury Regulations promulgated thereunder. No distribution under this provision shall be made after December 31, 1988 from any income allocable to Elective Contributions (or, to the extent provided in regulations, from any Company Contributions, Matching Contributions, or income allocable thereto).

(d) *Termination of Elective Contributions.* A Participant shall no longer have the right to make Elective Contributions upon the first to occur of: (i) the Participant's withdrawal from the plan; or (ii) termination of the Participant's employment with the Company.

5.03. *Maximum Amount of Contributions.* In no event will the Total Contribution to be made for any Plan Year: (a) be in an amount which would cause the Annual Addition for any Participant to exceed the amount permitted under Section 7.03, or (b) exceed the maximum amount deductible under the applicable provisions of the Code.

5.04 *Contributions Conditioned On Deductibility.* All Company Contributions, Matching Contributions, and deemed Company Contributions under the Plan are hereby conditioned on their deductibility under Section 404 of the Code, regardless of whether such deductions are actually taken (in view of the Company's tax-exempt status). In the event the amounts to be contributed for any Participant will cause his or her Annual Addition to exceed the amount permitted under Section 7.03, such contributions shall be reduced in the manner and order described in Section 7.04 In the event the Total Contributions to be made under this Article V would exceed the limitation described in clause (b) above, the Company shall reduce its Company Contributions and any applicable Matching Contributions and Elective Contributions in such order and manner as the Company determines in its discretion, under rules uniformly applicable to similarly situated Participants, with any reductions in Elective Contributions to be paid to the affected Participants in cash.

5.05. *Time for Making Contributions.* All contributions to be made under Sections 5.01 and 5.02 for any Plan Year shall be contributed in cash to the Trust and credited to the Participants' accounts as soon as practicable, and in all events not later than the time prescribed by law (including extensions thereof) for making such contributions on a pre-tax basis.

5.06. *Return of Company or Matching Contributions.* If a Company or Matching Contribution to the Trust is: (a) made by reason of a good faith mistake of fact, or (b) believed by the Company in good faith to be deductible under Section 404 of the Code, but the deduction is disallowed, the Trustees shall, upon request by the Company, return to the Company the excess of the amount contributed over the amount, if any, that would have been contributed had there not occurred a mistake of fact or a mistake in determining the deduction. In no event shall the return of a contribution hereunder cause any Participant's Accounts to be reduced to less than they would have been had the mistaken or nondeductible amount not been contributed. No return of a contribution hereunder shall be made more than one year after the mistaken payment of the contribution, or disallowance of the deduction, as the case may be.

5.07. *Nondiscrimination Requirements.*

(a) Elective Contributions and Matching Contributions for any Plan Year must satisfy at least one of the following tests: (1) The average of the individual ratios of such contributions to Total Compensation (the "deferral ratios") for the Plan Year for all Highly Compensated Participants does not exceed the product of 1.25 and the average of the deferral ratios for all other Participants, or (2) The excess of the average of the deferral ratios for all Highly Compensated Participants over that for all other Participants does not exceed two percentage points, and the average of the deferral ratios for all Highly Compensated Participants does not exceed twice the average of the deferral ratios for all other Participants, or (3) Clause (1) or (2) is satisfied after taking into account Company Contributions for the Plan Year, as if they were additional Elective Contributions, in determining each Participant's deferral ratio.

Clause (3) above shall be subject to such conditions as may be prescribed by regulations. Contributions under other plans of the Company or any Affiliated Company may also be taken into account under Clause (3) to the extent permitted by regulations.

(b) If any individual employed by the Company or any Affiliated Company is a member of the family (as defined in Section 414(q)(6)(B) of the Code) of a Highly Compensated Employee who is either: (1) a 5-percent owner (as defined in Section 416(i)(1) of the Code) of the Company, or (2) among the 10 individuals receiving the greatest Total Compensation during the Plan Year, such individual shall not be taken into account separately under this Section 5.07. Instead, the Total Compensation of such individual, any Elective Contributions, Matching Contributions, and any Company Contributions made for the individual's benefit, shall be aggregated with the Total Compensation for the Highly Compensated Employee in applying this Section 5.07, as if the two individuals were a single individual.

5.08. *Adjustments by Administrator.*

(a) The Administrator may, in its sole discretion, decrease the amount of the Elective Contribution to be made for the benefit of any Participant, and pay the amount of the decrease to the Participant in cash, if the Administrator deems such a decrease to be necessary in order to satisfy any of the following: (i) the nondiscrimination requirement of Section 5.07, (ii) the limitations described in Sections 5.03, and (iii) the limitations described in section 5.04.

If the Administrator decreases any Elective Contribution to meet the nondiscrimination requirements of Section 5.07, such decrease shall be made first in the Elective Contributions for the Highly Compensated Participants whose Elective Contributions represent the highest percentage of Total Compensation, so that no reduction is made in the Elective Contribution for any Highly Compensated Participant as long as any other Highly Compensated Participant has a higher percentage of Elective Contributions to Total Compensation.

(b) The Administrator may, in its sole discretion, decrease the amount of Company Contributions and/or Matching Contributions to be made for the benefit of Highly Compensated Participants if the Administrator deems such decrease to be necessary in order to satisfy the nondiscrimination requirements of Section 5.07. Any such decrease shall be made only after any adjustments under Section 5.07 or Section 7.04 have been made. Any decrease in Company Contributions or Matching Contributions in order to satisfy Section 5.07 shall be made first in the Company Contributions and/or Matching Contributions for the Highly Compensated Participants whose Company Contributions and/or Matching Contributions represent the highest percentage of Total Compensation, so that no reduction is made in the Company Contribution or Matching Contribution for any Highly Compensated Participant as long as any other Highly Compensated Participant had a higher percentage of Company Contribution to Total Compensation. If Elective Contributions are taken into account under Section 5.07(b)(3) in order to satisfy either Section 5.07(b)(1) or Section 5.07(b)(2), then such Elective Contributions shall be proportionately reduced along with the Company Contributions and/or Matching Contributions to the extent the Administrator deems necessary in order to satisfy Section 5.07(b)(3).

5.09. *Distribution of Excess Contributions.* If, after all contributions for a Plan Year have been made, the nondiscrimination requirements of Section 5.07 have not been satisfied for the Plan Year, the Administrator shall, as soon as practicable (but in no event later than the close of the following Plan Year), distribute the excess contributions (and income allocable to such excess) to Highly Compensated Participants, in accordance with Section 401(k)(8) of the Code, to the extent necessary to satisfy Section 5.07. If there has been a net investment loss instead of income allocable to excess contributions, the amount of excess contributions to be distributed hereunder shall be reduced by such loss to the extent permitted by Section 401(k)(8) or regulations thereunder.

5.10. *Distribution of Excess Deferrals.* If, on or before March 1 of any year, a Participant notifies the Administrator, in accordance with Section 402(g)(2)(A) of the Code and regulations thereunder, that all or a specified part of an Elective Contribution made or to be made on his or her benefit represents an excess deferral for the preceding taxable year of the Participant, the Administrator shall make every reasonable effort to cause such excess deferral to be distributed to the Participant no later than the April 15 following such notification. If the Participant's Elective Contribution has not yet been contributed to the Trust, the Elective Contribution shall be reduced by the amount of the excess deferral and such amount shall be paid to the Participant in cash. Except to the extent otherwise provided in regulations, any amount paid to the Trust and distributed under this Section 5.10 shall be taken into account in applying Sections 5.07, 5.08 and 5.09 as if it had not been distributed, except that any decrease in the Elective Contribution for a Participant under Section 5.08 or distribution of an excess Elective Contribution to a Participant under Section 5.09 shall be reduced by the amount of any distribution to the Participant under this Section 5.10.

ARTICLE VI. TRUST FUND

6.01. *Appointment of Trustees.* There shall be ________ Trustees hereunder, to be named by the Company's Board of Directors. These individuals shall serve as Trustees until they resign or are replaced by the Board of Directors. If there is a vacancy among the Trustees the

Company's Board of Directors shall appoint a successor Trustee to fill the vacancy.

6.02. *Investment of the Trust Fund.* All contributions to the Trust for a Participant's benefit shall be held by the Trustees in the Trust Fund and invested by the Trustees solely for the benefit of Participants and their Beneficiaries and in accordance with the provisions of the trust document and in compliance with ERISA. Nothing in this provision, however, shall preclude the Trustees from investing Plan assets in one or more insurance contracts, such as individual or group annuity contracts, provided such investment is permissible under ERISA.

ARTICLE VII. PARTICIPANT ACCOUNTS

7.01. *Accounts.* The Trustees shall maintain on their books for each Participant an Elective Contribution Account and a Company Contribution Account, together with such other accounts and sub-accounts as the Trustees in their discretion deem appropriate.

7.02. *Adjustment of Accounts.* With respect to the Accounts required by Section 7.01, the Trustees shall, as of each Valuation Date,

(a) First, reduce the balance of each Participant's Elective Contribution Account by the aggregate amount of all distributions or withdrawals made from each such Account since the preceding Valuation Date;

(b) Second, adjust the balance of each Participant's Elective Account to reflect the current fair market value of the assets in which such Account is invested;

(c) Third, in the case of the last Valuation Date of each Plan Year, credit each Participant's Elective Contribution Account with any Elective Contribution made for the benefit of the Participant for such Plan Year.

For purposes of this Section 7.02, the word "Participant" shall include a former Participant if amounts remain credited him or her under this Plan.

7.03. *Limitations.* Notwithstanding any other provisions of the Plan, the Annual Addition to a Participant's Accounts under the Plan for any Limitation Year, when added to the Annual Additions to his or her accounts for such Year under all other defined contribution plans maintained by the Company or any Affiliated Company, shall not exceed the lesser of: (a) $30,000 (or, if greater, one-fourth of the limitation in effect for the Limitation Year under Section 415(b)(1)(A) of the Code), or (b) 25 percent of the Participant's Taxable Compensation for such Limitation Year. In the case of a Participant who also participates in a defined benefit plan maintained by the Company or an Affiliated Company, the Annual Addition for a Limitation Year will, if necessary, be further limited so that the sum of the Participant's "defined contribution fraction" (as determined under Section 415(e) of the Code and the regulations promulgated thereunder, including any special transition rules) and his or her "defined benefit plan fraction" (as determined under Section 415(e) of the Code and the regulations promulgated thereunder) for such Limitation Year does not exceed 1.0. In determining such fractions, 1.0 shall replace 1.25 each time it appears in Section 415(e) of the Code, unless the requirements of Code Section 416(h)(2) are satisfied.

7.04. *Order of Adjustments to Satisfy Limitations.* To the extent necessary to satisfy the limitations of Section 7.03 for any Participant, the Participant's Annual Addition under this Plan shall be reduced before any reduction in his or her Annual Addition under any other defined contribution plan or his or her benefit under any defined benefit plan. The Participant's Annual Addition under this Plan shall be reduced, first, by reducing and refunding to the Participant his or her Elective Contributions, if any, for the Limitation Year, to the extent such reduction has the effect of reducing such Participant's Annual Addition. If further adjustments are necessary, the Participant's Company Contribution for the Limitation Year shall be reduced.

ARTICLE VIII. BENEFITS UPON RETIREMENT OR DEATH

8.01. *Vesting.* Each Participant will at all times have a fully vested and nonforfeitable interest in his Accounts.

8.02. *Retirement or Other Termination of Employment.* Each Participant will be eligible for normal retirement upon attaining his or her Normal Retirement Age. Each Participant will be eligible for early retirement upon attaining his or her Early Retirement Age. Upon becoming disabled, a Participant shall be entitled to receive a Disability retirement benefit upon submission of credible medical evidence, including a requirement that the Employee submit to an examination by a physician of the Company's choice, that the Participant has incurred a Disability. If a Participant retires or ceases to be an Employee for any other reason except death, he or she shall be entitled under this Section 8.02 to a benefit equal to the value of his or her Accounts, which shall be distributed in accordance with the provisions of this Article VIII.

If an Employee becomes Disabled and begins to receive Disability retirement benefits and later recovers so that he or she is no longer disabled, Disability retirement benefits will cease, and benefit payments will not recommence until the Employee again qualifies for benefit payments under the terms of the Plan.

8.03. *Death.*

(a) If a Participant dies before the distribution of his or her Accounts has been completed, upon the Participant's death his or her designated Beneficiary will have a fully vested and nonforfeitable interest in, and will be entitled to receive, the value of his or her Accounts, including the proceeds of any life insurance contract held by the Plan on the Participant's life, provided that, in no event, shall the Plan purchase life insurance coverage on any Participant that would provide a death benefit that is more than "incidental" as that term is interpreted by the Internal Revenue Service for purposes of qualified profit-sharing plans. Distribution to the Beneficiary will be made in accordance with the applicable provisions of this Article VIII and a non-spousal Beneficiary (or a spousal Beneficiary if the Participant and the Participant's spouse have voluntarily waived the Qualified Joint and Survivor Annuity or Preretirement Survivor Annuity form of benefit hereunder, whichever applies) shall be entitled to elect to receive such death benefits in accordance with any optional mode of benefit payment provided under section 8.04, provided that the requirements of section 8.06 are satisfied. In the event the Participant's spouse is entitled to Qualified Joint and Survivor Annuity or a Preretirement Survivor Annuity, such annuity shall be offset against the amount which the Participant's Beneficiary would otherwise be entitled to receive as a death benefit hereunder so that the survivor annuity, if any, to which a participant's spouse is entitled, when added to the death benefit hereunder, will not cause the death benefit to be more than "incidental," as that term is defined above.

(b) If a Participant was married at the time of death, he or she shall be deemed to have designated his or her surviving spouse as Beneficiary unless:

(1) prior to the Participant's death, he or she designated as his or her Beneficiary a person other than such surviving spouse, such designation to be made in writing at such time and in such manner as the Administrator shall approve or prescribe; and

(2) either (i) the Participant's surviving spouse consents in writing to the designation described in (1) above, such consent acknowledges the effect of such designation and the specific non-spouse Beneficiary (including any class of Beneficiaries or any contingent Beneficiaries) or authorizes the Participant to designate Beneficiaries without further consent, and such consent is witnessed by a Plan representative or a notary public, or (ii) it is established to the satisfaction of the Administrator that the consent required under (i) above may not be obtained because there is no spouse, because the

spouse cannot be located, or because of such other circumstances as the Secretary of the Treasury may prescribe; and

(3) the non-spouse Beneficiary designated in accordance with the provisions of this Section survives the Participant.

Any consent by a spouse under (2)(i) above, or a determination by the Administrator with respect to such spouse under (2)(ii) above, shall be effective only with respect to such spouse. Any such consent shall be irrevocable, but shall be effective only with respect to the specific Beneficiary designation unless the consent expressly permits designations by the Participant without any requirement of further consent.

(c) A Participant who is not married may designate a Beneficiary in writing at such time and in such manner as the Administrator shall approve or prescribe.

(d) A Participant who has designated a Beneficiary in accordance with this Section 8.03 may change such designation at any time by giving written notice to the Administrator, subject to the conditions of this Section 8.03 and such additional conditions and requirements as the Administrator may prescribe in accordance with applicable law.

(e) If a Participant dies without a surviving Beneficiary, the full amount payable upon his or her death will be paid to the Participant's issue per stirpes. If any of such issue is a minor, the Trustees may deposit such minor's share in a savings account to the minor's credit in a savings bank or other financial institution for his or her benefit. If there is no surviving issue, then the amount may be paid to the Participant's executor or administrator or applied to the payment of the Participant's debts and funeral expenses, all as the Administrator shall determine.

8.04. *Form of Distributions*. Distributions under this Article VIII may be paid in cash or in kind, as the Participant (or, if Section 8.03 applies, the Beneficiary) shall elect, except as otherwise provided herein.

(a) Qualified Joint and Survivor Annuity.

(1) For each married Participant, the benefit, in case of retirement, shall be paid as a Qualified Joint and Survivor Annuity. Each Participant who is entitled to receive a Qualified Joint and Survivor Annuity under this section 8.04 may elect in writing, and may subsequently revoke such election in writing, to waive the Qualified Joint and Survivor Annuity form of benefit. Each such Participant must be furnished within a reasonable period of time before the Participant's Annuity Starting Date, a written explanation, in a manner calculated to be understood by him or her, of: (i) the terms and conditions of the Qualified Joint and Survivor Annuity, (ii) the Participant's right to make, and the effect of an election to waive the Qualified Joint and Survivor Annuity form of benefit, (iii) the rights of the Participant's spouse regarding the requirement that such spouse consent in writing to any election to waive the Qualified Joint and Survivor Annuity form of benefit, and (iv) the right to make, and the effect of, a revocation of an election to waive the Qualified Joint and Survivor Annuity form of benefit. If a Participant makes such an election within the Applicable Election Period described below, such election shall not take effect unless: (I) the Participant's spouse consents in writing to such election, and the spouse's consent acknowledges the effect of such election and is witnessed by a plan representative or a notary public; or (II) it is established to the satisfaction of the Trustees that the consent required by the spouse may not be obtained because there is no spouse, because the spouse cannot be located, or because of such other circumstances as the Treasury Secretary may prescribe by regulations (consent by a spouse, or establishment that consent cannot be obtained shall be effective only with respect to such spouse).

(2) If the election to waive the Qualified Joint and Survivor Annuity form of benefit is effective, then the Participant's benefit shall be paid by means of one of the other payment options specified in this section 8.04. In the event a Married Participant does not make an effective election, distribution of such Participant's benefits shall be in the form of a Qualified Joint and Survivor Annuity.

(3) The Applicable Election Period shall be the 90-day period ending on the Annuity Starting Date.

b. Qualified Preretirement Survivor Annuity

(1) In the event a Participant dies before his or her Annuity Starting date and leaves a surviving spouse, such spouse shall receive a Qualified Preretirement Survivor Annuity except as otherwise provided herein.

(2) Each Married Participant whose spouse would be entitled to receive a Qualified Preretirement Survivor Annuity under this section 8.04(b) may elect in writing, and may subsequently revoke such election in writing at any time during the Applicable Election Period described in this section 8.04(b) not to have death benefits paid in the form of a Preretirement Survivor Annuity.

(3) Each Married Participant must be furnished, within the period beginning with the first day of the Plan Year in which the Participant attains age 32 and ending with the close of the Plan Year preceding the Plan Year in which the Participant attains age 35 (and consistent with such regulations as the Secretary of the Treasury may prescribe), a written explanation of the provision for the Preretirement Survivor Annuity.

(4) If a Participant makes such an election within the Applicable Election Period, such election shall not take effect unless: (i) the Participant's spouse consents in writing to such election, and the spouse's consent acknowledges the effect of such election and is witnessed by a plan representative or notary public; or (ii) it is established to the Trustees' satisfaction that the consent required by the spouse may not be obtained because there is no spouse, because the spouse cannot be located, or because of such circumstances as the Treasury Secretary has prescribed by regulations. Consent by a spouse or establishment that consent may not be obtained shall be effective only with respect to such spouse.

(5) The "Applicable Election Period" begins on the first day of the Plan Year in which the Participant attains age 35 and ends on the date of the Participant's death, provided that, if the Participant separates from the Company's service, the "Applicable Election Period" shall begin on the date of separation from service with respect to benefits accrued before the separation from service.

c. Optional Forms of Benefit Distribution.

A Participant not subject to, or who has validly elected out of, the requirements of (a) and/or (b), above, may elect to have his or her benefit distributed: (1) In a single payment (except that Employees receiving distributions on account of disability shall not be entitled to receive benefits in this form unless and until such disabled Employee reaches Early or Normal Retirement Age under this Plan or otherwise separates from the Employer's service in a manner that would entitle such Employee to begin to receive benefits under this Plan (other than benefits in respect of disability); (2) In substantially equal installments over a fixed period not to exceed the life expectancy of the Participant or the joint life and last survivor expectancy of the Participant and his or her Beneficiary. If distributions are being made pursuant to Section 8.03, the fixed period shall not exceed the life expectancy of the Beneficiary; (3) In the form of a Joint and Survivor Annuity, except that the Beneficiary may be someone other than the Participant's spouse and, at the Participant's election, the survivor benefit shall be equal to 50%, of the life annuity benefit of the Participant and the Participant's spouse; or (4) In the form of a Qualified Joint and Survivor Annuity, except that the survivor benefit shall be equal to 75% or 100% (at the Participant's option) of the life annuity benefit of the Participant and the Participant's spouse.

If the Participant's Beneficiary is not his or her spouse, the present value of the installments payable to the Participant, determined at the time installments commence, shall in all cases be greater than 50% of the present value of all installments to be paid.

All optional forms of benefits provided hereunder shall be the actuarial equivalent to the benefits provided pursuant to section 8.04(a) and/or (b), above, whichever is applicable.

8.05. *Time of Distributions — Termination of Employment.*

Distributions to a Participant under Section 8.02 will be made or commence not later than the 60th day after the date on which the Participant incurs a Disability, or attains Early, Normal, or actual Retirement Age, whichever applies, or separates from the Employer's service, unless the distributee elects in writing to have distributions commence at a later time. The foregoing is subject to the following special rules:

(a) Notwithstanding any election to the contrary, payment of benefits to a Participant shall commence not later than the April 1 next following the later of: (1) the close of the calendar year in which he or she attains age 70-1/2, or (2) the earlier of December 31, 1988 or the close of the calendar year in which he or she retires.

However, clause (2) shall not apply, and payment of benefits shall commence no later than April 1 next following the close of the calendar year in which the Participant attains age 70½, if the Participant is a 5-percent owner of the Company (as defined in Section 416(i)(1)(B) of the Code) at any time during the five Plan Year period ending with such calendar year.

(b) No distribution shall be made to a Participant before his or her incurring a Disability, or attaining his or her Early or Normal Retirement Date (or actual retirement date, if later), whichever applies, unless: (1) the Participant's prior written consent to the distribution has been obtained by the Administrator, or (2) the value of the Participant's Accounts does not exceed $3,500. If the Participant's consent is required under this Section 8.05(b) but is not provided prior to the time distributions are to be made under the first sentence of this Section 8.05, distribution shall be made or commence within 60 days after the earliest of: (i) the Participant's incurring a Disability, or reaching his or her Early, Normal, or actual Retirement Date, whichever applies, or (ii) the date the Administrator is notified of the Participant's death.

8.06. *Time of Distributions — Death.* Distributions at death shall be made of any remaining amounts to the Participant's credit to such Participant's Beneficiary, in accordance with the following requirements.

(a) If a Participant dies before payment of his or her benefits have commenced, distributions must either: (1) be made in their entirety within 5 years after the Participant's death, or (2) be made over a period not extending beyond the recipient's life expectancy.

(b) If a Participant dies after his or her benefits has commenced, but before such distribution has been completed, the remaining benefits shall be distributed at least as rapidly as under the method of distribution under which the Participant was receiving his or her benefits as of the date of death.

8.07. *Former Participants.* For purposes of this Article VIII, the word "Participant" shall include a former Participant.

ARTICLE IX. TOP-HEAVY PLAN RULES

9.01. If the Plan is or becomes Top-Heavy in any Plan Year beginning after December 31, 1983, the provisions of this article will supersede any conflicting provisions in the Plan.

9.02. *Top-Heavy Definitions.*

For purposes of this article, the following terms shall have the following meanings:

(a) "Key Employee" means any Employee or former Employee (and the beneficiaries of such Employee who at any time during the determination period was: (1) an officer of the Company if such individual's annual compensation exceeds 150 percent of the dollar limitation under Code section 415(c)(1)(A), (2) an owner (or one considered an owner under Code section 318) of one of the 10 largest interests in the Company if such individual's compensation exceeds 100 percent of such dollar limitation, (3) a 5-percent owner of the Company, or (4) a 1-percent owner of the Company who has an annual compensation of more than $150,000.

The determination period is the Plan Year containing the Determination Date and the four preceding Plan Years.

The determination of who is a Key Employee will be made under Code section 416(i)(1) and the regulations thereunder.

(b) "Top-Heavy Plan" means, for any Plan Year beginning after December 31, 1983, this Plan if any of the following conditions exist: (1) If the Top-Heavy Ratio for this Plan exceeds 60 percent and this Plan is not part of a Required Aggregation Group or Permissive Aggregation Group of plans, (2) If this Plan is a part of a Required Aggregation Group of plans but not part of a Permissive Aggregation Group and the Top-Heavy Ratio for the group of plans exceeds 60 percent, or (3) If this Plan is a part of a Required Aggregation Group and part of a Permissive Aggregation Group of plans and the Top-Heavy Ratio for the Permissive Aggregation Group exceeds 60 percent.

(c) "Top-Heavy Ratio:"

(1) If the Company maintains one or more defined contribution plans (including any simplified employee pension plan) and the Company has not maintained any defined benefit plan which, during the five-year period ending on the Determination Date(s) has or has had accrued benefits, the Top-Heavy Ratio for this Plan alone or for the Required or Permissive Aggregation Group as appropriate is a fraction, the numerator of which is the sum of the account balances of all Key Employees as of the Determination Date(s) (including any part of any account balance distributed in the five-year period ending on the Determination Date(s), both computed in accordance with Code section 416 and the regulations thereunder. Both the numerator and the denominator of the Top-Heavy Ratio are adjusted to reflect any contribution not actually made as of the Determination Date, but which is required to be taken into account on that date under Code section 416 and the regulations thereunder.

(2) If the Company maintains one or more defined contribution plans (including simplified employee pension plans) and the Company maintains or has maintained one or more defined benefit plans which, during the five-year period ending on the Determination Date(s) has or has had any accrued benefits, the Top-Heavy Ratio for any Required or Permissive Aggregation Group as appropriate is a fraction, the numerator of which is the sum of the account balances under the aggregated defined contribution plan or plans for all Key Employees, determined in accordance with (1) above, and the present value of accrued benefits under the aggregated defined benefit plan or plans for all Key Employees as of the Determination Date(s), and the

denominator of which is the sum of the account balances under the aggregated defined contribution plan or plans for all Participants as of the Determination Date(s), all determined in accordance with Code section 416 and the regulations thereunder. The accrued benefits under a defined benefit plan in both the numerator and the denominator of the Top-Heavy Ratio are adjusted for any distribution of an accrued benefit made in the five-year period ending on the Determination Date.

(3) For purposes of (1) and (2) above, the value of account balances and the present value of accrued benefits will be determined as of the most recent valuation date that falls within or ends with the 12-month period ending on the Determination Date, except as provided in Code section 416 and the regulations thereunder for the first and second years of a defined benefit plan. The account balances and accrued benefits of a Participant: (i) who is not a Key Employee but who was a Key Employee in a prior year, or (ii) who has not received any compensation from any Company maintaining the plan at any time during the five-year period ending on the Determination Date will be disregarded.

The calculation of the Top-Heavy Ratio, and the extent to which distributions, rollovers, and transfers are taken into account will be made in accordance with Code section 416 and the regulations thereunder. Deductible Employee contributions will not be taken into account for purposes of determining the Top-Heavy Ratio. When aggregating plans, the value of account balances and accrued benefits will be calculated with reference to the Determination Dates that fall within the same calendar year.

(d) "Permissive Aggregation Group:" The Required Aggregation Group of plans plus any other plan or plans of the Company which, when considered as a group with the Required Aggregation Group, would continue to satisfy the requirements of Code sections 401(a)(4) and 410.

(e) "Required Aggregation Group:" (i) Each qualified plan of the Company in which at least one Key employee participates, and (ii) any other qualified plan of the Company which enables a plan described in (ii), above, to meet the requirements of Code sections 401(a)(4) or 410.

(f) "Determination Date:" For any Plan Year subsequent to the first Plan Year, the last day of the preceding Plan Year. For the first Plan Year of the Plan, the last day of that year.

(g) "Valuation Date:" The date which is used to calculate the value of account balances or accrued benefits for purposes of determining the Top-Heavy Ratio. In the case of this Plan, the Valuation Date shall be the Determination Date.

(h) "Present Value:" For purposes of calculating the present value of any accrued benefit in determining the Top-Heavy Ratio, the actuarial assumptions employed shall be those that are specified in the plan under consideration.

9.03. *Minimum Contribution Requirement.*

(a) Except as otherwise provided in (c) and (d), below, the Company Contributions and forfeitures allocated on behalf of any Participant who is not a Key Employee shall not be less than the lesser of 3 percent of such Participant's Taxable Compensation or, in the case where the Company has no defined benefit plan which designates this Plan to satisfy Code section 401, the largest percentage of Company Contributions and forfeitures, as a percentage of the first $200,000 of the Key Employee's Taxable Compensation, allocated on behalf of any Key Employee for that year. The minimum allocation is determined without regard to any Social Security contribution. This minimum allocation shall made even though under other Plan provisions, the Participant would not otherwise be entitled to receive an allocation, or would have received a lesser allocation for the year because of: (i) the Participant's failure to complete 1,000 Hours of Service (or any equivalent provided in the Plan), (ii) the Participant's failure to make mandatory Employee contributions to the Plan, or (iii) compensation less than a stated amount.

(b) For purposes of computing the minimum allocation, Compensation will mean Taxable Compensation as defined in Article II hereof.

(c) the provision in (a) above shall not apply to any Participant who was not employed by the Company on the last day of the Plan Year.

(d) The provision in (a), above, shall not apply to any Participant to the extent the Participant is covered under any other plan or plans of the Company, if such plan provides that the minimum allocation or benefit requirement applicable to top-heavy plans will be met in the other plan or plans.

9.05. For any Plan Year in which the Plan is top-heavy, only the first $200,000 (or such amount as may be taken into account for purposes of determining Company Contributions under the Plan shall be taken into account.

ARTICLE X. PURCHASE AND HOLDING OF LIFE INSURANCE CONTRACTS

10.01. To the extent this Plan purchases or carries any life insurance policy on the life of a Participant, it shall do so only to the extent that such insurance is incidental to the main purpose of this Plan, i.e., to provide retirement income to Participants and their designated beneficiaries.

10.02. For purposes of these incidental insurance provisions, ordinary life insurance contracts are contracts with both nondecreasing death benefits and nonincreasing premiums. If such contracts are purchased, less than one-half of the aggregate Company Contributions and Matching Contributions allocated to any Participant will be used to pay the premiums attributable to them.

10.03. No more than one-fourth of the aggregate Company Contributions and Matching Contributions allocated to any Participant will be used to pay the premium on term life insurance contracts, universal life insurance contracts, and all other life insurance contracts which are not ordinary life.

10.04. In the event that this Plan purchases or carries a combination of ordinary life insurance and term and universal life, it shall do so only to the extent that the sum of one-half of the ordinary life insurance premiums and all other life insurance premiums will not exceed one-fourth of the aggregate Company Contributions and Matching Contributions allocated to any Participant.

10.05. To the extent that this Plan purchases or carries any life insurance on the life of a Participant, the contracts on a Participant's life will be converted to cash or an annuity or distributed to the Participant upon commencement of benefits.

ARTICLE XI. ANNUAL VALUATION OF ASSETS — ALLOCATION OF TRUST EARNINGS AND LOSSES

11.01. The assets of the Trust will be valued annually at fair market value as of the last day of the Plan Year. On such date, the earnings and losses of the Trust will be allocated to each Participant's account in the ratio that such account balance bears to all account balances.

11.02. Any dividends or credits earned on insurance contracts will be allocated to the Participant's account derived from Company Contributions for whose benefit the contract is held.

ARTICLE XII. AMENDMENT AND TERMINATION

12.01. *Amendment.* The Company reserves the power at any time or times to amend the provisions of the Plan and Trust to any extent and in any manner that it may deem advisable by delivery to the Trustees of a written instrument executed by the Company providing for such amendment. Upon the delivery of such instrument to the Trustees, such instrument will become effective in accordance with its terms as to all Participants and all persons having or claiming any interest hereunder; provided, however, that the Company will not have the power:

(a) to amend the Plan or Trust in such manner as would cause or permit any part of the assets of the Trust to be diverted to purposes other than for the exclusive benefit of each Participant and his or her Beneficiary (except as permitted by Sections 5.06, 12.03, and 12.05), unless such amendment is permitted by law, governmental regulation or ruling;

(b) to amend the Plan or Trust retroactively in such a manner as would deprive any Participant of any benefit to which he or she was entitled under the Plan by reason of contributions made prior to the amendment, unless such amendment is necessary to conform the Plan or Trust to, or satisfy the conditions of, any law, governmental regulation or ruling, or to permit the Trust and the Plan to meet the requirements of Sections 401(a) and 501(a) of the Code; or

(c) to amend the Plan or Trust in such manner as would increase the duties or liabilities of the Trustees or affect their fee for services hereunder, unless the Trustees consent thereto in writing.

12.02. *Termination.* The Company has established the Plan and authorized the establishment of the Trust with the bona fide intention and expectation that contributions will be continued indefinitely, but the Company will have no obligation or liability whatsoever to maintain the Plan for any given length of time and may discontinue contributions under the Plan or terminate the Plan at any time by written notice delivered to the Trustees without liability whatsoever for any such discontinuance or termination. The Plan will be deemed terminated: (a) if and when the Company is judicially declared bankrupt, (b) if and when the Company is a party to a merger in which it is not the surviving corporation or sells all or substantially all of its assets, unless the surviving corporation or the purchaser adopts the Plan by an instrument in writing delivered to the Trustees within 60 days after the merger or sale, or (c) upon dissolution of the Company.

12.03. *Distributions Upon Termination of the Plan.* Upon termination or partial termination of the Plan or complete discontinuance of contributions thereunder, each Participant will continue to have a fully vested and nonforfeitable interest in his or her Accounts. Upon termination of the Plan, the Trustees will distribute to each Participant (or other person entitled to distribution) the value of the Participant's Accounts in a single lump sum payment or shall apply the Participant's Accounts to purchase an annuity contract on such Participant's behalf and shall distribute such annuity contract. However, if a successor plan is established within the meaning of Section 401(k)(2)(B)(i)(II) of the Code, Accounts shall be distributed to Participants and their Beneficiaries only in accordance with Article VIII. Upon the completion of distributions to all Participants, the Trust will terminate, the Trustees will be relieved from all liability under the Trust, and no Participant or other person will have any claims thereunder, except as required by applicable law.

12.04. *Merger or Consolidation of Plan; Transfer of Plan Assets.* In case of any merger or consolidation of the Plan with, or transfer of assets and liabilities of the Plan to, any other plan, provision must be made so that each Participant would, if the Plan then terminated, receive a benefit immediately after the merger, consolidation or transfer which is equal to or greater than the benefit he or she would have been entitled to receive immediately before the merger, consolidation or transfer if the Plan had then terminated.

ARTICLE XIII. VESTING UPON PLAN TERMINATION OR COMPLETE DISCONTINUANCE OF CONTRIBUTIONS

13.01. In the event of the termination or partial termination of the Plan, the account balance of each affected Participant will be nonforfeitable.

13.02. In the event of a complete discontinuance of contributions under the Plan, the account balance of each affected Participant will be nonforfeitable.

ARTICLE XIV. INALIENABILITY OF BENEFITS

14.01. No benefit or interest available hereunder will be subject to assignment or alienation, either voluntarily or involuntarily. The preceding sentence shall also apply to the creation, assignment, or recognition of a right to any benefit payable with respect to a Participant with respect to a domestic relations order, unless such order is determined to be a qualified domestic relations order, as defined in Code section 414(p), or any domestic relations order entered before January 1, 1985.

ARTICLE XV. PARTICIPANT LOANS

15.01. No Participant loans shall be allowed under this Plan.

ARTICLE XVI. EXCLUSIVE BENEFIT

16.01. The corpus or income of the Plan's Trust may not be diverted to or used for any purpose other than the exclusive benefit of Participants or their beneficiaries.

16.02. Notwithstanding the foregoing, any contribution made by mistake of fact will be returned to the Company within one year of the contribution. Further, in the event that the IRS Commissioner determines that the Plan does not initially qualify under Code section 401(a), any contribution made incident to that initial qualification by the Company must be returned to the Company within one year after the date the initial qualification is denied. In the event a contribution is made to the Plan conditioned upon qualification of the Plan as amended, such contribution must be returned to the Company upon a determination that the amended Plan fails to qualify under the Code, provided that: (a) the Plan amendment is submitted to the IRS for qualification within one year form the date the amendment is adopted, and (b) such contribution that was made conditioned on plan requalification is returned to the Company within one year after the date the Plan's requalification is denied.

ARTICLE XVII. MISCELLANEOUS

17.01. *Limitation of Rights.* Neither the establishment of the Plan or the Trust, nor any amendment thereof, nor the creation of any fund or account, nor the payment of any benefits, will be construed as giving to any Participant or other person any legal or equitable right against the Company, Administrator or Trustees, except as provided herein, and in no event will the terms of employment or service of any Participant be modified or in any way be affected hereby. It is a condition of the Plan, and each Participant expressly agrees by his or her participation herein, that each Participant will look solely to the assets held in the Trust for the payment of any benefit to which he or she is entitled under the Plan.

17.02. *Nonalienability of Benefits*. The benefits provided hereunder will not be subject to alienation, assignment, garnishment, attachment, execution or levy of any kind, and any attempt to cause such benefits to be so subjected will not be recognized, except to such extent as may be required by law. The provisions of the preceding sentence shall apply in general to the creation, assignment or recognition of a right to any benefit payable with respect to a Participant pursuant to a domestic relations order, except that if such order is a Qualified Domestic Relations Order, the provisions of the preceding sentence shall not apply.

17.03. *Failure to Qualify Initially*. If it is determined that the Plan or the Trust does not qualify initially under Section 401 or 501 of the Code, the Administrator will direct the Trustees to return to the Company all assets then held by the Trustees under the Plan within one year of such determination. Upon such payment, the Plan will be considered to be rescinded and to be of no force or effect. Any amounts returned to the Company under this Section 17.03 which are attributable to Elective Contributions of a Participant shall be paid by the Company to such Participant.

17.04. *Information Between Administrator and Trustees*. The Administrator and Trustees will furnish each other such information relating to the Plan and Trust as may be required under the Code and any regulations issued or forms adopted by the Treasury Department thereunder or under the provisions of ERISA and any regulations issued or forms adopted by the Labor Department thereunder.

17.05. *Payment Under Qualified Domestic Relations Orders*. Notwithstanding any provisions of the Plan to the contrary, if there is entered any Qualified Domestic Relations Order that affects the payment of benefits hereunder, such benefits shall be paid in accordance with the applicable requirements of such Order.

17.06. *Governing Law*. The Plan and Trust will be construed, administered and enforced according to the laws of the [insert name of state] to the extent such laws are not inconsistent with and preempted by ERISA.

17.07. *Rollovers from Qualified Plans*.

(a) With the Plan Administrator's permission, and without regard to any limit on contributions to the Plan or allocations to a Participant's account, the Plan may either receive directly any lump sum distribution for the benefit of a Participant from any qualified section 401(a) plan, or receive a lump sum distribution received by a Participant from such a plan, either directly within 60 days after such receipt or through the medium of an Individual retirement Account (IRA), provided such IRA contains no assets other than those representing employer contributions to a qualified section 401(a) plan, any earnings thereon, and any earnings from employee contributions to that plan.

(b) Such lump sum distribution shall be held by the Plan Administrator and a separate accounting shall be made for it. All such amounts shall be fully vested and their value shall be paid to the Participant in addition to any other benefits under this Plan in the manner the Participant elects at his or her retirement, upon termination or death.

17.08. *Predecessor Plan Assets*. The Plan may receive assets for a Participant from a predecessor plan. Such assets shall be accounted for separately unless such assets are transferred from a Plan in which there is no curtailment of benefits or rights and vesting remains the same.

ARTICLE XVIII. TRUST

18.01 *Purpose*. This Trust is established solely for the purposes of:

(a) the investment of contributions made by the Company and the contributions made by Participants and any income thereon; and

(b) the holding of such investments, dividends, or distributions thereon, life insurance policies and annuity contracts in the Trust until distributed in accordance with the provisions of the Plan upon written instructions delivered to the Trust by the Company.

18.02 *Contributions*. The Plan assets shall never inure to the benefit of the Company and shall be held by the Trustees solely in the interest of, and for the exclusive purpose of, providing benefits to Participants and their Beneficiaries and defraying expenses of administering the Plan, subject, however, to the following:

(a) return of mistake of fact contributions pursuant to section 16.02, above, and

(b) return of contributions predicated on the Plan's initial qualification pursuant to section 17.03, above.

(c) return of excess plan assets upon plan termination to the extent permitted by ERISA.

All contributions made to the Trust shall be made in accordance with the provisions of the Plan. The Trustees shall be accountable for all contributions received by them, but the Trustees shall have no obligation to verify the propriety of such contributions under the Plan any may rely solely on the Company's representation with respect thereto. Contributions under the Plan shall be accepted by the Trustees only when made through the Company (except for rollover contributions and asset transfers described in sections 17.07 and 17.08, above).

18.03 *Accounts*. The Trust shall maintain the Accounts called for under this Plan. The Company shall verify from time-to-time to the Trustees the names of Participants and such other information as the Trustees may request. All investments, annuity contracts, and life insurance policies purchased or acquired under the Plan with contributions made by or on behalf of a Participant or with income thereon or proceeds thereof shall be held in the name of the Trustees for the benefit of the Participant and his or her Beneficiaries.

18.04. *Prohibited Diversion*. No distributions from the Trust shall be made which are prohibited by the provisions of the Plan. At no time shall it be possible for any part of the Trust's assets to be used for, or revert back to, the Company or to be diverted to purposes other than the exclusive benefit of Participants and their Beneficiaries, other than mistake-of-fact contributions as described in section 16.03, contributions conditioned on the Plan's initial qualification as described in section 17.03, and any reversion of excess assets permitted by ERISA upon plan termination. Payment of the administrative expenses of the Trust, including Trustee fees, from Trust corpus is permitted.

18.05. *Investment of Trust Fund*. Except as otherwise directed by the Company under the Plan, the Trustees shall invest the amount of each contribution made hereunder in any type of asset they see fit so long as the investment does not violate ERISA. The Trustees are authorized to invest the Trust Fund in such bonds, notes, debentures, mortgages, equipment, trust certificates, investment trust certificates, preferred or common stocks including Company securities to the extent permitted by the Plan and by ERISA, or in such other property, real or personal, subject to the jurisdiction of the United States District Courts as the Trustees may deem advisable, subject to the requirements of ERISA. The Trustees, in their discretion, may hold in cash such portion of the Trust Fund as shall be reasonable under the circumstances, pending investment or payment of expenses or distribution of benefits. The Trustees may make plan loans to Participants to the extent, and under the terms, provided in the Plan other than in this Article XVIII.

18.06 *Distribution of the Trust.* In connection with the making of any distribution from the Trust, the Trustees may rely solely on the accuracy of all facts supplied at any time by the Company. On receipt of a written request from the Company certifying that a Participant's benefit is payable pursuant to the Plan, the Trustees shall distribute or apply the assets credited to such Participant's accounts at the time or times, in the manner, and to the Participant or designated Beneficiary, specified by the Company.

18.07. *Compensation of the Trustees.* The Trustees shall not be entitled to compensation for their services under this Article, but may be compensated at the discretion of the Company's Board of Directors.

18.08. *Expenses of the Trust.* All charges attributable to the acquisition of assets and any income taxes or other taxes of any kind whatsoever that may be levied or assessed upon, or in respect of, the Trust shall be paid from the assets of the Trust. Any transfer taxes incurred in connection with the investment and reinvestment of the assets of the Trust, all other administrative expenses incurred by the Trustees in the performance of their duties, including fees for legal services rendered to the Trustees in respect of the Trust created hereunder and such compensation of the Trustees as may be agreed on in writing from time to time between the Trustees and the Company shall be chargeable to the Trust or to the Company at the discretion of the Board of Directors of the Company.

18.09 *Removal of Trustees.* The Company shall, at any time, have the right to remove a Trustee by delivering to such Trustee a notice in writing to that effect, which notice shall also designate a successor Trustee. Upon receipt by a Trustee of written acceptance by a successor Trustee, the removal of the Trustee shall be effective. If all of the Trustees are removed, they shall forthwith transfer and pay over to their successor Trustee or Trustees the assets of the Trust and all records pertaining thereto. Trustees may, however, reserve such assets as may be required for the payment of all their fees, compensation, costs, and expenses, and for the payment of all liabilities of or against the assets of the Trust or Trustees and, where necessary, may liquidate such reserved assets. Any balance of such reserve remaining after the payment of all such items shall be paid over to the successor Trustee or trustees.

18.10. *Resignation of a Trustee.* A Trustee shall, at any time, have the right to resign as a trustee under this Article XVIII by delivering to the Company a notice in writing to that effect. Upon receiving such notice, the Company shall forthwith appoint a successor Trustee and, upon receipt of such an appointment, the successor Trustee is authorized to act in the same manner as provided for in this Article XVIII. If the Company fails to appoint a successor Trustee within thirty days of receiving a Trustee's resignation, the remaining Trustees may appoint a successor Trustee.

18.11 *Records, Information.*

(a) The Trustees shall keep accurate and detailed accounts of all contributions, receipts, investments, distributions, disbursements, and all other transactions. The Trustees shall cause to be prepared and filed any returns required to be filed under the Code and shall supply to the Internal Revenue Service, the Labor Department, and the Pension Benefit Guaranty Corporation (if applicable) any other information as may be required by Trustees under ERISA.

(b) The Company agrees to file in a timely manner for each taxable year any required Form 5500 series reports (or any form designated by the IRS in lieu thereof) and, upon request, to supply a copy of such reports to the Trustees.

(c) The Trustees shall cause to have prepared and delivered to the Company a receipt for each contribution received, showing the investment thereof and current cumulative status of the account or accounts to which contributions or forfeitures are credited, and forfeitures and other distributions charged. Each year the Trustees shall cause to have furnished to the Company a transcript of all activity in each account, which shall be deemed to be the sole accounting by the Trustees necessary under this Article.

(d) Each receipt, statement, and report furnished by the Trustees to the Company shall be open to inspection by any Participant named therein for a period of sixty days immediately following the date on which it is filed with the Company. Upon the expiration of such sixty days, the Trustees and all administrative agents and other parties who are, or may become, involved in the administration of this Trust shall be forever released and discharged from all liability and accountability to anyone with respect to their acts, transactions, duties, obligations, or responsibilities as shown in, or reflected by, such receipt, statement, or report, except with respect to any such acts or transactions as to which the Company shall have filed written objections with the Trustees during such period.

18.12. *Voting of Stock.* The Trustees shall deliver to the Company, at its request, all notes, prospectuses, financial statements, proxies, and proxy soliciting material relating to the stock held by it. The Trustees shall not vote any of the stock held thereunder except in accordance with the Company's written instructions. The Trustees may delegate their obligations hereunder to the administrative agent referred to in section 18.15.

18.13. *Responsibility for Certain Acts.*

(a) The Trustees shall not be responsible in any way for the collection of contributions provided for under the Plan, the purpose or propriety of any distribution made pursuant to the terms hereof, or any other action taken at the Company's request.

(b) The Trustees shall be responsible for the administration of the Plan but not for its validity or effect, or the qualification of the Plan or of this Trust under the Code.

(c) The Company shall at all times fully indemnify and save harmless the Trustees, their successors and assigns, from any liability arising from distributions made, and actions taken, and from any other liability which may arise in connection with this agreement, except that the Company shall not be required to indemnify and save harmless the Trustees for any liability arising out of their willful misconduct or gross negligence.

(d) The Trustees shall be under no duty to take any action other than as herein specified with respect to the Trust unless the Company furnishes the Trustees with instructions in proper form and the Trustees specifically agree to such instructions in writing. Further, the Trustees shall be under no duty to defend, or engage in, any suit with respect to the Trust unless the Trustees shall be protected in acting upon any written order from the Company or any other notice, request, consent, certificate, or other written instrument believed by them to be genuine and to have been properly executed and, so long as they act in good faith, and not in a manner that is grossly negligent, in taking or omitting to take any other action.

(e) The Company shall have the sole authority to enforce the provisions of this Trust Article on behalf of any and all persons having or claiming any interest in the Trust by virtue of this Article or the Plan as a whole. To protect the Trust from the expenses which might otherwise be incurred, it is imposed as a condition to the acquisition of any interest in the Trust, and it is hereby agreed that no person other than the Company may institute or maintain any action or proceeding against the Trustees in the absence of written authority from the Company or a determination by a court of competent jurisdiction that, in refusing such authority, the Company has acted fraudulently or in bad faith.

18.14. *Amendment.* This Trust, as part of the Plan, may be amended in accordance with the provisions in the Plan document for amending the Plan.

18.15. *Designation of Agent.* The Trustees may designate an administrative agent to receive and invest pursuant to the Plan the contribution made thereunder in accordance with the Company's written instructions; to reinvest in the account of a Participant all dividends and capital gain distributions payable on the assets held herein; to keep and regularly furnish to the Trustees and the Company a detailed cumulative statement of each Participant's account, showing contributions and earnings thereto, assets purchased therewith and the number and cost of the same, each redemption or distribution therefrom made for any reason, including fees and benefits; to make investments including life insurance policies or annuity contracts providing benefits to any Participant and/or such Participant's Beneficiary; to reallocate forfeitures under the Plan, and furnish to the Trustees any necessary information required by the Plan or the Internal Revenue Code and ERISA and the regulations promulgated thereunder, and to prepare for the Trustees such returns, reports, or forms as the Trustees shall be required to furnish to the Company, the IRS, the Labor Department, and the PBGC; and, in general, to do any and all such administrative acts under the Plan including, without limitation, the acts specified in section 18.12, as the Trustees may do through such agent, and the Trustees shall be fully protected in relying on the contents of statements and reports furnished to them by said administrative agent unless the Trustees know, or have reason to know, that such statements and/or reports are erroneous.

18.16. *Powers of Trustees.* In addition to, and not in modification or limitation of, their common law and statutory authority, the Trustees shall have the following powers and authority in the administration of the Trust Fund, all of which may be exercised without the order of any court:

(a) to receive and take title to any and all assets and property of the Trust by instrument executed in the name of the Trustees or in the name of their nominee with or without any fiduciary relationship, provided that the books of the Trust reflect actual ownership and the Trust shall be liable for the acts of their nominee;

(b) to sell any Trust property, real or personal, for cash or credit, at public or private sale; to exchange any Trust property for other property; to grant options to purchase or acquire any Trust property for other property; to grant options to purchase or acquire any Trust property; and to determine the prices and terms of any such sales, exchanges, and options;

(c) to execute leases and subleases for any length of time, even though the terms of such leases or subleases may extend beyond the termination of the Trust; to subdivide or improve real estate and tear down or alter improvements; to grant easements, give consents, and make contracts relating to real estate or its use; and to release or dedicate any interest in real estate;

(d) to take any action with respect to conserving or realizing upon the value of any Trust property and with respect to foreclosures, reorganizations, or other changes affecting Trust property; to collect, pay, contest, compromise, or abandon demands of, or against, the Trust property wherever situated, and to execute contracts, notes, conveyances, and other instruments, including instruments containing covenants and warranties binding upon and creating a charge against the Trust Fund, and containing provisions excluding personal liability;

(e) to exercise any conversion privilege or subscription right available in connection with any securities or other property at any time held by the Trustees; and to vote, personally or by proxy, any shares of stock which may be held by the Trustees at any time;

(f) to borrow money from any person (other than a "party in interest," as defined in section 3(14) of ERISA), firm, or corporation, including Trustees, binding the Trust for the payment thereof, and to secure any money so borrowed by a pledge, an assignment, a mortgage, or a conveyance covering any real or personal property, with such provisions protecting the lender as the Trustees may agree upon;

(g) to hold part or all of the Trust Fund in cash;

(h) to employ agents, attorneys, auditors, depositories, and proxies, with or without discretionary powers;

(i) to adopt an accrual method of accounting and of determining net profits or losses; to amortize any part or all of any premium or discount; to treat any dividend or other distribution on any investment as income or principal; to charge any expense against income or principal or apportion it between income and principal; to apportion the sales price of any asset between income and principal; and to provide, or fail to provide, a reasonable reserve against depreciation or obsolescence, but in the exercise of these powers, the trustees shall use reasonable accounting principals and act fairly and equitably;

(j) to determine the market value of account balances and assets, whenever such determination is required in connection with the administration of the Plan;

(k) to maintain all books and records of the trust and to perform clerical, bookkeeping, and accounting work in connection with the management and administration of the Trust; and

(l) to make, execute, and deliver all instruments in writing necessary or proper for the accomplishment of any of the foregoing powers and no person dealing with the Trustees shall be required to inquire into the validity of any such instrument or see to the application by the Trustees of any money or other property paid or delivered to the Trustees pursuant to the terms of any such instrument.

18.17. *Fiduciary Responsibilities and Duties.* A fiduciary shall discharge his or her duties, including the allocation of duties with respect to the Plan, solely by exercising the care, skill, prudence, and diligence under the circumstances then prevailing that a prudent person acting in a like capacity and familiar with such matters would use in the conduct of an enterprise of like character and with like aims; by diversifying Plan investments so as to minimize the risk of large losses, unless, under the circumstances, it is clearly prudent not to do so; all subject to the terms of the Plan documents insofar as the same are consistent with the provisions of Title I of ERISA. Further:

(a) Any person who is a fiduciary with respect to the Plan who breaches any of the responsibilities, obligations, or duties imposed upon fiduciaries by Title I of ERISA shall be personally liable to make good to the Plan any losses to the Plan resulting from each such breach and to restore to the Plan any profits from such fiduciary which have been made through use of assets of the Plan by the fiduciary and shall be subject to such other equitable or remedial relief as a court of competent jurisdiction may deem appropriate; however, no fiduciary shall be liable with respect to a breach of fiduciary duty committed before he or she became a fiduciary or after he or she ceased to be a fiduciary;

(b) Where there are co-fiduciaries, they shall act jointly in exercising their fiduciary duties, unless the fiduciary responsibilities have been otherwise delegated among them in accordance with the provisions of this Plan for delegating such responsibilities (if any); however, in addition to any liability of a fiduciary for his or her own breaches of fiduciary responsibility under (a), above, a fiduciary shall be liable for the breach for the breach of responsibility of another fiduciary to the Plan if:(1) he or she knowingly participates in or conceals an act or omission of a co-fiduciary knowing the same to be a breach; (2) by failure to carry out his or her own specific administrative responsibilities, a fiduciary enables another fiduciary of the Plan to commit a breach; or (3) he or she has knowledge of a breach by a fiduciary of the Plan and makes no reasonable effort under the circumstances to remedy the breach.

18.18 *Prohibited Transactions.* A fiduciary shall not (unless exempted by the Secretary of Labor or Secretary of the Treasury) cause the Plan to engage in any of the following transactions with a party in interest: (a) the sale or exchange of Plan property; (b) the loan of money or extension of credit; (c) the furnishing of goods, services, or facilities; (d) the transfer of Plan assets to or use by or for, the benefit of such person, except in the form of benefits to which he or she is entitled as a Plan Participant.

For this purpose, the term "party in interest" shall mean:

(a) any fiduciary (including, but not limited to, any administrator, officer, trustee, or custodian), counsel, or employee of the Plan;

(b) a person providing services to the Plan;

(c) an employer whose employees are covered by the Plan;

(d) an employee organization, any of the members of which are covered by the Plan;

(e) an owner, directly or indirectly, of 50% or more of the following: (1) the combined voting power of all classes of voting stock or the total value of all classes of stock of a corporation; (2) the capital or profits from an interest in a partnership; (3) the beneficial interest in a trust or unincorporated organization, which is the employer under (c), above, or the employee organization under (d), above;

(f) a relative (meaning spouse, ancestor, lineal descendant, or spouse of a lineal descendant) of any person described in (a), (b), (c), or (d);

(g) a corporation, partnership, trust, or estate in which 50% or more of (e)(1) or (2), above, is owned, directly or indirectly, or held, by a person described in (a) through (e), above.

(h) an employee, officer, director, or persons having powers or responsibilities similar to those of officers or directors, or a 10%-or-more shareholder, directly or indirectly, of a person described in (b), (c), (d), (e), or (g), above, or of the Plan;

(i) a 10%-or-more (directly or indirectly in capital or profits) partner or joint venturer of a person described in (b), (c), (d), (e), or (g), above.

18.19. *Savings Clause.* Nothing in this Article shall preclude:

(a) the Plan from purchasing insurance for itself to cover losses by reason of the act or omission of a fiduciary, provided that the insurer has recourse against the fiduciary in case of his or her breach of fiduciary obligation;

(b) a fiduciary from purchasing insurance to cover liability from and for his or her own account; or

(c) the Company from purchasing insurance to cover liability of one or more persons who serve as named fiduciaries under the Plan.

18.20. *Bonding.* Unless exempted by the Secretary of Labor, every fiduciary of the Plan (other than a trustee-/custodian which is a bank that meets the requirements of section 412(a)(2) of ERISA), shall be bonded by a surety bond in an amount determined at the beginning of each year which is the greater of 10% of the amount of the funds handled or $1,000, but, in all events, not more than $500,000.

18.21. *Miscellaneous.* Any notices from the Trustees to the Company provided for in this Article shall be effective if sent by first class mail to the Company's last known address of record.

18.22. *Standard of Care.* Except as otherwise specifically provided herein, the Trustees shall discharge their duties as set forth in this Plan and Trust solely in the interest of Participants and their beneficiaries, and:

(a) for the exclusive purpose of (1) providing benefits to Participants and their Beneficiaries, and (2) defraying the reasonable expenses of administering the Plan;

(b) with the care, skill, prudence, and diligence under the circumstances then prevailing that a prudent person acting in a like capacity and familiar with such matters would use in the conduct of an enterprise of like character and with like aims; and

(c) by diversifying the investments of the Plan so as to minimize the risk of large losses, unless, under the circumstances, it is clearly prudent not to do so.

FIRST AMENDMENT TO PROFIT SHARING PLAN

Note: IRS Notice 87-2 contains model amendments for qualified plans to bring them into compliance with certain provisions of the 1986 Tax Reform Act that are effective forplan years beginning before 1989. Notice 87-2 also contains certain optional amendments that plans may adopt. The amendment below is derived from Model Amendment IV of IRS Notice 87-2 (for defined contribution plans, including target benefit plans, that allocate employee contributions, matching employer contributions, or elective deferrals under a cash-or-deferred arrangement to participants' accounts in plan years beginning after 1986. Where a provision is required (R) appears next to the title. Optional provisions are marked with the letter (O). Required provisions must be adopted verbatim in order for a plan to rely on a favorable determination letter that was obtained before the 1986 Tax Reform Act. Plan sponsors that adopt the model amendments before the last day of the first plan year beginning after December 31, 1988 retroactive to December 31, 1986 and administer their plans after December 31, 1986 as if the required provisions were fully effective may rely on prior (*i.e.*, post-REA) favorable determination letters provided that the plan sponsor does not receive notice from the Service within 120 days of the adoption of the amendments that it may not rely on the amendments. Full text of the other model amendments in Notice 87-2, including Model Amendment III relating to defined contribution plans that do not allocate employee contributions, matching employer contributions, or elective deferrals under a cash-or-deferred arrangement to participants' accounts in plan years beginning after 1986, appears in Worksheet 17 to 351 T.M., *Pension Plans—Qualification.*

SECTION I: PURPOSE AND EFFECTIVE DATE (R)

1.1. *Purpose.* It is the intention of the Employer to amend the plan to comply with those provisions of the Tax Reform Act of 1986 that are effective prior to the first Plan Year beginning after December 31, 1988. Nothing contained in this amendment shall permit or require Elective Deferrals, Matching Employer Contributions, or Employee Contributions under the plan unless such Elective Deferrals, Matching Employer Contributions, or Employee Contributions have been authorized by the Employer under other provisions of the plan or under other amendments thereto.

1.2. *Effective Date.* Except as otherwise provided, this amendment shall be effective as of the first day of the first Plan Year beginning after December 31, 1986.

SECTION II: DEFINITIONS (R)

For purposes of this amendment only, the following definitions shall apply.

2.1. "Adjustment Factor" shall mean the cost of living adjustment factor prescribed by the Secretary of the Treasury under Section 415(d) of the Code for years beginning after December 31, 1987, as applied to such items and in such manner as the Secretary shall provide.

2.2. "Affiliated Employer" shall mean the Employer and any corporation which is a member of a controlled group of corporations (as defined in Section 414(b) of the Code) which includes the Employer; any trade or business (whether or not incorporated) which is under common control (as defined in Section 414(c) of the Code) with the Employer; any organization (whether or not incorporated) which is a member of an affiliated service group (as defined in Section 414(m) of the Code) which includes the Employer; and any other entity required to be aggregated with the Employer pursuant to regulations under Section 414(o) of the Code.

2.3. "Code" shall mean the Internal Revenue Code of 1986 and amendments thereto.

2.4. "Compensation" shall mean compensation paid by the Employer to the Participant during the taxable year ending with or within the Plan Year which is required to be reported as wages on the Participant's Form W-2 and, if the provisions of the plan other than this amendment so provide, shall also include compensation which is not currently includible in the Participant's gross income by reason of the application of sections 125, 402(a)(8), 402(h)(1)(B) or 403(b) of the Code.

2.5. "Elective Deferrals" shall mean contributions made to the plan during the Plan Year by the Employer, at the election of the Participant, in lieu of cash compensation and shall include contributions made pursuant to a salary reduction agreement.

2.6. "Employee" shall mean employees of the Employer and shall include leased employees within the meaning of Section 414(n)(2) of the Code. Notwithstanding the foregoing, if such leased employees constitute less than twenty percent of the Employer's non-highly compensated work force within the meaning of Section 414(n)(1)(C)(ii) of the Code, the term "Employee" shall not include those leased employees covered by a plan described in Section 414(n)(5) of the Code unless otherwise provided by the terms of this plan other than this amendment.

2.7. "Employee Contributions" shall mean contributions to the plan made by a Participant during the Plan Year.

2.8. "Employer" shall mean the entity that establishes or maintains the plan; any other organization which has adopted the plan with the consent of such establishing employer; and any successor of such employer.

2.9. "Family Member" shall mean an individual described in Section 414(q)(6)(B) of the Code.

2.10. "Highly Compensated Employee" shall mean an individual described in Section 414(q) of the Code.

2.11. "Inactive Participant" shall mean any Employee or former Employee who has ceased to be a Participant and on whose behalf an account is maintained under the plan.

2.12. "Matching Contribution" shall mean any contribution to the Plan made by the Employer for the Plan Year and allocated to a Participant's account by reason of the Participant's Employee Contributions or Elective Deferrals.

2.13. "Non-Highly Compensated Employee" shall mean an Employee of the Employer who is neither a Highly Compensated Employee nor a Family Member.

2.14. "Participant" shall mean any Employee of the Employer who has met the eligibility and participation requirements of the plan.

2.15. "Qualified Nonelective Contributions" shall mean contributions (other than Matching Contributions) made by the Employer and allocated to Participants' accounts that the Participant may not elect to receive in cash until distributed from the plan; that are 100 percent vested and nonforfeitable when made; and that are not distributable under the terms of the plan to Participants or their beneficiaries earlier than the earlier of:

(i) separation from service, death, or disability of the Participant;

(ii) attainment of the age 59 1/2 by the Participant;

(iii) termination of the plan without establishment of a successor plan;

(iv) the events specified in those of Sections XIII, XIV or XV of this amendment adopted by the Employer; or

(v) for Plan Years beginning before January 1, 1989, upon hardship of the Participant.

2.16. "Plan Year" shall mean the plan year otherwise specified in the plan.

SECTION III: PROVISIONS RELATING TO LEASED EMPLOYEES (R)

3.1. *Safe-Harbor.* Notwithstanding any other provisions of the Plan, for purposes of determining the number or identity of Highly Compensated Employees or for purposes of the pension requirements of Section 414(n)(3) of the Code, the employees of the Employer shall include individuals defined as Employees in Section 2.6 of this amendment.

3.2. *Participation and Accrual.* A leased employee within the meaning of Section 414(n)(2) of the Code shall become a Participant in and accrue benefits under, the plan based on service as a leased employee only as provided in provisions of the plan other than this Section III.

3.3. *Effective Date.* This Section III shall be effective for services performed after December 31, 1986.

SECTION IV: LIMITATIONS ON CONTRIBUTIONS AND BENEFITS (R)

4.1. *Revised Contribution Limitations Under Defined Contribution Plan.*

4.1(a). *Definition of Annual Additions.* For purposes of the plan, "Annual Addition" shall mean the amount allocated to a Participant's account during the Limitation Year that constitutes:

(i) Employer contributions,

(ii) Employee Contributions,

(iii) Forfeitures, and

(iv) Amounts described in Sections 415(1)(1) and 419(A)(d)(2) of the Code.

4.1(b). *Maximum Annual Addition.* The maximum Annual Addition that may be contributed or allocated to a Participant's account under the Plan for any Limitation Year shall not exceed the lesser of:

(i) the Defined Contribution Dollar Limitation, or

(ii) 25 percent of the Participant's compensation, within the meaning of Section 415(c)(3) of the Code for the Limitation Year.

4.1(c). Special Rules. The compensation limitation referred to in Section 4.1(b)(ii) shall not apply to:

(i) Any contribution for medical benefits (within the meaning of Section 419A(f)(2) of the Code) after separation from service which is otherwise treated as an Annual Addition, or

(ii) Any amount otherwise treated as an Annual Addition under Section 415(1)(1) of the Code.

4.1(d). *Definitions.* For purposes of Section 4.1, "Defined Contribution Dollar Limitation" shall mean $30,000 or, if greater, one- fourth of the defined benefit dollar limitation set forth in Section 415(b)(1) of the Code as in effect for the Limitation Year.

4.2. *Special Rules for Plans Subject to Overall Limitations Under Code Section 415(e).*

4.2(a). *Recomputation Not Required.* The Annual Addition for any Limitation Year beginning before January 1, 1987 shall not be recomputed to treat all Employee Contributions as an Annual Addition.

4.2(b). *Adjustment of Defined Contribution Plan Fraction.* If the plan satisfied the applicable requirements of Section 415 of the Code as in effect for all Limitation Years beginning before January 1, 1987, an amount shall be subtracted from the numerator of the defined contribution plan fraction (not exceeding such numerator) as prescribed by the Secretary of the Treasury so that the sum of the defined benefit plan fraction and defined contribution plan fraction computed under Section 415(e)(1) of the Code (as revised by this Section IV) does not exceed 1.0 for such Limitation Year.

4.3. *Limitation Year.* For purposes of this Section IV, "Limitation Year" shall mean the limitation year specified in the plan, or if none is specified, the calendar year.

4.4 *Effective Date of Section IV Provisions.* The provisions of this Section IV shall be effective for Limitation Years beginning after December 31, 1986.

SECTION V: ELECTIVE DEFERRALS

(R — For Plans with Cash or Deferred Arrangement)

5.1. *Maximum Amount of Elective Deferrals.* Effective as of January 1, 1987, no Employee shall be permitted to have Elective Deferrals made under this plan during any calendar year in excess of $7000 multiplied by the Adjustment Factor as provided by the Secretary of the Treasury. The foregoing, limit shall not apply to Elective Deferrals of amounts attributable to service performed in 1986 and described in Section 1105(c)(5) of the Tax Reform Act of 1986.

5.2. *Average Actual Deferral Percentage.*

(a) The Average Actual Deferral Percentage for Eligible Participants who are Highly Compensated Employees for the Plan Year shall not exceed the Average Actual Deferral Percentage for Eligible Participants who are Non-highly Compensated Employees for the Plan Year multiplied by 1.25; or

(b) the Average Actual Deferral Percentage for Eligible Participants who are Highly Compensated Employees for the Plan Year shall not exceed the Average Actual Deferral Percentage for Eligible Participants who are Non-highly Compensated Employees for the Plan Year multiplied by 2, provided that the Average Actual Deferral Percentage for Eligible Participants who are Highly Compensated Employees does not exceed the Average Actual Deferral Percentage for Eligible Participants who are Non-highly Compensated Employees by more than two (2) percentage points or such lesser amount as the Secretary of the Treasury shall prescribe to prevent the multiple use of this alternative limitation with respect to any Highly Compensated Employee.

5.3. *Definitions.* For purposes of this section V and for purposes of Sections X and XI of this Amendment, the following definitions shall be used:

5.3(a). "Actual Deferral Percentage" shall mean the ratio (expressed as a percentage), of Elective Deferrals and Qualified Employer Deferral Contributions on behalf of the Eligible Participant for the Plan Year to the Eligible Participant's Compensation for the Plan Year.

5.3(b). "Average Actual Deferral Percentage" shall mean the average (expressed as a percentage) of the Actual Deferral Percentages of the Eligible Participants in a group.

5.3(c). "Qualified Employer Deferral Contributions" shall mean Qualified Nonelective Contributions taken into account under the terms of the plan without regard to this amendment in determining the Actual Deferral Percentage.

5.3(d). "Eligible Participant" shall mean any Employee of the Employer who is otherwise authorized under the terms of the Plan to have Elective Deferrals or Qualified Employer Deferral Contributions allocated to his account for the Plan Year.

5.4. *Special Rules.*

5.4(a). For purposes of this Section V, the Actual Deferral Percentage for any Eligible Participant who is a Highly Compensated Employee for the Plan Year and who is eligible to have Elective Deferrals or Qualified Employer Deferral Contributions allocated to his account under two or more plans or arrangements described in Section 401(k) of the Code that are maintained by the Employer or an Affiliated Employer shall be determined as if all such Elective Deferrals and Qualified Employer Deferral Contribution were made under a single arrangement.

5.4(b). For purposes of determining the Actual Deferral Percentage of,a Participant who is a Highly Compensated Employee, the Elective Deferrals, Qualified Employer Deferral Contributions and Compensation of such Participant shall include the Elective Deferrals, Qualified Employer Deferral Contributions and Compensation of Family Members, and such Family Members shall be disregarded in determining the Actual Deferral Percentage for Participants who are Non-highly Compensated Employees.

5.4(c). The determination and treatment of the Elective Deferrals, Qualified Nonelective Contributions and Actual Deferral Percentage of any Participant shall satisfy such other requirements as may be prescribed by the Secretary of the Treasury.

SECTION VI. LIMITATIONS ON EMPLOYEE CONTRIBUTIONS AND MATCHING EMPLOYER CONTRIBUTIONS

(R — For Plans That Provide For Employee Contributions or Employer Matching Contributions)

6.1. *Contribution Percentage.*

6.1(a). The Average Contribution Percentage for Eligible Participants who are Highly Compensated Employees for the Plan Year shall not exceed the Average Contribution Percentage for Eligible Participants who are Non-highly Compensated Employees for the Plan Year multiplied by 1.25; or

6.1(b). The Average Contribution Percentage for Eligible Participants who are Highly Compensated Employees for the Plan Year shall not exceed the Average Contribution Percentage for Eligible Participants who are Non-highly Compensated Employees the Plan Year multiplied by 2, provided that the Average Contribution Percentage for Eligible Participants who are Highly Compensated Employees does not exceed the Average Contribution Percentage for Eligible Participants who are Non-highly Compensated Employees by more than two (2) percentage points or such lesser amount as the Secretary of the Treasury shall prescribe to prevent the multiple use of this alternative limitation with respect to any Highly Compensated Employee.

6.2. *Definitions.* For purposes of this Section VI, and for purposes of Section XII of this amendment, the following definitions shall apply.

6.2(a). "Average Contribution Percentage" shall mean the average (expressed as percentage) of the Contribution Percentages of the Eligible Participants in a group.

6.2(b). "Contribution Percentage" shall mean the ratio (expressed as a percentage), of the sum of the Employee Contributions and Matching Contributions under the plan on behalf of the Eligible Participant for the Plan Year to the Eligible Participant's Compensation for the Plan Year.

6.2(c). "Eligible Participant" shall mean any employee of the Employer who is otherwise authorized under the terms of the plan to have Employee Contributions or Matching Contributions allocated to his account for the Plan Year.

6.3. *Special Rules.*

6.3(a). For purposes of this section VI, the Contribution Percentage for any Eligible Participant who is a Highly Compensated Employee for the Plan Year and who is eligible to make Employee Contributions, or to receive Matching Contributions, Qualified Nonelective Contributions or Elective Deferrals allocated to his account under two or more plans described in Section 401(a) of the Code or arrangements described in Section 401(k) of the Code that are maintained by the Employer or an Affiliated Employer shall be determined as if all such contributions and Elective Deferrals were made under a single plan.

6.3(b). In the event that this plan satisfies the requirements of Section 410(b) of the Code only if aggregated with one or more other plans, or if one or more other plans satisfy the requirements of Section 410(b) of the Code only if aggregated with this plan, then this Section VI shall be applied by determining the Contribution Percentages of Eligible Participants as if all such plans were a single plan.

6.3(c). For purposes of determining the Contribution Percentage of an Eligible Participant who is a Highly Compensated Employee, the Employee Contributions, Matching Employer Contributions and Compensation of such Participant shall include the Employee Contributions, Matching Employer Contributions and Compensation of Family Members, and such Family Members shall be disregarded in determining the Contribution Percentage for Eligible Participants who are Non-highly Compensated Employees.

6.3(d). The determination and treatment of the Contribution Percentage of any Participant shall satisfy such other requirements as may be prescribed by the Secretary of the Treasury.

SECTION VII: QUALIFIED VOLUNTARY EMPLOYEE CONTRIBUTIONS NOT PERMITTED
(R — For Plans with Qualified Voluntary Employee Contributions)

The plan shall accept no Employee Contributions designated by the Participant as deductible employee contributions (within the meaning of Section 72(o)(5)(A) of the Code) for a taxable year of the Participant beginning after December 31, 1986.

SECTION VIII: SPECIAL PROVISIONS FOR EMPLOYEE STOCK OWNERSHIP PLANS AND STOCK BONUS PLANS
(R — For TCESOPs, ESOPs and stock bonus plans)

8.1. *Definitions.* For purposes of this amendment only, the following definitions shall apply.

8.1(a). "ESOP" shall mean an "Employee Stock Ownership Plan" as defined in Section 4975(e)(7) of the Code.

8.1(b). "TCESOP" shall mean a "Tax Credit Employee Stock Ownership Plan" as defined in Section 409(a) of the Code.

8.1(c). "Total Distribution" shall mean a distribution to a Participant or a Participant's beneficiary, within one taxable year of such recipient, of the entire balance to the credit of the Participant.

8.1(d). "Employer Securities" shall mean:

(i) In the case of a TCESOP, common stock issued by the Employer (or by a corporation which is a member of the same controlled group of corporations as the Employer as that term is defined in Section 409(1)(4) of the Code) which is readily tradable on an established securities market, or stock which satisfies the requirements of Section 409(1)(2) or (3) of the Code;

(ii) In the case of an ESOP which is not a TCESOP, stock described in Section 4975(e)(8) of the Code or in Treas. Reg. §54.4975-12;

(iii) In the case of a stock bonus plan which is not a TCESOP or an ESOP, any securities of the Employer held by the plan.

8.1(e). "Qualified Participant" shall mean a Participant who has attained age 55 and who has completed at least 10 years of participation.

8.1(f). "Qualified Election Period" shall mean the five Plan Year period beginning with the later of:

(i) the Plan Year after the Plan Year in which the Participant attains age 55; or,

(ii) the Plan Year after the Plan Year in which the Participant first becomes a Qualified Participant.

8.2. *Special Distribution and Payment Requirements.*

8.2(a). *In General.* This Section 8.2 shall apply to TCESOPs, ESOPs, and stock bonus plans and shall not eliminate any form or time of distribution available under the plan prior to adoption of this amendment.

8.2(b). *Time of Distribution.* Notwithstanding any other provision of the plan, other than such provisions as require the consent of the Participant and the Participant's spouse to a distribution with a present value in excess of $3,500, a Participant may elect to have the portion of the Participant's account attributable to Employer Securities acquired by the plan after December 31, 1986, distributed as follows:

(i) If the Participant separates from service by reason of the attainment of normal retirement age under the plan, death, or disability, the distribution of such portion of the Participant's account balance will begin not later than one year after the close of the Plan Year in which such event occurs unless the Participant otherwise elects under the provisions of the plan other than this Section 8.2.

(ii) If the Participant separates from service for any reason other than those enumerated in paragraph (i) above, and is not reemployed by the Employer at the end of the fifth Plan Year following the Plan Year of such separation from service, distribution of such portion of the Participant's account balance will begin not later than one year after the close of the fifth Plan Year following the Plan Year in which the Participant separated from service unless the Participant otherwise elects under the provisions of this plan other than this Section 8.2.

(iii) If the Participant separates from service for a reason other than those described in paragraph (i) above, and is employed by the Employer as of the last day of the fifth Plan Year following the Plan Year of such separation from service, distribution to the Participant, prior to any subsequent separation from service, shall be in accordance with terms of the plan other than this Section 8.2.

For purposes of this Section 8.2, Employer Securities shall not include any Employer Securities acquired with the proceeds of a loan described in Section 404(a)(9) of the Code until the close of the Plan Year in which such loan is repaid in full.

8.2(c) *Period for Payment.* Distributions required under Section 8.2 shall be made in substantially equal annual payments over a period of five years unless the Participant otherwise elects under provisions of this plan other than this Section 8.2. In no event shall such distribution period exceed the period permitted under Section 401(a)(9) of the Code.

8.2(d). *Determination of Amount Subject to Special Distribution and Payment Requirements.* The portion of a Participant's account balance attributable to Employer Securities which were acquired by the plan after December 31, 1986, shall be determined by multiplying the number of shares of such securities held in the account by a fraction, the numerator of which is the number of shares acquired by the plan after December 31, 1986, and allocated to Participants' accounts (nor to exceed the number of shares held by the plan on the date of distribution) and the denominator of which is the total number of such shares held by the plan at the date of the distribution.

8.3. *Put Option Requirements.*

8.3(a). *In General.* This Section 8.3 shall apply to distributions of Employer Securities which are acquired after December 31, 1986, by TCESOPs, ESOPs, and stock bonus plans and shall not eliminate any time or form of distribution available under the plan prior to adoption of this amendment.

8.3(b). *Put Option Payment.* Notwithstanding any other provisions of the plan regarding a Participant's right to exercise a put option, in the case of a distribution of Employer Securities which are not readily tradable on an established securities market, the plan shall provide the

Participant with a put option that complies with the requirements of Section 409(h) of the Code. Such put option shall provide that if an employee exercises the put option, the Employer, or the plan if the plan so elects, shall repurchase the Employer Securities as follows:

(i) If the distribution constitutes a Total Distribution, payment of the fair market value of a Participant's account balance shall be made in five substantially equal annual payments. The first installment shall be paid not later than 30 days after the Participant exercises the put option. The plan will pay a reasonable rate of interest and provide adequate security on amounts not paid after 30 days.

(ii) If the distribution does not constitute a Total Distribution, the plan shall pay the Participant an amount equal to the fair market value of the Employer Securities repurchased no later than 30 days after the Participant exercises the put option.

8.4. *Diversification of Investments.*

8.4(a). *In General.* This section 8.4 shall apply to TCESOPs and ESOPs.

8.4(b). *Election By Qualified Participant.* Each Qualified Participant shall be permitted to direct the plan as to the investment of 25 percent of the value of the Participant's account balance attributable to Employer Securities which were acquired by the plan after December 31, 1986, within 90 days after the last day of each Plan Year during the Participant's Qualified Election Period. Within 90 days after the close of the last Plan Year in the Participant's Qualified Election Period, a Qualified Participant may direct the plan as to the investment of 50 percent of the value of such account balance.

8.4(c). *Method of Directing Investment.* The Participant's direction shall be provided to the Plan Administrator in writing; shall be effective no later than 180 days after the close of the Plan Year to which the direction applies; and shall specify which, if any, of the options set forth in Section 8.4(d) the Participant selects.

8.4(d). *Investment Options.*

8.4(d)(i). At the election of the Qualified Participant, the plan shall distribute (notwithstanding section 409(d) of the Code) the portion of the Participant's account that is covered by the election within 90 days after the last day of the period during which the election can be made. Such distribution shall be subject to such requirements of the plan concerning put options as would otherwise apply to a distribution of Employer Securities from the plan. This Section 8.4(d)(i) shall apply notwithstanding any other provision of the plan other than such provisions as require the consent of the Participant and the Participant's spouse to a distribution with a present value in excess of $3500. If the Participant and the Participant's spouse do not consent, such amount shall be retained in this plan.

8.4(d)(ii). In lieu of distribution under Section 8.4(d)(i), the Qualified Participant who has the right to receive a cash distribution under Section 8.4(d)(i) may direct the plan to transfer the portion of the Participant's account that is covered by the election to another qualified plan of the Employer which accepts such transfers, provided that such plan permits employee-directed investment and does not invest in Employer Securities to a substantial degree. Such transfer shall be made no later than ninety days after the last day of the period during which the election can be made.

8.4(d)(iii). If the plan is a TCESOP, any distribution or transfer under this Section 8.4(d) shall be made first from Employer Securities allocated to the Participant's account at least 84 months before the month in which the distribution or transfer occurs.

8.4(e). Determination of Amount Subject to Diversification Requirements. The portion of a Participant's account balance attributable to Employer Securities which were acquired by the plan after December 31, 1986, shall be determined by multiplying the number of shares of such securities held in the account by a fraction, the numerator of which is the number of shares acquired by the plan after December 31, 1986, and allocated to Participants' accounts (not to exceed the number of shares held by the plan on the date the individual becomes a Qualified Participant) and the denominator of which is the total number of shares held by the plan at the date the individual becomes a Qualified Participant.

8.5. *Voting Rights of Participants*

8.5(a). *In General.* This Section 8.5 shall apply to TCESOPs, ESOPs, and stock bonus plans which are required to comply with Section 409(e) of the Code through the operation of Section 401(a)(22) of the Code.

8.5(b). Issues Where Pass-Through Required. Notwithstanding any other provision of the plan, if the plan has any class of securities which is not a registration-type class of securities (as defined in section 409(e)(4) of the Code), a Participant shall be entitled to direct the trustee as to the manner in which voting rights will be exercised with respect to any corporate matter which involves the voting of such shares allocated to the Participant's account with respect to the approval or disapproval of any corporate merger or consolidation, recapitalization, reclassification, liquidation, dissolution, sale of substantially all assets of a trade or business, or such similar transaction as may be prescribed in Treasury regulations.

8.6. *Independent Appraiser.*

8.6(a). *In General.* This Section 8.6 shall apply to TCESOPs and ESOPs.

8.6(b). *Independent Appraisals.* All valuations of Employer Securities which are not readily tradable on an established securities market with respect to activities carried on by the plan shall be made by an independent appraiser meeting requirements similar to those contained in Treasury regulations under Section 170(a)(1) of the Code.

SECTION IX: DETERMINATION OF TOP-HEAVY STATUS

(R — If plan is a target benefit plan or if the Employer or Affiliated Employers maintain, in addition to the defined contribution plan, a defined benefit or target benefit plan in which one or more key employees participate, or any other plan on which such a defined or target benefit plan depends to meet coverage and nondiscrimination requirements.)

Solely for the purpose of determining if the plan, or any other plan included in a required aggregation group of which this plan is a part, is top-heavy (within the meaning of Section 416(g) of the Code) the accrued benefit of an Employee other than a key employee (within the meaning of Section 416(i)(1) of the Code) shall be determined under (a) the method, if any, that uniformly applies for accrual purposes under all plans maintained by the Affiliated Employers, or (b) if there is no such method, as if such benefit accrued not more rapidly than the slowest accrual rate permitted under the fractional accrual rate of Section 411(b)(1)(C) of the Code.

SECTION X: DISTRIBUTION OF EXCESS DEFERRALS

(O — For Plans with Cash or Deferred Arrangement)

10.1. *In General.* Notwithstanding any other provision of the plan, Excess Deferral Amounts and income allocable thereto shall be distributed no later than April 15, 1988, and each April 15 thereafter to Participants who claim such Allocable Excess Deferral Amounts for the preceding calendar year.

10.2. *Definitions.* For purposes of this amendment, "Excess Deferral Amount" shall mean the amount of Elective Deferrals for a calendar year that the Participant allocates to this plan pursuant to the claim procedure set forth in Section 10.3.

10.3. *Claims*. The Participant's claim shall be in writing, shall be submitted to the plan administrator no later than March 1; shall specify the Participant's Excess Deferral Amount for the preceding calendar year; and shall be accompanied by the Participant's written statement that if such amounts are not distributed, such Excess Deferral Amount, when added to amounts deferred under other plans or arrangements described in Sections 401(k), 408(k) or 403(b) of the Code, exceeds the limit imposed on the Participant by Section 402(g) of the Code for the year in which the deferral occurred.

10.4. *Maximum Distribution Amount*. The Excess Deferral Amount distributed to a Participant with respect to a calendar year shall be adjusted for income and, if there is a loss allocable to the Excess Deferral, shall in no event be less than the lesser of the Participant's account under the plan or the Participant's Elective Deferrals for the Plan Year.

SECTION XI: DISTRIBUTION OF EXCESS CONTRIBUTIONS
(O — For Plans with Cash or Deferred Arrangement)

11.1. *In General*. Notwithstanding any other provision of the plan, Excess Contributions and income allocable thereto shall be distributed no later than the last day of each plan year beginning after December 31, 1987, to Participants on whose behalf such Excess Contributions were made for the preceding Plan Year.

11.2. *Excess Contributions*. For purposes of this amendment, "Excess Contributions" shall mean the amount described in Section 401(k)(8)(B) of the Code.

11.3. *Excess Contribution of Income*. The income allocable to Excess Contributions shall be determined by multiplying income allocable to the Participant's Elective Deferrals and Qualified Employer Deferral Contributions for the Plan Year by a fraction, the numerator of which is the Excess Contribution on behalf of the Participant for the preceding Plan Year and the denominator of which is the sum of the Participant's account balances attributable to Elective Deferrals and Qualified Employer Deferral Contributions on the last day of the preceding Plan Year.

11.4. *Maximum Distribution Amount*. The Excess Contributions which would otherwise be distributed to the Participant shall be adjusted for income; shall be reduced, in accordance with regulations, by the amount of Excess Deferrals distributed to the Participant; shall, if there is a loss allocable to the Excess Contributions, in no event be less than the lesser of the Participant's account under the plan or the Participant's Elective Deferrals and Qualified Employer Deferral Contributions for the Plan Year.

11.5. *Accounting for Excess Contributions*. Amounts distributed under this Section XI shall first be treated as distributions from the Participant's Elective Deferral account and shall be treated as distributed from the Participant's Qualified Employer Deferral Contribution account only to the extent such Excess Contributions exceed the balance in the Participant's Elective Deferral account.

SECTION XII: DISTRIBUTION OF EXCESS AGGREGATE CONTRIBUTIONS
(O — For Plans with Employee Contributions or Matching Employer Contributions)

12.1. *In General*. Excess Aggregate Contributions and income allocable thereto shall be forfeited, if otherwise forfeitable under the terms of this Plan, or if not forfeitable, distributed no later than the last day of each Plan Year beginning after December 31, 1987, to Participants to whose accounts Employee Contributions or Matching Contributions were allocated for the preceding Plan Year.

12.2. *Excess Aggregate Contributions*. For purposes of this amendment, "Excess Aggregate Contributions" shall mean the amount described in Section 401(m)(6)(B) of the Code.

12.3. *Determination of Income*. The income allocable to Excess Aggregate Contributions shall be determined by multiplying the income allocable to the Participant's Employee Contributions and Matching Employer Contributions for the Plan Year by a fraction, the numerator of which is the Excess Aggregate Contributions on behalf of the Participant for the preceding Plan Year and the denominator of which is the sum of the Participant's account balances attributable to Employee Contributions and Matching Employer Contributions on the last day of the preceding Plan Year.

12.4. *Maximum Distribution Amount*. The Excess Aggregate Contributions to be distributed to a Participant shall be adjusted for income, and, if there is a loss allocable to the Excess Aggregate Contribution, shall in no event be less than the lesser of the Participant's account under the plan or the Participant's Employee Contributions and Matching Contributions for the Plan Year.

12.5. *Accounting for Excess Aggregate Contributions*. Excess Aggregate Contributions shall be distributed from the Participant's Employee Contribution account, and forfeited if otherwise forfeitable under the terms of the plan (or, if not forfeitable, distributed) from the Participant's Matching Contribution account in proportion to the Participant's Employee Contributions and Matching Contributions for the Plan Year.

12.6. *Allocation of Forfeitures*.

12.6(a). Amounts forfeited by Highly Compensated Employees under this Section XII shall be:

(i) Treated as Annual Additions under Section 4.1(a) of this amendment and either;

(ii) Applied to reduce employer contributions if forfeitures of Matching Contributions under the Plan are applied to reduce employer contributions; or

(iii) Allocated, after all other forfeitures under the plan, and subject to Section 12.6(b) of this amendment, to the same Participants and in the same manner as such other forfeitures of Matching Contributions, are allocated to other Participants under the Plan.

12.6(b) Notwithstanding the foregoing, no forfeitures arising under this Section XII shall be allocated to the account of any Highly Compensated Employee.

SECTION XIII: DISTRIBUTIONS UPON PLAN TERMINATION
(O — For Plans with Cash or Deferred Arrangement).

Effective as of January 1, 1985 or such later date as the employer shall specify upon adoption of this Section XIII, Elective Deferrals, Qualified Employer Deferral Contributions, and income attributable thereto, shall be distributed to Participants or their beneficiaries as soon as administratively feasible after the termination of the plan, provided that neither the Employer nor an Affiliated Employer maintains a successor plan.

SECTION XIV: DISTRIBUTIONS UPON SALE OF ASSETS
(O — For Plans with Cash or Deferred Arrangement).

Effective as of January 1, 1985, or such later date as the Employer shall specify upon adoption of this Section XIV, all Elective Deferrals, Qualified Employer Deferral Contributions, and income attributable thereto, shall be distributed to Participants as soon as administratively feasible after the sale, to an entity that is not an Affiliated Employer, of substantially all of the assets used by the Employer in the trade or business in which the Participant is employed.

SECTION XV. DISTRIBUTIONS UPON SALE OF SUBSIDIARY
(O — For Plans with Cash or Deferred Arrangement)

Effective as of January 1, 1985, or such later date as the Employer specifies upon adoption of this Section XV, all Elective Deferrals, Qualified Employer Deferral Contributions, and income attributable thereto, shall be distributed, as soon as administratively feasible after the sale, to an entity that is not an Affiliated Employer, of an incorporated Affiliated Employer's interest in an subsidiary to Participants employed by such subsidiary.

SECTION XVI: DISTRIBUTIONS ON TERMINATION OF TAX CREDIT EMPLOYEE STOCK OWNERSHIP PLANS
(O — For Tax Credit ESOPs as defined in Section 409(a) of the Code)

Notwithstanding any other provisions of the plan, Employer Securities allocated to a Participant's account under the portion of the plan intended to meet the requirements of Section 401(a)(9) of the Code may not be distributed to any Participant before the 84th month after the month in which such Employer Securities were allocated to the such accounts, except that such securities may be distributed before the 84th month after such allocation in the case of:

(a) death, disability or separation from service;

(b) a transfer of a Participant to the employment of an acquiring employer from the employment of the selling corporation in the case of a sale to the acquiring corporation of substantially all of the assets used by the selling corporation in a trade or business conducted by the selling corporation;

(c) with respect to the stock of the selling corporation, a disposition of such selling corporation's interest in a subsidiary when the participant continues employment with such subsidiary; or,

(d) termination of the plan occurring after December 31, 1984, or such later date as the Employer shall specify upon adoption of this Section XVI.

SECTION XVII: BENEFIT FORFEITURES
(O — For Money Purchase Plans Other Than Target Benefit Plans Only)

17.1. *In General.* Notwithstanding any other provision of the plan, forfeitures occurring in Plan Years beginning after December 31, 1985, or such later date as the Employer specifies upon adoption of this Section XVII, shall be allocated to those Participants entitled to an allocation of Matching Contributions or other employer contributions for the Plan Year in which the forfeiture occurs. Forfeitures shall be allocated to such Participants in proportion to their compensation for the Plan Year.

17.2. *Forfeitures.* For purposes of this Section XVII, "forfeitures" shall mean those nonvested amounts allocated to Participants' accounts that, under the terms of this plan immediately prior to adoption of this amendment, would have been applied, if forfeited, to reduce Matching Contributions or other employer contributions under the plan.

17.3. *Limitations on Allocation of Forfeitures.*

17.3(a). Forfeitures allocated to the account of a Participant during the plan's Limitation Year under this Section XVII shall be treated as an Annual Addition for such Limitation Year for purposes of Section IV of this amendment.

17.3(b). If, as a result of such allocation of forfeitures, the Annual Addition under the plan for a Participant would exceed the limits specified in Section 415(c)(1) of the Code, such excess shall be allocated and reallocated to the accounts of other Participants in the manner described in Section 17.1 to the extent such allocations and reallocations, when added to other Annual Additions for such Participants, do not exceed the limits specified in Section 415(c)(1) of the Code. If, after such allocation and reallocation, there remains an amount that cannot be allocated to the accounts of Participants, such excess shall be held unallocated in a suspense account, and shall be allocated and reallocated among the accounts of Participants (subject to the limitations of Section 415(c)(1) of the Code) before any employer contributions, including Matching Contributions, or Employee Contributions may be made to the plan for the succeeding Limitation Year.

17.3(c). If at any time during the Limitation Year, a suspense account is in existence pursuant to this Section 17.3, investment gains and losses and other income shall be allocated to the suspense account, and the entire amount allocated to the Participants from such suspense account shall be considered as an Annual Addition for purposes of Section 415(c)(1) of the Code. Upon termination of the plan, unallocated amounts in the suspense account shall, notwithstanding any other provision of this plan, revert to the Employer.

17.4. *Nature of Plan.* Notwithstanding the adoption of this Section XVII, the plan shall continue to be designed to qualify as a money purchase pension plan for purposes of Sections 401(a), 402, 412 and 417 of the Code.

SECTION XVIII: PROFITS NOT REQUIRED
(O — Profit-Sharing Plans Only)

Effective for Plan Years beginning after December 31, 1985, or each later date as the Employer specifies when adopting this Section XVIII, the Employer shall, notwithstanding any other provision of the plan, make all contributions to the plan without regard to current or accumulated earnings and profits for the taxable year or years ending with or within such Plan Year. Notwithstanding the foregoing, the plan shall continue to be designed to qualify as a profit-sharing plan for purposes of Sections 401(a), 402, 412, and 417 of the Code.

SECTION XIX: PERIOD OF PAYMENT FOR DISTRIBUTIONS UNDER SECTION 8.2 OF MODEL AMENDMENTS
(O — For TCESOPs, ESOPs, and Stock Bonus Plans)

19.1(a). *Period For Payment.* Notwithstanding Section 8.2(c) of this amendment, if the fair market value of a Participant's account attributable to Employer Securities is in excess of $500,000 (multiplied by the Adjustment Factor as prescribed by the Secretary of the Treasury) as of the date distribution is required to begin under Section 8.2(b), distributions required under Section 8.2 shall be made in substantially equal annual payments over a period not longer than five years plus an additional one year (up to an additional five years) for each $100,000 increment, or fraction of such increment, by which the value of the Participant's account exceeds $500,000, unless the Participant otherwise elects under the provisions of the plan other than this Section 19.1. In no event shall such distribution period exceed the period permitted under Section 401(a)(9) of the Code.

19.2(b). *Effective Date.* This Section XIX shall apply to distributions of the value of a Participant's account attributable to Employer Securities acquired by the plan after December 31, 1986, or such later date as the Employer shall specify upon adoption of this Section XIX.

SECTION XX: DETERMINATION OF AMOUNT SUBJECT TO SPECIAL DISTRIBUTION AND PAYMENT REQUIREMENTS
(O — For TCESOPs, ESOPs, and Stock Bonus Plans)

20.1(b). *Determination of Amount Subject To Distribution, Payment and Diversification Requirements.* Effective as of January 1, 1987, or such later date as the Employer shall specify upon adoption of this Section XX, the provisions of Sections VIII and XIX (if adopted by the Employer) shall apply to the entire portion of a Participant's account attributable to Employer Securities.

SUMMARY PLAN DESCRIPTION OF THE ABC CORP. SECTION 401(K) PROFIT SHARING PLAN *

HIGHLIGHTS

All employees of the ABC Corp. (referred to herein as the "Company") are eligible to participate in the Plan (which is formally known as the ABC Corp. Section 401(k) Profit-Sharing Plan).

PLAN NUMBER

The number assigned to this plan by the Company is 001.

PLAN YEAR

The plan year-end for purposes of maintaining the plan's fiscal records is ______________.

PLAN ADMINISTRATOR

The name, business address and telephone number of the Plan Administrator(s) are: James Smith, 1000 Main St., Smithville, PA. 12234.

PLAN SPONSOR'S NAME AND ADDRESS

The name, business address and telephone number of the Plan Sponsor are: ABC Corp. 1000 Main St., Smithville, PA. 12234. (123)-456-7890.

PLAN SPONSOR'S EMPLOYER IDENTIFICATION NUMBER

The Plan sponsor's Employer Identification Number for Federal Income Tax purposes is: 54-1234567.

TRUSTEE'S NAME AND ADDRESS

The Plan Trustee's name and address are: The Jones Trust Company, 1111 North Drive, Southville, PA. 12345.

DESIGNATED AGENT FOR RECEIPT OF PROCESS

The name and address of the registered agent for receipt of process for the Plan is: James Smith, 1000 Main St., Smithville, PA. 12234.

TYPE OF PLAN

The Plan is a profit-sharing plan with a cash-or-deferred arrangement.

TYPE OF ADMINISTRATION

The Plan is administered through a trust arrangement. Trust assets are invested for the exclusive purpose of providing benefits to participants and their beneficiaries. Distributions of benefits to participants are made from trust assets. The trust is administered by the trustees named above.

WHAT BENEFITS DOES THE PLAN PROVIDE?

The Plan provides benefits upon: (1) retirement; (2) disability; or (3) death.

The benefits under the Plan are in addition to any Social Security benefits to which an employee or an employee's beneficiary may be entitled and are not offset by such Social Security benefits.

In addition to the employer-provided benefit, the Plan permits employees to save money by making elective contributions. Participants making elective contributions are eligible to receive matching contributions, provided by the company, as described below.

An employee's plan benefit is measured by the amount held in his or her accounts at any point in time.

Participants may have as many as three accounts under this Plan:

(1) An elective contribution account (consisting of elective contributions plus any investment growth thereon);

(2) A matching contribution account (consisting of any matching contributions plus investment growth thereon); and

(3) A Company contribution account (consisting of any Company contributions plus investment growth thereon).

These accounts will be kept by the Plan Administrator on the Plan's books, but the monies in these accounts may be commingled, and combined with the accounts of other participants by the trustees for purposes of investing the plan's assets.

WHEN DOES AN EMPLOYEE BECOME ELIGIBLE TO PARTICIPATE?

An employee will be allowed to make elective contributions and receive employer and matching contributions on the entry date next following the date he or she satisfies the Plan's age and length-of-service requirements. The Plan's age and service requirements are age 21 and one year of service, respectively. The plan has two annual entry dates: January 1st and July 1st.

HOW ARE PLAN BENEFITS FUNDED?

The Plan is funded with a combination of Company and employee contributions.

For each plan year the Company will contribute to the Plan on a participant's behalf:

(1) The amount of all elective contributions he or she made,

(2) A Company contribution of ____________% of the participant's taxable compensation paid during the year, plus

(3) A matching contribution, equal to one-half the amount he or she validly contributed as an elective contribution for the year, except that the total matching contribution a participant may receive in a year may not exceed ____________% of his or her taxable compensation for the year.

The total of (1) through (3), above is called the "total contribution."

WHAT ARE ELECTIVE CONTRIBUTIONS?

Elective contributions are amounts that a participant agrees to have withheld from his or her salary and contributed to the Plan. If an employee has been admitted to participation, he or she will receive matching contributions to his or her elective contributions as described above.

On or before ______ of a calendar year, employees who have been admitted to participation (or are expected to do so by the beginning of the next calendar year) may enter into an agreement with the Company under which part of their compensation for the next plan year will be contributed by the Company to the Plan's trust as an elective contribution in lieu of being paid to the employee in cash, subject to the limitations below.

A participant may specify what portion of his or her compensation will be contributed to the trust but it may not exceed the lesser of:

(1) $7,000 (or such higher limit as may be in effect for the plan year under Section 402(g)(1) of the Internal Revenue Code), reduced by any other elective deferrals (as defined in Code Section 402(g)(3)), or

(2) 15 percent of the participant's total compensation from the Company for the year.

*Reprinted from 352 T.M., *Pension Plans—Qualification.*

The Administrator may reduce a participant's allowable amount of elective contributions if the participant is a "highly compensated employee," so that it will not exceed the highest allowable "actual deferral percentage" allowed under Internal Revenue Code Section 401(k) for such employees for the plan year. (The Administrator may also reduce matching and Company contributions if this is necessary to satisfy applicable Internal Revenue Code requirements).

All Elective Contributions and any investment growth thereon will be fully vested and nonforfeitable at all times (as is the case with Company contributions and matching contributions).

If an amount from an employee's authorized salary in excess of that allowed is inadvertently deferred on an employee's behalf, the Administrator will, as soon as possible but in no event later than the last day of the next plan year, distribute the excess plus any investment growth thereon to the employee. These amounts will be taxed to the employee as compensation income.

Elective contributions will generally be subject to Federal employment taxes, but, in general, will not be subject to Federal or State income taxes until an employee's benefits are distributed.

WHEN DOES A PARTICIPANT'S RIGHT TO MAKE ELECTIVE CONTRIBUTIONS EXPIRE?

A participant will no longer have the right to make Elective Contributions upon the first to occur of:

(1) the participant's withdrawal from the Plan; or

(2) termination of the participant's employment with the Company.

WHEN DOES A PARTICIPANT'S RIGHT TO RECEIVE COMPANY CONTRIBUTIONS AND MATCHING CONTRIBUTIONS EXPIRE?

A participant will no longer be eligible to receive Company contributions or matching contributions for any year in which the participant has no compensation from the Company upon which a contribution may be based.

WHAT IS THE MAXIMUM TOTAL CONTRIBUTION THAT CAN BE MADE TO AN EMPLOYEE'S PLAN ACCOUNTS FOR ANY PLAN YEAR?

In no event will the total contribution to be made to all of an employee's accounts under this Plan and all qualified defined contribution plans maintained by the Company for any plan year:

(1) exceed the maximum "annual addition" that may be made to the employee's accounts under Internal Revenue Code Section 415 (in 1988 this amount was the lesser of 25% of compensation or $30,000, but the dollar limit is to be adjusted for the cost of living in future years) or

(2) with respect to Company contributions, exceed the maximum amount deductible by the Company under the applicable provisions of the Internal Revenue Code (determined as if the Company was a taxable entity).

WHAT IS THE MAXIMUM AMOUNT OF ANNUAL COMPENSATION THAT MAY BE CONSIDERED IN DETERMINING HOW MUCH MAY BE CONTRIBUTED TO AN EMPLOYEE'S PLAN ACCOUNTS?

In determining how much may be contributed to an employee's plan accounts for a year, annual compensation in excess of $200,000 will be disregarded.

WHEN DO A PARTICIPANT'S BENEFITS BECOME NONFORFEITABLE?

All amounts credited to a participant's Plan accounts will be fully vested and nonforfeitable at all times. This rule applies regardless of whether the Plan is a top-heavy plan for the plan year.

WHAT SERVICE WILL BE COUNTED IN DETERMINING AN EMPLOYEE'S PLAN BENEFITS?

An employee's service for purposes of computing benefits under the Plan is generally the total period of the employee's employment (but an employee will be entitled to no plan benefits before he or she is admitted to participation in the plan). To be credited with a year of service for participation, benefit accrual, or vesting purposes an employee must complete at least 1,000 Hours of Service during the applicable 12-month computation period.

For a new employee, the initial 12-month computation period is the 12 months immediately following his or her "employment commencement date." The "employment commencement date" is the first day in which the employee performed an "hour of service" for the Company. After an employee has completed his or her "initial eligibility computation period," service will be counted based on the plan year for eligibility purposes. If an employee completes 1,000 hours of service in both the initial computation period and the overlapping "first regular computation period," the employee will be credited with two Years of Service for eligibility purposes.

For purposes of benefit accrual and vesting, the computation period will always be the plan year.

If an employee leaves the Company and later returns to work there, he or she will be admitted to participation immediately if the employee was a participant before leaving. If the employee was not a participant before leaving, he or she will have to satisfy the Plan's eligibility requirements before being entitled to participate. For this purpose, participation after a return to work will be computed by substituting the employee's "reemployment commencement date" for the "employment commencement date" in the above formulation.

WHAT HOURS OF SERVICE WILL BE COUNTED UNDER THE PLAN?

Employees will be credited with an hour of service for:

(1) Each hour for which the employee is directly or indirectly compensated or entitled to compensation by the Company for performing duties during the applicable computation period;

(2) Each hour for which the employee is directly or indirectly compensated or entitled to compensation from the Company for reasons other than the performance of duties, such as vacation, holidays, sickness, disability, layoff, military duty or leave of absence;

(3) Each hour for which back pay is awarded to the employee or agreed to by the Company, without regard to mitigation of damages.

Notwithstanding the above rules:

(1) No more than 501 hours of service must be credited to an employee on account of any continuous period during which the employee performs no duties (regardless of whether this occurs in a single computation period);

(2) Any hour for which the employee is directly or indirectly paid or entitled to payment on account of a period during which no duties are performed will not be credited to the employee if the payment is made or due under a plan maintained solely for the purpose of complying with applicable workers' compensation or unemployment compensation or disability insurance law; and

(3) Hours of service do not have to be credited for a payment which solely reimburses an employee for medical or medically-related expenses.

For purposes of these rules, a payment will be considered to be made by, or due from, the Company regardless of whether it is made by or due from the Company directly or indirectly through, among others, mediums such as a trust, fund, or insurer to which the Company contributes or pays premiums and regardless of whether contributions made or due to such trust, fund, or other entity are for the benefit of particular employees or are on behalf of a group of employees.

An hour of service must be counted for purposes of determining:

(1) a year of service,

(2) a one-year break in service, (if applicable) and

(3) an employee's employment commencement date (or reemployment commencement date).

Department of Labor Regulations 29 C.F.R. Section 2530.200b-2(b) and (c) are incorporated herein by reference.

Hours of service will be credited for employment with other members of an affiliated service group (under Internal Revenue Code Section 414(m)), a controlled group of corporations (under Code Section 414(b)), or a group of trades or businesses under common control (under Code Section 414(c)), of which the Company is a member.

Hours of service will also be credited for any individual considered an employee under Code Section 414(n).

Notwithstanding the above rules, hours of service will be credited to an individual who is absent from work for maternity or paternity reasons as described below.

Solely for purposes of determining whether a break in service for participation and vesting purposes has occurred in a computation period, an employee who is absent from work for maternity or paternity reasons will receive credit for hours of service which would otherwise have been credited to the employee but for such absence or, in any case in which such hours cannot be determined, eight hours of service per day of such absence.

For purposes of this rule, an absence from work for maternity or paternity reasons means an absence:

(1) by reason of the pregnancy of the employee,

(2) by reason of a birth of a child of the employee,

(3) by reason of the placement of a child with the employee in connection with the adoption of such child by the employee, or

(4) for purposes of caring for such child for a period beginning immediately following such birth or placement.

The hours of service credited under this provision shall be credited:

(1) in the computation period in which the absence begins if the crediting is necessary to prevent a break in service for that period, or

(2) in all other cases, in the following computation period.

WHAT IS A YEAR OF SERVICE?

A year of service is a 12-month computation period during which an employee completes at least 1,000 hours of service.

WHEN MAY AN EMPLOYEE MAKE IN-SERVICE WITHDRAWALS FROM HIS OR HER MY PLAN ACCOUNTS?

An employee may not make withdrawals from his or her Plan accounts (other than hardship withdrawals as described below) until the employee qualifies for benefit payments under the Plan. There are no exceptions to this rule, so employees may wish to consider this in deciding whether, and to what extent, to make employee contributions.

WHEN MAY A PARTICIPANT RECEIVE A HARDSHIP WITHDRAWAL?

If a participant suffers a financial hardship, as defined below, the participant may request a withdrawal from his or her Plan accounts. This request must be made in writing to the Administrator, and must set forth the amount requested and the facts establishing the existence of such hardship. When the Administrator receives such a request, the Administrator will determine whether a financial hardship exists. If the Administrator determines that a hardship does exist, the Administrator will next determine what portion of the amount requested is needed to meet the need created by the hardship, and will direct the trustees to distribute to the participant this amount.

A "financial hardship" includes any financial need arising from:

(1) the education of a dependent of the participant,

(2) the purchase of a primary residence for the participant,

(3) major medical expenses the participant or a dependent of the participant incurs if the expenses are not covered by insurance, or

(4) any other cause which, in the Administrator's judgment, has produced an immediate and heavy financial need.

No hardship distribution may be made after December 31, 1988 from any income allocable to elective contributions (or, to the extent provided in regulations, from any Company contributions, matching contributions, or income allocable thereto).

WHAT IS THE DEFINITION OF DISABILITY FOR PURPOSES OF DETERMINING ELIGIBILITY FOR DISABILITY RETIREMENT BENEFITS?

"Disability" means the inability to engage in any substantial gainful activity, considering the employee's age, education, and work experience, by reason of any medically determined physical or mental impairment which can be expected to result in death or which can be expected to last for a continuous period of not less than 12 months.

If an employee seeks to receive disability retirement benefits, the Company may require the employee to submit proof of disability before beginning to make disability retirement benefit payments. This may include a requirement that the employee submit to a medical examination by a qualified physician selected by the Company. The Company may also require that, as a condition of continuing to receive disability retirement benefits, the employee submit proof of the continuing nature of the disability. This may include requiring the employee to submit to a physical examination by a physician selected by the Company. Such an examination cannot be required more frequently than annually.

If an employee is receiving disability retirement benefits and the disability ceases, Plan benefit payments will stop until the employee again qualifies for benefit payments under the provisions of the Plan.

WHAT IS EARLY RETIREMENT AGE UNDER THE PLAN?

"Early Retirement Age" means, before your Normal Retirement Date:

(1) If an employee was hired by the Company before the Effective Date of this Plan, the later of attaining age 55 or completing six years of participation,

(2) If an employee was hired by the Company after the Effective Date of this Plan, the later of attaining age 55 or completing 10 years of participation.

WHAT EARLY RETIREMENT BENEFITS WILL AN EMPLOYEE BE ENTITLED TO?

If an employee is eligible for early retirement, the employee will receive a retirement benefit based on the balance of the employee's Plan accounts at the time the employee takes early retirement.

WHAT IS NORMAL RETIREMENT AGE UNDER THE PLAN?

Normal retirement age is the later of:

(1) the employee's 65th birthday,

(2) if the employee begin participation at age 60 or over, the fifth anniversary of the date the employee began participation; or

(3) if the employee did not begin participation at age 60 or over, the 10th anniversary of the date the employee began participation.

WHAT IS THE NORMAL RETIREMENT BENEFIT PROVIDED UNDER THE PLAN?

The normal retirement benefit provided under the Plan is based on the employee's balance in the employee's Plan accounts when the employee retires under the normal retirement provisions of the Plan.

MAY AN EMPLOYEE CONTINUE TO EARN BENEFITS IF HE OR SHE REMAINS EMPLOYED AFTER REACHING NORMAL RETIREMENT AGE?

Yes. The employee will continue to earn benefits so long as the employee is employed with the Company. There is no maximum retirement age under the Plan. Employees are subject to whatever rules the Company has adopted concerning compulsory retirement.

WHAT DEATH BENEFITS ARE PROVIDED UNDER THE PLAN?

If the employee dies before the distribution of the employee's accounts has been completed, the employee's designated beneficiary will be entitled to receive the value of the employee's Plan accounts, including the proceeds of any life insurance contract held by the Plan on the employee's life.

Distribution to the beneficiary will be made in accordance with the applicable provisions of the Plan and a non-spousal beneficiary (or a spousal beneficiary if the participant and the participant's spouse have voluntarily waived the qualified joint and survivor annuity or preretirement survivor annuity form of benefit, whichever applies) may elect to receive such death benefits in accordance with any optional mode of benefit payment provided under the Plan, subject to certain minimum distribution requirements set forth in the Plan.

If the employee's spouse is entitled to "qualified joint and survivor annuity" or a "preretirement survivor annuity," such annuity will be offset against the amount which the employee's beneficiary would otherwise be entitled to receive as a death benefit to the extent necessary to satisfy IRS requirements concerning "incidental" death benefits.

If a participant is married at the time of death, the participant will be deemed to have designated his or her surviving spouse as beneficiary unless:

(1) before death, the participant designated as his or her beneficiary someone other than the surviving spouse, in writing at such time and in manner as the Administrator prescribes; and

(2) either: (i) the surviving spouse consents in writing to the designation described in (1) above, and such consent acknowledges the effect of such designation and the specific non-spouse beneficiary or authorizes the participant to designate Beneficiaries without further consent, and such consent is witnessed by a Plan representative or a notary public, or (ii) the participant establishes that the consent required under (i) above may not be obtained because there is no spouse, because the spouse cannot be located, or because of certain other circumstances which the IRS may specify and,

(3) such non-spouse beneficiary survives the participant.

Any consent by a spouse under (2)(i) above, or a determination by the Administrator with respect to such spouse under (2)(ii) above, will only apply to that spouse. Any such consent shall be irrevocable, but will only apply to the specific beneficiary designation unless the consent expressly permits the participant to make designations without any further consent.

If an employee is not married, he or she may designate a beneficiary in writing at such time and in such manner as the Administrator prescribes.

If an employee has designated a beneficiary, the employee may change his or her designation at any time by giving written notice to the Administrator, subject certain conditions as specified in the Plan.

If an employee dies without a surviving spouse or other designated beneficiary, the full amount payable upon the employee's death will be paid to the employee's children (if any). If any of the employee's children is a minor, the trustees may deposit such minor's share in a savings account to the minor's credit in a savings bank or other financial institution for his or her benefit. If there are no surviving children, the amount may be paid to the employee's executor or administrator or applied to the payment of the employee's debts and funeral expenses, all as the Administrator shall determine.

WHAT METHODS ARE AVAILABLE FOR PAYMENT OF PLAN BENEFITS?

The normal method of payment of an employee's benefit at retirement is a "qualified joint and survivor annuity" if the employee is married. An employee may elect "out" of qualified joint and survivor annuity retirement benefits and select another available form of benefit during the "applicable election period" if he or she does so in writing and such election is accompanied by a waiver of joint and survivor benefits by the employee's spouse that satisfies certain criterion.

A qualified joint and survivor annuity is, basically, an annuity for the employee's life or life expectancy followed by, upon the employee's death, an annuity for the life or life expectancy of the employee's spouse calling for payments of 50% to 100% (50% in this Plan unless elected otherwise) of the amounts that were payable during the spouses' joint lives.

If an employee is not married and makes no election to the contrary, the normal form of retirement benefit will be a life annuity.

A "preretirement survivor annuity" is a benefit that is similar to the qualified joint and survivor annuity, except that it is payable upon an employee's death if the employee was still employed with the Company at the time of death and had earned a vested benefit under the Plan.

Specifically, a "preretirement survivor annuity" is a survivor annuity for the life of the employee's surviving spouse, the actuarial equivalent of which is not less than 50% of the employee's benefit as of the date of the employee's death. If an employee has earned a benefit but dies before becoming entitled to payments, the normal form of benefit will be a preretirement survivor annuity.

This presumption in favor of preretirement survivor annuity benefits does not apply if an employee is not married. Further, as is the case with the qualified joint and survivor annuity, an employee may elect "out" of receiving benefits in this form if the employee makes a valid election during the applicable election period and this election is accompanied by a valid written waiver of the right to receive preretirement survivor annuity benefits by the employee's spouse.

If the joint and survivor or preretirement survivor annuity requirements apply to an employee, the employee's retirement benefits will be paid in this form unless the employee elects not to receive benefits in this form and the employee's spouse joins the employee in a valid written waiver of the right to receive such benefits.

Where the qualified joint and survivor annuity or the preretirement survivor annuity requirements either do not apply or have been the subject of a valid election "out" accompanied by a spousal waiver, the employee may choose to receive benefits in one of the optional forms described below in the section on optional forms of benefits. All optional benefit forms are the actuarial equivalent of the regular benefit form to which an employee would otherwise be entitled.

WHAT IS THE APPLICABLE ELECTION PERIOD FOR ELECTING "OUT" OF QUALIFIED JOINT AND SURVIVOR OR PRERETIREMENT SURVIVOR ANNUITY BENEFITS?

For electing "out" of qualified joint and survivor annuity benefits, the applicable election period is the 90-day period ending on the employee's "annuity starting date" (the first day of the first period during which annuity benefits are payable — thus, if a monthly annuity were payable, an employee's annuity starting date would be the first day of the first month during which annuity payments were received).

For electing "out" of preretirement survivor annuity benefits, the applicable election period begins on the first day of the plan year in which an employee attains age 35 and ends on the employee's date of death, provided that, if the employee leaves the Company, the applicable election period will begin on the date the employee left the Company with respect to benefits earned before the employee left.

The Administrator will provide each employee with information explaining the effect of electing "in" or "out" of qualified joint and survivor and/or preretirement survivor annuity benefits.

WHAT OPTIONAL FORMS OF BENEFIT PAYMENT ARE OFFERED UNDER THE PLAN?

Optional benefit forms offered under this Plan are:

(1) A single payment of the employee's entire benefit;

(2) Payments in substantially equal installments over a fixed period that may not exceed the employee's life expectancy or the joint and last survivor expectancy of the employee and the employee's beneficiary (if death benefits are being paid, the fixed period may not exceed the beneficiary's life expectancy);

(3) Payments in the form of a joint and survivor annuity with the survivor portion equal to 50%, 75% or 100% of the amount payable during the employee's life. If this option is elected, and the employee's beneficiary is not the employee's spouse, the present value of installments payable to the beneficiary may not be greater than 50% of the present value of all installments to be paid.

WHEN WILL RETIREMENT BENEFITS BE DISTRIBUTED?

Retirement benefit distributions will begin no later than the 60th day after the close of the plan year in which the employee incurs a disability, separates from the Company's service, or attains early, normal, or actual retirement age, whichever applies, unless the employee elects in writing to have distributions commence later. Regardless of any election an employee may have made, however, payment of retirement benefits will begin no later than the April 1 next following the later of:

(1) the close of the calendar year in which the employee reaches age 70-1/2, or

(2) the earlier of December 31, 1988 or the close of the calendar year in which the employee retires.

Under a special rule, no distribution will be made before an employee incurs a disability, or attains early or normal retirement age (or actual retirement age, if later), whichever applies, unless:

(1) the Administrator obtains the employee's prior written consent to the distribution, or

(2) the value of all of the employee's accounts under this Plan does not exceed $3,500.

If an employee's consent is required but is not provided before distributions are to begin, distributions will begin within 60 days after the earliest of:

(1) The employee's incurring a disability, or reaching early, normal, or actual retirement date, whichever applies, or

(2) the date the Administrator is notified of the employee's death.

WHEN WILL POST-DEATH DISTRIBUTIONS BE MADE?

Distributions at death will be made of any remaining amounts to an employee's credit to the employee's beneficiary, in accordance with the following requirements.

(1) If the employee dies before payment of benefits begin, distributions must either: (a) be made in their entirety within five years after the participant's death, or (b) be made over a period not extending beyond the recipient's life expectancy.

(2) If a participant dies after his or her benefits have commenced, but before distribution has been completed, the remaining benefits will be distributed at least as rapidly as under the method of distribution under which the participant was receiving benefits as of the date of death.

WHEN WILL THE PLAN BE CONSIDERED TO BE TOP-HEAVY AND WHAT ARE THE CONSEQUENCES OF THIS?

This Plan will be top-heavy for a plan year if, as of the "determination date" (the last day of the preceding plan year), more than 60% of the Plan's benefits are held for the benefit of certain highly-compensated individuals and officers known as "key employees." If this Plan is top-heavy for a plan year, each non-key employee will receive a Company contribution on their behalf to the Plan equal to 3% of his or her compensation, except that, if the highest contribution percentage for all key employees for the year is less than 3%, each non-key employee will receive only the percentage of his or her compensation that corresponds to the highest percentage of compensation allocated to the account of any key employee for the year. If non-key employees are already receiving benefits under the Plan, the required top-heavy contribution will be reduced dollar-for-dollar by any such contributions in accordance with Treasury regulations. Further, if a non-key employee participates in more than one qualified plan maintained by the Company, the Company will only have to provide such employee with minimum contributions (or minimum benefits if the other plan is a defined benefit pension plan) for any top-heavy plan year under one plan, even if both plans are top-heavy, to the extent permitted under IRS regulations.

IS A PARTICIPANT'S INTEREST IN TRUST SUBJECT TO CREDITORS' CLAIMS?

Except to the extent required by law, none of the benefits, payments, proceeds, or rights of any participant under the Plan will be subject to the claims of creditors, or to attachment or garnishment or other legal process, or to alienation, sale, transfer, pledge, encumbrance, or assignment, and the attempt by a participant to alienate, sell, transfer, pledge, encumber, or assign any of the benefits, payments, or proceeds which he or she may expect to receive under the Plan shall be void. This rule will also apply to the creation, assignment, or recognition of a right to any benefit payable with respect to a participant under a domestic relations order unless such order is determined to be a "qualified domestic relations order" (as defined in Internal Revenue Code Section 414(p)).

MAY THE COMPANY AMEND OR TERMINATE THE PLAN?

Yes. The provisions of this Plan are subject to change at the sole discretion of the Company and the Company reserves the right to terminate the Plan at any time. The Company, however, intends the Plan to be a permanent program and that any changes, required by law or otherwise, will not deprive any employee of any benefit to which he or she had become entitled unless such benefit mav be reduced in accordance with the Employee Retirement Income Security Act of 1974, as amended.

WHAT ARE THE PLAN'S CLAIMS AND REVIEW PROCEDURES?

(a) *Claims Procedure.* If an employee (or beneficiary) believes he or she is being denied any rights or benefits under the Plan, such individual may file a claim in writing with the Administrator. If any such claim is wholly or partially denied, the Administrator will notify the claimant of the decision in writing. Such notification will contain:

(1) specific reasons for the denial,

(2) specific reference to pertinent plan provisions,

(3) a description of any additional material or information necessary for the claimant to perfect the claim and an explanation of why such material or information is necessary, and

(4) information as to the steps to be taken if the claimant wishes to submit a request for review.

Such notification will be given within 90 days after the claim is received by the Administrator (or within 180 days, if special circumstances require an extension of time for processing the claim, and if written notice of such extension and circumstances is given to the claimant within the initial 90-day period). If such notification is not given within such period, the claim will be considered denied as of the last day of such period and the claimant may request a review of the claim.

(b) *Review Procedure.* Within 60 days after the date on which a claimant receives written notice of a denied claim (or, if applicable, within 60 days after the date on which such denial is considered to have occurred) the claimant (or the claimant's authorized representative) may:

(1) file a written request with the Administrator for a review of the denied claim and of pertinent documents, and

(2) submit written issues and comments to the Administrator.

The Administrator will notify the claimant of the decision on a claim in writing. Such notification will be written in a manner calculated to be understood by persons with no specialized knowledge about employee benefit plans and will contain specific reasons for the decision as well as specific references to pertinent plan provisions. The decision on review will be made within 60 days after the request for review is received by the Administrator (or within 120 days, if special circumstances require an extension of time for processing the request, such as an election by the Administrator to hold a hearing, and if written notice of such extension and circumstances is given to the claimant within the initial 60-day period). If the decision on review is not made within such period, the claim will be considered denied.

WHAT ARE THE RIGHTS OF PARTICIPANTS AND BENEFICIARIES?

Participants and beneficiaries in this Plan are entitled to certain rights and protections under the Employee Retirement Income Security Act of 1974 (ERISA), as amended. Title I of ERISA generally applies to plans as to which the employer or the employees have the necessary connection with interstate commerce.

Title I of ERISA provides that all plan participants are entitled to:

(1) Examine, without charge, at the plan administrator's office and at other locations such as worksites and union halls, all plan documents, including insurance contracts, collective bargaining agreements, and copies of all documents filed with by the plan administrator with the U.S. Department of Labor, such as annual reports and plan descriptions.

(2) Obtain written copies of all plan documents and other plan information upon written request to the plan administrator. The administrator may make a reasonable charge for these copies.

(3) Receive a summary of the plan's annual financial report. The plan administrator is required by law to furnish each participant with a copy of this summary annual report.

(4) Obtain, once a year, a statement of the total plan benefits accrued and non-forfeitable (vested), if any, or the earliest date on which benefits will become non-forfeitable (vested). The plan may require a written request for this statement, but it must provide the statement free of charge.

In addition to creating rights for plan participants, Title I of ERISA imposes duties upon the people who are responsible for the operation of the plan. The people who operate this Plan, called "fiduciaries" of the plan, have a duty to do so prudently and in the interest of plan participants and beneficiaries.

No one, including the Company, a union, or any other person may fire someone or otherwise discriminate against them in any way to prevent someone from obtaining a plan benefit or exercising their rights under ERISA.

As previously indicated, if a claim for a plan benefit is denied in whole or in part, the claimant must receive a written explanation of the reason for the denial. Also, as indicated above, if a claim is denied in whole or in part, the claimant has the right to have the plan review and reconsider the claim.

Under Title I of ERISA there are steps that individuals can take to enforce the above rights. For instance, if an individual entitled to such materials requests materials from the plan administrator and does not receive them within 30 days, the individual may file a suit in a federal court. In such a case, the court may require the plan administrator to provide the materials and pay the individual up to $100 a day until he or she receives the materials, unless the materials were not sent because of reasons beyond the control of the administrator. If an individual has a claim for benefits which is ignored in whole or in part, such individual may file suit in a state or federal court. The court will decide who should pay court costs and legal fees. If the claimant is successful the court may order the person sued to pay these costs and fees. If the claimant loses, the court may order the claimant to pay these costs and fees, for example, if it finds the claim is frivolous.

If employees or their beneficiaries have any questions about this plan, they should consult the plan administrator.

If employee or beneficiaries have any questions about this statement or their rights under ERISA, they should contact the plan administrator or the nearest Area Office of the U.S. Labor-Management Services Administration, Department of Labor.

Appendix B

IRS Forms

Form **5300** (Rev. August 1988)
Department of the Treasury
Internal Revenue Service

Application for Determination for Defined Benefit Plan

For Pension Plans Other Than Money Purchase Plans
(Under sections 401(a) and 501(a) of the Internal Revenue Code)

OMB No. 1545-0197
Expires 6-30-91

For IRS Use Only
File folder number ▶
Case number ▶

▶ Church and governmental plans not subject to ERISA need not complete lines 10, 11, 12b, 12c, and 15.
▶ **Caution:** All other plans must complete all lines except as indicated on specific lines. For example, if you answer "No" to line 7, you need not complete lines 7a and 7b since they require responses only if you answer "Yes" to line 7. N/A is only an acceptable answer if an N/A block is provided. All applications are now computer screened, therefore it is important that you provide all the information requested and have the application signed by the employer, plan administrator, or authorized representative. Otherwise, we may need to correspond with you or return your application for completion, which will delay its processing.

1 a Name of plan sponsor (employer if single employer plan)
1 b Employer identification no.
Address (number and street)
1 c Employer's tax year ends
Month ☐ N/A
City or town, state, and ZIP code
Telephone number
(   )

2 Person to be contacted if more information is needed (see Specific Instructions). If same as 1a, enter "same as 1a."
Name
Telephone number
(   )
Address

3 a Determination requested for (check applicable box(es)): See Instruction B. "What To File."
(i) ☐ Initial qualification—Date plan signed .... Date plan effective ....
(ii) ☐ Amendment after initial qualification—Is plan restated? ☐ Yes ☐ No Date amendment signed ....
Date amendment effective .... Date plan effective ....
(iii) ☐ Affiliated service group status (section 414(m))— Date effective .... Date plan effective ....
(iv) ☐ Partial termination— Date effective .... Date plan effective ....
b Enter IRS file folder number shown on the last determination letter issued to the plan sponsor .... ☐ N/A
c Is this application also expected to satisfy the notice requirement for this plan for merger, consolidation, or transfer of plan assets or liabilities involving another plan? See Specific Instructions. . . . . ☐ Yes ☐ No
d Were employees who are interested parties given the required notification of the filing of this application? . . . . ☐ Yes ☐ No
e Is this plan or trust currently under examination, or is any issue related to this plan or trust currently pending before the Internal Revenue Service, the Department of Labor, the Pension Benefit Guaranty Corporation, or any court?. . . . ☐ Yes ☐ No
If "Yes," attach explanation.

4 a Name of plan
b Plan number ▶ ....
c Plan year ends ▶

5 Are there other qualified plans? (Do not consider plans that were established under union-negotiated agreements that involved other employers.) . . . . ☐ Yes ☐ No
If "Yes," enter for each other qualified plan you maintain:
a Name of plan ▶ ....
b Type of plan ▶ ....
c Rate of employer contribution ▶ .... ☐ N/A
d Allocation formula ▶ .... ☐ N/A
e Benefit formula or monthly benefit ▶ .... ☐ N/A
f Number of participants ▶

6 Type of entity (check only one box). (If **b**, **c**, or **d** is checked, see instructions.):
a ☐ Corporation **b** ☐ Subchapter S corporation **c** ☐ Sole proprietor **d** ☐ Partnership
e ☐ Tax exempt organization **f** ☐ Church **g** ☐ Governmental organization
h ☐ Other (specify) ▶

7 Is this an adoption of a master or prototype plan? . . . . ☐ Yes ☐ No
If "Yes," complete **a** and **b**.
a Name of plan
b Notification letter no.

8 a Type of plan: (i) ☐ Fixed benefit (ii) ☐ Unit benefit
(iii) ☐ Flat benefit (iv) ☐ Other (specify) ▶
b Does plan provide for variable benefits? . . . . ☐ Yes ☐ No
c Is this a defined benefit plan covered under the Pension Benefit Guaranty Corporation insurance program? . . . . ☐ Yes ☐ No ☐ Not determined

Under penalties of perjury, I declare that I have examined this application, including accompanying statements, and to the best of my knowledge and belief, it is true, correct, and complete.

Signature **Title** **Date**

For Paperwork Reduction Act Notice, see page 1 of the instructions.
Form **5300** (Rev. 8-88)

Form 5300 (Rev. 8-88) Page **2**

(Section references are to the Internal Revenue Code, unless otherwise noted.)

Where applicable, indicate the article or section and page number of the plan or trust where the following provisions are contained. N/A (not applicable) is an appropriate response only if an "N/A" block is provided.

		Section and Page Number
9 a	General eligibility requirements: (Check box (i), (ii), (iii), or (iv), and complete (v), (vi), and (vii).) (i) ☐ All employees (ii) ☐ Hourly rate employees only (iii) ☐ Salaried employees only (iv) ☐ Other (specify) ▶ (v) Length of service (number of years) ▶ ☐ N/A (vi) Minimum age (specify) ▶ ☐ N/A (vii) Maximum age (specify) ▶ ☐ N/A	
b	Does any plan amendment since the last determination letter change the method of crediting service for eligibility? ☐ Yes ☐ No ☐ N/A	

10	Participation (see Specific Instructions):	**Yes**	**No**	**Not certain**
a (i)	Is the employer a member of an affiliated service group? If your answer is "No," go to 10b.			
(ii)	Did a prior ruling letter rule on what organizations were members of the employer's affiliated service group, or did the employer receive a determination letter on this plan that considered the effect of section 414(m) on this plan?			
(iii)	If (ii) is "Yes," have the facts on which that letter was based materially changed?			
b	Is the employer a member of a controlled group of corporations or a group of trades or businesses under common control?			

11	Coverage of plan at (give date) .... (Attach Form(s) 5302 as necessary—see instructions.) (If the employer is a member of an affiliated service group, controlled group of corporations, or a group of trades or businesses under common control, employees of all members of the group must be considered in completing the following schedule.)		**Number** Enter "0" if N/A
a	Total employed (see Specific Instructions) (include all self-employed individuals)		
b	Statutory exclusions under this plan (do not count an employee more than once):		
	(i) Number excluded because of age or years of service required		
	(ii) Number excluded because of employees included in collective bargaining		
	(iii) Number of other employees excluded (specify)		
c	Total statutory exclusions under this plan (add lines b(i) through (iii))		
d	Employees not excluded under the statute (subtract line c from line a)		
e	Other employees ineligible under terms of this plan (do not count an employee included in line b)		
f	Employees eligible to participate (subtract line e from line d)		
g	Number of employees participating in this plan		
h	Percent of nonexcluded employees who are participating (divide line g by line d) If line h is 70% or more, go to line k.	%	
i	Percent of nonexcluded employees who are eligible to participate (divide line f by line d)	%	
j	Percent of eligible employees who are participating (divide line g by line f) If lines h and i are less than 70% or line j is less than 80%, see Specific Instructions and attach schedule of information.	%	
k	Total number of participants in this plan (include certain retired and terminated employees (see Specific Instructions))		
l	Has a plan amendment since the last determination letter resulted in exclusion of previously covered employees? ☐ Yes ☐ No ☐ N/A		

12	Does the plan define the following terms:	**Yes**	**No**	**N/A**	**Section and Page Number**
a	Compensation (earned income if applicable)?				
b	Break in service?				
c	Hour of service (under Department of Labor Regulations)?				
d	Joint and survivor annuity?				
e	Normal retirement age?				
f	Year of service?				
g	Entry date?				

		Yes	No	N/A	Section and Page Number
13	Employee contributions:				
a	(i) Does the plan document allow voluntary deductible employee contributions?				
	(ii) If "Yes," are the voluntary deductible employee contributions appropriately limited?				
b	Are voluntary nondeductible contributions limited for all qualified plans to 10% or less of compensation?				
c	Are employee contributions nonforfeitable?				
14	Integration: Is this plan integrated with social security or railroad retirement? If "Yes," attach a schedule of compliance with Rev. Rul. 71-446 (see Specific Instructions).				
15	Vesting:				
a	Are years of service with other members of a controlled group of corporations, trades or businesses under common control, or an affiliated service group counted for vesting and eligibility to participate?				
b	Is employee's right to normal retirement benefits nonforfeitable on reaching normal retirement age as defined in section 411(a)(8)?				
c	Does any amendment to the plan decrease any participant's accrued benefit?				
d	Does any amendment to the plan directly or indirectly affect the computation of the nonforfeitable percentage of a participant's accrued benefit?				
e	Does the plan preclude forfeiture of an employee's vested benefits for cause?				
f	Check only one of these boxes to indicate the vesting provisions of the plan: (i) ☐ Full and immediate. (ii) ☐ Full vesting after 10 years of service, i.e., no vesting for the first 9 years, 100% vesting after 10 years (section 411(a)(2)(A)). (iii) ☐ 5- to 15-year vesting (section 411(a)(2)(B)). (iv) ☐ Rule of 45 (section 411(a)(2)(C)). (v) ☐ 4/40 vesting (Rev. Procs. 75-49 and 76-11). (vi) ☐ 10% vesting for each year of service (not to exceed 100%). (vii) ☐ Other (specify—see Specific Instructions and attach schedule).				
16	Administration:				
a	Type of funding entity: (i) ☐ Trust (benefits provided in whole from trust funds). (ii) ☐ Custodial account described in section 401(f) and not included in (iv) below. (iii) ☐ Trust or arrangement providing benefits partially through insurance and/or annuity contracts. (iv) ☐ Trust arrangement providing benefits exclusively through insurance and/or annuity contracts. (v) ☐ Other (specify) ►				
b	Does the trust agreement prohibit reversion of funds to the employer (Rev. Rul. 77-200)?				
17	Benefits and requirements for benefits:				
a	Normal retirement age is ► ...... If applicable, years of service/participation required				
b	Does the plan contain an early retirement provision?				
	If "Yes," (i) Early retirement age is ►				
	(ii) Years of service/participation required ►				
c	Does the plan provide for payment of benefits according to section 401(a)(14)?				
d	Method of determining accrued benefit ►				
	(i) Benefit formula at normal retirement age is ►				
	(ii) Benefit formula at early retirement age is ►				
	(iii) Normal form of retirement benefits is ►				
e	Does the plan comply with the payment of benefits provisions of section 401(a)(11)?				
f	Are benefits under the plan definitely determinable at all times (section 401(a)(25))?				
g	Are benefits computed on the basis of total compensation? If "No," see instructions and attach schedule.				
h	If participants may withdraw their mandatory contributions or earnings, may withdrawal be made without forfeiting vested benefits based on employer contributions?				

Form 5300 (Rev. 8-88) Page 4

		Yes	No	N/A	Section and Page Number
17	Benefits and requirements for benefits—*(Continued)*				
i	Does the plan disregard service attributable to a distribution in computing the employer-derived accrued benefit?				
j	If line i is "Yes," does the plan contain provisions that satisfy Regulations section 1.411(a)-7(d)(4) or (6)?				
k	Are distributions limited so that no more than incidental death benefits are provided?				
l	Does the plan provide for maximum limitation under section 415?				
m	Does the plan meet the requirements of section 401(a)(12)?				
n	Does the plan prohibit the assignment or alienation of benefits?				
o	Does the plan prohibit distribution of benefits except for retirement, disability, death, plan termination, or termination of employment?				
p	As a result of a plan amendment, has the amount of benefit or rate of accrual of the benefit been reduced?				
18	Termination of plan or trust:				
a	Are the participants' rights to benefits under the plan nonforfeitable (to the extent funded) on termination or partial termination of the plan?				
b	Has the early termination rule been included in the plan (Regulations section 1.401-4(c))?				

Caution: The following Procedural Requirements Checklist identifies certain basic data that will facilitate the processing of your application. While no response is required to the questions, you may find that answering them will ensure that your application is processed without the need for contact to obtain missing information. If the answer to any of the questions is "No," your application is incomplete. Incomplete applications are identified through a computer screening system for return to the applicant. **This checksheet should be detached before submitting the application.**

Procedural Requirements Checklist

	Yes	No	N/A
1 General requirements			
a If this application is made by a representative on behalf of the employer or plan administrator, has a current power of attorney been submitted with this application (see "Signature" under General Information)?			
b If notices or other communications are to be sent to someone other than the employer, have you provided proper authorization by attaching a completed **Form 2848**, Power of Attorney and Declaration of Representative, or by attaching a statement that contains all the information required (see Specific Instructions)?			
c Have you completed and attached Form(s) 5302?			
d Have you signed the application?			
e Have you completed and attached Schedule T (Form 5300)?			
2 Specific requirements			
a If this is a request for a determination letter on initial qualification of the plan, have the following documents been attached:			
(i) Copies of all instruments constituting the plan?			
(ii) Copies of trust indentures, group annuity contracts, or custodial agreements?			
b If this is a request for a determination letter on the effect of an amendment on the plan after initial qualification, have the following documents been attached:			
(i) A copy of the plan amendment(s)?			
(ii) A description of the amendment covering the changes to the plan sections?			
(iii) An explanation of the plan sections before the amendment?			
(iv) An explanation of the effect of the amendment on the provisions of the plan?			
c If this is a request for a determination letter on the qualification of the entire plan, as amended after initial qualification, have the following documents been included:			
(i) A copy of the plan incorporating all amendments made to the date of the application?			
(ii) A statement indicating that the copy of the plan is complete in all respects and that a determination letter is being requested on the qualification of the entire plan?			
(iii) A copy of trust indentures, group annuity contracts, or custodial agreements if there has been any change since copies were last furnished to IRS?			
d For partial termination:			
(i) Have you completed line 3a according to the Specific Instructions?			
(ii) Have you attached the information requested for a partial termination in General Instruction B?			
e For a plan adopted by one or more members of a controlled group:			
(i) Have you attached the statements requested in the Specific Instructions for line 10b?			
(ii) Have you completed line 11 according to General Instruction B and the Specific Instructions?			
f For a multiple-employer plan that does not involve collective bargaining:			
(i) Have you submitted one fully completed application (Form 5300 or 5301, whichever is appropriate) for all adopting employers?			
(ii) Have you attached a Form 5300 or 5301 (as applicable) with only lines 1 through 11 completed, and a Form 5302 for each employer who adopted the plan?			
g For a plan that contains a cash or deferred arrangement, have you submitted the appropriate information requested for line 11?			
h For governmental and church plans, have you completed Form 5300 or 5301 according to General Instruction B?			
i For notice of merger, consolidation, or transfer of plan assets or liabilities, have you submitted the information requested in the Specific Instructions for line 3c?			
j For a plan that is or may be sponsored by a member of an affiliated service group:			
(i) Have you completed lines 3a, 10, and 11 according to the Specific Instructions?			
(ii) Have you attached the information requested in the Specific Instructions for lines 10a(ii) and (iii)?			
3 Miscellaneous requirements:			
a Have you entered the plan sponsor's 9-digit employer identification number on line 1b?			
b If a determination letter was previously issued to this sponsor for any plan, have you entered the file folder number on line 3b?			
c Have you answered line 3d?			
d If this plan has been amended at least four times since the last determination letter on the entire plan was issued, have you attached a copy of the plan that includes all amendments made to the plan since that determination letter was issued?			
e Have you entered the effective date of the plan in the space provided by the block you checked for line 3a?			
f If applicable, have you attached schedules or other documentation required by:			
(i) Form 5300, lines 2, 3e, 6, 11j, 14, 15f(vii), and 17g?			
(ii) Form 5301, lines 2, 3e, 11j, 14, 15f(viii), 17k, 17l, 17m, and 17s?			

Form **5301** (Rev. August 1988)
Department of the Treasury
Internal Revenue Service

Application for Determination for Defined Contribution Plan

For Profit-sharing, Stock Bonus and Money Purchase Plans

(Under Sections 401(a), 401(k), and 501(a) of the Internal Revenue Code)

OMB No. 1545-0197
Expires 6-30-91

For IRS Use Only
File folder number ▶
Case number ▶

Caution: Church and governmental plans not subject to ERISA need not complete items 10, 11, 12b, 12c, 15, 17g, 17l, and 18b. All other plans must complete all items except as indicated on specific lines. For example, if you answer "No" to line 7, you need not complete lines 7a and 7b since they require responses only if you answer "Yes" to line 7. N/A is only an acceptable answer if an N/A block is provided. All applications are now computer screened, therefore it is important that you provide all the information requested and have the application signed by the employer, plan administrator, or authorized representative. Otherwise, we may need to correspond with you or return your application for completion, which will delay its processing.

1 a Name of plan sponsor (employer if a single employer plan)
Address (number and street)
City or town, state and ZIP code

1b Employer identification number

1c Employer's tax year ends
Month ☐ N/A
Telephone number
( )

2 Person to be contacted if more information is needed (If same as 1a, enter "same as 1a"). (See Specific Instructions.)
Name
Address
Telephone number
( )

3 a Determination requested for (check applicable boxes): (See Instruction B. "What To File.")
- *(i)* ☐ Initial qualification—Date plan signed ________ Date plan effective ________
- *(ii)* ☐ Amendment after initial qualification—Is plan restated? ☐ Yes ☐ No Date amendment signed ________
  Date amendment effective ________ Date plan effective ________
- *(iii)* ☐ Affiliated service group status (section 414(m))—Date effective ________ Date plan effective ________
- *(iv)* ☐ Partial termination—Date effective ________ Date plan effective ________

b Enter IRS file folder number shown on the last determination letter issued to the plan sponsor ________ ☐ N/A

c Is this application also expected to satisfy the notice requirement for this plan for merger, consolidation, or transfer of plan assets or liabilities involving another plan? (See Specific Instructions.) . . . ☐ Yes ☐ No

d Were employees who are interested parties given the required notification of the filing of this application? . . ☐ Yes ☐ No

e Is this plan or trust currently under examination or is any issue related to this plan or trust currently pending before the Internal Revenue Service, the Department of Labor, the Pension Benefit Guaranty Corporation, or any court? . . . . ☐ Yes ☐ No
If "Yes," attach explanation.

f Does your plan contain cash or deferred arrangements described in section 401(k)? . . . ☐ Yes ☐ No
If "Yes," is a determination also requested on the qualification of those provisions? (See Instruction B.) . . . ☐ Yes ☐ No

4 a Name of Plan
b Plan number ▶
c Plan year ends ▶

5 Are there other qualified plans? (Do not consider plans that were established under union-negotiated agreements that involved other employers.) . . . ☐ Yes ☐ No
- **a** Name of plan ▶
- **b** Type of plan ▶
- **c** Rate of employer contribution ▶
- **d** Allocation formula ▶ ☐ N/A
- **e** Benefit formula or monthly benefit ▶ ☐ N/A
- **f** Number of participants ▶ ☐ N/A

6 Type of entity (check only one box):
a ☐ Corporation **b** ☐ Subchapter S corporation **c** ☐ Sole proprietor **d** ☐ Partnership
e ☐ Tax exempt organization **f** ☐ Church **g** ☐ Governmental organization
h ☐ Other (specify) ▶

7 Is this an adoption of a master or prototype plan? ☐ Yes ☐ No. If "Yes," complete **a** and **b**
a Name of plan **b** Notification letter no.

8 Type of plan: **a** ☐ Profit-sharing **b** ☐ Stock bonus **c** ☐ Money purchase **d** ☐ Target benefit
e ☐ Other (specify) ▶

Under penalties of perjury, I declare that I have examined this application, including accompanying statements, and to the best of my knowledge and belief, it is true, correct, and complete.

Signature ▶ **Title** ▶ **Date** ▶

For Paperwork Reduction Act Notice, see page 1 of the instructions.

Form **5301** (Rev. 8-88)

Form 5301 (Rev. 8-88) Page 2

(Section references are to the Internal Revenue Code, unless otherwise noted.)

Where applicable, indicate the article or section and page number of the plan or trust where the following provisions are contained. N/A (not applicable) is an appropriate response only if an N/A block is provided.

		Section and Page Number
9 a	General eligibility requirements: (Check box (i), (ii), (iii) or (iv), and complete (v), (vi) and (vii).) (i) ☐ All employees (ii) ☐ Hourly rate employees only (iii) ☐ Salaried employees only (iv) ☐ Other (specify) ► (v) Length of service (number of years) ► ☐ N/A (vi) Minimum age (specify) ► ☐ N/A (vii) Maximum age (specify) ► ☐ N/A	
b	Does any plan amendment since the last determination letter change the method of crediting service for eligibility? ☐ Yes ☐ No ☐ N/A	

		Yes	No	Not Certain
10	Participation (see Specific Instructions):			
a	(i) Is the employer a member of an affiliated service group? If your answer is "No," go to 10b.			
	(ii) Did a prior ruling letter rule on what organizations were members of the employer's affiliated service group or did the employer receive a determination letter that considered the effect of section 414(m) on this plan?			
	(iii) If (ii) is "Yes," have the facts on which that letter was based materially changed?			
b	Is the employer a member of a controlled group of corporations or a group of trades or businesses under common control?			

			Number
11	Coverage of plan at (give date) .... (attach Form(s) 5302—see instructions) (If the employer is a member of an affiliated service group, a controlled group of corporations, or a group of trades or businesses under common control, employees of all members of the group must be considered in completing the following schedule.) If your plan contains cash or deferred arrangements described in section 401(k), see the Specific Instructions for line 11.		Enter "0" if N/A
a	Total employed (see Specific Instructions) (include all self-employed individuals)		
b	Statutory exclusions under this plan (do not count an employee more than once)		
	(i) Number excluded because of age or years of service required		
	(ii) Number excluded because of employees included in collective bargaining		
	(iii) Number of other employees excluded (specify)		
c	Total statutory exclusions under this plan (add lines b(i) through (iii))		
d	Employees not excluded under the statute (subtract line c from line a)		
e	Other employees ineligible under terms of this plan (do not count an employee included in line b)		
f	Employees eligible to participate (subtract line e from line d)		
g	Number of employees participating in this plan		
h	Percent of nonexcluded employees who are participating (divide line g by line d) If line h is 70% or more, go to line k.	%	
i	Percent of nonexcluded employees who are eligible to participate (divide line f by line d)	%	
j	Percent of eligible employees who are participating (divide line g by line f) If lines h and i are less than 70% or line j is less than 80%, see Specific Instructions and attach schedule of information.	%	
k	Total number of participants (include certain retired and terminated employees (see Specific Instructions)).		
l	Has a plan amendment since the last determination letter resulted in exclusion of previously covered employees? ☐ Yes ☐ No ☐ N/A		

		Yes	No	N/A	Section and Page Number
12	Does the plan define the following terms—				
a	Compensation (earned income if applicable)?				
b	Break in service?				
c	Hour of service (under Department of Labor Regulations)?				
d	Joint and survivor annuity?				
e	Normal retirement age?				
f	Year of service?				
g	Entry date?				
13 a	Employee contributions:				
	(i) Does the plan allow voluntary deductible employee contributions?				
	(ii) If "Yes," are the voluntary deductible employee contributions appropriately limited?				
	(iii) Are voluntary nondeductible contributions limited for all qualified plans to 10%, or less, of compensation?				
	(iv) Are employee contributions nonforfeitable?				

		Yes	No	N/A	Section and Page Number
13	*(Continued)*				
b	Employer contributions: (Response required in either (i), (ii), (iii) or (iv).)				
	(i) Profit-sharing or stock bonus plan contributions are determined under: ☐ A definite formula ☐ An indefinite formula ☐ Both				
	(ii) Profit-sharing or stock bonus plan contributions are limited to: ☐ Current earnings ☐ Accumulated earnings ☐ Combination				
	(iii) Money purchase—Enter rate of contribution ►				
	(iv) State target benefit formula, if applicable ►				
14	Integration:				
	Is this plan integrated with social security or railroad retirement?				
	If "Yes" and this is a target benefit plan, attach a schedule of compliance with Rev. Rul. 71-446 (see Specific Instructions).				
15	Vesting:				
a	Are years of service with other members of a controlled group of corporations, trades or businesses under common control, or an affiliated service group counted for vesting and eligibility to participate?				
b	Are employee's rights to normal retirement benefits nonforfeitable on reaching normal retirement age as defined in section 411(a)(8)?				
c	Does any amendment to the plan decrease any participant's accrued benefit?				
d	Does any amendment to the plan directly or indirectly affect the computation of the nonforfeitable percentage of a participant's accrued benefit?				
e	Does the plan preclude forfeiture of an employee's vested benefits for cause?				
f	Check only one of the boxes to indicate the vesting provisions of the plan:				
	(i) ☐ Full and immediate.				
	(ii) ☐ Full vesting after 10 years of service; i.e., no vesting for the first 9 years, 100% after 10 years (section 411(a)(2)(A)).				
	(iii) ☐ 5- to 15-year vesting (section 411(a)(2)(B)).				
	(iv) ☐ Rule of 45 (section 411(a)(2)(C)).				
	(v) ☐ 4/40 vesting (Rev. Procs. 75-49 and 76-11).				
	(vi) ☐ 10% vesting for each year of service (not to exceed 100%).				
	(vii) ☐ 100% vesting within 5 years after contributions are made (class year plans only).				
	(viii) ☐ Other (specify—see Specific Instructions and attach schedule).				
16	Administration: **a** Type of funding entity:				
	(i) ☐ Trust (benefits provided in whole from trust funds).				
	(ii) ☐ Custodial account described in section 401(f) and not included in (iv) below.				
	(iii) ☐ Trust or arrangement providing benefits partially through insurance and/or annuity contracts.				
	(iv) ☐ Trust or arrangement providing benefits exclusively through insurance and/or annuity contracts.				
	(v) ☐ Other (specify) ►				
b	Does the trust agreement prohibit reversion of funds to the employer? (Rev. Rul. 77-200)				
c	Are limits placed on the purchase of insurance contracts?				
	If "Yes," complete (i), (ii) or (iii), below				
	(i) Ordinary life ►				
	(ii) Term insurance ►				
	(iii) Other (specify) ►				
d	If the trustees may earmark specific investments, including insurance contracts, are such investments subject to the employee's consent, or purchased ratably when employee consent is not required?				
e	Are loans to participants limited to their vested interests?				
17	Requirements for benefits—distributions—allocations:				
a	Normal retirement age is ► ______ If applicable, years of service/participation required ►				
b	Does the plan contain an early retirement provision?				
	If "Yes," (i) Early retirement age is ►				
	(ii) Years of service participation required ►				
c	Does the plan provide for payment of benefits according to section 401(a)(14)?				

	Yes	No	N/A	Section and Page Number
17 *(Continued)*				
d Distribution of account balances may be made in: *(i)* ☐ Lump sum *(ii)* ☐ Annuity contracts *(iii)* ☐ Substantially equal annual installments—not more than ▶ .... years *(iv)* ☐ Other (specify) ▶				
e If distributions are made in installments, they are credited with: *(i)* ☐ Fund earnings *(ii)* ☐ Interest at a rate of ▶ .... % per year *(iii)* ☐ Other (specify) ▶				
f Does the plan comply with the payment of benefits provisions of section 401(a)(11)?				
g If this is a stock bonus plan, are distributions made in employer stock?				
h If this is a pension plan, does it permit distribution only on death, disability, plan termination, or termination of employment?				
i If this is a profit-sharing or stock bonus plan, what other events permit distributions?				
j If participants withdraw their mandatory contributions or earnings, may withdrawal be made without forfeiting vested benefits based on employer contributions?				
k Are contributions allocated on the basis of total compensation? If "No," see Specific Instructions and attach schedule.				
l Are forfeitures allocated, in case of a profit-sharing or stock bonus plan, on basis of total compensation? If "No," explain how they are allocated				
m Are trust earnings and losses allocated on the basis of account balances? If "No," explain how they are allocated.				
n For target benefit or other money purchase plan, are forfeitures applied to reduce employer contributions?				
o Does the plan provide for maximum limitation under section 415?				
p Does the plan prohibit the assignment or alienation of benefits?				
q Does the plan meet the requirements of section 401(a)(12)?				
r Are trust assets valued at fair market value?				
s Are trust assets valued at least annually on a specific date? If "No," explain.				
18 Termination of plan or trust:				
a Are the participants' rights to benefits under the plan nonforfeitable (to the extent funded) upon termination or partial termination of the plan?				
b Are employees' rights under the plan nonforfeitable on complete discontinuance of contributions under a profit-sharing or stock bonus plan?				

Procedural Requirements Checklist

Caution: The following Procedural Requirements Checklist identifies certain basic data that will facilitate the processing of your application. While no response is required to the questions, you may find that answering them will ensure that your application is processed without the need for contact to obtain missing information. If the answer to any of the questions is "No," your application may be incomplete. Incomplete applications are identified through a computer screening system for return to the applicant. **This checksheet should be detached before submitting the application.**

		Yes	No	N/A
1	General requirements			
a	If this application is made by a representative on behalf of the employer or plan administrator, has a current power of attorney been submitted with this application (see "Signature" under General Information)?			
b	If notices or other communications are to be sent to someone other than the employer, have you provided proper authorization by attaching a completed **Form 2848**, Power of Attorney and Declaration of Representative, or by attaching a statement that contains all the information required (see Specific Instructions)?			
c	Have you completed and attached Form(s) 5302?			
d	Have you signed the application?			
e	Have you completed and attached Schedule T (Form 5300)?			
2	Specific requirements			
a	If this is a request for a determination letter on initial qualification of the plan, have the following documents been attached:			
	(i) Copies of all instruments constituting the plan?			
	(ii) Copies of trust indentures, group annuity contracts, or custodial agreements?			
b	If this is a request for a determination letter on the effect of an amendment on the plan after initial qualification, have the following documents been attached:			
	(i) A copy of the plan amendments?			
	(ii) A description of the amendment covering the changes to the plan sections?			
	(iii) An explanation of the plan sections before the amendment?			
	(iv) An explanation of the effect of the amendment on the provisions of the plan sections?			
c	If this is a request for a determination letter on the qualification of the entire plan, as amended after initial qualification, have the following documents been included:			
	(i) A copy of the plan incorporating all amendments made to the date of the application?			
	(ii) A statement indicating that the copy of the plan is complete in all respects and that a determination letter is being requested on the qualification of the entire plan?			
	(iii) A copy of trust indentures, group annuity contracts, or custodial agreements, if there has been any change since copies were last furnished to IRS?			
d	For partial termination:			
	(i) Have you completed line 3a according to the Specific Instructions?			
	(ii) Have you attached the information requested for a partial termination in General Instruction B?			
e	For a plan adopted by one or more members of a controlled group:			
	(i) Have you attached the statement requested in the Specific Instructions for line 10b?			
	(ii) Have you completed line 11 according to General Instruction B and the Specific Instructions?			
f	For a multiple-employer plan that does not involve collective bargaining:			
	(i) Have you submitted one fully completed application (Form 5300 or 5301, whichever is appropriate) for all adopting employers?			
	(ii) Have you attached a Form 5300 or 5301 (as applicable) with only line items 1 through 11 completed, and a Form 5302 for each employer who adopted the plan?			
g	For a plan that contains a cash or deferred arrangement, have you submitted the appropriate information requested for line 11?			
h	For governmental and church plans, have you completed Form 5300 or 5301 according to General Instruction B?			
i	For notice of merger, consolidation, or transfer of plan assets or liabilities, have you submitted the information requested in the Specific Instructions for line 3c?			
j	For a plan that is or may be sponsored by a member of an affiliated service group:			
	(i) Have you completed lines 3a, 10, and 11 according to the Specific Instructions?			
	(ii) Have you attached the information requested in the instructions for lines 10a(ii) and (iii)?			
3	Miscellaneous requirements—			
a	Have you entered the plan sponsor's 9-digit employer identification number in line 1b?			
b	If a determination letter was previously issued to this sponsor for any plan, have you entered the file folder number on line 3b?			
c	Have you answered line 3d?			
d	If this plan has been amended at least four times since the last determination letter on the entire plan was issued, have you attached a copy of the plan that includes all amendments made to the plan since that determination letter was issued?			
e	Have you entered the effective date of the plan in the space provided by the block you checked for line 3a?			
f	If applicable, have you attached schedules or other documentation as required by:			
	(i) Form 5301—Lines 2, 3e, 11j, 14, 15f(viii), 17k, 17l, 17m, and 17s?			
	(ii) Form 5300—Lines 2, 3e, 6, 11j, 14, 15f(viii), and 17g?			

Department of the Treasury
Internal Revenue Service

Instructions for Forms 5300 and 5301

(Revised August 1988)

Application for Determination for Defined Benefit Plan and for Defined Contribution Plan

(Section references are to the Internal Revenue Code, unless otherwise noted.)

General Information

Paperwork Reduction Act Notice.—We ask for this information to carry out the Internal Revenue laws of the United States. We need it to determine whether you meet the legal requirements for plan approval. If you want to have your plan approved by IRS, you are required to give us this information.

The estimated average times needed to complete these forms, depending on individual circumstances, are as follows:

Form 5300 – 5 hours and 19 minutes
Schedule T (Form 5300) – 2 hours and 40 minutes
Form 5301 – 6 hours and 34 minutes

If you have comments concerning the accuracy of these time estimates or suggestions for making these forms more simple, we would be happy to hear from you. You can send your comments to the Internal Revenue Service, Washington, DC 20224, Attention: IRS Reports Clearance Officer TR:FP; or the Office of Information and Regulatory Affairs, Office of Management and Budget, Washington, DC 20503, Attention: Desk Officer for Internal Revenue Service.

Purpose of Forms.—Forms 5300 and 5301 may be used for the following reasons:

1. To request a determination letter on initial qualification; on amendment after initial qualification; on affiliated service group status; or on the effect of section 414(m) on the plan.
2. To request a determination letter regarding the effect of a potential partial termination on the plan's qualification.
3. To give notice of merger, consolidation, or transfer of plan assets or liabilities (required by section 6058(b)) and request a determination on the remaining plan(s). (See Instruction B. "What To File.", and item 3c under Specific Instructions.)

Form 5301 may also be used to obtain a determination letter on whether a defined contribution plan contains a qualified cash or deferred arrangement within the meaning of section 401(k).

User Fees.—The Revenue Act of 1987 requires payment of a user fee for determination letter requests submitted to the Internal Revenue Service. Use **Form 8717**, User Fee for Employee Plan Determination Letter Request, to make payment of the fee. Form 8717 must accompany each determination letter request submitted after January 31, 1988.

Public Inspection.—The application is open to public inspection if there are more than 25 participants. Therefore, it is important that the total number of participants be shown on line 11k. See the Specific Instructions for line 11k for the definition of participant.

Disclosure Requested by Taxpayers.—See item 2 under Specific Instructions for the information the request should include.

Signature.—The application must be signed by the employer, plan administrator, or an authorized representative who must be either an attorney, a certified public accountant, or a person enrolled to practice before the IRS. (See Treasury Department Circular No. 230 (Revised).) An application made by a representative on behalf of an employer or plan administrator must be accompanied by:

1. a power of attorney specifically authorizing representation in this matter (you may use **Form 2848**, Power of Attorney and Declaration of Representative); or
2. a written declaration that the representative is a currently qualified attorney, certified public accountant, or is currently enrolled to practice before the IRS (include either the enrollment number or the expiration date of the enrollment card); and is authorized to represent the employer or plan administrator.

General Instructions

A determination letter may be requested from the IRS for the qualification of a defined benefit plan or a defined contribution plan and the exempt status of any related trust. A defined contribution plan is a plan that provides for an individual account for each participant and for benefits based solely on the amount contributed to the participant's account, and any income, expenses, gains and losses, and any forfeitures of accounts of other participants which may be allocated to the participant's account. A defined benefit plan is any plan that is not a defined contribution plan.

Determination applications are now screened for completeness by computer. For this reason, it is important that an appropriate response be entered for each line item except as indicated in 5 below. In completing the application, be sure to pay careful attention to the following:

1. N/A (not applicable) is accepted as a response only if an N/A block is provided.
2. If an item requests a numeric response, a number must be entered.
3. If an item provides a choice of boxes to be checked, only one box should be checked unless instructed otherwise.
4. If an item provides a box or boxes to be checked, written responses are not acceptable.
5. If the Church or Governmental organization block is checked for line item 6, certain line items need not be completed. In this regard, please refer to General Instruction B. "What To File.", to determine which items to complete if this application is for a church or government plan.

Only one copy of the application must be filed. ATTACH ONLY ONE COPY OF EACH DOCUMENT AND STATEMENT REQUESTED BY THE FORM OR INSTRUCTIONS (SEE THE PROCEDURAL REQUIREMENTS CHECKLIST). If more space is needed for any item, attach additional sheets, preferably of the same size as the form.

The key district office may request additional information or return the application for completion if the application and attachments do not contain enough information to make a determination. In either case, the result will be a delay in issuing a determination letter.

A. Who May File.—1. Any employer, including a sole proprietor, a partnership which has adopted an individually designed plan, a plan sponsor or a plan administrator desiring a determination letter on an initial qualification, amendment, partial termination of a plan, affiliated services group status, or the effect of section 414(m) on the plan (all five items referred to as "determination request").

2. Any plan sponsor or plan administrator desiring a determination letter for a "determination request" that involves a plan of a controlled group of corporations (section 414(b)), or trades or businesses under common control (section 414(c)), hereafter referred to as "controlled group," or an affiliated service group (section 414(m)).

3. Any plan sponsor or plan administator desiring a determination letter for a "determination request" of a multiple-employer plan (a plan maintained by more than one employer but not a controlled group nor an affiliated service group).

4. Any employer, plan sponsor, or plan administrator desiring a determination letter for compliance with the applicable requirements of a foreign situs trust for the taxability of beneficiaries (section 402(c)) and deductions for employer contributions (section 404(a)(4)).

Note: *This form may not be filed by anyone desiring approval of a plan that covers only employees covered by a collective-bargaining agreement, including employees of the representative labor union or any plan(s) for union members or a multiemployer plan. Also, it may not be filed by anyone desiring approval of the adoption of a master or prototype plan, or a uniform plan.*

B. What To File.—Any plan sponsor or plan administrator making a determination request for a plan of a single employer should file one Form 5300 or 5301 with one **Form 5302**, Employee Census. A **Schedule T (Form 5300)**, Supplemental Application for Approval of Employee Benefit Plans Under TEFRA, TRA 1984, REA and TRA 1986, should be attached to each application. Only one application should be filed for each plan maintained by a single employer, i.e., if there are two separate plans, two separate applications should be filed, etc. A separate application must also be filed for each defined benefit plan and for each defined contribution plan.

The following specifies what to file when requesting a determination letter:

For initial qualification (Rev. Proc. 80-30, 1980-1 C.B. 685), file the application form and a copy of the appropriate documents and statements summarized in items 1, 2a(i), and 3 of the Procedural Requirements Checklist.

For the effect of an amendment on the plan (Rev. Proc. 81-19, 1981-1 C.B. 689), file the application form and a copy of the appropriate documents and statements summarized in items 1, 2b(iii), and 3 of the Procedural Requirements Checklist. A restated plan is required if four or more amendments have been made since the last restated plan was submitted. For restatement purposes, an amendment making only non-substantive plan changes need not be counted as a plan amendment. A non-substantive change will not affect the plan's qualification, for example: a change in name, address, or trustee of a corporate type plan.

Note: *In lieu of Form 5300 or 5301, a* **Form 6406**, *Short Form Application for Determination for Amendment of Employee Benefit Plan, may be used when requesting a determination letter on the effect of an amendment on a plan which received or was issued a favorable determination letter under the Employee Retirement Income Security Act of 1974 (ERISA). See Rev. Proc. 81-19 for further explanation on who may file Form 6406.*

For qualification of the entire plan as amended after initial qualification (Rev. Proc. 81-19), file the application form and a copy of the appropriate documents and statements summarized in items 1, 2b(iii), and 3 of the Procedural Requirements Checklist.

For partial termination (Rev. Proc. 80-30), file the application form and the appropriate documents and statements summarized in items 1, 2, and 3 of the Procedural Requirements Checklist (see the Specific Instructions and the Note for line 3a).

In addition:

(a) Attach a statement indicating whether a partial termination may have occurred or might occur as a result of proposed actions.

(b) Using the format that follows, submit a schedule of information for the plan year in which the partial (or potential partial) termination began or during which the multiemployer plan terminated. Also, submit a schedule for the next plan year, as well as for the two prior plan years, to the extent the information is available. If this is a plan maintained by more than one employer (when all employers in each affiliated service group or controlled group are considered one employer), in addition to completing (i)(e) for the entire plan, on an attached sheet show this information for each such single employer in the same format as (i)(e).

	19	19	Year of partial termination 19	19 ....
(i) Participants employed:				
(a) Number at beginning of plan year				
(b) Number added during the plan year				
(c) Total, add lines (a) and (b)				
(d) Number dropped during the plan year				
(e) Number at end of plan year, subtract (d) from (c)				
(f) Total number of participants in this plan separated from service without full vesting				
(ii) Present value (as of a date during the year) of:				
(a) Plan assets				
(b) Accrued benefits				
(c) Vested benefits				

(c) Submit a description of the actions that may have resulted or might result in a partial termination. Include an explanation of how the plan meets the requirements of section 411(d)(3).

For a plan sponsored by a member of an affiliated service group (Rev. Proc. 85-43, 1985-2 C.B. 501), file the application and a copy of the appropriate documents and statements listed in lines 10a(ii) and (iii) of these instructions, as well as any of the appropriate items summarized in the Procedural Requirements Checklist.

For a plan adopted by one or more members of a controlled group, file the appropriate documents and statements as summarized in the Procedural Requirements Checklist. In addition, attach a list of the member employers and explain in detail their relationship, the types of plans each member has, and the plans common to all member employers (See instructions for line 10b). For purposes of these instructions, a controlled group is considered a single entity.

Line 11 on Form 5300 or 5301 for a plan which includes one or more members of a controlled group must be completed as if the group were a single entity. If more than one member of a controlled group adopts the same plan, only one application for determination should be submitted for the controlled group. The controlled group should designate the parent corporation or a member of the group to act as the applicant for the controlled group and to furnish the names of the members who adopt the plan. The parent corporation or a member of the controlled group must have employees who are eligible to participate before adopting the qualified plan of the group.

For a multiple-employer plan that does not involve collective bargaining, file one application. In addition, attach a Form 5300 or 5301 (complete only lines 1 through 11) and a Form 5302 for each employer who adopted the plan, when all employers in each affiliated service group or controlled group are considered one employer. The applications for the individual employers must be signed by the respective employers.

For a plan that contains a cash or deferred arrangement (section 401(k)), file the appropriate documents and statements summarized in the Procedural Requirements Checklist. Also submit the information requested for line 11. See the Specific Instructions for that line.

For governmental and church plans, the plan administrator may request a determination by filing the appropriate application. If the request is for a plan that is subject to ERISA, complete all items of the application. If the request is for a plan that is not subject to ERISA, omit the following lines on the appropriate application form:

On Form 5300, omit lines 10, 11, 12b, 12c, and 15.

On Form 5301, omit lines 10, 11, 12b, 12c, 15, 17g, 17l, and 18b.

For merger, consolidation, or transfer of plan assets or liabilities, if this application is also intended to satisfy the notice requirement of section 6058(b), attach the information requested in line 3c of the Specific Instructions.

For terminations, file Form 5310, Application for Determination Upon Termination, to request a determination letter for the complete termination of a defined benefit plan or a defined contribution plan, except that Form 5303 should be filed to request a determination letter involving the complete termination of a multiemployer plan covered by the PBGC insurance program.

Note: *If a defined benefit plan is amended to become a defined contribution plan, or if the merger of a defined benefit plan with a defined contribution plan results solely in a defined contribution plan, the defined benefit plan is considered terminated.*

C. Where To File.—File this form as follows:

(i) Single Employer Plans.—Send the forms to the District Director for the key district in which the employer's or employee organization's principal place of business is located.

(ii) Plan Maintained by More Than One Employer.—Send the forms to the District Director for the key district in which the principal place of business of the plan sponsor is located. This means the principal place of business of the association, committee, joint board of trustees, or other similar group or representatives of those who established or maintain the plan.

If the principal office of the plan sponsor is located in the following IRS District ▼	Send your fee and application to the address below ▼
Brooklyn, Albany, Augusta, Boston, Buffalo, Burlington, Hartford, Manhattan, Portsmouth, Providence	Internal Revenue Service EP/EO Division P. O. Box 1680, GPO Brooklyn, NY 11202
Baltimore, District of Columbia, Pittsburgh, Richmond, Newark, Philadelphia, Wilmington, any U.S. possession or foreign country	Internal Revenue Service EP/EO Division P. O. Box 17010 Baltimore, MD 21203
Cincinnati, Cleveland, Detroit, Indianapolis, Louisville, Parkersburg	Internal Revenue Service EP/EO Division P. O. Box 3159 Cincinnati, OH 45201
Dallas, Albuquerque, Austin, Cheyenne, Denver, Houston, Oklahoma City, Phoenix, Salt Lake City, Wichita	Internal Revenue Service EP/EO Division Mail Code 4950 DAL 1100 Commerce Street Dallas, TX 75242
Atlanta, Birmingham, Columbia, Ft. Lauderdale, Greensboro, Jackson, Jacksonville, Little Rock, Nashville, New Orleans	Internal Revenue Service EP/EO Division Room 1112 P.O. Box 941 Atlanta, GA 30301
Honolulu, Laguna Niguel, Las Vegas, Los Angeles, San Jose,	Internal Revenue Service EP Application Receiving Room 5127, P. O. Box 536 Los Angeles, CA 90053-0536
Chicago, Aberdeen, Des Moines, Fargo, Helena, Milwaukee, Omaha, St. Louis, St. Paul, Springfield	Internal Revenue Service EP/EO Division 230 S. Dearborn DPN 20-6 Chicago, IL 60604
Sacramento, San Francisco	Internal Revenue Service EP Application Receiving Stop SF 4446 P. O. Box 36001 San Francisco, CA 94102
Anchorage, Boise, Portland, Seattle	Internal Revenue Service EP Application Receiving P. O. Box 21224 Seattle, WA 98111

Domestic employers adopting foreign situs trusts should file with the District Director for the key district in which the principal place of business of the employer is located.

Foreign employers should file with the Baltimore key district.

Determination requests for industry plans established or proposed by subscribing employers with principal places of business located within the jurisdiction of more than one District Director, should be addressed to the Director for the key district where the trustee's principal place of business is located. If the plans have more than one trustee, the request should be filed with the Director for the key district where the trustees usually meet.

Specific Instructions

Use the following instructions to complete Forms 5300 and 5301. If any item requests a date or number, the RESPONSE MUST BE A DATE OR A NUMBER. N/A (not applicable) IS ACCEPTABLE ONLY IF AN N/A BLOCK IS PROVIDED.

The following instructions are keyed to the line items on the forms.

1a. Enter the name and address of the plan sponsor. If a plan covers the employees of only one employer, "plan sponsor" means the employer. For plans maintained by two or more employers (other than a plan sponsored by two or more members of a controlled group of corporations), plan sponsor means the association, committee, joint board of trustees or other similar group of representatives of those who established or maintain the plan.

For a plan sponsored by two or more members of a controlled group of corporations, "plan sponsor" means one of the members participating in the plan.

Be sure to include enough information in 1a to describe the sponsor accurately.

1b. Enter the 9-digit employer identification number (EIN) assigned to the plan sponsor. This should be the same EIN that was used or will be used when Form 5500 series returns/reports are filed for the plan.

Controlled groups of corporations whose sponsor is more than one of the members of the controlled group should insert only the EIN of one of the sponsoring members. This EIN must be used in all subsequent filings of determination letter requests for the controlled group. This is also the EIN used for filing annual returns/reports.

1c. If this application is for a single employer plan, enter the month the employer's tax year ends. For plans of more than one employer, check the N/A box.

2. The Tax Reform Act of 1976 permits a taxpayer to request IRS to disclose and discuss his or her return and/or return information with any person(s) the taxpayer designates in a written request. If you want to designate a person or persons to assist in matters relating to an application for a determination, you must give the IRS office of jurisdiction a written statement containing certain information:

(i) Your name, address, employer identification number, and plan number(s).

(ii) A paragraph that clearly identifies the person or persons you have authorized to receive the return and/or return information. It must include the name, address, and telephone number(s), and social security number(s) of the authorized person(s).

(iii) A paragraph that clearly and explicitly describes the return and/or return information that you authorize the IRS to discuss.

(iv) You must sign the request as the taxpayer making the authorization. As an alternative to providing the statement, you may substitute **Form 2848**, Power of Attorney and Declaration of Representative, or **Form 2848-D**, Tax Information Authorization and Declaration of Representative.

3a. Check applicable box(es). In the place indicated, enter the date the plan or amendment was signed. If a determination is requested based on a proposed plan or amendment, enter 9/9/99. Enter the effective date where requested. The term "effective date" means the date the plan, amendment, affiliated service group status, or partial termination becomes operative, takes effect, or changes. The EFFECTIVE DATE OF THE PLAN is a required entry for all submissions. For example, if a determination is requested for an amendment to the plan, enter the date the plan is effective as well as the date the amendment is effective.

(i) Check this box if the IRS has not previously issued a determination letter for this plan.

(ii) Check this box if this application is for an amendment to a plan for which the IRS has previously issued a determination letter.

(iii) Check this box if a determination letter is desired with regard to the effect of section 414(m) on the plan being submitted. This box should also be checked if a determination letter is desired because of a change in the affiliated service group membership.

(iv) Check this box if a determination letter is desired on the effect of a potential partial termination on the plan's qualification.

Note: *For 3a(iii) and (iv), also check box 3a(i) or (ii), as applicable, unless: (1) IRS has previously issued a determination letter on this plan, and (2) an amendment is not involved in this request for a determination letter.*

3b. Enter the file folder number shown on the last determination letter, if any, issued to this sponsor. For example, if the sponsor maintains two plans and previously received a determination letter for plan number 001, the file folder number shown on that determination letter should be entered on line 3b when an application is submitted with regard to plan number 002.

3c. This form may be used for applications for a determination letter only in the situations provided in line 3a. However, in the case of a merger, consolidation, or transfer of plan assets or liabilities, a plan sponsor may request a determination letter on a plan involved in such activity and may simultaneously give notice of the merger, consolidation, or transfer of plan assets or liabilities as required by section 6058(b). Each sponsor or administrator of a plan involved in a merger, consolidation, or transfer of plan assets or liabilities must provide the notice 30 days before such event takes place. If the plan sponsor does not desire a determination letter on such a plan, Form 5310 must be filed to provide this notice. A plan sponsor who requests a determination letter on the qualified status of a plan that was involved in a merger, consolidation, or transfer of plan assets or liabilities may use Form 5300, 5301, or 5303 to simultaneously give the required notice and request a determination letter for that plan by:

(1) submitting this application not less than 30 days prior to the date of the merger, consolidation, or transfer of plan assets or liabilities, and

(2) attaching a statement containing the plan name(s) and number(s), the name(s) of the plan sponsor(s), and the employer identification number(s) for the other plan(s) involved in the merger, consolidation, or transfer. The statement should include the date of the transaction and, for a defined benefit plan, an actuarial statement of valuation for the plan showing compliance with the requirements of sections 401(a)(12) and 414(l) and the related regulations.

3d. Section 3001 of ERISA states that the applicant must provide evidence that each employee who qualifies as an interested party has been notified of the application. Check "Yes" only if you have notified each employee as required by regulations under section 7476. Rules defining "interested parties" and providing for the form of notification are contained in the regulations. **Note:** An example of an acceptable format can be found in Rev. Proc. 80-30.

4a. Enter the name you designated for your plan.

4b. You should assign a three-digit number beginning with "001", and continuing in numerical sequence, to each plan you adopt. This numbering will differentiate your plans. Enter your three-digit number here. The number that is assigned to a plan must not be changed or used for any other plan.

4c. Plan year means the calendar, policy, or fiscal year on which the records of the plan are kept.

6. Check only one box. All subchapter S corporations, check box (b). If the plan involves more than one employer, check box (h) and enter an appropriate explanation, i.e., controlled group of corporations, employers under common control, or non-controlled group of employers, such as multiple employers.

10. You should complete line 10 for the plan sponsor filing this application. However, for a multiple-employer plan, consider line 10 separately for each employer to determine the employers for whom information must be attached. In addition, answer line 10a(i) "Yes" if the answer is yes for any employer participating in the plan.

If the plan sponsor is a member of an affiliated service group described in section 414(m), all employees of the affiliated service group members will be treated as employed by a single employer for purposes of certain qualification requirements such as coverage. See Rev. Proc. 85-43, 1985-2 C.B. 501, for procedures on submission of an application to the key district office for a determination letter on the effect of section 414(m). Also see Rev. Rul. 81-105, 1981-1 C.B. 256, regarding the application of section 414(m).

10a(ii) and (iii). If you or any member (or possible member) of the affiliated service group received a ruling or determination letter regarding section 414(m), attach a copy of the letter to the application. If you are uncertain as to whether or not you are a member of an affiliated service group, and no affiliated service group ruling or determination letter is available, or if the facts have changed since the ruling or determination letter was issued, attach the following information:

(1) A description of the nature of the business of the employer, specifically discussing whether it is a service organization or an organization whose principal business is the performance of management functions for another organization, including the reasons therefor;

(2) The identification of other members (or possible members) of the affiliated service group;

(3) A description of the nature of the business of each member (or possible member) of the affiliated service group describing the type of organization (corporation, partnership, etc.) and indicating whether such member is a service organization or an organization whose principal business is the performance of management functions for the other group member(s);

(4) The ownership interests between the employer and the members (or possible members) of the affiliated service group (including ownership interests as described in section 414(m)(2)(B);

(5) A description of services performed for the employers by the members (or possible members) of the affiliated services group, or vice versa (including the percentage of each member's or possible member's gross receipts and service receipts provided by such services, if available, and data as to whether their services are a significant portion of the member's business) and whether or not, as of December 13, 1980, it was unusual for the services to be performed by employees of organizations in that service field in the United States;

(6) A description of how the employer and the members (or possible members) of the affiliated service group associate in performing services for other parties;

(7) A description of management functions, if any, performed by the employer for the member(s) (or possible member(s)) of the affiliated service group, or received by the employer from any other member(s) (or possible member(s)) of the group (including data as to whether such management functions are performed on a regular and continuous basis) and whether or not it is unusual for such management functions to be performed by employees of organizations in the employer's business field in the United States;

(8) If management functions are performed by the employer for the member(s) (or possible member(s)) of the affiliated service group, a description as to what part of the employer's business constitutes the performance of management functions for the member(s) (or possible member(s)) of the group (including the percentage of gross receipts derived from management activities as compared to the gross receipts from other activities);

(9) A brief description of any other plan(s) maintained by the member(s) (or possible member(s)) of the affiliated service group, if such other plan(s) is designated as a unit for qualification purposes with the plan for which a determination letter has been requested;

(10) A description of how the plan(s) satisfies the coverage requirements of section 410(b) if the member(s) (or possible member(s)) of the affiliated service group is considered part of an affiliated service group with the employer.

10b. If the adopting employer is a member of a controlled group, attach a statement showing in detail all members of the group, their relationship to the adopting employer, the types of plans each member has, and the plans common to all members.

11. Enter the total number of employees as of the date given on line 11. Include all self-employed individuals. If the answer to 10a is "Yes," or "Not certain," or the answer to 10b is "Yes," complete the coverage information (line 11) as if the employees of all the member(s) (or possible member(s)) of the controlled group or affiliated service group are employees of a single employer. If the plan involves more than one such group, a separate line 11 should be attached for each such group. Total employed should include any individual considered a leased employee of the employer within the meaning of section 414(n). For a plan in which more than one employer participates (a multiple-employer plan) that does not involve a controlled group or an affiliated service group, answer a through l of line 11 separately for each employer participating in the plan. For a plan that contains a cash or deferred arrangement (section 401(k)), complete line 11 as stated above. In addition, if the plan does not contain a provision for fail-safe devices or other mechanisms that will assure compliance with the antidiscrimination requirements of section 401(k) (including provisions in the Tax Reform Act of 1984), submit a demonstration of how the discrimination tests in section 401(a)(4) and 410(b) will be satisfied. This may require a schedule of the proposed employee allocations as of the end of the plan year in which the cash or deferred arrangements will become effective, or a schedule of the actual allocations as of the end of the latest year of operation.

11b. *Employees included in collective bargaining.*—Section 410(b)(3)(A) provides that a plan may exclude certain employees who are included in a unit of employees covered by an agreement which the Secretary of Labor finds to be a collective bargaining agreement between employee representatives and one or more employers, if there is evidence that retirement benefits were the subject of good faith bargaining between such employee representatives and such employer or employers.

Nonresident aliens. Section 410(b)(3) provides that a plan may exclude nonresident alien employees who receive no earned income from the employer which constitutes income from sources within the United States.

11e. Enter the number of employees ineligible under the terms of the plan for reasons such as minimum pay, hourly pay, maximum age, etc. Do not include persons excluded under line 11b. Also, do not include individuals who are ineligible solely because they elect not to be covered by the plan, or do not make mandatory contributions to the plan, or those who are not eligible because they are employed by a member of a controlled group or affiliated service group that has not adopted the plan.

11j. The percentage test of section 410(b)(1)(A) is met only if: (1) line 11h is 70% or more; or (2) line 11i is 70% or more and line 11j is 80% or more.

If the plan does not meet the percentage test, you must submit a schedule using the format below to show that the plan meets the requirements of section 410(b)(1)(B). The question of acceptable classification is a continuing one and must be met in all following years as well. You should review your classification at the time you submit your annual return/report. If the plan does not, by itself, satisfy the coverage requirements, other plans may be designated as a unit for this purpose. If any other plan is considered in combination with this plan, attach a schedule that follows the format of line 11. Complete the schedule as though the combined plans were a single plan. Also attach a brief description of the other plans considered.

1		2	3	4	5
*Compensation range		Employees not excluded (see note)	Employees ineligible to participate	Employees participating	Participants who are officers or shareholders
At least	But not more than				
Totals					

*The compensation brackets used must reflect the employer's pay pattern.
Note: *In column 2, enter the total number of employees less exclusions under section 410(b)(2) if provided in the plan.*

11k. The term "participant" includes retirees and other former employees and the beneficiaries of both who are receiving benefits under the plan, or will at some future date receive benefits under the plan. Thus, the figure to enter on this line is the total of: the number of employees who are participating in the plan, (2) former employees who are receiving benefits under the plan, or will at some future date receive benefits under the plan, and (3) beneficiaries of former employees who are receiving benefits under the plan. This means one beneficiary for each former employee regardless of the number of individuals receiving benefits. For example, payment of a former employee's benefits to three children is considered as a payment to one beneficiary.

14, Form 5300—all integrated plans. Form 5301—integrated target benefit plans. Show that the integration limit actually used by the plan cannot exceed the allowable plan integration limit. In determining the allowable integration limit, take into account all plan features that require an adjustment (for example, preretirement death benefit, normal form of payment other than life annuity, average compensation of less than 5 years).

15a. For a definition of a controlled group or trades or businesses under common control, see sections 414(b) and (c). For a definition of an affiliated service group, see section 414(m).

15d. This includes any amendment to a vesting schedule or any plan amendment that directly or indirectly affects the computation of the nonforfeitable percentage of a participant's accrued benefit, for example, each change in the plan which affects either the vesting percentages for years of service or the computation of years of service. See Regulations section 1.411(a)-8(c).

15f(vii), Form 5301. A class year plan is a plan in which the amount of vesting is determined separately with respect to each year's contributions and each contribution becomes 100% vested no later than the 5th plan year following the plan year for which the contributions were made.

15f(vii), Form 5300 and 15f(viii), Form 5301. Check one box to indicate the regular (not top-heavy) vesting schedule used in the plan. If box "Other" is checked and the vesting schedule is less rapid than 15f(v), submit a schedule of turnover of employees or provide enough facts upon which a determination can be made that the vesting schedule of the plan is satisfactory. See Rev. Proc. 76-11, 1976-1 C.B. 550, or its successor, if any. Note that this is a requirement for all initial qualifications.

17g, Form 5300. If compensation other than "total compensation" (generally Form W-2 pay) is used to determine benefits, you must submit with this application a schedule similar in format to the one in 17k (below) if there are more than 25 participants in the plan.

17l, Form 5301. See Regulations sections 1.401-1(b)(1)(ii) and (iii) for an explanation of distributions that will not affect the qualified status of a profit-sharing or stock bonus plan. An example of another event permitting distributions in a profit-sharing or stock bonus plan would be a hardship distribution within two years from the date of the contribution.

17k, Form 5301. If other than "total compensation" (generally Form W-2 pay) is used as the basis for allocating the employer's contributions, you must submit with this application a schedule in similar format to the following, if there are more than 25 participants in the plan.

1		2	3	4	5
*Brackets based on total compensation		Number of employees in bracket	Total compensation for employees included in compensation bracket	Amount of compensation used to determine benefits	Percentage of total (col. 4 divided by col. 3)
At least	But not more than				
Totals					

*The compensation brackets used must reflect the employer's pay pattern.

Before submitting your application, be sure that it conforms to the Procedural Requirements Checklist in the Form 5300 or 5301.

SCHEDULE T
(Form 5300)
(Rev. August 1988)
Department of the Treasury
Internal Revenue Service

Supplemental Application for Approval of Employee Benefit Plans Under TEFRA, TRA 1984, REA, and TRA 1986

▶ **Section references are to the Internal Revenue Code unless otherwise noted.**

OMB No. 1545-0197
Expires 6-30-91

For IRS Use Only
File Folder Number

Caution: Schedule T must be attached to all determination requests made on Form 5300, 5301, 5303, 5307, or 6406, including requests by adopters of master or prototype plans of self-employed individuals except: (1) adopters of master or prototype plans who received favorable opinion letters after June 19, 1984, that have only one plan, or (2) adopters of uniform plans who received notification letters after December 31, 1984, the effective date of Revenue Procedure 84-86, and that have only one plan.
This form is designed to get a response of "N/A" if a line would otherwise be answered "No," and to get an entry in the "Article or Section and Page Number" column if the answer would be "Yes."

1a Name of plan sponsor (employer if single employer) | **1b** Employer Identification Number

Address (number and street)

City or town, state, and ZIP code

Answer items 2 through 27 either by checking "N/A" if the item does not apply, or by entering the Article or Section and Page Number of the plan where the provision is found in the plan.	**N/A**	**Article or Section and Page Number**
2a Is the plan:		
(i) A collectively bargained plan that has never been top-heavy as defined in section 416, and that covers only employees who are covered by a collective bargaining agreement under which retirement benefits were the subject of good faith bargaining, or employees of employee representatives, or		
(ii) A governmental plan?		
If (i) or (ii) is "Yes," do not complete items 3–11 or 24e.		
b Is the plan:		
(i) A master or prototype plan which received a favorable opinion letter after June 19, 1984, and the applicant has more than one plan, or		
(ii) A uniform plan which received a notification letter after December 31, 1984, and the applicant has more than one plan?		
If (i) or (ii) is "Yes," complete only items 10, 24c, and 24d.		
3a Does the plan limit the compensation that can be taken into account for any employee to $200,000 for any year in which the plan is top-heavy?		
b Does the plan provide vesting which is at least as favorable as is required under section 416(b)?		
4 For a defined benefit plan:		
a Are minimum benefits provided for each non-key employee which are not less than 2% of the employee's average high 5 consecutive years of compensation per year of service (not to exceed 20% in total)?		
b Does each non-key employee obtain the minimum benefit if such non-key employee has 1,000 hours of service during an accrual computation period without exception?		
5 For defined contribution plans only:		
a Does the plan provide for a minimum contribution (allocation) which is not less than the lower of 3% of compensation or the highest rate of contribution applicable to any key employee?		
b Does the plan provide that, in determining the highest rate of contribution applicable to any key employee, amounts that a key employee elects to defer under a qualified section 401(k) arrangement are counted for purposes of section 416?		
c Will a non-key employee receive a minimum contribution if that employee has not separated from service at the end of the plan year?		
6 Are account balances attributable to minimum contributions fully nonforfeitable even though a non-key employee withdraws mandatory contributions?		
7 Are the plan provisions described in item 4 or 5 (whichever is applicable) and items 3 and 6 operative for each year regardless of whether the plan is actually top-heavy?		
If "Yes," do not complete items 8 and 9.		
8 Testing for top-heaviness:		
a Does the plan define:		
(i) Determination date?		
(ii) Valuation date?		
(iii) Required aggregation?		

Schedule T (Form 5300) (Rev. 8-88) Page 2

Answer all items either by checking "N/A" if the item does not apply, or by entering the Article or Section and Page Number of the plan where the provision is found in the plan.	**N/A**	**Article or Section and Page Number**
8 Testing for top-heaviness (continued):		
(iv) Permissive aggregation?		
(v) Top-heavy ratio?		
(vi) Key employee?		
(vii) Non-key employee?		
b If this is a defined benefit plan, are the actuarial assumptions used to determine the present value of accrued benefits:		
(i) Specified in the plan?		
(ii) Identical for all defined benefit plans being tested?		
9 Does the plan provide that the accrued benefits and account balances that are to be taken into account in order to determine top-heaviness must relate to the proper determination date (see instructions)?		
10 Answer 10 only if the employer maintains or has maintained more than one plan.		
a If this plan is a defined benefit plan, does it provide the top-heavy minimum benefit?		
b If both defined contribution and defined benefit plans have been or are being maintained, is the top-heavy minimum contribution for each non-key employee participating in both plans comparable to the top-heavy minimum benefit?		
c Does a floor offset arrangement apply with the floor being the top-heavy defined benefit minimum?		
d If both defined contribution and defined benefit plans have been or are being maintained, is a minimum 5% of compensation provided for each non-key employee participating in both plans?		
e If both defined contribution and defined benefit plans have been or are being maintained, is a minimum 2% of compensation provided for each non-key employee who participates solely in the defined benefit plan?		
11a Does this plan always use a factor for purposes of determining the fractions under section 415(e) of 1.0 times the applicable dollar limitation? If "Yes," do not answer 11b or c		
b Does this plan use a limitation of 1.0 times the dollar limitation if the top-heavy ratio is greater than 90%?		
c If the top-heavy ratio is between 60% and 90%, and the plan uses a factor of 1.25 times the dollar limitation, does the plan provide for one of the following:		
(i) If this is a defined benefit plan, a defined benefit minimum of 3% in lieu of the 2% minimum described in 4a (not to exceed 30% in total)?		
(ii) If this is a defined contribution plan, a defined contribution minimum of 4% in lieu of the 3% described in 5a?		
d When a non-key employee is covered by both a defined benefit plan and a defined contribution plan, both of which are top-heavy, and the employer wants to use the 1.25 factor, then does such an employee receive one of the following:		
(i) A defined contribution minimum comparable to a 3% defined benefit minimum?		
(ii) A floor offset in a defined benefit plan with the floor being a 3% minimum described in 11c(i)?		
(iii) If this is a defined contribution plan, and this plan and a defined benefit plan of the employer are both top-heavy, a defined contribution minimum of 7½% of compensation for each non-key employee covered under both plans?		
12 If this is a profit-sharing plan, are employer contributions on behalf of permanently and totally disabled employees nonforfeitable when made?		
13 Does the plan provide that the minimum age required for participation may not exceed age 21?		
14 Does the plan count years of service upon attainment of age 18 for vesting purposes?		
15 Does the plan require at least five consecutive 1-year breaks in service in order to disregard:		
a Post-break service for pre-break vested accrued benefits (see instructions)?		
b In the case of a nonvested participant, pre-break service for participation or vesting?		
16 Are hours of service credited, during maternity or paternity absence, for purposes of determining whether a break in service has occurred?		
17 If the plan provides for disregarding service attributable to a cash out, does it meet the requirements of Code section 411(a)(7)(C)?		
18 Does the plan (if a pension plan) provide for the payment of benefits in the form of a qualified joint and survivor annuity and a qualified preretirement survivor annuity?		
19 If the answer to 18 is "N/A," and this is a profit-sharing or stock bonus plan, does it provide that:		
a The participant's nonforfeitable account balance will be paid on the death of the participant to the surviving spouse or, if the surviving spouse consents or if there is no surviving spouse, to a designated beneficiary of the participant?		

Answer all items either by checking "N/A" if the item does not apply, or by entering the Article or Section and Page Number of the plan where the provision is found in the plan.	**N/A**	**Article or Section and Page Number**
19 (Continued):		
b If a life annuity is offered and elected by the participant, the participant's benefits will be paid in the form of a qualified joint and survivor annuity?		
c If the plan is, or may become, a direct or indirect transferee, the survivor annuity benefit described in 18 will be provided with respect to the participant who received the transfer?		
20 Does the plan provide a procedure for the participant to waive the qualified joint and survivor annuity and the qualified preretirement survivor annuity during the election period?		
a In the case of the qualified joint and survivor annuity, does the election period begin no later than 90 days before the annuity starting date?		
b In the case of a qualified preretirement survivor annuity, does the election period begin on the first day of the plan year in which the participant attains age 35 and end on the date of the plan participant's death?		
c Does any waiver require the written consent of the participant's spouse to the waiver?		
21 Does the plan provide that if the present value of the vested accrued benefit of a participant exceeds $3,500, then the benefit cannot be paid out immediately without the consent of the participant?		
22 If this is a defined benefit plan, are the actuarial assumptions used to determine the amount of any benefit specified in the plan so as to preclude employer discretion?		
23 If this application relates to an amendment to an existing plan, does the amendment preclude either:		
a The elimination or reduction of an early retirement benefit or a subsidy that continues after retirement?		
b Elimination of an optional form of benefit?		
24 Does the plan provide for the following within the limitations of section 415:		
a For a defined contribution plan:		
(i) Definition and limitation of annual additions according to the Code and regulations?		
(ii) A mechanism by which excess annual additions due to a reasonable estimate of a participant's annual compensation or an allocation of forfeitures are reduced according to one of the methods described in the regulations?		
b For a defined benefit plan:		
(i) An annual benefit to which a participant may be entitled, limited to the lesser of (a) 100% of the participant's average compensation for his or her high 3 years of service, or (b) $90,000 (or other amounts as adjusted for cost of living increases under section 415(d))?		
(ii) If the plan provides a retirement benefit beginning on or after age 55 but before social security retirement age, is the benefit limited to the actuarial equivalent of a $90,000 (or the adjusted dollar limitation in item 24b(i) above) annual benefit beginning at social security retirement age?		
(iii) If the plan provides a retirement benefit beginning before age 55, is the benefit limited to the actuarial equivalent of a $90,000 (or the adjusted dollar limitation in 24b(i) above) annual benefit beginning at social security retirement age?		
(iv) Are the actuarial equivalents in 24b(ii) and (iii) based on an interest rate not less than the greater of 5% or the rate specified in the plan?		
(v) If the retirement benefit under the plan begins after social security retirement age, provision for an increase in the maximum dollar limitation on benefits to the actuarial equivalent of a $90,000 (or the adjusted dollar limitation in 24b(i) above) annual benefit beginning at social security retirement age, using an interest assumption no greater than the lesser of 5% or the rate specified in the plan?		
(vi) If the employer maintains, or at one time maintained, another qualified defined benefit plan, the plan or plans preclude the possibility that the limitations of 24b(i)-(v) will be exceeded when all such defined benefit plans are treated as one plan?		
(vii) If the plan is a pre-TEFRA defined benefit plan, does it preserve a participant's accrued benefit that was properly accrued under pre-TEFRA law?		
c If the employer maintains another qualified defined contribution plan (or a defined benefit plan to which nondeductible employee contributions are made), the plan or plans preclude the possibility that the limitations of 24a(i) and/or 24b(i) will be exceeded when all such defined contribution plans and/or defined benefit plans are treated as one plan?		

Answer all items either by checking "N/A" if the item does not apply, or by entering the Article or Section and Page Number of the plan where the provision is found in the plan.	**N/A**	**Article or Section and Page Number**
24 (Continued):		
d If this plan is a defined contribution plan and the employer maintains, or at any time maintained, a qualified defined benefit plan, or if this plan is a defined benefit plan and the employer maintains, or at any time maintained, a qualified defined contribution plan, do the provisions of the plan preclude the possibility that, with respect to any participant for a limitation year, the sum of the defined benefit plan fraction and the defined contribution plan fraction will exceed 1.0?		
e If the plan is or becomes a top-heavy plan subject to the requirement of section 416(h)(1), the required adjustment to the computation of the defined benefit and defined contribution fraction denominators will be made?		
25 If this is an integrated defined contribution plan, does the contribution rate satisfy section 401(l)?		
26a Does the employer receive services from any leased employees within the meaning of section 414(n)?		
b If "Yes," are the leased employees included as employees in the employee data given for the plan?		
27a Distributions before death:		
(i) Does the plan require that distributions to a participant other than a 5% owner begin not later than April 1 of the calendar year following the later of the calendar year in which the participant attains age 70½ or the calendar year in which the participant retires?		
(ii) Does the plan require that distributions to a 5% owner begin not later than April 1 following the calendar year in which he or she attains age 70½?		
(iii) Will distribution(s) of the participant's entire interest be made in one of the following ways: in a lump sum; over the life of the participant; over the life of the participant and a designated beneficiary; over a period certain not extending beyond the life expectancy of the participant; or over a period certain not extending beyond the joint life and last survivor expectancy of the participant and a designated beneficiary?		
b Distributions after death:		
(i) Does the plan provide that if distribution has started before the participant's death, the remaining interest will be distributed at least as rapidly as under the method being used as of the date of the participant's death?		
(ii) Does the plan provide that if the participant dies before distribution begins, the portion of the participant's interest that is not payable to a beneficiary designated by the participant will be distributed within 5 years after such participant's death?		
(iii) Does the plan provide that if the participant dies before distribution begins, any portion of the participant's interest that is payable to a beneficiary designated by the participant will be distributed over the life of such beneficiary (or over a period not to exceed the life expectancy of the beneficiary) beginning not later than the later of one year after the participant's death, or, if the designated beneficiary is the participant's surviving spouse, the date on which the participant would have attained age 70½?		
c Transitional rule:		
If the plan permits an employee to designate before January 1, 1984, a method of distribution that does not satisfy section 401(a)(9), as in effect on January 1, 1985, does the method satisfy the requirements of section 401(a) as in effect before January 1, 1984?		

Reminder: *If this request relates to the adoption of a master or prototype or uniform plan, you must attach the latest opinion or notification letter issued to the sponsor. If this request relates to an amendment of an individually designed plan, you must attach a copy of the latest determination letter.*

Instructions

(Section references are to the Internal Revenue Code unless otherwise noted.)

Purpose of Form.—Schedule T (Form 5300) is used by applicants requesting a favorable determination letter on the qualified status of certain retirement plans to provide information under the Tax Equity and Fiscal Responsibility Act of 1982 (TEFRA), the Tax Reform Act of 1984 (TRA 1984), Retirement Equity Act of 1984 (REA), and the Tax Reform Act of 1986 (TRA 1986).

It should be attached to a Form 5300, 5301, 5303, 5307, or 6406 (whichever is appropriate) in order for the application to be complete. However, if you previously submitted a Schedule T with an application covering amendments under TEFRA, TRA of 1984, and REA, and received a favorable determination letter covering the amendments, and you are now making amendments not under these laws, attach a photocopy of the previous Schedule T and a brief explanation that your amendments under these laws have been approved by IRS (give date approved) and a new Schedule T is not required under these circumstances.

Note: *Determination letters pursuant to the submission of this form apply to changes under the Tax Reform Act of 1986 only to the extent that they are made to incorporate changes under sections 415(b)(2) and 416(g)(4) as amended by TRA of 1986.*

1. Enter the name, address, and EIN of the plan sponsor as shown on the Form 5300, 5301, 5303, 5307, or 6406 to which this schedule is attached.

2. Plans are not required to contain section 416 provisions, except for 416(h) in cases of multiple plans, if the plans contain a single benefit structure that satisfies the requirements of section 416(b), (c), and (d). Also, certain collectively bargained plans and government plans need not contain section 416 provisions. See T-36, T-37, and T-38 of Section 1.416-1 of the Income Tax Regulations. Unless the above applies, the plan must contain provisions that are effective in any plan year in which the plan is top-heavy. The contributions must satisfy the vesting requirement of section 416(b), the minimum benefit provision of section 416(c), the compensation limits of section 416(d), and the adjustment to section 415 limits in section 416(h). The plan must also preclude any change in the plan's benefit structure (including vesting) resulting from a change in the plan's top-heavy status from violating section 411(a)(10).

4a. See sections 416(c)(1)(A) and (B).

4b. See M-4 of Regulations section 1.416-1, effective for plan years beginning after December 31,1983.

5b. Effective for plan years beginning after December 31, 1984, see T-29 of Regulations section 1.416-1.

8. A qualified plan must contain some mechanism by which the plan administrator can implement the section 416 minimum requirements if the plan becomes top-heavy. A defined benefit plan is top-heavy when the ratio of the present value of accrued benefits for key employees to the present value of accrued benefits for all employees (including beneficiaries but excluding former key employees who are now non-key employees) exceeds 60%. All distributions that were made during the 5-year period ending on the most recent determination date must be taken into account. For plan years beginning after December 31, 1984, if an individual has not received compensation as an employee with respect to any plan of the employer at any time during the five-year period ending on the determination date for such (top-heaviness) testing, then any accrued benefit or account balance of the individual is disregarded.

Employee contributions, whether mandatory or voluntary, must be taken into account (except for deductible employee contributions).

If the employer maintains other qualified plans (including a Simplified Employee Plan), benefits from all plans in the required aggregation group must be taken into account for purposes of determining the top-heavy ratio.

For more complete definitions of the terms in Item 8, see section 416 and Regulations section 1.416-1.

9. For plan years beginning after December 31, 1986, accrued benefits will be treated as accruing ratably for purposes of determining whether the plan is top-heavy.

10. See M-12 of Regulations section 1.416-1.

11. See T-37, M-12, and M-14 of Regulations section 1.416-1.

12. This item is effective for tax years beginning after 1981.

13. REA amended section 410(a)(1)(A)(i) to provide that a plan cannot exclude from participation employees who have attained age 21, effective for plan years beginning after December 31, 1984.

14. REA amended section 411(a)(4)(A) to provide that a plan must count, for vesting purposes, years of service completed after the employee has attained age 18. This change is effective for plan years beginning after December 31, 1984.

15. See sections 410(a)(5)(D) and 411(a)(6)(C) and (D) as amended by REA; effective for plan years beginning after December 31, 1984.

16. Sections 410(a)(5)(E) and 411(a)(6)(E) were added to the Code by REA to provide, in general, that a maximum of 501 hours of service must be credited to an individual who is on maternity or paternity leave, effective for plan years beginning after December 31, 1984.

18–20. See section 401(a)(11) as amended by REA, effective for plan years beginning after December 31, 1984.

21. See section 411(a)(7)(B) as amended by REA and effective for plan years beginning after December 31, 1984.

22. See section 401(a)(25) and Rev. Rul. 79-90, 1979-1 C.B. 155.

23. See section 411(d)(6) and Rev. Rul. 81-12, 1981-1 C.B. 228.

24. TEFRA decreased the maximum dollar limitations applicable to qualified defined contribution and defined benefit plans. These new limits apply to limitation years ending after July 1, 1982, for plans not in existence on that date, and apply to limitation years beginning after December 31, 1982, for all other plans. Plans may continue to have "Cost of Living" language even though no adjustments will be made with respect to any calendar year beginning before 1988. See T-1 and T-7 of Notice 83-10, 1983-1 C.B. 536. Also see sections 415, 415(b)(2)(C), (D), and (E); and 415(d)(2)(A) and 415(d)(3) as amended by TRA of 1984.

26. Section 414(n) (added by TEFRA) deals with persons who are the employees of any employee leasing organization, but who perform services during the course of their employment for a separate trade or business (a recipient organization). Such leased employees are to be considered employees of the recipient organization at certain times and for certain qualification requirements unless the leasing organization adopts and maintains the type of qualified plan specified in section 414(n)(5).

Section 414(n)(5) provides a safe harbor for a recipient organization if the leasing organization maintains a qualified, nonintegrated, money purchase pension plan that provides for immediate participation, full and immediate vesting, and an annual contribution of at least 7½% of compensation. In general, if these requirements are met, the leased employee does not have to be counted for any purpose pertaining to the qualified plans of the recipient organization. However, the TRA of 1984 clarified section 414(n) to emphasize that common-law employer-employee principles are applicable in this area.

27a and b. The TRA of 1984 amended section 401(a)(9), as in effect prior to the amendments made by TEFRA. This means that for distributions in calendar years prior to calendar year 1985, distributions will be made according to section 401(a)(9) as constituted prior to TEFRA. For plan years beginning after 12/31/84, the TRA of 1984 distribution rules are effective. Also, if an employee designated a method of distribution before January 1, 1984, as allowed by TEFRA, which met the requirements of section 401(a)(9) as in effect on December 31, 1983, then it will be considered a valid method.

Form **5302**
(Rev. November 1987)
Department of the Treasury
Internal Revenue Service

Employee Census

▶ **Attach to application for determination—defined benefit and defined contribution plans.** **(Round off to nearest dollar)**

Schedule of 25 highest paid participating employees for 12-month period ended ▶

OMB No. 1545-0416
Expires 11-30-90

This Form is NOT Open to Public Inspection

Name of employer

Employer identification number

Line no.	Participant's last name and initials (See instructions)	Check				Annual Nondeferred Compensation				Defined Benefit		Defined Contribution			
		Officer, shareholder, or self-employed	Percent of voting stock or business owned	Age	Years of service	Used in computing benefits or employee's share of contributions	Excluded	Total	Employee contributions under the plan	Annual benefit expected under this plan	Annual benefit under each other qualified defined benefit plan of deferred compensation	Employer contribution allocated	Number of units, if any	Forfeitures allocated in the year	Amount allocated under each other defined contribution plan of deferred compensation
	(a)	(b)	(c)	(d)	(e)	(f)	(g)	(h)	(i)	(j)	(k)	(l)	(m)	(n)	(o)
1															
2															
3															
4															
5															
6															
7															
8															
9															
10															
11															
12															
13															
14															
15															
16															
17															
18															
19															
20															
21															
22															
23															
24															
25															
Total for above															
Totals for all others (specify number ▶)															
Total for all participants															

For Paperwork Reduction Act Notice, see back of this form.

See instructions on the back of this form.

Form **5302** (Rev. 11-87)

General Information

(Section references are to the Internal Revenue Code unless otherwise noted.)

Paperwork Reduction Act Notice.—We ask for this information to carry out the Internal Revenue laws of the United States. We need it to determine whether taxpayers meet the legal requirements for plan approval. If you want to have your plan approved by IRS, you are required to give us this information.

Purpose of Form.—This schedule is to be used by the Internal Revenue Service in its analysis of an application for determination as to whether a plan of deferred compensation qualifies under section 401(a) and 401(k), if applicable.

Public Inspection.—Section 6104(a)(1)(B) provides, generally, that applications filed for the qualification of a pension, profit-sharing, or stock bonus plan will be open to public inspection. However, section 6104(a)(1)(C) provides that information concerning the compensation of any participant will not be open to public inspection. Consequently, the information contained in this schedule will not be open to public inspection, including inspection by plan participants and other employees of the employer who established the plan.

General Instructions

Prepare the employee census for a current 12-month period. Generally the 12-month period should be the employer's tax year, a calendar year, or the plan year. If the actual information is not available, compensation, contributions, etc., may be projected for a 12-month period. However, such projection must be clearly identified.

Who Must File.—Every employer or plan administrator who files an application for determination for a defined benefit or a defined contribution plan is required to attach this schedule, complete in all details.

For collectively bargained plans a Form 5302 is required only if the plan covers employees of the representative labor union(s) or of any plan(s) for union members, and, if so, a separate Form 5302 is required for each such union or plan. For a plan, other than a collectively bargained plan, maintained by more than one employer (where all employers in each affiliated service group, controlled group of corporations, or group of trades or businesses under common control are considered one employer) a separate Form 5302 is required for each such employer.

Specific Instructions

Column (a), first list any participant who at any time during the 5-year period prior to the start of the current 12-month period owned directly or indirectly 10% or more of the voting stock or 10% or more of the business. Next, list the remaining participants in order of current compensation (see Note 2 and instructions for column (h), below) starting with the highest paid, followed by the next highest paid and so on. If there are fewer than 25 participants, list all the participants. Otherwise, only the first 25 who fall under the priorities listed above need be listed on lines 1 through 25.

Note 1: *For purposes of this form, "participant" means any employee who satisfies the participation requirements prescribed by the plan.*

Column (b), enter a check mark or an "X" to indicate that a participant is either an officer, a shareholder, or self-employed. If a participant is none of the above, enter N/A in this column for that participant.

Column (c), (i) enter the percentage of voting stock owned by a participant. For example, participant "P" owns 200 shares of voting stock of the employer's 5,000 shares outstanding. The percentage is 4% (200 ÷ 5,000). If a participant owns only nonvoting stock of the employer, make no entry in this column.

(ii) if an unincorporated business, enter the percentage of the business owned by the participant.

If a participant owns neither of the above, enter N/A.

Column (d), enter the attained age of each participant as of the end of the year for which this schedule applies. For example, if a participant's 47th birthday was on January 7, 1988, and the schedule covers the calendar year 1988, enter 47 for that participant.

Column (e), enter the number of full years of service each participant has been employed by the employer, and any prior employer if such employment is recognized for plan purposes.

Column (f), enter the amount of each participant's compensation that is recognized for plan purposes in computing the benefit (for a defined benefit plan) or in computing the amount of employer contribution that is allocated to the account of each participant (for a defined contribution plan). Do not include any portion of the employer contributions to this or any other qualified plan as compensation for any participant.

Column (g), enter the amount of compensation that is not recognized for purposes of column (f). For example, if a participant received $12,500 compensation for the year, $1,000 of which was a bonus and the plan does not recognize bonuses for plan purposes, enter $11,500 in column (f) and $1,000 in column (g).

Note 2: *"Compensation" for purposes of column (h) is defined as all amounts (including bonuses and overtime) paid to the participant for services rendered the employer. Do not enter employer contributions made to this or any other qualified plan.*

Column (h), enter the total amount of compensation for the year for each participant. The amount entered in this column will be the sum of the amounts entered in columns (f) and (g) for each participant.

Column (i), enter the total amount of mandatory and voluntary contributions made by each participant. If the plan does not provide for employee contributions of any kind, enter "N/A."

Column (j), enter the amount of benefit each participant may expect to receive at normal retirement age based on current information, assuming no future compensation increases. For example, under a 30% benefit plan, a participant whose benefit is based on annual compensation of $10,000 may expect an annual benefit of $3,000 ($10,000 × 30%) at retirement. In this case enter $3,000.

Column (k), enter the amount of benefit each participant may expect to receive under other qualified defined benefit plan(s) of deferred compensation of the employer.

Column (l), enter the amount of the employer's contribution that is allocated to the account of each participant.

Column (m), enter the number of units, if any, used to determine the amount of the employer contribution that is allocated to each participant.

Column (n), enter the amount of the forfeitures that is allocated to each participant, unless forfeitures are allocated to reduce employer contributions.

Column (o), enter the portion of the employer's contribution that is attributable to the cost for providing each participant's benefits under all defined contribution plans of the employer other than this plan.

Caution: *Before submitting this schedule, be sure that all relevant items are complete. Failure to meet this requirement may result in a request for the missing information or return of the schedule for completion, in which event there will be a delay in processing your application.*

Form **5303** (Rev. March 1986)

Department of the Treasury
Internal Revenue Service

Application for
Determination for Collectively Bargained Plan
(Under Sections 401(a) and 501(a) of the Internal Revenue Code)
(Section references are to the Internal Revenue Code.)

OMB No. 1545-0534
Expires 3-30-89

For IRS Use Only
File folder number ▶
Case number ▶

Church and governmental plans not subject to ERISA need not complete items 9, 10b, 10c, 13, 15g, 15l, and 17c.

All other plans must complete all items except as indicated on specific lines. For example, if you answer "No" to line 7b, you need not complete line 11b since it requires a response only if you answer "Yes" to line 7b. N/A is only an acceptable answer if an N/A block is provided. All applications are now computer screened, therefore it is important that you provide all the information requested and have the application signed by the employer, plan administrator, or authorized representative. Otherwise, we may need to correspond with you or return your application for completion, which will delay its processing.

1a Name of plan sponsor (employer if a single employer plan)
Address (number and street)
City or town, state and ZIP code

1b Employer identification number

1c Employer's tax year ends
Month ☐ N/A
Telephone number
( )

2 Person to be contacted if more information is needed. (If same as 1a, enter "same as 1a.") (See Specific Instructions.)
Name
Address
Telephone number
( )

3a Determination requested for (Check applicable boxes): (See Instruction B. "What to File.")
(i) ☐ Initial qualification—Date plan signed ________ Date plan effective ________
(ii) ☐ Amendment after initial qualification—Is plan restated? ☐ Yes ☐ No Date amendment signed ________
Date amendment effective ________ Date plan effective ________
(iii) ☐ Partial termination—Date effective ________ Date plan effective ________
(iv) ☐ Termination of multiemployer plan covered by PBGC insurance . . . . . Date effective ________
Date plan effective ________

b Enter IRS file folder number shown on the last determination letter issued to the plan sponsor ________ ☐ N/A

c Is this application also expected to satisfy the notice requirement for this plan for merger, consolidation, or transfer of plan assets or liabilities involving another plan (see Specific Instructions)? . . . ☐ Yes ☐ No

d Were employees who are interested parties given the required notification of the filing of this application? . . . ☐ Yes ☐ No

e Is this plan or trust currently under examination or is any issue related to this plan or trust currently pending before the Internal Revenue Service, the Department of Labor, the Pension Benefit Guaranty Corporation, or any court? . . . ☐ Yes ☐ No
If "Yes," attach explanation.

f Does your plan contain cash or deferred arrangements described in section 401(k)? . . . ☐ Yes ☐ No

g If 3f is "Yes," is a determination also requested with regard to the qualifications of those provisions (see Instruction B)? . . . ☐ Yes ☐ No

4a Name of plan
b Plan number ▶ ________
c Plan year ends ▶

5 Check proper box for the type of plan entity:
a ☐ Single employer plan
b ☐ Plan of controlled group of corporations or trades or businesses under common control
c ☐ Multiemployer plan
d ☐ Multiple-employer-collectively-bargained plan (other than a multiemployer plan)
e ☐ Church plan
f ☐ Governmental plan
g ☐ Other (specify) ▶

6 Is this an adoption of a master or prototype plan? ☐ Yes ☐ No—If "Yes," complete 6a and 6b
a Name of plan
b Letter serial number

7a Is this a defined benefit plan? . . . ☐ Yes ☐ No—If "Yes," indicate whether:
(i) ☐ Unit benefit (ii) ☐ Fixed benefit (iii) ☐ Flat benefit (iv) ☐ Other (specify) ________

b Is this a defined contribution plan? . . . ☐ Yes ☐ No—If "Yes," indicate whether: (i) ☐ Profit-sharing
(ii) ☐ Stock bonus (iii) ☐ Money purchase (iv) ☐ Target benefit (v) ☐ Other (specify) ________

c Does plan provide for variable benefits? ☐ Yes ☐ No ☐ N/A

d Is this plan, or was this plan before amendment, a defined benefit plan covered under the Pension Benefit Guaranty Corporation termination insurance program? . . . ☐ Yes ☐ No ☐ Not determined

Under penalties of perjury, I declare that I have examined this application, including accompanying statements, and to the best of my knowledge and belief it is true, correct, and complete.

Signature ▶ ________ **Title** ▶ ________ **Date** ▶ ________

Signature ▶ ________ **Title** ▶ ________ **Date** ▶ ________

For Paperwork Reduction Act Notice, see page 1 of the instructions.

Form **5303** (Rev. 3-86)

Where applicable, indicate the article or section and page number of the plan or other document (trust or collective-bargaining agreement) where the following provisions are contained. N/A is an appropriate response only if a check block is provided.

	Section and Page Number
8a General eligibility requirements: (Check box (i), (ii), (iii) or (iv), and complete (v), (vi) and (vii).)	
(i) ☐ All employees *(ii)* ☐ Hourly rate employees only *(iii)* ☐ Salaried employees only	
(iv) ☐ Other (specify) ▶	
(v) Length of service (number of years) ▶ ☐ N/A	
(vi) Minimum age (specify) ▶ ☐ N/A	
(vii) Maximum age (specify) ▶ ☐ N/A	
b Does any plan amendment since the last determination letter alter the method of crediting service for eligibility? ☐ Yes ☐ No ☐ N/A	

	Number Enter "0" if N/A (see instructions)
9 Coverage of plan at (give date) ▶	
a *(i)* Total number of participants, including certain retired and terminated employees (see Specific Instructions).	
(ii) Participants whose benefits or accounts are fully vested	
(iii) Number of contributing employers	
b Does this plan cover employees of the representative labor union(s) or of any plan(s) for union members? ☐ Yes ☐ No	
c Complete only if **b** is "Yes" (see Specific Instructions).	
(i) Total employed by union or plan	
(ii) Exclusions—	
a. Minimum age or years of service required (specify which) ▶	
b. Nonresident aliens who receive no earned income from United States sources	
c. Other (specify) ▶	
(iii) Total exclusions (add (ii) a through c)	
(iv) Employees not excluded under the statute (subtract (iii) from (i))	
(v) Employees who do not meet plan eligibility requirements	
(vi) Employees eligible to participate (subtract (v) from (iv)).	
(vii) Employees participating in the plan	
d If **b** is "Yes," attach a separate completed Form 5302 for employees of such union or plan.	
e Has a plan amendment since the last determination letter resulted in exclusion of previously covered employees? ☐ Yes ☐ No ☐ N/A	

	Yes	No	N/A	Section and Page Number
10 Does the plan define the following terms—				
a Compensation?				
b Break in service?				
c Hour of service (under Department of Labor Regulations)?				
d Joint and survivor annuity?				
e Normal retirement age?				
f Year of service?				
g Entry date?				
11a Employee contributions:				
(i) Does the plan document allow voluntary deductible employee contributions?				
(ii) If "Yes," are the voluntary deductible employee contributions appropriately limited?				
(iii) Are voluntary nondeductible contributions limited for all qualified plans to 10%, or less, of compensation?				
(iv) Are employee contributions nonforfeitable?				
b Employer contributions: If line 7b is "Yes," complete (i), (ii), (iii), or (iv) below:				
(i) Profit-sharing or stock bonus plan contributions are determined under: ☐ A definite formula ☐ An indefinite formula ☐ Both				
(ii) Profit-sharing or stock bonus plan contributions are limited to: ☐ Current earnings ☐ Accumulated earnings ☐ Combination				
(iii) Money purchase—Enter rate of contribution ▶				
(iv) State target benefit formula, if applicable ▶				
12 Integration:				
Is this plan integrated with social security or railroad retirement?				
If "Yes," and this is a defined benefit plan or a target benefit plan, attach a schedule of compliance with Rev. Rul. 71-446 (see Specific Instructions).				

Form 5303 (Rev. 3-86) Page **3**

	Yes	No	N/A	Section and Page Number
13 Vesting:				
a Are years of service with other members of a controlled group of corporations, trades or businesses under common control, or an affiliated service group counted for purposes of vesting and eligibility to participate?.				
b Are employee's rights to normal retirement benefits nonforfeitable on reaching normal retirement age as defined in section 411(a)(8)?				
c Does any amendment to the plan decrease any participant's accrued benefits?				
d Does any amendment to the plan directly or indirectly affect the computation of the nonforfeitable percentage of a participant's accrued benefit?				
e Does the plan preclude forfeiture of an employee's vested benefits for cause?				
f Check only one of the boxes to indicate the vesting provisions of the plan: *(i)* ☐ Full and immediate. *(ii)* ☐ Full vesting after 10 years of service; i.e., no vesting for the first 9 years, 100% after 10 years (section 411(a)(2)(A)). *(iii)* ☐ 5- to 15-year vesting as defined in section 411(a)(2)(B). *(iv)* ☐ Rule of 45 (section 411(a)(2)(C)). *(v)* ☐ 4/40 vesting (Rev. Procs. 75-49 and 76-11). *(vi)* ☐ 10% vesting for each year of service (not to exceed 100%). *(vii)* ☐ 100% vesting within 5 years after contributions are made (class year plans only). *(viii)* ☐ Other (specify—see Specific Instructions and attach schedule).				
14 Administration: **a** Type of funding entity: *(i)* ☐ Trust (benefits provided in whole from trust funds). *(ii)* ☐ Custodial account described in section 401(f) and not included in (iv) below. *(iii)* ☐ Trust or arrangement providing benefits partially through insurance and/or annuity contracts. *(iv)* ☐ Trust or arrangement providing benefits exclusively through insurance and/or annuity contracts. *(v)* ☐ Other (specify). ▶				
b Does the trust agreement prohibit reversion of funds to the employer?				
c Are limits placed on the purchase of insurance contracts? If "Yes," specify the limits in (i), (ii) or (iii).				
(i) Ordinary life ▶				
(ii) Term insurance ▶				
(iii) Other (specify) ▶				
d If the trustees may earmark specific investments including insurance contracts, are such investments subject to the employee's consent, or purchased ratably when employee consent is not required?				
e Are loans to participants limited to their vested interests?				
15 Requirements for benefits—distributions—allocations:				
a Normal retirement age is ▶ ...... If applicable, years of service/participation required ▶				
b Does the plan contain an early retirement provision? If "Yes,"				
(i) Early retirement age is ▶				
(ii) Years of service/participation required ▶				
c Does the plan provide for payment of benefits according to section 401(a)(14)?				
Note: *Complete* **d** *and* **e** *only if this plan is a defined contribution plan.* **d** Distribution of account balances may be made in: *(i)* ☐ Lump-sum *(ii)* ☐ Annuity contracts *(iii)* ☐ Substantially equal annual installments—not more than ▶ .... years *(iv)* ☐ Other (specify) ▶ **e** If distributions are made in installments, they are credited with: *(i)* ☐ Fund earnings *(ii)* ☐ Interest at a rate of ▶ .... % per year *(iii)* ☐ Other (specify) ▶				
f Does this plan comply with the payment of benefits provisions of section 401(a)(11)?				
g If this is a stock bonus plan, are distributions made in employer stock?				
h If this is a pension plan, does it permit distribution before normal retirement age only on death, disability, plan termination, or termination of employment?				
i If this is a profit-sharing or stock bonus plan, what other events permit distributions?				

		Yes	No	N/A	Section and Page Number
15	Requirements for benefits—distributions—allocations: (continued)				
j	If participants may withdraw their mandatory contributions or earnings, may withdrawal be made without forfeiting vested benefits based on employer contributions?				
k	Are contributions allocated or benefits computed on the basis of total compensation? If "No," see instructions and attach schedule.				
l	Are forfeitures allocated, in case of a profit-sharing or stock bonus plan, on the basis of total compensation? If "No," explain how they are allocated.				
m	Are trust earnings and losses allocated on the basis of account balances? If "No," explain how they are allocated.				
n	In case of target benefit or other money purchase plan, are forfeitures applied to reduce employer contributions?				
o	Does the plan provide for maximum limitation under section 415?				
p	Does the plan prohibit the assignment or alienation of benefits?				
q	Does the plan meet the requirements of section 401(a)(12)?				
r	Are trust assets valued at fair market value?				
s	Are trust assets valued at least annually on a specified date? If "No," explain.				
16	Additional information for defined benefit plans only:				
a	Method of determining accrued benefit ▶				
	(i) Benefit formula at normal retirement age is ▶				
	(ii) Benefit formula at early retirement age is ▶				
	(iii) Normal form of retirement benefits is ▶				
b	Are benefits under the plan definitely determinable at all times (see Rev. Rul. 79-90)?				
c	Does the plan disregard service attributable to a distribution in computing the employer-derived accrued benefit?				
d	If **c** is "Yes," does the plan contain provisions that satisfy regulations section 1.411(a)-7(d)(4) or (6)?				
e	Are distributions limited so that no more than incidental death benefits are provided?				
f	As a result of a plan amendment, has the amount of benefit or rate of accrual of the benefit been reduced?				
17	Termination of plan or trust:				
a	Are the participants' rights to benefits under the plan nonforfeitable (to the extent funded) upon termination or partial termination of the plan?				
b	If this is a defined benefit plan, has the early termination rule been included in the plan (see regulations section 1.401-4(c))?				
c	Upon complete discontinuance of contributions under a profit-sharing or stock bonus plan are the employees' rights under the plan nonforfeitable?				

Form 5303 (Rev. 3-86) Page **6**

Caution

The following Procedural Requirements Checklist identifies certain basic data that will facilitate the processing of your application. While no response is required to the questions, you may find that answering them will ensure that your application is processed without the need for contact to obtain missing information. If the answer to any of the questions is "No," your application may be incomplete. INCOMPLETE APPLICATIONS ARE IDENTIFIED THROUGH A COMPUTER SCREENING SYSTEM FOR RETURN TO THE APPLICANT. Detach this checksheet before submitting the application. You may wish to keep it for your records. DO NOT SEND THIS CHECKSHEET TO IRS.

Procedural Requirements Checklist

	Yes	No	N/A
1 General requirements:			
a If this application is made by a representative on behalf of the plan sponsor or plan administrator, has a current power of attorney been submitted with this application (see "Signature" under General Information)?			
b If notices or other communications are to be sent to someone other than the plan sponsor, have you provided proper authorization by attaching a completed **Form 2848**, Power of Attorney and Declaration of Representative, or by attaching a statement that contains all the information required (see Specific Instructions)?			
c If applicable, have you completed and attached Form(s) 5302?			
d Have you signed the application?			
e Have you completed and attached Schedule T (Form 5300)?			
2 Specific requirements:			
a If this is a request for a determination letter on initial qualification of the plan, have you attached the following documents:			
(i) Copies of all instruments constituting the plan?			
(ii) Copies of trust indentures, group annuity contracts, or custodial agreements?			
b If this is a request for a determination letter on the effect an amendment will have on the plan after initial qualification, have you attached the following documents:			
(i) A copy of the plan amendments?			
(ii) A description of the amendment covering the changes to the plan sections?			
(iii) An explanation of the plan sections before the amendment?			
(iv) An explanation of the effect of the amendment on the provisions of the plan sections?			
c If this is a request for a determination letter on the qualification of the entire plan, as amended after initial qualification, have you included the following documents:			
(i) A copy of the plan incorporating all amendments made to the date of the application?			
(ii) A statement indicating that the copy of the plan is complete in all respects and that a determination letter is being requested on the qualification of the entire plan?			
(iii) A copy of trust indentures, group annuity contracts, or custodial agreements, if there has been any change since copies were last furnished to IRS?			
d For partial termination:			
(i) Have you completed line 3a according to the Specific Instructions?			
(ii) Have you attached the information for a partial termination requested in General Instruction B?			
e For a plan that contains a cash or deferred arrangement, have you submitted the appropriate information requested for line 9?			
f For governmental and church plans, have you completed Form 5303 according to General Instruction B?			
g For notice of merger, consolidation, or transfer of plan assets or liabilities, have you submitted the information requested in the Specific Instructions for line 3c?			
3 Miscellaneous requirements:			
a Have you entered the plan sponsor's 9-digit employer identification number in item 1b?			
b If a determination letter was previously issued to this sponsor for any plan, have you entered the file folder number on line 3b?			
c Have you answered item 3d?			
d If this plan has been amended at least four times since the last determination letter on the entire plan was issued, have you attached a copy of the plan that includes all amendments made to the plan since that determination letter was issued?			
e Have you entered the effective date of the plan in the space provided by the block you checked for line 3a?			
f If applicable, have you attached schedules or other documentation as required by line items 2, 3e, 9d, 12, 13f(viii), 15k, 15l, 15m, and 15s?			

Department of the Treasury
Internal Revenue Service

Instructions for Form 5303

(Revised March 1986)

Application for Determination for Collectively Bargained Plan

(Section references are to the Internal Revenue Code, unless otherwise noted.)

General Information

Paperwork Reduction Act Notice.—We ask for this information to carry out the Internal Revenue laws of the United States. We need it to determine whether you meet the legal requirements for plan approval. If you want to have your plan approved by IRS, you are required to give us this information.

Purpose.—The Employee Retirement Income Security Act of 1974 (ERISA) provides special rules for qualifying a plan maintained under an agreement which the Secretary of Labor finds to be a collective-bargaining agreement between employee representatives and one or more employers. In determining whether there is a collective-bargaining agreement between employee representatives and 1 or more employers, the term "employee representative" will not include any organization more than one-half of the members of which are employees who are owners, officers, or executives of the employer.

Form 5303 may be used by a sponsor of a collectively bargained plan that covers only employees covered by a collective-bargaining agreement, including employees of the representative labor union(s) or of any plan(s) for union members or by a sponsor of a multiemployer plan, for the following reasons:

1. To request a determination letter on initial qualification or on amendment after initial qualification.

2. To request a determination letter regarding the effect of a potential partial termination on the plan's qualification.

3. To give notice of merger, consolidation, or transfer of plan assets or liabilities (required by section 6058(b)) and request a determination on the plan. (See Instruction B. "What to File." and item 3c under Specific Instructions.)

4. To request a determination letter regarding termination of a multiemployer plan covered by PBGC insurance.

Form 5303 may also be used to obtain a determination on whether a defined contribution plan contains a qualified cash or deferred arrangement within the meaning of section 401(k).

Disclosure Requested by Taxpayer.—See Item 2 under Specific Instructions for the information the request should include.

Public Inspection.—The application is open to public inspection if there are more than 25 participants. Therefore, it is important that the total number of participants be shown on line 9a(i). See the Specific Instructions for the definition of participant.

Signature.—The application must be signed by the employer, plan administrator or an authorized representative who must be either an attorney, a certified public accountant or a person enrolled to practice before the IRS. (See Treasury Department Circular No. 230 (Revised).) An application made by a representative on behalf of an employer or plan administrator must be accompanied by:

1. A power of attorney specifically authorizing representation in this matter (you may use **Form 2848**, Power of Attorney and Declaration of Representative); or

2. A written declaration that the representative is a currently qualified attorney, certified public accountant, or is currently enrolled to practice before the IRS (include either the enrollment number or the expiration date of the enrollment card) and is authorized to represent the employer or plan administrator.

General Instructions

A determination letter may be requested from the Internal Revenue Service for the qualification of a defined benefit plan or a defined contribution plan and the exempt status of any related trust. A defined contribution plan is a plan that provides for an individual account for each participant and for benefits based solely on the amount contributed to the participant's account, and any income, expenses, gains and losses, and any forfeitures of accounts of other participants which may be allocated to the participant's account. A defined benefit plan is any plan that is not a defined contribution plan.

Determination applications are now screened for completeness by computer. For this reason, it is important that an appropriate response be entered for each line item, except as indicated in item 5 below. In completing the application, be sure to pay careful attention to the following:

1. N/A (Not Applicable) is accepted as a response only if an N/A block is provided.

2. If an item requests a numerical response, a number must be entered.

3. If an item provides a choice of boxes to be checked, only one box should be checked unless instructions tell you to do otherwise.

4. If an item provides a box or boxes to be checked, written responses are not acceptable.

5. If the Church or Governmental organization block is checked for line item 5, certain line items need not be completed. In this regard, refer to instruction B. "What to File." below, to determine which items to complete if this application is for a church or governmental plan.

Only one copy of the application must be filed. Attach only one copy of each document and statement requested on the form or in the instructions. (See the Procedural Requirements Checklist attached to Form 5303.) Please refer to Instruction B. "What to File." below, to determine which items to complete if this application is for a church or governmental plan or the termination of certain multi-employer plans. For all other plans, all items must be completed.

The key district office may request additional information or return the application for completion if the application and attachments do not contain enough information to make a determination. In either case, the result will be a delay in issuing a determination letter. The Procedural Requirements Checklist will help you ensure that your application is complete.

A. Who May File.—This form may be filed by the employer or plan administrator of a plan maintained under a collective-bargaining agreement between employee representatives and one or more employers desiring a determination letter for initial qualification, amendment, partial termination of a plan, or termination of a multiemployer plan covered by PBGC insurance.

B. What to File.—Any plan administrator making a determination request for a plan should file one Form 5303. Only one application should be filed for each plan maintained by a single employer; i.e., if there are two separate plans, then two separate applications should be filed, etc.

Note: *Do not file* **Form 5302**, Employee Census, *with this application, except as required by line 9d for the employees of each union and/or each plan.*

A separate application must be filed for each defined benefit plan and for each defined contribution plan.

The following specifies what to file when requesting a determination letter:

For initial qualification (Rev. Proc. 80-30, 1980-1 C. B. 685), file the application form and a copy of the appropriate documents and statements summarized in items 1, 2a, and 3 of the Procedural Requirements Checklist.

For the effect of an amendment on the plan (Rev. Proc. 81-19, 1981-1 C.B. 689), file the application form and a copy of the appropriate documents and statements summarized in items 1, 2b, and 3 of the Procedural Requirements Checklist. A restated plan is required if four or more amendments have been made since the last restated plan was submitted. For restatement purposes, an amendment making only nonsubstantive plan changes need not be counted as a plan amendment. A nonsubstantive change will not affect the plan's qualification, i.e., a change in name, address, or trustee of a corporate type plan.

Note: In lieu of Form 5303, **Form 6406,** Short Form Application for Determination for Amendment of Employee Benefit Plan, may be used when requesting a determination letter on the effect of an amendment on a plan on which a favorable determination letter has been issued under ERISA. See Rev. Proc. 81-19, for further explanation on who may file Form 6406.

For qualification of the entire plan, as amended after initial qualification (Rev. Proc. 81-19), file the application form and a copy of the appropriate documents and statements summarized in items 1, 2c, and 3 of the Procedural Requirements Checklist.

For adoption of uniform plans (Rev. Proc. 84-86, 1984-2 C.B. 787), or master or prototype plans (Rev. Proc. 84-23, 1984-1 C.B. 457), file the application form and appropriate documents and statements required in these Revenue Procedures.

For partial termination (Rev. Proc. 80-30), or for termination of a multiemployer plan covered by PBGC insurance, file the application form and the appropriate documents and statements summarized in items 1, 2d, and 3 of the Procedural Requirements Checklist. See the Specific Instructions and Note for item 3a. In addition:

(a) Attach a statement (1) indicating whether a partial termination may have occurred or might occur as a result of proposed actions or (2) describing the termination of a multiemployer plan covered by PBGC insurance;

(b) Using the format that follows, submit a schedule of information for the plan year in which the partial (or potential partial) termination began or during which the multiemployer plan terminated. Also, submit a schedule for the next plan year, as well as for the two prior plan years, to the extent the information is available.

(i) Participants employed:	19..	19..	Year of termination or partial termination	19..
(a) Number at beginning of plan year				
(b) Number added during the plan year				
(c) Total, add lines (a) and (b)				
(d) Number dropped during the plan year				
(e) Number at end of plan year, subtract (d) from (c)				
(f) Total number of participants in this plan separated from service without full vesting				
(ii) Present value (as of a date during the year) of:				
(a) Plan assets				
(b) Accrued benefits				
(c) Vested benefits				

If this is a plan with more than one benefit computation formula, in addition to completing line (i)(e) of this schedule for the entire plan, attach a sheet showing the information separately in the same format as line (i)(e) for each benefit computation formula.

(c) Submit a description of the actions that may have resulted or might result in a partial termination.

(d) Include an explanation of how the plan meets the requirements of section 411(d)(3).

For a plan that contains a cash or deferred arrangement (section 401(k)), file the appropriate documents and statements summarized in items 1, 2a, 2b, or 2c, and 3 of the Procedural Requirements Checklist. In addition, if the plan does not contain a provision for fail-safe devices or other mechanisms that will assure compliance with the antidiscrimination requirements of section 401(k)(3), submit a demonstration of how the discrimination tests in section 401(a)(4) and 410(b) will be satisfied. This may require a schedule of the proposed employee allocations as of the end of the plan year in which the cash or deferred arrangements will become effective or a schedule of the actual allocations as of the end of the latest year of operation.

For governmental and church plans, if the request is for a plan that is subject to ERISA, complete all items of the application. If the request is for a plan that is not subject to ERISA, do not complete line items 9, 10b, 10c, 13, 15g, 15l, and 17c.

For merger, consolidation or transfer of plan assets or liabilities, if this application is also intended to satisfy the notice required by section 6058(b), attach the information requested in item 3c of the Specific Instructions, below.

Plans being amended to comply with The Tax Equity and Fiscal Responsibility Act, The Tax Reform Act of 1984, or The Retirement Equity Act of 1984 generally should have attached a **Schedule T (Form 5300)**, Supplemental Application for Approval of Employee Benefit Plans Under TEFRA, TRA 1984, and REA. See the instructions for that form to be sure whether you should attach one to the Form 5303.

For terminations, file **Form 5310**, Application for Determination Upon Termination; Notice of Merger, Consolidation or Transfer of Plan Assets or Liabilities; Notice of Intent to Terminate, to request a determination letter for the complete termination of a defined benefit or defined contribution plan. File Form 5303 to request a determination letter involving the complete termination of a multiemployer plan covered by the PBGC insurance program.

C. Where to File.—File this form as follows:

(1) Single Employer Plans.—Send the forms to the District Director for the key district in which the employer's or employee organization's principal place of business is located.

(2) Plan Maintained by More Than One Employer.—Send the forms to the District Director for the key district in which the principal place of business of the plan sponsor is located. This means the principal place of business of the association, committee, joint board of trustees, or other similar group of representatives of those who established or maintain the plan.

If the principal place of business, or office of the plan sponsor or plan administrator is in one of the districts or locations shown ▼	Send your application to the District Director for the Key District listed below ▼
Atlanta, Birmingham, Columbia, Greensboro, Jackson, Jacksonville, Little Rock, Nashville, New Orleans	Internal Revenue Service EP/EO Unit P.O. Box 941 Atlanta, GA 30370
Baltimore, Pittsburgh, Richmond, U.S. possessions, or a foreign country	Internal Revenue Service EP/EO Division P.O. Box 17010 Baltimore, MD 21203
Brooklyn, Albany, Augusta, Boston, Buffalo, Burlington, Hartford, Manhattan, Portsmouth, Providence	Internal Revenue Service EP/EO Division P. O. Box C-9050 General Post Office Brooklyn, NY 11202
Chicago, Aberdeen, Des Moines, Fargo, Helena, Milwaukee, Omaha, St. Louis, St. Paul, Springfield	Internal Revenue Service EP/EO Division P.O. Box A-3617 Chicago, IL 60690
Cincinnati, Cleveland, Detroit, Indianapolis, Louisville, Parkersburg	EP/EO Division P.O. Box 3159 Cincinnati, OH 45201
Dallas, Albuquerque, Austin, Cheyenne, Denver, Houston, Oklahoma City, Phoenix, Salt Lake City, Wichita	Internal Revenue Service EP/EO Division Mail Code 306 1100 Commerce St. Dallas, TX 75242
Los Angeles, Honolulu, Laguna Niguel	Internal Revenue Service EP Application Receiving P.O. Box 536 Los Angeles, CA 90053-0536
Newark, Philadelphia, Wilmington	Internal Revenue Service EP/EO Division P.O. Box 1680 Newark, NJ 07101
San Francisco, Las Vegas, Sacramento, San Jose	Internal Revenue Service EP/EO Division Box 36040, Stop 3-2-29 450 Golden Gate Ave. San Francisco, CA 94102
Seattle, Anchorage, Boise, Portland	Internal Revenue Service EP/EO Division 915 Second Ave. Mail Stop 554 Seattle, WA 98174

Domestic employers adopting foreign situs trusts should file with the District Director for the key district in which the principal place of business of the employer is located.

Foreign employers should file with the Baltimore Key District.

Determination requests for industry plans established or proposed by subscribing employers with principal places of business located within the jurisdiction of more than one District Director, should be addressed to the District Director for the key district where the trustee's principal place of business is located. If the plans have more than one trustee, the request should be filed with the District Director for the key district where the trustees usually meet.

Specific Instructions

Please follow the instructions below when completing this form. If any item requests a date or number, the response must be a date or number. N/A (not applicable) is acceptable only if an N/A block is provided.

The items below are keyed to the line items on the form.

1a. Enter the name and address of the plan sponsor. If a plan covers only the employees of one employer, "plan sponsor" means the employer. For plans maintained by two or more employers (other than a plan sponsored by two or more members of a controlled group of corporations), "plan sponsor" means the association, committee, joint board of trustees, or other similar group of representatives of those who established or maintain the plan. For a plan sponsored by two or more members of a controlled group of corporations, "plan sponsor" means one of the members participating in the plan.

Be sure to include enough information in line item 1a to identify the sponsor adequately.

1b. Enter the 9-digit employer identification number (EIN) assigned to the plan sponsor. This should be the same EIN that was used or will be used when Form 5500 series returns/reports are filed for the plan. Controlled groups of corporations whose sponsor is more than one of the members of the controlled group should insert only the EIN of one of the sponsoring members. This EIN must be used in all subsequent filings of determination letter requests for the controlled group. This EIN is also the EIN used for filing annual returns/reports.

1c. If this form is for a single employer plan, enter the month the employer's tax year ends. For all plans of more than one employer, check the N/A block.

2. The Tax Reform Act of 1976 permits a taxpayer to request IRS to disclose and discuss his or her return and/or return information with any person(s) the taxpayer designates in a written request. If you want to designate a person or persons to assist in matters relating to an application for a determination, you must give the IRS office of jurisdiction a written statement that must contain certain information:

(i) Your name, address, employer identification number, and plan numbers,

(ii) A paragraph that clearly identifies the person or persons you have authorized to receive the return and/or return information. This must include the name(s), address(es), telephone number(s) and social security number(s) of the authorized person(s),

(iii) A paragraph that clearly and explicitly describes the return and/or return information that you authorize IRS to disclose,

(iv) You must sign the request as the taxpayer making the authorization.

As an alternative to providing the above statement, **Form 2848**, Power of Attorney and Declaration of Representative, or **Form 2848-D**, Tax Information Authorization and Declaration of Representative, may be submitted.

3a. Check applicable box(es):

In the place indicated, enter the date the plan or amendment was signed. If a determination is requested based on a proposed plan or amendment, enter "9/9/99". Enter the effective date where requested. The term "effective date" means the date the plan, amendment, partial termination, or termination of a multiemployer plan covered by PBGC insurance becomes operative or takes effect. The effective date of the plan is a required entry for all submissions. For example, if a determination is requested for an amendment to the plan, enter the date the plan was effective.

(i) Check this box if the IRS has not previously issued a determination letter for this plan.

(ii) Check this box if this application is for an amendment to a plan for which the IRS has previously issued a determination letter.

(iii) Check this box if a determination letter is desired on the effect of a potential partial termination of the plan.

(iv) Check this box if a determination letter is requested regarding termination of a multiemployer plan covered by PBGC insurance. A multiemployer plan described above may not use a Form 5310 to request a determination letter upon plan termination.

Note: *For 3a(iii) or (iv) above, also check box 3a(i) or (ii), as applicable, unless (1) IRS has previously issued a determination letter on this plan and (2) an amendment is not involved in this request for a determination letter.*

3b. Enter the file folder number shown on the last determination letter issued to this sponsor. For example, if the sponsor maintains two plans and previously received a determination letter for plan number 001, the file folder number reflected on that determination letter should be entered on line 3b when an application is submitted with regard to plan number 002.

3c. This form may be used for applications for a determination letter only in the situations provided in item 3a. However, in the case of a merger, consolidation, or transfer of plan assets or liabilities, a plan sponsor may request a determination letter on a plan involved in such actions and may simultaneously give notice of the merger, consolidation, or transfer of plan assets or liabilities, as required by section 6058(b). Each sponsor or administrator of a plan (except a multiemployer plan covered by PBGC insurance) involved in a merger, consolidation, or transfer of plan assets or liabilities must provide the notice 30 days before such event takes place. If the plan sponsor does not desire a determination letter on such a plan, Form 5310 must be filed to provide this notice. A plan sponsor who requests a determination letter on the qualified status of a plan that was involved in a merger, consolidation, or transfer of plan assets or liabilities may use Forms 5300, 5301, or 5303 to simultaneously give the required notice and request a determination letter for that plan by:

(1) submitting this application not less than 30 days prior to the date of the merger, consolidation, or transfer of plan assets or liabilities and (2) attaching a statement containing the plan name(s) and number(s), the name(s) of the plan sponsor(s) and the employer identification number(s) for the other plan(s) involved in the merger, consolidation, or transfer. The statement should also include the date of the transaction. For a defined benefit plan also include an actuarial statement of valuation for the plan showing compliance with the requirements of sections 401(a)(12) and 414(l) and the related regulations.

3d. Section 3001 of ERISA states that the applicant must provide evidence that each employee who qualifies as an interested party has been notified of the filing of the application. Check "Yes" only if you have notified each employee as required by regulations under section 7476. Rules defining "interested parties" and providing for the form of notification are contained in the regulations.

4a. Enter the name you designated for your plan.

4b. You should assign a three-digit number, beginning with "001" and continuing in numerical sequence, to each plan you adopt. This numbering will differentiate your plans. Enter your three-digit number here. The number that is assigned to a plan must not be changed or used for any other plan.

4c. "Plan year" means the calendar, policy, or fiscal year on which the records of the plan are kept.

5. Check only one box. A single employer plan is a plan that is maintained by one employer. See sections 414(b), (c), (d), (e), and (f) for definitions of entities other than single employer.

6. Each opinion letter issued for a master or prototype plan will have a letter serial number.

9a(i). The term "participant" includes retirees and other former employees and the beneficiaries of both who are receiving benefits under the plan or will at some future date receive benefits under the plan. Thus, the figure to enter on this line is the sum of: (1) the number of employees who are participating in the plan, (2) former employees who are receiving benefits under the plan or will at some future date receive benefits under the plan, and (3) beneficiaries of former employees who are receiving benefits under the plan. This means one beneficiary for each former employee regardless of the number of individuals receiving benefits. For example, payment of a former employee's benefit to three children is considered as a payment to one beneficiary.

See Instruction B, "What to File," for more information on completing line 9 if the plan contains a cash or deferred arrangement under section 410(k).

9c. If this application covers the employees of more than one union or plan, complete a separate schedule for each plan or union using the format of 9c.

12. For all integrated defined benefit plans and integrated target benefit plans, show that the integration limit actually used by the plan cannot exceed the allowable plan integration limit. In determining the allowable integration limit, take into account all plan features that require an adjustment (for example, preretirement death benefit, normal form of payment other than life annuity, average compensation of less than 5 years).

13a. For a definition of a controlled group or trades or businesses under common control, see sections 414(b) and (c). For a definition of an affiliated service group, see section 414(m).

13d. This includes any amendment to a vesting schedule or any plan amendment that indirectly or directly affects the computation of the nonforfeitable percentage of a participant's accrued benefit, for example, each change in the plan which affects either the plan's computation of years of service or of vesting percentages for years of service. See regulations section 1.411(a)–8(c).

13f(vii). A class year plan is a plan in which the amount of vesting is determined separately with respect to each year's contributions and each contribution becomes 100% vested no later than the 5th plan year following the plan year for which the contributions were made.

13f(viii). If box "Other" is checked and the vesting schedule is less rapid than 13f(v), submit a schedule of turnover of employees or provide enough facts upon which a determination can be made that the vesting schedule of the plan is satisfactory. See Rev. Proc. 76-11, 1976-1 C.B. 550 or its successor, if any. Please note that this is a requirement for all initial qualifications.

15k. Attach a schedule similar in format to the schedule that follows, if an amount other than "total compensation" (generally W-2 pay) is used as the basis for allocating employer contributions or figuring benefits. If this is a plan with more than one benefit computation formula, complete a schedule for each of the benefit computation formulas.

1		2	3	4	5
*Brackets based on total compensation		Number of employees in bracket	Total compensation for employees included in compensation brackets	Amount of compensation used in figuring benefits or allocating employer contributions	Percent of total (Column 4 divided by column 3)
At least	But not more than				
Totals					

*The compensation brackets used must reflect the pay pattern of the employer.

Form **5305-SEP**
(Rev. June 1988)
Department of the Treasury
Internal Revenue Service

Simplified Employee Pension-Individual Retirement Accounts Contribution Agreement

(Under Section 408(k) of the Internal Revenue Code)

OMB No. 1545-0499
Expires 7-31-91

Do NOT File with Internal Revenue Service

______________________________ makes the following agreement under the terms of section 408(k) of
(Business name—employer)
the Internal Revenue Code and the instructions to this form.

The employer agrees to provide for discretionary contributions in each calendar year to the Individual Retirement Accounts or Individual Retirement Annuities (IRA's) of all eligible employees who are at least ________ years old (not over 21 years old) (see instruction "Who May Participate") and worked in at least ________ years (enter 1, 2, or 3 years) of the immediately preceding 5 years (see instruction "Who May Participate"). This ☐ includes ☐ does not include employees covered under a collective bargaining agreement and ☐ includes ☐ does not include employees whose total compensation during the year is less than $300.

The employer agrees that contributions made on behalf of each eligible employee will:

- Be made only on the first $200,000 of compensation (as adjusted per Code section 408(k)(8)).
- Be made in an amount that is the same percentage of total compensation for every employee.
- Be limited to the smaller of $30,000 (or if greater, ¼ of the dollar limitation in effect under section 415(b)(1)(A)) or 15% of compensation.
- Be paid to the employee's IRA trustee, custodian, or insurance company (for an annuity contract).

______________________________ Signature of employer

______________________________ Date

______________________________ By

Instructions for the Employer

(Section references are to the Internal Revenue Code, unless otherwise noted.)

Paperwork Reduction Act Notice.—The Paperwork Reduction Act of 1980 says we must tell you why we are collecting this information, how it is to be used, and whether you have to give it to us. The information is used to determine if you are entitled to a deduction for contributions made to a SEP. Your completing this form is only required if you want to establish a Model SEP.

Purpose of Form.—Form 5305-SEP (Model SEP) is used by an employer to make an agreement to provide benefits to all employees under a Simplified Employee Pension (SEP) plan described in section 408(k). This form is NOT to be filed with IRS.

What Is a SEP Plan?—A SEP provides an employer with a simplified way to make contributions toward an employee's retirement income. Under a SEP, the employer is permitted to contribute a certain amount (see below) to an employee's Individual Retirement Account or Individual Retirement Annuity (IRA's). The employer makes contributions directly to an IRA set up by an employee with a bank, insurance company, or other qualified financial institution. When using this form to establish a SEP, the IRA must be a model IRA established on an IRS form or a master or prototype IRA for which IRS has issued a favorable opinion letter. Making the agreement on Form 5305-SEP does not establish an employer IRA as described under section 408(c).

This form may not be used by an employer who:

- Currently maintains any other qualified retirement plan.
- Has maintained in the past a defined benefit plan, even if now terminated.
- Has any eligible employees for whom IRA's have not been established.
- Uses the services of leased employees (as described in section 414(n)).
- Is a member of an affiliated service group (as described in section 414(m)), a controlled group of corporations (as described in section 414(b)), or trades or businesses under common control (as described in section 414(c)), UNLESS all eligible employees of all the members of such groups, trades, or businesses, participate under the SEP.
- This form should only be used if the employer will pay the cost of the SEP contributions. This form is not suitable for a SEP that provides for contributions at the election of the employee whether or not made pursuant to a salary reduction agreement.

Who May Participate.—Any employee who is at least 21 years old and has performed "service" for you in at least 3 years of the immediately preceding 5 years must be permitted to participate in the SEP. However, you may establish less restrictive eligibility requirements if you choose. "Service" is any work performed for you for any period of time, however short. Further, if you are a member of an affiliated service group, a controlled group of corporations, or trades or businesses under common control, "service" includes any work performed for any period of time for any other member of such group, trades, or businesses. Generally, to make the agreement, all eligible employees (including all eligible employees, if any, of other members of an affiliated service group, a controlled group of corporations, or trades or businesses under common control) must participate in the plan. However, employees covered under a collective bargaining agreement and certain nonresident aliens may be excluded if section 410(b)(3)(A) or 410(b)(3)(C) applies to them. Employees whose total compensation for the year is less than $300 may be excluded.

Amount of Contributions.—You are not required to make any contributions to an employee's SEP-IRA in a given year. However, if you do make contributions, you must make them to the IRA's of all eligible employees, whether or not they are still employed at the time contributions are made. The contributions made must be the same percentage of each employee's total compensation (up to a maximum compensation base of $200,000 as adjusted per section 408(k)(8) for cost of living changes). The contributions you make in a year for any one employee may not be more than the smaller of $30,000 or 15% of that employee's total compensation (figured without considering the SEP-IRA contributions).

For this purpose, compensation includes:

- Amounts received for personal services actually performed (see section 1.219-1(c) of the Income Tax Regulations); and
- Earned income defined under section 401(c)(2).

In making contributions, you may not discriminate in favor of any employee who is highly compensated.

Under this form you may not integrate your SEP contributions with, or offset them by, contributions made under the Federal Insurance Contributions Act (FICA).

Currently, employers who have established a SEP using this agreement and have provided each participant with a copy of this form, including the questions and answers, are not required to file the annual information returns, Forms 5500, 5500-C, 5500-R, or 5500EZ for the SEP.

Deducting Contributions.—You may deduct all contributions to a SEP subject to the limitations of section 404(h). This SEP is maintained on a calendar year basis and contributions to the SEP are deductible for your taxable year with or within which the calendar year ends. Contributions made for a particular taxable year and contributed by the due date of your income tax return (including extensions) shall be deemed made in that taxable year.

Making the Agreement.— This agreement is considered made when (1) IRA's have been established for all of your eligible employees, (2) you have completed all blanks on the agreement form without modification, and (3) you have given all your eligible employees copies of the agreement form, instructions, and questions and answers.

Keep the agreement form with your records; do not file it with IRS.

Information for the Employee

The information provided explains what a Simplified Employee Pension plan is, how contributions are made, and how to treat your employer's contributions for tax purposes.

Please read the questions and answers carefully. For more specific information, also see the agreement form and instructions to your employer on this form.

Questions and Answers

1. Q. What is a Simplified Employee Pension, or SEP?

A. A SEP is a retirement income arrangement under which your employer may contribute any amount each year up to the smaller of $30,000 or 15% of your compensation into **your own** Individual Retirement Account/Annuity (IRA).

Your employer will provide you with a copy of the agreement containing participation requirements and a description of the basis upon which employer contributions may be made to your IRA.

All amounts contributed to your IRA by your employer belong to you, even after you separate from service with that employer.

The $30,000 limitation referred to above may be increased by ¼ of the dollar limitation in effect under section 415(b)(1)(A).

2. Q. Must my employer contribute to my IRA under the SEP?

A. Whether or not your employer makes a contribution to the SEP is entirely within the employer's discretion. If a contribution is made under the SEP, it must be allocated to all the eligible employees according to the SEP agreement. The Model SEP specifies that the contribution on behalf of each eligible employee will be the same percentage of compensation (excluding compensation higher than $200,000) for all employees.

3. Q. How much may my employer contribute to my SEP-IRA in any year?

A. Under the Model SEP **(Form 5305-SEP)** that your employer has adopted, your employer will determine the amount of contribution to be made to your IRA each year. However, the contribution for any year is limited to the smaller of $30,000 or 15% of your compensation for that year. The compensation used to determine this limit does not include any amount which is contributed by your employer to your IRA under the SEP. The agreement does not require an employer to maintain a particular level of contributions. It is possible that for a given year no employer contribution will be made on an employee's behalf.

Also see Question 5.

4. Q. How do I treat my employer's SEP contributions for my taxes?

A. The amount your employer contributes for years beginning after 1986 is excludable from your gross income subject to certain limitations including the lesser of $30,000 or 15% of compensation mentioned in 1.A. above and is not includible as taxable wages on your Form W-2.

5. Q. May I also contribute to my IRA if I am a participant in a SEP?

A. Yes. You may still contribute the lesser of $2,000 or 100% of your compensation to an IRA. However, the amount which is deductible is subject to various limitations.

Also see Question 11.

6. Q. Are there any restrictions on the IRA I select to deposit my SEP contributions in?

A. Under the Model SEP that is approved by IRS, contributions must be made to either a Model IRA which is executed on an IRS form or a master or prototype IRA for which IRS has issued a favorable opinion letter.

7. Q. What if I don't want a SEP-IRA?

A. Your employer may require that you become a participant in such an arrangement as a condition of employment. However, if the employer does not require all eligible employees to become participants and an eligible employee elects not to participate, all other employees of the same employer may be prohibited from entering into a SEP-IRA arrangement with that employer. If one or more eligible employees do not participate and the employer attempts to establish a SEP-IRA agreement with the remaining employees, the resulting arrangement may result in adverse tax consequences to the participating employees.

8. Q. Can I move funds from my SEP-IRA to another tax-sheltered IRA?

A. Yes, it is permissible for you to withdraw, or receive, funds from your SEP-IRA, and no more than 60 days later, place such funds in another IRA, or SEP-IRA. This is called a "rollover" and may not be done without penalty more frequently than at one-year intervals. However, there are no restrictions on the number of times you may make "transfers" if you arrange to have such funds transferred between the trustees, so that you never have possession.

9. Q. What happens if I withdraw my employer's contribution from my IRA?

A. If you don't want to leave the employer's contribution in your IRA, you may withdraw it at any time, but any amount withdrawn is includible in your income. Also, if withdrawals occur before attainment of age 59 ½, and not on account of death or disability, you may be subject to a penalty tax.

10. Q. May I participate in a SEP even though I'm covered by another plan?

A. An employer may not adopt this IRS Model SEP **(Form 5305-SEP)** if the employer maintains another qualified retirement plan or has ever maintained a qualified defined benefit plan. However, if you work for several employers you may be covered by a SEP of one employer and a different SEP or pension or profit-sharing plan of another employer.

Also see Questions 11 and 12.

11. Q. What happens if too much is contributed to my SEP-IRA in one year?

A. Any contribution that is more than the yearly limitations may be withdrawn without penalty by the due date (plus extensions) for filing your tax return (normally April 15th), but is includible in your gross income. Excess contributions left in your SEP-IRA account after that time may have adverse tax consequences. Withdrawals of those contributions may be taxed as premature withdrawals.

Also see Question 10.

12. Q. Do I need to file any additional forms with IRS because I participate in a SEP?

A. No.

13. Q. Is my employer required to provide me with information about SEP-IRA's and the SEP agreement?

A. Yes, your employer must provide you with a copy of the executed SEP agreement **(Form 5305-SEP)**, these Questions and Answers, and provide a statement each year showing any contribution to your IRA.

Also see Question 4.

14. Q. Is the financial institution where I establish my IRA also required to provide me with information?

A. Yes, it must provide you with a disclosure statement which contains the following items of information in plain, nontechnical language:

(1) the statutory requirements which relate to your IRA;

(2) the tax consequences which follow the exercise of various options and what those options are;

(3) participation eligibility rules, and rules on the deductibility and nondeductibility of retirement savings;

(4) the circumstances and procedures under which you may revoke your IRA, including the name, address, and telephone number of the person designated to receive notice of revocation **(this explanation must be prominently displayed at the beginning of the disclosure statement);**

(5) explanations of when penalties may be assessed against you because of specified prohibited or penalized activities concerning your IRA; and

(6) financial disclosure information which:

(a) either projects value growth rates of your IRA under various contribution and retirement schedules, or describes the method of computing and allocating annual earnings and charges which may be assessed;

(b) describes whether, and for what period, the growth projections for the plan are guaranteed, or a statement of the earnings rate and terms on which the projection is based;

(c) states the sales commission to be charged in each year expressed as a percentage of $1,000; and

(d) states the proportional amount of any nondeductible life insurance which may be a feature of your IRA.

See **Publication 590,** Individual Retirement Arrangements (IRA's), available at most IRS offices, for a more complete explanation of the disclosure requirements.

In addition to this disclosure statement, the financial institution is required to provide you with a financial statement each year. It may be necessary to retain and refer to statements for more than one year in order to evaluate the investment performance of the IRA and in order that you will know how to report IRA distributions for tax purposes.

Form **5305A-SEP**
(Rev. October 1987)
Department of the Treasury
Internal Revenue Service

Salary Reduction and Other Elective Simplified Employee Pension-Individual Retirement Accounts Contribution Agreement
(Under Section 408(k) of the Internal Revenue Code)

OMB No. 1545-1012
Expires 9-30-90
Do NOT File with Internal Revenue Service

Caution: *This form may only be used if the three conditions found at Article III, items E, F, and G are met.*

______________________________ establishes the following arrangement under the terms of section
(Business name—employer)
408(k) of The Internal Revenue Code and the instructions to this form.

Article I—Eligibility Requirements

Provided the requirements of Article III are met, the employer agrees to permit elective deferrals to be made in each calendar year to the Individual Retirement Accounts or Individual Retirement Annuities (IRA), established by or on behalf of all employees who are at least ________ years old (see instructions) and have performed services for the employer in at least ________ years (see instructions) of the immediately preceding 5 years. This ☐ includes ☐ does not include employees covered under a collective bargaining agreement and ☐ includes ☐ does not include employees whose total compensation during the year is less than $300.

Article II—Elective Deferrals

A. Salary Reduction Option. A participant may elect to have his or her compensation reduced by the following percentage or amount per pay period, as designated in writing to the employer (check appropriate box, or boxes, and fill in the blanks):

1. ☐ An amount not in excess of ________ % (enter a specified percent of 15% or less) of a participant's compensation.
2. ☐ An amount not in excess of $ ________ (not to exceed $7,000 per year as adjusted per Code section 415(d)).

B. Cash Bonus Option. A participant may base elective deferrals on bonuses that, at the participant's election, may be contributed to the SEP or received by the participant in cash during the calendar year. Check here ☐ if such elective deferrals may be made to this SEP.

Article III—SEP Requirements

The employer agrees that each employee's elective deferrals to this SEP will:

A. Be based only on the first $200,000 of compensation (as adjusted annually per Code section 408(k)(8)).

B. Be limited annually to the lesser of:

1. 15% of compensation (see instructions for Article III); **or**
2. $7,000 (as adjusted annually per Code section 415(d)).

Amounts in excess of these limits will be treated as excess SEP deferrals.

C. Be further reduced, as necessary in accordance with Code section 415, if the employer also maintains a SEP to which non-elective SEP employer contributions are made for a calendar year.

D. Be paid to the employee's IRA trustee, custodian, or insurance company (for an annuity contract) or, if necessary, an IRA established for an employee by an employer.

E. Be made only if at least 50% of the employer's employees eligible to participate elect to have amounts contributed to the SEP.

F. Be made only if the employer had 25 or fewer employees eligible to participate at all times during the prior calendar year.

G. Be adjusted only if deferrals to this SEP for any calendar year do not meet the "ADP" requirements described in the instructions on page 3.

Article IV—Excess SEP Contributions

The employer agrees to notify each employee by March 15 of each year of any excess SEP contributions to the employee's SEP-IRA for the preceding calendar year.

Article V—Top-heavy Requirements

A. Unless paragraph B below is checked, the minimum top-heavy contribution for each year must be allocated to the SEP-IRA of each non-key employee eligible to participate in this SEP in accordance with Code section 416. This allocation may not be less than the smaller of: **(1)** 3% of the non-key employee's compensation; **or (2)** the largest percentage of elective deferrals, as a percentage of the first $200,000 of the key employee's compensation, deferred by any key employee for that year.

B. ☐ The top-heavy requirements of section 416 will be satisfied through contributions to this employer's non-elective SEP-IRA.

______________________________ ________________
Signature of employer Date

____
By

Form **5305A-SEP** (Rev. 10-87)

Instructions for the Employer

(Section references are to the Internal Revenue Code, unless otherwise noted.)

Paperwork Reduction Act Notice.—The Paperwork Reduction Act of 1980 says we must tell you why we are collecting this information, how it is to be used, and whether you must give it to us. The information is used to determine if you are entitled to a deduction for contributions made to a SEP. Completion of this form is required only if you want to establish a Model Elective SEP.

Purpose of Form.—Form 5305A-SEP (model elective SEP) is used by an employer to permit employees to make elective deferrals to a Simplified Employee Pension (SEP) described in section 408(k). This form is NOT to be filed with IRS.

What is a SEP?—A SEP is a plan that provides an employer with a simplified way to enhance the employee's retirement income. Under an elective SEP, employees may choose whether or not to make elective deferrals to the SEP. The employer puts the amounts deferred by employees directly into an IRA set up by or on behalf of the employee with a bank, insurance company, or other qualified financial institution. When using this form to establish a SEP, the IRA established by or on behalf of an employee must be a model IRA or a master or prototype IRA for which IRS has issued a favorable opinion letter. Making the agreement on Form 5305A-SEP does not establish an employer IRA as described under section 408(c).

This form may NOT be used by an employer who:

1. Currently maintains any other qualified retirement plan. This does not prevent an employer from also maintaining a Model SEP (Form 5305-SEP) or other SEP to which either elective or non-elective contributions are made.

2. Has maintained in the past a defined benefit plan, even if now terminated.

3. Has any eligible employees by or for whom IRAs have not been established.

4. Has only highly compensated employees.

5. Is a member of one of the groups described in the Specific Instructions for Article III, G. 2 below, UNLESS all eligible employees of all the members of such groups, trades, or businesses are eligible to make elective deferrals to this SEP, and PROVIDED that in the prior calendar year there were never more than 25 employees eligible to participate in this SEP, in total, of all the members of such groups, trades, or businesses.

6. Is a state or local government or a tax-exempt organization.

This form should be used only if the employer intends to permit elective deferrals to a SEP. If the employer wishes to establish a SEP to which non-elective employer contributions may be made, Form 5305-SEP or a non-model SEP should be used instead of, or in addition to, this form.

Making the Agreement.—This agreement is considered made when:

1. IRAs have been established by or for all of your eligible employees;

2. You have completed all blanks on the agreement form without modification; **and**

3. You have given all your eligible employees copies of the agreement form, instructions, and questions and answers.

Keep the agreement form with your records; do NOT file it with IRS.

Currently, employers who have established a SEP using this agreement and have provided each participant with a copy of this form, including the questions and answers, are not required to file the annual information returns, Forms 5500, 5500-C, 5500-R, or 5500EZ for the SEP.

Deducting Contributions.—You may deduct contributions made by the due date of the employer's tax return, and extensions thereof, to a SEP subject to the limitations of section 404(h). This SEP is maintained on a calendar year basis, and contributions to the SEP are deductible for your taxable year with or within which the calendar year ends.

However, please see the Actual Deferral Percentage worksheet on page 6 in this booklet.

Specific Instructions

Article I.—Eligibility Requirements

Any employee who is at least 21 years old and has performed "service" for you in at least 3 years of the immediately preceding 5 years must be permitted to participate in the SEP. However, you may establish less restrictive eligibility requirements if you choose. Service is any work performed for you for any period of time, however short. Further, if you are a member of one of the groups described in Article III, G. 2 below, service includes any work performed for any period of time for any other member of such group, trades, or businesses. Generally, to make the agreement, all eligible employees, including leased employees within the meaning of section 414(n), of the affiliated employer must be permitted to make elective deferrals to the SEP. However, employees covered under a collective bargaining agreement and certain nonresident aliens may be excluded if section 410(b)(3)(A) or 410(b)(3)(C) applies to them. Employees whose total compensation for the year is less than $300 also may be excluded.

Article II.—Elective Deferrals

You may permit your employees to make elective deferrals through salary reduction or on the basis of bonuses that, at the participant's option, may be contributed to the SEP or received by the participant in cash during the calendar year.

You are responsible for telling your employees how they may make, change, or terminate elective deferrals based on either salary reduction or cash bonuses. You must also provide a form on which they may make their deferral elections. (This requirement may be satisfied by use of the model form provided on page 5 of this booklet or by use of a form setting forth, in a manner calculated to be understood by the average plan participant, the information contained in the "Model SEP Deferral Form.") No deferral election may be made with respect to compensation already received.

Article III.—SEP Requirements

A. Elective deferrals may not be based on more than $200,000 of compensation, as adjusted per section 408(k)(8) for cost of living changes. Compensation is the employee's compensation from the employee (figured without including the SEP-IRA contributions) and includes:

- Amounts received for personal services actually performed (see section 1.219-1(c) of the Income Tax Regulations), **and**
- Earned income defined under section 401(c)(2).

Note: *The deferral limit of 15% of compensation (less employer SEP-IRA contributions) is computed using the following formula: (compensation including employer SEP-IRA contribution ÷ 115%) × .15 = 15% of compensation limitation.*

B. The maximum limit on the amount of compensation an employee may elect to defer under a SEP for a calendar year is the lesser of:

- 15% of the employee's compensation; or
- $7,000, adjusted as explained below.

Amounts deferred for a year in excess of $7,000 as adjusted are considered excess deferrals and are subject to the consequences described below.

The $7,000 limit on the amount an employee may elect to defer in each year applies to the total elective deferrals the employee makes for the year under the following arrangements:

1. Elective SEPs under section 408(k)(6);
2. Cash or deferred arrangements under section 401(k); and
3. Salary reduction arrangements under section 403(b).

Thus, the employee may have excess deferrals even if the amount deferred under this SEP does not exceed $7,000.

The $7,000 limit will be indexed according to the cost of living. In addition, the limit may be increased to $9,500 if the employee makes elective deferrals to a salary reduction arrangement under section 403(b).

If an employee who elects to defer compensation under this SEP has made excess deferrals for a year, he or she must withdraw those excess deferrals by April 15 following the year of the deferral. Excess deferrals not withdrawn by April 15 following the year of the deferral may also be subject, when withdrawn, to the 10% tax on early distributions under section 72(t).

C. If you also maintain a Model SEP or any other SEP to which you make non-elective contributions, contributions to the two SEPs together may not exceed the lesser of $30,000 or 15% of compensation for any employee. If these limits are exceeded on behalf of any employee for a particular calendar year, that employee's elective deferrals for that year must be reduced to the extent of the excess.

E. and F. Each of these calculations is made after first excluding employees who do not meet the eligibility requirements of Article I, including employees covered under a collective bargaining agreement and nonresident aliens.

F. New employers who had no employees during the prior calendar year will meet this requirement if they have 25 or fewer employees throughout the first 30 days that the employer is in existence.

G. Actual Deferral Percentage (ADP) Requirements. An excess SEP contribution for the calendar year is the amount of each highly compensated employee's elective deferrals that exceeds the ADP for a calendar year. In order to meet the ADP requirements for a calendar year, the following test must be satisfied. The ADP of any "highly compensated employee" eligible to participate in this SEP may not be more than the product obtained by multiplying the average of the ADPs for that year of all non-highly compensated employees eligible to participate by 1.25. Only elective deferrals count for this test; non-elective SEP contributions may not be included.

For purposes of making this computation, the calculation of a highly compensated employee's ADP is made on the basis of the entire "affiliated employer." The determination of the number and identity of highly compensated employees is also made on the basis of the affiliated employer.

In addition, for purposes of determining the ADP of a highly compensated individual, the elective deferrals and compensation of the employee will also include the elective deferrals and compensation of any "family member." This special rule applies, however, only if the highly compensated employee is a 5% owner and is one of a group of the ten most highly compensated employees. The elective deferrals and compensation of family members used in this special rule do not count in computing the ADP of individuals who do not fall into this group.

The following definitions apply for purposes of this ADP computation:

1. ADP—the ratio of an employee's elective deferrals for a calendar year to the employee's compensation (as defined in III A. above) for that year. The ADP of an employee who is eligible to make an elective deferral, but who does not make a deferral during the year, is zero.

2. Affiliated employer—the employer and any member of an affiliated service group (as described in section 414(m)), a controlled group of corporations (as described in section 414(b)) or trades or businesses as described in section 414(c), or any other entity required to be aggregated with the employer under section 414(o).

3. Family member—an individual who is related to a highly compensated individual as a spouse, or as a lineal ascendant, such as a parent or grandparent, or a descendent such as a child or grandchild, or spouse of either of those.

4. Highly compensated individual—an individual who (as described in section 414(q)) during the current or preceding calendar year:

(i) was a 5% or more owner;

(ii) received compensation in excess of $75,000;

(iii) received compensation in excess of $50,000 and was in the top-paid group (the top 20% of employees, by compensation); **or**

(iv) was an officer and received compensation in excess of 150% of the section 415 dollar limit for defined contribution plans. (No more than 3 employees need be taken into account under this rule. At least one officer, the highest-paid officer if no one else meets this test, however, must be taken into account.)

A worksheet to calculate the ADP test and excess SEP contributions is provided on page 6.

Article IV.—Excess SEP Contributions

A. As stated above, a worksheet to calculate excess SEP contributions is provided on page 6 of this booklet. This worksheet should be used to determine the amount of excess SEP contributions to be reported to employees with respect to a calendar year. The employer is responsible for notifying each employee by March 15 of the amount, if any, of any excess SEP contributions to that employee's SEP-IRA for the preceding calendar year. If you do not notify any of your employees by March 15, you must pay a tax equal to 10% of the excess SEP contributions for the preceding calendar year. If you fail to notify your employees by December 31 of the calendar year following the year of the excess SEP contributions, your SEP no longer will be considered to meet the requirements of section 408(k)(6). This means that the earnings on the SEP are subject to tax immediately, that no more deferrals can be made under the SEP, and that deferrals of all employees in the uncorrected excess are includible in their income in that year.

Your notification to each affected employee of the excess SEP contributions must specifically state in a manner calculated to be understood by the average plan participant: (i) the amount of the excess contributions attributable to that employee's elective deferrals; (ii) the calendar year for which the excess contributions were made; (iii) that the excess contributions are includible in the affected employee's gross income for the specified calendar year; and (iv) that failure to withdraw the excess contributions and income attributable thereto by the due date (plus extensions) for filing the affected employee's tax return for the preceding calendar year may result in significant penalties, with a reference to Question 6 of Form 5305A-SEP for further information concerning possible penalties. If you wish, you may use the model form we have included for this purpose on page 5 following the "Model Elective SEP Deferral Form." If you already have issued W-2s to your employees by the time of the notification of the excess SEP contributions, you must also issue to the affected employees any required forms that reflect the fact that excess SEP contributions must be included in an employee's taxable income.

Example: Employee "A," a highly-compensated employee of employer "X," elects to defer $4,000 for calendar year 1987 to his SEP-IRA. A's compensation for 1987, excluding his SEP contribution, was $60,000. On January 15, 1988, X issues to A a W-2 stating that A's taxable income for 1987 was $60,000.

In February of 1988 X calculates the ADP test for 1987 for the SEP and discovers that A's maximum permissible SEP-IRA contribution for 1987 was $3,500. A is the only employee of X with excess SEP contributions. Therefore, on February 20, 1988, X notifies A that A had an excess SEP contribution of $500 for 1987. In addition, X issues the required form to A on that date that specifies that A's corrected taxable income for 1987 was $60,500. X is not liable for the 10% tax on excess SEP-IRA contributions because he notified A of the excess SEP-IRA contributions by March 15, 1988.

In order to avoid excess SEP contributions with respect to which you must notify employees you may want to institute a mechanism that would monitor elective deferrals on a continuing basis throughout the calendar year to insure that the deferrals comply with the limits as they are paid into each employee's SEP-IRA.

Article V.—Top-heavy Requirements

A. For purposes of determining whether a plan is top-heavy under section 416, elective deferrals are considered employer contributions. Elective deferrals may not be used, however, to satisfy the minimum contribution requirement under section 416. Thus, in any year in which a key employee makes an elective deferral, this Model SEP is deemed top-heavy for purposes of section 416 and the employer is required to make the minimum contribution to the SEP-IRA of each non-key employee eligible to participate in the SEP.

A key employee under section 416(i)(1) is any employee or former employee (and the beneficiaries of these employees) who, at any time during the "determination period," was:

1. an officer of the employer (if the employee's compensation exceeds 150% of the limit under section 415(c)(1)(A));

2. an owner of one of the ten largest interests in the employer (if the employee's compensation exceeds 100% of the limit under section 415(c)(1)(A));

3. a 5% or more owner of the employer; **or**

4. a 1% owner of the employer (if the employee has compensation in excess of $150,000).

The "determination period" is the current calendar year and the four preceding years.

B. The employer may satisfy the minimum contribution requirement of section 416 by making the required contributions through a non-elective SEP.

Information for the Employee

The following information explains what a Simplified Employee Pension plan is, how contributions are made, and how to treat these contributions for tax purposes.

Please read the questions and answers carefully. For more specific information, also see the agreement form and instructions to your employer on this form.

Questions and Answers

1. Q. What is a Simplified Employee Pension, or SEP?

A. A SEP is a retirement income arrangement. In this particular "elective" SEP, you may choose to defer compensation to your own Individual Retirement Account/Annuity (IRA). These elective deferrals may be based either on a salary reduction arrangement or on bonuses that, at your election, may be contributed to your IRA or received by you in cash. This type of elective SEP is available only to an employer with 25 or fewer eligible employees.

Your employer will provide you with a copy of the agreement containing eligibility requirements and a description of the basis upon which contributions may be made to your IRA.

All amounts contributed to your IRA belong to you, even after you separate from service with that employer.

2. Q. Must I make elective deferrals to an IRA?

A. No. However, if more than half of the eligible employees choose not to make elective deferrals in a particular year, then no employee may participate in an elective SEP of that employer for the year.

3. Q. How much may I elect to defer to my SEP-IRA in a particular year?

A. The amount that may be deferred to this SEP for any year is limited to the lesser of:

(1) 15% of compensation; **or**

(2) $7,000 (as adjusted for increases in the cost of living).

These limits may be reduced if your employer also maintains a SEP to which non-elective contributions are made. In that case, total contributions on your behalf to both SEPs may not exceed the lesser of $30,000 or 15% of your compensation. If these limits are exceeded, the amount you may elect to contribute to this SEP for the year will be correspondingly reduced.

The $7,000 is an overall cap on the maximum amount you may defer in each calendar year to all elective SEPs and cash-or-deferred arrangements under section 401(k), regardless of how many employers you may have worked for during the year.

The $7,000 will be indexed according to the cost of living and is increased to $9,500 (more in some cases) if you make salary reduction contributions under a section 403(b) arrangement of another employer.

If you are a highly compensated employee there may be a further limit on the amount you may contribute to a SEP-IRA for a particular year. This limit is calculated by your employer and is based on a special kind of non-discrimination test known as an ADP test. This test is based on a mathematical formula that limits the percentage of pay that highly compensated employees may elect to defer to a SEP-IRA. As discussed below, your employer will notify you if you have exceeded the ADP limits.

4. Q. How do I treat elective deferrals for tax purposes?

A. The amount you elect to defer to your SEP-IRA is excludible from your gross income, subject to the limitations discussed above, and is not includible as taxable wages on your Form W-2. These amounts are treated as amounts subject to FICA taxes.

5. Q. How will I know if too much is contributed to my SEP-IRA in one year?

A. There are two different ways in which you may contribute too much to your SEP-IRA. One way is to make "excess elective deferrals," i.e., exceed the $7,000 limitation described above. The second way is to make "excess SEP contributions," i.e., violate the "ADP" test, as discussed above. You are responsible for calculating whether or not you have exceeded the $7,000 limitation. Your employer is responsible for determining whether you have made any excess SEP contributions.

Your employer is required to notify you by March 15 if you have made any excess SEP contributions for the preceding calendar year. Your employer will notify you of an excess SEP contribution by providing you with any required form for the preceding calendar year.

6. Q. What must I do about excess deferrals to avoid adverse tax consequences?

A. Excess deferrals are includible in your gross income in the year of the deferral. You should withdraw excess deferrals under this SEP and any income allocable to the excess deferrals from your SEP-IRA by April 15. These amounts cannot be transferred or rolled over to another SEP-IRA.

If you fail to withdraw your excess deferrals and any income allocable thereto by April 15 of the following year, your excess deferrals will be subject to a 6% excise tax for each year they remain in the SEP-IRA.

If you have both excess deferrals and excess SEP contributions (as described in 6a below), the amount of excess deferrals you withdraw by April 15 will reduce your excess SEP contributions.

6a. Q: What must I do about excess SEP contributions to avoid adverse tax consequences?

A. Excess SEP contributions are includible in your gross income in the year of the deferral. You should withdraw excess SEP contributions for a calendar year and any income allocable to the excess SEP contributions by the due date (including extensions) for filing your income tax return for the year. These amounts cannot be transferred or rolled over to another SEP-IRA.

If you fail to withdraw your excess SEP contributions and income allocable thereto by the due date (including extensions) for filing your income tax return, your excess SEP contributions will be subject to a 6% excise tax for each year they remain in the SEP-IRA.

7. Q. Can I reduce excess elective deferrals or excess SEP contributions by rolling over or transferring amounts from my SEP-IRA to another IRA?

A. No. Excess elective deferrals or excess SEP contributions may be reduced only by a distribution to you. Excess amounts rolled over or transferred to another IRA will be includible in income and subject to the penalties discussed above.

8. Q. How do I know how much income is allocable to my excess elective deferrals or any excess SEP contributions?

A. The rules for determining and allocating income to excess elective deferrals or SEP contributions are the same as those governing regular IRA contributions. The trustee or custodian of your SEP-IRA may be able to inform you of the amount of income allocable to your excess amounts.

9. Q. May I also contribute to my IRA if I am a participant in a SEP?

A. Yes. You may still contribute the lesser of $2,000 or 100% of compensation to an IRA. However, the amount that is deductible is subject to various limitations. See Publication 590 for more specific information.

10. Q. Are there any restrictions on the IRA I select to deposit my SEP contributions in?

A. Under the Model Elective SEP that is approved by IRS, contributions must be made either to a Model IRA that is executed on an IRS form or a master or prototype IRA for which IRS has issued a favorable opinion letter.

11. Q. Can I move funds from my SEP-IRA to another tax-sheltered IRA?

A. Yes. It is permissible for you to withdraw, or receive, funds from your SEP-IRA, and no more than 60 days later, place such funds in another IRA or SEP-IRA. This is called a "rollover" and may not be done without penalty more frequently than at one-year intervals. However, there are no restrictions on the number of times you may make "transfers" if you arrange to have such funds transferred between the trustees, so that you never have possession.

12. Q. What happens if I withdraw my elective deferrals to my SEP-IRA?

A. If you don't want to leave the money in the IRA, you may withdraw it at any time, but any amount withdrawn is includible in your income. Also, if withdrawals occur before you are 59½, and not on account of death or disability, you may be subject to a 10% penalty tax. (As discussed above, different rules apply to the removal of excess amounts contributed to your SEP-IRA.)

13. Q. May I participate in a SEP even though I'm covered by another plan?

A. An employer may adopt this IRS Model Elective SEP (Form 5305A-SEP) and at the same time maintain an IRS Model SEP (Form 5305-SEP) or other non-elective SEP. However, an employer may not adopt this IRS Model Elective SEP if the employer maintains any qualified retirement plan or has ever maintained a qualified defined benefit plan. If you work for several employers, however, you may be covered by a SEP of one employer and a different SEP or pension or profit-sharing plan of another employer.

You should remember, however, as discussed in Question 3 above, that your elective deferrals to all plans or arrangements, even if maintained by unrelated employers, are subject to a $7,000 limit (more if one is a section 403(b) annuity). If you participate in two arrangements that permit elective deferrals, you should take care that this limit is not exceeded for any calendar year.

14. Q. Do I need to file any additional forms with IRS because I participate in a SEP?

A. No.

15. Q. Is my employer required to provide me with information about SEP-IRAs and the SEP agreement?

A. Yes. Your employer must provide you with a copy of the executed SEP agreement (Form 5305A-SEP), these Questions and Answers, the form used by the employee to defer amounts to the SEP, the notice of excess SEP contributions, if applicable, and a statement each year showing any contribution to your SEP-IRA.

16. Q. Is the financial institution where my IRA is established also required to provide me with information?

A. Yes. It must provide you with a disclosure statement that contains the following items of information in plain, nontechnical language:

(1) the statutory requirements that relate to your IRA;

(2) the tax consequences that follow the exercise of various options and what those options are;

(3) participation eligibility rules, and rules on the deductibility and nondeductibility of retirement savings;

(4) the circumstances and procedures under which you may revoke your IRA, including the name, address, and telephone number of the person designated to receive notice of revocation (this explanation must be prominently displayed at the beginning of the disclosure statement);

(5) explanations of when penalties may be assessed against you because of specified prohibited or penalized activities concerning your IRA; and

(6) financial disclosure information which:

(a) either projects value growth rates of your IRA under various contribution and retirement schedules, or describes the method of computing and allocating annual earnings and charges which may be assessed;

(b) describes whether, and for what period, the growth projections for the plan are guaranteed, or a statement of earnings rate and terms on which these projections are based; and

(c) states the sales commission to be charged in each year expressed as a percentage of $1,000.

See Publication 590, Individual Retirement Arrangements (IRAs), available at most IRS offices, for a more complete explanation of the disclosure requirements.

In addition to this disclosure statement, the financial institution is required to provide you with a financial statement each year. It may be necessary to retain and refer to statements for more than one year in order to evaluate the investment performance of the IRA and in order that you will know how to report IRA distributions for tax purposes.

Model Elective SEP Deferral Form

I. Salary reduction deferral

Subject to the requirements of the Model Elective SEP of ______________ (insert name of employer), I authorize the following amount or percentage of my compensation to be withheld from each of my paychecks and contributed to my SEP-IRA:

(a) ________ percent of my salary (not in excess of 15%); or **(b)** ________ dollar amount.

This salary reduction authorization shall remain in effect until I give a written modification or termination of its terms to my employer.

II. Cash bonus deferral

Subject to the requirements of the Model Elective SEP of ______________ (insert name of employer), I authorize the following amount to be contributed to my SEP-IRA rather than being paid to me in cash: ________ dollar amount.

III. Amount of deferral

I understand that the total amount I defer in any calendar year to this SEP may not exceed the lesser of: **(a)** 15% of my compensation; or **(b)** $7,000 (as adjusted per Code section 415(d)).

IV. Commencement of deferral

The deferral election specified in either I. or II. above shall not become effective before: ______________ (Month, Day, Year)

(Specify a date no earlier than the next payday beginning after this authorization.)

Signature ► Date ►

Notification of Excess SEP Contributions

To: ______________ (Name of employee)

Our calculations indicate that the elective deferrals you made to your SEP-IRA for calendar year ______ exceed the maximum permissible limits under section 408(k)(6) of the Internal Revenue Code. You made excess SEP contributions of $________ for that year.

These excess SEP contributions are includible in your gross income for the calendar year specified above.

These excess SEP contributions must be distributed from your IRA by the due date (plus extensions) for filing your tax return for the preceding calendar year (normally April 15th) in order to avoid significant penalties. Income allocable to the excess amounts must be withdrawn at the same time and is includible in income along with the excess contributions. Excess contributions left in your SEP-IRA account after that time are subject to a 6% excise tax.

Signature ► Date ►

Form 5305A-SEP (Rev. 10-87) Page **6**

Elective SEP Actual Deferred Percentage Worksheet

a Employee Name	**b** Status H = Highly compensated F = Family 0 = Other	**c** Compensation (Including compensation from related employers and compensation of family.)	**d** Deferrals (Add all SEP deferrals; add deferrals of family to HCE*)	**e** Ratio (if family member enter N.A. - otherwise d ÷ c)	**f** Permitted ratio (for HCE* only from below)	**g** Permitted amount (for HCE* only) c X f	**h** Excess (for HCE* only) d minus g
1.							
2.							
3.							
4.							
5.							
6.							
7.							
8.							
9.							
10.							
11.							
12.							
13.							
14.							
15.							
16.							
17.							
18.							
19.							
20.							
21.							
22.							
23.							
24.							
25.							

Permitted Ratio Computation for column f:

A. Enter the total of all the ratios of the employees marked as "-0-" in column b ____________

B. Divide line A by the number of employees marked as "-0-" in column b ____________

C. Permitted ratio—Multiply line B by 1.25 and enter the permitted ratio here ____________

* Highly compensated employee

☆U.S. Government Printing Office: 1987—201-993/60118

Form **5306-SEP**
(Rev. March 1987)
Department of the Treasury
Internal Revenue Service

Application for
Approval of Prototype Simplified Employee Pension-SEP
(Under Section 408 of the Internal Revenue Code)

OMB No. 1545-0199
Expires 2-29-90

Please complete all items on this form. If an item does not apply, enter "N/A."

For IRS Use Only
File folder number ▶

1 Approval requested for:

a ☐ Initial application

b ☐ Amendment—Enter ▶ (i) Latest letter serial number | (ii) Date letter issued | (iii) File folder no. | (iv) Plan number

2a Name of applicant

2b Applicant's employer identification number

Address (number and street)

City or town, state, and ZIP code

3a Name of person to be contacted

3b Telephone number
(   )

4 Type of sponsoring organization:
a ☐ Insurance company
b ☐ Trade or professional organization
c ☐ Savings and loan association that qualifies as a bank
d ☐ Bank
e ☐ Regulated investment company
f ☐ Federally insured credit union
g ☐ Other (specify) ▶ ....

5 Attach a copy of the documents to be used and indicate the article or section and the page number where the following provisions may be found. If not applicable, insert "N/A."	Article or section	Page number	For IRS Use Only
a Participation requirements—Plan covers each employee (see instructions) who has:			
(i) Reached age 21			1
(ii) Performed service for the employer during 3 of the immediately preceding 5 years. **And,**			1
(iii) Received at least $300 in compensation from the employer for the year. **Plan excludes:**			1
(i) Nonresident alien employees **Or,**			
(ii) Employees covered by a collective bargaining agreement whose retirement benefits have been the subject of good faith collective bargaining with the employer			1
b Definite written allocation formula—			
(i) Provision stating the requirements that employees must satisfy to share in an allocation			2
(ii) Provision stating how the amount allocated is figured			3
(iii) Provision that only the first $200,000 of each employee's compensation be included in total compensation used in the allocation formula			3
c Provision that the allocation formula is integrated with social security (if not, enter "N/A")			3
d Provision that the plan must be used with a prototype IRA that has a favorable opinion letter from IRS or with an IRS model IRA			5

6 Withdrawals—	Yes	No
a Are future employer contributions conditioned on prior contributions being kept in the IRA, that is, not withdrawn by the participants?		
b Does the SEP impose any prohibition on withdrawals?		

Under penalties of perjury, I declare that I have examined this application, including accompanying statements, and to the best of my knowledge and belief it is true, correct, and complete.

Signature ▶ **Title ▶** **Date ▶**

For Paperwork Reduction Act Notice, see instructions on back of Form. Form **5306** (3-87)

Instructions

(Section references are to the Internal Revenue Code, unless otherwise noted.)

General Information

Paperwork Reduction Act Notice.—We ask for this information to carry out the Internal Revenue laws of the United States. We need it to determine if your prototype simplified employee pension (SEP) meets the requirements of the IRC. If you want this approval, you are required to give us this information.

Purpose of Form

Form 5306-SEP is used by program sponsors who want to get IRS approval of their prototype simplified employee pension agreements.

General Instructions

Who May File

You may use this application to request a favorable opinion letter if: (1) you are a bank, federally insured credit union, savings and loan association that qualifies as a bank, insurance company, regulated investment company, or trade or professional society or association (other than an employee association); and (2) you want to get a favorable opinion letter that a SEP agreement to be used by more than one employer is acceptable in form.

Who Does Not Need To File

Instead of designing their own SEP, sponsors of programs may use IRS **Form 5305-SEP**, Simplified Employee Pension—Individual Retirement Accounts Contribution Agreement, to establish a SEP. Sponsors who use Form 5305-SEP with individual retirement accounts or annuities on which IRS has issued a favorable opinion or ruling letter, or with model individual retirement accounts issued by IRS, are considered to have established a SEP that meets the requirements of section 408(k). This applies even if you have reproduced the provisions of Form 5305-SEP on your own letterhead or in pamphlets that omit all references to IRS or its forms. Therefore, these sponsors should not file Form 5306-SEP for approval of their SEP by IRS.

IRS will not issue an opinion letter on a document submitted with Form 5306-SEP that is a combination of a prototype SEP and a prototype individual retirement account or annuity.

What To File

File this application and one copy of all documents that make up the SEP agreement. If this is an amendment, include a copy of the amendment and an explanation of its effect on the SEP agreement.

Where To File

File this application with the Commissioner of Internal Revenue, 1111 Constitution Avenue, NW., Attention: OP:E:EP:Q, Washington, DC 20224.

Signature

An officer who is authorized to sign or another person authorized under a power of attorney must sign this application. (Send the power of attorney, Form 2848 or Form 2848-D, with this application when you file it.)

Specific Instructions

Line 1(b)(iii)

If you are amending your SEP, enter the file folder number from the latest opinion letter you received for your SEP.

Line 1(b)(iv)

In order to distinguish between the SEP's of the same sponsor, the sponsor must designate a different three-digit SEP number beginning with the number 001 for each separate plan of the sponsor. The second SEP submitted by a sponsor should be designated 002 and so forth. Enter here the plan number assigned to the plan covered by this application.

Line 5(a)

The term "Employees" includes all employees of: a controlled group of corporations (section 414(b)); a group of businesses under common control (section 414(c)); an affiliated service group (section 414(m)); and certain leased employees required to be treated as the employer's own employees under section 414(n).

Form **5307** (Rev. July 1987)
Department of the Treasury
Internal Revenue Service

Short Form Application for Determination for Employee Benefit Plan
(Other than Collectively Bargained Plans)
(Under sections 401(a) and 501(a) of the Internal Revenue Code)

OMB No. 1545-0200
Expires 5-31-90

For IRS Use Only
File folder number ▶
Case number ▶

Church and governmental plans not subject to ERISA need not complete items 16, 17, 18, 19, and 20.

All other plans must complete all items except as indicated on the specific lines. For example, if you answer "No" to line 16a(i), you need not complete lines 16a(ii) and (iii) since they require responses only if you answer "Yes" to line 16a(i). "N/A" is only an acceptable answer if an N/A block is provided. All applications are now computer screened; therefore, it is important that you provide all the information requested and have the application signed by the employer, plan administrator, or authorized representative. Otherwise, we may need to correspond with you or return your application for completion, which will delay its processing.

1 a Name, address, and ZIP code of sponsor (employer if single employer plan)

Telephone number ▶ (   )

2 a Employer identification number

b Employer's tax year ends
Month ☐ N/A

3 Name, address, ZIP code, and phone number of person to be contacted if more information is needed. (See Specific Instructions.) (If same as 1a, enter "same as 1a.")

Name ▶ ______ Telephone number ▶ (   )
Address ▶

4 Determination requested for—(Check applicable box):

a *(i)* ☐ Initial qualification—date plan adopted ▶
(ii) ☐ Amendment—date adopted ▶
(iii) If (ii) is checked, enter file folder number ▶

b Were employees who are interested parties given the required notification of the filing of this application? ☐ **Yes** ☐ **No**

5 Check appropriate box to indicate the type of plan entity:

a ☐ Single employer plan
b ☐ Plan of controlled group of corporations, common control employers, or affiliated service group
c ☐ Multiple-employer plan
d ☐ Church plan
e ☐ Governmental plan
f ☐ Other (specify) ▶

6 a Name of plan

b Plan number ▶
c Plan year ends ▶

7 a This is a:
(i) ☐ Master or prototype plan
(ii) ☐ Field prototype plan
(iii) ☐ Uniform plan (see instructions)

b Letter serial number or notification letter number

8 a Is this a defined benefit plan? ☐ **Yes** ☐ **No**—If "Yes," indicate whether:
(i) ☐ Unit benefit
(ii) ☐ Fixed benefit
(iii) ☐ Flat benefit
(iv) ☐ Other (specify) ▶

b Is this a defined contribution plan? ☐ **Yes** ☐ **No**—If "Yes," indicate whether:
(i) ☐ Profit-sharing
(ii) ☐ Money purchase
(iii) ☐ Stock bonus
(iv) ☐ Target benefit

c *(i)* If 8a (i), (ii), (iii), or (iv) is checked, is this a defined benefit plan covered under the Pension Benefit Guaranty Corporation termination insurance program?
☐ **Yes** ☐ **No** ☐ **Not determined**

(ii) If 4a (ii) and 8b (i), (ii), (iii), or (iv) are checked and the plan was a defined benefit plan before the amendment, was the plan covered by the termination insurance program before the amendment? ☐ **Yes** ☐ **No** ☐ **N/A**

9 Effective date of plan

10 Effective date of amendment ☐ **N/A**

11 Date plan was communicated to employees ▶
How communicated ▶

12 Integration: Is this plan integrated with social security or railroad retirement (see instructions)? ☐ **Yes** ☐ **No**

13 Type of funding entity:
a ☐ Trust
b ☐ Custodial account
c ☐ Nontrusteed
d ☐ Trust with insurance contracts

14 a Does plan provide for maximum limitation under section 415 (see instructions)? ☐ **Yes** ☐ **No**
b Do you maintain any other qualified plan(s) (see instructions)? ☐ **Yes** ☐ **No**

Under penalties of perjury, I declare that I have examined this application, including accompanying statements, and to the best of my knowledge and belief it is true, correct, and complete.

Signature ▶ ______ **Title ▶** ______ **Date ▶** ______

Signature ▶ ______ **Title ▶** ______ **Date ▶** ______

For Paperwork Reduction Act Notice, see page 1 of the instructions.

Form **5307** (Rev. 7-87)

Form 5307 (Rev. 7-87) **Page 2**

15 Is any issue relating to this plan or trust currently pending before the Internal Revenue Service, the Department of Labor, the Pension Benefit Guaranty Corporation, or any court? . . . ☐ Yes ☐ No
If "Yes," attach explanation.

	Yes	No	Not Certain
16 a *(i)* Is the employer a member of an affiliated service group? . . .			
If there is uncertainty whether the employer is a member of an affiliated service group, check the "Not Certain" column.			
(ii) If 16a(i) is "Yes" or "Not Certain," did a prior ruling or determination letter rule on what organizations were members of the employer's affiliated service group? (See instructions.) . . .			
(iii) If 16a(ii) is "Yes," have the facts on which that letter was based materially changed? (See instructions.) . . .			
b Is the employer a member of a controlled group of corporations or a group of trades or businesses under common control? . . .			

	Number Enter "0" if N/A
17 Coverage of plan at (give date) ▶ ________	
a Total employed . . .	
b Exclusions under plan because of (do not count an employee more than once):	
(i) Minimum age (specify) ▶ ______ ☐ N/A Years of service (specify) ▶ ______ ☐ N/A	
(ii) Employees included in collective bargaining . . .	
(iii) Nonresident aliens who receive no earned income from United States sources . . .	
c Total exclusions (add b(i) through (iii)) . . .	
d Employees not excluded under the statute (subtract c from a) . . .	
e Ineligible under plan because of (do not count an employee included in b):	
(i) Minimum pay (specify) ▶ ______ ☐ N/A	
(ii) Hourly-paid . . .	
(iii) Maximum age (specify) ▶ ______ ☐ N/A	
(iv) Other (specify) ▶ ______ ☐ N/A	
f Total employees ineligible (add e(i) through (iv)) . . .	
g Employees eligible to participate (subtract f from d) . . .	
h Number of employees participating in plan . . .	
i Percent of nonexcluded employees who are participating (divide h by d) . . . % If line i is 70% or more, go to line l.	
j Percent of nonexcluded employees who are eligible to participate (divide g by d) . . . %	
k Percent of eligible employees who are participating (divide h by g) . . . % If i and j are less than 70%, or k is less than 80%, see instructions.	
l Total number of participants, including certain retired and terminated employees (see instructions) . . .	

18 Vesting—Check only one of the boxes for the vesting provisions of the plan:

a ☐ Full and immediate
b ☐ Full vesting after 10 years of service (see instructions)
c ☐ 5- to 15-year vesting, i.e., 25% after 5 years of service, 5% additional for each of the next 5 years, then 10% additional for each of the next 5 years (see instructions)
d ☐ Rule of 45 (section 411(a)(2)(C)) (see instructions)
e ☐ For each year of employment, beginning with the 4th year, vesting not less than 40% after 4 years of service, 5% additional for each of the next 2 years, and 10% additional for each of the next 5 years
f ☐ Other (specify and see instructions) ▶

19 Complete only for a plan of more than one employer:

a Total number of participants (including certain retired and terminated employees) . . .	
b Participants whose benefits or accounts are fully vested . . .	
c Number of contributing employers . . .	

20 Is the plan sponsor an S Corporation? . . . ☐ Yes ☐ No

Instructions for Form 5307

(Revised July 1987)

Short Form Application for Determination for Employee Benefit Plan

(Section references are to the Internal Revenue Code unless otherwise noted.)

General Information

Paperwork Reduction Act Notice.—We ask for this information to carry out the Internal Revenue laws of the United States. We need it to determine whether you meet the legal requirements for plan approval. If you want to have your plan approved by IRS, you are required to give us this information.

You may request an advance determination from the Internal Revenue Service for the qualification of a defined benefit plan or a defined contribution plan and the exempt status of any related trust.

The application is open to public inspection if there are more than 25 participants. Therefore, it is important that the total number of participants be shown on line 17(l). See the Specific Instructions for definition of "participant."

General Instructions

Determination applications are now screened for completeness by computer. For this reason, it is important that an appropriate response be entered for each line item (except as indicated in 5, below). **In completing the application, be sure to pay careful attention to the following:**

1. N/A (not applicable) is accepted as a response only if an N/A block is provided.
2. If an item requests a numeric response, a numeric response must be entered.
3. If an item provides a choice of boxes to be checked, only one box should be checked unless instructed otherwise.
4. If an item provides a box or boxes to be checked, written responses are not acceptable.
5. If the Church or Governmental plan box is checked for line 5, certain line items may not need to be completed. In this regard, please refer to the heading on page 1 of the form to determine which items to complete if this application is for a church or governmental plan.

A. Who May File.—This form may be filed by a plan sponsor who has adopted a master or prototype plan that was approved by the National Office, or a uniform plan that was approved by a key District Director. It may also be used by a plan sponsor who has adopted any other plan that has been approved by the key District Director to whom this application is submitted, but only if the key District Director has approved the use of this form for that plan.

If a plan sponsor adopts a master or prototype standardized plan and has had another qualified plan, adopts one or more nonstandardized plans, or adopts a master or prototype standardized plan and any other qualified plan, then an application for a determination letter must be filed by the plan sponsor (see Rev. Proc. 84-23, 1984-1 C.B. 457).

This form may not be used for collectively bargained plans.

B. What To File.—Whether the application is for an initial qualification or for an amendment, attach a completed **Form 5302**, Employee Census, and a copy of the joinder agreement. **Schedule T (Form 5300),** Supplemental Application for Approval of Employee Benefit Plans Under TEFRA, TRA 1984, REA, and TRA 1986, must be attached to each application except: (1) adopters of master or prototype plans who received favorable opinion letters after June 19, 1984, that have only one plan; or (2) adopters of uniform plans who received notification letters after December 31, 1984, the effective date of Rev. Proc. 84-86, that have only one plan.

A copy of the opinion letter or notification letter should be filed with the application.

A copy of the plan or trust instrument should not be filed with this application. However, the key district office may request additional information if the application and attachments do not contain enough information to make a determination. For plans of controlled groups of corporations, trades or businesses under common control, and affiliated service groups, submit the documents and statements listed above. In addition, attach a list of the member employers. Explain in detail their relationship, the types of plans each member has and the plans common to all member employers. (See instructions for line 17.)

C. Where To File.—

(i) *Single-Employer Plans.*—Send the forms to the key District Director for the district in which the employer's or employee organization's principal place of business is located.

(ii) *Plan Maintained by More Than One Employer.*—Send the forms to the key District Director for the district in which the principal place of business of the plan sponsor is located. This means the principal place of business of the association, committee, joint board of trustees, or other similar group of representatives of those who established or maintain the plan.

If the principal office of the plan sponsor is located in the following IRS District: ▼	Send your application to the address below: ▼
Cincinnati, Cleveland, Detroit, Indianapolis, Louisville, or Parkersburg	EP/EO Division P.O. Box 3159 Cincinnati, OH 45201
Baltimore, Pittsburgh, Richmond, any U.S. possession or foreign country	IRS, EP/EO Division P.O. Box 17010 Baltimore, MD 21203
Chicago, Aberdeen, Des Moines, Fargo, Helena, Milwaukee, Omaha, Springfield, St. Louis, or St. Paul	IRS, EP/EO Division P.O. Box A-3617 Chicago, IL 60960
Brooklyn, Albany, Buffalo, Manhattan, Augusta, Boston, Burlington, Hartford, Portsmouth, or Providence	IRS, EP/EO Division P.O. Box C-9050, GPO Brooklyn, NY 11202
Atlanta, Birmingham, Columbia, Greensboro, Jackson, Jacksonville, Little Rock, Nashville, or New Orleans	IRS, EP/EO Division P.O. Box 941; Room 310 Atlanta, GA 30370
Dallas, Albuquerque, Austin, Cheyenne, Denver, Oklahoma City, Houston, Phoenix, Salt Lake City, or Wichita	IRS, EP/EO Division 1100 Commerce Street Mail Code 306 Dallas, TX 75242
Los Angeles, Honolulu, or Laguna Niguel	IRS EP Application Receiving P.O. Box 486 Los Angeles, CA 90053-0486
San Francisco, Las Vegas, Sacramento, or San Jose	IRS, EP/EO Division Box 36040, Stop 3-2-29 450 Golden Gate Ave San Francisco, CA 94102
Seattle, Anchorage, Boise, or Portland	IRS, EP/EO Division 915 Second Ave. Mail Stop 554 Seattle, WA 98174

D. Disclosure Requested by Taxpayers.—A taxpayer may request IRS to disclose and discuss his or her return and/or return information with any person(s) the taxpayer designates in a written request. If you want to designate a person or persons to assist in matters relating to an application for a determination, you must give the IRS office of jurisdiction a written statement that must contain:

1. Your name, address, employer identification number, and plan numbers.
2. A paragraph that clearly identifies the person or persons you have authorized to receive the return and/or return information. This must include the name, address, telephone number(s), and social security number(s) of the authorized person(s).
3. A paragraph that clearly and explicitly describes the return and/or return information that you authorize IRS to disclose.
4. Your signature as the taxpayer making the authorization.

As an alternative to providing the above statement, you may submit **Form 2848,** Power of Attorney and Declaration of Representative, or **Form 2848-D,** Tax Information Authorization and Declaration of Representative.

Specific Instructions

1a. Enter the name and address of the plan sponsor. If a plan covers only the employees of one employer, "plan sponsor" means the employer. For plans maintained by two or more employers (other than a plan sponsored by two or more members of a controlled group of corporations), plan sponsor means the association, committee, joint board of trustees or other similar group of representatives of those who established or maintain the plan. For a plan sponsored by two or more members of a controlled group of corporations, plan sponsor means one of the members participating in the plan. This should be the same name that was used or will be used when Form 5500 series returns/reports are filed for the plan.

2a. Enter the nine-digit employer identification number (EIN) assigned to the plan sponsor. This should be the same EIN that was used or will be used when Form 5500 series returns/reports are filed for the plan.

2b. Complete for single-employer plans. For plans of more than one employer, check the "N/A" block.

3. See the instructions under "Disclosure Requested by Taxpayers," above.

4a. You must check box *(i)* or *(ii)*. If the plan or amendment was executed, enter the date signed. If a determination is requested based on a proposed plan or amendment, enter "9/9/99."

4a(iii). Enter the folder number if shown on the last determination letter for this plan.

4b. Section 3001 of the Employee Retirement Income Security Act of 1974 states that the applicant must provide evidence that each employee who qualifies as an interested party has been notified of the filing of the application. If you check "Yes," it means that you have notified each employee as required by regulations under section 7476. Rules defining "interested parties" and providing for the form of notification are contained in the regulations. An example of an acceptable format can be found in Rev. Proc. 80-30, 1980-1 C.B. 685.

5. Check only one box. A single-employer plan is a plan that is maintained by one employer. See sections 414(b), (c), and (m) for definitions of entities other than single employer.

6a. Enter the name you designated for your plan.

6b. You should assign a three-digit number, beginning with "001" and continuing in numerical sequence, to each plan you adopt. This numbering will differentiate your plans. Enter your three-digit number here. The number that is assigned to a plan must not be changed or used for any other plan.

6c. Plan year means the calendar, policy, or fiscal year on which the records of the plan are kept.

7a(i). Check for a master or prototype plan identified by letter serial number prefixed by a letter.

7a(iii). Check for a uniform plan identified by a notification letter number prefixed by a letter. Rev. Proc. 84-86, 1984-2 C.B. 787, sets forth procedures for issuing notification and determination letters relating to the qualification of uniform plans.

7b. Enter the appropriate letter serial number or notification letter number, e.g., A300001A.

11. You are required to notify all employees of the existence of a benefit plan and the important provisions of that plan. (See Rev. Rul. 71-90, 1971-1 C.B. 115.)

12. Attach a schedule of compliance with Rev. Rul. 71-446, 1971-2 C.B. 187.

Page 2

14a. Your plan(s) must meet the section 415 limitations by the effective dates prescribed by law.

14b. If you maintain any other qualified plan(s), attach a list for each plan which includes the following information: name of plan, type of plan, form of plan (standardized or nonstandardized) and indicate if the plan is paired, rate of employer contributions, allocation formula, benefit formula or monthly benefit, and number of participants (if paired, indicate the letter serial number of the paired plan).

16. If the plan sponsor is a member of an affiliated service group as defined in section 414(m), all employees of the affiliated service group members will be treated as employed by a single employer for purposes of certain qualification requirements such as coverage. See Rev. Proc. 85-43, 1985-2 C.B. 501, for procedures on submission to the key district office for a determination letter on the effect of section 414(m). Also see Rev. Rul. 81-105, 1981-1 C.B. 256, regarding the application of section 414(m).

16a(ii) and (iii). If you or any member (or possible member) of the affiliated service group received a ruling or determination letter regarding section 414(m), attach a copy of the letter to the application. If you are uncertain as to whether or not you are a member of an affiliated service group and no affiliated service group ruling or determination letter is available, or if the facts have changed since the ruling or determination letter was issued, attach the following information:

(1) A description of the nature of the business of the employer, specifically discussing whether it is a service organization or an organization whose principal business is the performance of management functions for another organization, including the reasons therefor;

(2) The identification of other members (or possible members) of the affiliated service group;

(3) A description of the nature of the business of each member (or possible member) of the affiliated service group describing the type of organization (corporation, partnership, etc.) and indicating whether such member is a service organization or an organization whose principal business is the performance of management functions for the other group member(s);

(4) The ownership interests between the employer and the members (or possible members) of the affiliated service group (including ownership interests as described in section 414(m)(2)(B)(ii));

(5) A description of the services performed for the employer by the members (or possible members) of the affiliated service group, or vice versa (including the percentage of each member's or possible member's gross receipts and service receipts provided by such services, if available, and data as to whether the services are a significant portion of the member's business) and whether or not, as of December 13, 1980, it was unusual for the services to be performed by employees of organizations in that service field in the United States;

(6) A description of how the employer and the members (or possible members) of the affiliated service group associate in performing services for other parties.

(7) A description of management functions, if any, performed by the employer for the member(s) (or possible member(s)) of the affiliated service group or received by the employer from any other member(s) (or possible member(s)) of the group (including data as to whether such management functions are performed on a regular and continuing basis) and whether or not it is unusual for such management functions to be performed by employees of organizations in the employer's business field in the United States;

(8) If management functions are performed by the employer for the member(s) (or possible member(s)) of the affiliated service group, a description as to what part of the employer's business constitutes the performance of management functions for the member(s) (or possible member(s)) of the group (including the percentage of gross receipts derived from management activities as compared to the gross receipts from other activities);

(9) A brief description of any other plan(s) maintained by the members (or possible members) of the affiliated service group if such other plan(s) is designated as a unit for qualification purposes with the plan for which a determination letter has been requested;

(10) A description of how the plan(s) satisfies the coverage requirements of section 410(b) if the members (or possible members) of the affiliated service group are considered part of an affiliated service group with the employer.

17. Enter the total number of employees as of the date given on line 17. Members of a controlled group of corporations, commonly controlled employers (whether or not incorporated), or affiliated service groups must include all the employees of the entire group in line 17. Total employees should include any individual considered a leased employee of the employer within the meaning of section 414(n).

17b(ii). Section 410(b)(3)(A) provides that a plan may exclude certain employees who are included in a unit of employees covered by an agreement which the Secretary of Labor finds to be a collective bargaining agreement between employee representatives and one or more employers, if there is evidence that retirement benefits were the subject of good faith bargaining between the employee representatives and the employer or employers.

17b(iii). Section 410(b)(3)(C) provides that a plan may exclude nonresident alien employees who receive no earned income from the employer that is income from sources within the United States.

17k. The percentage test of section 410(b)(1)(A) is met if, and only if: (1) line i is 70% or more; or (2) line j is 70% or more, and line k is 80% or more.

If the plan does not meet the percentage test, you must submit a schedule using the format on the next page to show that the plan meets the requirements of section 410(b)(1)(B). The question of acceptable classification is a continuing one and must be met in all later years as well. You should review your classification at the time you submit your annual return/report.

1		2	3	4	5
*Compensation range		Employees not excluded (See note)	Employees ineligible to participate	Employees participating	Participants who are officers or shareholders
At least	But not more than				
Totals					

*The compensation brackets used must reflect the pay pattern of the employer.

Note: *Enter in column 2 the total number of employees less exclusions under section 410(b)(3) if provided in the plan.*

17l. The term "participant" includes retirees and other former employees and the beneficiaries of both who are receiving benefits under the plan or will at some future date receive benefits under the plan. The figure to enter on this line is the total of: (1) the number of employees who are participating in the plan, (2) former employees who are receiving benefits under the plan or will at some future date receive benefits under the plan, and (3) beneficiaries of former employees who are receiving benefits under the plan. (This means one beneficiary for each former employee regardless of the number of individuals receiving benefits. For example, payment of a former employee's benefit to three children is considered as a payment to one beneficiary.)

18. If box b, c, d, or f is checked and the vesting schedule is less rapid than 18e, submit a schedule of turnover of employees or provide enough facts upon which a determination can be made that the vesting schedule of the plan is satisfactory. See Rev. Proc. 76-11, 1976-1 C.B. 550. Uniform plans must provide for a vesting schedule which is at least as favorable as the top-heavy schedule set forth in section 416(b)(1)(A) or (B).

Caution

The following Procedural Requirements Checklist identifies certain basic data that will facilitate the processing of your application. While no response is required to the questions, you may find that answering them will ensure that your application is processed without the need for contact to obtain missing information. If the answer to any of the questions is "No," your application may be incomplete. **Incomplete applications are identified through a computer screening system for return to the applicant.**

Procedural Requirements Checklist

	Yes	No	N/A
1. General requirements			
a If this application is made by a representative on behalf of the plan sponsor or plan administrator, has a current power of attorney been submitted with this application?			
b If notices or other communications are to be sent to someone other than the plan sponsor, have you provided proper authorization by attaching a completed Form 2848, 2848-D, or statement that contains all the information required?			
c Have you completed and attached Form(s) 5302?			▨
d Have you signed the application?			▨
e If applicable, have you completed and attached Schedule T (Form 5300)?			
2. Specific requirements			
a Have you attached an executed adoption agreement?			▨
b Have you attached a copy of the opinion or notification letter issued for the plan you adopted?			▨
c If this application is for the adoption of a uniform plan, have you attached a certification that the notification letter has not been withdrawn and is still in effect for the plan being submitted?			
d For a plan adopted by one or more members of a controlled group:			
(i) Have you attached the information outlined in General Instruction B?			
(ii) Have you completed line 17 according to the Specific Instructions?			
e For a plan that is or may be sponsored by a member of an affiliated service group:			
(i) Have you completed lines 16 and 17 according to the Specific Instructions?			
(ii) Have you attached the information requested in the instructions for lines 16a(ii) and (iii)?			
3. Miscellaneous requirements			
a Have you entered the plan sponsor's 9-digit employer identification number in line 2a?			▨
b Have you checked the appropriate block in line 4?			▨
c Have you entered the effective date of the plan in line 9?			▨

Form **5309** (Rev. June 1988)
Department of the Treasury
Internal Revenue Service

Application for Determination of Employee Stock Ownership Plan

(Under section 409 or 4975(e)(7) of the Internal Revenue Code)
File with Form 5301, 5303, or 5307, whichever applies.

OMB No. 1545-0284
Expires 5-31-91

For IRS Use Only
File folder number ▶

1 Name, address, and ZIP code of employer

Telephone number ▶ ( )

2 Employer's identification number

3 Date plan was adopted
Mo. Day Yr.

4 This application is for (complete one):

- a ☐ A tax credit employee stock ownership plan under section 409
- b ☐ An employee stock ownership plan under section 4975(e)(7)

5 Type of plan:

- a ☐ Profit-sharing
- b ☐ Stock bonus
- c ☐ Money purchase and stock bonus

Indicate the section and page number in the plan document where the following provisions will be found.	Section and page number
6 Complete the following for all plans:	
a The plan is designed to invest primarily in employer securities	
b Each participant must be entitled to direct the plan to vote the allocated securities as required in section 409(e)	
c A participant entitled to a distribution from the plan has a right to demand the entire distribution in employer securities, and if the securities are not readily marketable, the employer will repurchase the securities under a fair valuation formula	
d A participant is entitled to the election to diversify a portion of his or her account's investment in employer securities as required under section 401(a)(28)	
e A participant is entitled to commence distribution of his or her account balance after attaining normal retirement age, or after death, disability, or separation from service not later than required by section 409(o)	
7 Only plans applying under section 409 complete the following:	
a All employer securities transferred to or purchased by the plan for the employee plan credit or employee stock ownership credit shall be allocated for the plan year to the accounts of all participants who are entitled to share in these allocations	
b The allocation to each participant of the employer securities transferred or purchased for the employee plan credit or employee stock ownership credit is in substantially the same proportion as each employee's compensation is to the total compensation of all participants. For this allocation, compensation of any participant in excess of the first $100,000 per year shall be disregarded	
c No allocated securities as described in section 409(d) may be distributed to any participant before the end of the 84th month after the month of allocation of such securities except for separation from service, death, disability, termination of the plan, or as otherwise stated in section 409(d)	
d The right of all participants to the securities allocated to them must be nonforfeitable	
e If any part of the employee plan credit or employee stock ownership credit is recaptured or redetermined, amounts transferred to the plan for such credit shall remain in the plan and if allocated shall remain allocated	
8 Only plans applying under section 4975(e)(7) complete the following:	
a The plan is designated as an employee stock ownership plan within the meaning of section 4975(e)(7)	
b The plan provides for the establishment and maintenance of a suspense account as required under regulations section 54.4975-11(c)	
c Participants' rights to plan assets acquired by use of the exempt loan are protected as specified in regulations section 54.4975-11(a)(3)(i) and (ii)	
9 If the plan is applying under section 409(n) with respect to transactions under section 1042 or section 2057, the plan provides that the assets of the plan attributable to employer securities acquired by the plan in a sale to which section 1042 or section 2057 applies cannot accrue for the benefit of the persons specified in section 409(n) during the nonallocation period	

Under penalties of perjury, I declare that I have examined this application, including accompanying statements, and to the best of my knowledge and belief it is true, correct, and complete.

Signature ▶ **Title ▶** **Date ▶**

For Paperwork Reduction Act Notice, see back of form. Form **5309** (Rev. 6-88)

Instructions

(Section references are to the Internal Revenue Code.)

General Information

Use this form to apply for a determination letter for either a Tax Credit Employee Stock Ownership Plan that meets the requirements of section 409, or an Employee Stock Ownership Plan (ESOP) that meets the requirements of section 4975(e)(7). Use the form in conjunction with Form 5301, 5303, or 5307, whichever applies.

The plan you establish must be designed to invest primarily in employer securities. For a definition of employer securities as it pertains to your plan, see section 409(l) or section 4975(e)(8). Also see regulations section 1.46-8(d) for the formal plan requirements.

Paperwork Reduction Act Notice.— The Paperwork Reduction Act of 1980 says that we must tell you why we are collecting this information, how it is to be used, and whether your response is voluntary, required to obtain a benefit, or mandatory. The information is used to determine whether you meet the legal requirements for the plan approval you request. Your filing of this information is only required if you wish IRS to determine if your plan qualifies under section 409 or 4975(e)(7).

General Instructions

A. Who May File

1. Any corporate employer who elects to have an employee plan credit apply which was earned under section 48(n) as in effect prior to the enactment of the Tax Reform Act of 1984 and has been properly carried from such prior year and establishes a plan intended to meet the requirements under section 409.

2. Any corporate employer who has established an ESOP intended to meet the requirements under section 4975(e)(7).

3. Any corporate employer who amends an ESOP under sections 409 or 4975.

B. What To File

To receive a determination on whether a plan, initially or as a result of a plan amendment, meets the requirements of section 409 or 4975(e)(7), submit Forms 5309 and 5301, 5303, or 5307 plus a copy of all documents and statements required by those forms.

C. How To File

Attach the completed Form 5309 to Form 5301, 5303, or 5307 (whichever applies) and file with that form.

D. Signature

The application must be signed by the principal officer authorized to sign.

Form **5310** (Rev. April 1988)

Department of the Treasury
Internal Revenue Service

Pension Benefit Guaranty Corporation

Application for Determination Upon Termination; Notice of Merger, Consolidation or Transfer of Plan Assets or Liabilities; Notice of Intent To Terminate

(Under sections 401(a) and 6058(b) of the Internal Revenue Code and section 4041(a) of the Employee Retirement Income Security Act of 1974)

OMB No. 1545-0202
Expires 4-30-91

For Agency Use Only

Complete every applicable part of this form. If an item in an applicable part does not apply, enter N/A. Multiemployer plans covered by PBGC insurance program, see Purpose on page 1 of the instructions.

Reason for filing (check applicable box(es); see General Instructions):

A ☐ Notice of plan—(i) Merger, (ii) Consolidation, or (iii) Transfer of plan assets or liabilities to another plan.

B ☐ Application for ONLY an Internal Revenue Service (IRS) determination letter regarding a plan termination. (This is NOT a notice of intent to terminate for the Pension Benefit Guaranty Corporation.)

C ☐ Defined benefit plan filing "ONE STOP" for:
(i) Notice of intent to terminate under the Pension Benefit Guaranty Corporation (PBGC) termination insurance program AND
(ii) Application for an IRS determination letter upon plan termination.
(One-Stop filing is a voluntary choice in lieu of separate filings under B and D. It is NOT available when the Enrolled Actuary Certification Program is being used.)

D ☐ Defined benefit plan filing ONLY a notice of intent to terminate under the PBGC termination insurance program. (This is NOT a request for an IRS determination letter.)

E ☐ Enrolled Actuary Certification for a defined benefit plan filing ONLY a notice of intent to terminate under the PBGC termination insurance program

Part I All Filers Complete This Part

1 (a) Name of plan sponsor (see instructions):	**1 (b)** Employer identification number
Address (number and street)	**1 (c)** Sponsor's telephone number ( )
City or town, state, and ZIP code	**1 (d)** Employer's tax year ends Month Day Year 19
2 (a) Name of plan administrator (if same as 1(a), enter "same")	**1 (e)** Business code number
Address (number and street)	**1 (f)** Date business incorporated or began
City or town, state, and ZIP code	
2 (b) Administrator's employer identification number	**2 (c)** Administrator's telephone number ( )

2 (d) Name, address, and telephone number of person to be contacted if more information is needed (see instructions):
Name ____________ Telephone number ( )
Address

2 (e) Office of the District Director of the key district where sponsor is located (see instructions):

3 If you checked reason for filing B, C, D, or E, has each party who is required to be notified been properly informed of this filing (see instructions)? . . . . . ☐ Yes ☐ No

4 Type of plan entity (check only one box; see instructions):
(a) ☐ Single-employer plan
(b) ☐ Plan of controlled group of corporations or trades or businesses under common control
(c) ☐ Multiple-employer-collectively-bargained plan (other than a multiemployer plan)
(d) ☐ Multiple-employer plan (other)
(e) ☐ Other (specify) ______

5 (a) Plan name	**(b)** Plan number	**(c)** Plan year ends

6 (a) Is this a defined benefit plan covered under the Pension Benefit Guaranty Corporation termination insurance program (see Part IV instructions)? . . *(i)* ☐ Yes *(ii)* ☐ No *(iii)* ☐ Not determined

(b) If you checked "Yes" or "Not determined," have you ever used an employer identification number or plan number in any prior filing with PBGC other than the ones entered on lines 1(b) or 5(b) above? . . . . ☐ Yes ☐ No
If "Yes," enter the number(s) previously reported. ▶

7 Indicate type of plan (see General Instruction E):
(a) ☐ Defined benefit *(i)* ☐ Fixed benefit *(ii)* ☐ Unit benefit *(iii)* ☐ Flat benefit
(b) ☐ Money purchase **(c)** ☐ Profit-sharing **(d)** ☐ Other (specify) ▶

Under penalties of perjury, I declare that I have examined this application, including accompanying statements, and to the best of my knowledge and belief it is true, correct and complete.

Signature ▶ ______ Title ▶ ______ Date ▶ ______
Signature ▶ ______ Title ▶ ______ Date ▶ ______

For Paperwork Reduction Act Notice, see page 1 of the instructions.

Form **5310** (Rev. 4-88)

Form 5310 (Rev. 4-88) — If more space is needed for any item, attach additional sheets the same size as this form. Identify each sheet with the plan sponsor's name and EIN and identify each item. — Page 2

Part II **Complete This Part If You Checked Reason for Filing A**

8 Other plan(s) involved in transaction (see instructions):
(a) Plan name ____
(b) Name of employer ____
(c) Employer identification number ____
(d) Plan number ____
(e) Date of merger, consolidation or transfer ____
(f) If the plan listed in 5(a) is a defined benefit plan, attach an actuarial statement of valuation evidencing compliance with the requirements of Code section 401(a)(12) and the Income Tax Regulations under Code section 414(l).

Part III **Complete This Part If You Checked Reason for Filing B, C, D, or E**
If you checked reason for filing E, complete only 9, 10(a), (b), 11(a) and 12

9 Effective date of plan

		Yes	No
10 (a)	Has the plan ever received an IRS determination letter?		
(b)	If (a) is "Yes," enter the file folder number and date of the most recent determination letter and complete (d) through (g). File folder No. ____ Date ▶ ____		
(c)	If (a) is "No" and your reason for filing is B or C, attach a copy of the executed original plan document or joinder/adoption agreement, all plan amendments, trust agreement, group annuity contracts and custodial agreements (do not complete (d) through (g)).		
(d)	If (a) is "Yes," has the plan been amended since the last determination letter?		
(e)	If (d) is "Yes," and your reason for filing is B or C, attach a copy of the amendment(s) and complete (f) and (g).		
(f)	Do any of the amendments alter the plan's vesting provisions?		
(g)	Do any of the amendments (including the termination) decrease plan benefits? (see instructions)		

11 (a) Proposed date of plan termination ▶ ____
(b) Attach copies of records of all actions taken to terminate the plan (see instructions).
(c) Last contribution to the plan:
(i) Date (ii) Amount (see instructions) $ (iii) For plan year ended

12 Reason for termination (check only one box to indicate primary reason for termination):
(a) ☐ Change in ownership by merger
(b) ☐ Liquidation or dissolution of employer
(c) ☐ Change in ownership by sale or transfer
(d) ☐ Adverse business conditions (see instructions and attach explanation)
(e) ☐ Adoption of new plan (see instructions and attach explanation)
(f) ☐ Other (specify) ▶

13 Indicate funding arrangement:
(a) ☐ Trust (benefits provided in whole from trust funds)
(b) ☐ Trust or other arrangement providing benefits partially through insurance and/or annuity contracts
(c) ☐ Trust or other arrangement providing benefits exclusively through insurance and/or annuity contracts
(d) ☐ Custodial account described in Code section 401(f) and not included in (c) above
(e) ☐ Other (specify) ▶

14 (a) Name(s) of trustee(s) or custodian(s) — (b) Date trust's accounting period ends
Address (number and street)
City or town, state, and ZIP code

		Yes	No	Not Certain
15	Participation (see instructions): Collectively bargained plans and plans filing only a notice of intent to terminate (reason for filing D) do not complete (a) and (c).			
(a) (i)	Is the employer a member of an affiliated service group? If there is uncertainty whether the employer is a member of an affiliated service group, check the "Not Certain" column.			
(ii)	If (i) is "Yes" or "Not Certain," did a prior ruling letter rule on what organizations were members of the employer's affiliated service group or did the employer receive a determination letter on this plan that considered the effect of Code section 414(m)?			
(iii)	If (ii) is "Yes," have the facts on which that letter was based materially changed?			
(b)	Is the employer a member of a controlled group of corporations or a group of trades or businesses under common control?			

Form 5310 (Rev. 4-88) Page **3**

15 (Continued):

(c) Complete the following as of the proposed date of plan termination (current year) and as of the end of the 2 prior plan years:

	19		19		Current year 19	
	Yes	**No**	**Yes**	**No**	**Yes**	**No**
(i) Did the plan satisfy the percentage tests of Code section 410(b)(1)(A)?						
(ii) Total number of employees (if more than 100 enter "100 plus")						

(d) Enter the total number of participants employed for the current plan year and each of the 5 prior plan years on the schedule below:

	19	19	19	19	19	Current year 19 .....
(i) Number at beginning of plan year						
(ii) Number added during the plan year						
(iii) Total (add lines (i) and (ii))						
(iv) Number dropped during the plan year						
(v) Number at end of plan year (subtract (iv) from (iii))						
(vi) Total number of participants in this plan separated from service during the plan year without full vesting						

16 Summary of participants or claimants by category:	Total number	Amount of monthly benefits as of the most recent payment date
(a) Retirees and beneficiaries (including disability retirees) receiving benefits		
(b) Active participants eligible for normal retirement		
(c) Active participants eligible for early (but not normal) retirement		
(d) Active participants vested before termination (other than normal or early retirement)		
(e) All other active participants		
(f) Participants separated from service with deferred vested benefits		
(g) Total (add lines (a) through (f))		

17 Miscellaneous:	**Yes**	**No**	**Not Applicable**
(a) As a result of the termination, are accrued benefits or account balances nonforfeitable as required under Code section 411(d)(3)?			
(b) For each participant, do the accrued benefits upon termination include the subsidized benefits that the participant may become entitled to receive subsequent to the termination? (See instructions)			
(c) Will the trust continue to operate after termination of the plan? (See instructions)			
(d) Were any funds contributed in the form of, or invested in, obligations or property of the employer or any group of corporations or group of trades or businesses under common control?			
(e) Will distribution include property other than cash?			
(f) For a defined benefit or money purchase plan, do you estimate there will be an accumulated funding deficiency as of the end of the plan year during which the proposed termination date occurs if no additional plan contributions are made?			
If "Yes," enter the estimated accumulated funding deficiency $			
(g) *(i)* If there are unallocated funds which can be reallocated to participants without exceeding the limitations of Code section 415, have these funds been reallocated?			
(ii) If (i) is "Yes," did the plan originally contain a provision allowing this allocation?			
(iii) If (ii) is "No," was the plan amended to provide for this allocation?			
(h) Will any funds be, or have any funds been, returned to the employer? (See specific instructions)			
If "Yes," enter the estimated amount ▶ $			
Complete (i) through (ix) only if 17(h) is "Yes."			
(i) Has the terminating plan been involved in a spinoff or other transfer of assets or liabilities, subject to Code section 414(l), within 60 months preceding the proposed date of termination? If "Yes," attach a list and explanation of the transaction(s) involved that have occurred within the 60 month period preceding the proposed date of termination			
(ii) If (i) is "Yes," answer (A) and (B).			
(A) Are the accrued benefits of all participants, in the other plan(s) included in (i), fully vested and nonforfeitable as of the date of this plan termination? (See instructions)			
(B) Have cash distributions or guaranteed annuity contracts been provided for all accrued benefits, as of the date of this termination, of all participants in the other plan(s) included in (i)? (See instructions)			
Note: *Distributions may not be made to employed participants in nonterminating plans.*			
(iii) Have cash distributions or guaranteed annuity contracts been provided for all accrued benefits of all participants in this plan?			
(iv) Attach a statement providing the dates and amounts of these cash distributions or purchase of annuity contracts.			

	Yes	No	Not Applicable
17 (v) If this is a defined benefit plan, is it intended or is it a fact that any or all of the participants in the terminating plan will be covered by a new or existing defined benefit plan of the employer?			
(vi) If "Yes," does the new plan give full prior service credit for vesting and entitlement purposes?			
(vii) If (i) or (v) is "Yes," then			
(A) Has a Form 5300 been submitted for a determination letter for the other plan(s) involved? If "Yes," attach plan numbers.			
(B) Has the IRS granted approval for a change in funding method in connection with this termination for the other plan(s) involved? If "Yes," attach a copy of such approval letter(s)			
(viii) Has the employer previously received a reversion of assets upon termination of a defined benefit plan in the past 15 years? If "Yes," attach explanation			
(ix) If the plan was ever a contributory plan, were distributions of employee contributions made within the 12 month period immediately preceding the date of plan termination?			
(i) Is this plan or trust currently under examination or is any issue relating to this plan or trust currently pending before the Internal Revenue Service, the Department of Labor, the Pension Benefit Guaranty Corporation or any court? If "Yes," attach a statement naming the agency(s) and/or court and briefly describe the issues			
(j) Did any plan participant during the current plan year or in the 5 prior plan years receive a lump-sum distribution (see instructions) or have an annuity contract purchased by the plan from an insurance company on his or her behalf?			
If "Yes," state the largest amount so distributed or applied to purchase an annuity contract $			
(k) Does the plan have ESOP/TRASOP features?			
(l) Were plan benefits not required to be provided in annuity form valued as of the proposed distribution date in accordance with PBGC Regulation 29 CFR 2619.26(b) and (c)? (Attach an explanation of how lump sum values were determined.)			
(m) Does the plan require appropriate written participant and/or spousal consent(s) for distributions where the present value of the nonforfeitable accrued benefit exceeds $3,500? (See instructions.)			
(n) In the case of a distribution from a defined benefit plan, is the interest rate used to determine the present value of the accrued benefit and the amount to be distributed not greater than the PBGC interest rate for valuing immediate annuities?			

18 Defined contribution plans (other than money purchase plans) such as profit-sharing, stock bonus, or other such plans where forfeitures are credited to individual account balances, enter the information for the current plan year and the 5 prior plan years on the following schedule:

	19 ----	19 ----	19 ----	19 ----	19 ----	Current year 19 ----
(a) Employer contributions						
(b) Forfeitures						

(c) Attach a statement explaining bases on which forfeitures were allocated.

19 Indicate how distributions will be made on termination (check applicable box(es)):

(a) ☐ Lump-sum distribution **(b)** ☐ Annuity contract **(c)** ☐ Periodic payments from trust
(d) ☐ Transfer of assets and liabilities to another plan **(e)** ☐ Other (specify) ▶

20 Statement of net assets available to pay benefits as of the proposed date of plan termination. Read specific instruction 20, and if you checked Reason for Filing C or D, read specific instruction 25(c) before completing this item.

Assets	
(a) Cash and cash equivalents	
(b) Receivables—	
(i) Employer contributions	
(ii) Other	
(c) Party-in-interest investments—	
(i) Loans to employer	
(ii) Employer securities	
(iii) Other	
(d) Other investments—	
(i) Government securities	
(ii) Pooled funds/mutual funds	
(iii) Corporate (debt and equity instruments)	
(iv) Real estate and mortgages	
(v) Other	
(e) Buildings and other depreciable property	
(f) Unallocated insurance contracts	
(g) Other assets	
(h) Total assets (add lines (a) through (g))	

Form 5310 (Rev. 4-88) Page **5**

	Liabilities and Net Assets	
20 (i)	Accounts and notes payable—	
	(i) Past due benefits	
	(ii) Employer	
	(iii) Other	
(j)	Accrued expenses	
(k)	Mortgages payable	
(l)	Acquisition indebtedness	
(m)	Other liabilities	
(n)	Total liabilities (add lines (i) through (m))	
(o)	Net assets available to pay benefits (subtract line (n) from line (h))	

Part IV **Complete This Part If You Checked Reason for Filing C or D and Checked "Yes" on Line 6(a).**

If you checked Reason for filing C or D and "Not determined" on line 6(a), completion of this part is optional. However, if you do not complete this part, you must file the plan document, any amendments to the plan document, and the IRS determination letter(s) for the plan as described for lines 22(b), (c), and (g). If PBGC later determines that the termination insurance program covers the plan, you must file the remainder of the information required by this Part (see Part IV instructions).

21 (a) Name(s) of labor organization(s) representing plan participants	**(b)** Telephone number ( )
Address (number and street)	**(c)** Name of principal officer
City or town, state, and ZIP code	**(d)** Title of principal officer

22 Indicate the applicability of items (a) through (i) by checking the appropriate column. Attach each item that is applicable (see instructions):	**Applicable**	**Not applicable**
(a) Power of attorney. File 2 copies if you are filing "one-stop" (see General Instruction H)		
(b) Copy of executed plan document		
(c) Copy of executed amendment(s) to the plan document		
(d) Copy of executed group annuity or group insurance contract(s)		
(e) Copy of executed trust agreement(s)		
(f) Copy of executed collective bargaining agreement(s)		
(g) Copy of IRS determination letter(s)		
(h) Copy of the most recent actuarial report		
(i) Copy of the most recent financial statement of plan assets		

23 Indicate the sufficiency of plan assets (see instructions):	**Yes**	**No**
(a) Are any participants entitled to receive benefits assigned to categories 1 through 4 under ERISA section 4044?		
If "Yes," complete (b); if "No," enter N/A in (b), (c), (d), and (e).		
(b) Do you estimate that plan assets (excluding any amount described in (d) below) are adequate to provide all the benefits assigned to categories 1 through 4 on the proposed date of plan termination?		
If "Yes," enter N/A in (c) and complete item (d); if "No," complete (c) and (d).		
(c) Indicate the estimated amount by which the value of benefits in categories 1 through 4 exceeds the value of plan assets on the proposed date of plan termination ▶ $ ____		
(d) Is the employer making a commitment (in the form prescribed in the PBGC regulation on determination of plan sufficiency) to pay, on or before the date assets are distributed, the amount needed to provide all benefits in categories 1 through 4?		
If "Yes," attach a signed copy of the commitment; if "No," complete (e).		
(e) Has the plan sponsor paid or does the plan sponsor intend to pay employer liability as prescribed in the PBGC regulation on employer liability before PBGC's request for payment?		
Note: Interest on employer liability will accrue from the date of plan termination.		

24 Submit participant data schedules in the format shown in the instructions for the following groups of participants:

(a) Retired participants and beneficiaries receiving benefits from the plan;

(b) Participants separated from service not yet receiving vested benefits from the plan; and

(c) All other participants with vested or nonvested accrued benefits.

25 Indicate the information you are filing with this notice by checking one of the following boxes (see instructions):

(a) ☐ I am filing a complete Form 5310 including required attachments.

(b) ☐ I am filing a complete Form 5310 except the information showing plan assets allocated to participants (see note below).

(c) ☐ I am filing a complete Form 5310 except plan asset information (line 20) and participant data schedules (line 24). I will file the information required by lines 20 and 24 within 90 days after the date of this filing. (See note below.) By not filing lines 20 and 24 with the form, I am agreeing to extend the 90-day period prescribed by ERISA section 4041(a) during which I will not make any distributions pursuant to the proposed termination of the plan.

(d) ☐ With this form I am filing a request for an extension of time to file the information required by line(s) ____________ (other than the information required by lines 20 and 24). (See note below.) For more information about extensions see the instructions.

Note: If you checked reason for filing C and you are not sending all the information required in Parts I, III, IV, and either completed Form(s) 6088 or a second copy of the complete participant data schedules described in the line 24 instructions of Form 5310, the 270-day period prescribed by Code section 7476(b)(3) will not commence until you file the remaining required information.

Department of the Treasury
Internal Revenue Service

Pension Benefit
Guaranty Corporation

Instructions for Form 5310

(Revised April 1988)

Application for Determination Upon Termination; Notice of Merger, Consolidation, or Transfer of Plan Assets or Liabilities; Notice of Intent To Terminate

(Section references are to the Internal Revenue Code. ERISA refers to the Employee Retirement Income Security Act of 1974.)

Paperwork Reduction Act Notice.—We need this information to carry out the laws of the United States as defined in the Internal Revenue Code and Title IV of the Employee Retirement Income Security Act of 1974. You are required to give us this information.

Purpose of Form.—

Form 5310 is used by plans, other than multiemployer plans covered by PBGC insurance, for the following reasons:

1. To give notice of merger, consolidation, or transfer of plan assets or liabilities to another plan (required by Code section 6058(b));

2. To apply for a determination upon termination of a plan (under Code section 401(a));

3. To give notice of intent to terminate a defined benefit pension plan (required by ERISA section 4041(a)).

Special Filing Information for Multiemployer Plans Covered by the PBGC Insurance Program.—A multiemployer plan covered by PBGC insurance that is merging with or transferring assets or liabilities to another multiemployer plan is required to notify PBGC but is NOT to use this form. The plan must file as required by ERISA section 4231.

A terminating multiemployer plan covered by PBGC insurance is required to notify PBGC but is NOT to use this form. The plan must file as required by the PBGC regulation on termination for multiemployer plans (29 CFR Part 2673).

If you want a determination letter for a multiemployer plan described above, request it from IRS on Form 5303.

General Instructions

A. Who Must File.—

1. *Pension Plan, Profit-Sharing Plan, and Other Deferred Compensation Plan.*—Any sponsor or plan administrator of a pension, profit-sharing, or other deferred compensation plan (except any multiemployer plan covered by PBGC insurance) should file this form for a plan merger, a plan consolidation, or a transfer of plan assets or liabilities to another plan. See Code section 6058(b).

Note: *When assets or liabilities are transferred from one plan to another, a Form 5310 should be filed for each plan.*

2. *Defined Benefit Pension Plan Covered Under the PBGC Termination Insurance Program.*—Any plan administrator of a defined benefit pension plan (other than a multiemployer plan) covered under the PBGC termination insurance program must file this form for a plan termination. If the Enrolled Actuary Certification Program is being used, only Part I and Part III, questions 9, 10(a), (b), 11(a) and 12 must be completed.

Note: *If the merger of a defined benefit plan with a defined contribution plan results solely in a defined contribution plan, the defined benefit plan is considered terminated. If the defined benefit plan is covered under the PBGC termination insurance program, this form must be filed with PBGC as a notice of intent to terminate.*

If the Enrolled Actuary Certification Program described in PBGC's regulation on Determination of Plan Sufficiency and Termination of Sufficient Plans (29 CFR 2617) is being used with this filing, one-stop filing is not permitted. An Enrolled Actuary's certification of sufficiency may not be used when the plan administrator intends to ask PBGC to provide early retirement benefits pursuant to PBGC Regulation 29 CFR 2617.30. Also, the certification may not be used in the case of plans in which assets are expected to exceed all plan liabilities (and excess assets will revert to the employer) if the following conditions apply (see PBGC Regulation 29 CFR 2617 for further details).

(i) The plan has been involved in a spin-off or other transfer of assets or liabilities within a 36-month period immediately preceding the proposed date of termination, unless the total value of the assets or liabilities transferred was less than 20% of the present value of the accrued benefits of the transferring plan as of any day during the year that the transfer occurred (with all transfers aggregated and treated as if they occurred in the first plan year in which a transfer occurred).

Reason for Filing (These reasons correspond to the reasons at the top of page 1 of Form 5310)	Where to File (See General Instruction D)	What to File	When to File
1. Plans (except multiemployer plans covered by PBGC insurance) that are going to merge, consolidate or transfer plan assets or liabilities to another plan. Reason For Filing A.	IRS	One copy of Form 5310 Parts I, II, and attachments. If a determination letter is being requested for the plan as amended, the applicable Form 5300, 5301, 5303, or 5307 and the actuarial statement asked for on line 8(f) of Form 5310 are to be filed in lieu of Form 5310.	At least 30 days before the merger, consolidation, or transfer.
2. Terminations: a. Plans (except multiemployer plans covered by PBGC insurance) that are requesting only a determination letter from IRS. Reason For Filing B.	IRS [1]	One copy of Form 5310 Parts I, III, and attachments and Form(s) 6088.	Any time a determination letter upon termination is requested.
b. Defined benefit plans covered by PBGC termination insurance [2] (other than multiemployer plans) filing a notice of intent to terminate with PBGC and requesting a determination letter upon termination from IRS, "One-Stop." Reason For Filing C. **Note:** *One-Stop filing may not be used where the Enrolled Actuary Certification Program is being used.*	PBGC [3]	Two copies of Form 5310 Parts I, III, IV[2], attachments as specified (never more than 2 copies of any attachment), and one copy of Form(s) 6088. Also submit one copy of your most recent PBGC Form 1.	At least 10 days before the proposed date of plan termination.
c. Defined benefit plans covered by PBGC termination insurance [2] (other than multiemployer plans) filing a notice of intent to terminate with PBGC and NOT requesting a determination letter upon termination from IRS. Reason For Filing D.	PBGC	One copy of Form 5310 Parts I, III, IV, and attachments. Also submit one copy of your most recent PBGC Form 1.	At least 10 days before the proposed date of plan termination.
d. Defined benefit plans covered by PBGC termination insurance (other than multiemployer plans) filing a notice of intent to terminate with PBGC under the Enrolled Actuary Certification Program. Reason for filing E.	PBGC	One copy of Form 5310 completed as follows: Part I, and Part III, question 9, 10(a),(b), 11(a), and 12; Plan Administrator Certification, Enrolled Actuary Certification and Checklist and a copy of your most recent PBGC Form 1. PBGC forms may be obtained from PBGC by calling 202-254-4817. Hearing impaired persons may call 202-254-8010.	Form 5310, at least 10 days before the proposed date of plan termination. See instructions to PBGC forms for other filing information.

[1] For a defined benefit plan covered by PBGC termination insurance, a notice of intent to terminate must be submitted to PBGC at least 10 days before the proposed termination date of the plan.

[2] If you are unsure as to whether the PBGC termination insurance program covers the plan, you are not required to complete all of Part IV. See optional filing requirements in the instructions for Part IV.

[3] If you do not choose to file "One-Stop," file separately with PBGC and IRS. Do NOT check Reason For Filing C. File with PBGC according to 2c of this chart. File with IRS according to 2a.

(ii) The plan sponsor will or intends to cover the same employees participating in the plan to be terminated under a new or existing defined benefit plan.

(iii) The plan requires or permits employee contributions and a method other than that contained in PBGC Regulation 29 CFR 2618.31(b) is requested for computing the portion of the excess assets attributable to employee contributions.

If the plan does not have excess assets, or if the plan has excess assets but the above three conditions do not apply, the Enrolled Actuary Certification Program may be used.

B. Who May File Voluntarily.—Any sponsor or plan administrator of any pension, profit-sharing or other deferred compensation plan (other than a multiemployer plan covered under PBGC insurance) may file this form to ask the IRS to make a determination on the plan's qualification status upon the plan's termination. Those wishing to file requesting a determination as to the plan's qualification status upon a partial termination should file Form 5300, 5301, 5303, or 5307 as applicable.

C. What, Where and When to File.—The chart on page one describes what forms to use and where and when to file them.

D. Where to File.—

1. Forms That Must Be Filed With PBGC.—Send or take these forms, including attachments, to the Pension Benefit Guaranty Corporation, Insurance Operations Department, Room 5300-A, Code 542, 2020 K Street, NW, Washington, DC 20006-1806. If you have any questions, please call PBGC at 202-254-4817. Hearing impaired persons may call PBGC's Superphone at 202-254-8010.

2. Forms That Must Be Filed With IRS.—File these forms as follows:

(i) Single Employer Plans.—Send the forms to the District Director, EP/EO Division, for the key district in which the employer's principal place of business is located.

(ii) Plan Maintained by More Than One Employer.—Send the forms to the District Director, EP/EO Division, for the key district in which the principal place of business of the plan sponsor or administrator is located. This means the principal place of business of the association, committee, joint board of trustees, or other similar group of representatives of those who established or maintain the plan. All forms and attachments to be filed with IRS should be filed with the key district indicated below:

If entity is in this IRS District ▼	Send fee and request for determination letter or notification letter to this address ▼
Brooklyn, Albany, Augusta, Boston, Buffalo, Burlington, Hartford, Manhattan, Portsmouth, Providence	Internal Revenue Service EP/EO Division P.O. Box 1680, GPO Brooklyn, NY 11202
Baltimore, District of Columbia, Pittsburgh, Richmond, Newark, Philadelphia, Wilmington, any U.S. possession or foreign country	Internal Revenue Service EP/EO Division, P.O. Box 17010, Baltimore, MD 21203
Cincinnati, Cleveland, Detroit, Indianapolis, Louisville, Parkersburg	Internal Revenue Service EP/EO Division, P. O. Box 3159, Cincinnati, OH 45201
Dallas, Albuquerque, Austin, Cheyenne, Denver, Houston, Oklahoma City, Phoenix, Salt Lake City, Wichita	Internal Revenue Service EP/EO Division Mail Code 4950 DAL 1100 Commerce Street Dallas, TX 75242
Atlanta, Birmingham, Columbia, Ft. Lauderdale, Greensboro, Jackson, Jacksonville, Little Rock, Nashville, New Orleans	Internal Revenue Service EP/EO Division Room 1112 P.O. Box 941 Atlanta, GA 30301
Honolulu, Laguna Niguel, Las Vegas, Los Angeles, San Jose	Internal Revenue Service EP Application Receiving Room 5127 P.O. Box 536 Los Angeles, CA 90053-0536
Chicago, Aberdeen, Des Moines, Fargo, Helena, Milwaukee, Omaha, St. Louis, St. Paul, Springfield	Internal Revenue Service EP/EO Division 230 S. Dearborn DPN 20-6 Chicago, IL 60604
Sacramento, San Francisco	Internal Revenue Service EP Application Receiving Stop SF 4446 P.O. Box 36001 San Francisco, CA 94102
Anchorage, Boise, Portland, Seattle	Internal Revenue Service EP Application Receiving P.O. Box 21224 Seattle, WA 98111

E. Definitions.—

1. Defined Contribution Plan.—This is a plan that provides for an individual account for each participant. Benefits are based solely on the amount contributed to the participant's account and any income, expenses, gains and losses and any forfeitures of accounts of other participants that may be allocated to the participant's account. Profit-sharing plans, stock bonus plans, and money purchase plans are defined contribution plans. See Code section 414(i) and ERISA section 3(34).

2. Defined Benefit Plan.—This is any plan that is not a defined contribution plan. These plans include unit benefit, fixed benefit, and flat benefit plans, and plans defined in Code section 414(k). Also, see ERISA section 3(35).

F. Failure to File a Notice of Intent to Terminate (Reasons for Filing C, D and E).—It is a violation of the provisions of Title IV of ERISA not to file the notice of intent to terminate at least 10 days before the proposed termination date of a plan (other than a multiemployer plan) covered under the PBGC termination insurance program. The PBGC may declare a notice of intent to terminate void if any required information is not filed. If you checked reason for filing "E" and are not submitting the enrolled actuary certification and check list, you must file a request for an extension of time to file them or the notice will be invalid. The instructions for line 25 explain how to obtain an extension of time to complete a filing.

G. Penalties.—If you are filing Form 5310 to report a plan merger, consolidation, or transfer of plan assets or liabilities, there is a penalty for late filing. The penalty is $25 for each day Form 5310 is late (up to a maximum of $15,000). The form is late if it is not filed at least 30 days before the plan merger, consolidation, or transfer of assets or liabilities.

H. Signature.—In general, the plan administrator must sign the form. For single employer plans the plan administrator and the employer are generally the same person. When the plan administrator is a joint employer—union board or committee, at least one employer representative and one union representative must sign. Both copies of the form submitted for a "One-Stop" filing (Reason for Filing C) must be signed. A Form 5310 filed with IRS or IRS and PBGC by a representative on behalf of an employer or plan administrator must be accompanied by:

(1) a power of attorney specifically authorizing such representation in this matter (you may use Form 2848, Power of Attorney), or

(2) a written declaration that the representative is a currently qualified attorney, certified public accountant, enrolled actuary, or is currently enrolled to practice before the IRS (include either the enrollment number or the expiration date of the enrollment card); and is authorized to represent the employer or plan administrator.

(File 2 copies of the above if you are filing "One-Stop.")

If you are an authorized representative other than an attorney-at-law and you are submitting this form only to PBGC, you must send in a notarized power of attorney specifically stating that you are authorized to represent the employer or plan administrator.

Specific Instructions

Please follow the instructions below when completing this form. If any item in a Part of this form you are required to complete does not apply, enter N/A.

Part I

1(a). Enter the name and address of the plan sponsor. If a plan covers only the employees of one employer enter the name of the employer. Otherwise, "plan sponsor" means the following:

(i) For a plan established or maintained by an employee organization, the employee organization.

(ii) For a plan established or maintained jointly by one or more employers and one or more employee organizations or by two or more employers, the association, committee, joint board of trustees, or other similar group of representatives of those who established or maintain the plan.

Be sure to include enough information in 1(a) to describe the sponsor adequately.

1(b). Enter the 9-digit employer identification number (EIN) assigned to the plan sponsor. This should be the same EIN that was used when the plan filed Form 5500, 5500-C, or 5500-R.

1(d). If this form is for a single employer plan, enter the date the employer's tax year ends. For all plans of more than one employer, enter N/A.

1(e). Enter the same business code that you entered on your most recently filed Form 5500, 5500-C, or 5500-R, whichever applies.

2(d). If you complete 2(d) and this is a filing for IRS, you must attach a written statement that contains:

(i) Your name, address, employer identification number, and plan number.

(ii) A paragraph that clearly identifies the person or persons you have authorized to receive the return and/or return information. This must include the name, address, telephone number(s) and social security number(s) of the authorized person(s).

(iii) A paragraph that clearly and explicitly describes the return and/or return information that you authorize IRS to disclose.

(iv) You must sign the request as the taxpayer making the authorization.

Note: *Forms sent to PBGC will be treated by PBGC under the Freedom of Information Act and the Privacy Act, as applicable.*

2(e). If you are filing for a defined benefit plan, enter the District Director's office for the key district where the plan sponsor's principal place of business is located.

3. If you checked Reason for Filing B or C, each person who qualifies as an interested party must be notified that the applicant has asked for a determination letter. Rules defining "interested parties" and providing for the form of notification are contained in the Income Tax regulations section 1.7476. Any delay in the start of the 270-day period under Code section 7476(b)(3) because all the information required in Parts I, III, IV, and either completed Form(s) 6088 or a second copy of the complete participant data schedules described for line 24 is not initially submitted for a "One-Stop" filing (Reason for filing C) does not affect the date the application for determination is made for satisfying the requirements for notice to interested parties in accordance with Code section 7476(b)(2).

If you checked Reason for Filing C, D, or E, individuals entitled to benefits under the plan and any union representing the individuals must be notified that the plan administrator or duly authorized representative has filed a notice of intent to terminate. The notification must be given in the manner and must contain the information prescribed in the PBGC regulation on notice of intent to terminate (29 CFR Part 2616).

4(a). Check for a single-employer plan, that is, a plan which is maintained by one employer, or one employee organization. Also check if more than one employer is contributing and an individual employer's contributions are available to pay benefits only for that employer's employees who are covered by the plan. Also check for a single-employer plan that is collectively bargained.

4(b). Check if more than one employer participates in a plan where all the participating employers are members of the same controlled group of corporations (Code section 414(b)). Also check if more than one employer participates in a plan where all the participating employers are members of the same group of employers under common control (Code section 414(c)).

4(c). Check for a plan of more than one employer (other than a multiemployer plan) that is collectively bargained, is collectively funded, and is not a plan of trades or businesses under common control.

4(d). Check for plan of more than one employer that is not collectively bargained, other than a plan defined in (b) above.

5(b). Enter the 3-digit number that the employer or plan administrator has assigned to the plan. This number should be the same as the 3-digit number entered on the latest Form 5500, 5500-C, or 5500-R filed for this plan.

Part II

If you checked Reason for Filing A, complete (a) through (f) for the plan(s) with which the plan named in line 5 is being merged or consolidated or the plan(s) to which the assets or liabilities of the plan are being transferred.

8(a). List the name of the plan(s), other than the plan named in 5(a), involved in this transaction.

8(b), (c), (d), and (e) should be completed for the plan(s) listed in 8(a).

8(f). No actuarial statement is required where all of a defined benefit plan's assets and liabilities are being merged into a multiemployer plan covered by the PBGC insurance program.

Part III

If you checked Reason for Filing B, C, or D, complete all questions in Part III. If you are filing with PBGC and checked Reason for Filing E, complete only questions 9, 10(a), (b), 11(a) and 12 of Part III.

10(g). A plan is not a qualified plan if a plan amendment, including the amendment to terminate the plan, directly or indirectly decreases the accrued benefit of any plan participant. Section 411(d)(6), section 1.411(d)-3(b) of the Income Tax Regulations and Rev. Rul. 85-6, 1985-1 C.B. 133.

11(b). If filing One-Stop (Reason for Filing C) attach 2 copies of records of all actions taken to terminate the plan, such as board of directors' resolutions, notification to participants, notification to trustees, etc. If you checked Reason for Filing B or D, attach only one copy of the required records.

11(c)(ii). If the date shown in 11(c)(i) is later than the date shown in 11(a), indicate the amount of contribution for each plan year beginning after the date shown in 11(a). Otherwise, do not complete 11(c)(ii) or 11(c)(iii).

12(d). If the plan termination is due to adverse business conditions, attach an explanation of the conditions and why the conditions require that this plan be terminated.

12(e). If the plan termination is due to the adoption of a new plan, attach an explanation briefly describing the type of the new plan.

15(a). For a plan maintained by more than one employer (other than a collectively bargained plan), consider 15(a) separately for each employer to determine for which employers information must be attached.

15(a)(i). If any organization maintaining this plan is a member of an affiliated service group as described in Code section 414(m), all employees of the affiliated service group will be treated as employed by a single employer for purposes of certain qualification requirements. See Rev. Proc. 81-12, 1981-1 C.B. 652 and Rev. Rul. 81-105, 1981-1 C.B. 256, regarding the application of Code section 414(m).

15(a)(ii) and (iii). If you checked (ii) "No," or if you checked (iii) "Yes" or "Not certain," attach the following information:

(1) a description of the business of the employer specifically discussing whether and why it is a service organization,

(2) the identification of other members (or possible members) of the affiliated service group,

(3) a description of the nature of the business of each member (or possible member) of the affiliated service group, specifically discussing whether and why each member is a service organization,

(4) the ownership interests between the employer and the members (or possible members) of the affiliated service group (including ownership interests described in Code sections 414(m)(2)(B)(ii) and 414(m)(5)(B)),

(5) a description of the services performed for the employer by the member (or possible members) of the affiliated service group, or vice versa (including an opinion whether the services are a significant portion of the member's business, and are of a type historically performed in the employer's service field by employers),

(6) a description of how the employer and the members (or possible members) of the affiliated service group associate in performing services for other parties, and

(7) if known, a copy of any affiliated service group ruling or determination letter issued to any other member (or possible members) of the affiliated service group. Also state whether the facts have materially changed since that letter was issued.

15(b). For a plan maintained by more than one employer, answer "Yes," if any employer maintaining the plan is a member of such a group.

15(c). If 15(a)(i) is "Yes" or "Not certain," or if 15(b) is "Yes," items 15(c)(i) and (ii) should be completed assuming the employees of all the members (or possible members) of the applicable group are employees of a single "employer." If all the employers maintaining the plan are not members of the same single "employer" or the plan involves more than one single "employer"; (1) answer "Yes" to 15(c)(i) only if the test is satisfied for each such single "employer," and (2) complete 15(c)(ii) separately for each such single "employer" by attaching a sheet with the information for each such "employer" in the same format as 15(c)(ii) (see instruction 15(d)(v) on page 4).

The following schedule is to help you determine if your plan meets the percentage test of Code section 410(b)(1)(A).

The percentage test of section 410(b)(1)(A) is met if, and only if:
(1) line (i) of the schedule below is 70% or larger, or *(2)* line (j) is 70% or larger and line (k) is 80% or larger.

		Number
(a)	Total employed	
(b)	Exclusions under plan (do not count an employee more than once):	
	(i) Minimum age and years of service	
	(ii) Employees included in collective bargaining	
	(iii) Nonresident aliens who receive no earned income from United States sources	
(c)	Total exclusion (add (b)(i) through (iii))	
(d)	Employees not excluded under the statute (subtract (c) from (a))	
(e)	Ineligible under plan on account of (do not count an employee included in (b)):	
	(i) Minimum pay	
	(ii) Hourly pay	
	(iii) Maximum age	
	(iv) Other	
(f)	Employees ineligible, add (e)(i) through (iv)	
(g)	Employees eligible to participate (subtract (f) from (d))	
(h)	Number of employees participating in the plan	
(i)	Percent of nonexcluded employees who are participating (divide (h) by (d))	%
	Complete (j) only if (i) is less than 70% and complete (k) only if (j) is 70% or more	
(j)	Percent of nonexcluded employees who are eligible to participate (divide (g) by (d))	%
(k)	Percent of eligible employees who are participating (divide (h) by (g))	%

If the plan does not meet the percentage test, you must submit a schedule using the format below to show that the plan meets the requirements of Code section 410(b)(1)(B). If the plan does not, by itself, satisfy the coverage requirements, other plans may be designated as a unit for this purpose. If any other plan is considered in combination with this plan, fill out item 15(c) as though the combined plans were a single plan. Also attach a brief description of the other plan(s) considered.

1		2	3	4	5
*Compensation range		Employees not excluded (See note)	Employees ineligible to participate	Employees participating	Participants who are officers or shareholders
At least	But not more than				
Totals					

*The compensation brackets used must reflect the pay pattern of the employer.
Note: *Enter in column 2, the total number of employees less exclusions under Code section 410(b)(3) if provided in the plan.*

15(d)(v). If 15(c)(ii) is required to be completed separately for more than one single "employer" under the plan, in addition to completing this line for the entire plan on the form, on an attached sheet show this information for each such single "employer" in the same format as 15(d)(v).

15(d)(vi). Enter the number of employees separated from service with less than 100% vesting in their accrued benefit or account balance. If more than 10, enter "10 plus." Only consider vesting in employer contributions.

17(b). The accrued benefits of a plan participant may not be reduced upon plan termination. Among other things, this means that a plan amendment that effectively eliminates or reduces an early retirement benefit or a retirement type subsidy with respect to benefits attributable to pre-amendment service is treated as reducing the accrued benefit of a participant if subsequent to termination the participant could satisfy the condition necessary to receive such benefits. See sections 411(d)(6) and 1.411(d)-3 of the Income Tax Regulations, and Rev. Rul. 85-6.

17(c). If the trust continues to operate after the termination of the plan, the employer or plan administrator must file an annual information return on Form 5500, 5500-C, or 5500-R.

17(h). Check "No," only if you are certain that there will be no reversion of assets to the employer.

17(h)(i). The list must include the name(s) of the sponsor(s) involved; the identification number(s) of the sponsor(s); the plan administrator(s) name(s) and identification number(s) and name(s) of the plan(s), and be accompanied by a description of the transaction(s).

17(h)(ii) and (iii). All plan benefits must be satisfied before assets can revert to the employer upon termination of the plan. All liabilities will not be satisfied if the value of retirement-type subsidies are not provided with respect to participants who, after the date of the proposed termination, satisfy certain pretermination conditions necessary to receive such benefits. Code sections 401(a)(2) and 1.401-2(a)(1) of the regulations and Rev. Rul. 85-6.

17(h)(iii) and (iv). The annuity contracts purchased must be guaranteed for each participant. However, to maintain qualification of a continuing pension plan, the contracts covering participants' accrued benefits in such plan must not be distributed except in accordance with section 1.401-1(b)(1)(i) of the Income Tax Regulations.

17(h)(viii). If the answer to this item is "Yes," attach a list which includes the name(s) of the plan sponsor(s), employer or sponsor's identification number(s), administrator's identification number(s), plan number(s) and an explanation of the termination(s) including the amount(s) of the reversion(s), the date(s) of termination and the reason(s) for termination.

17(j). For this question only, "lump-sum distribution" will mean a single payment of the value of a participant's benefits or a series of payments that do not provide substantially equal payments (either alone or in conjunction with other benefit payments) over the life of the participant.

17(m). Regardless of the form of benefit, if the present value of a participant's nonforfeitable accrued benefit exceeds $3,500, then neither part nor all of the present value may be distributed unless the participant and the spouse, if applicable, consent in writing. Spousal consent is required in all defined benefit plans, all money purchase plans (except if an ESOP) and certain profit-sharing and stock bonus plans (see section 401(a)(11)). In addition, for plans subject to section 417, no distribution is permissible after the annuity starting date, regardless of amount, unless the requisite written consents are given. No consent is needed for distribution of a participant's nonforfeitable accrued benefit in the form of a qualified joint and survivor annuity after the later of the normal retirement age (as defined in section 411(a)(8)) or age 62.

Note: *The interest rate, as determined in 17(n) below, must be used both for the $3,500 threshold test and for determining the amount of the distribution. See Code sections 401(a)(11), 411(a)(11) and 417(e).*

17(n). See Code sections 411(a)(11) and 417(e) and Income Tax Regulations section 1.417(e)-1T(a), (b), and (c).

20. Complete the statement showing the estimated fair market value of the plan assets and liabilities as of the proposed date of termination.

If you are filing this form as a notice of intent to terminate and plan assets include items which are not publicly traded, submit an explanation of how the fair market value was determined. Some examples of assets not publicly traded are: insurance contracts, real estate, pooled funds, mortgages, or depreciable property. Do not include the value of a sponsor's commitment (see line 23(d)) to make the plan sufficient.

Include and clearly identify all liabilities (other than liabilities for benefit payments due after the date of plan termination) that are unpaid as of the proposed termination date or that are paid or payable from plan assets under the provisions of the plan after the proposed date of plan termination. Liabilities include expenses, fees, other administrative costs, and benefit payments due and not paid before the proposed termination date.

Part IV

This part applies to a plan filing a notice of intent to terminate under the PBGC termination insurance program (Reason for Filing C or D). See also 29 CFR Part 2616. If the Enrolled Actuary Certification Program is used, do not complete this part.

If you have any questions concerning this part of the form, contact the Pension Benefit Guaranty Corporation, Insurance Operations Department, Room 5300-A, Code 542, 2020 K Street, N.W., Washington, D.C. 20006-1806 or call 202-254-4817.

If your answer to line 6(a) is "Yes," you must complete and file all information required by Part IV.

If your answer to line 6(a) is "No," do not complete Part IV.

If you checked "Not determined" on line 6(a), completion of Part IV is optional. However, if you do not complete Part IV you must submit a copy of the plan document and a copy of the IRS determination letter(s) for the plan as described in the instructions for lines 22(b), (c), and (g). If you do not complete Part IV and it is later determined that the plan is covered under the PBGC termination insurance program, the plan administrator will be deemed to have agreed that the 90-day period prescribed in ERISA section 4041(a), during which no plan assets may be distributed under the plan termination, will be extended until a date 90 days after the day on which a complete Part IV is filed with PBGC. If you fail to file a complete Part IV within 90 days after the PBGC notifies you that this is a covered plan or if you fail to request an extension of time to complete the filing within that period, the notice of intent to terminate will be voidable at the option of the PBGC. If the plan sponsor wishes to make a commitment to make the plan sufficient in the event that the plan is covered, he or she must do so in accordance with the instruction for line 23(d).

22(b) through (f). The documents described in (b) through (f) below must have been executed, i.e., signed by the person(s) authorized to adopt them. Each document must include its text, the effective date and the date it was adopted. The PBGC will accept a clear reproduction of any required document that includes this information.

22(b). If your plan was adopted and has been in effect for 5 or more years, submit the plan document(s) showing the provisions of the plan adopted and effective at the beginning of the 5-year period ending on the proposed date of plan termination. Otherwise, submit the document establishing the plan.

22(c). Attach each amendment to the plan that was adopted and effective after the document described in line 22(b) and before the proposed date of termination.

Note: *If you estimate that plan assets will be sufficient to pay all vested benefits and the plan has been restated within the 5 years before termination, you may satisfy the requirements of 22(b) and 22(c) by submitting the restated plan document and any subsequent amendments adopted and effective before the proposed date of plan termination.*

22(d). Attach each group annuity or group insurance contract that provides for the management of plan assets, plan administration, or the payment of benefits under the plan.

22(e). Attach each trust agreement that provides for management of plan assets, plan administration, or payment of benefits under the plan.

22(f). Attach each collective bargaining agreement that contains provisions relating to the plan.

22(g). Attach letters of determination issued by the IRS that relate to the establishment of the plan, amendments to the plan, partial termination of the plan, disqualification of the plan, and any later requalification.

23(a). See 29 CFR Part 2618, the PBGC regulation on allocating assets, for an explanation of which benefits are to be assigned to categories 1 through 4 of ERISA section 4044.

23(b). When establishing whether plan assets will be adequate to provide plan benefits, base your estimate on the most recent actuarial report, financial statements, and other pertinent information which supports your claim. Attach a summary statement or analysis which supports your estimate and include the actuarial assumptions used in making the determinations as of the proposed date of plan termination.

If plan assets are determined to be clearly insufficient, PBGC will issue a notice of inability to determine sufficiency and proceed to place the plan into trusteeship. (PBGC will require the submission of periodic financial statements for the plan between the date of termination and the date the plan is placed into trusteeship.) Otherwise, PBGC will direct you to proceed according to Subpart B of 29 CFR Part 2617, the PBGC regulation on determination of sufficiency.

23(d). An employer may determine that it is in the employer's best interest to make or ensure that a terminating plan is sufficient. Therefore, the PBGC will consider a commitment to contribute an amount necessary to make the plan sufficient as a plan asset unless it appears that the employer will not be able to satisfy its commitment. The commitment must be:

(i) Made by the employer(s) maintaining the plan;

(ii) Made in the form prescribed in 29 CFR Part 2617; and

(iii) Made and submitted to PBGC before the proposed termination date of the plan. (Such a commitment may be made and submitted after the date of plan termination only with the consent of the PBGC.)

The amount of the contribution will be determined when plan assets are distributed.

24. Submit participant data schedules in a format like or similar to the example shown on page 6. PBGC will accept copies of workpapers as long as the data and supporting information submitted clearly show the calculation of each participant's total accrued and vested accrued monthly benefits. (If the schedules are not complete when the notice is filed, see instructions for line 25.) Include all participants entitled to benefits, grouped as follows:

(a) Retired participants and beneficiaries receiving benefits from the plan;

(b) Participants separated from service not yet receiving vested benefits from the plan; and

(c) All other participants with vested or nonvested accrued benefits.

For collectively bargained plans covering employees of representative labor union(s) or employees of any plan(s) for union members, attach a list of the union(s) and plan(s), assign an identification code to each union or plan and enter the appropriate code for each participant after the participant's name in column (a) of the line 24 participant data schedules.

For a plan, other than a collectively bargained plan, maintained by more than one employer (where all employers in each affiliated service group, controlled group of corporations or group of trades or businesses under common control are considered one employer) attach a list of employers, assign an identification code to each employer, and enter the appropriate code for each participant after the participant's name in column (a) of the line 24 participant data schedules.

unless the requisite written consents are given. No consent is needed for distribution of a participant's nonforfeitable accrued benefit in the form of a qualified joint and survivor annuity after the later of the normal retirement age (as defined in section 411(a)(8)) or age 62.

Note: *The interest rate, as determined in 17(n) below, must be used both for the $3,500 threshold test and for determining the amount of the distribution. See Code sections 401(a)(11), 411(a)(11) and 417(e).*

17(n). See Code sections 411(a)(11) and 417(e) and Income Tax Regulations section 1.417(e)-1T(a), (b), and (c).

20. Complete the statement showing the estimated fair market value of the plan assets and liabilities as of the proposed date of termination.

If you are filing this form as a notice of intent to terminate and plan assets include items which are not publicly traded, submit an explanation of how the fair market value was determined. Some examples of assets not publicly traded are: insurance contracts, real estate, pooled funds, mortgages, or depreciable property. Do not include the value of a sponsor's commitment (see line 23(d)) to make the plan sufficient.

Include and clearly identify all liabilities (other than liabilities for benefit payments due after the date of plan termination) that are unpaid as of the proposed termination date or that are paid or payable from plan assets under the provisions of the plan after the proposed date of plan termination. Liabilities include expenses, fees, other administrative costs, and benefit payments due and not paid before the proposed termination date.

Part IV

This part applies to a plan filing a notice of intent to terminate under the PBGC termination insurance program (Reason for Filing C or D). See also 29 CFR Part 2616. If the Enrolled Actuary Certification Program is used, do not complete this part.

If you have any questions concerning this part of the form, contact the Pension Benefit Guaranty Corporation, Insurance Operations Department, Room 5300-A, Code 542, 2020 K Street, N.W., Washington, D.C. 20006-1806 or call 202-254-4817.

If your answer to line 6(a) is "Yes," you must complete and file all information required by Part IV.

If your answer to line 6(a) is "No," do not complete Part IV.

If you checked "Not determined" on line 6(a), completion of Part IV is optional. However, if you do not complete Part IV you must submit a copy of the plan document and a copy of the IRS determination letter(s) for the plan as described in the instructions for lines 22(b), (c), and (g). If you do not complete Part IV and it is later determined that the plan is covered under the PBGC termination insurance program, the plan administrator will be deemed to have agreed that the 90-day period prescribed in ERISA section 4041(a), during which no plan assets may be distributed under the plan termination, will be extended until a date 90 days after the day on which a complete Part IV is filed with PBGC. If you fail to file a complete Part IV within 90 days after the PBGC notifies you that this is a covered plan or if you fail to request an extension of time to complete the filing within that period, the notice of intent to terminate will be voidable at the option of the PBGC. If the plan sponsor wishes to make a commitment to make the plan sufficient in the event that the plan is covered, he or she must do so in accordance with the instruction for line 23(d).

22(b) through (f). The documents described in (b) through (f) below must have been executed, i.e., signed by the person(s) authorized to adopt them. Each document must include its text, the effective date and the date it was adopted. The PBGC will accept a clear reproduction of any required document that includes this information.

22(b). If your plan was adopted and has been in effect for 5 or more years, submit the plan document(s) showing the provisions of the plan adopted and effective at the beginning of the 5-year period ending on the proposed date of plan termination. Otherwise, submit the document establishing the plan.

22(c). Attach each amendment to the plan that was adopted and effective after the document described in line 22(b) and before the proposed date of termination.

Note: *If you estimate that plan assets will be sufficient to pay all vested benefits and the plan has been restated within the 5 years before termination, you may satisfy the requirements of 22(b) and 22(c) by submitting the restated plan document and any subsequent amendments adopted and effective before the proposed date of plan termination.*

22(d). Attach each group annuity or group insurance contract that provides for the management of plan assets, plan administration, or the payment of benefits under the plan.

22(e). Attach each trust agreement that provides for management of plan assets, plan administration, or payment of benefits under the plan.

22(f). Attach each collective bargaining agreement that contains provisions relating to the plan.

22(g). Attach letters of determination issued by the IRS that relate to the establishment of the plan, amendments to the plan, partial termination of the plan, disqualification of the plan, and any later requalification.

23(a). See 29 CFR Part 2618, the PBGC regulation on allocating assets, for an explanation of which benefits are to be assigned to categories 1 through 4 of ERISA section 4044.

23(b). When establishing whether plan assets will be adequate to provide plan benefits, base your estimate on the most recent actuarial report, financial statements, and other pertinent information which supports your claim. Attach a summary statement or analysis which supports your estimate and include the actuarial assumptions used in making the determinations as of the proposed date of plan termination.

If plan assets are determined to be clearly insufficient, PBGC will issue a notice of inability to determine sufficiency and proceed to place the plan into trusteeship. (PBGC will require the submission of periodic financial statements for the plan between the date of termination and the date the plan is placed into trusteeship.) Otherwise, PBGC will direct you to proceed according to Subpart B of 29 CFR Part 2617, the PBGC regulation on determination of sufficiency.

23(d). An employer may determine that it is in the employer's best interest to make or ensure that a terminating plan is sufficient. Therefore, the PBGC will consider a commitment to contribute an amount necessary to make the plan sufficient as a plan asset unless it appears that the employer will not be able to satisfy its commitment. The commitment must be:

(i) Made by the employer(s) maintaining the plan;

(ii) Made in the form prescribed in 29 CFR Part 2617; and

(iii) Made and submitted to PBGC before the proposed termination date of the plan. (Such a commitment may be made and submitted after the date of plan termination only with the consent of the PBGC.)

The amount of the contribution will be determined when plan assets are distributed.

24. Submit participant data schedules in a format like or similar to the example shown on page 6. PBGC will accept copies of workpapers as long as the data and supporting information submitted clearly show the calculation of each participant's total accrued and vested accrued monthly benefits. (If the schedules are not complete when the notice is filed, see instructions for line 25.) Include all participants entitled to benefits, grouped as follows:

(a) Retired participants and beneficiaries receiving benefits from the plan;

(b) Participants separated from service not yet receiving vested benefits from the plan; and

(c) All other participants with vested or nonvested accrued benefits.

For collectively bargained plans covering employees of representative labor union(s) or employees of any plan(s) for union members, attach a list of the union(s) and plan(s), assign an identification code to each union or plan and enter the appropriate code for each participant after the participant's name in column (a) of the line 24 participant data schedules.

For a plan, other than a collectively bargained plan, maintained by more than one employer (where all employers in each affiliated service group, controlled group of corporations or group of trades or businesses under common control are considered one employer) attach a list of employers, assign an identification code to each employer, and enter the appropriate code for each participant after the participant's name in column (a) of the line 24 participant data schedules.

Provide the information in columns (a) through (t) for all participants; provide the information in columns (u) and (v) for retired participants and beneficiaries only. List basic data for each participant and determine benefit entitlements and benefit amounts as of the proposed date of plan termination. Report all benefits as monthly amounts.

The following instructions describe the information to be entered in each column of the sample format:

Columns (a), (b), and (c): Name, sex and birth date of each participant including beneficiaries in pay status. (If the participant is entitled to a benefit form that provides an annuity or lump-sum death benefit to a surviving beneficiary, e.g., qualified J & S benefit, enter the name, sex and birth date of the beneficiary in parentheses on the line under that of the participant.)

Column (d): Date employment began for purposes of computing benefits.

Column (e): Date participation in the plan began.

Column (f): Earlier of the date employment ended or the proposed date of plan termination.

Column (g): Credited service as defined in the plan document.

Column (h): The highest percentage of ownership during the 5 years before the date of plan termination for each substantial owner, as defined in ERISA section 4022(b)(5)(A).

Columns (i) through (n): Specific data used to compute the accrued benefit under the provisions of the plan. Use as many columns as necessary to show the determination of each participant's accrued benefit.

The following are examples of the types of data that must be reported:

(i) if the plan is contributory, show the amount of employee contributions with and without interest as of the date of plan termination.

(ii) if compensation is a factor in the benefit formula, show the applicable compensation figure(s) as defined in the plan document. If the benefit formula provides that past service and future service are determined using different compensation figures, enter the compensation for past service in one column and for future service in another.

(iii) if you are filing One-Stop (Reason for Filing C), and compensation is not required to determine plan benefits, and you are not filing Form(s) 6088, Distributable Benefits from Employee Pension Benefit Plans, enter the compensation as described in the instructions for columns (i) and (j) of Form 6088.

(iv) if the benefit under the plan is offset by a flat amount or by a percentage of the Social Security benefit, show the offset and the data used in the determination.

Participant Data Schedule

Name of plan:

Proposed date of termination: Proposed date of distribution:

Name of participant (beneficiary) (Put an asterisk (*) in front of the name of each officer and/or owner-employee, including partners)	Sex	Dates									
		Birth	Employment began	Participation began	Earlier of: 1. Employment terminated 2. Plan terminated	Credited service	Percent of business owned				
(a)	(b)	(c)	(d)	(e)	(f)	(g)	(h)	(i)	(j)	(k)	(l)

		Accrued monthly benefit	Vesting percent	Vested accrued monthly benefit	Form of annuity	Monthly benefit provided under an ERISA section 4044 asset allocation	Cost or value of benefit in col.(s)	Pay Status Only	
								Benefit commencement date	Type of benefit
(m)	(n)	(o)	(p)	(q)	(r)	(s)	(t)	(u)	(v)

Note: *If you checked Reason for Filing C and you are not sending all the information required in Parts I, III, IV, and either completed Form(s) 6088 or a second copy of the complete participant data schedules described in the line 24 instructions of Form 5310, the 270-day period prescribed by Code section 7476(b)(3) will not start until you file the remaining required information.*

(v) if, before retirement, the benefit is determined from the cash value of insurance or annuity contracts, show the cash value.

(vi) if you are filing One-Stop (Reason for Filing C) and you are not filing Form(s) 6088, complete an additional column entering the value of the accrued benefits shown in column (o), and attach a statement explaining the basis of the valuation.

Column (o): Accrued monthly benefit in the normal annuity form under the plan.

Column (p): Vesting percentage computed without regard to any increase in vesting due to the termination. (For contributory plans, enter the percentage applicable to the portion of the accrued benefit provided by employer contributions.)

Column (q): Amount of vested accrued benefits.

Column (r): Form of annuity that is payable (normal form payable under the terms of the plan or an optional form elected before the proposed date of plan termination) or that would be payable if the benefit were vested. For example, J & 50% S represents a joint and 50% survivor annuity.

Column (s): Benefit provided as a result of the allocation of assets prescribed by ERISA section 4044. Adjust the amount of the benefit, if necessary, for the annuity form and the age at which it is assumed to be payable. If this amount is less than a participant's vested benefits, provide an explanation as to how it was determined in a footnote to the schedule OR show its determination using additional columns.

Column (t): Value of the benefit in column (s) as of proposed date of distribution. If annuities will be purchased from an insurance carrier, attach a copy of the annuity bid. If an early retirement benefit will be purchased from PBGC, identify these benefits in a footnote to the schedule. If participants elect a lump-sum payment, explain in a footnote how the lump sums were calculated and include a statement of the actuarial assumptions (applying expected early retirement age where appropriate) used to determine the amount of the distributions. If the sum of the amounts in column (t) does not equal line 20(o) of Form 5310 attach an explanation of the difference.

Column (u): The date benefits commenced.

Column (v): The type of benefit (normal, early, late, or disability).

25(a). Check this box if you are filing a complete Form 5310 including required attachments. You may shorten the amount of time necessary to process the termination by filing all of the required information at one time.

25(b). Check this box if you are filing Form 5310 complete except for information showing the estimated plan assets allocated to individual participants, i.e., the information described in the instructions for columns (s) and (t) of the sample participant data schedules. On receipt of a filing, PBGC will determine whether or not plan assets are clearly insufficient and will inform the plan administrator of its determination.

If you are filing One-Stop (Reason for Filing C) and you choose to use Form 6088, rather than a second copy of Form 5310, line 24 participant data schedules to request an IRS determination, you need only complete columns (a) through (j) of Form(s) 6088. When you file the proposed distribution data with PBGC, you should file another Form(s) 6088 completing columns (a), (k), (l), and (m) only.

25(c). Check this box if you are filing under an automatic extension of time to prepare participant data and plan asset information. Under this method, you must include all of the information required for a complete Form 5310 except:

(i) Plan asset information (line 20); and/or

(ii) Participant data schedules (line 24) and, if applicable, Form(s) 6088.

When you file under this method, you are agreeing to an extension of the 90-day period in ERISA section 4041(a), during which you may not make any distributions under the proposed termination of the plan. The extension allows you an additional 90 days to submit the plan asset and participant information. If you are unable to submit the information within 90 days of the filing of the incomplete notice, you must apply for an extension of time to complete the notice. You must file this request no later than 10 days before the end of the 90-day period which begins on the date you filed the incomplete notice. Instructions for line 25(d) explain how to request an extension of time to complete a filing.

25(d). Check this box if you are filing with Form 5310 a request for an extension of time to file any of the information (other than the information described in 25(c)) or a waiver of the obligation to file any of the information required by the form. It must be a written request explaining why you need the extension or waiver and the relief sought. The request for an extension of time must be accompanied by 2 copies of an agreement, each signed by the plan administrator or his or her representative, whereby the plan administrator agrees that if PBGC grants the request, the 90-day period specified in ERISA section 4041(a), during which the plan administrator may not make any distributions, may be automatically extended by a period of time equal to the extension of time granted by PBGC. If PBGC grants the request for an extension of time, PBGC will sign the agreement submitted and return one copy to the plan administrator or his or her representative. When PBGC grants or denies a request to waive the filing of required information, PBGC will notify the plan administrator or his or her representative in writing.

Note: *Whether or not an extension or waiver is granted, a commitment to make a plan sufficient as provided in line 23(d) generally must be made and submitted to PBGC before the proposed date of plan termination in accordance with 29 CFR Part 2617 of the PBGC regulations.*

Form **5500**
Department of the Treasury, Internal Revenue Service
Department of Labor, Pension and Welfare Benefits Administration
Pension Benefit Guaranty Corporation

Annual Return/Report of Employee Benefit Plan (With 100 or more participants)

This form is required to be filed under sections 104 and 4065 of the Employee Retirement Income Security Act of 1974 and sections 6039D, 6057(b), and 6058(a) of the Internal Revenue Code, referred to as the Code.

► **For Paperwork Reduction Act Notice, see page 1 of the instructions.**

OMB No 1210-0016

1988

This form is open to public inspection.

For the calendar plan year 1988 or fiscal plan year beginning , 1988, and ending , 19

If your plan year changed since the last return/report filed, check this box ► ☐

Type or print in ink all entries on the form, schedules, and attachments. If an item does not apply, enter "N/A." File the originals.

If *(i)* through *(iii)* do not apply to this year's return/report, leave the boxes unmarked. This return/report is:
(i) ☐ the first return/report filed for the plan; (ii) ☐ an amended return/report; or (iii) ☐ the final return/report filed for the plan.

► Welfare benefit plans and fringe benefit plans need only complete certain items—see the instructions "What To File."

► If you have been granted an extension of time to file this form, you must attach a copy of the approved extension to this form.

Use IRS label. Otherwise, please print or type.	**1a** Name of plan sponsor (employer if for a single-employer plan)	**1b** Employer identification number
	Address (number and street)	**1c** Telephone number of sponsor ( )
	City or town, state, and ZIP code	**1d** Business code number
2a	Name of plan administrator (if same as plan sponsor, enter "Same")	**1e** CUSIP issuer number
	Address (number and street)	**2b** Administrator's employer identification no.
	City or town, state, and ZIP code	**2c** Telephone number of administrator ( )

3 Are the name, address, and employer identification number (EIN) of the plan sponsor and/or plan administrator the same as they appeared on the last return/report filed for this plan? ☐ Yes ☐ No. If "No," enter the information from the last return/report in **a** and/or **b**, and complete **c**.

a Sponsor ► .... EIN .... Plan number ....

b Administrator ► .... EIN ....

c If **a** indicates a change in the sponsor's name and EIN, is this a change in sponsorship only? (See specific instructions for definition of sponsorship.) ☐ Yes ☐ No

4 Check the appropriate box to indicate the type of plan entity (check only one box):

a ☐ Single-employer plan
b ☐ Plan of controlled group of corporations or common control employers
c ☐ Multiemployer plan
d ☐ Multiple-employer-collectively-bargained plan
e ☐ Multiple-employer plan (other)
f ☐ Group insurance arrangement (of welfare plans)

5a *(i)* Name of plan ► ....

(ii) ☐ Check if name of plan changed since last return/report

5b Effective date of plan ►

5c Enter three-digit plan number ►

6a ☐ Welfare benefit plan (plan numbers 501 through 999) must check applicable items (A) through (P) and 6c.

(i) ☐ Type

(A) ☐ Health (other than dental or vision)
(B) ☐ Life insurance
(C) ☐ Supplemental unemployment
(D) ☐ Dental
(E) ☐ Vision
(F) ☐ Temporary disability (accident & sickness)
(G) ☐ Prepaid legal
(H) ☐ Long-term disability
(I) ☐ Severance pay
(J) ☐ Apprenticeship & training
(K) ☐ Scholarship (funded)
(L) ☐ Death benefits other than life insurance
(M) ☐ Code section 120 (group legal services plan)
(N) ☐ Code section 125 (cafeteria plan)
(O) ☐ Code section 127 (educational assistance program)
(P) ☐ Other (specify) ► ....

(ii) If you checked (M), (N), or (O), check if plan is: ☐ funded or ☐ unfunded.

6b ☐ Pension benefit plan (plan numbers 001 through 500) must check applicable items in *(i)* through *(vii)* and answer 6c through 6f.

(i) ☐ Defined benefit plan

(ii) ☐ Defined contribution plan—(indicate type of defined contribution): (A) ☐ Profit-sharing (B) ☐ Stock bonus (C) ☐ Target benefit (D) ☐ Other money purchase (E) ☐ Other (specify) ► ....

(iii) ☐ Defined benefit plan with benefits based partly on balance of separate account of participant (Code section 414(k))

(iv) ☐ Annuity arrangement of certain exempt organizations (Code section 403(b)(1))

(v) ☐ Custodial account for regulated investment company stock (Code section 403(b)(7))

(vi) ☐ Pension plan utilizing individual retirement accounts or annuities (described in Code section 408) as the sole funding vehicle for providing benefits

(vii) ☐ Other (specify) ►

► Caution: A penalty for the late or incomplete filing of this return/report will be assessed unless reasonable cause is established.

Under penalties of perjury and other penalties set forth in the instructions, I declare that I have examined this return/report, including accompanying schedules and statements, and to the best of my knowledge and belief, it is true, correct, and complete.

Date ► .... Signature of employer/plan sponsor ► ....

Date ► Signature of plan administrator ►

Form **5500** (1988)

6c Other plan features: *(i)* ☐ ESOP *(ii)* ☐ Leveraged ESOP *(iii)* ☐ Participant-directed account plan
(iv) ☐ Pension plan maintained outside the United States *(v)* ☐ Master trust (see instructions)
(vi) ☐ 103-12 investment entity (see instructions) *(vii)* ☐ Common/collective trust *(viii)* ☐ Pooled separate account

		Yes	No
d Single-employer plans enter the tax year end of the employer in which this plan year ends ▶ Month ...... Day ...... Year			
e Is the employer a member of an affiliated service group?			
f Does this plan contain a cash or deferred arrangement described in Code section 401(k)?			

7 Number of participants as of the end of the plan year (welfare plans complete only a(iv), b, c, and d):

a Active participants: *(i)* Number fully vested	a(i)	
(ii) Number partially vested	(ii)	
(iii) Number nonvested	(iii)	
(iv) Total	(iv)	
b Retired or separated participants receiving benefits	b	
c Retired or separated participants entitled to future benefits	c	
d Subtotal (add a(iv), b, and c)	d	
e Deceased participants whose beneficiaries are receiving or are entitled to receive benefits	e	
f Total (add d and e)	f	

		Yes	No
g *(i)* Was any participant(s) separated from service with a deferred vested benefit for which a Schedule SSA (Form 5500) is required to be attached to this form?	g(i)		
(ii) If "Yes," enter the number of separated participants required to be reported ▶			
8a Were any plan amendments adopted during the plan year?	8a		
b Did any amendment result in the retroactive reduction of accrued benefits for any participant?	b		
c Enter the date the most recent amendment was adopted ▶ Month .... Day .... Year			
d If **a** is "Yes," did any amendment change the information contained in the latest summary plan descriptions or summary description of modifications available at the time of the amendment?	d		
e If **d** is "Yes," has a summary plan description or summary description of modifications that reflects the plan amendments referred to in **d** been furnished to participants and filed with the Department of Labor?	e		
9a Was this plan terminated during this plan year or any prior plan year? If "Yes," enter the year ▶	9a		
b Were all plan assets either distributed to participants or beneficiaries, transferred to another plan, or brought under the control of PBGC?	b		
c Was a resolution to terminate this plan adopted during this plan year or any prior plan year?	c		
d If **a** or **c** is "Yes," have you received a favorable determination letter from IRS for the termination?	d		
e If **d** is "No," has a determination letter been requested from IRS?	e		
f If **a** or **c** is "Yes," have participants and beneficiaries been notified of the termination or the proposed termination?	f		
g If **a** is "Yes" and the plan is covered by PBGC, is the plan continuing to file a PBGC Form 1 and pay premiums until the end of the plan year in which assets are distributed or brought under the control of PBGC?	g		
h During this plan year, did any trust assets revert to the employer for which the Code section 4980 excise tax is due?	h		
i If **h** is "Yes," enter the amount of tax paid with your Form 5330 ▶			

10a In this plan year, was this plan merged or consolidated into another plan(s), or were assets or liabilities transferred to another plan(s)? ☐ **Yes** ☐ **No**

If "Yes," identify other plan(s)

b Name of plan(s) ▶	**c** Employer identification number(s)	**d** Plan number(s)

e Has Form 5310 been filed? ☐ **Yes** ☐ **No**

11 Enter the plan funding arrangement code (see instructions)	**12** Enter the plan benefit arrangement code (see instructions)

		Yes	No
13a Is this a plan established or maintained pursuant to one or more collective bargaining agreements?	13a		
b If **a** is "Yes," enter the appropriate six-digit LM number(s) of the sponsoring labor organization(s) (see instructions): ▶ *(i)* *(ii)* *(iii)*			
14 If any benefits are provided by an insurance company, insurance service, or similar organization, enter the number of **Schedules A** (Form 5500), Insurance Information, that are attached. If none, enter "-0-." ▶			

Form 5500 (1988) Page **3**

WELFARE PLANS DO NOT COMPLETE ITEMS 15 THROUGH 27. GO TO ITEM 28

			Yes	No
15a	If this is a defined benefit plan, is it subject to the minimum funding standards for this plan year? If "Yes," attach **Schedule B** (Form 5500).	15a		
b	If this is a defined contribution plan, i.e., money purchase or target benefit, is it subject to the minimum funding standards? (If a waiver was granted, see instructions.) If "Yes," complete *(i)*, *(ii)*, and *(iii)* below:	b		
	(i) Amount of employer contribution required for the plan year under Code section 412 — **b(i)** $			
	(ii) Amount of contribution paid by the employer for the plan year — **b(ii)** $ Enter date of last payment by employer ▶ Month ______ Day ______ Year ______			
	(iii) If *(i)* is greater than *(ii)*, subtract *(ii)* from *(i)* and enter the funding deficiency here; otherwise, enter zero. (If you have a funding deficiency, file Form 5330.) — **b(iii)** $			
16	Has the plan been top-heavy at any time beginning with the 1984 plan year?	16		
17	Has the plan accepted any transfers or rollovers with respect to a participant who had attained age 70½?	17		
18a	If the plan distributed any annuity contracts this year, did these contracts contain a requirement that the spouse consent before any distributions under the contract are made in a form other than a qualified joint and survivor annuity?	18a		
b	Did the plan make distributions to participants or spouses in a form other than a qualified joint and survivor annuity (a life annuity if a single person) or qualified preretirement survivor annuity (exclude deferred annuity contracts)?	b		
c	Did the plan make distributions or loans to married participants and beneficiaries without the required consent of the participant's spouse?	c		
d	Upon plan amendment or termination, do the accrued benefits of every participant include the subsidized benefits that the participant may become entitled to receive subsequent to the plan amendment or termination?	d		
19	Were the spousal consent requirements for distributions under Code section 417(e) complied with?	19		
20	Have any contributions been made or benefits accrued in excess of the Code section 415 limits, as amended by the Tax Reform Act of 1986?	20		
21	Has the plan made the required distributions in 1988 under Code section 401(a)(9)?	21		
22a	Does the plan satisfy the percentage test of Code section 410(b)(1)(A)? If **a** is "Yes," complete **b** through **i**. If "No," complete only **b** and **c** below and see specific instructions.	22a		

			Number
b	*(i)* Number of employees who are aggregated with employees of the employer as a result of the employer being aggregated with any employer covered by this plan under Code section 414(b), (c), or (m)	b(i)	
	(ii) Number of individuals who performed services as leased employees under Code section 414(n) including leased employees of employers in *(i)*	b(ii)	
c	Total number of employees (including any employees aggregated in **b**)	c	
d	Number of employees excluded under the plan because of *(i)* minimum age or years of service, *(ii)* employees on whose behalf retirement benefits were the subject of collective bargaining, or *(iii)* nonresident aliens who receive no earned income from United States sources	d	
e	Total number of employees not excluded (subtract **d** from **c**)	e	
f	Employees ineligible (specify reason) ▶	f	
g	Employees eligible to participate (subtract **f** from **e**)	g	
h	Employees eligible but not participating	h	
i	Employees participating (subtract **h** from **g**)	i	

			Yes	No
23a	Is it intended that this plan qualify under Code section 401(a)? If "Yes," complete **b** and **c**.	23a		
b	Enter the date of the most recent IRS determination letter — Month ______ Year ______			
c	Is a determination letter request pending with IRS?	c		
24a	If this is a plan with Employee Stock Ownership features, was a current appraisal of the value of the stock made immediately before any contribution of stock or the purchase of the stock by the trust for the plan year covered by this return/report?	24a		
b	If **a** is "Yes," was the appraisal made by an unrelated third party?	b		
25	Is this plan integrated with social security or railroad retirement?	25		
26	Does the employer/sponsor listed in **1a** of this form maintain other qualified pension benefit plans? If "Yes," enter the total number of plans, including this plan ▶	26		
27	If this plan is an adoption of a master, prototype, or uniform plan, indicate which type by checking the appropriate box: **a** ☐ Master **b** ☐ Prototype **c** ☐ Uniform			

		Yes	No
28a Did any person who rendered services to the plan receive directly or indirectly $5,000 or more in compensation from the plan during the plan year (except for employees of the plan who were paid less than $1,000 in each month)? If "Yes," complete Part I of **Schedule C** (Form 5500).	28a		
b Did the plan have any trustees who must be listed in Part II of Schedule C (Form 5500)?	b		
c Has there been a termination in the appointment of any person listed in **d** below?	c		
d If **c** is "Yes," check the appropriate box(es), answer **e** and **f**, and complete Part III of Schedule C (Form 5500): *(i)* ☐ Accountant *(ii)* ☐ Enrolled actuary *(iii)* ☐ Insurance carrier *(iv)* ☐ Custodian *(v)* ☐ Administrator *(vi)* ☐ Investment manager *(vii)* ☐ Trustee			
e Have there been any outstanding material disputes or matters of disagreement concerning the above termination?	e		
f If an accountant or enrolled actuary has been terminated during the plan year, has the terminated accountant/actuary been provided a copy of the explanation required by Part III of Schedule C (Form 5500) with a notice advising them of their opportunity to submit comments on the explanation directly to DOL?	f		
g Enter the number of Schedules C (Form 5500) that are attached. If none, enter -0- ▶			
29a Is this plan exempt from the requirement to engage an independent qualified public accountant?	29a		
b If a is "No," attach the accountant's opinion to this return/report and check the appropriate box. This opinion is: *(i)* ☐ Unqualified *(ii)* ☐ Qualified/disclaimer per Department of Labor Regulations 29 CFR 2520.103-8 and/or 2520.103-12(d) *(iii)* ☐ Qualified/disclaimer other *(iv)* ☐ Adverse *(v)* ☐ Other (explain)			
c If **a** is "No," do the financial statements or notes to the financial statements attached to this return/report disclose *(i)* a loss contingency indicating that assets are impaired or liability incurred; *(ii)* significant real estate or other transactions in which the plan and (A) the sponsor, (B) plan administrator, (C) the employer(s), or (D) the employee organization(s) are jointly involved; *(iii)* that the plan has participated in any related party transactions; or, *(iv)* any unusual or infrequent events or transactions occurring subsequent to the plan year-end that might significantly affect the usefulness of the financial statements in assessing the plan's present or future ability to pay benefits?	c		
d If **c** is "Yes," provide the total amount involved in such disclosure ▶			
30 If **29a** is "No," during the plan year:			
a Did the plan have assets held for investment?	30a		
b Were any loans by the plan or fixed income obligations due the plan in default as of the close of the plan year or classified during the year as uncollectible?	b		
c Were any leases to which the plan was a party in default or classified during the year as uncollectible?	c		
d Were any plan transactions or series of transactions in excess of 5% of the current value of plan assets?	d		
e Do the notes to the financial statements accompanying the accountant's opinion disclose any nonexempt transactions with parties-in-interest?	e		
f Did the plan engage in any nonexempt transactions with parties-in-interest not reporte	f		
g Did the plan hold qualifying employer securities that are not publicly traded?	g		
h Did the plan purchase or receive any nonpublicly traded securities that were not writing by an unrelated third party within 3 months prior to their receipt?	h		
i Did any person manage plan assets who had a financial interest worth more than 10% in any party providing services to the plan or receive anything of value from any party providing services to the plan? If **a, b, c, d, e,** or **f** is checked "Yes," schedules of those items in the format set forth in the instructions are required to be attached to this return/report.	i		
31 Did the plan acquire individual whole life insurance contracts during the plan year?	31		
32 During the plan year:			
a *(i)* Was this plan covered by a fidelity bond?	32a		
(ii) If **(i)** is "Yes," enter amount of bond ▶			
b *(i)* Was there any loss to the plan, whether or not reimbursed, caused by fraud or dishonesty?	b		
(ii) If **(i)** is "Yes," enter amount of loss ▶			

33a Is the plan covered under the Pension Benefit Guaranty Corporation termination insurance program?
☐ Yes ☐ No ☐ Not determined

b If **a** is "Yes" or "Not determined," enter the employer identification number and the plan number used to identify it.
Employer identification number ▶ Plan number ▶

Form 5500 (1988) Page **5**

34 Current value of plan assets and liabilities at the beginning and end of the plan year. Combine the value of plan assets held in more than one trust. Allocate the value of the plan's interest in a commingled trust containing the assets of more than one plan on a line-by-line basis unless the trust meets one of the specific exceptions described in the instructions. Do not enter the value of that portion of an insurance contract which guarantees, during this plan year, to pay a specific dollar benefit at a future date. **Round off amounts to the nearest dollar.** Plans with no assets at the beginning and the end of the plan year, enter zero on line 34f.

Assets		**(a)** Beginning of year	**(b)** End of Year
a Total noninterest-bearing cash	**a**		
b Receivables (net):			
(i) Employer contributions	**b(i)**		
(ii) Participant contributions	**(ii)**		
(iii) Income	**(iii)**		
(iv) Other	**(iv)**		
(v) Total	**(v)**		
c General investments:			
(i) Interest-bearing cash (including money market funds)	**c(i)**		
(ii) Certificates of deposit	**(ii)**		
(iii) U.S. Government securities	**(iii)**		
(iv) Corporate debt instruments	**(iv)**		
(v) Corporate stocks:			
(A) Preferred	**(v)(A)**		
(B) Common	**(B)**		
(vi) Partnership/joint venture interests	**(vi)**		
(vii) Real estate:			
(A) Income-producing	**(vii)(A)**		
(B) Nonincome-producing	**(B)**		
(viii) Loans (other than to participants) secured by mortgages:			
(A) Residential	**(viii)(A)**		
(B) Commercial	**(B)**		
(ix) Loans to participants:			
(A) Mortgages	**(ix)(A)**		
(B) Other	**(B)**		
(x) Other loans	**(x)**		
(xi) Value of interest in certain investment arrangements (see instructions)	**(xi)**		
(xii) Value of funds held in insurance company general account (unallocated contracts)	**(xii)**		
(xiii) Other	**(xiii)**		
(xiv) Total	**(xiv)**		
d Employer-related investments:			
(i) Employer securities	**d(i)**		
(ii) Employer real property	**(ii)**		
e Buildings and other property used in plan operation	**e**		
f Total assets	**f**		
Liabilities			
g Benefit claims payable	**g**		
h Operating payables	**h**		
i Acquisition indebtedness	**i**		
j Other liabilities	**j**		
k Total liabilities	**k**		
Net Assets			
l Line **f** minus line **k**	**l**		

Form 5500 (1988) Page 6

35 Plan income, expenses, and changes in net assets for the plan year.
Include all income and expenses of the plan, including any trust(s) or separately maintained fund(s), and any payments/receipts to/from insurance carriers. **Round off amounts to the nearest dollar.**

Income		(a) Amount	(b) Total
a Contributions:			
(i) Received or receivable from:			
(A) Employers	a(i)(A)		
(B) Participants	(B)		
(C) Others	(C)		
(ii) Noncash contributions	(ii)		
b Earnings on investments:			
(i) Interest:			
(A) Interest-bearing cash (including money market funds)	b(i)(A)		
(B) Certificates of deposit	(B)		
(C) U.S. Government securities	(C)		
(D) Corporate debt instruments	(D)		
(E) Mortgage loans	(E)		
(F) Other loans	(F)		
(G) Other	(G)		
(ii) Dividends:			
(A) Preferred stock	b(ii)(A)		
(B) Common stock	(B)		
(iii) Rents	(iii)		
(iv) Net gain (loss) on sale of assets:			
(A) Aggregate proceeds	b(iv)(A)		
(B) Aggregate costs	(B)		
(v) Unrealized appreciation (depreciation) of assets	(v)		
(vi) Net investment gain (loss) from certain investment arrangements—see instructions	(vi)		
c Other income	c		
d Total income (add **a**, **b**, and **c**)	d		
Expenses			
e Benefit payment and payments to provide benefits:			
(i) Directly to participants or beneficiaries	e(i)		
(ii) To insurance carriers for the provision of benefits	(ii)		
(iii) Other	(iii)		
f Interest expense	f		
g Administrative expenses:			
(i) Salaries and allowances	g(i)		
(ii) Accounting fees	(ii)		
(iii) Actuarial fees	(iii)		
(iv) Contract administrator fees	(iv)		
(v) Investment advisory and management fees	(v)		
(vi) Legal fees	(vi)		
(vii) Valuation/appraisal fees	(vii)		
(viii) Trustees fees/expenses (including travel, seminars, meetings, etc.)	(viii)		
(ix) Other	(ix)		
h Total expenses (add **e**, **f**, and **g**)	h		
i Net income (loss) (**d** minus **h**)	i		
j Transfers to (from) the plan (see instructions)	j		
k Net assets at beginning of year (line **34l**, column (a))	k		
l Net assets at end of year (line **34l**, column (b))	l		

	Yes	No
36 Did any employer sponsoring the plan pay any of the administrative expenses of the plan that were not reported in **35g**?		

Department of the Treasury
Internal Revenue Service

Department of Labor
Pension and Welfare Benefits Administration

Pension Benefit Guaranty Corporation

1988 Instructions for Form 5500

Annual Return/Report of Employee Benefit Plan (With 100 or more participants)

(Code references are to the Internal Revenue Code. ERISA refers to the Employee Retirement Income Security Act of 1974.)

Paperwork Reduction Act Notice.—We ask for this information to carry out the law as specified in ERISA and Code section 6039D. We need it to determine whether the plan is operating according to the law. You are required to give us this information.

The time needed to complete and file the forms listed below reflect the combined requirements of the Internal Revenue Service, Department of Labor, Pension Benefit Guaranty Corporation, and the Social Security Administration. These times will vary depending on individual circumstances. The estimated average times are:

	Recordkeeping	Learning about the law or the form	Preparing the form	Copying, assembling, and sending the form to IRS
Form 5500	82 hrs., 2 min.	9 hrs., 3 min.	13 hrs., 34 min.	49 min.
Schedule A(Form 5500)	17 hrs., 28 min.	28 min.	1hr., 42 min.	16 min.
Schedule B(Form 5500)	25 hrs., 50 min.	1 hr.,	1 hr., 27 min.	
Schedule C(Form 5500)	5 hrs., 1 min.	6 min.	11 min.	
Schedule P(Form 5500)	2hrs., 9 min.	1 hr., 24 min.	1 hr., 29 min.	
Schedule SSA(Form 5500)	6 hrs., 42 min.	12 min.	19 min.	

If you have comments concerning the accuracy of these time estimates or suggestions for making these forms more simple, we would be happy to hear from you. You can write to the **Internal Revenue Service,** Washington, DC 20224, Attention: IRS Reports Clearance Officer, TR:FP; or the **Office of Management and Budget,** Paperwork Reduction Project, Washington, DC 20503.

File 1988 forms for plan years that started in 1988. If the plan year differs from the calendar year, fill in the fiscal year space just under the form title. For a short plan year, see Section 1, instruction B.

Reminder: In addition to filing this form with IRS, plans covered by the Pension Benefit Guaranty Corporation termination insurance program must file their Annual Premium Payment, PBGC Form 1, directly with that agency.

Penalties.—ERISA and the Code provide for the assessment or imposition of penalties for not giving complete information and not filing statements and returns/reports. Certain penalties are administrative; that is, they may be imposed or assessed by one of the governmental agencies delegated to administer the collection of Form 5500 series data. Others require a legal conviction.

A. Administrative Penalties.—Listed below are various penalties for not meeting the Form 5500 series filing requirements. One or more of the following five penalties may be imposed or assessed in the event of incomplete filings or filings received after the date they are due unless it is determined that your explanation for failure to file properly is for reasonable cause:

1. A penalty of up to $1,000 a day for each day a plan administrator fails or refuses to file a complete return/report. See ERISA section 502(c)(2) and 29 CFR 2560.502c-2.
2. A penalty of $25 a day (up to $15,000) for not filing returns for certain plans of deferred compensation, certain trusts and annuities, and bond purchase plans by the due date(s). See Code section 6652(e). This penalty also applies to returns required to be filed under Code section 6039D.
3. A penalty of $1 a day (up to $5,000) for each participant for whom a registration statement (Schedule SSA (Form 5500)) is required but not filed. See Code section 6652(d)(1).
4. A penalty of $1 a day (up to $1,000) for not filing a notification of change of status of a plan. See Code section 6652(d)(2).
5. A penalty of $1,000 for not filing an actuarial statement. See Code section 6692.

B. Other Penalties.—

1. Any individual who willfully violates any provision of Part 1 of Title I of ERISA shall be fined not more than $5,000 or imprisoned not more than 1 year, or both. See ERISA section 501.
2. A penalty of up to $10,000, 5 years imprisonment, or both, for making any false statement or representation of fact, knowing it to be false, or for knowingly concealing or not disclosing any fact required by ERISA. See section 1027, Title 18, U.S. Code, as amended by section 111 of ERISA.

How To Use This Instruction Booklet

The instructions are divided into four main sections.

Section 1

A. Who Must File.—Any administrator or sponsor of an employee benefit plan subject to ERISA must file information about each such plan **every year** (Code section 6058 and ERISA sections 104 and 4065). Also required to file, for each year, is every employer maintaining a specified fringe benefit plan as described in Code section 6039D. The Internal Revenue Service (IRS), Department of Labor (DOL), and Pension Benefit Guaranty Corporation (PBGC) have consolidated their returns and report forms to minimize the filing burden for plan administrators and employers. The chart on page 7 gives a brief guide to the type of return/report to be filed.

B. When To File.—File all required forms and schedules by the last day of the 7th month after the plan year ends. For a short plan year, file the form and applicable schedules by the last day of the 7th month after the short plan year ends. For purposes of this return/report, the short plan year ends upon the date of the change in accounting period or upon the complete distribution of the assets of the plan. (Also see Section 3.) If the current year Form 5500 is not available before the due date of your short plan year return/report, use the latest year form available and change the date printed on the return/report to the current year. Also show the dates your short plan year began and ended.

Request for Extension of Time To File.—A one time extension of time up to 2½ months may be granted for filing returns/reports if **Form 5558,** Application for Extension of Time To File Certain Employee Plan Returns, is filed **before the normal due date of the return/report.**

Exception: *Single-employer plans and plans of a controlled group of corporations which file consolidated Federal income tax returns are automatically granted an extension of time to file Form 5500, 5500-C, or 5500-R to the due date of the Federal income tax return of the single employer or controlled group of corporations if all the following conditions are met:*

1. The plan year and the tax year coincide.

2. The single employer or the controlled group has been granted an extension of time to file its Federal income tax return to a date later than the normal due date for filing the Form 5500, 5500-C, or 5500-R.

3. A copy of the IRS extension of time to file the Federal income tax return is attached to each Form 5500, 5500-C, or 5500-R filed with IRS.

Note: *An extension of time to file the return/report does not operate as an extension of time to file the PBGC Form 1.*

C. Where To File.—Please file the return/report with the Internal Revenue Service Center indicated below. No street address is needed.

See page 5 for the filing address for investment arrangements filing directly with DOL.

If the principal office of the plan sponsor or the plan administrator is located in ▼	Use the following Internal Revenue Service Center address ▼
Connecticut, Delaware, District of Columbia, Foreign Address, Maine, Maryland, Massachusetts, New Hampshire, New Jersey, New York, Pennsylvania, Puerto Rico, Rhode Island, Vermont, Virginia	Holtsville, NY 00501
Alabama, Alaska, Arkansas, California, Florida, Georgia, Hawaii, Idaho, Louisiana, Mississippi,Nevada, North Carolina, Oregon, South Carolina, Tennessee, Washington	Atlanta, GA 39901
Arizona, Colorado, Illinois, Indiana, Iowa, Kansas, Kentucky, Michigan, Minnesota, Missouri, Montana, Nebraska, New Mexico, North Dakota, Ohio, Oklahoma, South Dakota, Texas, Utah, West Virginia, Wisconsin, Wyoming	Memphis, TN 37501
All Form 5500EZ filers	Andover, MA 05501

Section 2

A. Kinds of Plans.—Employee benefit plans include pension benefit plans and welfare benefit plans. File the applicable return/report for any of the following plans.

(a) Pension benefit plan.—This is an employee pension benefit plan covered by ERISA. The return/report is due whether or not the plan is qualified and even if benefits no longer accrue, contributions were not made this plan year, or contributions are no longer made ("frozen plan" or "wasting trust"). See, Section 3 "Final Return/Report" on page 6.

Pension benefit plans required to file include defined benefit plans and defined contribution plans (e.g., profit-sharing, stock bonus, money purchase plans, etc.). The following are among the pension benefit plans for which a return/report must be filed:

(i) Annuity arrangements under Code section 403(b)(1).

(ii) Custodial account established under Code section 403(b)(7) for regulated investment company stock.

(iii) Individual retirement account established by an employer under Code section 408(c).

(iv) Pension benefit plan maintained outside the United States primarily for nonresident aliens if the employer who maintains the plan is:

(A) a domestic employer, or

(B) a foreign employer with income derived from sources within the U.S. (including foreign subsidiaries of domestic employers) and deducts contributions to the plan on its U.S. income tax return. See "Plans Excluded From Filing" below.

(v) Church plans electing coverage under Code section 410(d).

(vi) A plan that covers residents of Puerto Rico, the Virgin Islands, Guam, Wake Island, or American Samoa. This includes a plan that elects to have the provisions of section 1022(i)(2) of ERISA apply.

See "Items To Be Completed on Form 5500" on page 4 for more information about what questions need to be completed by pension plans.

(b) Welfare benefit plan.—This is an employee welfare benefit plan covered by Part 1 of Title I of ERISA. Welfare plans would provide benefits such as medical, dental, life insurance, apprenticeship training, educational assistance, severance pay, disability, etc.

See "Items To Be Completed on Form 5500" on page 4 for more information about what questions need to be completed for welfare benefit plans.

(c) Fringe benefit plan.—Group legal services plans described in Code section 120, cafeteria plans described in Code section 125, and educational assistance programs described in Code section 127 are considered fringe benefit plans and generally are required to file the annual information specified by Code section 6039D. However, Code section 127 educational assistance programs which provide only job-related training which is deductible under Code section 162 do not need to file Form 5500.

See "Items To Be Completed on Form 5500" on page 4 for more information about how to complete this form for a fringe benefit plan.

B. Plans Excluded From Filing (this does not apply if you are a fringe benefit plan required to file by Code section 6039D).—Do not file a return/report for an employee benefit plan that is any of the following:

(a) A welfare benefit plan which covered fewer than 100 participants as of the beginning of the plan year and is: (i) fully insured, (ii) unfunded, or (iii) a combination of insured and unfunded.

(1) An unfunded welfare benefit plan has its benefits paid as needed directly from the general assets of the employer or the employee organization that sponsors the plan.

(2) A fully insured welfare benefit plan has its benefits provided exclusively through insurance contracts or policies, the premiums of which must be paid directly by the employer or employee organization from its general assets or partly from its general assets and partly from contributions by its employees or members (which the employer or organization forwards within 3 months of receipt).

(3) A combination unfunded/insured welfare plan has its benefits provided partially as an unfunded plan and partially as a fully insured plan. An example of such a plan is a plan which requires the employer to reimburse an employee for hospital expenses with the first $1,000 per year of benefits paid from the general assets of the employer and any benefits above $1,000 paid from a stop loss insurance contract.

The insurance contracts or policies discussed above must be issued by an insurance company or similar organization (such as Blue Cross, Blue Shield or a health maintenance organization) that can legally do business in any state. A plan meeting (1) cannot have any assets at any time during the plan year.

"Directly," as used in (1) above, means that the plan cannot use a trust or separately maintained fund (including a Code section 501(c)(9) trust) to hold plan assets or to act as a conduit for the transfer of plan assets.

See 29 CFR 2520.104-20.

Note: *An "employees' association" as used in Code section 501(c)(9) should not be confused with the employee organization or employer which establishes and maintains (i.e., sponsors) the welfare benefit plan.*

(b) An unfunded pension benefit plan or an unfunded or combination unfunded and insured welfare benefit plan: (1) whose benefits go only to a select group of management or highly compensated employees, and (2) which meets the terms of Department of Labor Regulations 29 CFR 2520.104-23 (including the requirement that a notification statement be filed with DOL) or 29 CFR 2520.104-24.

(c) Plans maintained only to comply with workers' compensation, unemployment compensation, or disability insurance laws.

(d) An unfunded excess benefit plan.

(e) A welfare benefit plan maintained outside the United States primarily for persons substantially all of whom are nonresident aliens.

(f) A pension benefit plan maintained outside the United States if it is a qualified foreign plan within the meaning of Code section 404A(e) that does not qualify for the treatment provided in Code section 402(c).

(g) An annuity arrangement described in 29 CFR 2510.3-2(f).

(h) A simplified employee pension (SEP) described in Code section 408(k) which conforms to the alternative method of compliance described in 29 CFR 2520.104-48 or 29 CFR 104-49. A SEP is a pension plan which meets certain minimum qualifications regarding eligibility and employer contributions.

(i) A church plan not electing coverage under Code section 410(d) or a governmental plan.

(j) A welfare plan (other than a fringe benefit plan) that participates in a group insurance arrangement that files a return/report Form 5500 on behalf of the welfare plan. See 29 CFR 2520.104-43.

C. Kinds of Filers.—Item 4 on the Form 5500, 5500-C and 5500-R lists the different types of entities which file the forms. These entities are described below.

(a) Single-employer plan.—If one employer or one employee organization maintains a plan, file a separate return/report for the plan. If the employer

or employee organization maintains more than one such plan, file a separate return/report for each plan.

If a member of either a controlled group of corporations or a group of trades or businesses under common control maintains a plan that does not involve other group members, file a separate return/report as a single-employer plan.

If several employers participate in a program of benefits wherein the funds attributable to each employer are available only to pay benefits to that employer's employees, each employer must file a separate return/report.

(b) Plan for controlled group of corporations or group of trades or businesses under common control.— These groups are defined in Code sections 414(b) and (c), and are referred to as controlled groups.

If the benefits are payable to participants from the plan's total assets without regard to contributions by each participant's employer, file one return/report for the plan. On the return/report for the plan, complete item 22 only for the controlled group's employees.

Exception: Employers who participate in a plan of one of the groups listed above but who are not members of the group must file a separate return/report. The return/report should be filed on Form 5500-C or 5500-R, as applicable (see "What To File" on page 4). On Form 5500-C complete only items 1, 2, 3, 4f, 5, 6, 9, and 22. On Form 5500-R complete only items 1 through 3, 4f and 5 through 8b.

If several employers participate in a program of benefits wherein the funds attributable to each employer are available only to pay benefits to that employer's employees, each employer must file a separate return/report as a single employer plan.

(c) Multiemployer plan.— Multiemployer plans are plans: (1) to which more than one employer is required to contribute; (2) which are maintained pursuant to one or more collective bargaining agreements, and (3) have not made the election under Code section 414(f)(5) and ERISA section 3(37)(E). File one return/report for each such plan. Contributing employers do not file individually with respect to such plans. See Code section 414 for more information.

(d) Multiple-employer-collectively-bargained plan.—A multiple-employer-collectively-bargained plan involves more than one employer, is collectively bargained and collectively funded, and, if covered by PBGC termination insurance, has properly elected before 9-27-81 not to be treated as a multiemployer plan under Code section 414(f)(5) or ERISA sections 3(37)(E) and 4001(a)(3). File one return/report for each such plan. Participating employers do not file individually for these plans.

(e) Multiple-employer plan (other).—A multiple-employer plan (other) involves more than one employer and is not one of the plans already described. A multiple-employer plan (other) includes only plans whose contributions from individual employers are available to pay benefits to all participants. File one return/report for each such plan.

In addition, for pension benefit plans, each participating employer files either a Form 5500-C, regardless of the number of participants, or Form 5500-R . On Form 5500-C complete only items 1, 2, 3, 4f, 5, 6, 9, and 22. On Form 5500-R complete only items 1 through 3, 4f, and 5 through 8b.

Note: *If a participating employer is also the sponsor of the multiple-employer plan (other), the plan number on the return/report filed for the plan should be 333.*

The Form 5500-C or Form 5500-R filed by the participating employer should list his or her appropriate plan number.

If more than one employer participates in the plan and the plan provides that each employer's contributions are available to pay benefits only for that employer's employees who are covered by the plan, one annual return/report must be filed for each participating employer. These filers will be considered single employers and should complete the entire form.

(f) Group insurance arrangement.— A group insurance arrangement is an arrangement which provides benefits to the employees of two or more unaffiliated employers (not in connection with a multi-employer plan or a multiple-employer-collectively-bargained plan), fully insures one or more welfare plans of each participating employer, and uses a trust (or other entity such as a trade association) as the holder of the insurance contracts and the conduit for payment of premiums to the insurance company.

You do not need to file a separate return/report for a welfare benefit plan that is part of a group insurance arrangement if a consolidated return/report for all the plans in the arrangement was filed by the trust or other entity according to 29 CFR 2520.104-43. Form 5500 is required by 29 CFR 2520.103-2 to be part of the consolidated report.

D. Investment Arrangements Filing Directly With DOL.—Some plans invest in certain trusts, accounts, and other investment arrangements which may file information concerning itself and its relationship with employee benefit plans (as specified on page 5) directly with DOL. Plans participating in an investment arrangement as described in paragraphs **a** through **c** below are required to attach certain additional information to the return/report filed with IRS as specified below.

a. Common/Collective Trust and Pooled Separate Account

(i) Definition. For reporting purposes, a common/collective trust is a trust maintained by a bank, trust company, or similar institution which is regulated, supervised, and subject to periodic examination by a state or Federal agency for the collective investment and reinvestment of assets contributed thereto from employee benefit plans maintained by more than one employer or controlled group of corporations, as the term is used in Code section 1563. For reporting purposes, a pooled separate account is an account maintained by an insurance carrier which is regulated, supervised, and subject to periodic examination by a state or Federal agency for the collective investment and reinvestment of assets contributed thereto from employee benefit plans maintained by more than one employer or controlled group of corporations, as the term is used in Code section 1563. See 29 CFR sections 2520.103-3, 2520.103-4, 2520.103-5, and 2520.103-9.

Note: *For reporting purposes, a separate account which is not considered to be holding plan assets pursuant to 29 CFR 2510.3-101(h)(1)(iii), shall not constitute a pooled separate account.*

(ii) Additional Information Required To Be Attached to the Form 5500 for Plans Participating in Common/Collective Trusts and Pooled Separate Accounts. A plan participating in a common/collective trust or pooled separate account must complete the annual return/report and attach either (1) the most recent statement of the assets and liabilities of any common/ collective trust or pooled separate account, or (2) a certification that: (A) the statement of the assets and liabilities of the common/ collective trust or pooled separate account has been submitted directly to DOL by the financial institution or insurance carrier; (B) the plan has received a copy of the statement; and (C) includes the EIN and other numbers used by the financial institution or insurance carrier to identify the trusts or accounts in the direct filing made with DOL.

b. Master Trust

(i) Definition. For reporting purposes, a master trust is a trust for which a regulated financial institution (as defined below) serves as trustee or custodian (regardless of whether such institution exercises discretionary authority or control with respect to the management of assets held in the trust), and in which assets of more than one plan sponsored by a single employer or by a group of employers under common control are held.

A "regulated financial institution" means a bank, trust company, or similar financial institution which is regulated, supervised, and subject to periodic examination by a state or Federal agency. Common control is determined on the basis of all relevant facts and circumstances (whether or not such employers are incorporated). See 29 CFR 2520.103-1(e).

For reporting purposes, the assets of a master trust are considered to be held in one or more "investment accounts." A master trust investment account may consist of a pool of assets or a single asset.

Each pool of assets held in a master trust must be treated as a separate master trust investment account if each plan which has an interest in the pool has the same fractional interest in each asset in the pool as its fractional interest in the pool, and if each such plan may not dispose of its interest in any asset in the pool without disposing of its interest in the pool. A master trust may also contain assets which are not held in such a pool. Each such asset must be treated as a separate master trust investment account.

Financial information must generally be provided with respect to each master trust investment account as specified on page 5.

(ii) Additional Information Required To Be Attached to the Form 5500 for Plans Participating in Master Trusts. A plan participating in a master trust must complete the annual return/report and attach a list of each master trust investment

account in which the plan has an interest indicating the plan's name, EIN, and plan number and the name of the master trust used in the master trust information filed with DOL (see page 5). In tabular format, show the net value of the plan's interest in each investment account at the beginning and end of the plan year and the net investment gain (or loss) allocated to the plan for the plan year from the investment account (see instructions for item 34c(xi) on page 15).

Note: *If a master trust investment account consists solely of one plan's asset(s) during the reporting period, the plan may report the(se) asset(s) either as an investment account to be reported as part of the master trust report filed directly with DOL or as a plan asset(s) which is not part of the master trust (and therefore subject to all instructions pertaining to assets not held in a master trust).*

c. 103-12 Investment Entities

Definition. 29 CFR 2520.103-12 provides an alternative method of reporting for plans which invest in an entity (other than an investment arrangement filing with DOL described in **a** or **b** above), the underlying assets of which include "plan assets" (within the meaning of 29 CFR 2510.3-101) of two or more plans which are not members of a "related group" of employee benefit plans. For reporting purposes, a "related group" consists of each group of two or more employee benefit plans (1) each of which receives 10 percent or more of its aggregate contributions from the same employer or from a member of the same controlled group of corporations (as determined under Code section 1563(a), without regard to Code section 1563(a)(4) thereof); or (2) each of which is either maintained by, or maintained pursuant to a collective bargaining agreement negotiated by, the same employee organization or affiliated employee organizations. For purposes of this paragraph, an "affiliate" of an employee organization means any person controlling, controlled by, or under common control with such organization. See 29 CFR 2520.103-12.

For reporting purposes, the investment entities described above with respect to which the required information is filed directly with DOL constitute "103-12 investment entities" (103-12 IEs).

E. What To File.—This section describes the different categories of the 5500 series of forms and schedules. In addition, this section also lists items to be completed by different types of Form 5500 filers. This section also contains a description of the special filing requirements for plans that invest in certain investment arrangements. Finally, a brief guide illustrating which forms and schedules are required by different types of plans and filers may be found on page 7.

Forms

Form 5500.—File **Form 5500**, Annual Return/Report of Employee Benefit Plan, annually for each plan with 100 or more participants at the beginning of the plan year.

Form 5500-C.—File **Form 5500-C**, Return/Report of Employee Benefit Plan, for each pension benefit plan, welfare benefit plan, and fringe benefit plan (unless otherwise exempted) with fewer than 100 participants (one-participant plans see "Form 5500EZ" below) at the beginning of the plan year. File Form 5500-C for the first plan year, the year for which the final return/report is due, and for plan years in which a Form 5500-R is not filed as explained below.

Form 5500-R.—**Form 5500-R**, Registration Statement of Employee Benefit Plan (with fewer than 100 participants), may be filed instead of a Form 5500-C for this plan year provided: (a) this is not the first plan year, (b) this is not a year for which the final return/report is due, and (c) a Form 5500-C has been filed for one of the prior 2 plan years. The Form 5500-R should not be filed if (a) this plan year is the first plan year, (b) this is the plan year for which a final return/report is due, or (c) the Form 5500-R has been filed for both of the prior 2 plan years.

Any plan may choose not to file the Form 5500-R if the plan files the Form 5500-C instead.

Note: *Generally, under the filing requirements explained above, if the number of plan participants increases from under 100 to 100 or more, or decreases from 100 or more to under 100, from one year to the next, you would have to file a different form from that filed the previous year. However, there is an exception to this rule. You may file the same form you filed last year, even if the number of participants changed, provided that at the beginning of this plan year the plan had at least 80 participants, but not more than 120.*

Form 5500EZ.—**Form 5500EZ**, Annual Return of One-Participant Pension Benefit Plan, should be filed by most one-participant plans.

A one-participant plan is: (1) a pension benefit plan that covers only an individual or an individual and his or her spouse who wholly own a trade or business, whether incorporated or unincorporated; or (2) a pension benefit plan for a partnership that covers only the partners or the partners and the partners' spouses.

See Form 5500EZ and its instructions to see if the plan meets the requirements for filing the form.

Items To Be Completed on Form 5500

Certain kinds of plans and certain kinds of filers that are required to submit an annual Form 5500 are not required to complete the entire form. These are described below, by type of plan. Check the list of headings to see if your plan is affected.

1. Welfare Benefit Plans—Welfare benefit plans generally must complete the following items on the Form 5500 : 1 through 6c; 7a(iv), b, c, and d; 8a, c, d, and e; 9a, b, c, and f; 10a through d; 11 through 14; 28 through 32; and 34 through 36.

Note: *If one Form 5500 is filed for both a welfare plan and a fringe benefit plan, items 22c, 22g, and 22i must be completed in addition to the items listed above for welfare plans.*

Exception for unfunded, fully insured and unfunded /insured welfare plans—Welfare benefit plans that are unfunded, fully insured or combination unfunded/insured need not complete items 34 and 35 unless the Form 5500 also serves as a return/report under Code section 6039D (fringe benefit plan) in which case items 35g and 35h must be completed. See page 2, Section 2 B(a) for definition of (1) unfunded, (2) fully insured, and (3) combination of unfunded/insured.

2. Fringe Benefit Plans—A Form 5500 filed only because of Code section 6039D (i.e., for a fringe benefit plan) need complete only items 1 through 6a, 7a(iv), 7b, 9a, 9b, 22c, 22g, 22i, 35e, 35g, and 35h.

If the annual return/report is also for a welfare benefit plan (see "Who Must File" on page 1), complete the above items and those specified for welfare benefit plans in "1" above.

3. Pension Plans—In general, most pension plans (defined benefit and defined contribution) are required to complete all items on the form. However, some items need not be completed by certain types of pension plans, as described below.

a. Plans exclusively using a tax deferred annuity arrangement under Code section 403(b)(1). These plans (see "Who Must File" on page 1), need only complete items 1 through 5, 6b(iv), and 9.

b. Plans exclusively using a custodial account for regulated investment company stock under Code section 403(b)(7).These plans need only complete items 1 through 5, 6b(v), and 9.

c. Individual Retirement Account Plan.—A pension plan utilizing individual retirement accounts or annuities (as described in Code section 408) as the sole funding vehicle for providing benefits need only complete items 1 through 5, 6b(vi), and 9.

d. Fully Insured Pension Plan.—A pension benefit plan providing benefits exclusively through an insurance contract, or contracts that are fully guaranteed, and which meets all of the conditions of 29 CFR 2520.104-44 need only complete items 1 through 29, 32, and 33.

A pension plan which includes both insurance contracts of the type described in 29 CFR 2520.104-44 as well as other assets should limit its reporting in items 34 and 35 to those other assets.

Note: *For purposes of the annual return/report and the alternative method of compliance set forth in 29 CFR 2520.104-44, a contract is considered to be "allocated" only if the insurance company or organization that issued the contract unconditionally guarantees, upon receipt of the required premium or consideration, to provide a retirement benefit of a specified amount, without adjustment for fluctuations in the market value of the underlying assets of the company or organization, to each participant, and each participant has a legal right to such benefits which is legally enforceable directly against the insurance company or organization.*

e. Nonqualified plans maintained outside the U.S.—Nonqualified pension benefit plans maintained outside the United States primarily for nonresident aliens required to file a return/report (see "Who Must File" on page 1) need only complete items 1 through 8c, 9 through 12, and 15 through 17.

4. Plans of More Than One Employer—All plans of more than one employer (plans of a controlled group, multiemployer plans, multiple-employer-collectively-bargained plans, and multiple-employer-plan (other)) generally should complete all applicable (welfare or pension) items on the form except for item 6d. Only single-employer pension plans must complete this item. In addition, multiemployer and multiple-employer-collectively-bargained plans need not complete item 22 on the Form 5500.

Schedules

The various schedules to be attached to the return/report are listed below.

Note: *All attachments to the Forms 5500, 5500-C, and 5500-R must include the name of the plan and the EIN and plan number (PN) as found in items 5a, 1b, and 5c, respectively.*

Attach Schedule A (Form 5500), Insurance Information, to Form 5500, 5500-C, or 5500-R if any benefits under the plan are provided by an insurance company, insurance service, or other similar organization (such as Blue Cross, Blue Shield, or a health maintenance organization).

Exception: *Schedule A (Form 5500) is not needed if the plan covers: (1) only an individual, or an individual and his or her spouse, who wholly owns a trade or business, whether incorporated or unincorporated; or (2) a partner in a partnership, or a partner and his or her spouse.*

Do not file a Schedule A (Form 5500) with a Form 5500EZ.

Attach Schedule B (Form 5500), Actuarial Information, to Forms 5500, 5500-C, 5500-R, or 5500EZ for most defined benefit pension plans. See the instructions for Schedule B.

Attach Schedule C (Form 5500), Service Provider and Trustee Information, to Form 5500. See item 28 and the instructions to Schedule C.

Schedule SSA (Form 5500), Annual Registration Statement Identifying Separated Participants With Deferred Vested Benefits, may be needed for separated participants. See "When To Report Separated Participants" in the instructions for Schedule SSA.

Schedule P (Form 5500), Annual Return of Fiduciary of Employee Benefit Trust.—Any fiduciary (trustee or custodian) of an organization that is qualified under Code section 401(a) and exempt from tax under Code section 501(a) who wants to protect the organization under the statute of limitations provided in Code section 6501(a) must file a Schedule P (Form 5500).

File the Schedule P (Form 5500) as an attachment to Form 5500, 5500-C, 5500-R, or 5500EZ for the plan year in which the trust year ends.

Other Filings

Reporting Requirements for Investment Arrangements Filing Directly with DOL

Certain investment arrangements for employee benefit plans file financial information directly with DOL. These arrangements include common/collective trusts, pooled separate accounts, master trusts, and 103-12 IEs. Definitions of these investment arrangements may be found on pages 3 and 4. Their DOL filing requirements are described below.

1. Common/Collective Trust and Pooled Separate Account Information To Be Filed Directly With DOL

Financial institutions and insurance carriers filing the statement of the assets and liabilities of a common/collective trust or pooled separate account should identify the trust or account by providing the EIN of the trust or account, or (if more than one trust or account is covered by the same EIN) both the EIN and any additional number assigned by the financial institution or insurance carrier (such as: 99-1234567 Trust No. 1); and a list of all plans participating in the trust or account, identified by the plan number, EIN, and name of the plan sponsor. The direct filing should be addressed to:

Common/Collective Trust (OR)
Pooled Separate Account
Pension and Welfare Benefits
Administration
U.S. Department of Labor, Room N5644
200 Constitution Avenue, NW.
Washington, DC 20210

2. Master Trust Information To Be Filed Directly With DOL

The following information with respect to a master trust must be filed with DOL by the plan administrator or by a designee, such as the administrator of another plan participating in the master trust or the financial institution serving as trustee of the master trust, no later than the date on which the plan's return/report is due. While only one copy of the required information should be filed for all plans participating in the master trust, the information is an integral part of the return/report of each participating plan, and the plan's return/report will not be deemed complete unless all the information is filed within the prescribed time.

Note: *If a master trust investment account consists solely of one plan's asset(s) during the reporting period, the plan may report the(se) asset(s) either as an investment account to be reported as part of the master trust report filed directly with DOL* ***or*** *as a plan asset(s) which is not part of the master trust (and therefore subject to all instructions pertaining to assets not held in a master trust).*

Each of the following statements and schedules must indicate the name of the master trust and the name of the master trust investment account. The information shall be filed with DOL by mailing it to:

Master Trust
Pension and Welfare Benefits
Administration
U.S. Department of Labor, Room N5644
200 Constitution Avenue, NW.
Washington, DC 20210

a. The name and fiscal year of the master trust and the name and address of the master trustee.

b. A list of all plans participating in the master trust, showing each plan's name, EIN, PN, and its percentage interest in each master trust investment account as of the beginning and end of the fiscal year of the master trust ending with or within the plan year.

c. A statement, in the same format as Part I of Schedule C (Form 5500), for each master trust investment account showing amounts of compensation paid during the fiscal year of the master trust ending with or within the plan year to persons providing services with respect to the investment account and subtracted from the gross income of the investment account in determining the net increase (decrease) in net assets of the investment account.

d. A statement for each master trust investment account showing the assets and liabilities of the investment account at the beginning and end of the fiscal year of the master trust ending with or within the plan year, grouped in the same categories as those specified in item 34 of Form 5500.

e. A statement for each master trust investment account showing the income and expenses, changes in net assets, and net increase (decrease) in net assets of each such investment account during the fiscal year of the master trust ending with or within the plan year, in the categories specified in item 35 of Form 5500. In place of item 35a, show the total of all transfers of assets into the investment account by participating plans. In place of item 35j, show the total of all transfers of assets out of the investment account by participating plans.

f. Schedules, in the format set forth in the instructions for item 30 of Form 5500, of the following items with respect to each master trust investment account for the fiscal year of the master trust ending with or within the plan year: assets held for investment, nonexempt party-in-interest transactions, defaulted or uncollectible loans and leases, and 5% transactions involving assets in the investment account. The 5% figure shall be determined by comparing the current value of the transaction at the transaction date with the current value of the investment account assets at the beginning of the applicable fiscal year of the master trust.

3. 103-12 IE Information To Be Filed Directly With DOL

The information described below must be filed with the DOL by the sponsor of the 103-12 IE no later than the date on which the plan's return/report is due before the plan administrator can elect the alternative method of reporting. While only one copy of the required information should be filed for the 103-12 IE, the information is an integral part of the return/report of each plan electing the alternative method of compliance.

The filing address is:

103-12 Investment Entity
Pension and Welfare Benefits
Administration
U. S. Department of Labor, Room N5644
200 Constitution Avenue NW.
Washington, DC 20210

a. The name, fiscal year, and EIN of the 103-12 IE and the name and address of the sponsor of the 103-12 IE. If more than one 103-12 IE is covered by the same EIN, they shall be sequentially numbered as follows: 99-1234567 Entity No. 1.

b. A list of all plans participating in the 103-12 IE, showing each plan's name, EIN, PN, and its percentage interest in the 103-12 IE as of the beginning and end of the fiscal year of the 103-12 IE ending with or within the plan year.

c. A statement, in the same format as Part I of Schedule C (Form 5500), for the 103-12 IE showing amounts of compensation paid during the fiscal year of the 103-12 IE ending with or within the plan year to persons providing services to the 103-12 IE.

d. A statement showing the assets and liabilities at the beginning and end of the fiscal year of the 103-12 IE ending with or within the plan year, grouped in the same categories as those specified in item 34 of Form 5500.

e. A statement showing the income and expenses, changes in net assets, and net increase (decrease) in net assets during the fiscal year of the 103-12 IE ending with or within the plan year, grouped in the same categories as those specified in item 35 of Form 5500. In place of item 35a, show the total of all transfers of assets into the 103-12 IE by participating plans. In place of item 35j, show the total of all transfers of assets out of the 103-12 IE by participating plans.

f. Schedules, in the format set forth in the instructions for item 30 of Form 5500 (except item 30c) with respect to the 103-12 IE for the fiscal year of the 103-12 IE investment entity ending with or within the plan year. Substitute the term "103-12 IE" in place of the word "plan" when completing the schedules.

g. A report of an independent qualified public accountant regarding the above items and other books and records of the 103-12 IE that meets the requirements of 29 CFR 2520.103-1(b)(5).

Section 3

General Information

Final Return/Report.—If all assets under the plan (including insurance/annuity contracts) have been distributed to the participants and beneficiaries or distributed to another plan (and when all liabilities for which benefits may be paid under a welfare plan have been satisfied), check the "final return/report" box at the top of the form filed for such plan. The year of complete distribution is the last year a return/report must be filed for the plan. For purposes of this paragraph, a complete distribution will occur in the year in which the assets of a terminated plan are brought under the control of PBGC.

For a defined benefit plan covered by PBGC, a PBGC Form 1 must be filed and a premium must be paid until the end of the plan year in which the assets are distributed or brought under the control of PBGC.

Filing the return/report marked "final return" and indicating that the plan terminated satisfies the notification requirement of Code section 6057(b)(3).

Signature and Date.—The plan administrator must sign and date all returns/reports filed. In addition, the employer must sign a return/report filed for a single-employer plan or a plan required to file only because of Code section 6039D.

When a joint employer-union board of trustees or committee is the plan sponsor or plan administrator, at least one employer representative and one union representative must sign and date the return/report.

Participating employers in a multiple-employer plan (other), who are required to file Form 5500-C or 5500-R, are required to sign the return/report. The plan administrator need not sign the Form 5500-C or 5500-R filed by the participating employer.

Reproductions.—Original forms are preferable, but a clear reproduction of the completed form is acceptable. Sign the return/report after it is reproduced. All signatures must be original.

Change in Plan Year.—Generally only defined contribution pension benefit plans need to get prior approval for a change in plan year. (See Code section 412(c)(5).) Rev. Proc. 87-27, 1987-1 C.B. 769 explains the procedure for automatic approval of a change in plan year. A pension benefit plan that would ordinarily need to obtain approval for a change in plan year under Code section 412(c)(5) is granted an automatic approval for a change in plan year if all the following criteria are met:

1. No plan year is more than 12 months long.

2. The change will not delay the time when the plan would otherwise have been required to conform to the requirements of any statute, regulation, or published position of the IRS.

3. The trust, if any, retains its exempt status for the short period required to effect the change, as well as for the taxable year immediately preceding the short period.

4. All actions necessary to implement the change in plan year, including plan amendment and a resolution of the board of directors (if applicable), have been taken on or before the last day of the short period.

5. No change in plan year has been made for any of the preceding plan years.

6. In the case of a defined benefit plan, deductions are taken in accordance with section 5 of Rev. Proc. 87-27.

For the first return/report that is filed following the change in plan year, check the box indicated on the second line under the title at the top of the form (or item 1d if Form 5500R is being filed).

Amended Return/Report.—If you file an amended return/report, check the "(ii) an amended return/report" box at the top of the form. When filing an amended return, be sure to answer all questions and put a circle around the numbers of the items that have been amended.

How The Annual Return/Report Information May Be Used.—All Form 5500 series return/reports will be subjected to a computerized review. It is, therefore, in the filer's best interest that the responses accurately reflect the circumstances they were designed to report. Annual reports filed under Title I of ERISA must be made available by plan administrators to plan participants and by the Department of Labor to the public pursuant to ERISA section 104.

Section 4

Specific Instructions for Form 5500

Important: Answer all items on the Form 5500 with respect to the plan year, unless otherwise explicitly stated in the item-by-item instructions or on the form itself. Therefore, your responses usually apply to the year entered or printed at the top of the first page of the form. Yes and no questions are to be marked either "Yes" or "No" but not both. If neither "Yes" nor "No" applies, enter "NA."

Information To Be Completed at the Top of the Form

First Line at the top of the form—Complete the space for dates when: (1) the 12-month plan year is not a calendar year, or (2) the plan year is less than 12 months (a short plan year).

Second Line— Check the box if the plan year has been changed since the last return/report was filed.

Fifth Line—Check box (i) if this is the initial filing for this plan. Do not check this box if you have ever filed for this plan even if it was on a different form (Form 5500 vs. Form 5500-C or Form 5500-R).

Check box (ii) if you have already filed for the 1988 plan year and are now submitting an amended return/report to reflect errors and/or omissions on the previously filed return/report.

Check box (iii) if the plan no longer exists to provide benefits. See section 3 for instructions concerning the requirement to file a final return/report.

The numbers of the following instructions are the same as the item numbers on the return/report.

1a. If you did not receive a preaddressed mailing label, enter the name and address of the plan sponsor. If the plan covers only the employees of one employer, enter the employer's name.

If you received a Form 5500 with a preaddressed mailing label, please attach it in the name and address area of the form you file. If the name or address on the label is wrong, draw a line through the incorrect part and correct it.

The term "plan sponsor" means—

(i) the employer, for an employee benefit plan that a single employer established or maintains;

(ii) the employee organization in the case of a plan of an employee organization; or

(iii) the association, committee, joint board of trustees, or other similar group of representatives of the parties who establish or maintain the plan, if the plan is established or maintained jointly by one or more employers and one or more employee organizations, or by two or more employers.

Include enough information in 1(a) to describe the sponsor adequately. For example, "Joint Board of Trustees of Local 187 Machinists" rather than just "Joint Board of Trustees."

For group insurance arrangements, enter the name of the trust or other entity that holds the insurance contracts. In addition, attach a list of all participating employers and their EINs.

A group insurance arrangement is an arrangement which provides benefits to the employees of two or more unaffiliated employers (not in connection with a multiemployer plan or a mutiple-employer-collectively-bargained plan), fully insures one or more welfare plans of each participating employer, and uses a trust (or other entity such as a trade association) as the holder of the insurance contracts and the conduit for payment of premiums to the insurance company.

1b. Enter the 9-digit employer identification number (EIN) assigned to the plan sponsor/employer. For example, 00-1234567.

Employers and plan administrators who do not have an EIN should apply for one on Form SS-4, available from most IRS or Social Security Administration offices. Send Form SS-4 to the same Internal Revenue Service Center to which this form will be sent.

Plan sponsors are reminded that they should use the trust EIN when opening a bank account or conducting other transactions for a plan that requires an employer identification number. The trust may apply for an EIN as explained in the preceding paragraph.

A plan of a controlled group of corporations whose sponsor is more than one of the members of the controlled group should insert only the EIN of one of the sponsoring members. This EIN must be used in all subsequent filings of the annual returns/reports for the controlled group unless there is a change in the sponsor.

If the plan administrator is a group of individuals, get a single EIN for the group. When you apply for a number, enter on line 1 of Form SS-4 the name of the group, such as "Joint Board of Trustees of the Local 187 Machinists' Retirement Plan."

Note: *Although Employer Identification Numbers (EINs) for funds (trusts or custodial accounts) associated with plans are not required to be furnished on the Form 5500 series returns/reports, the IRS will issue EINs for such funds for other reporting purposes. EINs may be obtained by filing Form SS-4 as explained above.*

1d. From the list of business codes on pages 18 and 19, enter the one that best describes the nature of the employer's business. If more than one employer is involved, enter the business code for the main business activity.

1e. Plans checking item 4a or 4b must enter the first six digits of the CUSIP (Committee on Uniform Securities Identification Procedures) number, "issuer number," if one has been assigned to the plan sponsor for purposes of issuing corporate securities. CUSIP issuer numbers are assigned to corporations and other entities which issue public securities listed on stock exchanges or traded over the counter. The CUSIP issuer number is the first six digits of the number assigned to the individual securities which are traded. If the plan sponsor has no CUSIP issuer number, enter "N/A."

2a. If the document constituting the plan appoints or designates a plan administrator other than the sponsor, enter the administrator's name and address. If the plan administrator is also the sponsor, enter "Same." If filing as a group insurance arrangement, enter "Same." If 2a is the "Same," then items 2b and 2c should be left blank.

The term "administrator" means—

(i) the person or group of persons specified as the administrator by the instrument under which the plan is operated;

(ii) the plan sponsor/employer if an administrator is not so designated; or

(iii) any other person prescribed by regulations of the Secretary of Labor if an administrator is not designated and a plan sponsor cannot be identified.

2b. A plan administrator must have an EIN for reporting purposes. Enter the plan administrator's 9-digit EIN here. If the plan administrator has no EIN, apply for one as explained in 1b above.

Employees of an employer are not plan administrators unless so designated in the plan document, even though they engage in administrative functions of the plan. If an employee of the employer is designated as the plan administrator, that employee must get an EIN.

3. If you answer "No," enter the name, address, and EIN of the plan sponsor and/or the plan administrator shown on the prior return/report.

3c. Indicate if the change in 3a is only a change in sponsorship. "Change in sponsorship" means the plan's sponsor has been changed but no assets or liabilities have been transferred to another plan(s), the plan has not terminated or merged with any other plan, and so forth.

4a. Check for a single-employer plan. See "Kinds of Filers" for what is considered a single-employer plan.

4b. Check for a plan in which more than one employer participates, and some of the employers are members of a controlled group of corporations (Code section 414(b)) or members of a group of employers under common control (Code section 414(c)).

4c. Check for a multiemployer plan as defined in Code section 414(f) and ERISA sections 3(37) and 4001(a)(3).

4d. Check for a multiple-employer-collectively-bargained plan as described under "Kinds of Filers."

4e. Check for a multiple-employer plan (other) if the plan administrator is filing for the plan as a whole.

4f. Check for a consolidated filing (pursuant to 29 CFR 2520.104-43) that a trust or other entity makes on behalf of welfare benefit plans that participate in a group insurance arrangement.

5a. Enter the formal name of the plan, group insurance arrangement, or enough information to identify the plan.

5b. Enter the date the plan first became effective.

5c. Enter the 3-digit number the employer or plan administrator assigned to the plan. All welfare plan numbers and Code section 6039D plan numbers start at 501. All other plans start at 001.

Once you use a plan number, continue to use it for that plan on all future filings with IRS, DOL and PBGC. Do not use it for any other plan even if you terminated the first plan.

Group Insurance Arrangement.—For entities filing as a group insurance arrangement, enter the name of the arrangement and enter the next 3-digit plan number available to the plan sponsor in the 500 series (i.e., 501, 502 etc.).

6a. Check every box that describes the welfare benefit plan for which this return/report is being filed. Example: If your plan provides health insurance, dental insurance, eye examinations, and life insurance, four boxes should be checked—6a(i)(A), 6a(i)(B), 6a(i)(D), and 6a(i)(E).

If you checked box (M), (N), or (O), you must check one box in 6a(ii). Check unfunded if the plan is (1) unfunded, (2) fully insured, or (3) a combination of unfunded/insured as defined on page 2, Section 2B(a).

6b(i). For a defined benefit plan, check the box.

Summary of Filing Requirements for Employers and Plan Administrators
(File forms ONLY with IRS)

Type of plan	What to file	When to file
Most pension plans with only one participant or one participant and that participant's spouse	Form 5500EZ	File all required forms and schedules for each plan by the last day of the 7th month after the plan year ends.
Pension plan with fewer than 100 participants	Form 5500-C or 5500-R	
Pension plan with 100 or more participants	Form 5500	
Annuity under Code section 403(b)(1) or trust under Code section 408(c)	Form 5500, 5500-C, or 5500-R	
Custodial account under Code section 403(b)(7)	Form 5500, 5500-C, or 5500-R	
Welfare benefit plan with 100 or more participants*	Form 5500	
Welfare benefit plan with fewer than 100 participants (see exception on page 1 of these instructions)*	Form 5500-C or 5500-R	
Pension or welfare plan with 100 or more participants (see instructions for item 29)	Financial statements, schedules, and accountant's opinion	
Pension or welfare plan with benefits provided by an insurance company	Schedule A (Form 5500)	
Pension plan that requires actuarial information	Schedule B (Form 5500)	
Plan with 100 or more participants	Schedule C (Form 5500)	
Pension plan filing a registration statement identifying separated participants with deferred vested benefits from a pension plan	Schedule SSA (Form 5500)	

*This includes Code section 6039D filers.

6b(ii). Check (C) for a money purchase plan if the contribution is determined by a target benefit calculation. Check (D) for all money purchase plans that do not have a target benefit calculation.

6c(ii). Check this box for an ESOP which acquires employer securities with borrowed money or other debt-financed techniques.

6c(iii). Check if the plan is a pension plan that provides for individual accounts and permits a participant or beneficiary to exercise independent control over the assets in his or her account (see ERISA section 404(c)).

6c(iv). Check this box for pension benefit plans maintained outside the United States primarily for nonresident aliens. See "Kinds of Filers" for more information.

6c(v). In the space provided following 6c(viii), enter name of the trust and bank or financial institution. Also enter city and state where the trust is maintained. (See page 3 for master trust instructions.)

6c(vi). In the space provided following 6c(viii), enter name and address of the 103-12 IE. (See page 4.)

6d. For single-employer plans enter the date the employer's tax year ends. For example, if the tax year is a calendar year, enter 12-31-88. For all plans with more than one employer, enter "N/A."

6e. Definition of Affiliated Service Group.—In general, Code section 414(m)(2) defines an affiliated service group as a first service organization (FSO) that has:

(1) a service organization (A-ORG) that is a shareholder or partner in the FSO and that regularly performs services for the FSO, or is regularly associated with the FSO in performing services for third persons, and/or

(2) any other organization (B-ORG) if:

(a) a significant portion of the business of that organization consists of performing services for the FSO or A-ORG of a type historically performed by employees in the service field of the FSO or A-ORG, and

(b) 10% or more of the interest of the B-ORG is held by persons who are highly compensated employees of the FSO or A-ORG.

An affiliated service group also includes a group consisting of an organization whose principal business is performing management functions for another organization (or one organization and other related organizations) on a regular and continuing basis, and the organization for which such functions are so performed by the organization. For a plan maintained by more than one employer, check "Yes" if any such employer is a member of an affiliated service group.

6f. A cash or deferred arrangement described in Code section 401(k) is a part of a qualified defined contribution plan which provides for an election by employees to defer part of their compensation or receive these amounts in cash.

7. The description of "participant" in the instructions below is only for purposes of item 7 of this form.

For welfare plans, dependents are considered to be neither participants nor beneficiaries. For pension benefit plans, "alternate payees" entitled to benefits under a qualified domestic relations order are not to be counted as participants for this item.

"Participant" means any individual who is included in one of the categories below.

7a. Active participants include any individuals who are currently in employment covered by a plan and who are earning or retaining credited service under a plan. This category includes any individuals who are: (i) currently below the integration level in a plan that is integrated with social security, and/or (ii) eligible to elect to have the employer make payments to a Code section 401(k) qualified cash or deferred arrangement. Active participants also include any nonvested individuals who are earning or retaining credited service under a plan. This category does not include nonvested former employees who have incurred the greater of 5 consecutive one year breaks in service or the break in service period specified in the plan.

For determining if active participants are fully vested, partially vested, or nonvested, consider vesting in employer contributions only.

For purposes of Code section 6039D, "participant" means any individual who, for a plan year, has had at least one dollar excluded from income by reason of Code section 120, 125, or 127. If you are filing Form 5500 for a welfare plan that is required to file under Title I of ERISA and under Code section 6039D, the preceding sentence does not apply.

7b. Inactive participants receiving benefits are any individuals who are retired or separated from employment covered by the plan and who are receiving benefits under the plan. This includes former employees who are receiving group health continuation coverage benefits pursuant to Part 6 of ERISA who are covered by the employee welfare benefit plan. This category does not include any individual to whom an insurance company has made an irrevocable commitment to pay all the benefits to which the individual is entitled under the plan.

7c. Inactive participants entitled to future benefits are individuals who are retired or separated from employment covered by the plan and who are entitled to begin receiving benefits under the plan in the future. This category does not include any individual to whom an insurance company has made an irrevocable commitment to pay all the benefits to which the individual is entitled under the plan.

7e. Deceased participants are any deceased individuals who have one or more beneficiaries who are receiving or are entitled to receive benefits under the plan. This category does not include an individual if an insurance company has made an irrevocable commitment to pay all the benefits to which the beneficiaries of that individual are entitled under the plan.

7g(i). If "Yes," file Schedule SSA (Form 5500) as an attachment to Form 5500. Plan administrators: Code section 6057(e) provides that the plan administrator must give each participant a statement showing the same information for that participant as is reported on Schedule SSA.

8a. Check "Yes" if an amendment to the plan was adopted in this plan year, regardless of the effective date of the amendment.

8b. Check "Yes" only if the accrued benefits were retroactively reduced. For example, a plan provides a benefit of 2% for each year of service, but the plan is amended to change the benefit to 1½% a year for all years of service under the plan.

8c. Enter the date the most recent amendment was adopted regardless of the date of the amendent or the effective date of the amendment.

8d. Check "Yes" only if an amendment changed the information previously provided to participants by the summary plan description or summary description of modifications.

8e. A revised summary plan description or summary description of modifications must be filed with DOL and distributed to all participants and pension plan beneficiaries no later than 210 days after the close of the plan year in which the amendment(s) was adopted. If the material was distributed and filed since the amendments were adopted (even if after the end of the plan year), check "Yes" to item 8e.

9a. Check "Yes" if the plan was terminated or if the plan was merged or consolidated into another plan. Enter year of termination if applicable. If you checked 6a(i)(M), (N), or (O) and indicated that this is an unfunded plan and you also answered 9a "Yes," you must also check 9b "Yes."

9b. If the plan was terminated and all plan assets were not distributed, file a return/report for each year the plan has assets. In that case, the return/report must be filed by the plan administrator, if designated, or by the person or persons who actually control the plan's property.

If all plan assets were used to buy individual annuity contracts and the contracts were distributed to the participants, check "Yes."

If all the trust assets were transferred to another plan, check "Yes."

Do not check "Yes" for a welfare plan which is still liable to pay benefits for claims which were incurred prior to the termination date, but not yet paid. See 29 CFR 2520.104b-2(g)(2)(ii).

9h. The Code provides for a nondeductible excise tax on a reversion of assets from a qualified plan. The tax is effective for reversions after December 31, 1985, unless the plan termination date is prior to January 1986.

9i. The employer must report the reversion by filing Form 5330 and pay any applicable tax. The tax will not be imposed upon employers who are tax-exempt entities under Code section 501(a). See instructions for Form 5330.

10a. If this plan was merged or consolidated into another plan(s), or plan assets or liabilities were transferred to another plan(s), indicate which other plan or plans were involved.

10c. Enter the EIN of the sponsor (employer, if for a single-employer plan) of the other plan.

10e. Pension benefit plans must file Form 5310 at least 30 days before any plan merger or consolidation or any transfer of plan assets or liabilities to another plan. **Caution:** *There is a penalty for not filing Form 5310 on time.*

11. Enter the code for the **funding arrangement** used by the plan from the list below.

The "funding arrangement" is the method used for the receipt, holding, investment, and transmittal of plan assets prior to the time the plan actually provides the benefits promised under the plan. For purposes of items 11 and 12, the term "trust" includes any fund or account which receives, holds, transmits, or invests plan assets other than an account or policy of an insurance company.

	Funding Arrangement Codes
Trust	1
Trust and insurance	2
Insurance	3
Exclusively from general assets of sponsor (unfunded)	4
Partially insured and partially from general assets of sponsor	5
Other	6

12. Enter the code for the **benefit arrangement** used by the plan from the list below.

The "benefit arrangement" is the method by which benefits are actually provided to participants by the plan. For example, when a participant retires, the plan might purchase an annuity from an insurance company for that individual to provide the actual benefits promised by the plan. In this example, the annuity would be the benefit arrangement.

Using the chart below, the plan in the above example would enter a "3" to indicate the benefit arrangement.

	Benefit Arrangement Codes
Trust	1
Trust and insurance	2
Insurance	3
Exclusively from general assets of sponsor (unfunded)	4
Partially insured and partially from general assets of sponsor	5
Other	6

13a. Enter "Yes," if either the contributions to the plan or the benefits paid by the plan are subject to the collective bargaining process, even if the plan is not established and administered by a joint board of trustees. Enter "Yes" even if only some of those covered by the plan are members of a collective bargaining unit which negotiates benefit levels on its own behalf. The benefit schedules need not be identical for all employees under the plan.

13b. All plans checking items 4c or 4d must enter the 6-digit LM number to identify each sponsoring labor organization which is a party to the collective bargaining agreement. Other plans which are maintained pursuant to collective bargaining agreements should enter the appropriate LM number, if available. The "LM number" is the six-digit Labor-Management disclosure number entered by the sponsoring labor organization in item 1 of the Form LM-2 or LM-3 (Labor Organization Annual Report) filed with the Department of Labor. Accordingly, the LM number(s) should be readily available from the sponsoring labor organization(s). If all sponsoring labor organizations' LM numbers cannot be entered in the spaces provided in item 13b on the form, enter the additional LM numbers on a supplemental sheet to accompany the Form 5500.

14. If the funding arrangement code (item 11) and/or the benefit arrangement code (item 12) is 2,3, or 5, at least one Schedule A (Form 5500) must be attached to the Form 5500 filed for pension and welfare plans. The insurance company (or similar organization) which provides benefits is required to provide the plan administrator with the information needed to complete the return/report, pursuant to ERISA section 103 (a)(2). If you do not receive this information in a timely manner, contact the insurance company (or similar organization). If information is missing on Schedule A due to a refusal to provide this information, note this on the Schedule A. If there are no Schedule(s) A attached, enter "0."

15b. If a waived funding deficiency is being amortized in the current plan year, do not complete (i), (ii), and (iii), but complete 1, 2, 3, 7, and 9 of Schedule B (Form 5500). An enrolled actuary need not sign Schedule B under these circumstances.

15b(iii). File Form 5330 with IRS to pay the excise tax on any funding deficiency. **Caution:** *There is a penalty for not filing Form 5330 on time.*

16. A "top-heavy plan" is a plan which during any plan year is:

(1) any defined benefit plan if, as of the determination date, the present value of the cumulative accrued benefits under the plan for key employees exceeds 60% of the present value of the cumulative accrued benefits under the plan for all employees; and

(2) any defined contribution plan if, as of the determination date, the aggregate of the accounts of key employees under the plan exceeds 60% of the aggregate of the accounts of all employees under the plan.

Each plan of an employer included in a required aggregation group is to be treated as a top-heavy plan if such group is a top-heavy group. See definitions of required aggregation group and top-heavy group, below.

Key Employee —A key employee is any participant in an employer plan who at any time during the plan year, or any of the 4 preceding years, is:

(1) an officer of the employer having an annual compensation greater than 50% of the amount in effect under Code section 415(c)(1)(A) for any such plan year,

(2) one of the 10 employees having annual compensation from the employer of more than the limitation in effect under Code section 415(c)(1)(A) and owning (or considered as owning within the meaning of Code section 318) both more than ½% interest and the largest interests in the employer,

(3) a 5% owner of the employer, or

(4) a 1% owner of the employer having an annual compensation from the employer of more than $150,000.

In determining whether an individual is an officer of the employer, no more than 50 employees, or, if less, the greater of 3 employees or 10% of the employees, are to be treated as officers. See Code section 416(i) and T-12 of Regulations section 1.416. A key employee will not include any officer or employee of a governmental plan under Code section 414(d).

Required Aggregation Group—A required aggregation group consists of:

(1) each plan of the employer in which a key employee is or was a participant, and

(2) each other plan of the employer which enables a plan to meet the requirements for nondiscrimination in contributions or benefits under Code section 401(a)(4), or the participation requirements under Code section 410.

Top-Heavy Group—A top-heavy group is an aggregation group if, as of the determination date, the sum of the present value of the cumulative accrued benefits for key employees under all defined benefit plans included in such group and the aggregate of the accounts of key employees under all defined contribution plans in such group exceeds 60% of a similar sum determined for all employees. To determine if a plan is top-heavy, include distributions made in the 5-year period ending on the determination date. However, do not take into account accrued benefits for an individual who hasn't performed services for the employer during the 5-year period ending on the determination date.

18a. If the plan distributes an annuity contract, whether or not deferred and whether or not upon termination, that contract must provide that all distributions from it will meet the participant and spousal consent requirements of Code section 417. Consent is not needed for the distribution of the contract itself. Check "No" if the plan did not distribute any annuity contracts.

18b. In general, distributions must be made in the form of a qualified joint and survivor annuity for life or a qualified preretirement survivor annuity. An annuity distribution to a single individual is a qualified joint and survivor annuity. Check "Yes" if distributions in other forms were made, even if such distributions were permissible, e.g., because consent was obtained or was not needed.

18c. Generally, within the 90 days prior to the date of any benefit payment or the making of a loan to a participant, you must get the spouse's consent to the payment of the benefit or the use of the accrued benefit for the making of the loan. However, there are some circumstances where obtaining this spousal consent is not required. The following is a partial listing of circumstances where spousal consent is not required:

(1) The participant is not married and no spouse is required to be treated as a current spouse under a qualified domestic relations order issued by a court.

(2) The participant's accrued benefit in the plan never had a present value of more than $3,500.

(3) The benefit is paid in the form of a qualified joint and survivor annuity, i.e., an annuity for the life of the participant with a survivor annuity for the life of the spouse which is not less than 50% of (and is not greater than 100% of) the amount of the

annuity which is payable during the joint lives of the participant and the spouse. See Code section 417(b).

(4) The payout is from a profit-sharing or stock bonus plan that pays the spouse the participant's full account balance upon the participant's death, an annuity payment is not elected by the participant, and the profit-sharing or stock bonus plan is not a transferee plan with respect to the participant (i.e., had not received a transfer from a plan that was subject to the consent requirements with respect to the participant).

(5) The participant had no service under the plan after August 22, 1984.

18d. A plan may not eliminate a subsidized benefit or a retirement option by plan amendment or plan termination.

19. For purposes of determining the present value of a participant's accrued benefits and the amount of any distribution, a qualified plan must use a rate no higher than "the applicable interest rate." The "applicable interest rate" means the interest rate which would be used (as of the date of distributions) by the PBGC for determining the present value of a lump sum distribution on termination of the plan.

a. If the present value of the vested accrued benefit is no more than $25,000, the amount to be distributed is calculated using the PBGC rate.

b. If the present value of the vested accrued benefit exceeds $25,000 (using the PBGC rate), the total amount to be distributed is determined using an interest rate no greater than 120% of the applicable interest rate that would be used by the PBGC upon the plan's termination. In such a case the value will be no less than $25,000.

20. The Tax Reform Act of 1986 amended Code section 415 to provide that the maximum annual benefit that may be provided under a defined benefit plan may not exceed the lesser of $90,000 or 100% of compensation. However, if benefits begin before the social security retirement age, the $90,000 limit must be reduced as described in Notice 87-21, 1987-1 C.B. 458.

In addition, the dollar limitations will be reduced for participants with fewer than 10 years of participation in a defined benefit plan, i.e., a 10% reduction for each year under 10 years of participation.

For defined contribution plans, Code section 415 now provides that the dollar limit on annual additions to a qualified plan may not exceed the greater of $30,000 or 25% of the defined benefit dollar limit for such limitation year. The defined contribution dollar limit will not be increased until the defined benefit dollar limit, as increased by cost of living adjustments, equals or exceeds $120,000. (For years beginning after December 31, 1987, the $90,000 defined benefit limit will be adjusted to reflect post-1986 cost of living increases.) The defined contribution dollar limit will then be increased to an amount equal to 25% of the defined benefit limit.

Annual additions to a defined contribution plan will, for years beginning after December 31, 1986, include 100% of all after-tax employee contributions. For participants participating in plans of tax-exempt organizations, the pre-Tax Reform Act limits remain in effect.

The Tax Reform Act of 1986 also provides that a participant's previously accrued benefit won't be reduced merely because of the reduction in dollar limits or increases in required periods of participation. The transitional rule applies to an individual who was a participant prior to January 1, 1987, in a plan in existence on May 5, 1986. If this participant's current accrued benefit exceeds the dollar limit under the Tax Reform Act of 1986, but complies with prior law, then the applicable dollar limit for the participant is equal to the current accrued benefit. The term "current accrued benefit" is defined as the participant's accrued benefit as of the close of the last limitation year beginning before January 1, 1987, and expressed as an annual benefit. To compute the defined benefit fraction, the current accrued benefit would replace the dollar limit otherwise used in the denominator of the fraction. The current accrued benefit is also reflected in the numerator of the defined benefit fraction.

21. In the calendar year in which the employee attains age 70 ½, the employee must begin to receive minimum distributions pursuant to Code section 401(a)(9) by April 1 of the following calendar year. Once begun, minimal distributions must continue each calendar year.

22. For purposes of filing required only because of Code section 6039D, complete only items 22c, 22g, and 22i.

22a. If you do not claim to meet the percentage tests of Code section 410(b)(1)(A), attach an explanation indicating how your plan meets the coverage requirements of Code section 410(b)(1)(B).

22b. Provide information for all employers of a controlled group, a group under common control, or an affiliated service group even if they do not participate in the plan. Also, leased employees (described in Code section 414(n)(2)) of any such employer(s) are to be included as employees unless the leasing organization maintains a "safe harbor" plan described in Code section 414(n)(5) for the leased employees. See below for more information regarding a "safe harbor" plan.

Generally, leased employees are individuals who are employees of a leasing organization, but who during the course of their employment perform services for a trade or business other than the leasing organization on a substantially full-time basis for a period of at least one year.

Service is to include any period during which the employee would have been a leased employee, but for the requirement that substantially full-time service be performed for at least one year. Such leased employees are to be considered employees of their recipient organization at certain times and for certain qualification requirements unless the leasing organization adopts and maintains the type of qualified plan specified in Code section 414(n)(5).

A *safe harbor plan* is a money purchase pension plan maintained by the leasing organization that provides with respect to a leased employee:

(A) a nonintegrated employer contribution rate of at least 10%, and

(B) immediate participation and full and immediate vesting.

The plan must cover all employees of the leasing organization other than those who are not "leased out" and cover those whose compensation from the leasing organization is less than $1,000 per year during a plan year and each of the prior 3 plan years. The safe harbor plan must provide the 10% of compensation allocation regardless of the number of hours of service during the year, age, or whether the employee is employed on a specific date.

In general, if leased employees make up more than 20% of the nonhighly compensated work force of the recipient, such employees must be covered by the recipient's pension plan regardless of the safe harbor plan. Recipient includes employers aggregated under Code section 414(b), (c), or (m). Under the 20% rule, "leased employees" include all persons who performed services as a "nonemployee."

Therefore, the total number of employees entered in 22c, the breakdown of excluded employees shown in 22d, and the ineligible employees shown in 22f should also include the employees of the controlled group, employees of employers under common control, or other employees in the affiliated service group or leased employees as described above.

Do not complete 22 for multiemployer plans described in Code section 414(f) or for multiple-employer-collectively-bargained plans.

24b. An independent appraiser must be used to ascertain the value of securities, acquired by a plan after December 31, 1986, if the securities aren't readily tradeable on an established securities market.

28a. Check "Yes" if any person (including, when applicable, a corporation or partnership) received, directly or indirectly, $5,000 or more during the plan year for providing services to the plan. For exceptions, see instructions to Part I of Schedule C (Form 5500). If you checked "Yes," complete Part I of Schedule C (Form 5500), which must then be attached to the Form 5500. Include payments from the plan sponsor which are reimbursable by the plan.

28b. Include all trustees in office during the plan year. List these trustees on Part II of Schedule C (Form 5500) and attach it to the Form 5500.

28c. Check "Yes," if there has been a termination in the appointment of any person for which a box must be checked in item 28d. In the case where the service provider is not an individual (i.e., when the service provider is a legal entity such as a corporation, partnership, etc.), check "Yes" when the service provider (not the individual) has been terminated. If item 28c is checked "Yes," complete Part III of Schedule C (Form 5500) and attach the Schedule C to the Form 5500. Otherwise, check "No" and skip to item 28g.

28d. Check all appropriate boxes and complete Part III of Schedule C (Form 5500). At least one box must be checked if 28c is answered "Yes."

28e. If item 28c is checked "Yes," check 28e "Yes" if, during the two most recent plan years preceding the termination and any subsequent interim period preceding such termination, resignation, or dismissal, there were any disagreements (whether or not the disagreements were a factor in the termination) on any matter of professional judgment that, if not resolved to the satisfaction of the former appointee, would have caused (or did cause) the former appointee to take some action, such as including the subject matter of the disagreement within a written report. For example, check "Yes," if the accountant was terminated as a result of a disagreement over the valuation of plan assets and the accountant would have required that the matter be disclosed in a note to the financial statements. Disagreements not involving a matter of professional judgement, such as the payment or nonpayment of fees, or the amount of the fee charged should not be included.

28f. If items 28d(i) or 28d(ii) has been checked, indicating that an independent qualified public accountant or enrolled actuary has been terminated, the plan administrator must provide the terminated accountant or enrolled actuary with a copy of the explanation of the reason for the termination provided in Part III of Schedule C (Form 5500), along with a completed copy of the notice which follows.

Notice To Terminated Accountant or Enrolled Actuary

An explanation of the reasons for the termination of an accountant or enrolled actuary (terminated party) must be provided as part of the annual report (Part III of Schedule C). The plan administrator of the employee benefit plan is also required to provide the terminated party with a copy of this explanation and a notification that the terminated party has the opportunity to comment directly to the Department of Labor concerning any aspect of this explanation.

In accordance with this requirement, I, as plan administrator, verify that the explanation that is either reproduced below or attached to this notice is the explanation concerning your termination as reported on the Schedule C (Form 5500) attached to the 1988 Annual Return/Report Form 5500 for the (enter name of plan). This return/report is identified in item 1b by the nine-digit EIN – (enter Employer Identification Number) and in item 5c by the three-digit PN (enter plan number).

Signed

Dated

Any comments concerning this explanation should include the name, EIN, and PN of the plan and be submitted directly to:

Office of Enforcement
Pension and Welfare Benefits Administration
U. S. Department of Labor
200 Constitution Avenue, NW.
Washington, DC 20210

28g. A Schedule C (Form 5500) must be attached if item 28a, 28b, and/or 28c is checked "Yes." More than one Schedule C may be required if additional space is required to complete any part of the Schedule C. If no Schedule(s) C is required to be attached, enter "0".

29. Employee benefit plans filing the Annual Return/Report Form 5500 are generally required to engage an independent qualified public accountant pursuant to ERISA section 103(a)(3)(A). An independent qualified public accountant's opinion must be attached to Form 5500 unless: (i) the plan is an employee welfare benefit plan which is unfunded, fully insured, or a combination of unfunded and insured as described in 29 CFR 2520. 104-44(b)(1) ; (ii) the plan is an employee pension benefit plan whose sole asset(s) consists of insurance contracts which provide that, upon receipt of the premium payment, the insurance carrier fully guarantees the amount of benefit payments attributable to plan participants for that plan year as specified in 29 CFR 2520.104-44(b)(2); or (iii) the plan has elected to defer attaching the accountant's opinion for the first of two plan years, one of which is a short plan year of 7 months or less as allowed by 29 CFR 2520.104-50. (Also see the instructions for item 29a below.)

Single employer welfare plans using a 501(c)(9) trust are generally not exempt from the requirement of engaging an independent qualified public accountant.

29a. Plans meeting (i) or (ii) above should check "Yes" for item 29a and skip to item 31. Plans meeting (iii) must attach the required explanation and statements in lieu of the opinion and should check "No" to item 29a and "Other" to item 29b, and specify, in the space provided, that "the opinion is to be attached to the next Form 5500 pursuant to 29 CFR 2520.104-50." All other plans should check "No." "N/A" is NOT an acceptable response to this item. If the required accountant's opinion is not attached to the Form 5500, the filing is subject to rejection as incomplete and penalties may be imposed (see page 1).

29b(i). Generally, an unqualified opinion is issued when the auditor concludes that the plan's financial statements present fairly, in all material respects, the financial status of the plan as of the end of the period audited, and the changes in its financial status for the period under audit in conformity with generally accepted accounting principles. Check this box if the plan received an unqualified opinion.

29b(ii). Department of Labor regulations 29 CFR 2520.103-8 and 2520.103-12(d) generally state that the examination and report of an independent qualified public accountant need not extend to: (1) information prepared and certified to by a bank or similar institution or by an insurance carrier which is regulated and supervised and subject to periodic examination by a state or Federal agency, or (2) information concerning a 103-12 IE which is reported directly to the Department of Labor. Check this box if the plan received an accountant's opinion as discussed in 29b(i) above except for the information not audited pursuant to the above regulations.

29b(iii). Generally a qualified opinion is issued by an independent qualified public accountant when the plan's financial statements present fairly, in all material respects, the financial position of the plan as of the end of the audit period and the results of its operations for the audit period in conformity with generally accepted accounting principles except for the effects of one or more matters which are described in the opinion. A disclaimer of opinion is issued when the independent qualified public accountant does not express an opinion on the financial statements because he has not performed an audit sufficient in scope to enable him to form an opinion of the financial statements. Check this block if the plan received a qualified opinion or if a disclaimer of opinion was issued. If the audit was of limited scope pursuant to 29 CFR 2520.103-8 and/or 2520.103-12(d), and no other limitations as to scope or procedures were in effect, then check the box in item 29b(ii).

29b(iv). Generally an adverse opinion is issued by an independent qualified public accountant when the plan's financial statements do not present fairly, in all material respects, the financial position of the plan as of the end of the audit period and the results of its operations for the audit period in conformity with generally accepted accounting principles. Check this box if the plan received an adverse accountant's opinion.

29b(v). Generally, an independent qualified public accountant's opinion will be described by one of the categories in 29b(i)–(iv). Check this box if the accountant's opinion received by the plan is not described by one of the categories in 29b(i)–(iv). Explain the nature of the opinion in the space next to this box. In the event the explanation requires more space, enter "See attached" and on a separate sheet of paper explain in detail the nature of the accountant's opinion. Any attachments should identify the item number and include the plan's name, EIN and PN.

29c and d. These items must be answered by all plans required to engage an independent qualified public accountant (item 29a is "No"). The disclosure of the transactions and financial conditions listed in 29c are some of the disclosures required to be made when a plan's financial statements are presented in accordance with generally accepted accounting principles. (Usually these disclosures are contained in the notes to the financial statements.) If you are unsure as to whether the disclosures presented in or accompanying the plans' financial statements fall within one of the disclosures described in 29c, you should consult with the plan's independent qualified public accountant.

Check "Yes" to 29c and provide the amount involved in 29d if the financial statements or the notes to the statements contain any of the disclosures listed in 29c. The amount should be determined by adding the amounts of all of the applicable disclosures. For example, if two significant transactions are disclosed between the plan and the sponsor, the amounts, if any, disclosed in the notes should be added together and the total reported.

If you confirm, through consultation with the accountant, if necessary, that the accountant's report, including any applicable financial statements or notes, does not contain any of the disclosures noted in 29c, check "No" to item 29c and enter '0' in 29d.

30. Plans with assets held in a master trust and/or 103-12 IE (see pages 3 and 4 for the definition of these terms) should complete items 30a, b, c, and d to report information relating to assets held and transactions occurring outside the master trust and/or 103-12 IE. In determining the 5% figure for item 30d, subtract the value of plan assets held in the master trust or 103-12 IE from the current value of the plan's total assets at the beginning of the plan year.

Do not complete sub-items 30a through 30f if all plan funds are held in a master trust.

If "Yes" is checked for item(s) 30a, b, c, d, e, and/or f, schedules must be completed and attached to the Form 5500. If the required schedule is not attached to the Form 5500, the filing is subject to rejection as incomplete and penalties may be imposed (see page 1). Any attachments should identify the item number and include the plan's name, EIN, and PN.

30a–30d. If the assets or investment interests of two or more plans are maintained in one trust (except investment arrangements reported in 34c(xi) (see page 15)), all entries in the schedules included under items 30a, b, and c which relate to the trust shall be completed by including the plan's allocable portion of the trust. For purposes of item 30d, the plan's allocable portion of the transactions of the trust shall be combined with the other transactions of the plan, if any, to determine which transactions (or series of transactions) are reportable. Do not include individual transactions of investment arrangements reported in 34c(xi).

For purposes of this form, party-in-interest is deemed to include a disqualified person—see Code section 4975(e)(2). The term "party-in-interest" means, as to an employee benefit plan—

(A) any fiduciary (including, but not limited to, any administrator, officer, trustee or custodian), counsel, or employee of the plan;

(B) a person providing services to the plan;

(C) an employer, any of whose employees are covered by the plan;

(D) an employee organization, any of whose members are covered by the plan;

(E) an owner, direct or indirect, of 50% or more of—(i) the combined voting power of all classes of stock entitled to vote, or the total value of shares of all classes of stock of a corporation, (ii) the capital interest or the profits interest of a partnership, or (iii) the beneficial interest of a trust or unincorporated enterprise that is an employer or an employee organization described in (C) or (D);

(F) a relative of any individual described in (A), (B), (C), or (E);

(G) a corporation, partnership, or trust or estate of which (or in which) 50% or more of: (i) the combined voting power of all classes of stock entitled to vote or the total value of shares of all classes of stock of such corporation, (ii) the capital interest or profits interest of such partnership, or (iii) the beneficial interest of such trust or estate is owned directly or indirectly, or held by, persons described in (A), (B), (C), (D) or (E);

(H) an employee, officer, director (or an individual having powers or responsibilities similar to those of officers or directors), or a 10% or more shareholder, directly or indirectly, of a person described in (B), (C), (D), (E), or (G), or of the employee benefit plan; or

(I) a 10% or more (directly or indirectly in capital or profits) partner or joint venturer of a person described in (B), (C), (D), (E), or (G).

30a. Check "Yes" and attach one or both of the following two schedules to the Form 5500 if the plan had any assets held for investment purposes at any time during the plan year. Assets held for investment purposes shall include:

1 Any investment asset held by the plan on the last day of the plan year; and

2 Any investment asset purchased during the plan year and sold before the end of the plan year except:

(i) Debt obligations of the U.S. or any U.S. agency.

(ii) Interests issued by a company registered under the Investment Company Act of 1940 (e. g.., a mutual fund).

(iii) Bank certificates of deposit with a maturity of one year or less.

(iv) Commercial paper with a maturity of 9 months, or less, if it is valued in the highest rating category by at least two nationally recognized statistical rating services and is issued by a company required to file reports with the Securities and Exchange Commission under section 13 of the Securities Exchange Act of 1934.

(v) Participations in a bank common or collective trust.

(vi) Participations in an insurance company pooled separate account.

(vii) Securities purchased from a broker-dealer registered under the Securities Exchange Act of 1934 and either:

(A) listed on a national securities exchange registered under section 6 of the Securities Exchange Act of 1934, or (B) quoted on NASDAQ.

Assets held for investment purposes shall not include any investment which was not held by the plan on the last day of the plan year if that investment is reported in the annual report for that plan year in any of the following:

1 The schedule of loans or fixed income obligations in default required by item 30b;

2 The schedule of leases in default or classified as uncollectible required by item 30c;

3 The schedule of reportable transactions required by item 30d; and

4 The schedule of party-in-interest transactions required by items 30e and f.

The first schedule required to be attached to the Form 5500 is a schedule of all assets held for investment purposes at the end of the plan year, aggregated and identified by issue, maturity date, rate of interest, collateral, par or maturity value, cost and current value, and, in the case of a loan, the payment schedule. The schedule should use the following or a similar format and the same size paper as the Form 5500.

Note: *In column (a), place an asterisk (*) on the line of each identified person known to be a party-in-interest to the plan. In column (c), include any restriction on transferability of corporate securities. (Include lending of securities permitted under Prohibited Transactions Exemption 81-6.)*

(a)	**(b)** Identity of issue, borrower, lessor, or similar party	**(c)** Description of investment including maturity date, rate of interest, collateral, par or maturity value	**(d)** Cost	**(e)** Current value

The second schedule required to be attached to the Form 5500 is a schedule of investment assets which were both acquired and disposed of within the plan year (see 29 CFR 2520.103-11). The schedule should use the following or a similar format and the same size paper as the Form 5500.

(a) Identity of issue, borrower, lessor, or similar party	**(b)** Description of investment including maturity date, rate of interest, collateral, par or maturity value	**(c)** Costs of acquisitions	**(d)** Proceeds of dispositions

30b. Check "Yes," and attach the following schedule to the Form 5500 if the plan had any loans or fixed income obligations in default or determined to be uncollectible as of the end of the plan year. Include obligations where the required payments have not been made by the due date. With respect to notes and loans, the due date, payment amount and conditions for default are usually contained in the note or loan documents. Defaults can occur at any time for those obligations which require periodic repayment. Generally loans and fixed income obligations are considered uncollectible when payment has not been made and there is little probability that payment will be made. A loan by the plan is in default when the borrower is unable to pay the obligation upon maturity. A fixed income obligation has a fixed maturity date at a specified interest rate. List any loans by the plan which are in default and any fixed income obligations which have matured, but have not been paid, for which it has been determined that payment will not be made. The schedule should be in the following or similar format, use the same size paper as the Form 5500.

Note: *In column (a), place an asterisk (*) on the line of each identified person known to be a party-in-interest to the plan. Include all loans that were renegotiated during the plan year. Also, explain what steps have been taken or will be taken to collect overdue amounts for each loan listed.*

(a)	(b) Identity and address of obligor	(c) Original amount of loan	Amount received during reporting year		(f) Unpaid balance at end of year	(g) Detailed description of loan including dates of making and maturity, interest rate, the type and value of collateral, any renegotiation of the loan and the terms of the renegotiation and other material items	Amount overdue	
			(d) Principal	(e) Interest			(h) Principal	(i) Interest

30c. Check "Yes," and attach to the Form 5500 the following schedule if the plan had any leases in default or classified as uncollectible. The schedule should use the following or a similar format and the same size paper as the Form 5500.

A lease is an agreement conveying the right to use property, plant or equipment for a stated period. A lease is in default when the required payment(s) has not been made. An uncollectible lease is one where the required payments have not been made and for which there is little probability that payment will be made *Also. explain what steps have been taken or will be taken to collect overdue amounts for each lease listed.*

(a)	(b) Identity of lessor/lessee	(c) Relationship to plan, employer, employee organization or other party-in-interest	(d) Terms and description (type of property, location and date it was purchased, terms regarding rent, taxes, insurance, repairs, expenses, renewal options, date property was leased)	(e) Original cost	(f) Current value at time of lease	(g) Gross rental receipts during the plan year	(h) Expenses paid during the plan year	(i) Net receipts	(j) Amount in arrears

30d. Check "Yes" and attach to the Form 5500 the following schedule if the plan had any reportable transactions (see 29 CFR 2520 103-6). The schedule should use the following or a similar format and the same size paper as the Form 5500 A reportable transaction includes:

1. A single transaction within the plan year in excess of 5% of the current value of the plan assets;

2. Any series of transactions with, or in conjunction with, the same person, involving property other than securities, which amount in the aggregate within the plan year (regardless of the category of asset and the gain or loss on any transaction) to more than 5% of the current value of plan assets;

3. Any transaction within the plan year involving securities of the same issue if within the plan year any series of transactions with respect to such securities amount in the aggregate to more than 5% of the current value of the plan assets; and

4. Any transaction within the plan year with respect to securities with, or in conjunction with, a person if any prior or subsequent single transaction within the plan year with such person, with respect to securities, exceeds 5% of the current value of plan assets

The 5% figure is determined by comparing the current value of the transaction at the transaction date with the current value of the plan assets at the beginning of the plan year

If the assets of two or more plans are maintained in one trust, the plan's allocable portion of the transactions of the trust shall be combined with the other transactions of the plan, if any, to determine which transactions (or series of transactions) are reportable (5%) transactions. This does not apply to investment arrangements whose current value is reported in 34c(xi). Instead, for investments in common/collective trusts, pooled separate accounts, 103-12 IEs and registered investment companies, determine the 5% figure by comparing the transaction date value of the acquisition and/or disposition of units of participation or shares in the entity with the current value of the plan assets at the beginning of the plan year. Do not complete item 30d if all plan funds are held in a master trust. Plans with assets in a master trust which have other transactions should determine the 5% figure by subtracting the current value of plan assets held in the master trust from the current value of all plan assets at the beginning of the plan year. Do not include individual transactions of investment arrangements reported in 34c(xi).

In the case of a purchase or sale of a security on the market, do not identify the person from whom purchased or to whom sold.

(a) Identity of party involved	(b) Description of asset (include interest rate and maturity in case of a loan)	(c) Purchase price	(d) Selling price	(e) Lease rental	(f) Expense incurred with transaction	(g) Cost of asset	(h) Current value of asset on transaction date	(i) Net gain or (loss)

30e and f. Check "Yes," and attach the following schedule to the Form 5500 if the plan had any non-exempt transactions with a party-in-interest. For purposes of this form, party-in-interest is deemed to include a disqualified person (see Code section 4975(e)(2)). The term "party-in-interest" is defined on page 12 . Non-exempt transactions with a party-in-interest include any direct or indirect:

1. Sale or exchange, or leasing, of any property between the plan and a party-in-interest.
2. Lending of money or other extension of credit between the plan and party-in-interest.
3. Furnishing of goods, services, or facilities between the plan and a party-in-interest.
4. Transfer to, or use by or for the benefit of, a party-in-interest, of any income or assets of the plan.
5. Acquisition, on behalf of the plan, of any employer security or employer real property in violation of Code section 407(a).
6. Dealing with the assets of the plan for a fiduciary's own interest or own account.
7. Acting in a fiduciary's individual or in any other capacity in any transaction involving the plan on behalf of a party (or represent a party) whose interests are adverse to the interests of the plan or the interests of its participants or beneficiaries.

8. Receipt of any consideration for his or her own personal account by a party-in-interest who is a fiduciary for any party dealing with the plan in connection with a transaction involving the income or assets of the plan.

Do not check "Yes" for items 30e or 30f, or list transactions that are statutorily exempt under Part 4 of Title I of ERISA, or administratively exempt under ERISA section 408(a), or exempt under Code sections 4975(c) and 4975(d), or include transactions of a 103-12 IE with parties other than the plan. You may indicate that an application for an administrative exemption is pending.

If you are unsure as to whether a transaction is exempt or not, you should consult with either the plan's independent qualified public accountant or legal counsel or both.

Set out each transaction with the information set forth below in the following or similar format using the same size paper as the Form 5500.

If a nonexempt prohibited transaction occurred with respect to a disqualified person, file Form 5330 with IRS to pay the excise tax on the transaction.

(a) Identity of party involved	(b) Relationship to plan, employer or other party-in-interest	(c) Description of transactions including maturity date, rate of interest, collateral, par or maturity value	(d) Purchase price	(e) Selling price	(f) Lease rental	(g) Expenses incurred in connection with transaction	(h) Cost of asset	(i) Current value of asset	(j) Net gain or (loss) on each transaction

30g. Employer Security.—An employer security is any security issued by an employer (including affiliates of employees) covered by the plan. These may include common stocks, preferred stocks, bonds, zero coupon bonds, debentures, convertible debentures, notes, and commercial paper. Generally, a publicly traded security is a security which is bought and sold on a recognized market (e.g., NYSE, AMEX, over the counter, etc.) for which there is a pool of willing buyers and sellers. Securities which are listed on a market but for which there does not exist a pool of willing buyers and sellers are not publicly traded.

Qualifying Employer Security.—An employer security which is a stock or a "marketable obligation" is considered a qualifying employer security. For purposes of this definition, the term "marketable obligation" means a bond, debenture, note, certificate, or other evidence of indebtedness (obligation) if:

(i) such obligation is acquired —

(A) on the market, either: (1) at the price of the obligation prevailing on a national securities exchange which is registered with the Securities and Exchange Commission, or (2) if the obligation is not traded on such a national securities exchange, at a price not less favorable to the plan than the offering price for the obligation as established by current bid and asked prices quoted by persons independent of the issuer;

(B) from an underwriter, at a price: (1) not in excess of the public offering price for the obligation as set forth in a prospectus or offering circular filed with the Securities and Exchange Commission, and (2) at which a substantial portion of the same issue is acquired by persons independent of the issuer; or

(C) directly from the issuer, at a price not less favorable to the plan than the price paid currently for a substantial portion of the same issue by persons independent of the issuer;

(ii) immediately following the acquisition of such obligation—

(A) not more than 25% of the aggregate amount of obligations issued in such issue and outstanding at the time of acquisition is held by the plan, and

(B) at least 50% of the aggregate amount referred to in subparagraph (A) is held by persons independent of the issuer; and

(iii) immediately following the acquisition of the obligation, not more than 25% of the assets of the plan is invested in obligations of the employer or an affiliate of the employer.

For purposes of the qualifying employer security definition, the term "stock" must meet the following conditions:

1. No more than 25% of the aggregate amount of stock of the same class issued and outstanding at the time of acquisition is held by the plan, and

2. At least 50% of the aggregate amount of stock described in the preceding paragraph is held by persons independent of the issuer.

For exceptions to the above, see ERISA section 407(f).

30h. Generally, as it relates to this question, an appraisal by an unrelated third party is an evaluation of the value of a security prepared by an individual or firm who knows how to judge the value of securities and does not have an ongoing relationship with the plan or plan fiduciaries except for preparing the appraisal. Non-publicly traded securities are generally held by few people and not traded on a stock exchange.

32a(i). Generally, every plan official of an employee benefit plan who handles funds or other property of such plan must be bonded. A plan administrator, officer, or employee shall be deemed to be handling funds or other property of a plan, so as to require bonding, whenever his or her duties or activities with respect to given funds are such that there is a risk that such funds could be lost in the event of fraud or dishonesty on the part of such person, acting either alone or in collusion with others. Section 412 of ERISA and the regulations found at 29 CFR 2580 provide the bonding requirements, including the definition of "handling" (29 CFR 2580.412-6), the permissible forms of bonds (29 CFR 2580.412-10), and certain exemptions such as the exemption for unfunded plans, certain banks and insurance companies (ERISA section 412), and the exemption allowing plan officials to purchase bonds from surety companies authorized by the Secretary of the Treasury as acceptable reinsurers on Federal bonds (29 CFR 2580.412-23).

Check "Yes" only if the plan itself (as opposed to the plan sponsor) is a named insured under a fidelity bond covering plan officials.

Plans are permitted under certain conditions to purchase fiduciary liability insurance. These policies do not protect the plan from dishonest acts and are not bonds which should be reported in question 32.

32a(ii). Indicate the aggregate amount of coverage available for all claims.

32b(i). Check "Yes" if the plan has suffered or discovered any loss as the result of a dishonest or fraudulent act(s).

32b(ii). If item 32b(i) has been answered "Yes," enter the full amount of the loss. If the full amount of the loss has not yet been determined, provide and disclose that the figure is an estimate, such as "Approximately $1,000."

Note: *Willful failure to report is a criminal offense. See ERISA section 501.*

33a. If you are uncertain as to whether the plan is covered under the PBGC termination insurance program check the box "Not determined" and contact the PBGC and request a coverage determination. Welfare and fringe benefit plans do not complete this item.

34 and 35. You can use either the cash, modified accrual, or accrual basis for recognition of transactions in items 34 and 35, as long as you use one method consistently.

Round off all amounts in items 34 and 35 to the nearest dollar. Be sure to check all sub-totals and totals carefully.

Caution: *Do not mark through the printed line descriptions and insert your own description as this may cause additional correspondence due to a new computerized review of the Form 5500.*

"Current value" means fair market value, where available. Otherwise, it means the fair value as determined in good faith under the terms of the plan by a trustee or a named fiduciary, assuming an orderly liquidation at the time of the determination.

If the assets of two or more plans are maintained in one trust, such as when an employer has two plans which are funded through a single trust (except investment arrangements reported in 34c(xi)), complete items 34 and 35 by entering the plan's allocable part of each line item.

If assets of one plan are maintained in two or more trust funds, report the combined financial information in items 34 and 35.

Fully insured, unfunded, and unfunded/insured welfare plans, and fully insured pension plans meeting the conditions of 29 CFR 2520.104-44, need not complete items 34 and 35. To determine if your welfare plan is fully insured, unfunded, or unfunded/insured, see page 2.

To determine if your pension plan is fully insured, see page 4.

Exception: *Plans which are both welfare and fringe benefit plans must complete items 35e, 35g and 35h.*

34. Column (a) should be used to enter the current value of plan assets and liabilities as of the beginning of the plan year. Column (b) should be used to enter the current value of plan assets and liabilities as of the end of the plan year.

Amounts reported in column (a) must be the same as reported for corresponding line items in column (b) of the return/report for the preceding plan year.

34a. Total noninterest-bearing cash includes, among other things, cash on hand or cash in a noninterest-bearing checking account.

34b. Subtract any allowance for doubtful accounts from each receivable to obtain the net receivable for that line item.

34b(i). Noncash basis filers should include contributions due the plan by the employer but not yet paid. Do not include other amounts due from the employer such as the reimbursement of an expense or the repayment of a loan.

34b(ii). Noncash basis filers should include contributions withheld by the employer from participants and amounts due directly from participants which have not yet been received by the plan. Do not include the repayment of participant loans.

34b(iii). Noncash basis filers should include income from investment income earned but not yet received by the plan.

34b(iv). Noncash basis filers should include amounts due to the plan which are not includable in items 34b(i)–(iii) above. These may include amounts due from the employer or another plan for expense reimbursement or from a participant for the repayment of an overpayment of benefits.

34b(v). Add 34b(i), 34b(ii), 34b(iii) and 34b(iv) and enter the total.

34c(i). Include all assets which earn interest in a financial institution account or in a money market fund, including, interest bearing checking accounts, passbook savings accounts, et al.

34c(iii). Include securities issued or guaranteed by the U.S. Government or its designated agencies such as U.S. Savings Bonds, Treasury bonds, Treasury bills, FNMA, and GNMA.

34c(iv). Include investment securities issued by a corporate entity at a stated interest rate repayable on a particular future date such as most bonds, debentures, convertible debentures, commercial paper and zero coupon bonds. Do not include debt securities of Governmental units or municipalities reported under 34c(iii) or 34c(xiii).

34c(v)(A). Include stock issued by corporations which is accompanied by preferential rights such as the right to share in distributions of earnings at a higher rate or has general priority over the common stock of the same entity. Include the value of warrants convertible into preferred stock.

34c(v)(B). Include any stock which represents regular ownership of the corporation and is not accompanied by preferential rights plus the value of warrants convertible into common stock.

34c(vi). Include the value of the plan's participation in a partnership or joint venture if the underlying assets of the partnership or joint venture are not considered to be plan assets under 29 CFR 2510.3-101. Do not include the value of a plan's interest in a partnership or joint venture which is a 103-12 IE (see 34c(xi), below).

34c(vii)(A). Include the current value of real property owned by the plan which produces income from rentals, etc. This property is not to be included in item 34e, buildings and other property used in plan operations.

34c(vii)(B). Include the current value of real property owned by the plan which is not producing income or used in plan operations.

34c(viii)(A). Include the current value of all loans made by the plan to provide mortgage financing to purchasers (other than plan participants) of residential dwelling units, either by making or participating in loans directly or by purchasing mortgage loans originated by a third party. (For participant loans, see 34c(ix), below.)

34c(viii)(B). Include the current value of all loans made by the plan to provide mortgage financing to purchasers (other than participants) of commercial real estate, either by making or participating in the loans directly or by purchasing mortgage loans originated by a third party. (For participant loans, see 34c(ix), below).

34c(ix)(A). Include the current value of all loans to participants which are made by the plan to provide mortgage financing to participants who were purchasers of real property, irrespective of whether the mortgage was for residential, commercial or farm property.

34c(ix)(B). Include the balance of any loans made to participants which were not reported in 34c(ix)(A).

34c(x). Include all loans made by the plan which are not to be reported elsewhere in item 34 such as loans for construction, securities loans, and other miscellaneous loans.

34c(xi). Enter the current value of the sum of the plan's interest in common/collective trusts, pooled separate accounts, master trusts, 103-12 IEs and registered investment companies (registered under the Investment Company Act of 1940) at the beginning and end of the plan year. If some plan funds are held in these investment arrangements, and other plan funds are held in other funding media, complete all applicable sub-items of item 34 with regard to assets held in other funding media.

A plan investing in common/collective trusts or pooled separate accounts should attach to the return/report either the statement of assets and liabilities of the common/collective trust or pooled separate account or the certification discussed on page 3 of these instructions.

The value of the plan's interest in a master trust is the sum of the net values of the plan's interest in master trust investment accounts. The net values of such interests are obtained by multiplying the plan's percentage interest in each master trust investment account by the net assets of the investment account (total assets minus total liabilities) at the beginning and end of the plan year.

34c(xii). You can use the same method for determining the value of the insurance contracts reported in 34c(xii) that you used for line 6e of the Schedule A (Form 5500) as long as the contract values are stated as of the beginning and end of the plan year.

34c(xiii). Other investments include options, index futures, repurchase agreements, and state and municipal securities among other things.

34c(xiv). Add items 34c(i) through 34c(xiii) and enter the total.

34d. See 30g on page 14 for the definition of employer security.

34e. Include the current (not book) value of the buildings and other property used in the operation of the plan. Buildings or other property held as plan investments should be reported in item 34c(vii)(A) or (B), or 34d(ii).

34f. Add items 34a, 34b(v), 34c(xiv), 34d(i), 34d(ii) and 34e and enter the total.

Do not include the value of future pension payments in 34g, 34h, 34i, 34j or 34k.

34g. Noncash basis plans should include the total amount of benefit claims which have been processed and approved for payment by the plan.

34h. Noncash basis plans should include the total amount of obligations owed by the plan which were incurred in the normal operations of the plan and have been approved for payment by the plan but have not been paid.

34i. Acquisition Indebtedness.—"Acquisition indebtedness," for debt-financed property other than real property, means the outstanding amount of the principal debt incurred:

(1) by the organization in acquiring or improving the property;

(2) before the acquisition or improvement of the property if the debt was incurred only to acquire or improve the property; or

(3) after the acquisition or improvement of the property if the debt was incurred only to acquire or improve the property and was reasonably foreseeable at the time of such acquisition or improvement.

For further explanation, see Code section 514(c).

34j. Noncash basis plans should include amounts owed for any liabilities which would not be classified as benefit claims payable, operating payables, or acquisition indebtedness.

35a(i). Include the total cash contributions received and/or (for accrual basis plans) due to be received.

35a(ii). Use the current value, at date contributed, of securities or other noncash property.

35b(i)(A). Include the interest earned on interest-bearing cash. This is derived from investments which are includable in 34c(i), including earnings from sweep accounts, STIF accounts, etc.

35b(i)(B). Include the interest earned on certificates of deposit. This is the interest earned on the investments which are reported on line 34c(ii).

35b(i)(C). Include the interest earned on U.S. Government securities. This is the interest earned on the investments which are reported on line 34c(iii).

35b(i)(D). Generally, this is the interest earned on securities which are reported on line(s) 34c(iv) and 34d(i).

35b(i)(E). Include the interest earned on the investments which are reported on line(s) 34c(viii)(A) and (B) and 34c(ix)(A).

35b(i)(F). Include the interest earned on the investments which are reported on lines(s) 34c(ix)(B) and 34c(x).

35b(i)(G). Include any interest not reported in 35b(i)(A)–(F).

35b(ii) (A) and (B). Generally, these dividends are from the investments which are reported in items 34c(v)(A) and (B) and 34d(i).

For accrual basis plans, include any dividends declared for stock held on the date of record, but not yet received as of the end of the plan year.

35b(iii). Generally, rents represent the income earned on the real property which is reported in items 34c(vii)(A) and 34d(ii). Rents should be entered as a "Net" figure. Net rents are determined by taking the total rent received and subtracting all expenses directly associated with the property. If the real property is jointly used as income producing property and for the operation of the plan, that portion of the expenses attributable to the income producing portion of the property should be netted against the total rents received.

35b(iv). Column (b), total of net gain (loss) on sale of assets, should reflect the sum of the net realized gain (or loss) on each asset held at the beginning of the plan year which was sold or exchanged during the plan year and each asset which was both acquired and disposed of within the plan year.

Note: *As current value reporting is required for the Form 5500, assets are revalued to current value at the end of the plan year. For the purposes of this form, the increase or decrease in the value of assets since the beginning of the plan year (if held on the first day of the plan year) or their acquisition date (if purchased during the plan year) is reported in item 35b(v) below, with two exceptions: (1) the realized gain (or loss) on each asset which was disposed of during the plan year is reported in 35b(iv) (NOT in 35b(v)), and (2) the net investment gain (or loss) from certain investment arrangements is reported in item 35b(vi).*

The sum of the realized gain (or loss) of all assets sold or exchanged during the plan year is to be calculated by—

(1) entering the sum of the amount received for these former assets in 35b(iv), column (a), line (A),

(2) entering in 35b(iv), column (a), line (B), the sum of the current value of these former assets as of the beginning of the plan year, for those assets on hand at the beginning of the plan year, or the purchase price for those assets acquired during the plan year, and

(3) subtracting (B) from (A) and entering this result in column (b).

A negative figure should be placed in parentheses.

35b(v). Subtract the current value of assets at the beginning of the year plus the cost of any assets acquired during the plan year from the current value of assets at the end of the year to obtain this figure. A negative figure should be placed in parentheses. Do not include assets which were disposed of within the plan year (reportable in 35b(iv) above) or certain investment arrangements (reportable in 35b(vi) below).

35b(vi). For purposes of this item, investment arrangements include investments includable in 34c(xi). Report all earnings, expenses, gains or losses, and unrealized appreciation or depreciation which were included in computing the net investment gain (or loss) from any such investment arrangement here. If some plan funds are held in any of these investment arrangements and other plan funds are held in other funding media, complete all applicable sub-items of item 35 to report plan earnings, and expenses, relating to the other funding media.

The net investment gain (or loss) allocated to the plan for the plan year from the plan's investment in these investment arrangements is equal to:

(A) the sum of the current value of the plan's interest in each investment arrangement at the end of the plan year,

(B) minus the current value of the plan's interest in each investment arrangement at the beginning of the plan year,

(C) plus any amounts transferred out of each investment arrangement by the plan during the plan year, and

(D) minus any amounts transferred into each investment arrangement by the plan during the plan year.

Enter the net gain as a positive number or the net loss in parentheses on line 35b(vi).

35c. Include any other plan income earned that is not included in 35a or 35b. Do not include transfers from other plans which should be reported in item 35j.

35d. Add items 35a, 35b, and 35c and enter the total income.

35e. If distributions include securities or other property, use the current value at date distributed for this item. See page 14 for the definition of current value. If this return/report is being filed only for a fringe benefit plan (or for both a fringe benefit plan and a welfare benefit plan which is exempt from completing item 35), you must complete items 35g and 35h (reasonable estimates will be acceptable for these figures).

35e(i). Include the current value of all cash, securities or other property at the date of distribution.

35e(ii). Include payments to insurance companies and similar organizations such as Blue Cross, Blue Shield and health maintenance organizations for the provision of plan benefits, e.g., paid-up annuities, accident insurance, health insurance, vision care, dental coverage, etc.

35e(iii). Include payments made to other organizations or individuals providing benefits. Generally, these are individual providers of welfare benefits such as legal services, day care services, training and apprenticeship services.

35f. Interest expense is a monetary charge for the use of money borrowed by the plan. This amount should include the total of interest paid or to be paid (for accrual basis plans) during the plan year.

35g. Expenses incurred in the general operations of the plan are classified as administrative expenses. Report all administrative expenses (by specified category) paid by or charged to the plan, including those which were not subtracted from the gross income of common/collective trusts, pooled separate accounts, master trust investment accounts, and 103-12 IEs in determining their net investment gain(s) or loss(es). If this return/report is filed only for a fringe benefit plan and NOT for a welfare benefit plan, do not include overhead expenses such as utilities and photocopying expenses. Also, if you are filing for an educational assistance program described in Code section 127, do not include expenses for job-related training which are deductible under Code section 162.

35g(i). Include all of the plan's expenditures such as salaries and the payment of premiums to provide benefits to plan employees (e.g., health insurance, life insurance, etc.).

35g(ii). Include the total fees paid (or in the case of accrual basis plans, costs incurred during the plan year but not paid as of the end of the plan year) by the plan for outside accounting services. These may include the fee(s) for the annual audit of the plan by an independent qualified public accountant, for payroll audits, and for accounting/bookkeeping services. These do not include amounts paid to plan employees to perform accounting functions.

35g(iii). Include the total fees paid (or in the case of accrual basis plans, costs incurred during the plan year but not paid as of the end of the plan year) to an actuary for services rendered to the plan.

35g(iv). Include the total fees paid (or in the case of accrual basis plans, costs incurred during the plan year but not paid as of the end of the plan year) to a contract administrator for performing administrative services for the plan. For purposes of the return/report, a contract administrator is any individual, partnership, or corporation, responsible for managing the clerical operations (e.g., handling membership rosters, claims payments, maintaining books and records) of the plan on a contractual basis. Do not include salaried staff or employees of the plan or banks, or insurance carriers.

35g(v). Include the total fees paid (or in the case of accrual basis plans, costs incurred during the plan year but not paid as of the end of the plan year) to an individual, partnership or corporation (or other person) for advice to the plan relating to its investment portfolio. These may include fees paid to manage the plan's investments, fees for specific advice on a particular investment, and fees for the evaluation of the plan's investment performance.

35g(vi). Include total fees paid (or in the case of accrual basis plans, costs incurred during the plan year but not paid as of the end of the plan year) to a lawyer for services rendered to the plan. Include fees paid for rendering legal opinions, litigation, and advice but not for providing legal services as a benefit to plan participants.

35g(vii). Include the total fees paid (or in the case of accrual basis plans, costs incurred during the plan year but not paid as of the end of the plan year) for valuations or appraisals to determine the cost, quality, or value of an item. These may include the fee(s) paid for appraisals of real property (real estate, gemstones, coins, etc.), and a valuation of closely held securities for which there is no ready market.

35g(viii). Include the total fees and expenses paid to or on behalf of plan trustees (or in the case of accrual basis plans, costs incurred during the plan year but not paid as of the end of the plan year). These may include reimbursement of expenses associated with trustees such as lost time, seminars, travel, meetings, etc.

35g(ix). Other expenses are those that cannot be associated definitely with items 35g(i) through 35g(viii). All miscellaneous expenses are also included in this figure. These may include expenses for office supplies and equipment, cars, telephone, postage, rent, and expenses associated with the ownership of a building used in the operation of the plan.

35h. Add column (b) of items 35e, 35f, and 35g.

35i. Subtract item 35h from item 35d

35j. Include in this reconciliation figure any transfers of assets into or out of the plan resulting from mergers and consolidations of plans or associated with benefit liabilities which are also being transferred. A transfer is not a shifting of assets or liabilities from one investment medium to another used for a single plan (e.g., between a trust and an annuity contract). Transfers out should be shown in parentheses.

35k. Include amount of net assets at the beginning of the year. This amount must equal item 34l, column (a).

35l. Include the amount of net assets at the end of the year. This amount must equal item 34l, column (b).

Codes for Principal Business Activity and Principal Product or Service

These industry titles and definitions are based, in general, on the Enterprise Standard Industrial Classification System authorized by the Regulatory and Statistical Analysis Division, Office of Information and Regulatory Affairs, Office of Management and Budget, to classify enterprises by type of activity in which they are engaged.

Code

AGRICULTURE, FORESTRY, AND FISHING

0120 Field crop.
0150 Fruit, tree nut, and vegetable.
0180 Horticultural specialty.
0230 Livestock.
0270 Animal specialty.

Agricultural services and forestry:

0740 Veterinary services.
0750 Animal services, except veterinary.
0780 Landscape and horticultural services.
0790 Other agricultural services.
0800 Forestry.

Farms:

Fishing, hunting, and trapping:

0930 Commercial fishing, hatcheries, and preserves.
0970 Hunting, trapping, and game propagation.

MINING

Metal mining:

1010 Iron ores.
1070 Copper, lead and zinc, gold and silver ores.
1098 Other metal mining.
1150 Coal mining.

Oil and gas extraction:

1330 Crude petroleum, natural gas, and natural gas liquids.
1380 Oil and gas field services.

Nonmetallic minerals (except fuels) mining:

1430 Dimension, crushed and broken stone; sand and gravel.
1498 Other nonmetallic minerals, except fuels.

CONSTRUCTION

General building contractors and operative builders:

1510 General building contractors.
1531 Operative builders.

Heavy construction contractors:

1611 Highway and street construction.
1620 Heavy construction, except highway.

Special trade contractors:

1711 Plumbing, heating, and air conditioning.
1721 Painting, paperhanging, and decorating.
1731 Electrical work.
1740 Masonry, stonework, and plastering.
1750 Carpentering and flooring.
1761 Roofing and sheet metal work.
1771 Concrete work.
1781 Water well drilling.
1790 Miscellaneous special trade contractors.

MANUFACTURING

Food and kindred products:

2010 Meat products.
2020 Dairy products.
2030 Preserved fruits and vegetables.
2040 Grain mill products.
2050 Bakery products.
2060 Sugar and confectionery products.
2081 Malt liquors and malt.
2088 Alcoholic beverages, except malt liquors and malt.
2089 Bottled soft drinks and flavorings.
2096 Other food and kindred products.
2100 Tobacco manufacturers.

Textile mill products:

2228 Weaving mills and textile finishing.
2250 Knitting mills.
2298 Other textile mill products.

Apparel and other textile products:

2315 Men's and boys' clothing.
2345 Women's and children's clothing.
2388 Hats, caps, millinery, fur goods, and other apparel and accessories.
2390 Misc. fabricated textile products.

Code

Lumber and wood products:

2415 Logging camps and logging contractors, sawmills, and planing mills.
2430 Millwork, plywood, and related products.
2498 Other wood products, including wood buildings and mobile homes
2500 Furniture and fixtures.

Paper and allied products:

2625 Pulp, paper, and board mills.
2699 Other paper products.

Printing, publishing, and allied industries:

2710 Newspapers.
2720 Periodicals.
2735 Books, greeting cards, and miscellaneous publishing.
2799 Commercial and other printing, and printing trade services.

Chemical and allied products:

2815 Industrial chemicals, plastics materials, and synthetics.
2830 Drugs.
2840 Soap, cleaners, and toilet goods.
2850 Paints and allied products.
2898 Agricultural and other chemical products.

Petroleum refining and related industries (including those integrated with extraction):

2910 Petroleum refining (including those integrated with extraction).
2998 Other petroleum and coal products.

Rubber and misc. plastics products:

3050 Rubber products, plastics footwear, hose, and belting.
3070 Misc. plastics products.

Leather and leather products:

3140 Footwear, except rubber.
3198 Other leather and leather products.

Stone, clay, glass, and concrete products:

3225 Glass products.
3240 Cement, hydraulic.
3270 Concrete, gypsum, and plaster products.
3298 Other nonmetallic mineral products.

Primary metal industries:

3370 Ferrous metal industries; miscellaneous primary metal products.
3380 Nonferrous metal industries.

Fabricated metal products, except machinery and transportation equipment:

3410 Metal cans and shipping containers.
3428 Cutlery, hand tools, and hardware; screw machine products, bolts, and similar products.
3430 Plumbing and heating, except electric and warm air.
3440 Fabricated structural metal products.
3460 Metal forgings and stampings.
3470 Coating, engraving, and allied services.
3480 Ordnance and accessories, except vehicles and guided missiles.
3490 Misc. fabricated metal products.

Machinery, except electrical:

3520 Farm machinery.
3530 Construction, mining and materials handling machinery, and equipment.
3540 Metalworking machinery.
3550 Special industry machinery, except metalworking machinery.
3560 General industrial machinery.
3570 Office, computing, and accounting machines.
3598 Engines and turbines, service industry machinery, and other machinery, except electrical.

Code

Electrical and electronic machinery, equipment, and supplies:

3630 Household appliances.
3665 Radio, television, and communication equipment.
3670 Electronic components and accessories.
3698 Other electric equipment.

Transportation equipment:

3710 Motor vehicles and equipment.
3725 Aircraft, guided missiles, and parts.
3730 Ship and boat building and repairing.
3798 Other transportation equipment.

Measuring and controlling instruments; photographic and medical goods, watches and clocks:

3815 Scientific instruments and measuring devices; watches, and clocks.
3845 Optical, medical, and ophthalmic goods.
3860 Photographic equipment and supplies.
3998 Other manufacturing products.

TRANSPORTATION, COMMUNICATION, ELECTRIC, GAS, SANITARY SERVICES

Transportation:

4000 Railroad transportation.

Local and interurban passenger transit:

4121 Taxicabs.
4189 Other passenger transportation.

Trucking and warehousing:

4210 Trucking, local and long distance.
4289 Public warehousing and trucking terminals.

Other transportation including transportation services:

4400 Water transportation.
4500 Transportation by air.
4600 Pipelines, except natural gas.
4722 Passenger transportation arrangement.
4723 Freight transportation arrangement.
4799 Other transportation services.

Communication:

4825 Telephone, telegraph, and other communication services.
4830 Radio and television broadcasting.

Electric, gas, and sanitary services:

4910 Electric services.
4920 Gas production and distribution.
4930 Combination utility services.
4990 Water supply and other sanitary services.

WHOLESALE TRADE

Durable:

5010 Motor vehicles and automotive equipment.
5020 Furniture and home furnishings.
5030 Lumber and construction materials.
5040 Sporting, recreational, photographic, and hobby goods, toys, and supplies.
5050 Metals and minerals, except petroleum and scrap.
5060 Electrical goods.
5070 Hardware, plumbing, and heating equipment.
5083 Farm machinery and equipment.
5089 Other machinery, equipment, and supplies.
5098 Other durable goods.

Nondurable:

5110 Paper and paper products.
5129 Drugs, drug proprietaries, and druggists' sundries.
5130 Apparel, piece goods, and notions.
5140 Groceries and related products, except meats and meat products.
5147 Meats and meat products.
5150 Farm product raw materials.
5160 Chemicals and allied products.
5170 Petroleum and petroleum products.
5180 Alcoholic beverages.
5190 Miscellaneous nondurable goods.

Code	
	RETAIL TRADE
	Building materials hardware, garden supply, and mobile home dealers:
5211	Lumber and other building materials dealers.
5231	Paint, glass and wallpaper stores.
5251	Hardware stores.
5261	Retail nurseries and garden stores.
5271	Mobile home dealers.
	General merchandise:
5331	Variety stores.
5398	Other general merchandise stores.
	Food stores:
5411	Grocery stores.
5420	Meat and fish markets and freezer provisioners.
5431	Fruit stores and vegetable markets.
5441	Candy, nut, and confectionery stores.
5451	Dairy products stores.
5460	Retail bakeries.
5490	Other food stores.
	Automotive dealers and service stations:
5511	New car dealers (franchised).
5521	Used car dealers.
5531	Auto and home supply stores.
5541	Gasoline service stations.
5551	Boat dealers.
5561	Recreational vehicle dealers.
5571	Motorcycle dealers.
5599	Aircraft and other automotive dealers.
	Apparel and accessory stores:
5611	Men's and boys' clothing and furnishings.
5621	Women's ready-to-wear stores.
5631	Women's accessory and specialty stores.
5641	Children's and infants' wear stores.
5651	Family clothing stores.
5661	Shoe stores.
5681	Furriers and fur shops.
5699	Other apparel and accessory stores.
	Furniture, home furnishings, and equipment stores:
5712	Furniture stores.
5713	Floor covering stores.
5714	Drapery, curtain, and upholstery stores.
5719	Home furnishings, except appliances.
5722	Household appliance stores.
5732	Radio and television stores.
5733	Music stores.
	Eating and drinking places:
5812	Eating places.
5813	Drinking places.
	Miscellaneous retail stores:
5912	Drug stores and proprietary stores.
5921	Liquor stores.
5931	Used merchandise stores.
5941	Sporting goods stores and bicycle shops.
5942	Book stores.
5943	Stationery stores.
5944	Jewelry stores.
5945	Hobby, toy, and game shops.
5946	Camera and photographic supply stores.
5947	Gift, novelty, and souvenir shops.
5948	Luggage and leather goods stores.
5949	Sewing, needlework, and piece goods stores
5961	Mail order houses.
5962	Merchandising machine operators.
5963	Direct selling organizations.
5982	Fuel and ice dealers (except fuel oil and bottle gas dealers).
5983	Fuel oil dealers.
5984	Liquefied petroleum gas (bottled gas).
5992	Florists.
5993	Cigar stores and stands.
5994	News dealers and newsstands.
5996	Other miscellaneous retail stores.

Code	
	FINANCE, INSURANCE, AND REAL ESTATE
	Banking:
6030	Mutual savings banks.
6060	Banking holding companies.
6090	Banks, except mutual savings banks and bank holding companies.
	Credit agencies other than banks:
6120	Savings and loan associations.
6140	Personal credit institutions.
6150	Business credit institutions.
6199	Other credit agencies.
	Security, commodity brokers, dealers, exchanges, and services:
6212	Security underwriting syndicates.
6218	Security brokers and dealers, except underwriting syndicates.
6299	Commodity contracts brokers and dealers; security and commodity exchanges; and allied services.
	Insurance:
6355	Life insurance.
6356	Mutual insurance, except life or marine and certain fire or flood insurance companies.
6359	Other insurance companies.
6411	Insurance agents, brokers, and services.
	Real estate:
6511	Real estate operators (except developers) and lessors of buildings.
6516	Lessors of mining, oil, and similar property.
6518	Lessors of railroad property and other real property.
6531	Real estate agents, brokers and managers.
6541	Title abstract offices.
6552	Subdividers and developers, except cemeteries.
6553	Cemetery subdividers and developers.
6599	Other real estate.
6611	Combined real estate, insurance, loans and law offices.
	Holding and other investment companies:
6742	Regulated investment companies.
6743	Real estate investment trusts.
6744	Small business investment companies.
6749	Holding and other investment companies, except bank holding companies.
	SERVICES
	Hotels and other lodging places:
7012	Hotels.
7013	Motels, motor hotels, and tourist courts.
7021	Rooming and boarding houses.
7032	Sporting and recreational camps.
7033	Trailer parks and camp sites.
7041	Organizational hotels and lodging houses on a membership basis.
	Personal services:
7215	Coin-operated laundries and dry cleaning.
7219	Other laundry, cleaning and garment services.
7221	Photographic studios, portrait.
7231	Beauty shops.
7241	Barber shops.
7251	Shoe repair and hat cleaning shops.
7261	Funeral services and crematories.
7299	Miscellaneous personal services.
	Business services:
7310	Advertising.
7340	Services to buildings.
7370	Computer and data processing services.
7392	Management, consulting, and public relations services.
7394	Equipment rental and leasing.
7398	Other business services.

Code	
	Automotive repair and services:
7510	Automotive rentals and leasing, without drivers.
7520	Automobile parking.
7531	Automobile top and body repair shops.
7538	General automobile repair shops.
7539	Other automobile repair shops.
7540	Automobile services, except repair.
	Miscellaneous repair services:
7622	Radio and TV repair shops.
7628	Electrical repair shops, except radio and TV.
7641	Reupholstery and furniture repair.
7680	Other miscellaneous repair shops.
	Motion pictures:
7812	Motion picture production, distribution, and services.
7830	Motion picture theaters.
	Amusement and recreation services:
7920	Producers, orchestras, and entertainers.
7932	Billiard and pool establishments.
7933	Bowling alleys.
7980	Other amusement and recreation services.
	Medical and health services:
8011	Offices of physicians.
8021	Offices of dentists.
8031	Offices of osteopathic physicians.
8041	Offices of chiropractors.
8042	Offices of optometrists.
8048	Registered and practical nurses.
8050	Nursing and personal care facilities.
8060	Hospitals.
8071	Medical laboratories.
8072	Dental laboratories.
8098	Other medical and health services.
	Other services:
8111	Legal services.
8200	Educational services.
8911	Engineering and architectural services.
8932	Certified public accountants.
8933	Other accounting, auditing, and bookkeeping services.
8999	Other services, not elsewhere classified.
	TAX-EXEMPT ORGANIZATIONS
9002	Church plans making an election under section 410(d) of the Internal Revenue Code.
9319	Other tax-exempt organizations.
9904	Governmental instrumentality or agency.

Form **5500-C**
Department of the Treasury
Internal Revenue Service
Department of Labor
Pension and Welfare Benefits Administration
Pension Benefit Guaranty Corporation

Return/Report of Employee Benefit Plan

(With fewer than 100 participants)

This form is required to be filed under sections 104 and 4065 of the Employee Retirement Income Security Act of 1974 and sections 6039D, 6057(b), and 6058(a) of the Internal Revenue Code, referred to as the Code.

OMB No. 1210-0016

1988

This Form Is Open to Public Inspection.

For the calendar plan year 1988 or fiscal plan year beginning , 1988, and ending , 19

If your plan year changed since the last return/report filed, check this box ▶ . . . ☐

Type or print in ink all entries on the form, schedules, and attachments. If an item does not apply, enter "N/A." File the originals.

If *(i)* through *(iii)* do not apply to this year's return/report, leave the boxes unmarked. This return/report is:

(i) ☐ the first return/report filed for the plan; *(ii)* ☐ an amended return/report; or *(iii)* ☐ the final return/report filed for the plan.

▶ Welfare benefit plans and fringe benefit plans need only complete certain items or may not be required to file—see instructions "What to File."

▶ One-participant plans file Form 5500EZ for 1988.

▶ If you have been granted an extension of time to file this form, you must attach a copy of the approved extension to this form.

Use IRS label. Otherwise, please print or type.

1a Name of plan sponsor (employer, if for a single-employer plan) | **1b** Employer identification number

Address (number and street) | **1c** Telephone number of sponsor ( )

City or town, state, and ZIP code | **1d** Business code number

1e CUSIP issuer number

2a Name of plan administrator (if same as plan sponsor, enter "Same")

Address (number and street) | **2b** Administrator's employer identification no.

City or town, state, and ZIP code | **2c** Telephone number of administrator ( )

3 Are the name, address, and employer identification number (EIN) of the plan sponsor and/or plan administrator the same as they appeared on the last return/report filed for this plan? ☐ Yes ☐ No If "No," enter the information from the last return/report in a and/or b, and complete c.

a Sponsor ▶ ______ EIN ______ Plan number ______

b Administrator ▶ ______ EIN ______

c If a indicates a change in the sponsor's name and EIN, is this a change in sponsorship only? (See specific instructions for definition of sponsorship.) ☐ Yes ☐ No

4 Check box to indicate the type of plan entity (check only one box):

a ☐ Single-employer plan

b ☐ Plan of controlled group of corporations or common control employers

c ☐ Multiemployer plan

d ☐ Multiple-employer-collectively-bargained plan

e ☐ Multiple-employer plan (other)

f ☐ Exceptions to (b) and (e). (See instructions for line 4f.)

5a *(i)* Name of plan ▶ ______

(ii) ☐ Check if name of plan changed since the last return/report

(iii) ☐ Check this box if this plan covers self-employed participants

5b Effective date of plan

5c Enter three-digit plan number . . . . ▶

6a ☐ Welfare benefit plan (plan numbers 501 through 999) must check applicable items A through P and 6c

(i) ☐ Type

A ☐ Health (other than dental or vision)
B ☐ Life insurance
C ☐ Supplemental unemployment
D ☐ Dental
E ☐ Vision
F ☐ Temporary disability (accident and sickness)
G ☐ Prepaid legal
H ☐ Long-term disability
I ☐ Severance pay
J ☐ Apprenticeship and training
K ☐ Scholarship (funded)
L ☐ Death benefits other than life insurance
M ☐ Code section 120 (group legal services plan)
N ☐ Code section 125 (cafeteria plan)
O ☐ Code section 127 (educational assistance plan)
P ☐ Other (specify) ______

(ii) If you checked M, N, or O, check if plan is: ☐ funded or ☐ unfunded

6b ☐ Pension benefit plan (plan numbers 001 through 500) must check applicable items in (i) through (vii) and answer 6c through 6f.

(i) ☐ Defined benefit plan

(ii) ☐ Defined contribution plan—(indicate type of defined contribution): (A) ☐ Profit-sharing (B) ☐ Stock bonus (C) ☐ Target benefit (D) ☐ Other money purchase (E) ☐ Other (specify) ▶ ______

(iii) ☐ Defined benefit plan with benefits based partly on balance of separate account of participant (Code section 414(k))

(iv) ☐ Annuity arrangement of certain exempt organizations (Code section 403(b)(1))

(v) ☐ Custodial account for regulated investment company stock (Code section 403(b)(7))

(vi) ☐ Pension plan utilizing individual retirement accounts or annuities (described in Code section 408) as the sole funding vehicle for providing benefits

(vii) ☐ Other (specify) ▶

Under penalties of perjury and other penalties set forth in the instructions, I declare that I have examined this return/report, including accompanying schedules and statements, and to the best of my knowledge and belief it is true, correct, and complete.

Date ▶ ______ Signature of employer/plan sponsor ▶ ______

Date ▶ ______ Signature of plan administrator ▶ ______

For Paperwork Reduction Act Notice, see page 1 of the Instructions.

Form **5500-C** (1988)

Form 5500-C (1988) Page **2**

		Yes	No
6c Other plan features: *(i)* ☐ ESOP *(ii)* ☐ Leveraged ESOP *(iii)* ☐ Participant-directed account plan *(iv)* ☐ Pension plan maintained outside the United States *(v)* ☐ Master trust (see instructions) *(vi)* ☐ 103-12 investment entity (see instructions) *(vii)* ☐ Common/Collective trust *(viii)* ☐ Pooled separate account			
d Single-employer plans enter the tax year end of the employer in which this plan year ends ▶ Month ______ Day ____ Year _____			
e Is the employer a member of an affiliated service group?	e		
f Does this plan contain a cash or deferred arrangement described in Code section 401(k)?	f		
7a Total participants: *(i)* Beginning of plan year __________ *(ii)* End of plan year __________			
b *(i)* Were any participants in the pension benefit plan separated from service with a deferred vested benefit for which a Schedule SSA (Form 5500) is required to be attached?	(i)		
(ii) If "Yes," enter the number of separated participants required to be reported ▶			
8a Were any plan amendments adopted during the plan year?	a		
b Did any amendment result in the retroactive reduction of accrued benefits for any participant?	b		
c Enter the date the most recent amendment was adopted ▶ Month ________ Day ______ Year ______			
d If a is "Yes," did any amendment change the information contained in the latest summary plan descriptions or summary description of modifications available at the time of the amendment?	d		
e Has a summary plan description or summary description of modifications that reflects the plan amendments referred to in d been furnished to participants and filed with the Department of Labor?	e		
9a Was this plan terminated during this plan year or any prior plan year? If "Yes," enter year ▶ ________	9a		
b Were all plan assets either distributed to participants or beneficiaries, transferred to another plan, or brought under the control of PBGC?	b		
c Was a resolution to terminate this plan adopted during this plan year or any prior plan year?	c		
d If a or c is "Yes," have you received a favorable determination letter from IRS for the termination?	d		
e If d is "No," has a determination letter been requested from IRS?	e		
f If a or c is "Yes," have participants and beneficiaries been notified of the termination or the proposed termination?	f		
g If a is "Yes" and the plan is covered by PBGC, is the plan continuing to file a PBGC Form 1 and pay premiums until the end of the plan year in which assets are distributed or brought under the control of PBGC?	g		
h During this plan year, did any trust assets revert to the employer for which the Code section 4980 excise tax is due?	h		
i If h is "Yes," enter the amount of tax paid with your Form 5330 ▶			
10a Was this plan merged or consolidated into another plan(s), or were assets or liabilities transferred to another plan(s) since the end of the plan year covered by the last return/report Form 5500 or 5500-C which was filed for this plan (or during this plan year if this is the initial return/report)?	10a		

If "Yes," identify the other plan(s):

b Name of plan(s) ▶	**c** Employer identification number(s)	**d** Plan number(s)

e Has Form 5310 been filed? ☐ Yes ☐ No

11 Enter the plan funding arrangement code (see instructions) ▶

12 Enter the plan benefit arrangement code (see instructions) ▶

		Yes	No
13 Is this a plan established or maintained pursuant to one or more collective bargaining agreements?	13		
14 If any benefits are provided by an insurance company, insurance service, or similar organization, enter the number of Schedules A (Form 5500), Insurance Information, that are attached. If none, enter "-0-" ▶			

Welfare Plans Do Not Complete Items 15 Through 28. Skip to item 29.

15a If this is a defined benefit plan, is it subject to the minimum funding standards for this plan year? If "Yes," attach Schedule B (Form 5500).		a	
b If this is a defined contribution plan, i.e., money purchase or target benefit, is it subject to the minimum funding standards (if a waiver was granted, see instructions)? If "Yes," complete *(i)*, *(ii)*, and *(iii)* below:		b	
(i) Amount of employer contribution required for the plan year under Code section 412	(i) $		
(ii) Amount of contribution paid by the employer for the plan year	(ii) $		
Enter date of last payment by employer ▶ Month ________ Day ______ Year ______			
(iii) If *(i)* is greater than *(ii)*, subtract *(ii)* from *(i)* and enter the funding deficiency here. Otherwise, enter zero. (If you have a funding deficiency, file Form 5330.)	(iii) $		
16 Has the plan been top-heavy at any time beginning with the 1984 plan year?		16	
17 Has the plan accepted any transfers or rollovers with respect to a participant who has attained age 70½?		17	

Form 5500-C (1988) Page 3

		Yes	No
18a If the plan distributed any annuity contracts this year, did these contracts contain a requirement that the spouse consent before any distributions under the contract are made in a form other than a qualified joint and survivor annuity?	18a		
b Did the plan make distributions to participants or beneficiaries in a form other than a qualified joint and survivor annuity (a life annuity if a single person) or qualified preretirement survivor annuity (exclude deferred annuity contracts)?	b		
c Did the plan make distributions or loans to married participants and beneficiaries without the required consent of the participant's spouse?	c		
d Upon plan amendment or termination, do the accrued benefits of every participant include the subsidized benefits that the participant may become entitled to receive subsequent to the plan amendment or termination?	d		
19 Were distributions made in accordance with the requirements of Code section 417(e)? (See instructions.)	19		
20 Have any contributions been made or benefits accrued in excess of the Code section 415 limits, as amended by the Tax Reform Act of 1986?	20		
21 Has the plan made the required distributions in 1988 under Code section 401(a)(9)?	21		
22a Does the plan satisfy the percentage test of Code section 410(b)(1)(A)?	22a		

If a is "Yes," complete b through i. If "No," complete only b and c below and see Specific Instructions.

		Number
b *(i)* Number of employees who are aggregated with employees of the employer as a result of being an affiliated service group under Code section 414(b), (c), or (m)	(i)	
(ii) Number of individuals who performed services as leased employees under Code section 414(n) including leased employees of employers in (i)	(ii)	
c Total number of employees (including any employees aggregated in b)	c	
d Number of employees excluded under the plan because of *(i)* minimum age or years of service, *(ii)* employees on whose behalf retirement benefits were the subject of collective bargaining, or *(iii)* nonresident aliens who received no earned income from United States sources	d	
e Total number of employees not excluded (subtract d from c)	e	
f Employees ineligible (specify reason)	f	
g Employees eligible to participate (subtract f from e)	g	
h Employees eligible but not participating	h	
i Employees participating (subtract h from g)	i	

		Yes	No
23a Is it intended that this plan qualify under Code section 401(a)? If "Yes," complete b and c.	23a		
b Enter the date of the most recent IRS determination letter—Month ________ Year ________			
c Is a determination letter request pending with IRS?	c		
24a If this is a plan with Employee Stock Ownership features, was a current appraisal of the value of the stock made immediately before any contribution of stock or the purchase of the stock by the trust for the plan year covered by this return/report?	24a		
b If a is "Yes," was the appraisal made by an unrelated third party?	b		
25 Is this plan integrated with social security or railroad retirement?	25		
26 Does the employer/sponsor listed in 1a of this form maintain other qualified pension benefit plans? If "Yes," enter the total number of plans including this plan ▶	26		

27 Is this plan an adoption of a master, prototype or uniform plan? Indicate which type by checking the appropriate box:
a ☐ Master **b** ☐ Prototype plan **c** ☐ Uniform plan

28a Is the plan covered under the Pension Benefit Guaranty Corporation termination insurance program? ☐ **Yes** ☐ **No** ☐ **Not determined**

b If a is "Yes" or "Not determined," enter the employer identification number and the plan number used to identify it.
Employer identification number ▶ Plan number ▶

29 During the plan year:		Yes	No	Amount
a Was this plan covered by a fidelity bond?	29a			
b Was there any loss to the plan, whether or not reimbursed, caused by fraud or dishonesty?	b			
c Was there any sale, exchange, or lease of any property between the plan and the employer, any fiduciary, any of the five most highly paid employees of the employer, any owner of a 10% or more interest in the employer, or relatives of any such persons?	c			
d Was there any loan or extension of credit by the plan to the employer, any fiduciary, any of the five most highly paid employees of the employer, any owner of a 10% or more interest in the employer, or relatives of any such persons?	d			
e Did the plan acquire or hold any employer security or employer real property?	e			
f Has the plan granted an extension on any delinquent loan owed to the plan?	f			
g Has the employer owed contributions to the plan which are more than 3 months overdue?	g			
h Were any loans by the plan or fixed income obligations due the plan classified as uncollectible or in default as of the close of the plan year?	h			

Form 5500-C (1988) Page 4

			Yes	No	Amount
i	Has any plan fiduciary had a financial interest in excess of 10% in any party providing services to the plan or received anything of value from any such party?	29i			
j	Did the plan at any time hold 20% or more of its assets in any single security, debt, mortgage, parcel of real estate, or partnership/joint venture interests?	j			
k	Did the plan at any time engage in any transaction or series of related transactions involving 20% or more of the current value of plan assets?	k			
l	Were there any noncash contributions made to the plan whose value was set without an appraisal by an independent third party?	l			
m	Were there any purchases of nonpublicly traded securities by the plan whose value was set without an appraisal by an independent third party?	m			
n	Has the plan failed to provide any benefit when due under the terms of the plan because of insufficient assets?	n			

30 Current value of plan assets and liabilities at the beginning and end of the plan year. Combine the value of plan assets held in more than one trust. Allocate the value of the plan's interest in a commingled trust containing the assets of more than one plan on a line-by-line basis unless the trust meets one of the specific exceptions described in the instructions. Do not enter the value of that portion of an insurance contract which guarantees during this plan year to pay a specific dollar benefit at a future date. Round off amounts to the nearest dollar.

Assets		(a) Beginning of year	(b) End of year
a Cash	a		
b Receivables	b		
c Investments:			
(i) U.S. Government securities	(i)		
(ii) Corporate debt and equity instruments	(ii)		
(iii) Real estate and mortgages (other than to participants)	(iii)		
(iv) Loans to participants:			
A Mortgages	A		
B Other	B		
(v) Other	(v)		
(vi) Total investments (add (i) through (v))	(vi)		
d Buildings and other property used in plan operations	d		
e Other assets	e		
f Total assets	f		
Liabilities			
g Payables	g		
h Acquisition indebtedness	h		
i Other liabilities	i		
j Total liabilities	j		
k Net assets (f minus j)	k		

31 Plan income, expenses, and changes in net assets for the plan year. Include all income and expenses of the plan including any trust(s) or separately maintained fund(s) and payments/receipts to/from insurance carriers.

Income		(a) Amount	(b) Total
a Contributions received or receivable in cash from:			
(i) Employer(s) (including contributions on behalf of self-employed individuals)	(i)		
(ii) Employees	(ii)		
(iii) Others	(iii)		
b Noncash contributions	b		
c Earnings from investments (interest, dividends, rents, royalties)	c		
d Net realized gain (loss) on sale or exchange of assets	d		
e Other income (specify) ▶	e		
f Total income (add a through e)	f		
Expenses			
g Distribution of benefits and payments to provide benefits:			
(i) Directly to participants or their beneficiaries	(i)		
(ii) Other	(ii)		
h Administrative expenses (salaries, fees, commissions, insurance premiums)	h		
i Other expenses (specify) ▶	i		
j Total expenses (add g through i)	j		
k Net income (loss) (subtract j from f)	k		

Department of the Treasury
Internal Revenue Service

Department of Labor
Pension and Welfare Benefits Administration

Pension Benefit Guaranty Corporation

1988 Instructions for Form 5500-C

Return/Report of Employee Benefit Plan (With fewer than 100 participants)

(Code references are to the Internal Revenue Code. ERISA refers to the Employee Retirement Income Security Act of 1974.)

Paperwork Reduction Act Notice.—We ask for this information to carry out the law as specified in ERISA and Code section 6039D. We need it to determine whether the plan is operating according to the law. You are required to give us this information.

The time needed to complete and file the forms listed below reflect the combined requirements of the Internal Revenue Service, Department of Labor, Pension Benefit Guaranty Corporation and the Social Security Administration. These times will vary depending on individual circumstances. The estimated average times are:

	Recordkeeping	Learning about the law or the form	Preparing the form	Copying, assembling, and sending the form to IRS
Form 5500-C	52 hrs., 37 min.	7 hrs., 12 min.	10 hrs., 13 min.	32 min.
Schedule A (Form 5500)	17 hrs., 28 min.	28 min.	1 hr., 42 min.	16 min.
Schedule B (Form 5500)	25 hrs., 50 min.	1 hr.	1 hr., 27 min.	-----
Schedule P (Form 5500)	2 hrs., 9 min.	1 hr., 24 min.	1 hr., 29 min.	-----
Schedule SSA (Form 5500)	6 hrs., 42 min.	12 min.	19 min.	-----

If you have comments concerning the accuracy of these time estimates or suggestions for making these forms more simple, we would be happy to hear from you. You can write to the **Internal Revenue Service,** Washington, DC 20224, Attention: IRS Reports Clearance Officer, TR:FP; or the **Office of Management and Budget,** Paperwork Reduction Project, Washington, DC 20503.

File 1988 forms for plan years that started in 1988. If the plan year differs from the calendar year, fill in the fiscal year space just under the form title. For a short plan year, see Section 1, instruction B.

Reminder: In addition to filing this form with IRS, plans covered by the Pension Benefit Guaranty Corporation termination insurance program must file their Annual Premium Payment, PBGC Form 1, directly with that agency.

Penalties.—ERISA and the Code provide for the assessment or imposition of penalties for not giving complete information and not filing statements and returns/reports. Certain penalties are administrative; that is, they may be imposed or assessed by one of the governmental agencies delegated to administer the collection of Form 5500 series data. Others require a legal conviction.

A. Administrative Penalties.—Listed below are various penalties for not meeting the Form 5500 series filing requirements. One or more of the following five penalties may be imposed or assessed in the event of incomplete filings and /or filings received after the date they are due unless it is determined that your explanation for failure to file properly is for reasonable cause:

1. A penalty of up to $1,000 a day for each day a plan administrator fails or refuses to file a complete return/report. See ERISA section 502(c)(2) and 29 CFR 2560.502c-2.
2. A penalty of $25 a day (up to $15,000) for not filing returns for certain plans of deferred compensation, certain trusts and annuities, and bond purchase plans by the due date(s). See Code section 6652(e). This penalty also applies to returns required to be filed under Code section 6039D.
3. A penalty of $1 a day (up to $5,000) for each participant for whom a registration statement (Schedule SSA (Form 5500)) is required but not filed. See Code section 6652(d)(1).
4. A penalty of $1 a day (up to $1,000) for not filing a notification of change of status of a plan. See Code section 6652(d)(2).
5. A penalty of $1,000 for not filing an actuarial statement. See Code section 6692.

B. Other Penalties.—

1. Any individual who willfully violates any provision of Part 1 of Title I of ERISA shall be fined not more than $5,000 or imprisoned not more than 1 year, or both. See ERISA section 501.
2. A penalty of up to $10,000, 5 years imprisonment, or both, for making any false statement or representation of fact, knowing it to be false, or for knowingly concealing or not disclosing any fact required by ERISA. See section 1027, Title 18, U.S. Code, as amended by section 111 of ERISA.

How To Use This Instruction Booklet

The instructions are divided into four main sections.

Section 1

A. Who Must File.—Any administrator or sponsor of an employee benefit plan subject to ERISA must file information about each such plan **every year** (Code section 6058 and ERISA sections 104 and 4065). Also required to file, for each year, is every employer maintaining a specified fringe benefit plan as described in Code section 6039D. The Internal Revenue Service (IRS), Department of Labor (DOL), and Pension Benefit Guaranty Corporation (PBGC) have consolidated their returns and report forms to minimize the filing burden for plan administrators and employers. The chart on page 7 gives a brief guide to the type of return/report to be filed.

B. When To File.—File all required forms and schedules by the last day of the 7th month after the plan year ends. For a short plan year, file the form and applicable schedules by the last day of the 7th month after the short plan year ends. For purposes of this return/report, the short plan year ends upon the date of the change in accounting period or upon the complete distribution of the assets of the plan. (Also see Section 3.) If the current year Form 5500-C is not available before the due date of your short plan year return/report, use the latest year form available and change the date printed on the return/report to the current year. Also show the dates your short plan year began and ended.

Request for Extension of Time To File.—A one time extension of time up to 2½ months may be granted for filing returns/reports if **Form 5558,** Application for Extension of Time to File Certain Employee Plan Returns, is filed **before the normal due date of the return/report.**

Exception: *Single-employer plans and plans of a controlled group of corporations which file consolidated Federal income tax returns are automatically granted an extension of time to file Form 5500, 5500-C, or 5500-R to the due date of the Federal income tax return of the single employer or controlled group of corporations if all the following conditions are met:*

1. The plan year and the tax year coincide.

2. The single employer or the controlled group has been granted an extension of time to file its Federal income tax return to a date later than the normal due date for filing the Form 5500, 5500-C, or 5500-R.

3. A copy of the IRS extension of time to file the Federal income tax return is attached to each Form 5500, 5500-C, or 5500-R filed with IRS.

Note: *An extension of time to file the return/report does not operate as an extension of time to file the PBGC Form 1.*

C. Where To File.—Please file the return/report with the Internal Revenue Service Center indicated below. No street address is needed.

See page 5 for the filing address for investment arrangements filing directly with DOL.

If the principal office of the plan sponsor or the plan administrator is located in ▼	Use the following Internal Revenue Service Center address ▼
Connecticut, Delaware, District of Columbia, Foreign Address, Maine, Maryland, Massachusetts, New Hampshire, New Jersey, New York, Pennsylvania, Puerto Rico, Rhode Island, Vermont, Virginia	Holtsville, NY 00501
Alabama, Alaska, Arkansas, California, Florida, Georgia, Hawaii, Idaho, Louisiana, Mississippi, Nevada, North Carolina, Oregon, South Carolina, Tennessee, Washington	Atlanta, GA 39901
Arizona, Colorado, Illinois, Indiana, Iowa, Kansas, Kentucky, Michigan, Minnesota, Missouri, Montana, Nebraska, New Mexico, North Dakota, Ohio, Oklahoma, South Dakota, Texas, Utah, West Virginia, Wisconsin, Wyoming	Memphis, TN 37501
All Form 5500EZ filers	Andover, MA 05501

Section 2

A. Kinds of Plans.—Employee benefit plans include pension benefit plans and welfare benefit plans. File the applicable return/report for any of the following plans.

(a) Pension benefit plan.—This is an employee pension benefit plan covered by ERISA. The return/report is due whether or not the plan is qualified and even if benefits no longer accrue, contributions were not made this plan year, or contributions are no longer made ("frozen plan" or "wasting trust"). See Section 3, "Final Return/Report" on page 6.

Pension benefit plans required to file include defined benefit plans and defined contribution plans (e.g., profit-sharing, stock bonus, money purchase plans, etc.). The following are among the pension benefit plans for which a return/report must be filed:

(i) Annuity arrangements under Code section 403(b)(1).

(ii) Custodial account established under Code section 403(b)(7) for regulated investment company stock.

(iii) Individual retirement account established by an employer under Code section 408(c).

(iv) Pension benefit plan maintained outside the United States primarily for nonresident aliens if the employer who maintains the plan is:

(A) a domestic employer, or

(B) a foreign employer with income derived from sources within the U.S. (including foreign subsidiaries of domestic employers) and deducts contributions to the plan on its U.S. income tax return. See "Plans Excluded From Filing" below.

(v) Church plans electing coverage under Code section 410(d).

(vi) A plan that covers residents of Puerto Rico, the Virgin Islands, Guam, Wake Island, or American Samoa. This includes a plan that elects to have the provisions of section 1022(i)(2) of ERISA apply.

See "Items To Be Completed on Form 5500-C" on page 4 for more information about what questions need to be completed by pension plans.

(b) Welfare benefit plan.—This is an employee welfare benefit plan covered by Part 1 of Title I of ERISA. Welfare plans would provide benefits such as medical, dental, life insurance, apprenticeship training, educational assistance, severance pay, disability, etc.

See "Items To Be Completed on Form 5500-C" on page 4 for more information about what questions need to be completed for welfare benefit plans.

(c) Fringe benefit plan.—Group legal services plans described in Code section 120, cafeteria plans described in Code section 125, and educational assistance programs described in Code section 127 are considered fringe benefit plans and generally are required to file the annual information specified by Code section 6039D. However, Code section 127 educational assistance programs which provide only job-related training which is deductible under Code section 162 do not need to file Form 5500-C.

See "Items To Be Completed on Form 5500-C" on page 4 for more information about how to complete this form for a fringe benefit plan.

B. Plans Excluded From Filing (this does not apply to a fringe benefit plan required to file by Code section 6039D).—Do not file a return/report for an employee benefit plan that is any of the following:

(a) A welfare benefit plan which covers fewer than 100 participants as of the beginning of the plan year and is: (i) fully insured, (ii) unfunded, or (iii) a combination of insured and unfunded.

(1) An unfunded welfare benefit plan has its benefits paid as needed directly from the general assets of the employer or the employee organization that sponsors the plan.

(2) A fully insured welfare benefit plan has its benefits provided exclusively through insurance contracts or policies, the premiums of which must be paid directly by the employer or employee organization from its general assets or partly from its general assets and partly from contributions by its employees or members (which the employer or organization forwards within 3 months of receipt).

(3) A combination unfunded/insured welfare plan has its benefits provided partially as an unfunded plan and partially as a fully insured plan. An example of such a plan is a plan which requires the employer to reimburse an employee for hospital expenses with the first $1,000 per year of benefits paid from the general assets of the employer and any benefits above $1,000 paid from a stop loss insurance contract.

The insurance contracts or policies discussed above must be issued by an insurance company or similar organization (such as Blue Cross, Blue Shield or a health maintenance organization) that can legally do business in any state. A plan meeting (1) cannot have any assets at any time during the plan year.

"Directly," as used in (1) above, means that the plan cannot use a trust or separately maintained fund (including a Code section 501(c)(9) trust) to hold plan assets or to act as a conduit for the transfer of plan assets.

See 29 CFR 2520.104-20.

Note: *An "employees' association" as used in Code section 501(c)(9) should not be confused with the employee organization or employer which establishes and maintains (i.e., sponsors) the welfare benefit plan.*

(b) An unfunded pension benefit plan or an unfunded or combination unfunded and insured welfare benefit plan: (1) whose benefits go only to a select group of management or highly compensated employees, and (2) which meets the terms of Department of Labor Regulations 29 CFR 2520.104-23 (including the requirement that a notification statement be filed with DOL) or 29 CFR 2520.104-24.

(c) Plans maintained only to comply with workers' compensation, unemployment compensation, or disability insurance laws.

(d) An unfunded excess benefit plan.

(e) A welfare benefit plan maintained outside the United States primarily for persons substantially all of whom are nonresident aliens.

(f) A pension benefit plan maintained outside the United States if it is a qualified foreign plan within the meaning of Code section 404A(e) that does not qualify for the treatment provided in Code section 402(c).

(g) An annuity arrangement described in 29 CFR 2510.3-2(f).

(h) A simplified employee pension (SEP) described in Code section 408(k) which conforms to the alternative method of compliance described in 29 CFR 2520.104-48 or 29 CFR 104-49. A SEP is a pension plan which meets certain minimum qualifications regarding eligibility and employer contributions.

(i) A church plan not electing coverage under Code section 410(d) or a governmental plan.

(j) A welfare plan (other than a fringe benefit plan) that participates in a group insurance arrangement that files a return/report Form 5500 on its behalf. A group insurance arrangement is an arrangement which provides benefits to the employees of two or more unaffiliated employers (not in connection with a multi-employer plan or a multiple-employer-collectively-bargained plan), fully insures one or more welfare plans of each participating employer, and uses a trust (or other entity such as a trade association) as the holder of the insurance contracts and the conduit for payment of premiums to the insurance company. For further details, see 29 CFR 2520.104-43.

C. Kinds of Filers.—Item 4 on the Form 5500, 5500-C, and 5500-R lists the different types of entities which file the forms. These entities are described below.

(a) Single-employer plan.—If one employer or one employee organization maintains a plan, file a separate return/report for the plan. If the employer or employee organization maintains more than one such plan, file a separate return/report for each plan.

If a member of either a controlled group of corporations or a group of trades or businesses under common control maintains a plan that does not involve other group members, file a separate return/report as a single-employer plan.

If several employers participate in a program of benefits wherein the funds attributable to each employer are available only to pay benefits to that employer's employees, each employer must file a separate return/report.

(b) Plan for controlled group of corporations or group of trades or businesses under common control.—These groups are defined in Code sections 414(b) and (c), and are referred to as controlled groups.

If the benefits are payable to participants from the plan's total assets without regard to contributions by each participant's employer, file one return/report for the plan. On the return/report for the plan, complete item 22 only for the controlled group's employees.

Exception: Employers who participate in a plan of one of the groups listed above but who are not members of the group must file a separate return/report. The return/report should be filed on Form 5500-C or 5500-R, as applicable (see "What To File" on page 4). On the Form 5500-C, complete only items 1, 2, 3, 4f, 5, 6, 9, and 22. On Form 5500-R, complete only items 1 through 3, 4f, and 5 through 8b.

If several employers participate in a program of benefits wherein the funds attributable to each employer are available only to pay benefits to that employer's employees, each employer must file a separate return/report as a single employer plan.

(c) Multiemployer plan.— Multiemployer plans are plans: (1) to which more than one employer is required to contribute; (2) which are maintained pursuant to one or more collective bargaining agreements, and (3) have not made the election under Code section 414(f)(5) and ERISA section 3(37)(E). File one return/ report for each such plan. Contributing employers do not file individually with respect to such plans. See Code section 414 for more information.

(d) Multiple-employer-collectively-bargained plan.—A multiple-employer-collectively-bargained plan involves more than one employer, is collectively bargained and collectively funded, and, if covered by PBGC termination insurance, has properly elected before 9-27-81 not to be treated as a multiemployer plan under Code section 414(f)(5) or ERISA sections 3(37)(E) and 4001(a)(3). File one return/report for each such plan. Participating employers do not file individually for these plans.

(e) Multiple-employer plan (other).—A multiple-employer plan (other) involves more than one employer and is not one of the plans already described. A multiple-employer plan (other) includes only plans whose contributions from individual employers are available to pay benefits to all participants. File one return/report for each such plan.

In addition, for pension benefit plans, each participating employer files either a Form 5500-C, regardless of the number of participants, or Form 5500-R. On Form 5500-C, complete only items 1, 2, 3, 4f, 5, 6, 9, and 22. On Form 5500-R, complete only items 1 through 3, 4f, and 5 through 8b.

Note: *If a participating employer is also the sponsor of the multiple-employer plan (other), the plan number on the return/report filed for the plan should be 333. The Form 5500-C or Form 5500-R filed by the participating employer should list his or her appropriate plan number.*

If more than one employer participates in the plan and the plan provides that each employer's contributions are available to pay benefits only for that employer's employees who are covered by the plan, one annual return/report must be filed for each participating employer. These filers will be considered single employers and should complete the entire form.

D. Investment Arrangements Filing Directly With DOL.—Some plans invest in certain trusts, accounts, and other investment arrangements which may file information concerning itself and its relationship with employee benefit plans (as specified on page 5) directly with DOL. Plans participating in an investment arrangement as described in paragraphs **a** through **c** below are required to attach certain additional information to the return/report filed with IRS as specified below.

a. Common/Collective Trust and Pooled Separate Account

(i) Definition. For reporting purposes, a common/collective trust is a trust maintained by a bank, trust company, or similar institution which is regulated, supervised, and subject to periodic examination by a state or Federal agency for the collective investment and reinvestment of assets contributed thereto from employee benefit plans maintained by more than one employer or controlled group of corporations, as the term is used in Code section 1563. For reporting purposes, a pooled separate account is an account maintained by an insurance carrier which is regulated, supervised, and subject to periodic examination by a state or Federal agency for the collective investment and reinvestment of assets contributed thereto from employee benefit plans maintained by more than one employer or controlled group of corporations, as the term is used in Code section 1563. See 29 CFR sections 2520.103-3, 2520.103-4, 2520.103-5, and 2520.103-9.

Note: *For reporting purposes, a separate account which is not considered to be holding plan assets pursuant to 29 CFR 2510.3-101(h)(1)(iii), shall not constitute a pooled separate account.*

(ii) Additional Information Required To Be Attached to the Form 5500-C for Plans Participating in Common/Collective Trusts and Pooled Separate Accounts. A plan participating in a common/collective trust or pooled separate account must complete the annual return/report in accordance with the specific instructions and attach either (1) the most recent statement of the assets and liabilities of any common/collective trust or pooled separate account, or (2) a certification that: (A) the statement of the assets and liabilities of the common/collective trust or pooled separate account has been submitted directly to DOL by the financial institution or insurance carrier; (B) the plan has received a copy of the statement; and (C) includes the EIN and other numbers used by the financial institution or insurance carrier to identify the trusts or accounts in the direct filing made with DOL.

b. Master Trust

(i) Definition. For reporting purposes, a master trust is a trust for which a regulated financial institution (as defined below) serves as trustee or custodian (regardless of whether such institution exercises discretionary authority or control with respect to the management of assets held in the trust), and in which assets of more than one plan sponsored by a single employer or by a group of employers under common control are held.

A "regulated financial institution" means a bank, trust company, or similar financial institution which is regulated, supervised, and subject to periodic examination by a state or Federal agency. Common control is determined on the basis of all relevant facts and circumstances (whether or not such employers are incorporated). See 29 CFR 2520.103-1(e).

For reporting purposes, the assets of a master trust are considered to be held in one or more "investment accounts." A master trust investment account may consist of a pool of assets or a single asset.

Each pool of assets held in a master trust must be treated as a separate master trust investment account if each plan which has an interest in the pool has the same fractional interest in each asset in the pool as its fractional interest in the pool, and if each such plan may not dispose of its interest in any asset in the pool without disposing of its interest in the pool. A master trust may also contain assets which are not held in such a pool. Each such asset must be treated as a separate master trust investment account.

Financial information must generally be provided with respect to each master trust investment account as specified on page 5.

(ii) Additional Information Required To Be Attached to the Form 5500-C for Plans Participating in Master Trusts. A plan participating in a master trust must complete the annual return/report and attach to it a schedule listing each master trust investment account in which the plan has an interest indicating the plan's name, EIN, and plan number and the name of the master trust used in the master trust information filed with DOL (see page 5). For each investment account you must show, in tabular format, the net value of the plan's interest in each investment account at the beginning and end of the plan year, and the net investment gain (or loss) allocated to the plan for the plan year from the investment account.

Note: *If a master trust investment account consists solely of one plan's asset(s) during the reporting period, the plan may report* *the(se) asset(s) either as an investment account to be reported as part of the master trust report filed directly with DOL or as a plan asset(s) which is not part of the master trust (and therefore subject to all instructions pertaining to assets not held in a master trust).*

c. 103-12 Investment Entities

Definition. 29 CFR 2520.103-12 provides an alternative method of reporting for plans which invest in an entity (other than an investment arrangement filing with DOL described in **a** or **b** above), the underlying assets of which include "plan assets" (within the meaning of 29 CFR 2510.3-101) of two or more plans which are not members of a "related group" of employee benefit plans. For reporting purposes, a "related group" consists of each group of two or more employee benefit plans (1) each of which receives 10 percent or more of its aggregate contributions from the same employer or from a member of the same controlled group of corporations (as determined under Code section 1563(a), without regard to Code section 1563(a)(4) thereof); or (2) each of which is either maintained by, or maintained pursuant to a collective bargaining agreement negotiated by, the same employee organization or affiliated employee organizations. For purposes of this paragraph, an "affiliate" of an employee organization means any person controlling, controlled by, or under common control with such organization. See 29 CFR 2520.103-12.

For reporting purposes, the investment entities described above with respect to which the required information is filed directly with DOL constitute "103-12 investment entities" (103-12 IEs).

E. What To File.—The circumstances that dictate which form should be filed are described below. In addition, there are schedules that may need to be attached to the return/report. These are also described below. Finally, this section also contains a description of special filing requirements for plans that invest in certain investment arrangements. A brief guide illustrating which forms and schedules are required by different types of plans and filers may be found on page 7.

Forms

Form 5500.—File **Form 5500**, Annual Return/Report of Employee Benefit Plan, annually for each plan with 100 or more participants at the beginning of the plan year.

Form 5500-C.—File **Form 5500-C**, Return/Report of Employee Benefit Plan, for each pension benefit plan, welfare benefit plan, and fringe benefit plan (unless otherwise exempted) with fewer than 100 participants (one-participant plans see "Form 5500EZ" below) at the beginning of the plan year. File Form 5500-C for the first plan year, the year for which the final return/report is due, and for plan years in which a Form 5500-R is not filed as explained below.

Form 5500-R.—**Form 5500-R**, Registration Statement of Employee Benefit Plan (with fewer than 100 participants), may be filed instead of a Form 5500-C for this plan year provided (a) this is not the first plan year, (b) this is not a year for which the final return/report is due, and (c) a Form 5500-C has been filed for one of the prior 2 plan years. The Form 5500-R should not be filed if (a) this plan year is the first plan year, (b) this is the plan year for which a final return/report is due, or (c) the Form 5500-R has been filed for both of the prior 2 plan years.

Any plan may choose not to file the Form 5500-R if the plan files the Form 5500-C instead.

Note: *Generally, under the filing requirements explained above, if the number of plan participants increases from under 100 to 100 or more, or decreases from 100 or more to under 100, from one year to the next, you would have to file a different form from that filed the previous year. However, there is an exception to this rule. You may file the same form you filed last year, even if the number of participants changed, provided that at the beginning of this plan year the plan had at least 80 participants, but not more than 120.*

Form 5500EZ.—**Form 5500EZ**, Annual Return of One-Participant Pension Benefit Plan, should be filed by most one-participant plans.

A one-participant plan is: (1) a pension benefit plan that covers only an individual or an individual and his or her spouse who wholly own a trade or business, whether incorporated or unincorporated; or (2) a pension benefit plan for a partnership that covers only the partners or the partners and the partners' spouses.

See Form 5500EZ and its instructions to see if the plan meets the requirements for filing the form.

Items To Be Completed on Form 5500-C

Certain kinds of plans and certain kinds of filers that are required to submit Form 5500-C are **not** required to complete the entire form. These are described below, by type of plan. Check the list of headings to see if your plan is affected.

1. Welfare Benefit Plans—Welfare benefit plans generally must complete the following items on the Form 5500-C: 1 through 6c; 7a; 8a, c, d, and e; 9a, b, c, and f; 10a through d; 11 through 14; and 29 through 31.

Note: *If one Form 5500-C is filed for both a welfare plan and a fringe benefit plan, items 22c, 22g, and 22i must be completed in addition to the items listed above for welfare plans.*

2. Fringe Benefit Plans—A Form 5500-C filed only because of Code section 6039D (i.e., for a fringe benefit plan) need complete only items 1 through 6a, 7a, 9a, 9b, 22c, 22g, 22i, 31h, and 31j.

If the annual return/report is also for a welfare benefit plan (see "Who Must File" on page 1), complete the above items and those specified for welfare benefit plans in "1" above.

3. Pension Plans—In general, most pension plans (defined benefit and defined contribution) are required to complete all items on the form. However, some items need not be completed by certain types of pension plans, as described below.

a. Plans exclusively using a tax deferred annuity arrangement under Code section 403(b)(1). These plans need only complete items 1 through 5, 6b(iv), and 9.

b. Plans exclusively using a custodial account for regulated investment company stock under Code section 403(b)(7). These plans need only complete items 1 through 5, 6b(v), and 9.

c. Individual Retirement Account Plan.—A pension plan utilizing individual retirement accounts or annuities (as described in Code section 408) as the sole funding vehicle for providing benefits need only complete items 1 through 5, 6b(vi), and 9.

d. Fully Insured Pension Plan.—A pension benefit plan providing benefits exclusively through an insurance contract, or contracts that are fully guaranteed, and which meets all of the conditions of 29 CFR 2520.104-44 need only complete items 1 through 29b. A pension plan which includes both insurance contracts of the type described in 29 CFR 2520.104-44 as well as other assets should limit its reporting in items 30 and 31 to those other assets.

Note: *For purposes of the annual return/report and the alternative method of compliance set forth in 29 CFR 2520.104-44, a contract is considered to be "allocated" only if the insurance company or organization that issued the contract unconditionally guarantees, upon receipt of the required premium or consideration, to provide a retirement benefit of a specified amount, without adjustment for fluctuations in the market value of the underlying assets of the company or organization, to each participant, and each participant has a legal right to such benefits which is legally enforceable directly against the insurance company or organization.*

e. Nonqualified Plans Maintained Outside the U.S.—Nonqualified pension benefit plans maintained outside the United States primarily for nonresident aliens required to file a return/report (see "Who Must File" on page 1) need only complete items 1 through 8c, 9 through 12, and 15 through 17.

4. Plans of More Than One Employer—All plans of more than one employer (plans of a controlled group, multiemployer plans, multiple-employer-collectively-bargained plans, and multiple-employer-plan (other)) generally should complete all applicable (welfare or pension) items on the form except for item 6d. Only single-employer pension plans must complete this item. In addition, multiemployer and multiple-employer-collectively-bargained plans need not complete item 22 on the Form 5500-C.

Schedules

The various schedules to be attached to the return/report are listed below.

Note: *All attachments to the Forms 5500, 5500-C, and 5500-R must include the name of the plan and the EIN and plan number (PN) as found in items 5a, 1b, and 5c, respectively.*

Attach Schedule A (Form 5500), Insurance Information, to Form 5500, 5500-C, or 5500-R if any benefits under the plan are provided by an insurance company, insurance service, or other similar organization (such as Blue Cross, Blue Shield, or a health maintenance organization).

Exception: *Schedule A (Form 5500) is not needed if the plan covers: (1) only an individual, or an individual and his or her spouse, who wholly owns a trade or business, whether incorporated or unincorporated; or (2) a partner in a partnership, or a partner and his or her spouse.*

Do not file a Schedule A (Form 5500) with a Form 5500EZ.

Attach Schedule B (Form 5500), Actuarial Information, to Forms 5500, 5500-C, 5500-R, or 5500EZ for most defined benefit pension plans. See instructions for Schedule B.

Schedule SSA (Form 5500), Annual Registration Statement Identifying Separated Participants With Deferred Vested Benefits, may be needed for separated participants. See "When To Report Separated Participants" in the instructions for Schedule SSA.

Schedule P (Form 5500), Annual Return of Fiduciary of Employee Benefit Trust.—Any fiduciary (trustee or custodian) of an organization that is qualified under Code section 401(a) and exempt from tax under Code section 501(a) who wants to protect the organization under the statute of limitations provided in Code section 6501(a) must file a Schedule P (Form 5500).

File the Schedule P (Form 5500) as an attachment to Form 5500, 5500-C, 5500-R, or 5500EZ for the plan year in which the trust year ends.

Other Filings

Reporting Requirements for Investment Arrangements Filing Directly With DOL

Certain investment arrangements for employee benefit plans file financial information directly with DOL. These arrangements include common/collective trusts, pooled separate accounts, master trusts, and 103-12 IEs. Definitions of these investment arrangements may be found on page 3. Their DOL filing requirements are described below.

A. Common/Collective Trust and Pooled Separate Account Information To Be Filed Directly With DOL

Financial institutions and insurance carriers filing the statement of the assets and liabilities of a common/collective trust or pooled separate account should identify the trust or account by providing the EIN of the trust or account, or (if more than one trust or account is covered by the same EIN) both the EIN and any additional number assigned by the financial institution or insurance carrier (such as: 99-1234567 Trust No. 1); and a list of all plans participating in the trust or account, identified by the plan number, EIN, and name of the plan sponsor. The direct filing should be addressed to:

Common/Collective Trust (OR)
Pooled Separate Account
Pension and Welfare Benefits
Administration
U.S. Department of Labor, Room N5644
200 Constitution Avenue, NW
Washington, DC 20210

B. Master Trust Information To Be Filed Directly With DOL

The following information with respect to a master trust must be filed with DOL by the plan administrator or by a designee, such as the administrator of another plan participating in the master trust or the financial institution serving as trustee of the master trust, no later than the date on which the plan's return/report is due. While only one copy of the required information should be filed for all plans participating in the master trust, the information is an integral part of the return/report of each participating plan, and the plan's return/report will not be deemed complete unless all the information is filed within the prescribed time.

Note: *If a master trust investment account consists solely of one plan's asset(s) during the reporting period, the plan may report the(se) asset(s) either as an investment account to be reported as part of the master trust report filed directly with DOL or as a plan asset(s) which is not part of the master trust (and therefore subject to all instructions pertaining to assets not held in a master trust).*

Each of the following statements and schedules must indicate the name of the master trust and the name of the master trust investment account. The information shall be filed with DOL by mailing it to:

Master Trust
Pension and Welfare Benefits
Administration
U.S. Department of Labor, Room N5644
200 Constitution Avenue, NW
Washington, DC 20210

1. The name and fiscal year of the master trust and the name and address of the master trustee.

2. A list of all plans participating in the master trust, showing each plan's name, EIN, PN, and its percentage interest in each master trust investment account as of the beginning and end of the fiscal year of the master trust ending with or within the plan year.

3. A statement, in the same format as Part I of Schedule C (Form 5500), for each master trust investment account showing amounts of compensation paid during the fiscal year of the master trust ending with or within the plan year to persons providing services with respect to the investment account and subtracted from the gross income of the investment account in determining the net increase (decrease) in net assets of the investment account.

4. A statement for each master trust investment account showing the assets and liabilities of the investment account at the beginning and end of the fiscal year of the master trust ending with or within the plan year, grouped in the same categories as those specified in item 34 of Form 5500.

5. A statement for each master trust investment account showing the income and expenses, changes in net assets, and net increase (decrease) in net assets of each such investment account during the fiscal year of the master trust ending with or within the plan year, in the categories specified in item 35 of Form 5500. In place of item 35a, show the total of all transfers of assets into the investment account by participating plans. In place of item 35j, show the total of all transfers of assets out of the investment account by participating plans.

6. Schedules, in the format set forth in the instructions for item 30 of Form 5500, of the following items with respect to each master trust investment account for the fiscal year of the master trust ending with or within the plan year: assets held for investment, nonexempt party-in-interest transactions, defaulted or uncollectible loans and leases, and 5% transactions involving assets in the investment account. The 5% figure shall be determined by comparing the current value of the transaction at the transaction date with the current value of the investment account assets at the beginning of the applicable fiscal year of the master trust.

C. 103-12 IE Information To Be Filed Directly With DOL

The information described below must be filed with the DOL by the sponsor of the 103-12 IE no later than the date on which the plan's return/report is due before the plan administrator can elect the alternative method of reporting. While only one copy of the required information should be filed for the 103-12 IE, the information is an integral part of the return/report of each plan electing the alternative method of compliance.

The filing address is:
103-12 Investment Entity
Pension and Welfare Benefits
Administration
U.S. Department of Labor, Room N5644
200 Constitution Avenue NW
Washington, DC 20210

1. The name, fiscal year, and EIN of the 103-12 IE and the name and address of the sponsor of the 103-12 IE. If more than one 103-12 IE is covered by the same EIN, they shall be sequentially numbered as follows: 99-1234567 Entity No. 1.

2. A list of all plans participating in the 103-12 IE, showing each plan's name, EIN, PN, and its percentage interest in the 103-12 IE as of the beginning and end of the fiscal year of the 103-12 IE ending with or within the plan year.

3. A statement, in the same format as Part I of Schedule C (Form 5500), for the 103-12 IE showing amounts of compensation paid during the fiscal year of the 103-12 IE ending with or within the plan year to persons providing services to the 103-12 IE.

4. A statement showing the assets and liabilities at the beginning and end of the fiscal year of the 103-12 IE ending with or within the plan year, grouped in the same categories as those specified in item 34 of Form 5500.

5. A statement showing the income and expenses, changes in net assets, and net increase (decrease) in net assets during the fiscal year of the 103-12 IE ending with or within the plan year, grouped in the same categories specified in item 35 of Form 5500. In place of item 35a, show the total of all transfers of assets into the 103-12 IE by participating plans. In place of item 35j, show the total of all transfers of assets out of the 103-12 IE by participating plans.

6. Schedules, in the format set forth in the instructions for item 30 of Form 5500 (except item 30c) with respect to the 103-12 IE for the fiscal year of the 103-12 IE investment entity ending with or within the plan year. Substitute the term "103-12 IE" in place of the word "plan" when completing the schedules.

7. A report of an independent qualified public accountant regarding the above items and other books and records of the 103-12 IE which meets the requirements of 29 CFR 2520.103-1(b)(5).

Section 3

General Information

Final Return/Report.—If all assets under the plan (including insurance/annuity contracts) have been distributed to the participants and beneficiaries or distributed to another plan (and when all liabilities for which benefits may be paid under a welfare plan have been satisfied), check the "final return/report" box at the top of the form filed for such plan. The year of complete distribution is the last year a return/report must be filed for the plan. For purposes of this paragraph, a complete distribution will occur in the year in which the assets of a terminated plan are brought under the control of PBGC.

For a defined benefit plan covered by PBGC, a PBGC Form 1 must be filed and a premium must be paid until the end of the plan year in which the assets are distributed or brought under the control of PBGC.

Filing the return/report marked "final return" and indicating that the plan terminated satisfies the notification requirement of Code section 6057(b)(3).

Signature and Date.—The plan administrator must sign and date all returns/reports filed. In addition the employer must sign a return/report filed for a single-employer plan or a plan required to file only because of Code section 6039D.

When a joint employer-union board of trustees or committee is the plan sponsor or plan administrator, at least one employer representative and one union representative must sign and date the return/report.

Participating employers in a multiple-employer plan (other), who are required to file Form 5500-C or 5500-R, are required to sign the return/report. The plan administrator need not sign the Form 5500-C or 5500-R filed by the participating employer.

Reproductions.—Original forms are preferable, but a clear reproduction of the completed form is acceptable. Sign the return/report after it is reproduced. All signatures must be original.

Change in Plan Year.—Generally only defined contribution pension benefit plans need to get prior approval for a change in plan year. (See Code section 412(c)(5).) Rev. Proc. 87-27, 1987-1 C.B. 769 explains the procedure for automatic approval of a change in plan year. A pension benefit plan that would ordinarily need to obtain approval for a change in plan year under Code section 412(c)(5) is granted an automatic approval for a change in plan year if all the following criteria are met:

1. No plan year is more than 12 months long.

2. The change will not delay the time when the plan otherwise would have been required to conform to the requirements of any statute, regulation, or published position of the IRS.

3. The trust, if any, retains its exempt status for the short period required to effect the change, as well as for the taxable year immediately preceding the short period.

4. All actions necessary to implement the change in plan year, including plan amendment and a resolution of the board of directors (if applicable), have been taken on or before the last day of the short period.

5. No change in plan year has been made for any of the preceding plan years.

6. In the case of a defined benefit plan, deductions are taken in accordance with section 5 of Rev. Proc. 87-27.

For the first return/report that is filed following the change in plan year, check the box indicated on the second line under the title at the top of the form (or item 1d if Form 5500-R is being filed).

Amended Return/Report.—If you file an amended return/report, check the "(ii) and amended return/report" box at the top of the form. When filing an amended return, be sure to answer all questions and put a circle around the numbers of the items that have been amended.

How the Annual Return/Report Information May Be Used.—All Form 5500 series return/reports will be subjected to a computerized review. It is, therefore, in the filer's best interest that the responses accurately reflect the circumstances they were designed to report. Annual reports filed under Title I of ERISA must be made available by plan administrators to plan participants and by the Department of Labor to the public pursuant to ERISA section 104.

Section 4

Specific Instructions for Form 5500-C

Important: Answer all items on the Form 5500-C with respect to the plan year, unless otherwise explicitly stated in the item-by-item instructions or on the form itself. Therefore, your responses usually apply to the year entered or printed at the top of the first page of the form. Yes and no questions are to be marked either "yes" or "no" but not both. If neither "yes" nor "no" apply, enter "N/A."

Information To Be Completed at the Top of the Form

First Line at the top of the form—Complete the space for dates when: (1) the 12-month plan year is not a calendar year, or (2) the plan year is less than 12 months (a short plan year).

Second Line—Check the box if the plan year has been changed since the last return/report was filed.

Fourth Line—Check box (i) if this is the initial filing for this plan. Do not check this box if you have ever filed for this plan even if it was on a different form (Form 5500 vs. Form 5500-C or Form 5500-R).

Check box (ii) if you have already filed for the 1988 plan year and are now submitting an amended return/report to reflect errors and/or omissions on the previously filed return/report.

Check box (iii) if the plan no longer exists to provide benefits. See Section 3 for instructions concerning the requirement to file a final return/report.

The numbers of the following instructions are the same as the item numbers on the return/report.

1a. If you did not receive a preaddressed mailing label, enter the name and address of the plan sponsor. If the plan covers only the employees of one employer, enter the employer's name.

If you received a Form 5500-C with a preaddressed mailing label, please attach it in the name and address area of the form you file. If the name or address on the label is wrong, draw a line through the incorrect part and correct it.

The term "plan sponsor" means—

(i) the employer, for an employee benefit plan that a single employer established or maintains;

(ii) the employee organization in the case of a plan of an employee organization; or

(iii) the association, committee, joint board of trustees, or other similar group of representatives of the parties who establish or maintain the plan, if the plan is established or maintained jointly by one or more employers and one or more employee organizations, or by two or more employers.

Include enough information in 1(a) to describe the sponsor adequately, for example, "Joint Board of Trustees of Local 187 Machinists" rather than just "Joint Board of Trustees."

1b. Enter the 9-digit employer identification number (EIN) assigned to the plan sponsor/employer, i.e., 00-1234567.

Employers and plan administrators who do not have an EIN should apply for one on Form SS-4, available from most IRS or Social Security Administration offices. Send Form SS-4 to the same Internal Revenue Service Center to which this form will be sent.

Plan sponsors are reminded that they should use the trust EIN when opening a bank account or conducting other transactions for a plan that requires an employer identification number. The trust may apply for an EIN as explained in the preceding paragraph.

A plan of a controlled group of corporations whose sponsor is more than one of the members of the controlled group should insert only the EIN of one of the sponsoring members. This EIN must be used in all subsequent filings of the annual returns/reports for the controlled group unless there is a change in the sponsor.

If the plan administrator is a group of individuals, get a single EIN for the group. When you apply for a number, enter on line 1 of Form SS-4 the name of the group, such as "Joint Board of Trustees of the Local 187 Machinists' Retirement Plan."

Note: *Although Employer Identification Numbers (EINs) for funds (trusts or custodial accounts) associated with plans are not required to be furnished on the Form 5500 series returns/reports, the IRS will issue EINs for such funds for other reporting purposes. EINs may be obtained by filing Form SS-4 as explained above.*

1d. From the list of business codes on pages 13 and 14, enter the one that best describes the nature of the employer's business. If more than one employer is involved, enter the business code for the main business activity.

1e. Plans checking item 4a or 4b must enter the first six digits of the CUSIP (Committee on Uniform Securities Identification Procedures) number, "issuer number," if one has been assigned to the plan sponsor for purposes of issuing corporate securities. CUSIP issuer numbers are assigned to corporations and other entities which issue public securities listed on stock exchanges or traded over the counter. The CUSIP issuer number is the first six digits of the number assigned to the individual securities which are traded. If the plan sponsor has no CUSIP issuer number, enter "N/A."

2a. If the document constituting the plan appoints or designates a plan administrator other than the sponsor, enter the administrator's name and address. If the plan administrator is also the sponsor, enter "Same." If 2a is the "Same," then items 2b and 2c should be left blank.

The term "administrator" means—

(i) the person or group of persons specified as the administrator by the instrument under which the plan is operated;

(ii) the plan sponsor/employer if an administrator is not so designated; or

(iii) any other person prescribed by regulations of the Secretary of Labor if an administrator is not designated and a plan sponsor cannot be identified.

2b. A plan administrator must have an EIN for reporting purposes. Enter the plan administrator's 9-digit EIN here. If the plan administrator has no EIN, apply for one as explained in 1b above.

Employees of an employer are not plan administrators unless so designated in the plan document, even though they engage in administrative functions of the plan. If an employee of the employer is designated as the plan administrator, that employee must get an EIN.

3. If you answer "No," enter the name, address, and EIN of the plan sponsor and/or the plan administrator shown on the prior return/report.

3c. Indicate if the change in 3a is only a change in sponsorship. "Change in sponsorship" means the plan's sponsor has been changed but no assets or liabilities have been transferred to another plan(s), the plan has not terminated or merged with any other plan, and so forth.

4a. Check for a single-employer plan. See "Kinds of Filers" for what is considered a single-employer plan.

4b. Check for a plan in which more than one employer participates, and some of the employers are members of a controlled group of corporations (Code section 414(b)) or a member of a group of employers under common control (Code section 414(c)).

4c. Check for a multiemployer plan as defined in Code section 414(f) and ERISA sections 3(37) and 4001(a)(3).

4d. Check for a multiple-employer-collectively-bargained plan as described under "Kinds of Filers."

4e. Check for a multiple-employer plan (other) if the plan administrator is filing for the plan as a whole.

4f. Exceptions to **b** and **e.** Each participating employer in a multiple-employer plan (other) pension benefit plan and nonmember employers participating in a plan of a controlled group of corporations or businesses need to file either the Form 5500-C or Form 5500-R, regardless of the number of participants. Complete items 1, 2, 3, 4f, 5, 6, 9, and 22 on the Form 5500-C, and items 1, 2, 3, 4f, 5, 6, 7, 8a, and 8b on the Form 5500-R.

5a. Enter the formal name of the plan or enough information to identify the plan.

5b. Enter the date the plan first became effective.

5c. Enter the 3-digit number the employer or plan administrator assigned to the plan. All welfare plan numbers and Code section 6039D plan numbers start at 501. All other plans start at 001.

Once you use a plan number, continue to use it for that plan on all future filings with IRS, DOL and PBGC reports. Do not use it for any other plan even if you terminated the first plan.

6a. Check every box that describes the welfare benefit plan for which this return/report is being filed. Example: If your plan provides health insurance, dental insurance, eye examinations, and life insurance, four boxes should be checked: 6a(i)(A), 6a(i)(B), 6a(i)(D), and 6a(i)(E).

If you checked box (M), (N), or (O), you must check one box in 6a(ii). Check "unfunded" if the plan is (1) unfunded, (2) fully insured, or (3) a combination of unfunded/insured as defined on page 2, Section 2B(a).

6b(i). For a defined benefit plan, check the box.

6b(ii). Check (C) for a money purchase plan if the contribution is determined by a target benefit calculation. Check (D) for all money purchase plans that do not have a target benefit calculation.

6c(ii). Check for an ESOP which acquires employer securities with borrowed money or other debt-financed techniques.

6c(iii). Check if the plan is a pension plan that provides for individual accounts and permits a participant or beneficiary to exercise independent control over the assets in his or her account (see ERISA section 404(c)).

6c(iv). Check this box for pension benefit plans maintained outside the United States primarily for nonresident aliens. See "Kinds of Filers" for more information.

6c(v). In the space provided following 6c(viii), enter name of the trust and bank or financial institution. Also enter city and state where the trust is maintained. (See page 3 for master trust instructions.)

6c(vi). In the space provided following 6c(viii), enter name and address of the 103-12 IE. (See page 5.)

6d. For single-employer plans enter the date the employer's tax year ends. For example, if the tax year is a calendar year, enter 12-31-88. For all plans with more than one employer, enter "N/A."

6e. Definition of Affiliated Service Group.—In general, Code section 414(m)(2) defines an affiliated service group as a first service organization (FSO) that has:

(1) a service organization (A-ORG) that is a shareholder or partner in the FSO and that regularly performs services for the FSO, or is regularly associated with the FSO in performing services for third persons, and/or

(2) any other organization (B-ORG) if:

(a) a significant portion of the business of that organization consists of performing services for the FSO or A-ORG of a type historically performed by employees in the service field of the FSO or A-ORG, and

(b) 10% or more of the interest of the B-ORG is held by persons who are highly compensated employees of the FSO or A-ORG.

An affiliated service group also includes a group consisting of an organization whose principal business is performing management functions for another organization (or one organization and other related organizations) on a regular and

Summary of Filing Requirements for Employers and Plan Administrators
(File forms ONLY with IRS)

Type of plan	What to file	When to file
Most pension plans with only one participant or one participant and that participant's spouse	Form 5500EZ	File all required forms and schedules for each plan by the last day of the 7th month after the plan year ends.
Pension plan with fewer than 100 participants	Form 5500-C or 5500-R	
Pension plan with 100 or more participants	Form 5500	
Annuity under Code section 403(b)(1) or trust under Code section 408(c)	Form 5500, 5500-C, or 5500-R	
Custodial account under Code section 403(b)(7)	Form 5500, 5500-C, or 5500-R	
Welfare benefit plan with 100 or more participants*	Form 5500	
Welfare benefit plan with fewer than 100 participants (see exception on page 1 of these instructions)*	Form 5500-C or 5500-R	
Pension or welfare plan with 100 or more participants (see Form 5500 instructions)	Financial statements, schedules, and accountant's opinion	
Pension or welfare plan with benefits provided by an insurance company	Schedule A (Form 5500)	
Pension plan that requires actuarial information	Schedule B (Form 5500)	
Plan with 100 or more participants	Schedule C (Form 5500)	
Pension plan filing a registration statement identifying separated participants with deferred vested benefits from a pension plan	Schedule SSA (Form 5500)	

*This includes Code section 6039D filers.

continuing basis, and the organization for which such functions are so performed by the organization. For a plan maintained by more than one employer, check "Yes" if any such employer is a member of an affiliated service group.

6f. A cash or deferred arrangement described under Code section 401(k) is a part of a qualified defined contribution plan which provides for an election by employees to defer part of their compensation or receive these amounts in cash.

7. The description of "participant" in the instructions below is only for purposes of item 7 of this form

For welfare plans, dependents are considered to be neither participants nor beneficiaries. For pension benefit plans, "alternate payees" entitled to benefits under a qualified domestic relations order are not to be counted as participants for this item.

"Participant" means any individual who is included in one of the categories below.

Active participants include any individuals who are currently in employment covered by a plan and who are earning or retaining credited service under a plan. This category includes any individuals who are: (i) currently below the integration level in a plan that is integrated with social security, and/or (ii) eligible to elect to have the employer make payments to a code section 401(k) qualified cash or deferred arrangement. Active participants also include any nonvested individuals who are earning or retaining credited service under a plan. This category **does not** include nonvested former employees who have incurred the greater of 5 consecutive one year breaks in service or the break in service period specified in the plan.

For determining if active participants are fully vested, partially vested, or nonvested, consider vesting in employer contributions only.

For purposes of Code section 6039D, "participant" means any individual who, for a plan year, has had at least one dollar excluded from income by reason of Code section 120, 125, or 127. If you are filing Form 5500-C for a welfare plan that is required to file under Title I of ERISA and under Code section 6039D, the preceding sentence does not apply.

Inactive participants receiving benefits are any individuals who are retired or separated from employment covered by the plan and who are receiving benefits under the plan. This includes former employees who are receiving group health continuation coverage benefits pursuant to Part 6 of ERISA and who are covered by the employee welfare benefit plan. This category does not include any individual to whom an insurance company has made an irrevocable commitment to pay all the benefits to which the individual is entitled under the plan.

Inactive participants entitled to future benefits are individuals who are retired or separated from employment covered by the plan and who are entitled to begin receiving benefits under the plan in the future. This category does not include any individual to whom an insurance company has made an irrevocable commitment to pay all the benefits to which the individual is entitled under the plan.

Deceased participants are any deceased individuals who have one or more beneficiaries who are receiving or are entitled to receive benefits under the plan. This category does not include an individual if an insurance company has made an irrevocable commitment to pay all the benefits to which the beneficiaries of that individual are entitled under the plan.

7b(i). If "Yes," file Schedule SSA (Form 5500) as an attachment to the Form 5500-C. **Plan administrators:** Code section 6057(e) provides that the plan administrator must give each participant a statement showing the same information for that participant as is reported on Schedule SSA.

8a. Check "Yes" if an amendment to the plan was adopted in this plan year, regardless of the effective date of the amendment.

8b. Check "Yes" only if the accrued benefits were retroactively reduced. For example, a plan provides a benefit of 2% for each year of service, but the plan is amended to change the benefit to 1½% a year for all years of service under the plan.

8c. Enter the date the most recent amendment was adopted regardless of the date of the amendent or the effective date of the amendment.

8d. Check "Yes" only if an amendment changed the information previously provided to participants by the summary plan description or summary description of modifications.

8e. A revised summary plan description or summary description of modifications must be filed with DOL and distributed to all participants and pension plan beneficiaries no later than 210 days after the close of the plan year, in which the amendment(s) was adopted. If the material was distributed and filed since the amendments were adopted (even if after the end of the plan year), check "Yes" to item 8e.

9a. Check "Yes" if the plan was terminated or if the plan was merged or consolidated into another plan. Enter year of termination if applicable. If you checked 6a(i)(M), (N), or (O) and indicated that this is an unfunded plan and you also answered 9a "Yes," you must also check 9b "Yes."

9b. If the plan was terminated and all plan assets were not distributed, file a return/report for each year the plan has assets. In that case, the return/report must be filed by the plan administrator, if designated, or by the person or persons who actually control the plan's property.

If all assets were used to buy individual annuity contracts and the contracts were distributed to the participants, check "Yes."

If all the trust assets were transferred to another plan, check "Yes."

Do not check "Yes" for a welfare plan which is still liable to pay benefits for claims which were incurred prior to the termination date but not yet paid. See 29 CFR 2520.104b-2(g)(2)(ii).

9h. The Code provides for a nondeductible excise tax on a reversion of assets from a qualified plan.

9i. The employer must report the reversion by filing Form 5330 and pay any applicable tax. The tax will not be imposed upon employers who are tax-exempt entities under Code section 501(a). See instructions for Form 5330.

10a. If this plan was merged or consolidated into another plan(s), or plan assets or liabilities were transferred to another plan(s), indicate which other plan or plans were involved.

10c. Enter the EIN of the sponsor (employer, if for a single-employer plan) of the other plan.

10e. Pension benefit plans must file Form 5310 at least 30 days before any plan merger or consolidation or any transfer of plan assets or liabilities to another plan.

Caution: *There is a penalty for not filing Form 5310 on time.*

11. Enter the code for the **funding arrangement** used by the plan from the list below.

The "funding arrangement" is the method used for the receipt, holding, investment, and transmittal of plan assets prior to the time the plan actually provides the benefits promised under the plan. For purposes of items 11 and 12, the term "trust" includes any fund or account which receives, holds, transmits, or invests plan assets other than an account or policy of an insurance company.

	Funding Arrangement Codes
Trust	1
Trust and insurance	2
Insurance	3
Exclusively from general assets of sponsor (unfunded)	4
Partially insured and partially from general assets of sponsor	5
Other	6

12. Enter the code for the **benefit arrangement** used by the plan from the list below.

The "benefit arrangement" is the method by which benefits are actually provided to participants by the plan. For example, when a participant retires, the plan might purchase an annuity from an insurance company for that individual to provide the actual benefits promised by the plan. In this example, the annuity would be the benefit arrangement.

Using the chart below, the plan in the above example would enter a "3" to indicate the benefit arrangement.

	Benefit Arrangement Codes
Trust	1
Trust and insurance	2
Insurance	3
Exclusively from general assets of sponsor (unfunded)	4
Partially insured and partially from general assets of sponsor	5
Other	6

13. Check "Yes" if either the contributions to the plan or the benefits paid by the plan are subject to the collective bargaining process, even if the plan is not established and administered by a joint board of trustees. Check "Yes" even if only some of those covered by the plan are members of a collective bargaining unit which negotiates benefit levels on its own behalf. The benefit schedules need not be identical for all employees under the plan.

14. If either the funding arrangement code (item 11) and/or the benefit arrangement code (item 12) is 2, 3, or 5, at least one Schedule A (Form 5500) must be attached to the Form 5500-C filed for pension and welfare plans. The insurance company (or similar organization) which provides benefits is required to provide the plan administrator with the information needed to complete the return/report, pursuant to ERISA section 103 (a)(2). If you do not receive this information in a timely manner, contact the insurance company (or similar organization). If information is missing on Schedule A (Form 5500) due to a refusal to provide this information, note this on the Schedule A. If there are no Schedule(s) A attached, enter "0."

15b. If a waived funding deficiency is being amortized in the current plan year, do not complete (i), (ii), and (iii), but complete 1, 2, 3, 7, and 9 of Schedule B (Form 5500). An enrolled actuary need not sign Schedule B under these circumstances.

15b(iii). File Form 5330 with IRS to pay the excise tax on the funding deficiency. **Caution:** *There is a penalty for not filing Form 5330 on time.*

16. A "top-heavy plan" is a plan which during any plan year is:

(1) any defined benefit plan if, as of the determination date, the present value of the cumulative accrued benefits under the plan for key employees exceeds 60% of the present value of the cumulative accrued benefits under the plan for all employees; and

(2) any defined contribution plan if, as of the determination date, the aggregate of the accounts of key employees under the plan exceeds 60% of the aggregate of the accounts of all employees under the plan.

Each plan of an employer included in a required aggregation group is to be treated as a top-heavy plan if such group is a top-heavy group. See definitions of required aggregation and top-heavy groups below.

Key Employee —A key employee is any participant in an employer plan who at any time during the plan year, or any of the 2 preceding years, is:

(1) an officer of the employer having an annual compensation greater than 50% of the amount in effect under Code section 415(c)(1)(A) for any such plan year,

(2) one of the 10 employees having annual compensation from the employer of more than the limitation in effect under Code section 415(c)(1)(A) and owning (or considered as owning within the meaning of Code section 318) both more than ½% interest and the largest interests in the employer,

(3) a 5% owner of the employer, or

(4) a 1% owner of the employer having an annual compensation from the employer of more than $150,000.

In determining whether an individual is an officer of the employer, no more than 50 employees, or, if less, the greater of 3 employees or 10% of the employees, are to be treated as officers. See Code section 416(i) and T-12 of Regulations section 1.416. A key employee will not include any officer or employee of a governmental plan under Code section 414(d).

Required Aggregation Group—A required aggregation group consists of:

(1) each plan of the employer in which a key employee is or was a participant, and

(2) each other plan of the employer which enables a plan to meet the requirements for nondiscrimination in contributions or benefits under Code section 401(a)(4), or the participation requirements under Code section 410.

Top-Heavy Group—A top-heavy group is an aggregation group if, as of the determination date, the sum of the present value of the cumulative accrued benefits for key employees under all defined benefit plans included in such group and the aggregate of the accounts of key employees under all defined contribution plans in such group exceeds 60% of a similar sum determined for all employees. To determine if a plan is top-heavy, include distributions made in the 5-year period ending on the determination date. However, do not take into account accrued benefits for an individual who hasn't performed services for the employer during the 5-year period ending on the determination date.

18a. If the plan distributes an annuity contract, whether or not deferred and whether or not upon termination, that contract must provide that all distributions from it will meet the participant and spousal consent requirements of Code section 417. Consent is not needed for the distribution of the contract itself. Check "No" if the plan did not distribute any annuity contracts.

18b. In general, distributions must be made in the form of a qualified joint and survivor annuity for life or a qualified preretirement survivor annuity. An annuity distribution to a single individual is a qualified joint and survivor annuity. Check "Yes" if distributions in other forms were made, even if such distributions were permissible, e.g., because consent was obtained or was not needed.

18c. Generally, within the 90 days prior to the date of any benefit payment or the making of a loan to a participant, you must get the spouse's consent to the payment of the benefit or the use of the accrued benefit for the making of the loan. However, there are some circumstances where obtaining this spousal consent is not required. The following is a partial listing of circumstances where spousal consent is not required:

(1) The participant is not married and no spouse is required to be treated as a current spouse under a qualified domestic relations order issued by a court.

(2) The participant's accrued benefit in the plan never had a present value of more than $3,500.

(3) The benefit is paid in the form of a qualified joint and survivor annuity, i.e., an annuity for the life of the participant with a survivor annuity for the life of the spouse which is not less than 50% of (and is not greater than 100% of) the amount of the annuity which is payable during the joint lives of the participant and the spouse. See Code section 417(b).

(4) The payout is from a profit-sharing or stock bonus plan that pays the spouse the participant's full account balance upon the participant's death, an annuity payment is not elected by the participant, and the profit-sharing or stock bonus plan is not a transferee plan with respect to the participant (i.e., had not received a transfer from a plan that was subject to the consent requirements with respect to the participant)

(5) The participant had no service under the plan after August 22, 1984.

18d. A plan may not eliminate a subsidized benefit or a retirement option by plan amendment or plan termination.

19. For purposes of determining the present value of a participant's accrued benefits and the amount of any distribution, a qualified plan must use a rate no higher than "the applicable interest rate." The "applicable interest rate" means the interest rate which would be used (as of the date of distributions) by the PBGC for determining the present value of a lump sum distribution on termination of the plan.

a. If the present value of the vested accrued benefit is no more than $25,000, the amount to be distributed is calculated using the PBGC rate.

b. If the present value of the vested accrued benefit exceeds $25,000 (using the PBGC rate), the total amount to be distributed is determined using an interest rate no greater than 120% of the applicable interest rate that would be used by the PBGC upon the plan's termination. In such a case the value will be no less than $25,000.

20. The Tax Reform Act of 1986 amended Code section 415 to provide that the maximum annual benefit that may be provided under a defined benefit plan may not exceed the lesser of $90,000 or 100% of compensation. However, if benefits begin before the social security retirement age, the $90,000 limit must be reduced as described in Notice 87-21, 1987-1 C.B. 458.

In addition, the dollar limitations will be reduced for participants with fewer than 10 years of participation in a defined benefit plan, i.e., a 10% reduction for each year under 10 years of participation.

For defined contribution plans, Code section 415 now provides that the dollar limit on annual additions to a qualified plan may not exceed the greater of $30,000 or 25% of the defined benefit dollar limit for such limitation year. The defined contribution dollar limit will not be increased until the defined benefit dollar limit, as increased by cost of living adjustments, equals or exceeds $120,000. (For years beginning after December 31, 1987, the $90,000 defined benefit limit will be adjusted to reflect post-1986 cost of living increases.) The defined contribution dollar limit will then be increased to an amount equal to 25% of the defined benefit limit.

Annual additions to a defined contribution plan will, for years beginning after December 31, 1986, include 100% of all after-tax employee contributions. For participants in plans of tax-exempt organizations, the pre-Tax Reform Act limits remain in effect.

The Tax Reform Act of 1986 also provides that a participant's previously accrued benefit won't be reduced merely because of the reduction in dollar limits or increases in required periods of participation. The transitional rule applies to an individual who was a participant prior to January 1, 1987, in a plan in existence on May 5, 1986. If this participant's current accrued benefit exceeds the dollar limit under the Tax Reform Act of 1986, but complies with prior law, then the applicable dollar limit for the participant is equal to the current accrued benefit. The term "current accrued benefit" is defined as the participant's accrued benefit as of the close of the last limitation year beginning before January 1, 1987, and expressed as an annual benefit. To compute the defined benefit fraction, the current accrued benefit would replace the dollar limit otherwise used in the denominator of the fraction. The current accrued benefit is also reflected in the numerator of the defined benefit fraction.

21. In the calendar year in which the employee attains age 70 ½, the employee must begin to receive minimum distributions pursuant to Code section 401(a)(9) by April 1 of the following calendar year. Once begun, minimal distributions must continue each calendar year.

22. For purposes of filing required only because of Code section 6039D, complete only items 22c, 22g, and 22i.

22a. If you do not claim to meet the percentage tests of Code section 410(b)(1)(A), attach an explanation indicating how your plan meets the coverage requirements of Code section 410(b)(1)(B).

22b. Provide information for all employers of a controlled group, a group under common control, or an affiliated service group even if they do not participate in the plan. Also, leased employees (described in Code section 414(n)(2)) of any such employer(s) are to be included as employees unless the leasing organization maintains a "safe harbor" plan described in Code section 414(n)(5) for the leased employees. See below for more information regarding a "safe harbor" plan.

Generally, leased employees are individuals who are employees of a leasing organization, but who during the course of their employment perform services for a trade or business other than the leasing organization on a substantially full-time basis for a period of at least one year.

Service is to include any period during which the employee would have been a leased employee, but for the requirement that substantially full-time service be performed for at least one year. Such leased employees are to be considered employees of their recipient organization at certain times and for certain qualification requirements unless the leasing organization adopts and maintains the type of qualified plan specified in Code section 414(n)(5).

A *safe harbor* plan is a money purchase pension plan maintained by the leasing organization which provides with respect to a leased employee:

(A) a nonintegrated employer contribution rate of at least 10%, and

(B) immediate participation and full and immediate vesting.

The plan must cover all employees of the leasing organization other than those who are not "leased out" and cover those whose compensation from the leasing organization is less than $1,000 per year during a plan year and each of the prior 3 plan years. The safe harbor plan must provide the 10% of compensation allocation regardless of the number of hours of service during the year, age, or whether the employee is employed on a specific date.

In general, if leased employees make up more than 20% of the nonhighly compensated work force of the recipient, such employees must be covered by the recipient's pension plan regardless of the safe harbor plan. Recipient includes employers aggregated under Code section 414(b), (c), or (m). Under the 20% rule, "leased employees" include all persons who performed services as a "nonemployee."

Therefore, the total number of employees entered in 22c, the breakdown of excluded employees shown in 22d, and the ineligible employees shown in 22f should also include the employees of the controlled group, employees of employers under common control, or other employees in the affiliated service group or leased employees as described above.

Do not complete 22 for multiemployer plans described in Code section 414(f) or for multiple-employer-collectively-bargained plans.

24b. An independent appraiser must be used to ascertain the value of securities acquired by a plan after December 31, 1986, if the securities aren't readily tradable on an established securities market.

28a. If you are uncertain as to whether the plan is covered under the PBGC termination insurance program, check the box "Not determined" and contact the PBGC and request a coverage determination.

29. Check "Yes" or "No" and enter the total amount (except 29i) for all "Yes" responses. Round off all amounts to the nearest dollar.

29a. Check "Yes" and indicate the aggregate amount of coverage available for all claims if every plan official who handles plan funds is covered by a bond. Otherwise, check "No." Generally, every plan official of an employee benefit plan who "handles" funds or other property of such plan must be bonded. A plan administrator, officer, or employee shall be deemed to be "handling" funds or other property of a plan, so as to require bonding, whenever his or her duties or activities with respect to given funds are such that there is a risk that such funds could be lost in the event of fraud or dishonesty on the part of such person, acting either alone or in collusion with others. Section 412 of ERISA and the regulations found at 29 CFR 2580 provide the bonding requirements including the definition of "handling" (29 CFR 2580.412-6), the permissible forms of bonds (29 CFR 2580.412-10), and certain exemptions such as the exemption for unfunded plans, banks and insurance companies (ERISA section 412) and the exemption allowing plan officials to purchase bonds from surety companies authorized by the Secretary of the Treasury as acceptable reinsurers on Federal bonds (29 CFR 2580.412-23).

Check "Yes" only if the plan itself (as opposed to the plan sponsor) is a named insured under a fidelity bond covering plan officials.

Plans are permitted under certain conditions to purchase fiduciary liability insurance. These policies do not protect the plan from dishonest acts and are not bonds which should be reported in item 29.

29b. If item 29a is answered "Yes," this must be answered. Check "Yes" to item 29b if the plan has suffered or discovered any loss as the result of a dishonest or fraudulent act(s). If "Yes," enter the full amount of the loss. If the full amount of the loss has not yet been determined, provide and disclose that the figure is an estimate, such as "approximately $1,000."

Note: *Wilful failure to report is a criminal offense. See ERISA section 501.*

29c. For purposes of item 29, the term "employer" includes affiliates of the employer. In determining the five most highly paid employees, use all compensation paid including cash, bonuses, and noncash payments (e.g., the use of a car). A fiduciary is a person with respect to a plan to the extent: (1) he or she exercises any discretionary authority or discretionary control with respect to the management of such plan or exercises any authority or control with respect to the management or disposition of its assets, (2) he or she renders investment advice for a fee or other compensation, direct or indirect, with respect to any moneys or other property of such plan, or has any authority or responsibility to do so, or (3) he or she has any discretionary authority or discretionary responsibility in the administration of such plan.

29d. Relatives include spouses, siblings, ancestors, lineal descendents (e.g., children, grandchildren, etc.) and spouses of lineal descendents. If 29c is answered "Yes," enter the total amount of these transactions.

29e. An "employer security" is a security issued by an employer (including affiliates of employees) covered by the plan. These may include common stocks, preferred stocks, bonds, zero coupon bonds, debentures, convertible debentures, notes, and commercial paper.

Employer real property is any real property (and related personal property) owned by the plan and leased to the employer of employees covered by the plan. This may include land, warehouses, office buildings, etc. If item 29e is "Yes," enter the total amount of employer securities and/or employer real property held or acquired.

29f. Generally, a loan requires that both the principal and interest be paid according to a pre-established repayment schedule. If the principal and/or interest has not been paid in accordance with the original repayment schedule and the period for repayment of the principal and/or interest has been extended, or the loan has been renegotiated after it has not met the original repayment schedule, a "Yes" must be checked and the total amount of the delinquent loan must be entered. Otherwise check "No."

29h. Check "Yes," for obligations where the required payments have not been made by the due date. With respect to notes and loans, the due date, payment amount and conditions for default are usually contained in the note or loan document. Defaults can occur at any time for those obligations that require periodic repayment. Generally, loans and fixed income obligations are considered uncollectible when payment has not been made and there is little probability that payment will be made. A loan by the plan is in default when the borrower is unable to pay the obligation upon maturity. A fixed income obligation has a fixed maturity date at a specified interest rate. If item 29h is "Yes," enter the total amount of loans by the plan or fixed income obligations that are uncollectible or in default as of the plan year end.

29i. Consider all fiduciaries and parties providing services to the plan, including: (1) persons who are fiduciaries by reason of their relationship to a master trust investment account or 103-12 IE in which the plan has an interest or the assets in such an investment account or 103-12 IE; and (2) parties providing services rendered with respect to assets held in master trusts and 103-12 IEs.

See item 29c above for the definition of fiduciary.

29j. Include as a single security all securities of the same issue. For the purposes of item 29j, do not check "Yes" for securities issued by the U.S. Government or its agencies. If item 29j is "Yes," enter the total.

29k. In determining the 20% figure, subtract the current value of plan assets held in any master trust or 103-12 IE from the current value of the plan's total assets at the beginning of the plan year. Check "Yes" if the plan had:

1. A single transaction within the plan year in excess of 20% of the current value of the plan assets;

2. Any series of transactions with, or in conjunction with, the same person, involving property other than securities, which amount in the aggregate within the plan year (regardless of the category of asset and the gain or loss on any transaction) to more than 20% of the current value of plan assets;

3. Any transaction within the plan year involving securities of the same issue if within the plan year any series of transactions with respect to such securities amount in the aggregate to more than 20% of the current value of the plan assets; or

4. Any transaction within the plan year with respect to securities with, or in conjunction with, a person if any prior or subsequent single transaction within the plan year with such person, with respect to securities, exceeds 20% of the current value of plan assets. The 20% figure is determined by comparing the current value of the transaction at the transaction date with the current value of the plan assets at the beginning of the plan year.

If the assets of two or more plans are maintained in one trust, the plan's allocable portion of the transactions of the trust shall be combined with the other transactions of the plan, if any, to determine which transactions (or series of transactions) are reportable (20%) transactions.

Exception: For investments in common/collective trusts, pooled separate accounts, 103-12 IEs, and registered investment companies, determine the 20% figure by comparing the transaction date value of the acquisition and/or disposition of units of participation or shares in the entity with the current value of the plan assets at the beginning of the plan year. Check "No" if all plan funds are held in a master trust. Do not include individual transactions of common/collective trusts, pooled separate accounts, 103-12 IEs and registered investment companies.

If item 29k is answered "Yes," enter the amount.

29l. Check "No" if the plan received all of its contributions in cash. Generally, as it relates to this question, an appraisal by an unrelated third party is an evaluation of the value of the asset contributed prepared by an individual or firm who knows how to judge the value of the asset and does not have an ongoing relationship with the plan or plan fiduciaries except for preparing the appraisal. If item 29l is checked "Yes," enter the value of the asset as established by the plan.

29m. Nonpublicly traded securities are generally held by few people and not traded on a stock exchange. Generally, as it relates to this question, an appraisal by an unrelated third party is an evaluation of the value of the security prepared by an individual or firm who knows how to judge the value of the security and does not have an ongoing relationship with the plan or plan fiduciaries except for preparing the appraisal. If item 29m is answered "Yes," enter the value of the security as established by the plan.

30 and 31. You can use either the cash, modified accrual, or accrual basis for recognition of transactions in items 30 and 31, as long as you use one method consistently.

"Current value" means fair market value where available. Otherwise, it means the fair value as determined in good faith under the terms of the plan by a trustee or a named fiduciary, assuming an orderly liquidation at the time of the determination.

If the assets of two or more plans are maintained in one trust, such as when an employer has two plans which are funded through a single trust (except investment arrangements filing with DOL as specified below), complete items 30 and 31 by entering the plan's allocable part of each line item.

If assets of one plan are maintained in two or more trust funds, report the combined financial information in 30 and 31.

A fully insured pension plan meeting the conditions of 29 CFR 2520.104-44 need not complete items 30 and 31. For more details, see page 4 of the instructions under "Items To Be Completed on Form 5500-C."

Plan assets may include, among other things:

(1) Cash both interest and noninterest bearing. This includes all cash on hand or in a financial institution including money market funds.

(2) All contributions due to the plan from the employer and participants, income earned, but not yet received by the plan and receivables from any other source.

(3) Investments securities (stocks, bonds, U. S. Government obligations, municipal obligations, etc.); real property (land, buildings, gold, furniture, equipment, etc.); loans (mortgages, promissory notes, etc.) and all other investments (certificates of deposit, repurchase agreements, land contracts, units of participation in common/collective trusts and pooled separate accounts, shares of registered investment companies (mutual funds), interests in master trusts and 103-12 IE's, etc.).

Plans holding units of participation in common/collective trusts and/or pooled separate accounts must attach to the return/report either the statement of assets and liabilities of the common/collective trust and/or pooled separate account or the certification discussed on page 3 of these instructions. For details, see 29 CFR sections 2520.103-3, 2520.103-4, 2520.103-5, and 2520.103-9.

Plans in a master trust must include the value of the plan's interest in the master trust which is the sum of the net values of the plan's interest in all of the master trust investment accounts (see page 3 for the definition of master trust investment account). The net values of such interests are obtained by multiplying the plan's percentage interest in each master trust investment account by the net assets of the investment account (total assets minus total liabilities) at the beginning and end of the plan year.

30c. Investments in securities of the U.S. Government should be included in c(i).

You can use the same method for determining the value of the insurance contracts reported in 30 that you used for line 6e of the Schedule A (Form 5500) as long as the contract values are stated as of the beginning and end of the plan year.

Liabilities include among other things:

(1) Benefit claims payable—claims that have been processed and approved for payment but have not been paid.

(2) Accounts payable—obligations owed by the plan that were incurred in the normal operations of the plan and have been approved for payment but not been paid.

(3) Other liabilities—such as acquisition indebtedness and any other amount owed by the plan.

Liabilities. Do not include the value of future pension payments .

30g. Enter total amount of claims which have been processed and approved for payment directly from the trust but have not been paid. Do not include the value of future pension payments.

30h. Acquisition Indebtedness.—Acquisition indebtedness, for debt-financed property other than real property, means the outstanding amount of the principal debt incurred:

(1) by the organization in acquiring or improving the property;

(2) before the acquisition or improvement of the property if the debt was incurred only to acquire or improve the property; or

(3) after the acquisition or improvement of the property if the debt was incurred only to acquire or improve the property and was reasonably foreseeable at the time of such acquisition or improvement.

For further explanation, see Code section 514(c).

31a(i). If the plan is on the accrual basis, enter the amount of contributions received or accrued.

31b. Show current value, at date contributed, of securities or other noncash property contributed to the plan.

31g. If distributions include securities or other property, show the current value at date distributed in this figure.

31h. Report all administrative expenses paid by or charged to the plan, including those which were not subtracted from the gross income of master trust investment accounts and 103-12 IEs in determining their net investment gain(s) or loss(es).

For purposes of a filing required only because of Code section 6039D, do not include overhead expenses such as utilities and photocopying expenses. Also, if filing for an educational assistance program described in Code section 127, do not include expenses for job-related training which are deductible under Code section 162.

Codes for Principal Business Activity and Principal Product or Service

These industry titles and definitions are based, in general, on the Enterprise Standard Industrial Classification System authorized by the Regulatory and Statistical Analysis Division, Office of Information and Regulatory Affairs, Office of Management and Budget, to classify enterprises by type of activity in which they are engaged.

Code

AGRICULTURE, FORESTRY, AND FISHING

0120 Field crop.
0150 Fruit, tree nut, and vegetable.
0180 Horticultural specialty.
0230 Livestock.
0270 Animal specialty.

Agricultural services and forestry:

0740 Veterinary services.
0750 Animal services, except veterinary.
0780 Landscape and horticultural services.
0790 Other agricultural services.
0800 Forestry.

Farms:

Fishing, hunting, and trapping:

0930 Commercial fishing, hatcheries, and preserves.
0970 Hunting, trapping, and game propagation.

MINING

Metal mining:

1010 Iron ores.
1070 Copper, lead and zinc, gold and silver ores.
1098 Other metal mining.
1150 Coal mining.

Oil and gas extraction:

1330 Crude petroleum, natural gas, and natural gas liquids.
1380 Oil and gas field services.

Nonmetallic minerals (except fuels) mining:

1430 Dimension, crushed and broken stone; sand and gravel.
1498 Other nonmetallic minerals, except fuels.

CONSTRUCTION

General building contractors and operative builders:

1510 General building contractors.
1531 Operative builders.

Heavy construction contractors:

1611 Highway and street construction.
1620 Heavy construction, except highway.

Special trade contractors:

1711 Plumbing, heating, and air conditioning.
1721 Painting, paperhanging, and decorating.
1731 Electrical work.
1740 Masonry, stonework, and plastering.
1750 Carpentering and flooring.
1761 Roofing and sheet metal work.
1771 Concrete work.
1781 Water well drilling.
1790 Miscellaneous special trade contractors.

MANUFACTURING

Food and kindred products:

2010 Meat products.
2020 Dairy products.
2030 Preserved fruits and vegetables.
2040 Grain mill products.
2050 Bakery products.
2060 Sugar and confectionery products.
2081 Malt liquors and malt.
2088 Alcoholic beverages, except malt liquors and malt.
2089 Bottled soft drinks and flavorings.
2096 Other food and kindred products.
2100 Tobacco manufacturers.

Textile mill products:

2228 Weaving mills and textile finishing.
2250 Knitting mills.
2298 Other textile mill products.

Apparel and other textile products:

2315 Men's and boys' clothing.
2345 Women's and children's clothing.
2388 Hats, caps, millinery, fur goods, and other apparel and accessories.
2390 Misc. fabricated textile products.

Code

Lumber and wood products:

2415 Logging camps and logging contractors, sawmills, and planing mills.
2430 Millwork, plywood, and related products.
2498 Other wood products, including wood buildings and mobile homes
2500 Furniture and fixtures.

Paper and allied products:

2625 Pulp, paper, and board mills.
2699 Other paper products.

Printing, publishing, and allied industries:

2710 Newspapers.
2720 Periodicals.
2735 Books, greeting cards, and miscellaneous publishing.
2799 Commercial and other printing, and printing trade services.

Chemical and allied products:

2815 Industrial chemicals, plastics materials, and synthetics.
2830 Drugs.
2840 Soap, cleaners, and toilet goods.
2850 Paints and allied products.
2898 Agricultural and other chemical products.

Petroleum refining and related industries (including those integrated with extraction):

2910 Petroleum refining (including those integrated with extraction).
2998 Other petroleum and coal products.

Rubber and misc. plastics products:

3050 Rubber products, plastics footwear, hose, and belting.
3070 Misc. plastics products.

Leather and leather products:

3140 Footwear, except rubber.
3198 Other leather and leather products.

Stone, clay, glass, and concrete products:

3225 Glass products.
3240 Cement, hydraulic.
3270 Concrete, gypsum, and plaster products.
3298 Other nonmetallic mineral products.

Primary metal industries:

3370 Ferrous metal industries; miscellaneous primary metal products.
3380 Nonferrous metal industries.

Fabricated metal products, except machinery and transportation equipment:

3410 Metal cans and shipping containers.
3428 Cutlery, hand tools, and hardware; screw machine products, bolts, and similar products.
3430 Plumbing and heating, except electric and warm air.
3440 Fabricated structural metal products.
3460 Metal forgings and stampings.
3470 Coating, engraving, and allied services.
3480 Ordnance and accessories, except vehicles and guided missiles.
3490 Misc. fabricated metal products.

Machinery, except electrical:

3520 Farm machinery.
3530 Construction, mining and materials handling machinery, and equipment.
3540 Metalworking machinery.
3550 Special industry machinery, except metalworking machinery.
3560 General industrial machinery.
3570 Office, computing, and accounting machines.
3598 Engines and turbines, service industry machinery, and other machinery, except electrical.

Code

Electrical and electronic machinery, equipment, and supplies:

3630 Household appliances.
3665 Radio, television, and communication equipment.
3670 Electronic components and accessories.
3698 Other electric equipment.

Transportation equipment:

3710 Motor vehicles and equipment.
3725 Aircraft, guided missiles, and parts.
3730 Ship and boat building and repairing.
3798 Other transportation equipment.

Measuring and controlling instruments; photographic and medical goods, watches and clocks:

3815 Scientific instruments and measuring devices; watches, and clocks.
3845 Optical, medical, and ophthalmic goods.
3860 Photographic equipment and supplies.
3998 Other manufacturing products.

TRANSPORTATION, COMMUNICATION, ELECTRIC, GAS, SANITARY SERVICES

Transportation:

4000 Railroad transportation.

Local and interurban passenger transit:

4121 Taxicabs.
4189 Other passenger transportation.

Trucking and warehousing:

4210 Trucking, local and long distance.
4289 Public warehousing and trucking terminals.

Other transportation including transportation services:

4400 Water transportation.
4500 Transportation by air.
4600 Pipelines, except natural gas.
4722 Passenger transportation arrangement.
4723 Freight transportation arrangement.
4799 Other transportation services.

Communication:

4825 Telephone, telegraph, and other communication services.
4830 Radio and television broadcasting.

Electric, gas, and sanitary services:

4910 Electric services.
4920 Gas production and distribution.
4930 Combination utility services.
4990 Water supply and other sanitary services.

WHOLESALE TRADE

Durable:

5010 Motor vehicles and automotive equipment.
5020 Furniture and home furnishings.
5030 Lumber and construction materials.
5040 Sporting, recreational, photographic, and hobby goods, toys, and supplies.
5050 Metals and minerals, except petroleum and scrap.
5060 Electrical goods.
5070 Hardware, plumbing, and heating equipment.
5083 Farm machinery and equipment.
5089 Other machinery, equipment, and supplies.
5098 Other durable goods.

Nondurable:

5110 Paper and paper products.
5129 Drugs, drug proprietaries, and druggists' sundries.
5130 Apparel, piece goods, and notions.
5140 Groceries and related products, except meats and meat products.
5147 Meats and meat products.
5150 Farm product raw materials.
5160 Chemicals and allied products.
5170 Petroleum and petroleum products.
5180 Alcoholic beverages.
5190 Miscellaneous nondurable goods.

Code

RETAIL TRADE

Building materials hardware, garden supply, and mobile home dealers:

5211 Lumber and other building materials dealers.
5231 Paint, glass and wallpaper stores.
5251 Hardware stores.
5261 Retail nurseries and garden stores.
5271 Mobile home dealers.

General merchandise:

5331 Variety stores.
5398 Other general merchandise stores.

Food stores:

5411 Grocery stores.
5420 Meat and fish markets and freezer provisioners.
5431 Fruit stores and vegetable markets.
5441 Candy, nut, and confectionery stores.
5451 Dairy products stores.
5460 Retail bakeries.
5490 Other food stores.

Automotive dealers and service stations:

5511 New car dealers (franchised).
5521 Used car dealers.
5531 Auto and home supply stores.
5541 Gasoline service stations.
5551 Boat dealers.
5561 Recreational vehicle dealers.
5571 Motorcycle dealers.
5599 Aircraft and other automotive dealers.

Apparel and accessory stores:

5611 Men's and boys' clothing and furnishings.
5621 Women's ready-to-wear stores.
5631 Women's accessory and specialty stores.
5641 Children's and infants' wear stores.
5651 Family clothing stores.
5661 Shoe stores.
5681 Furriers and fur shops.
5699 Other apparel and accessory stores.

Furniture, home furnishings, and equipment stores:

5712 Furniture stores.
5713 Floor covering stores.
5714 Drapery, curtain, and upholstery stores.
5719 Home furnishings, except appliances.
5722 Household appliance stores.
5732 Radio and television stores.
5733 Music stores.

Eating and drinking places:

5812 Eating places.
5813 Drinking places.

Miscellaneous retail stores:

5912 Drug stores and proprietary stores.
5921 Liquor stores.
5931 Used merchandise stores.
5941 Sporting goods stores and bicycle shops.
5942 Book stores.
5943 Stationery stores.
5944 Jewelry stores.
5945 Hobby, toy, and game shops.
5946 Camera and photographic supply stores.
5947 Gift, novelty, and souvenir shops.
5948 Luggage and leather goods stores.
5949 Sewing, needlework, and piece goods stores
5961 Mail order houses.
5962 Merchandising machine operators.
5963 Direct selling organizations.
5982 Fuel and ice dealers (except fuel oil and bottle gas dealers).
5983 Fuel oil dealers.
5984 Liquefied petroleum gas (bottled gas).
5992 Florists.
5993 Cigar stores and stands.
5994 News dealers and newsstands.
5996 Other miscellaneous retail stores.

Code

FINANCE, INSURANCE, AND REAL ESTATE

Banking:

6030 Mutual savings banks.
6060 Banking holding companies.
6090 Banks, except mutual savings banks and bank holding companies.

Credit agencies other than banks:

6120 Savings and loan associations.
6140 Personal credit institutions.
6150 Business credit institutions.
6199 Other credit agencies.

Security, commodity brokers, dealers, exchanges, and services:

6212 Security underwriting syndicates.
6218 Security brokers and dealers, except underwriting syndicates.
6299 Commodity contracts brokers and dealers; security and commodity exchanges; and allied services.

Insurance:

6355 Life insurance.
6356 Mutual insurance, except life or marine and certain fire or flood insurance companies.
6359 Other insurance companies.
6411 Insurance agents, brokers, and services.

Real estate:

6511 Real estate operators (except developers) and lessors of buildings.
6516 Lessors of mining, oil, and similar property.
6518 Lessors of railroad property and other real property.
6531 Real estate agents, brokers and managers.
6541 Title abstract offices.
6552 Subdividers and developers, except cemeteries.
6553 Cemetery subdividers and developers.
6599 Other real estate.
6611 Combined real estate, insurance, loans and law offices.

Holding and other investment companies:

6742 Regulated investment companies.
6743 Real estate investment trusts.
6744 Small business investment companies.
6749 Holding and other investment companies, except bank holding companies.

SERVICES

Hotels and other lodging places:

7012 Hotels.
7013 Motels, motor hotels, and tourist courts.
7021 Rooming and boarding houses.
7032 Sporting and recreational camps.
7033 Trailer parks and camp sites.
7041 Organizational hotels and lodging houses on a membership basis.

Personal services:

7215 Coin-operated laundries and dry cleaning.
7219 Other laundry, cleaning and garment services.
7221 Photographic studios, portrait.
7231 Beauty shops.
7241 Barber shops.
7251 Shoe repair and hat cleaning shops.
7261 Funeral services and crematories.
7299 Miscellaneous personal services.

Business services:

7310 Advertising.
7340 Services to buildings.
7370 Computer and data processing services.
7392 Management, consulting, and public relations services.
7394 Equipment rental and leasing.
7398 Other business services.

Code

Automotive repair and services:

7510 Automotive rentals and leasing, without drivers.
7520 Automobile parking.
7531 Automobile top and body repair shops.
7538 General automobile repair shops.
7539 Other automobile repair shops.
7540 Automobile services, except repair.

Miscellaneous repair services:

7622 Radio and TV repair shops.
7628 Electrical repair shops, except radio and TV.
7641 Reupholstery and furniture repair.
7680 Other miscellaneous repair shops.

Motion pictures:

7812 Motion picture production, distribution, and services.
7830 Motion picture theaters.

Amusement and recreation services:

7920 Producers, orchestras, and entertainers.
7932 Billiard and pool establishments.
7933 Bowling alleys.
7980 Other amusement and recreation services.

Medical and health services:

8011 Offices of physicians.
8021 Offices of dentists.
8031 Offices of osteopathic physicians.
8041 Offices of chiropractors.
8042 Offices of optometrists.
8048 Registered and practical nurses.
8050 Nursing and personal care facilities.
8060 Hospitals.
8071 Medical laboratories.
8072 Dental laboratories.
8098 Other medical and health services.

Other services:

8111 Legal services.
8200 Educational services.
8911 Engineering and architectural services.
8932 Certified public accountants.
8933 Other accounting, auditing, and bookkeeping services.
8999 Other services, not elsewhere classified.

TAX-EXEMPT ORGANIZATIONS

9002 Church plans making an election under section 410(d) of the Internal Revenue Code.
9319 Other tax-exempt organizations.
9904 Governmental instrumentality or agency.

Form **5500-R**
Department of the Treasury
Internal Revenue Service

Department of Labor
Pension and Welfare Benefits Administration

Pension Benefit Guaranty Corporation

Registration Statement of Employee Benefit Plan

(With fewer than 100 participants)

This form is required to be filed under sections 104 and 4065 of the Employee Retirement Income Security Act of 1974 and sections 6039D and 6058 of the Internal Revenue Code.

OMB No. 1210-0016

1988

Amended ☐

This Form is Open to Public Inspection

For the calendar plan year 1988 or fiscal plan year beginning , 1988, and ending 19

One-participant plans file Form 5500EZ (see the instructions).
Plans described in Code section 6039D, complete the applicable box 6d, 6e, or 6f, and see the instructions.
Do NOT file this form for the plan's first year or for the plan's final return/report. Instead file Form 5500-C.
Check this box if an extension of time to file this return is attached . . . . ▶ ☐

▶ If you have been granted an extension of time to file this form, you must attach a copy of the approved extension to this form.
▶ Type or complete in ink and file the original. If any item does not apply, enter "N/A."

Use IRS label. Otherwise, please print or type.

1a Name of plan sponsor (employer, if for a single employer plan)
Address (number and street)
City or town, state, and ZIP code

1b Employer identification number
1c Sponsor's telephone number ( )
1d If plan year changed since last return/report, check here . . ▶ ☐

2a Name of plan administrator (if same as plan sponsor, enter "Same")
Address (number and street)
City or town, state, and ZIP code

2b Administrator's employer identification number
2c Administrator's telephone number ( )

3 Are the name, address, and identification number of the plan sponsor and/or plan administrator the same as they appeared on the last return/report filed for this plan? . . . ☐ Yes ☐ No
If "No," enter the information from the last return/report in a and/or b, and complete c.
a Sponsor ▶ ________ EIN ________ Plan number ________
b Administrator ▶ ________ EIN ________
c If **a** is completed, is this a change in sponsorship only? (See specific instructions for definition of sponsorship.) ☐ Yes ☐ No

4 Check appropriate box to indicate the type of plan entity (check only one box):
a ☐ Single-employer plan
b ☐ Plan of controlled group of corporations or common control employers
c ☐ Multiemployer plan
d ☐ Multiple-employer-collectively-bargained plan
e ☐ Multiple-employer plan (other)
f ☐ Exceptions to (b) and (e). (See instructions for line 4f.)

5a(*i*) Name of plan ▶ ________
(*ii*) ☐ Check if name of plan changed since last return/report
(*iii*) ☐ Check this box if this plan covers self-employed participants

5b Effective date of plan ▶
5c Enter three-digit plan number . . . ▶

6 Type of plan (check applicable boxes):
a ☐ Defined benefit
b ☐ Defined contribution (money purchase or profit-sharing)
c ☐ Welfare benefit
d ☐ Code section 120 (group legal services plan)
e ☐ Code section 125 (cafeteria plan)
f ☐ Code section 127 (educational assistance program)
g ☐ Master trust
h ☐ Common/collective trust
i ☐ Pooled separate account
j ☐ Other (specify) ▶
k If you checked d, e, or f, check if plan is: ☐ funded or ☐ unfunded

		Yes	No
7a Total participants: (*i*) Beginning of plan year ________ (*ii*) End of plan year ________			
b (*i*) Was any pension benefit plan participant(s) separated from service with deferred vested benefits for which a Schedule SSA (Form 5500) is required to be attached to this form? . . .	7b(i)		
(*ii*) If "Yes," enter the number of separated participants required to be reported ▶			

Under penalties of perjury and other penalties set forth in the instructions, I declare that I have examined this return/report, including accompanying schedules and statements, and to the best of my knowledge and belief, it is true, correct and complete.

Date ▶ ________ Signature of employer/plan sponsor ▶ ________

Date ▶ ________ Signature of plan administrator ▶ ________

For Paperwork Reduction Act Notice, see page 1 of Form 5500-R instructions.

Form **5500-R** (1988)

Form 5500-R (1988) Page 2

			Yes	No
8a	Was this plan terminated during this plan year or any prior plan year? If "Yes," enter the year	8a		
b	Were all the plan assets either distributed to participants or beneficiaries, transferred to another plan, or brought under the control of PBGC?	8b		
c	If **a** is "Yes" and the plan is covered by PBGC, is the plan continuing to file PBGC Form 1 and pay premiums until the end of the plan year in which assets are distributed or brought under the control of PBGC?	8c		
9	Is this a plan established or maintained pursuant to one or more collective bargaining agreements?	9		
10	If any benefits are provided by an insurance company, insurance service, or similar organization, enter the number of Schedules A (Form 5500), Insurance Information, that are attached. (If none, enter "-0-") ▶			
11a	Were any plan amendments adopted during the plan year?	11a		
b	If **a** is "Yes," did any amendment result in a retroactive reduction of accrued benefits for any participant?	11b		
c	If **a** is "Yes," did any amendment change the information contained in the latest summary plan description or summary description of modifications available at the time of the amendment?	11c		
d	Has a summary plan description or summary description of modifications that reflects the plan amendments referred to in 11c been furnished to participants and filed with the Department of Labor?	11d		
12a	If this is a pension benefit plan subject to the minimum funding standards, has the plan experienced a funding deficiency for this plan year (defined benefit plans must answer this question and, attach Schedule B (Form 5500))?	12a		
b	If **a** is "Yes," have you filed Form 5330 to pay the excise tax?	12b		

13a Total plan assets as of the beginning .... and end .... of the plan year.
b Total liabilities as of the beginning .... and end .... of the plan year.
c Net assets as of the beginning .... and end .... of the plan year.

14 For this plan year, enter: **a** Plan income ....
b Expenses .... **c** Net income (loss) ....
d Plan contributions **e** Total benefits paid

			Yes	No	Amount
15	During this plan year:				
a	Was this plan covered by a fidelity bond?	15a			
b	Was there any loss to the plan, whether or not reimbursed, caused by fraud or dishonesty?	15b			
c	Was there any sale, exchange, or lease of any property between the plan and the employer, any fiduciary, any of the five most highly paid employees of the employer, any owner of a 10% or more interest in the employer, or relatives of any such persons?	15c			
d	Was there any loan or extension of credit by the plan to the employer, any fiduciary, any of the five most highly paid employees of the employer, any owner of a 10% or more interest in the employer, or relatives of any such persons?	15d			
e	Did the plan acquire or hold any employer security or employer real property?	15e			
f	Has the plan granted an extension on any delinquent loan owed to the plan?	15f			
g	Has the employer owed contributions to the plan which are more than 3 months overdue?	15g			
h	Were any loans by the plan or fixed income obligations due the plan classified as uncollectible or in default as of the close of the plan year?	15h			
i	Has any plan fiduciary had a financial interest in excess of 10% in any party providing services to the plan or received anything of value from any such party?	15i			
j	Did the plan hold at any time 20% or more of its assets in any single security, debt, mortgage, parcel of real estate, or partnership/joint venture interests?	15j			
k	Did the plan at any time engage in any transaction or series of related transactions involving 20% or more of the current value of plan assets?	15k			
l	Were there any noncash contributions made to the plan the value of which was set without an appraisal by an independent third party?	15l			
m	Were there any purchases of nonpublicly traded securities by the plan the value of which was set without an appraisal by an independent third party?	15m			
n	Has the plan failed to provide any benefit when due under the terms of the plan because of insufficient assets?	15n			

16a Is the plan covered under the Pension Benefit Guaranty Corporation termination insurance program?
☐ Yes ☐ No ☐ **Not determined**

b If **a** is "Yes" or "Not determined," enter the employer identification number and the plan number used to identify it.
Employer identification number ▶ Plan number ▶

Department of the Treasury
Internal Revenue Service

Department of Labor
Pension and Welfare Benefits Administration

Pension Benefit Guaranty Corporation

1988 Instructions for Form 5500-R

Registration Statement of Employee Benefit Plan (With fewer than 100 participants)

(Code references are to the Internal Revenue Code. ERISA refers to the Employee Retirement Income Security Act of 1974.)

Paperwork Reduction Act Notice.—We ask for this information to carry out the law as specified in ERISA and Code section 6039D. We need it to determine whether the plan is operating according to the law. You are required to give us this information.

The time needed to complete and file the forms listed below reflect the combined requirements of the Internal Revenue Service, Department of Labor, Pension Benefit Guaranty Corporation and the Social Security Administration. These times will vary depending on individual circumstances. The estimated average times are:

	Recordkeeping	Learning about the law or the form	Preparing the form	Copying, assembling, and sending the form to IRS
Form 5500-R	13 hrs., 26 min.	3 hrs., 37 min.	5 hrs., 50 min.	32 min.
Schedule A (Form 5500)	17 hrs., 28 min.	28 min.	1 hr., 42 min.	16 min.
Schedule B (Form 5500)	25 hrs., 50 min.	1 hr.	1 hr., 27 min.	-----
Schedule P (Form 5500)	2 hrs., 9 min.	1 hr., 24 min.	1 hr., 29 min.	-----
Schedule SSA (Form 5500)	6 hrs., 42 min.	12 min.	19 min.	-----

If you have comments concerning the accuracy of these time estimates or suggestions for making these forms more simple, we would be happy to hear from you. You can write to the **Internal Revenue Service,** Washington, DC 20224, Attention: IRS Reports Clearance Officer, TR:FP; or the **Office of Management and Budget,** Paperwork Reduction Project, Washington, DC 20503.

File 1988 forms for plan years that started in 1988. If the plan year differs from the calendar year, fill in the fiscal year space just under the form title. For a short plan year, see instruction B, Section 1.

Reminder: In addition to filing this form with IRS, plans covered by the Pension Benefit Guaranty Corporation termination insurance must file their Annual Premium Payment, PBGC Form 1, directly with that agency.

Penalties.—ERISA and the Code provide for the assessment and imposition of penalties for not giving complete information and not filing statements and returns/reports. Certain penalties are administrative; that is, they may be imposed or assessed by one of the governmental agencies delegated to administer the collection of Form 5500 series data. Others require a legal conviction.

A. Administrative Penalties.—Listed below are various penalties for not meeting the Form 5500 series filing requirements. One or more of the following five penalties may be imposed or assessed in the event of incomplete filings and/or filings received after the date they are due unless it is determined that your explanation for failure to file properly is for reasonable cause:

1. A penalty of up to $1,000 a day for each day a plan administrator fails or refuses to file a complete return/report. See ERISA section 502(c)(2) and 29 CFR 2560.502c-2.

2. A penalty of $25 a day (up to $15,000) for not filing returns for certain plans of deferred compensation, certain trusts and annuities, and bond purchase plans by the due date(s). See Code section 6652(e). This penalty also applies to returns required to be filed under Code section 6039D.

3. A penalty of $1 a day (up to $5,000) for each participant for whom a registration statement (Schedule SSA (Form 5500)) is required but not filed. See Code section 6652(d)(1).

4. A penalty of $1 a day (up to $1,000) for not filing a notification of change of status of a plan. See Code section 6652(d)(2).

5. A penalty of $1,000 for not filing an actuarial statement. See Code section 6692.

B. Other Penalties.

1. Any individual who willfully violates any provision of Part 1 of Title I of ERISA shall be fined not more than $5,000 or imprisoned not more than 1 year, or both. See ERISA section 501.

2. A penalty up to $10,000, 5 years imprisonment, or both, for making any false statement or representation of fact, knowing it to be false, or for knowingly concealing or not disclosing any fact required by ERISA. See section 1027, Title 18, U.S. Code, as amended by section 111 of ERISA.

How To Use This Instruction Booklet

The instructions are divided into four main sections.

Section 1

A. Who Must File.—Any administrator or sponsor of an employee benefit plan subject to ERISA must file information about each such plan **every year** (Code section 6058 and ERISA sections 104 and 4065). Also required to file, for each year, is every employer maintaining a specified fringe benefit plan as described in Code section 6039D. The Internal Revenue Service (IRS), Department of Labor (DOL), and Pension Benefit Guaranty Corporation (PBGC) have consolidated their returns and report forms to minimize the filing burden for plan administrators and employers. The chart on page 4 gives a brief guide to the type of return/report to be filed.

Reminder. Form 5500-R cannot be filed unless the plan has filed a Form 5500-C for at least one of the two immediately preceding plan years. The exclusions from the filing requirements for Form 5500-R and Form 5500-C are identical. See Form 5500-C instructions.

B. When To File.—File all required forms and schedules by the last day of the 7th month after the plan year ends. For a short plan year, file the form and applicable schedules by the last day of the 7th month after the short plan year ends. For purposes of this return/report, the short plan year ends upon the date of the change in accounting period or upon the complete distribution of the assets of the plan. (Also see Section 3.) If the current year Form 5500-R is not available before the due date of your short plan year return/report, use the latest year form available and change the date printed on the return/report to the current year. Also show the dates your short plan year began and ended.

Request for Extension of Time To File.—An extension of time up to 2½ months may be granted for filing returns/reports if **Form 5558,** Application for Extension of Time To File Certain Employee Plan Returns, is filed before the normal due date of the return/report.

Exception. *Single-employer plans and plans of a controlled group of corporations that file consolidated Federal income tax returns are automatically granted an extension of time to file Form 5500, 5500-C, or 5500-R to the due date of the Federal income tax return of the single employer or controlled group of corporations if all the following conditions are met:*

1. The plan year and the tax year coincide.

2. The single employer or the controlled group has been granted an extension of time to file its Federal income tax return to a date later than the normal due date for filing the Form 5500, 5500-C, or 5500-R.

3. A copy of the IRS extension of time to file the Federal income tax return is attached to each Form 5500, 5500-C, or 5500-R filed with IRS.

Note: *An extension of time to file the return/report does not operate as an extension of time to file the PBGC Form 1.*

C. Where To File.—Please file the return/report with the Internal Revenue Service Center indicated below. No street address is needed.

If the principal office of the plan sponsor or the plan administrator is located in	Use the following Internal Revenue Service Center address
Connecticut, Delaware, District of Columbia, Foreign Address, Maine, Maryland, Massachusetts, New Hampshire, New Jersey, New York, Pennsylvania, Puerto Rico, Rhode Island, Vermont, Virginia	Holtsville, NY 00501
Alabama, Alaska, Arkansas, California, Florida, Georgia, Hawaii, Idaho, Louisiana, Mississippi, Nevada, North Carolina, Oregon, South Carolina, Tennessee, Washington	Atlanta, GA 39901
Arizona, Colorado, Illinois, Indiana, Iowa, Kansas, Kentucky, Michigan, Minnesota, Missouri, Montana, Nebraska, New Mexico, North Dakota, Ohio, Oklahoma, South Dakota, Texas, Utah, West Virginia, Wisconsin, Wyoming	Memphis, TN 37501
All Form 5500EZ filers	Andover, MA 05501

Investment arrangements filing directly with DOL should file using the applicable address:

(1) Common/Collective Trust (OR)
Pooled Separate Account
Pension and Welfare Benefits Administration
U.S. Department of Labor
Room N5644
200 Constitution Avenue, NW.
Washington, DC 20210

(2) Master Trust
Pension and Welfare Benefits Administration
U. S. Department of Labor
Room N5644
200 Constitution Avenue, NW.
Washington, DC 20210

(3) 103-12 Investment Entity
Pension and Welfare Benefits Administration
U. S. Department of Labor
Room N5644
200 Constitution Avenue NW.
Washington, DC 20210

Section 2

What To File

The circumstances that dictate which form should be filed are described below. In addition, there are schedules that may need to be attached to the return/report. These are also described below. A brief guide illustrating which forms and schedules are required by different types of plans and filers may be found on page 4. Finally, this section also contains a description of special filing requirements for plans that invest in certain investment arrangements.

Forms

Form 5500.—File **Form 5500**, Annual Return/Report of Employee Benefit Plan, annually for each plan with 100 or more participants at the beginning of the plan year.

Form 5500-C.—File **Form 5500-C**, Return/Report of Employee Benefit Plan, for each pension benefit plan, welfare benefit plan, and fringe benefit plan (unless otherwise exempted) with fewer than 100 participants (one-participant plans see "Form 5500EZ", below) at the beginning of the plan year. File Form 5500-C for the first plan year, the year for which the final return/report is due, and for plan years in which a Form 5500-R is not filed as explained below.

Form 5500EZ.—**Form 5500EZ**, Annual Return of One-Participant Pension Benefit Plan, should be filed by most one-participant plans.

A one-participant plan is: (1) a pension benefit plan that covers only an individual or an individual and his or her spouse who wholly own a trade or business, whether incorporated or unincorporated; or (2) a pension benefit plan for a partnership that covers only the partners or the partners and the partners' spouses.

See Form 5500EZ and its instructions to see if the plan meets the requirements for filing the form.

Form 5500-R.—**Form 5500-R**, Registration Statement of Employee Benefit Plan (with fewer than 100 participants), may be filed instead of a Form 5500-C for this plan year provided: (a) this is not the first plan year, (b) this is not a year for which the final return/report is due, and (c) a Form 5500-C has been filed for one of the prior 2 plan years. The Form 5500-R should not be filed if: (a) this plan year is the first plan year, (b) this is the plan year for which a final return/report is due, or (c) the Form 5500-R has been filed for both of the prior 2 plan years.

Any plan may choose not to file Form 5500-R if the plan files the Form 5500-C instead.

Note: *Generally, under the filing requirements explained above, if the number of plan participants increases from under 100 to 100 or more, or decreases from 100 or more to under 100, from one year to the next, you would have to file a different form from that filed the previous year. However, there is an exception to this rule. You may file the same form you filed last year, even if the number of participants changed, provided that at the beginning of this plan year the plan had at least 80 participants, but not more than 120.*

Items To Be Completed on Form 5500-R

Certain kinds of plans and certain kinds of filers that are required to submit Form 5500-R are not required to complete the entire form. These are described below, by type of plan. Check the list of headings to see if your plan is affected.

1. Welfare Benefit Plans.—Welfare benefit plans must complete the following items on the Form 5500-R: 1 through 6c; 7a; 8a and b; 9; 10; 11; and 13 through 15.

2. Fringe Benefit Plans—A Form 5500-R filed only because of Code section 6039D (i.e., for a fringe benefit plan) need complete only items 1 through 6, 7a, and 14b.

If the plan is also a welfare benefit plan required to file a Form 5500-R (see "Who Must File" on page 1), complete the above items and those specified for welfare benefit plans in "1" above.

3. Pension Plans—In general, most pension plans (defined benefit and defined contribution) are required to complete all items on the form. However, some items need not be completed by certain types of pension plans, as described below.

a. Plans exclusively using a tax deferred annuity arrangement under Code section 403(b)(1). These plans need only complete items 1 through 5, 6b, and 8.

b. Plans exclusively using a custodial account for regulated investment company stock under Code section 403(b)(7). These plans need only complete items 1 through 5, 6b, and 8.

c. Individual retirement account plan. A pension plan utilizing individual retirement accounts or annuities (as described in Code section 408) as the sole funding vehicle for providing benefits need only complete items 1 through 5, 6b, and 8.

d. Fully insured pension plan. A pension benefit plan providing benefits exclusively through an insurance contract, or contracts that are fully guaranteed, and that meets all of the conditions of 29 CFR 2520.104-44 need only complete items 1 through 12, 14, and 15a and b. A pension plan that includes both insurance contracts of the type described in 29 CFR 2520.104-44 as well as other assets should limit its reporting in item 13 to those other assets.

For purposes of the annual return/report and the alternative method of compliance set forth in 29 CFR 2520.104-44, a contract is considered to be "allocated" only if the insurance company or organization that issued the contract unconditionally guarantees, upon receipt of the required premium or consideration, to provide a retirement benefit of a specified amount, without adjustment for fluctuations in the market value of the underlying assets of the company or organization, to each participant, and each participant has a legal right to such benefits that is legally enforceable directly against the insurance company or organization.

e. Nonqualified plans maintained outside the U.S. — Nonqualified pension benefit plans maintained outside the United States primarily for nonresident aliens required to file a return/report need only complete items 1 through 8 and 11 through 15.

Schedules

The various schedules to be attached to the return/report are listed below.

Note: *All attachments to the Forms 5500, 5500-C, and 5500-R must include the name of the plan and the EIN and plan number as found in items 5a, 1b, and 5c, respectively.*

Attach Schedule A (Form 5500), Insurance Information, to Form 5500, 5500-C, or 5500-R if any benefits under the plan are provided by an insurance company, insurance service, or other similar organization (such as Blue Cross, Blue Shield, or a health maintenance organization).

Exception. *Schedule A (Form 5500) is not needed if the plan covers: (1) only an individual, or an individual and his or her spouse, who wholly owns a trade or business, whether incorporated or* *unincorporated; or (2) a partner in a partnership, or a partner and his or her spouse.*

Do not file a Schedule A (Form 5500) with a Form 5500EZ.

Attach Schedule B (Form 5500), Actuarial Information, to Forms 5500, 5500-C, 5500-R, or 5500EZ for most defined benefit pension plans. See instructions for Schedule B.

Schedule SSA (Form 5500), Annual Registration Statement Identifying Separated Participants With Deferred Vested Benefits, may be needed for separated participants. See "When To Report Separated Participants" in the instructions for Schedule SSA.

Schedule P (Form 5500), Annual Return of Fiduciary of Employee Benefit Trust, Any fiduciary (trustee or custodian) of an organization that is qualified under Code section 401(a) and exempt from tax under Code section 501(a) who wants to protect the organization under the statute of limitations provided in Code section 6501(a) must file a Schedule P (Form 5500).

File the Schedule P (Form 5500) as an attachment to Form 5500, 5500-C, 5500-R, or 5500EZ for the plan year in which the trust year ends.

Other Filings

Reporting requirements for investment arrangements filing with the Department of Labor (master trusts, common/collective trusts, pooled separate accounts, etc.) are printed in the Form 5500-C instructions under "Other Filings."

Section 3
General Information

Final Return/Report.—If all assets under the plan (including insurance/annuity contracts) have been distributed to the participants and beneficiaries or distributed to another plan (and when all liabilities for which benefits may be paid under a welfare plan have been satisfied), check the "final return" box at the top of the Form 5500 or Form 5500-C filed for such plan. The year of complete distribution is the last year a return/report must be filed for the plan. For purposes of this paragraph, a complete distribution will occur in the year in which the assets of a terminated plan are brought under the control of PBGC.

For a defined benefit plan covered by PBGC, a PBGC Form 1 must be filed and a premium must be paid until the end of the plan year in which the assets are distributed or brought under the control of PBGC.

Filing the return/report marked "final return" and indicating that the plan terminated satisfies the notification requirement of Code section 6057(b)(3).

Signature and Date.—The plan administrator must sign and date all returns/reports filed. In addition the sponsoring employer must sign a return/report filed for a single-employer plan or a plan required to file only because of Code section 6039D.

When a joint employer-union board or committee is the plan sponsor or plan administrator, at least one employer representative and one union representative must sign and date the return/report.

Participating employers in a multiple-employer plan (other), who are required to file Form 5500-C or 5500-R, are required to sign the return/report. The plan administrator need not sign the Form 5500-C or 5500-R filed by the participating employer.

Reproductions.—Original forms are preferable, but a clear reproduction of the completed form is acceptable. Sign the return after it is reproduced. All signatures must be original.

Change in Plan Year.—Generally only defined benefit pension plans need to get prior approval for a change in plan year. (See Code section 412(c)(5).) Rev. Proc.87-27, 1987 CB-1 769 explains the procedure for automatic approval of a change in plan year. A pension benefit plan that would ordinarily need to obtain approval for a change in plan year under Code section 412(c)(5) is granted an automatic approval for a change in plan year if all the following criteria are met:

1. No plan year is more than 12 months long.

2. The change will not delay the time when the plan would otherwise have been required to conform to the requirements of any statute, regulation, or published position of the IRS.

3. The trust, if any, retains its exempt status for the short period required to effect the change, as well as for the taxable year immediately preceding the short period.

4. All actions necessary to implement the change in plan year, including plan amendment and a resolution of the board of directors (if applicable), have been taken on or before the last day of the short period.

5. No change in plan year has been made for any of the preceding plan years.

6. In the case of a defined benefit plan, deductions are taken in accordance with section 5 of Rev. Proc. 87-27.

For the first return/report that is filed following the change in plan year, check item 1d if Form 5500-R is being filed.

Amended Return/Report.—If you file an amended return/report, check the "amended" box at the top of the form. When filing an amended return, be sure to answer all questions and put a circle around the numbers of the items that have been amended.

How the Annual Return/Report Information May Be Used.—All Form 5500 series returns/reports will be subjected to a computerized review. It is, therefore, in the filer's best interest that the responses accurately reflect the circumstances they were designed to report. Annual reports filed under Title I of ERISA must be made available by plan administrators to plan participants and by the Department of Labor to the public pursuant to ERISA section 104.

Section 4
Specific Instructions for Form 5500-R

Important: Complete all items on the Form 5500-R with respect to the plan year, unless otherwise explicitly stated in these item-by-item instructions or on the form itself. Therefore, your responses usually apply to the year entered or printed at the top of the first page of the form.

First Item at the Top of the Form.—Complete the space for dates when:

(1) the 12-month plan year is not a calendar year, or (2) the plan year is less than 12 months (short plan year).

1a. If you did not receive a preaddressed mailing label, enter the name and address of the plan sponsor. If the plan covers only the employees of one employer, enter the employer's name.

If you received a Form 5500-R with a preaddressed mailing label, please attach it in the name and address area of the form you file. If the name or address on the label is wrong, draw a line through the incorrect part and correct it.

The term "plan sponsor" means—

(i) the employer, for an employee benefit plan that a single employer established or maintains;

(ii) the employee organization in the case of a plan of an employee organization; or

(iii) the association, committee, joint board of trustees, or other similar group of representatives of the parties who establish or maintain the plan, if the plan is established or maintained jointly by one or more employers and one or more employee organizations, or by two or more employers.

Include enough information in 1(a) to describe the sponsor adequately. For example, "Joint Board of Trustees of Local 187 Machinists" rather than just "Joint Board of Trustees."

1b. Enter the 9-digit employer identification number (EIN) assigned to the plan sponsor/employer. For example, 00-1234567.

Employers and plan administrators who do not have an EIN should apply for one on Form SS-4, available from most IRS or Social Security Administration offices. Send Form SS-4 to the same Internal Revenue Service Center to which this form will be sent.

Plan sponsors are reminded that they should use the trust EIN when opening a bank account or conducting other transactions for a plan that requires an employer identification number. The trust may apply for an EIN as explained in the preceding paragraph.

A plan of a controlled group of corporations whose sponsor is more than one of the members of the controlled group should insert only the EIN of one of the sponsoring members. This EIN must be used in all subsequent filings.

If the plan administrator is a group of individuals, get a single EIN for the group. When you apply for a number, enter on line 1 of Form SS-4 the name of the group, such as "Joint Board of Trustees of the Local 187 Machinists' Retirement Plan."

Note: *Although Employer Identification Numbers (EINs) for funds (trusts or custodial accounts) associated with plans are not required to be furnished on the Form 5500 series returns/reports, the IRS will issue EINs for such funds for other reporting purposes. EINs may be obtained by filing Form SS-4 as explained in 1b above.*

2a. If the document constituting the plan appoints or designates a plan administrator other than the sponsor, enter the administrator's name and address. If the plan administrator is also the sponsor, enter "Same." If filing as a group insurance arrangement, enter "Same." If 2a is the "Same," then items 2b and 2c should be left blank.

The term "administrator" means—

(i) the person or group of persons specified as the administrator by the instrument under which the plan is operated;

(ii) the plan sponsor/employer if an administrator is not so designated; or

(iii) any other person prescribed by regulations of the Secretary of Labor if an administrator is not designated and a plan sponsor cannot be identified.

2b. A plan administrator must have an EIN for reporting purposes. Enter the plan administrator's 9-digit EIN here. If the plan administrator has no EIN, apply for one as explained in 1b above.

Employees of an employer are not plan administrators unless so designated in the plan document, even though they engage in administrative functions of the plan. If an employee of the employer is designated as the plan administrator, that employee must get an EIN.

3. If you answer "No," enter the name, address, and EIN of the plan sponsor and/or the plan administrator shown on the prior return/report.

3c. Indicate if the change in 3a is only a change in sponsorship. "Change in sponsorship" means the plan's sponsor has been changed but no assets or liabilities have been transferred to another plan(s), the plan has not terminated or merged with any other plan, and so forth.

4b. Check for a plan in which more than one employer participates, and some of the employees are members of a controlled group of corporations (Code section 414(b)) or members of a group of employers under common control (Code section 414(c)).

4c. Check for a multiemployer plan as defined in Code section 414(f) and ERISA sections 3(37) and 4001(a)(3).

4e. Check for a multiple-employer plan (other) filed by the plan administrator for the plan as a whole.

4f. Exceptions to b and e. Each participating employer in a multiple-employer plan (other) pension benefit plan and nonmember employers participating in a plan of a controlled group of corporations or businesses need to file either Form 5500-C or Form 5500-R, regardless of the number of participants. Complete items 1, 2, 3, 4f, 5, 6, 9, and 22 on Form 5500-C, and items 1, 2, 3, 4f, 5, 6, 7, 8a, and 8b on Form 5500-R.

5a. Enter the formal name of the plan, or enough information to identify the plan.

5b. Enter the date the plan first became effective.

5c. Enter the 3-digit number the employer or plan administrator assigned to the plan. All welfare plan numbers and Code section 6039D plan numbers start at 501. All other plans start at 001.

Once you use a plan number, continue to use it for that plan on all future returns/reports. Do not use it for any other plan even if you terminated the first plan.

6a. Defined benefit plan means a pension benefit plan other than a defined contribution plan.

6b. Defined contribution plan means a plan which provides for an individual account for each participant and for benefits based solely on the amount contributed to the participant's account, and any income, expenses, gains and losses, and any forfeitures of accounts of other participants that may be allocated to such participant's account. Examples of defined contribution plans are profit-sharing, stock bonus, and money purchase plans.

6d, e, and f. Plans described in Code section 120 (group legal services plans), check box 6d. Plans described in Code section 125 (cafeteria plans), check box 6e. Programs described in Code section 127 (educational assistance programs), check box 6f.

6j. If your pension plan is not included in 6a or b, check j and specify the applicable Code section. For example, Code section 403(b)(1) annuity arrangements and Code section 408(c) individual retirement account trusts of employers, would check j and enter the applicable Code section 403(b)(1) or 408(c).

6k. Check "unfunded" if the plan is (1) unfunded, (2) fully insured, or (3) a combination of unfunded/insured. For further information, see page 2, section 2B(a) of the Form 5500-C instructions.

7. The definition of "participant" in the instructions below is only for purposes of item 7 of this form.

For welfare plans, dependents are considered to be neither participants nor beneficiaries. For pension benefit plans, "alternate payees" entitled to benefits under a qualified domestic relations order are not to be counted as participants for this item.

"Participant" means any individual who is included in one of the categories below.

(i) Active participants include any individuals who are currently in employment covered by a plan and who are earning or retaining credited service under a plan. This category includes any individuals who are: (A) currently below the integration level in a plan that is integrated with social security, and/or (B) eligible to elect to have the employer make payments to a Code section 401(k) qualified cash or deferred arrangement. Active participants also include any nonvested individuals who are earning or retaining credited service under a plan. This category does not include nonvested former employees who have incurred the greater of 5 consecutive 1 year breaks in service or the break in service period specified in the plan.

For determining if active participants are fully vested, partially vested, or nonvested, consider vesting in employer contributions only.

For purposes of Code section 6039D, "participant" means any individual who, for a plan year, has had at least one dollar excluded from income by reason of Code section 120, 125, or 127. If you are filing Form 5500-R for a plan that is required to file under Title I of ERISA and under Code section 6039D, the preceding sentence does not apply.

Summary of Filing Requirements for Employers and Plan Administrators
(File forms ONLY with IRS)

Type of plan	What to file	When to file
Most pension plans with only one participant or one participant and that participant's spouse	Form 5500EZ	File all required forms and schedules for each plan by the last day of the 7th month after the plan year ends.
Pension plan with fewer than 100 participants	Form 5500-C or 5500-R	
Pension plan with 100 or more participants	Form 5500	
Annuity under Code section 403(b)(1) or trust under Code section 408(c)	Form 5500, 5500-C, or 5500-R	
Custodial account under Code section 403(b)(7)	Form 5500, 5500-C, or 5500-R	
Welfare benefit plan with 100 or more participants*	Form 5500	
Welfare benefit plan with fewer than 100 participants (see exception on page 1 of these instructions)*	Form 5500-C or 5500-R	
Pension or welfare plan with 100 or more participants (see Form 5500 instructions)	Financial statements, schedules, and accountant's opinion	
Pension or welfare plan with benefits provided by an insurance company	Schedule A (Form 5500)	
Pension plan that requires actuarial information	Schedule B (Form 5500)	
Plans with 100 or more participants	Schedule C (Form 5500)	
Pension plan filing a registration statement identifying separated participants with deferred vested benefits from a pension plan	Schedule SSA (Form 5500)	

*This includes Code section 6039D filers.

(ii) Inactive participants receiving benefits are any individuals who are retired or separated from employment covered by the plan and who are receiving benefits under the plan. This includes former employees who are receiving group health continuation coverage benefits pursuant to Part 6 of ERISA who are covered by the employee welfare benefit plan. This category does not include any individual to whom an insurance company has made an irrevocable commitment to pay all the benefits to which the individual is entitled under the plan.

(iii) Inactive participants entitled to future benefits are individuals who are retired or separated from employment covered by the plan and who are entitled to begin receiving benefits under the plan in the future. This category does not include any individual to whom an insurance company has made an irrevocable commitment to pay all the benefits to which the individual is entitled under the plan.

(iv) Deceased participants are any deceased individuals who have one or more beneficiaries who are receiving or are entitled to receive benefits under the plan. This category does not include an individual if an insurance company has made an irrevocable commitment to pay all the benefits to which the beneficiaries of that individual are entitled under the plan.

7b(i). If "Yes," file Schedule SSA (Form 5500) as an attachment to Form 5500-R.

Plan administrators: Code section 6057(e) provides that the plan administrator must give each participant a statement showing the same information for that participant as is reported on Schedule SSA.

8a. Check "Yes" if the plan was terminated or if the plan was merged or consolidated into another plan. Enter year of termination if applicable.

8b. If the plan was terminated and all trust assets were not distributed, file a return/report for each year the trust has assets. In that case, the return/report must be filed by the plan administrator, if designated, or by the person or persons who actually control the plan's property.

If all assets were used to buy individual annuity contracts and the contracts were distributed to the participants, check "Yes."

If all the trust assets were transferred to another plan, check "Yes."

9. Check "Yes" if either the contributions to the plan or the benefits paid by the plan are subject to the collective bargaining process, even if the plan is not established and administered by a joint board of trustees. Check "Yes" even if only some of those covered by the plan are members of a collective bargaining unit which negotiates benefit levels on its own behalf. The benefit schedules need not be identical for all employees under the plan.

10. The insurance company (or similar organization) which provides benefits is required to provide the plan administrator with the information needed to complete the return/report, pursuant to ERISA section 103(a)(2). If you do not receive this information in a timely manner, contact the insurance company (or similar organization). If information is missing on Schedule A due to a refusal to provide this information, note this on Schedule A. If there are no Schedule(s) A attached, enter "0."

11a. Check "Yes" if an amendment to the plan was adopted in this plan year, regardless of the effective date of the amendment.

11b. Check "Yes" only if the accrued benefits were retroactively reduced. For example, a plan provides a benefit of 2% for each year of service, but the plan is amended to change the benefit to 1½% a year for all years of service under the plan.

11c. Check "Yes" only if an amendment changed the information previously provided to participants by the summary plan description or summary description of modifications.

11d. A revised summary plan description or summary description of modifications must be filed with DOL and distributed to all plan participants and pension plan beneficiaries no later than 210 days after the close of the plan year in which the amendment(s) was adopted. If the material was distributed and filed since the amendments were adopted (even if after the end of the plan year), check "Yes" to item 11d.

12a. Check "Yes" if this is a pension plan subject to minimum funding standards that has experienced a funding deficiency. If item 12a is answered "Yes," and item 6a indicates this is a defined benefit pension plan, complete and attach Schedule B (Form 5500) to this registration statement. All defined benefit plans are subject to minimum funding standards except fully insured plans, church plans, governmental plans, and certain other plans covered by Code section 412(h). Code section 412 describes the minimum funding standards applicable to defined contribution plans qualified under Code section 401(a) or 403(a). A funding deficiency occurs if the amount of required employer contribution for the plan year exceeds the actual contribution paid by the employer for the plan year.

12b. If item 12a is answered "Yes," this item must be answered. If a funding deficiency occurs, Form 5330 must be filed with the IRS to pay the excise tax on the amount of the deficiency.

13 and 14. Use either the cash, modified accrual, or accrual basis for recognition of transactions in items 13 and 14, as long as one method is used consistently. Round off all amounts in items 13 and 14 to the nearest dollar. Where it is used in these instructions, "current value" means fair market value where available. Otherwise, it means the fair value as determined in good faith under the terms of the plan by a trustee or a named fiduciary, assuming an orderly liquidation at the time of the determination.

If the assets of two or more plans are maintained in one trust, such as when an employer has two plans that are funded through a single trust (except investment arrangements filing directly with DOL), complete items 13 and 14 by entering the plan's allocable part of each line item.

If assets of one plan are maintained in two or more trust funds, report the combined financial information in 13 and 14. Fully insured defined benefit or defined contribution pension plans meeting the conditions of 29 CFR 2520.104-44 need not complete items 13 and 14.

For purposes of the annual return/report and the alternative method of compliance set forth in 29 CFR 2520.104-44, a contract is considered to be "allocated" only if the insurance company or organization that issued the contract unconditionally guarantees, upon receipt of the required premium or consideration, to provide a retirement benefit of a specified amount, without adjustment for fluctuations in the market value of the underlying assets of the company or organization, to each participant, and each participant has a legal right to such benefits which is legally enforceable directly against the insurance company or organization.

13a. Enter the total plan assets at the beginning and end of the plan year. Plan assets may include, among other things:

(1) Cash including both interest and noninterest bearing. This includes all cash on hand or in a financial institution including money market funds.

(2) Receivables including all contributions due to the plan from the employer and participants, income earned, but not yet received by the plan and receivables from any other source.

(3) Investments including securities (stocks, bonds, U.S. Government obligations, municipal obligations, etc.); real property (land, buildings, gold, furniture, equipment, etc.); loans (mortgages, promissory notes, etc.); and all other investments (certificates of deposit, repurchase agreements, land contracts, units of participation in common/collective trusts and pooled separate accounts, shares of registered investment companies (mutual funds), interests in master trusts and 103-12 IEs, etc.).

Plans holding units of participation in common/collective trusts and/or pooled separate accounts must attach to the Form 5500-R either the statement of assets and liabilities of the common/collective trust and/or pooled separate account or the required certification. For details, see 29 CFR sections 2520.103-3, 2520.103-4, 2520.103-5, and 2520.103-9.

Plans in a master trust must include the value of the plan's interest in the master trust which is the sum of the net values of the plan's interest in all of the master trust investment accounts. The net values of such interests are obtained by multiplying the plan's percentage interest in each master trust investment account by the net assets of the investment account (total assets minus total liabilities) at the beginning and end of the plan year.

13b. Enter the total liabilities at the beginning and end of the plan year. Liabilities to be entered here do not include the value of future pension payments to plan participants; however, the amount to be entered in item 13b for accrual basis filers includes, among other things:

(1) Benefit claims that have been processed but have not been paid,

(2) Accounts payable obligations owed by the plan that were incurred in the normal operations of the plan but have not been paid,

(3) Other liabilities such as acquisition indebtedness and any other amount owed by the plan.

13c. Enter the net assets as of the beginning and end of the plan year. Subtract item 13b from item 13a.

14a. Enter all plan income during the year. Plan income received and/or receivable may include, among other things:

(1) Interest on investments (including money market funds, sweep accounts, STIF accounts, etc.)

(2) Dividends. (Accrual basis plans should include dividends declared for all stock held by the plan even if the dividends have not been received as of the end of the plan year.)

(3) Rents from income producing property owned by the plan.

(4) Royalties.

(5) Contributions including securities or other noncash property contributed to the plan.

(6) Net gains or loss from the sale of assets.

(7) Other income such as unrealized appreciation (depreciation) in plan assets. To compute this amount subtract the current value of all assets at the beginning of the year plus the cost of any assets acquired during the plan year from the current value of all assets at the end of the year minus assets disposed of during the plan year. A negative figure should be placed in parentheses.

14b. Enter all the expenses of the plan during the year. Expenses (paid and/or payable) may include, among others:

(1) Direct payments made to participants or beneficiaries in cash, securities or other property. If the securities or other property are distributed to plan participants or beneficiaries, include the fair market value (or a good faith estimate if fair market value is not available) on the date the property was distributed.

(2) Payments to insurance carriers and similar organizations (including Blue Cross, Blue Shield and health maintenance organizations).

(3) Payments to provide benefits for such things as legal services, day care services, training and apprenticeship services.

(4) Administrative expenses including:

(A) Salaries to employees of the plan.

(B) Expenses for accounting, actuarial, legal, and investment services.

(C) Fees and expenses for trustees including reimbursement for travel, seminars and meeting expenses.

(D) Fees paid for valuations and appraisals.

If this Form 5500-R is filed only for purposes of fulfilling the requirements of Code section 6039D, i.e., for a fringe benefit plan but not for a welfare benefit plan, do not include overhead expenses such as utilities and photocopying expenses. If this filing is only for an educational assistance program described in Code section 127, do not include expenses for job-related training that are deductible under Code section 162.

14c. Enter the net income (loss). Subtract item 14b from item 14a. If the result is a negative number, enter it in parentheses.

14d. Enter the total cash contributions received and (for accrual basis plans) due to be received from the employer, participants and/or any other source.

14e. Include payments made (and for accrual basis filers payments due) to participants or beneficiaries in cash, securities or other property and to insurance carriers (or similar organizations such as Blue Cross, Blue Shield, and health maintenance organizations, etc.). If securities or other property are distributed to plan participants or beneficiaries, include the fair market value (or a good faith estimate if fair market value is not available) on the date of distribution.

15. Check "Yes" or "No" and enter the total amount (except 15i) for all "Yes" responses. Round off all amounts to the nearest dollar.

15a. Check "Yes" and indicate the aggregate amount of coverage available for all claims if every plan official who handles plan funds is covered by a bond. Otherwise, check "No." Generally, every plan official of an employee benefit plan who "handles" funds or other property of such plan must be bonded. A plan administrator, officer, or employee shall be deemed to be "handling" funds or other property of a plan, so as to require bonding, whenever his or her duties or activities with respect to given funds are such that there is a risk that such funds could be lost in the event of fraud or dishonesty on the part of such person, acting either alone or in collusion with others. Section 412 of ERISA and the regulations found at 29 CFR 2580 provide the bonding requirements including the definition of "handling" (29 CFR 2580.412-6), the permissible forms of bonds (29 CFR 2580.412-10), and certain exemptions such as the exemption for unfunded plans, banks and insurance companies (ERISA section 412) and the exemption allowing plan officials to purchase bonds from surety companies authorized by the Secretary of the Treasury as acceptable reinsurers on Federal bonds (29 CFR 2580.412-23).

Check "Yes" only if the plan itself (as opposed to the plan sponsor) is a named insured under a fidelity bond covering plan officials.

Plans are permitted under certain conditions to purchase fiduciary liability insurance. These policies do not protect the plan from dishonest acts and are not bonds which should be reported in item 15.

15b. If item 15a is answered "Yes," this must be answered. Check "Yes" to item 15b if the plan has suffered or discovered any loss as the result of a dishonest or fraudulent act(s). If "Yes," enter the full amount of the loss. If the full amount of the loss has not yet been determined, provide and disclose that the figure is an estimate, such as "approximately $1,000."

Note: *Willful failure to report is a criminal offense. See ERISA section 501.*

15c. For purposes of item 15, the term "employer" includes affiliates of the employer. In determining the five most highly paid employees, use all compensation paid including cash, bonuses, and noncash payments (e.g., the use of a car). A fiduciary is a person with respect to a plan to the extent: (1) he or she exercises any discretionary authority or discretionary control with respect to the management of such plan or exercises any authority or control with respect to the management or disposition of its assets, (2) he or she renders investment advice for a fee or other compensation, direct or indirect, with respect to any moneys or other property of such plan, or has any authority or responsibility to do so, or (3) he or she has any discretionary authority or discretionary responsibility in the administration of such plan.

15d. Relatives include spouses, siblings, ancestors, lineal descendents (e.g., children, grandchildren, etc.) and spouses of lineal descendents. If 15c is answered "Yes," enter the total amount of these transactions.

15e. An "employer security" is a security issued by an employer (including affiliates of employees) covered by the plan. These may include common stocks, preferred stocks, bonds, zero coupon bonds, debentures, convertible debentures, notes, and commercial paper.

Employer real property is any real property (and related personal property) owned by the plan and leased to the employer of employees covered by the plan. This may include land, warehouses, office buildings, etc. If item 15e is "Yes," enter the total amount of employer securities and/or employer real property held or acquired.

15f. Generally, a loan requires that both the principal and interest be paid according to a pre-established repayment schedule. If the principal and/or interest has not been paid in accordance with the original repayment schedule and the period for repayment of the principal and/or interest has been extended, or the loan has been renegotiated after the original repayment schedule has not been met, a "Yes" must be checked and the total amount of the delinquent loan must be entered. Otherwise check "No."

15h. Check "Yes" for obligations where the required payments have not been made by the due date. With respect to notes and loans, the due date, payment amount and conditions for default are usually contained in the note or loan document. Defaults can occur at any time for those obligations that require periodic repayment. Generally, loans and fixed income obligations are considered uncollectible when payment has not been made and there is little probability that payment will be made. A loan by the plan is in default when the borrower is unable to pay the obligation upon maturity. A fixed income obligation has a fixed maturity date at a specified interest rate. If item 15h is "Yes," enter the total amount of loans by the plan or fixed income obligations that are uncollectible or in default as of the plan year end.

15i. Consider all fiduciaries and parties providing services to the plan, including (1) persons who are fiduciaries by reason of their relationship to a master trust investment account or 103-12 IE in which the plan has an interest or the assets in such an investment account or 103-12 IE; and (2) parties providing services rendered with respect to assets held in master trusts and 103-12 IEs.

See item 15c above for the definition of fiduciary.

15j. Include as a single security all securities of the same issue. For the purposes of item 15j, do not check "Yes" for securities issued by the U.S. Government or its agencies. If item 15j is "Yes," enter the total.

15k. In determining the 20% figure, subtract the current value of plan assets held in any master trust or 103-12 IE from the current value of the plan's total assets at the beginning of the plan year. Check "Yes" if the plan had:

1. A single transaction within the plan year in excess of 20% of the current value of the plan assets;

2. Any series of transactions with, or in conjunction with, the same person, involving property other than securities, which amount in the aggregate within the plan year (regardless of the category of asset and the gain or loss on any transaction) to more than 20% of the current value of plan assets;

3. Any transaction within the plan year involving securities of the same issue if within the plan year any series of transactions with respect to such securities amount in the aggregate to more than 20% of the current value of the plan assets; or

4. Any transaction within the plan year with respect to securities with, or in conjunction with, a person if any prior or subsequent single transaction within the plan year with such person, with respect to securities, exceeds 20% of the current value of plan assets. The 20% figure is determined by comparing the current value of the transaction at the transaction date with the current value of the plan assets at the beginning of the plan year.

If the assets of two or more plans are maintained in one trust, the plan's allocable portion of the transactions of the trust shall be combined with the other transactions of the plan, if any, to determine which transactions (or series of transactions) are reportable (20%) transactions.

Exception. For investments in common/collective trusts, pooled separate accounts, 103-12 IEs, and registered investment companies, determine the 20% figure by comparing the transaction date value of the acquisition and/or disposition of units of participation or shares in the entity with the current value of the plan assets at the beginning of the plan year. Check "No" if all plan funds are held in a master trust. Do not include individual transactions of common/collective trusts, pooled separate accounts, 103-12 IEs, and registered investment companies.

If item 15k is answered "Yes," enter the amount.

15l. Check "No" if the plan received all of its contributions in cash. Generally, as it relates to this question, an appraisal by an unrelated third party is an evaluation of the value of the asset contributed prepared by an individual or firm who knows how to judge the value of the asset and does not have an ongoing relationship with the plan or plan fiduciaries except for preparing the appraisal. If item 15l is checked "Yes," enter the value of the asset as established by the plan.

15m. Non-publicly traded securities are generally held by few people and not traded on a stock exchange. Generally, as it relates to this question, an appraisal by an unrelated third party is an evaluation of the value of the security prepared by an individual or firm who knows how to judge the value of the security and does not have an ongoing relationship with the plan or plan fiduciaries except for preparing the appraisal. If item 15m is answered "Yes," enter the value of the security as established by the plan.

16a. If you are uncertain as to whether the plan is covered under the PBGC termination insurance program, check the box "Not determined" and contact the PBGC and request a coverage determination. Welfare and fringe benefit plans do not complete this item.

Form **2848**
(Rev. February 1988)
Department of the Treasury
Internal Revenue Service

Power of Attorney and Declaration of Representative

► **See separate instructions.**

OMB No. 1545-0150
Expires: 12-31-90

Part I **Power of Attorney**

(Please type or print)

Taxpayer(s) name(s)	Taxpayer identification number	For IRS Use Only		
		File So.		
		Level		
Address (number and street)	Plan number (if applicable)	Receipt		
		Powers		
City, state, and ZIP code	Telephone number	Blind T.		
		Action		
		Ret. Ind.		

hereby appoint(s) the following individual(s)*

Name	CAF Number	Address	New Address	Telephone Number

as attorney(s)-in-fact to represent the taxpayer(s) before any office of the Internal Revenue Service for the following tax matter(s) (specify the type(s) of tax and year(s) or period(s) (date of death if estate tax)):

Type of tax (Individual, corporate, etc.)	Federal tax form number (1040, 1120, etc.)	Year(s) or period(s) (Date of death if estate tax)

The attorney(s)-in-fact (or either of them) are authorized, subject to revocation, to receive confidential information and to perform any and all acts that the principal(s) can perform with respect to the above specified tax matters (excluding the power to receive refund checks and the power to sign the return, unless specifically granted below). See Regulations section 1.6012-1(a)(5) for information on returns made by agents. (List excludable powers below. Indicate if you are granting the power to sign the return.)

- -

- -

☐ Send originals of all notices and all other written communications in proceedings involving the above tax matters to the appointee first named above, and a duplicate copy of all notices and all other written communications to the taxpayer named above, or

☐ Send copies of all notices and all other written communications addressed to the taxpayer(s) in proceedings involving the above tax matters to:

1 ☐ the appointee first named above, or

2 ☐ (names of not more than two of the appointees named above) - - - - - - - - - - - - - - - -

Initial here ► - - - - - - if you are granting the power to receive, but not to endorse or cash, refund checks for the above tax matters to:

3 ☐ the appointee first named above, or

4 ☐ (name of one of the above designated appointees) ► - - - - - - - - - - - - - - - -

This power of attorney revokes all earlier powers of attorney and tax information authorizations on file with the Internal Revenue Service for the same tax matters and years or periods covered by this power of attorney, except the following:

- -

- -

(Specify to whom granted, date, and address including ZIP code, or refer to attached copies of earlier powers and authorizations.)

Signature of or for taxpayer(s)

(If signed by a corporate officer, partner, or fiduciary on behalf of the taxpayer, I certify that I have the authority to execute this power of attorney on behalf of the taxpayer.)

- - - - - - - - - - - - - - - - (Signature) - - - - - - - - - - (Title, if applicable) - - - - - - (Date)

(Also type or print your name below if signing for a taxpayer who is not an individual.)

- - - - - - - - - - - - - - - - (Signature) - - - - - - - - - - (Title, if applicable) - - - - - - (Date)

* You may authorize an organization, firm, or partnership to receive confidential information, but your representative must be an individual who must complete Part II.

For Privacy Act and Paperwork Reduction Act Notices, see page 1 of the separate instructions. Form **2848** (Rev. 2-88)

If the power of attorney is granted to a person other than an attorney, certified public accountant, enrolled agent, or enrolled actuary, the taxpayer(s) signature must be witnessed or notarized below. (The representative must complete Part II. List representatives there only if they are recognized to practice before the Internal Revenue Service.)

The person(s) signing as or for the taxpayer(s): (Check and complete one.)

☐ is/are known to and signed in the presence of the two disinterested witnesses whose signatures appear here:

____________________ (Signature of Witness) ________ (Date)

____________________ (Signature of Witness) ________ (Date)

☐ appeared this day before a notary public and acknowledged this power of attorney as a voluntary act and deed.

Witness: ________________ (Signature of Notary) ________ (Date)

NOTARIAL SEAL
(if required by state law)

Part II Declaration of Representative

I declare that I am not currently under suspension or disbarment from practice before the Internal Revenue Service; that I am aware of **Treasury Department Circular No. 230** (31 CFR, Part 10), as amended, regulations governing the practice of attorneys, certified public accountants, enrolled agents, enrolled actuaries, and others; and that I am one of the following:

a a member in good standing of the bar of the highest court of the jurisdiction shown below;
b duly qualified to practice as a certified public accountant in the jurisdiction shown below;
c enrolled as an agent under the requirements of Treasury Department Circular No. 230;
d a bona fide officer of the taxpayer organization;
e a full-time employee of the taxpayer;
f a member of the taxpayer's immediate family (spouse, parent, child, brother or sister);
g a fiduciary for the taxpayer;
h an enrolled actuary (the authority of an enrolled actuary to practice before the Service is limited by section 10.3(d)(1) of Treasury Department Circular No. 230);
i Commissioner's special authorization (see instructions for Part II, item i) ________________;

and that I am authorized to represent the taxpayer identified in Part I for the tax matters specified there.

Designation (insert appropriate letter from above list)	Jurisdiction (state, etc.) or Enrollment Card Number	Signature	Date

Instructions for Form 2848

(Revised February 1988)

Power of Attorney and Declaration of Representative

(Section references are to the Internal Revenue Code, unless otherwise noted.)

Privacy Act and Paperwork Reduction Act Notice.—We ask for this information to carry out the Internal Revenue laws of the United States. We need it to ensure that taxpayers are complying with these laws and to allow us to figure and collect the right amount of tax. You are required to give us this information.

Under section 6109, you must disclose your taxpayer identification number. The principal purpose is to secure proper identification of the taxpayer. If you do not disclose this number, IRS may suspend processing the power of attorney until you provide the number.

General Information

If you want a representative to perform certain acts on your behalf and to receive or inspect certain tax information, you must file a power of attorney. You may file a power of attorney without using Form 2848, but it must reflect the information that would be provided by using Form 2848. A representative must have a power of attorney (or tax information authorization, Form 2848-D) on file in order to receive or inspect certain tax information.

You may use Form 2848 as a power of attorney to appoint one or more individuals to represent you before the Internal Revenue Service. A firm, organization, or partnership may not be designated as a representative. You may use Form 2848 for any matters affecting any tax imposed by the Internal Revenue Code, except alcohol and tobacco taxes or firearms activities.

Form 2848 is for your convenience. Its use is voluntary, and you can file a power of attorney in other ways without using this form. If you wish to prepare a power of attorney without using Form 2848, see **Publication 216**, Conference and Practice Requirements of the Statement of Procedural Rules (Subpart E of Part 601 of Title 26 of the Code of Federal Regulations).

Powers Granted by Form 2848.—Your signature on Form 2848 authorizes the individual(s) you designate (your representative or "attorney-in-fact") to perform any act you can perform, except for the power to receive refund checks, and the power to sign tax returns. This includes executing waivers and offers of waivers of restrictions on assessment or collection of deficiencies in tax, and waivers of notice of disallowance of a claim for credit or refund. It also includes executing consents extending the statutory period for assessment or collection of taxes, executing closing agreements under section 7121, and delegating authority, or substituting another representative. A delegation or substitution must be evidenced by a statement signed by the representative named in the power of attorney.

If you want to exclude granting authority to perform any of these or other specific acts, insert language excluding these acts in the blank space provided.

If you want to include additional powers, such as authority to sign your return, insert language specifying the additional powers. See Regulations section 1.6012-1(a)(5) for the provisions permitting the use of agents to sign returns, such as disease or injury that prevents you from making your return, or your continuous absence from the United States for at least 60 days before the return due date.

If you want your representative to have authority only to receive confidential information and to make written or oral presentations of fact or argument on your behalf, you should use **Form 2848-D**, Tax Information Authorization and Declaration of Representative, instead of Form 2848.

Filing the Power of Attorney.—If you did not file a power of attorney previously, you must file the original or a photocopy with each IRS office in which your representative is to represent you. You do not have to file another copy with other IRS officers or counsel who later have the matter under consideration, unless you are specifically asked to provide an additional copy.

Revoking a Power of Attorney or Tax Information Authorization.—If you want to revoke an earlier power of attorney, you may use Form 2848 as a new authorization for your representative. This will authorize him or her to represent you in specified matters and years or periods before the office of IRS where you filed the earlier power. It will also revoke all earlier tax information authorizations for the same matters and years or periods filed in that office of IRS, unless you specifically state otherwise.

If you want to revoke a power of attorney without executing a new one, send a signed statement to each office of IRS where you filed each earlier power of attorney that you are now revoking. List in this statement the name and address of each representative whose authority is being revoked.

How To Complete Form 2848

Part I. Power of Attorney

Taxpayer's Name, Identification Number, and Address.—For individuals: Enter your name, social security number, and address in the space provided. If a joint return is involved, and you and your spouse are designating the same representative(s), also enter your spouse's name and social security number, and your spouse's address if different from yours.

For a corporation, partnership, or association: Enter the name, employer identification number, and business address. If the power of attorney for a partnership will be used in a tax matter in which the name and social security number of each partner have not previously been sent to IRS, list the name and social security number of each partner in the available space at the end of the form or on an attached sheet.

For an employee plan: Enter the name, employer identification number, 3-digit plan number, and business address.

For a trust: Enter the name, title, and address of the fiduciary, and the name and employer identification number of the trust.

For an estate: Enter the name, title, and address of the decedent's personal representative, and the name and identification number of the estate. The identification number for an estate includes both the employer identification number if the estate has one and the decedent's social security number.

Appointee.—Enter the name(s), CAF number(s) (if one has already been assigned), address(es), and telephone number(s) of the individual(s) you appoint. This may not be the name of a law firm, etc. See *Where You Want Original or Copies Sent*, below.

The CAF number is the unique number (not the social security number) that IRS will assign to a representative after he or she has filed a Form 2848 or 2848-D with an IRS office that is using the CAF system. After IRS tells the representative what his or her CAF number is, the representative is requested, but not required, to use the CAF number on all future Forms 2848 or 2848-D filed. Please check the box under *New Address*, if the appointee's address has changed since being assigned a CAF number. In the case of an employee plan administrator who is required to obtain an employer identification number in order to be recognized as the plan administrator, the CAF number is the employer identification number assigned to the administrator.

Internal Revenue Tax Matters and Years or Periods.—Consider the application of each tax imposed by the Internal Revenue Code for each tax period as a separate tax matter. In the columns provided, clearly identify the type of tax(es), the tax form number(s), and the year(s) or period(s) for which the power is granted. You may list any number of specified years or periods and types of taxes on the same power of attorney. For example, you may list income tax Form 1040 for calendar year 1988 and excise tax Form 720 for the 1st, 2nd, 3rd, and 4th quarters of 1988, but a general reference to "all years," "all periods," or "all taxes" is not acceptable. If the matter relates to estate tax, enter the date of the taxpayer's death instead of the year or period.

If the power of attorney will be used in connection with a penalty that is not related to a particular type of tax, such as individual or corporate, enter the Code section of the penalty involved in the type of tax column. If no tax form is involved, enter the name of the organization or investment in the space provided for the form number.

If the power of attorney is used for ruling requests, submit a copy with each request. If you want the original of the ruling mailed to your representative, see the next paragraph.

Where You Want Original or Copies Sent.—By checking the applicable box, you may have the original of all notices and all other written communications addressed and sent to your representative, or you may have the original addressed to you and have copies of all notices and all other written communications sent to your representative, but to no more than two representatives if they are located at different addresses. Please check box 1 if you want copies of all notices or all communications sent to the first appointee named at the top of the form. Check box 2 if you want them sent to someone other than the first named appointee or if you want them sent to two appointees. In that case, list the names of the appointees.

Refund Checks (Boxes 3 and 4).—Check box 3 or 4 and put your initials in the space provided if you want your refund checks mailed to your representative. Your representative may then receive but not endorse or cash refund checks.

Signature of Taxpayers.—For individuals: If a joint return is involved and both husband and wife will be represented by the same individual(s), then both must sign the power of attorney unless one spouse authorizes (in writing) the other to sign for both. In that case, attach a copy of the authorization. However, if they are to be represented by different individuals, each may execute his or her own power of attorney.

For a partnership: All partners must sign unless one partner is authorized to act in the name of the partnership. A partner is authorized to act in the name of the partnership if under state law the partner has authority to bind the partnership.

For a corporation or association: An officer having authority to bind the entity must sign.

If you are signing the power of attorney for a taxpayer who is not an individual, please type or print your name below the signature line at the bottom of the form.

Other: If the taxpayer has died, is insolvent, or is a dissolved corporation or partnership, or if a trustee, guardian, or other fiduciary is acting for the taxpayer, see section 601.504(b)(2) of Subpart E of the Conference and Practice Requirements for further instructions about executing a power of attorney.

Notarizing or Witnessing the Power of Attorney.—A notary public or two disinterested individuals must witness a power of attorney unless it is granted to an attorney, certified public accountant, enrolled agent, or enrolled actuary.

Part II. Declaration of Representative

Your representative must complete Part II to make a declaration containing the following:

(1) A statement that the representative is authorized to represent the taxpayer as a certified public accountant, attorney, enrolled agent, enrolled actuary, member of your immediate family, etc.

An actuary enrolled by the Joint Board for the Enrollment of Actuaries may represent a taxpayer before IRS. However, the actuary's representation is limited to certain areas of the Code. See section 10.3(d)(1) of Treasury Department Circular No. 230 for a list of the Code sections involved and the areas covered by them.

(2) The jurisdiction recognizing the representative. For an attorney or certified public accountant: Enter in the *Jurisdiction* column the state, District of Columbia, possession, or commonwealth that has granted the declared professional recognition. For an enrolled agent or actuary: Enter in the *Jurisdiction* column the enrollment card number.

(3) The signature of the representative and the date signed.

If the representative is a former employee of the Federal Government, he or she must be aware of the post-employment restrictions contained in the Ethics in Government Act, 18 USC 207, and in section 10.26 of Treasury Department Circular No. 230. Criminal penalties are provided for violation of the post-employment restrictions.

Unenrolled return preparers (see Treasury Department Circular No. 230, section 10.7(a)(7)) may NOT use Form 2848. They may use Form 2848-D for the limited practice without enrollment provided in Treasury Department Circular No. 230, section 10.7(a)(7).

Part II, Item i.—Use this item to explain a special authorization by the Commissioner, as described in Treasury Department Circular No. 230, section 10.7(b).

Form **8717**
(Rev. January 1989)
Department of the Treasury
Internal Revenue Service

User Fee for Employee Plan Determination Letter Request

Attach to determination letter applications.

For IRS Use Only
Control number ______
Amount paid ______
User fee screener ______

1 Sponsor's name

2 Sponsor's employer identification number

3 Plan name

4 Plan number

5 Type of request (check only one box and include a check or money order made payable to Internal Revenue Service for the amount indicated)

		Type of request	Fee
a	☐	Form 5300/5301 for plan with fewer than 100 participants	$ 450
b	☐	Form 5300/5301 for plan with 100 or more participants	750
c	☐	Form 5310 (for plan terminations only) with fewer than 100 participants	225
d	☐	Form 5310 (for plan terminations only) with 100 or more participants	450
e	☐	Form 5303	550
f	☐	Form 5307	100
g	☐	Form 6406	100
h	☐	Volume submitter lead or specimen plan (Form 5300, 5301, or 5303 for lead plan; letter request for specimen plan)	1,000
i	☐	Form 4461 or Form 4461-A (Uniform plan)	500
j	☐	Form 4461 or Form 4461-A (Regional Prototype Plan)	1,000
k	☐	Group trust	400

Instructions

The Revenue Act of 1987 requires payment of a user fee for determination letter requests submitted to the Internal Revenue Service. The fee must accompany each request submitted to a key district office. For more information see Rev. Proc. 89-4 1989-3 I.R.B. 18.

The fee for each type of request for an employee plan determination letter is listed in item 5 of this form. For determining the category when submitting Form 5300, 5301, or 5310, the term "participant" includes active employees participating in the plan as well as retirees, other former employees, and beneficiaries of both, who are receiving benefits under the plan. If the plan is adopted by multiple employers, the combined participants of all adopting employers must be considered. For a further definition of participant, see the instructions for Form 5300, 5301, or 5310.

Check the block that describes the type of request you are submitting, and attach this form to the front of your request form along with a check or money order for the amount indicated. Make the check or money order payable to the Internal Revenue Service.

Determination letter requests received with no payment or with an insufficient payment will be returned to the applicant and will have to be resubmitted with the proper fee.

To avoid delays in receiving a determination letter, please be sure that the proper application is sent to the appropriate address from the list shown below. Restated plans and plans amended to comply with the Tax Reform Act of 1986 will not be accepted on **Form 6406,** Short Form Application for Determination for Amendment of Employee Benefit Plan. Nor will a multiple plan (e.g., a profit-sharing and a money purchase plan) be accepted on one application form.

If entity is in this IRS District ▼	**Send fee and request for determination letter or notification letter to this address** ▼
Brooklyn, Albany, Augusta, Boston, Buffalo, Burlington, Hartford, Manhattan, Portsmouth, Providence	Internal Revenue Service EP/EO Division P. O. Box 1680, GPO Brooklyn, NY 11202
Baltimore, District of Columbia, Pittsburgh, Richmond, Newark, Philadelphia, Wilmington, any U.S. possession or foreign country	Internal Revenue Service EP/EO Division P. O. Box 17010 Baltimore, MD 21203
Cincinnati, Cleveland, Detroit, Indianapolis, Louisville, Parkersburg	Internal Revenue Service EP/EO Division P. O. Box 3159 Cincinnati, OH 45201
Dallas, Albuquerque, Austin, Cheyenne, Denver, Houston, Oklahoma City, Phoenix, Salt Lake City, Wichita	Internal Revenue Service EP/EO Division Mail Code 4950 DAL 1100 Commerce Street Dallas, TX 75242
Atlanta, Birmingham, Columbia, Ft. Lauderdale, Greensboro, Jackson, Jacksonville, Little Rock, Nashville, New Orleans	Internal Revenue Service EP/EO Division Room 1112 P. O. Box 941 Atlanta, GA 30301
Honolulu, Laguna Niguel, Las Vegas, Los Angeles, San Jose	Internal Revenue Service EP Application Receiving Room 5127 P. O. Box 536 Los Angeles, CA 90053-0536
Chicago, Aberdeen, Des Moines, Fargo, Helena, Milwaukee, Omaha, St. Louis, St. Paul, Springfield	Internal Revenue Service EP/EO Division 230 S. Dearborn DPN 20-6 Chicago, IL 60604
Sacramento, San Francisco	Internal Revenue Service EP Application Receiving Stop SF 4446 P. O. Box 36001 San Francisco, CA 94102
Anchorage, Boise, Portland, Seattle	Internal Revenue Service EP Application Receiving P. O. Box 21224 Seattle, WA 98111

Attach Check or Money Order Here

*U.S. Government Printing Office: 1989-242-473/80055

Glossary of ERISA Terms*

accrual the crediting of benefits to an employee by reason of his participation in a plan; accrued benefits can be forfeited until they are vested. *See* vesting and minimum accrual.

actuarial equivalent one amount to be received in the future is the actuarial equivalent of another if, using the same actuarial assumptions (such as rate of return, retirement age, and mortality), both have the same present value.

affiliated service group two or more service organizations which are related through ownership and provision of services for one another or in association for third parties, or two or more organizations which are related by performing management services for one another on a regular and continuing basis.

annuity a contract for the payment of specified or objectively determinable periodic payments over a specified period of time or for the lifetime of the recipient.

beneficiary the person who is eligible for benefits under a plan upon the death of the participant.

break in service a year in which an employee is credited with no more than 500 hours of service. *See* year of service.

cafeteria plan plan in which participants can choose among two or more benefits consisting either of cash and qualified benefits or of only qualified benefits.

church plan plan established and maintained by a church or association of churches exempt from taxation under Code §501.

cliff vesting schedule for vesting of benefits in which all accrued benefits become nonforfeitable at a specified length of service, such as five years.

COBRA Consolidated Omnibus Budget Reconciliation Act of 1985, P.L. 99-272.

CODA cash or deferred arrangement; *see* 401(k) plan.

collectively bargained plan plan that provides for retirement benefits specified in a collective bargaining agreement; can include more than one employer. *See* multiemployer plan.

common control unincorporated businesses are under common control if ownership of interests in the businesses is related in such a

---

*We gratefully acknowledge the assistance of Michael A. Schinabeck, Esq., a member of the staff of BNA's Tax Management, Inc., for his work in compiling this glossary. The Glossary also includes entries for pertinent statutes and their citations.

way that the businesses would be members of a controlled group if they were incorporated. *See* controlled group.

controlled group two or more corporations are in a controlled group if (a) one is the parent and the others are members of an 80% owned group (parent-subsidiary group), or (b) the same five or fewer persons own at least 80% of the voting power or value of each and there is identical ownership of at least 50% of the corporations (brother-sister group), or (c) each is a member of either a parent-subsidiary group or a brother-sister group and at least one is the common parent of a parent-subsidiary group and a member of a brother-sister group.

coverage requirement that plan benefit a minimum number of employees; to satisfy the requirement, must meet one of three percentage tests and benefit the lesser of 50 employees or 40% of all employees.

defined benefit plan a pension plan that pays a specified amount of benefits at retirement; contributions to the plan are based on the amount needed to provide the projected benefit.

defined contribution plan a pension or profit sharing plan in which the amount of contributions is specified and benefits under the plan are based on the amount contributed plus or minus any gains, income, or losses, that occur while the contributions are held by the plan.

dependent care assistance program plan in which the employer assists employees with respect to services to dependents which are necessary for the employee to engage in gainful employment by reimbursing the employee for expenses incurred, paying the service provider directly, or supplying the services directly to the employee's dependents.

discrimination the favoring of highly compensated employees, owners, or officers by the terms or operation of a plan.

disqualified person a person with a specified relationship to a plan, such as the fiduciary, the employer, and officers, directors, highly compensated employees, and certain owners of the employer.

educational assistance program a plan under which an employer provides instruction to or pays educational expenses of an employee.

employee an individual who performs services for compensation and who is under the employer's control.

entry date the date on which an employee must be permitted to participate in a plan; it must be the earlier of the first day of the first plan year after the employee satisfies participation requirements, or the date six months after the date the employee first satisfies those requirements.

equivalency a formula for crediting hours of service based on working time, periods of employment, earnings, or elapsed time.

ERISA the Employee Retirement Income Security Act of 1974, P.L. 93-403; the statute that established the basic requirements for qualified plans.

ERTA Economic Recovery Tax Act of 1981, P.L. 97-34.

ESOP employee stock ownership plan; a qualified stock bonus, profit sharing, or money purchase pension plan that must invest primarily in the employer's stock.

exclusive benefit rule rule requiring the fiduciary of a plan to provide benefits only to participants and their beneficiaries.

final pay the highest compensation received for any year within an employee's final five years of service.

5% owner person owning, directly or indirectly, more than 5% of the stock (or capital or profits interest) of an employer.

forfeiture loss of benefits resulting from leaving employment before all accrued benefits have vested.

forward averaging method of computing tax on a lump sum distribution in which the tax is determined in effect as if the distribution were received over a period of years.

401(k) plan stock bonus or profit sharing plan which allows the employee to elect to be paid in cash or to have the money placed in a trust under the plan

frozen plan a plan in which accrual of benefits has stopped, but which remains in existence to distribute its assets to participants and beneficiaries.

governmental plan plan established and maintained by the U.S. government, a state or political subdivision government, or an agency or instrumentality of such government.

graded vesting a vesting schedule in which an increasing percentage of accrued benefits become vested each year, until 100% has been reached.

group legal services plan a plan under which the employer provides specified legal services to employees through prepayment of legal fees for such services.

highly compensated employee employee who, in the current or preceding plan year, (a) was a 5% owner of the employer, (b) received $75,000 compensation (adjusted for inflation), (c) received $50,000 compensation (adjusted for inflation) and whose compensation was in the top 20% of compensation of all employees of the employer, (d) received compensation greater than 50% of the dollar limitation on annual benefits and was an officer of the employer, or (e) was a former employee who was highly compensated when separated from service or at any time after age 55.

hour of service an hour for which an employee is paid or entitled to pay for performing duties for an employer or for excused absences such as vacation, holiday, illness, incapacity, layoff, jury duty, military duty, or leave of absence, or an hour for which an employee is awarded back pay.

incentive stock option option granted under a plan which permits an employee to purchase employer stock within 10 years at a price equal to or greater than the fair market value of employer stock as of the date the option was granted.

insurance contract plan a plan that is funded entirely by insurance contracts.

integration reduction of benefits or contributions under a pension plan to take into account Social Security benefits or contributions to which the participant is entitled.

IRA/IRAN individual retirement arrangements, private pension arrangements permitted for individuals with earned income who are not covered by a pension plan of an employer.

J&S *see* qualified joint and survivor annuity.

Keogh plan a pension plan established by a self-employed person that is generally subject to the same requirements and limitations as a qualified pension plan.

key employee an employee who was (a) an officer with compensation more than 1.5 times the annual limit on contributions, (b) an owner of one of the 10 largest interests in the employer with compensation more than the annual limitation on contributions and with more than .5% ownership, (c) a 5% owner, or (d) a 1% owner with compensation of more than $150,000.

leased employee a person other than an employee who provides, under an agreement with a leasing organization and on a substantially full-time basis for more than one year, services that are historically provided by employees.

limitation on annual benefits in a defined benefit plan, the annual benefit paid cannot exceed the lesser of the employee's average compensation for the highest three consecutive years, or $90,000 (adjusted for inflation after 1987).

limitation on contributions in a defined contribution plan, the annual contribution to an employee's account cannot exceed the lesser of 25% of compensation or $30,000 (the dollar limit increases to 1/4 of the limitation on annual benefits when that limit has increased to more than $120,000).

lump sum distribution distribution of the entire balance of an employee's account within the same taxable year on the occurrence of the employee's retirement, death, separation from service, disability, or attaining age 59½.

master plan plan operated by a financial institution that an employer can adopt by executing a participation agreement.

minimum accrual a minimum percentage of benefits that must be accrued each year under a defined benefit plan; the plan must meet one of three tests designed to prevent undue delay in accruals. In a defined contribution plan, the minimum accrual is the employee's account balance. A top heavy plan must provide for additional accrual for both defined benefit and defined contribution plans.

minimum funding the minimum amount that an employer is required to contribute to a plan to cover all operating costs and plan liabilities.

minimum vesting employee contributions must be fully vested; accrued benefits from employer contributions must vest under one of two schedules: 100% after five years, or 20% after three years, with an additional 20% each year until fully vested. The minimum vesting schedule is accelerated in top heavy plans.

money purchase plan a defined contribution pension plan. *See* defined contribution plan.

MPPAA Multiemployer Pension Plan Amendments Act of 1980, P.L. 96-364.

multiemployer plan a collectively bargained pension plan that covers the employees of more than one employer.

normal retirement age the earlier of (a) the age specified in the plan as the normal retirement age, or (b) the later of 65 or the fifth anniversary of participation in the plan.

officer an executive who is in regular and continued service of the employer.

parity (1) rule providing that a former participant who returns to employment after a break in service need not be credited with prior service if the greater of five or the number of consecutive one-year breaks in service equals or exceeds the employee's aggregate number of years of service before the break. (2) equality of treatment of plans of unincorporated employers with plans of incorporated employers.

partial termination the ending of a portion of a plan because of cutting back of vesting, accrual of benefits, or eligibility for participation.

participation allowing an employee to be covered by a plan; must generally be allowed after one year of service; cannot exclude an employee because attaining a specified age, but can exclude based on reasonable classification, such as job description.

party-in-interest the ERISA term for what the Internal Revenue Code refers to as a disqualified person. *See* disqualified person.

PBGC Pension Benefit Guaranty Corporation, a corporation operated under the Department of Labor that insures pension plan benefits.

pension plan plan providing for definitely determinable retirement benefits for the livelihood of employees or beneficiaries; can be based on specific benefits (*see* defined benefit plan) or specific contributions to employee's account (*see* defined contribution plan).

plan a definite written program maintained by an employer for the benefit of employees or beneficiaries; must be permanent and must be communicated to employees.

plan year any period of 12 consecutive months chosen for keeping the records of the plan; need not coincide with the employer's taxable year.

profit-sharing plan a plan for enabling employees and beneficiaries to participate in the profits of the employer's business by means of recurring and substantial contributions by the employer to the employee's account under a definite predetermined formula for allocating contributions and making distributions.

prohibited group group in favor of which plans may not discriminate; includes highly compensated employees, officers, and owners.

prohibited transaction a transaction that is not allowed with respect to a plan, including (a) sale, exchange, or leasing of property between the plan and a disqualified person; (b) lending of money between the plan and a disqualified person; (c) furnishing of goods, services, or facilities between the plan and a disqualified person; (d) use by a disqualified person of plan income or assets; (e) dealing by the fiduciary for his own account with plan income of assets; and (f) receipt of consideration for his personal account by the fiduciary in connection with a transaction involving the income or assets of the plan.

prototype plan another term for a master plan. *See* master plan.

qualified domestic relations order (QDRO) order from state court that permits an alternate payee, other than the participant and the named beneficiary, to receive benefits from a plan.

qualified joint and survivor annuity (J&S) annuity, effective if the participant survives to retirement, for the life of the participant with a survivor annuity for the life of the participant's spouse.

qualified plan a plan that meets the requirements of the Internal Revenue Code, and therefore receives favorable tax treatment.

qualified preretirement survivor annuity annuity for the surviving spouse if the participant does not survive to retirement.

qualified stock option option granted generally before May 21, 1976, under a plan which permits an employee to purchase employer stock within five years at a price equal to or greater than the fair market value of the employer's stock as of the date the option was granted.

qualified trust the trust that holds the assets of a qualified plan.

rabbi trust a nonqualified arrangement in which the employer places funds for the employee's retirement in a trust which remains under the employer's control and subject to the claims of the employer's creditors.

REA Retirement Equity Act of 1984, P.L. 98-397.

reasonable compensation the amount paid to an employee for services that would be paid by a like enterprise under like circumstances.

required distribution amount that must be distributed by a plan, beginning no later than age 70½, over the life expectancy of the employee.

restricted stock option option granted generally before January 1, 1964, under a plan which permits an employee to purchase employer stock within 10 years at a price equal to 85% of the fair market value of the employer's stock as of the date the option was granted.

reversion the return to an employer of the portion of its contributions to a plan, usually on account of termination of the plan, in excess of the amount needed to satisfy all fixed and contingent liabilities of the plan.

rollover reinvestment in qualified plan, IRA, or Keogh plan of money or property received in a non-required distribution from another qualified plan; if the reinvestment is made within 60 days of the distribution, tax on the distribution is deferred.

salary reduction arrangement arrangement in which an employee can elect to have some salary, instead of being paid directly, contributed to a qualified plan.

section 89 Internal Revenue Code section prohibiting and providing tests for discrimination in eligibility and benefits under an accident or health plan, a group-term life insurance plan, and, if the employer so elects, a qualified group legal services plan, an educational assistance program, a dependent care assistance program, a cafeteria plan, miscellaneous fringe benefits, and benefits under a welfare benefit fund.

self-employed individual a sole proprietor, a partner in a partnership, and (for some purposes) a 2% shareholder in S corporation.

simplified employee pension plan (SEP) a retirement plan in which, in effect, the employer establishes individual retirement accounts (IRAs) for eligible employees.

SEPPAA Single Employer Pension Plan Amendments Act of 1986, P.L. 99-272.

stock bonus plan a plan established and maintained to provide benefits similar to a profit sharing plan, but benefits are generally paid in the employer's stock.

summary plan description a summary of the plan, written in language understandable by the average participant and sufficiently accurate and complete to apprise participants of their rights and obligations, that must be given to all participants and beneficiaries.

TAMRA Technical and Miscellaneous Revenue Act of 1988, P.L. 100-647.

target benefit plan a pension plan in which the amount of each year's contribution is determined by reference to the plan's original actuarial assumptions; treated as a defined contribution plan for limitation purposes.

tax-deferred annuity (TDA) an annuity used to fund retirement plans of colleges and universities, hospitals, and other tax-exempt employers or to fund the retirement savings of employees of those organizations.

TEFRA Tax Equity and Fiscal Responsibility Act of 1982, P.L. 97-248.

termination the ending of a pension plan by decision of the employer or by force of circumstances (such as bankruptcy) or the ending of a profit sharing plan by complete discontinuance of contributions.

top-heavy a plan that gives an undue proportion of its benefits to key employees; must use faster vesting schedule than other plans and must give non-key employees specified minimum benefits. *See* key employee.

vesting accrued benefits are considered to vest when they become nonforfeitable; benefits attributable to employee contributions must always be vested, while benefits attributable to employer contributions must vest in accordance with a schedule. *See* cliff vesting and graded vesting.

welfare benefit plan any plan, fund or program to provide employees and beneficiaries medical, surgical, or hospital benefits; benefits for sickness, accident, disability, death, or unemployment; vacation benefits; training programs; day care centers; scholarship funds; or prepaid legal services.

year of service any 12 month period in which the employee has 1,000 hours of service.

Index of Internal Revenue Code Sections

Index

C

D

E

F

G

H

I

J

K

L

M

N

O

R

S

T

U

V

W

Y

Z

About the Authors

MICHAEL G. KUSHNER, ESQ., received his J.D. from the University of Virginia and his LL.M. in Taxation from George Washington University. As a Tax Law Analyst for Tax Management Inc. in the area of ERISA and compensation planning, he analyzes developments and trends for a variety of practitioner-oriented publications. He is an Adjunct Professor at the Dickinson School of Law and has taught in the Certified Employee Benefits Specialist Program at Georgetown University. He is the author of *ERISA: Qualified Retirement Plans and Employee Fringe Benefits*, published by The Bureau of National Affairs, Inc. Mr. Kushner practices law in the ERISA area in Washington, D.C.

VIRGINIA L. BRIGGS, ESQ., received her J.D. from Cornell Law School. As a Tax Law Analyst for Tax Management Inc., she edits and updates Tax Management's compensation planning portfolio series and the *Tax Management Compensation Planning Journal*. She also edits *Business Tax Report*, in which she authors a biweekly column on business tax topics, including employee benefit issues.

PATRICK M. ROCKELLI, ESQ., received his LL.M. in Taxation from Georgetown University School of Law. As Director of the professional tax staff of Tax Management Inc., he oversees the work of attorneys and accountants in analyzing developments in all areas of federal income, estate, and gift tax. In addition, he coordinates the preparation of numerous portfolios written by leading practitioners and educators in law and accounting. Mr. Rockelli practices tax law in Washington, D.C. He has authored and edited numerous articles on taxation and is the co-author of *Legal Considerations in Choice of Business Entity*, published by The Bureau of National Affairs, Inc.